# The Herts Genealogist And Antiquary
# (Volume II)

Editor

William Brigg

Alpha Editions

This Edition Published in 2020

ISBN: 9789354307669

Design and Setting By
**Alpha Editions**
www.alphaedis.com
Email - info@alphaedis.com

As per information held with us this book is in Public Domain.
This book is a reproduction of an important historical work. Alpha Editions uses the best technology to reproduce historical work in the same manner it was first published to preserve its original nature. Any marks or number seen are left intentionally to preserve its true form.

## TABLE OF CONTENTS.

Abstracts of Wills. Consistory Court of London 9, 62. 102.
" Archdeaconry of Huntingdon (Hitchin) 29, 72, 155, 227, 310.
" Archdeaconry of Middlesex (Essex & Herts) 37, 84, 119, 179, 215, 318.
" Archdeaconry of St Albans 44, 90, 189, 236.
Feet of Fines for Herts (Tudor Period) 33, 76, 130, 172, 217, 253, 302, 337.
Marriage Licences. Archdeaconry of St Albans 5, 92, 135, 166, 238. 281, 328, 369.
" Archdeaconry of Huntingdon (Hitchin) 41, 141, 149, 208.
Subsidy Rolls 1545. Hundred of Dacorum 26.
" " " Braughing 272.
" " " Cashio 346.
Transcripts of Parish Registers. Northaw 48, 83.
" Wigginton 112, 159.
" Chipping Barnet 197, 242.
" Minsden 288.
" Ayot St Peter 354.
Church Terrors 19, 66, 105, 181, 224, 247, 296.
List of Chancery Inquisitiones post mortem 13, 54.
" Rentals & Surveys 116.
" Ministers Accounts 171.
Inquisitiones post mortem. 87, 122, 186, 205, 278.
Funeral Certificates. Sir Richard Anderson 241.
" Sir Edw. Barkham 336.
Humberstone of Walkern etc. 1, 49, 97.
Penn Family Notes 23.
" Wills 233.
Wyndowt Family 364.
Rowlett Wills 124, 184.
Amphillis Washington 47.
Herts Ancestory of the Hon. Richard Olney 376.
Will of John Thomas Hilocomius 316.
Rental of Sir John Say 145, 193.
Rental of St Mary's Sopwell 231.
Hitchin Parish Registers 165.
Deeds relating to Stone Hall in St Albans 259.
Court Rolls of Piggotts Manor in Bps. Stortford 266, 322, 377.
Monumental Inscriptions. Dagnall Street Chapel, St Albans 309.

# The Herts Genealogist and Antiquary.

## Humberstone of Walkern, etc.

WILLS AND ADMINISTRATIONS FROM THE PREROGATIVE COURT OF CANTERBURY.*

[*P.C.C. Wrastley* 52.]

JOHN HUMERSTONE of Walkerne in the diocese of Lincoln. (*Dat.* 12 Oct. 1557). Bur. in church or churchyard of Walkerne; Servants Margt. Pye, John Pennyngton & Richard Pennyngton; Wife Alice; My occupation of 'Tannyng'; Lease of Walkerne burye; Dau. Eliz.; Sons Wm., Leonard, John & Barnaba; Daus. Alice, Avice, Joane, Dorothee, Barbara & Margt.; The childn of my bro. Thomas; 'If my wife be now wt childe'; Friend Edw. Wilson & Wm. Hamonde exors. Wits:—James Halfhide, Rich. Pennyngton, Wm. Scapisworth & other. (*Pr.* 29 Nov. 1557).

[*P.C.C. Loftes* 2.]

THOMAS HUMBERSTONE of Stevenage, husbandman. (*Dat.* 6 Oct. 1560). Bur. at Stevenage; Wife Margt; My house called Netherwalles in Stevenage; Son Leonard; House called Bedwalles in Stevenage; Tenement at Stevenag church yarde gate; Daus. Joan & Beatris; Son Thos; Bro. John; Thos. Clarke of Stevenage & Robt. Andrew of same exors. Wits:—Wm. Gynne, Edw. Clarke, John Sayvll. (*Pr.* 22 Jan. 1560-1).

[*P.C.C. Bakon* 44.]

JOHN HUMBERSTONE of Little Amwell in psh. of Ware, innkeeper. (*Dat.* 5 Aug. 1579). Bur. at Ware; To wife Eliz. house in Gt. Amwell which I bought of Mr Purvey, for life, & after her decease to Tho. Hobsone of Cambridge; Eliz. Slater my brother's dau; Allse Hunte my sisters dau; Avis Hunte; Robert Slater my wifes brother; Agnes Wilson my wifes sister; Agnes Hunte my sister; Sist. Eliz. Peppercorne; Wm. Wilson my wifes sisters son;

* Abstracts of all Humberstone wills and admons. down to 1700 are here given.

Bro. Rich. Humberstone; Wife Eliz. & Nich. Thorowgood exors. Wit[s]:—Nich. Thorowgood. Robt. Wilsonne. (Pr. 4 Nov. 1579 by Eliz. relict, the other exor renouncing. A 'sententia pro valore' follows, the suit being between John Humberston natural bro. of the dec[d] of the one part & Eliz. the relict of the other part).

[P.C.C. Nevell 84.]

FRAUNCYS HUMBERSTON citizen & haberdasher of London. (Dat. 7 Nov. 1593). Bur. in church of S[t] Mildred's in London; Mistris Farthing widow; Johane Clarke serv[t] to M[r] Raynton; Ellen Willson serv[t] to M[rs] Farthinge; Tho. Rudd haberdasher & Temperance his wife; Rich. Rudd bro. of s[d] Thos; Jane Evans; Goodwife Wetherall; Johane Welles serv[t] to Tho. Rudd; Cous. Eliz. Humberston of Hales greene in Norf. & her two daus; Aunt Mistris Crathorne; M[r] Felton minister; M[r] Seracoale parson of S[t] Mildreds; Bro. John Humberston; Bro. Wm.; Sist. Mary Humberston; Bro. Henry Humberston exor. *By me Francys Humberston.* Wit[s]:—Zacharia Jackson scrivener, Wm. Brooke notary. (Pr. 5 Dec. 1593).

[P.C.C. Drake 57.]

THOMAS HUMBERSTONE of Hytchyn, yeoman. (Dat. 14 Jan. 1595). Bur. at Hitchin; Kinsman Gyles, son of my bro. Richard Humberston; Henry, Leonard, Edw. & Wm. sons of s[d] Richard; Gyles son of my kinsman John Humberston; Maid serv[t] Alice Woodlande; Dennys Seabrooke widow; Anne wife of Nich. Lyle; Avis wife of Mathewe Audeley; Mary wife of Wm. Chambers; Eliz. wife of Wm. Monke the younger; Frances Awdeley dau. of s[d] Matthew; Serv[t] John Copcott; Serv[t] Edw. Harrolde; Luce wife of John Lawe thelder; Tho. Chapman gent; Mathew Audeley yeoman; Legacy to poor of Hitchin; Dorothy wife of Robert Marvyle; Mary Lyle dau. of said Nicholas; My house to kinsman John Humberston now in the house with me; Agnes wife of John Cooke; Mary Chambers dau. of Wm. Chambers; Edw. & John sons of Matt. Audeley; Ralph son of Wm. Chambers; House in occupation of John Smithe; Ellen wife of John Hawfeheade; Robt. Draper; Lands in Wynnington co. Beds. now in occupation of Robt. Dukesoun of Northampton; Wm. Chambers of Hitchin yeoman; Alveraie Birtbye vicar of Hitchin; Joan wife of Tho. Chapman of Hitchin gent; Wm. Chambers exor; Tho. Chapman overseer. Wit[s]:—Alveraie Birtbye, Tho. Chapman, John Humberstone. (Pr. 2 July 1596.)

[P.C.C. Hele 71.]

WILLIAM HUMBERSTON of Stourton in psh. of Stowe, co. Linc., yeoman. (Dat. 29 June 1 Chas. 1625). Bur. in psh. church of Stowe; Legacies to poor of Stowe, Normanby, Stourton, Bransbye & Lyssington; John Yorke; Xpofer Stov'ing *als.* Stringer; Robt. Croftes; Wm. & Robt. sons of Alice Humberston; Mary, Susanna & Margt. daus. of s[d] Alice; Susanna Rowsom; Eliz. Rowsom; Dau-in-law Alice Humberston; My wifes sisters child[n] dwelling beyond Gaynsbroughe; Her [i.e., my wifes] sisters child[n] at Fillingham; John Eastgate & his child[n]; Eliz. Eastgate the younger; Eliz. Eastgate the elder my sister & her sons & her dau.; Child[n] of Wm. Humberston of Skellingthorpe; Goddau. Isabell Adkins; Wife Alice; Robt. Crofts living in Stourton; Robt. son of Alice Humberston; Lands in Stourton bought of John

Dawber: Henry Adkins: My now wife Alice: Son Thomas: Apprentice John Smithe: Lands in Lissington bought of Robt. Brice: Wife extrix: Alex. Cussen & Rich. Codd supervisors. (*Mark*). Wit$^s$:—Alex$^r$ Cussen, Henry Adkins, John Eastland, W$^m$. Lerie, Rich. Codd, Anth. Pennystone. (*Pr.* 5 May 1626).

[*P.C.C. Barrington* 28.]

GILES HUMBERSTONE of Walkerne, co. Herts., gent. (*Dat.* 29 Aug. 1627). Bur. in Walkern Church near my father; Legacy to poor of Walkern; To son Henry the tenement where Tho. Pett now dwells which I bought of W$^m$. Scarbrough containing 22 acr. called Coxes in Walkern, with remainders successively to sons Osmond, Edw$^d$ & W$^m$. and dau. Theodocia; To son Henry 4 acr. bought of my bro. John Humberston lying in Walkern called Wellfeild; To wife Mary for life, tenement called Garnars in Walkern containing 12 acr. bought of John Clarke & Matthew Howe, & after her decease to son Osmond; Tenement wherein Phillippe Cooke lately dwelt in Walkern, bought of bro. John Humberston; To son Edw. tenement called Cheney Hall in Walkern sometimes the lands of John Pake of Walkern; Messuage & lands in Puckeridge (which were sometime my wifes fathers & came by my wife) to s$^d$ wife; Bro. Tho. Humberston; Son Thomas long since by me advanced; Grandchild Edw. (son of my son Thos.); Dau. Mary Humberston; Tenement called Holmes in Walkern; Wife Mary extrix: Friends Geo. Barry, clerk, parson of Walkerne & W$^m$. Robins of London gent. overseers. *Gyles Humberstone.* Wit$^s$:—George Barry, W$^m$. Ling, Joseph Loveland, Edw. Lane. Re-delivered 6 Sep. 1627 in presence of W$^m$. Robyns. *Codicil* 9 Jan. 1627-8 names Joane Smartfoote my wifes mother. (*Pr.* 31 Mch. 1628).

[*P.C.C. Scroope* 35.]

THOMAS HUMBERSTON of Usselebie, co. Linc. yeoman (*Dat.* 4 May 1629). Daus. Anne & Marie (under 18); Child$^n$ of my bro. W$^m$. viz. Margt., Rich., & Sara; Dau. Eliz. wife of John Smith; Anne Smith dau. of son-in-law John Smith; The 4 child$^n$ of bro. Hugh viz. W$^m$., John, Marie & Anne; Sist. Anne Morris & Faith her dau; W$^m$. son of Edw$^d$ Humberston; W$^m$. Laminge; Wife Marie extrix; Bro. W$^m$. Humberston & son-in-law John Smith supervisors. Wit$^s$:—Moyses Walker, clk, Hen. Wrawby, John Millington. (*Pr.* 13 Apr. 1630).

[*P.C.C. Pile* 67.]

WILLIAM HUMBERSTON.[*] (*Dat.* 3 Feb. 1635). My true and trustie freind Thomas Midleton to dispose of such goods and Tobaccoes as I am possessed withall here in the Paule nowe beinge in Virginia if in case shee shall goe to anie other parte or place except London and to deliver the money which come of the p$^d$uce thereof vnto my very lovinge freind M$^r$ Raphe Baily beinge my vncle which is my vnckle dwelling vpon Whittington Colledge Hill but if in case that the shipp shall goe first to London That then I ordaine before her delivery that then the aforesaid goods and Tobaccoes with book$^s$ shalbe delivered vnto my aforesaid freind M$^r$ Raphe Bailie he payinge what debts shalbe found owinge by me William Humberston in the shipp Paule. Wearing apparel

---

[*] The probate act book describes testator as 'nuper in partibus transmarinis celebis defuncti'

to Wm. Burde now being in the ship Paule for his paines & care he hath had of me in my sicknes. Also I give my surgery cheste withall my instruments thereto belonging with the seabedd unto M^r Barth^w Vanderlus dwelling in Great Woodstreete with my wages, etc. *William Humberston.* Wit^s :—Thomas Midleton, Leonard Betts, Phillipp Dyer. (*Admon.* 7 May 1636 to Ralph Bailie principal legatee).

[*P.C.C. Lee* 174.]

GEORGE HUMBERSTONE of Stevenage, co. Herts, gent. (*Dat.* 7 Aug. 1637). To be buried in parish church of Walkerne. Bond for £120 due to me from Wm. Pratt clerk & £100 due from Tho. Garnons grocer, to my 2nd son Henry ; To son Henry a featherbed etc ; To Garnons my youngest son, annuity of 20*l.* for his life & to s^d son £50 more within 3 years of my decease ; Friend & cousin M^r Wm. Clarke & bro. M^r John Humberstone supervisors ; All lands, houses & goods not before bequeathed, to eldest son James whom I make exor. *George Humberstone.* Wit^s :—John Humberston, Jo. Humberston jun. (*Pr.* 5 Dec. 1638).

[*P.C.C. Bowyer* 59.]

EDMOND HUMBERSTON of the psh. of S^t Sepulchres, London. (*Dat.* 26 Sep. 1651). Bur^d in churchy^d of S^t Sepulchres ; Son Peter to have the profit of my land called Netherwells in psh. of Stevenag, co. Hertf., till such time that it please god hee may returne from the Barbadoes ; Cous. Thos. Humberston exor ; Jas. Weeden overseer ; To bro-in-law John Humberston if he be living after my decease 10*s.* ; To bro. Francis 10*s.* ; To sist. Eliz. Goodwin 20*s.* ; To sist. Margt. Fernes, widow, the little brasse morter which shee had to keepe for me ; To cous. Giles Humberston 5*s.* ; To cous. Wm. Humberston 5*s.* ; To cous. Ann Cutts 5*s.* ; To cous. Edmond Humberston the carpender 5*s.* & to his bro. Robt. 5*s.* ; To neph. Geo. Humberston 5*s.* ; If son Peter shall die & not come againe nor have any child, then neph. Tho. Humberston to enjoy his portion ; To Jas. Cressell one of 'my fellowes at stocke in Poultry London,' 5*s.* to spend with our other fellowes there ; To Goody Taylor one of my little brasse candsticks. *Edmond Humberston.* Wit^s :—Edw. Bush, Nich. Stanton. (*Pr.* 18 Mch. 1651-2).

[*P.C.C. Brent* 308.]

WILLIAM HUMBERSTON of Walesby, co. Linc., yeoman. (*Dat.* 14 May 1652). Bur. in church of Walesby ; Sons Thos. & Wm ; Dau. Margt. wife of Rich. Meares ; Dau. Sarah wife of John Manger ; My five grandchild^n ; My man Edwards ; Mary ; Sheepheards wife ; Widow Kinwood ; Widow Stafford ; Bro. Hugh ; Wm. Humberston of Tenbby ; Sist. Susan wife of Geo. Curtis ; Son Rich. exor. [*Mark.*] Wit^s :—Erasmus Sturton, Edw. Day. (*Pr.* 13 Sep. 1653).

[*P.C.C. Alchin* 104.]

EDWARD HUMERSTONE of Reauesbye, co. Linc. (*Dat.* 1 July 1653). Dau. Elline ; [? Dau.] Eliz. ; Dau. Anne ; Sist. Anne Knite & her 4 ch^n ; Sist. Humerston ; Bro. Wm. Humerston's child^n ; Henry Story ; Wm. Rusten ; Wife Elline extrix ; Bro. Wm. Humerstone & Wm. Pye supervisors. [*Mark*]. Wit^s :—Wm. Humerston, Wm. Pye. (*Pr.* 23 Aug. 1654).

*To be Continued.*

# Marriage Licences.
## Archdeaconry of St. Albans.
### By A. E. GIBBS.
(CONTINUED FROM VOL. I., PAGE 363).

1667-8

February 3. Thomas Townsend and Anna Bilson of St. Stephens: at St. Stephens. Griffin Aubon a surety.

February 28. Joseph Eaton of St. Peters, butcher, bachelor, and Anne Bradbury, maiden, of St. Albans. Robert Eaton of St. Albans, cordwainer, a surety.

[*No date or year. Endorsed* 1667]. William Chackley [*signed* Chakley] of Codicote, weaver, bachelor, and Susan Gurnett of Sandridge, maiden; at Sandridge. Thomas Seabrooke of Harding, yeoman, a surety.

[*Undated*]. William Eames of Dunstable, co. Bedford, bachelor, and Mary Bunby of Chipping Barnet, maiden; at the church in the licence specified. John Hare of St. Michaels, blacksmith, and George Barnes of St. Albans, plomer, sureties.

1668

March 26. John Coghill of Aldenham, bachelor, and Deborah Dudley of Idlestrey, maiden. Elisha Dudley of Idlestree, a surety.

April 1. Daniel Baker of St. Michaels, bachelor, and Martha Brouks of the same, maid. Edward Camfeild of St. Albans, tallow chandler, a surety.

April 20. John Draper of Storton, co. Northampton, husbandman, bachelor, and Mary Wilson of St. Albans, maiden. Edward Towensend of St. Albans, a surety.

May 9. James Turner of St. Albans, butcher, widower, and Anne Norris of Cheping Barnet, maiden; at Cheping Barnet or other church within the Archdeaconry.

May 9. Joseph Hodson of Luton, bachelor, and Hannah Rawlins late of the same but now of St. Albans, maiden; at St. Peters. Edmund Rawlins of Luton, her father, and Joseph Ewer of St. Albans, joiner, sureties.

May 23. Thomas Swenston of St. Peters, bachelor, and Mary Rickeson of the same, maiden; at St. Peters, St. Michaels or Redbourne. Robert Swenstone of St. Peters, tailor, and William Burton of Redbourne, collarmaker, sureties.

[*Undated, on same sheet as last*]. Thomas Latimore, of St. Peters, bachelor, and Mary Bird, of same, maiden; at East Barnet.

May 25. Edward Browne of Sarrat, widower, and Elizabeth Hunt of Rickmersworth, widow; at Sarrat or Rickmersworth. Henry Browne of Sarrat, a surety.

[*Undated*]. George Goodin of Hatfeild, bachelor, and Sarah Fissh, widow, of Northaw; at Northaw. Thomas Odell of Hatfeild, a surety.

June 11. Richard Preston of St. Michaels, carpenter, bachelor, and Elizabeth Ewer of St. Albans, maiden: at St. Michaels, the Abbey, or Redbourne. Richard Preston senr. of St. Michaels, a surety.

June 19. Edward Marshall of Kempton, brickmaker, widower, and Elizabeth Oxenfort of the Abbey parish, widow; at Sandridg or St. Peters. Thomas Hall of St. Albans, a surety.

June 20. Thomas Gregory of Chipping Barnet, bachelor, and Mary Woodroofe of South Mims; at Chipping Barnet. Daniel Gregory of Chipping Barnet, his father, collarmaker, and Peter Fullwood of St. Albans, sureties.

July 15. Christopher Taylor of St. Albans, tailor, bachelor, and Eliz. Jewet of the same, maid; at St. Michaels. James Hobley [*signed* Hopley] of the same, tailor, a surety.

July 22. Joseph Osbourne of Carington, yeoman, bachelor, and Elizabeth Birchmore late of the same but now of St. Albans, maiden; at St. Peters. Thomas Dunnill of St. Albans, innholder, a surety.

August 14. John Parrat of St. Albans, bachelor, and Anne Staple of the same, maiden; at Sandridge, Codicote, or Paules Walden. James Martin of St. Albans, a surety.

August 24. Searles Perkins of London, and Mary Lightfoote of St. Stephens, widow; at St. Stephens. William Dalemore of St. Stephens, a surety.

September 29. William Cater of Abbots Langley, bachelor, and Esther Long of Hemell Hempstead, maiden; at St. Albans or St. Peters.

September 30. William Thebridge of Sandridge, bachelor, and Elizabeth Nash of Kimpton, maiden; at Sandridge or any other church in the Archdeaconry. Thomas Thebridge of Sandridge, yeoman, his father, a surety.

November 12. Daniel Rofe of Watford, bachelor, and Mary Halsey of Luiton, maiden; at Sandridge. Gowing Crosfield of St. Albans, a surety.

November 18. Thomas Tufnell of Hertford and Dorothy Partridg of Hempstead; at St. Albans. James Ramridge of St. Albans, a surety.

1668-9

January 7. John Ray of Sandridge, bachelor, and Mary Dell of St. Stephens; at Sandridge, Redbourne, or St. Michaels. Richard Preston of St. Michaels, carpenter, a surety.

January 14. Edward Osman and Dorothy Evans; at St. Albans. John Groome and Griffin Jones, sureties.

January 14. Christopher Jackson of St. Michaels, tapster, bachelor, and Alice Moores of the same, maiden; at St. Albans. Christopher Browne of St. Albans, a surety.

February 20. John Edmonds of Great Gadesdon, bachelor, and Recka Packer; at St. Peters. Robert Scott, a surety.

[*Undated*]. James Royce of Redborne, blacksmith, widower, and Sarah Halsey of the same, widow; at Redborne. George Stepny of Redbourn, innholder, a surety.

[*Undated*]. John Williams of St. Albans, tapster, bachelor, and Martha Twiford of the same, maiden; at St. Stephens or St. Peters. William Bostocke, hostler, a surety.

[*Undated*]. William Skelton of Ridge, husbandman, and Ellin Sawer of the same, maid. Robert Smith of Tinnanger, a surety.

[*Undated*]. Richard Beamont of St. Michaels, yeoman, bachelor, and Mary Edmonds of Dunstable: at St. Peters. William Harrop of St. Michaels, tanner, a surety.

[*Blank*] 28. Robert Bellingham of Edmunton, co. Middlesex, bachelor, and Sarah Robinson of St. Albans, maiden; at St. Albans. Edward Bunyan of Edmunton, bachelor, a surety.

1669

June 8. Thomas Woodward of St. Albans, cordwinder, bachelor, and Katherine Rose of the same, maiden; at St. Albans. John New of St. Albans, innholder, a surety.

June 10. John Seabrooke of Redbourne, husbandman, widower, and Ann Grunnill of Sandridge, maiden; at Sandridg. Edward Seabrooke of Harding, husbandman, a surety.

June 21. Robert Chalkley of St. Stephens, yeoman, widower, and Mary Carpenter, maiden: at St. Peters or Sandridge. Joseph Ewer of St. Peters, cowper, a surety.

July 12. William Wethered of Harpesden but now of St. Albans, bachelor, and Anne Dixon of the same but now of St. Albans, maiden. Edward Dixon of Whethamsted, yeoman, a surety.

November 1. Thomas Tayler of Edger, co. Middlesex, wagoner, single man, and Elizabeth Page of St. Stephens, maiden, daughter of [*blank*] Page deceased, of St. Peters, her mother also deceased; at Ridge or St. Stephens. Joseph Marshall of St. Peters, a surety.

November 11. Thomas Preston of St. Michaels and Anne White, maiden; at Sandridge. Edward Fowk of St. Albans, gent., a surety.

December 11. Thomas Onge citizen and linen draper of London [a note on another obligation shows he was of St. Botolph's Without, Aldersgate], widower, and Abigael Grubb of St. Albans, maiden. Thomas Richards of St. Albans, gent., a surety. [This is the first printed form].

December 18. Thomas Legg of Redborne, husbandman, bachelor, and Elizabeth Redding of St. Michaels, maiden. John Pryor of St. Michaels, a surety.

December 20. William Beasley of Redborne, yeoman, widower, and Mary Foster of Berkhamsted, maiden. Thomas Deacon of Redborne, husbandman, a surety.

December 24. Henry Stevens of St. Albans, bachelor, and Anne Grube, maiden. Mark Armestronge of Ridge, husbandman, a surety.

1669-70

January 5. Edward Hope of St. Albans, gent., and Elizabeth Crosse of the same, widow. William Rance of St. Albans, gent., a surety.

January 8. Stephen Pecocke of Aiseworth in co. Bedford but now of St. Albans, bachelor, and Hannah Fells, daughter of William Fells, maiden. Nathaniel Pryor, of St. Michaels, a surety.

January 22. Isaac Halsey of Great Gaddesden, gent., bachelor, and Mary Gape, daughter of Mr. John Gape of St. Albans, maiden. John New of St. Albans, pewterer, a surety.

February 11. Isaack Finch of Watford, bachelor, and Susan Marsh of Ruslup, maiden. Joseph [*signed* Joshua] Carpenter of St. Albans, innholder, and Robert Robinson of the same, butcher, sureties.

[*Undated, on same sheet as last*]. Francis Chappell of Sandridge, blacksmith, and Margaret Thrale of the same, maiden. Thomas Meadow of St. Albans, joiner, a surety.

[*Blank*] 26. James Woodward of Little Harwood, co. Buckingham, yeoman, bachelor, and Alice Tatham, maiden. Abel Bennett of Watford, tailor, a surety.

1670

April 20. George Rose of Redburne, bachelor, and Anne Hall of Hemsteed. William Brand of St. Albans, widower, a surety.

April 23. James Funge of Rickemansworth, bachelor, and Hannah Hunt of the same, maiden. Daniel Baldwyn of the same, a surety.

May 16. Nathaneel Bacon of Friston, co. Suffolk, gent., bachelor, and Elizabeth Duke, daughter of Edward Duke of Bemhall, co. Suffolk, gent. Thomas Matthews of Friston, a surety.

June 27. Samuel Anderson of Watford, gent., and Margarett Bird, widow. Thomas Nicolls of Langley, a surety.

July 8. William Birch of Sarrott and Sarah How of the same. Thomas Hunt of the same, a surety.

July 16. Henry Boswell of Maverne Parva, co. Worcester, bachelor, and Mary Brewer. Francis Squire, a surety.

September 2. Henry Smith of Sarratt, yeoman, bachelor, and Mary Grove, maiden, daughter of Joseph Grove of Flawning. Edward Fowke of St. Albans, gent., a surety.

September 2. James Creeke of St. Albans, tailor, bachelor, and Mary Knevett of the same, maiden. John Wingfeild of the same, gent., a surety.

September 7. Thomas Halsey of Kimpton but now of St. Albans, husbandman, and Mary Hurst of Kimpton, widow. William Gibson of St. Albans, shoemaker, a surety.

September 29. Edward Strayne of St. Stephens, husbandman, bachelor, and Mary Martin of the same, maiden. John Martin of the same, husbandman, a surety.

September 30. Daniell Tarbox of Redborne, bachelor, and Martha Hamond of the same, maiden. Isaac Stepney [*signed* (?) Stagny] of the same, glover, and William Mores of St. Albans, felmonger, sureties.

October 7. Emanuell Clarke, widower, and Mary Howe, maiden. Thomas Royston of Harpenden, gent., and Edmund Fowke of St. Albans, gent., sureties.

October 11. William Owen of St. Albans, bachelor, and Mary Bigott of the same. Nicholas Whelpeley of the same, a surety.

October 15. William How of Abbots Langley, bachelor, and Sara Carter of the same, maiden. John How of the same, gent., a surety.

October 15. Thomas Seabrocke of Sandridge, yeoman, bachelor, and Mary Chalkley. Henry Chalkley of Kimpton, yeoman, her father, a surety.

October 25. Benjamin Geery [*signed* Geary] of Hempstedd, and Sara Holiday of St. Albans, maiden. William Morris of St. Albans, innholder, a surety.

[*Undated, on same sheet as last*]. Henry Bradwyn [or Bradwin, *signed* Braden] of St. Albans, cordwainer, widower, and Elizabeth Heyward of St. Stephens, widow. Martin Element of St. Albans, locksmith, a surety.

*To be Continued.*

# Abstracts of Wills.

**CONSISTORY COURT OF THE BISHOP OF LONDON.**

### REGISTER "SPERIN."

f. 1. JOHN HODGESON of Waltham Crosse in the psh. of Chesthunt. (*Dat.* 20 Sep. 1586). Bur. at Chesthunt; Daus. Eliz. & Hester; Wife Millicent extrix. Wit$^s$:—Robert Pettite, Edward White & Simon Williams vicar of Chesthunt. (*Pr.* 19 Apr. 1592).

f. 1. JOHN MALDON of Wormley, yeoman. (*Dat.* 12 Dec. 1591). Tenement called Fanners & 1 acr. land in Howsfeild & 1 orchard called the Moore all in Wormley & one Ayland called Bush Ayland in Cheston to use of wife Joane for life: after to my two daus. Joane & Alice equally; Son Wm.; Residue to bro. Wm. Cooke of Waltham to bestow at his discretion; Wife extrix. (*Mark*). Wit$^s$:—John Hawkins marke, Thomas Archers marke, William Cooke jun$^r$. (*Pr.* 12 May 1592).

f. 3. MARY ALEWOOD of Ware, spinster. (*Nunc. will dat.* Nov. 1590). Ellen Challas her keeper; Money due to her by the gift of Rob$^t$. Mitchell her uncle dec$^d$; Margery Wyley; Cous. Rob$^t$. Coates; Cous. Agnes Coates her children; 'And for my brother he shall have never one penny of it because I sent for him so often and he never came to me.' (Admon. with will annexed 5 June 1592 to Rob$^t$. Coates & Agnes his wife, next of kin, during minority of Rob$^t$. & Agnes Coates their child$^n$).

f. 21. JOHN JOHNSON of Wormeley, basketmaker. (*Dat.* 29 Mch. 1592). Bur. in churchyard of Wormeley; Sons Wm. & John; Joane Johnson my sons dau.; John Johnson & Richard 'my sonne sonnes'; Anne Johnson; Alice Johnson; Lease of 'ground of osyers' held of M$^r$ Tucke; Wm. Turner; John Bumsted; Wife Mary extrix. *Signu' Johannis Johnson.* Wit$^s$:—Richard King & Edw. Colt. (*Pr.* 7 Aug. 1592).

f. 27. WILLIAM HARTBARD *alias* ROGERS of psh. of Meesden, laborer. (*Dat.* 13 June 1592). Bur. in churchyard of Meesden; Henry Lodge; Land in Honnishfeild; Rich. Salmon of Meesden 'otemealeman' and Lettice his wife; Wm. son of s$^d$ Richard; Wm. son of Wm. Hartbard of Braughing my kinsman; Wife Clemence exor. *William Hartbard.* Wit$^s$:—William Cowell, Henry Totnam, John Kinge. (*Pr.* 13 Sep. 1592).

f. 28. RICHARD FAYRCLOUGH of Cufflay in psh of Northaw yeoman. (*Dat.* 24 May 1592). Bur. at Northaw; Son Giles Fayrclough's child$^n$; Richard Lowens child$^n$; Rob$^t$. Lowes child$^n$ of Hadley; Tho. Feeldes child$^n$ of Kempton; Son Geo. & dau. Margerie Fayrclough; Wife Agnes extrix. Wit$^s$:—Richard Newton, George Cooke marke, Rich. Lowen marke, (*Pr.* 22 Sep. 1592).

f. 29. LUCE HATTON in the psh. of Shepall, widow. (*Dat.* 22 May 1592). Bur. in Shepall churchyard: John Saburne the elder & John Saburne the younger of Watton: Eliz. Prior widow; Eliz. Kympton, dau. to Wm. Kimpton (under 16); Agnes Kempton sist to Eliz. (under 16); Margt. dau. to Wm. Kempton; Susan dau. of Wm. Kempton; Edw. Gue; Geo. Kempton of Shepall & Wm. Kempton of Shephall exors. *Wit*<sup>s</sup>:—Wm. Browne & John Mardoll & Robt. Wood vicar of Shepall. (*Pr.* 22 Sep. 1592).

f. 53. HENRY MYNOTT of Meseden, the elder. (*Dat.* 28 Apr. 1592). Bur. in churchyard of Meseden; Wife Margt; Sons Robert & Henry; Dau. Annis; My 5 child[n] Henry, Robert, Alice, Lettice & Anne: Son Henry exor: Son Robt. overseer. *Wit*<sup>s</sup>:—William Cowell, Henry Mynott, Evon Colt, Thomas Kinge & Henry Modle. (*Pr.* 13 Sep. 1592).

f. 56. AGNES CODGELL of Abbotts Langley, widow. (*Dat.* 12 July 1592). Henry Child my daughters son, & Bennet Child. Agnes & Margt. Child her daus; Dau. Ellins 7 child[n] viz:—Henry, Wm. Tho. John, Bennet, Agnes & Margt; Dau. Bennetts 4 child[n] viz:—Rob[t], Benj[n], John & Benett; Geo. Heywards wife; Rafe Parishe wife; Henry Dallinge my dau's son; Goddau. Agnes Heyward; Bennet Parish; Son in law Henry Childe exor. *Wit*<sup>s</sup>:—Anne Haward, Mary Rutter (*mark*), Alice Parishe (*mark*). (*Pr.* 17 Sep. 1592).

f. 58. JOHN CAMPION husbandman, in the towne of Anstie (*Dat.* 13 Aug. 1592). Bro. Wm; Sist Avis; Wife Alice extrix. *Wit*<sup>s</sup>:—Edmond Pelham, Hen. Bawcocke. (*Pr.* 13 Sep. 1592).

f. 65. EDWARD FERRIS of Wormeley, farrier. (*Dat.* 7 July 1592). Dau. Sus. Ferris; Dau. Jone; Dau. Alice; Frances Fynche & Joane Fynche my wifes daus; Bros. Samuel & Thos; Robt. Becke my neighbour & son in law John Fynche overseers; Wife Eliz. extrix; Lease from 'my worshipfull m[r] William Purvey Esquire' to me. *Edward Ferris.* *Wit*<sup>s</sup>:—Edward Cobett hujus script., Robt. Becke & John Fynche. (*Pr.* 4 Oct. 1592).

f. 68. WILLIAM LAWRENCE of S[t] Albans (*Dated* 'a day or two before the death, and in the spring time Anno d'ni 1584'). Wife Joane to have my farm at New Myll end for life & also house in Halliwell strete in St Albans. A lease to be made to W[m] Marston of S[t] Albans of a house in Halliwell streete for 20 or 21 years; Wife extrix. *Wit*<sup>s</sup>:—Andrew Coltman, Wm. Marston, Eliz. Marston his wife & Eliz. Marsey. (*Pr.* 8 May 1592. A 'sententia' follows, in which the executrix is named as Joan Lawrence *alias* Lansdale).

f. 73. JOHN BOXSTED of Hodsdon. (*Dat.* 31 May 1580). Bur. at Broxborne; Son John; Wife Grace extrix. (*Mark*). *Wit*<sup>s</sup>:—Wm. Swanson, John Founteine, Tim. Sharrenbrooke. (*Pr.* 26 Feb. 1592-3).

f. 74. WILLIAM SMEWYN. (*Dat.* 6 Sept. 1592). Bur. at Rickmansworthe; Wife Jane extrix.; Dau. Sara (under 14); Sist. Evelins two child[n]; Sist. Fraunces her two child[n]; Sist. Annis; Friends John Durrant & Tho. Ludlowe. (*Mark*). *Wit*<sup>s</sup>:—Rowland Beresforde, John Durrant, Tho. Ludlowe, Rich. Edmonds. (*Pr.* 15 Feb. 1592-3).

## ABSTRACTS OF WILLS.

f. 74. JOHN LONGE of Elstree. (*Undated*). Son Simon: The rest of my four small child<sup>n</sup> viz:—John, Annis, Marg<sup>t</sup>. & Marion: Father-in-law Tho. Codgell & his son my bro-in-law Thos. Codgell exors. (*Mark*). Wit<sup>s</sup>:—Tho. Codgell sen<sup>r</sup>, W<sup>m</sup>. Bat𝔢, Tho. Codgell, Gruf. Owen scr. (*Pr.* 9 Mch. 1592-3).

f. 79. ELIZABETH NICHOLLS of East Barnet. (*Dat.* 7 Sep. 1592). Eliz. Graye my son Robert's dau; Eliz. Rolfe my daughters dau; Rich. and Robt. Nicholls my son Robert's sons; Agnes Nicholls that now dwelleth with me; Joane Nicholls my son Roberts dau; Sara Nicholls; Sara Lame; Old Gilberte; son. Robt. Nicholls exor. Wit<sup>s</sup>:—Sim. Thomson, Tho. Rolfe and Margt. Thompson. (*Pr.* 11 May 1593).

f. 79. JOHN BEDWELL of S<sup>t</sup> Margettes als Stansted theale, labourer. (*Dat.* 21 Aug. 1592). Wife Eliz. extrix; Eldest son Anth.; Lands in Amwell marshe; Second son Andrew; Third son John; Fourth son Ambrose; Fifth son Edward; Lands in Hodgden feild; Dau. Eliz. (*Mark*). Wit<sup>s</sup>:—Robt. Boothe, Robt. Essex. (*Pr.* 19 May 1593).

f. 82. JOHN HEADLAMME parson of Raylegh in Essex. (*Dat.* 3 Dec. 1593). Bur. 'by my sonne John Headlamme in Braughing church neere by the chauncell wall'; Son W<sup>m</sup>; Dau. Bridget Headlamme; M<sup>r</sup> Otway; Serv<sup>t</sup> Johan; Serv<sup>t</sup> W<sup>m</sup>. and his sist. Sibill; Legacy to poor of Braughing & Raleigh; George Lottie; M<sup>r</sup> Brograve; M<sup>r</sup> Hanchett; Wife Kath extrix. *Per me Johannem Headlamm, rectorem de Ralegh predict*. (*Pr.* 4 Mch. 1593-4).

f. 83. JOHN WALKER of Wormeley. (*Dat.* 27 Apr. 1591). Eliz. Walker my sons dau; My sister; Kinsman Robt. King; W<sup>m</sup>. Walker my sons son; Tho. Burgin; John Chandler & W<sup>m</sup>. Swanson of Hogsdon; Tho. Lowin and Tho. Johnson of Wormeley. M<sup>r</sup> Walpoole pson of Wormeley; Dau-in-law Kath. Turner; John Walker my sons son; Harry Maunder of Pimbridge; Son Robt. father of s<sup>d</sup> Eliz. W<sup>m</sup>. & John Walker; Isabell Bird; Grandson John Walker exor. Wife Kath. (*Mark*). Wit<sup>s</sup>:—Cesar Walpoole parson of Wormley, Nich. Turner. (Admon. during minority of exor, to John Cordell of Chesthunt, collier, his uncle on the mothers side.)

f. 97. RANDALL CLAYE of Wormeley. (*Dat.* 3 Dec. 36 Eliz.) Wife Eliz. extrix. Wit<sup>s</sup>:—Ceasar Walpoole, John Bumsteade ju., W<sup>m</sup>. Turner. (*Pr.* 28 Mch. 1595).

f. 97. THOMAS GLADIN of Wormeley, basketmaker. (*Dat.* 29 June 1595). Son Tho; Dau. Joane; Son W<sup>m</sup>. exor; My master Bumsted overseer. (*Mark*). Wit<sup>s</sup>:—W<sup>m</sup>. Malldon, W<sup>m</sup>. Warde, Tho. Bumstede. (*Pr.* 18 July 1595).

f. 99. RICHARD BENNINGE of Sarret, yeoman. (*Dat.* 16 July 1594). Second son Tho.; My new house in a piece of land called Longe Wheelers, lying between Great Wheelers & Wallnut tree close; Close called Woodfeild; Third son Robt; Two closes called Wheelers lying between Sarret greene and Woodfeild; Fourth son Geo. Benninge; Land called Hasardes in psh. of Watford; Fifth son Henry; Lands in psh. of Rickmansworth; Sixth son John; Close called Nutthazell close; Eldest dau. Mary Benninge; Second dau. Anne B; Third dau.

Ales B: Fourth dau. Eliz. B: Fifth dau. Johane B; Eldest son Richard: Wife Agnes extrix: Close called Chuise feilde; Tho. Hobbes & John Randall overseers. *Signum Richardi Bennynge.* *Wit*<sup>s</sup>:—John Ibotsonue, Nich. Cock. (*Pr.* 16 Sep. 1595).

f. 100. **THOMAS TYMBERLAK** of Rickmansworth, husbandman. (*Dat.* 4 May 1595). Son Thos.; Jerom Webbe my daughters son (under 16); Son in law Robt. Webbe; Dau. Susan wife of Rich. Hampton; Sons Ezechiell & Robert; Chalfont Warren; Richard Tyler; Wife Christian; Susan & Thos. Webbe my daughters ch<sup>n</sup>; Dau. Hampton's ch<sup>n</sup>; Serv<sup>t</sup> Geo. Huff; Serv<sup>t</sup> maid Sara; Edw. Harbinger of Chalfont; Wife & son Ezechiell exors; Neighbours Nich. Gybbe & Tho. Fotherley overseers. *Mark.* *Wit*<sup>s</sup>:—Tho. Fotherley, Nich. Gibbe. *Codicil dat.* 1 Sep. 1595 names Grace Hampton, serv<sup>ts</sup> Nich. Gibbe & Joane Pratt. *Wit*<sup>s</sup>:—Tho. Fotherley writer hereof, Nich. Gybbe, John Worrell & Richard Pye. (*Pr.* 17 Sep. 1595).

f. 103. **THOMAS SNELL** *alias* **WHEELER** of Ware. (*Dat.* 8 Aug. 1593). Wife Margt. extrix; Lease to one Evans; Houses & lands at Hartford; John Throughgood & Robt. Lilly my neighbours overseers; Three eldest sons Thos, Nich. & Randoll Snell; Dau. Johane; My two youngest sons (Dated 22 Aug. 1595). *Wit*<sup>s</sup>:—John Thorowgood, Robt. Lylly, Christr. Beadle, Tho. Snell, Tho. Feild, John Huchin. (*Pr.* 18 Sep. 1595).

f. 108. **JOHN RUSHLEY** of Ricmansworth, yeoman. (*Dat.* 2 Aug. 1595). Daus. Venice, Marye, Anne & Bettresse (minors); Tenement in Bachworth, parcel of the manor of Moore, situate over against the mill there; Sons John & Geo. (minors); Wife Mary extrix; Bro. Jerom Rusley & bro-in-law Jonas Robsonne. *Wit*<sup>s</sup>:—Tho. Fotherley, Wm. Winchester, John Rushley, Jonas Robson, Jarame Rusley, Wm. Brainch. (*Pr.* 4 Oct. 1595).

f. 109. **ALICE HEYDON** of Wattforde, widow. (*Dat.* 16 Aug. 1595). Son Geo. Reade & Susan his wife; Sons Hugh, Edw. & Wm. Reade; Dau. Anne Clarke; Son-in-law Geo. Knevett; Eldest son Rich. Reade; Lease called the White Harte in Wattforde; Brothers Thos. & Wm. Duck gents exors; Serv<sup>t</sup> Sibell Downes. *Wit*<sup>s</sup>:—Nich. Cowlburne the wrighter, Jas. Baldwin, Tho. Knevet. (*Pr.* 8 Oct. 1595).

f. 125. **WILLIAM EDLIN** the elder of Harewoodes in psh. of Watforde, yeoman. (*Dat.* 10 July 1595). Wife Sicelye; Messuage in Watford wherein Lewes Grave tanner dwells, which I lately bought of Poule Stepneth gent & Sara his wife, John Duncombe gent & Judeth his wife & Rich. Cuppedge gent & Sibill his wife; Son Wm; Dau. Susan Edlyn (under 21); Dau. Alice Baldwin; Son Jas; John Edlin son of my son Wm; House & lands called Bellwastes in Oxhey in psh. of Watford, in occ. of Giles Chaundeler & Robt. Hayward; House called Bellcroftes; Wm. Kentish; Isack Chettells; Drew Baldwin husband of dau. Alice; John Beckett of Watford, taylor; Jas. son of s<sup>d</sup> Drew Baldwin; Cicely Hall now dwelling with John Reddwood; The two sons of John Ablet; Daus. Rose Edlyn, Agnes Kentish, Alice Baldwin & Dorothie Gren; Wife extrix: Wm. Kentish & Raphe Gunthorpe overseers. *Mark.* *Wit*<sup>s</sup>:—Wm. Leonardes, Robt. Pratt, Raphe Gunthorpe, Geo. Readhead, Wm. Kentishe. (*Pr.* 12 Dec. 1595).

*To be Continued.*

# A List of Inquisitiones Post Mortem,

RELATING TO THE COUNTY OF HERTS, RETURNED INTO THE COURT OF CHANCERY.

## HENRY VII. TO CHARLES I.

| Name | Reign | Number |
|---|---|---|
| Adams, Robert | 20 Eliz. pt. 1 | number 65 |
| Adelmare, *alias* Cæsar, Julius knt. | 13 Car. I. pt. 4 | 159 |
| Alexander *alias* Milward, Wm. | 7 Eliz. | 100 |
| Alington, Philip | 37 Eliz. pt. 2 | 71 |
| Allen, Christr. | 30 Eliz. pt. 1 | 63 |
| Allen, Margery | 4 Eliz. | 100 |
| Alley, Francis | 42 Eliz. pt. 2 | 49 |
| Alley, Francis | 43 Eliz. pt. 2 | 55 |
| Alley, John | 42 Eliz. pt. 2 | 77 |
| Allington, Giles knt. | 28 Eliz. | 163 |
| Allington, Wm. | 1 Hen. VII. | 34 |
| Altham, Edward | 6 Jas. I. pt 2 | 74 |
| Altham, Jas. | 25 Eliz. | 176 |
| Altham, Jas. knt. | 8 Jas I. pt. 2 | 201 |
| Anderson, Rich. knt. | 11 Car. I. pt. 2 | 156 |
| Appleyarde, Roger | 21 Henry VIII. | 37 |
| Appowell, Margaret | 9 Jas. I. pt. 1. | 120 |
| Aprice, Wm. | 4 Edw. VI. pt. 1 | 122 |
| Arnold, Thomas 'fatuus' | 9 Jas I. pt. 2 | 50 |
| Arthure *alias* Fawsette, Anthony | Eliz. v. o. 1st bund. | 555 |
| Audeley, Henry | 37 Hen. VIII. pt. 2 | 84 |
| Audeley, Thomas, lord | 2 Edw. VI. pt. 1 | 100 |
| Audley, Margt. dau. of Thos. lord Audley | 14 Eliz. | 167 |
| Auncell, Thomas | 5 Jas. I. pt. 1 | 146 |
| Ayleworth, Humph. | 10 Car. I. pt. 1 | 117 |
| Babthorp, Ralph, knt. | 6 Hen. VII. | 66 |
| Bacon, Francis lord, visc. St. Albans | 10 Car. I. pt. 3 | 75 |
| Baeshe, Ralph | 40 Eliz. pt. 1 | 81 |
| Bailye, John | 10 Jas. I. pt. 1 | 141 |
| Baldrey, Geo. | 31 Hen. VIII. | 46 |
| Barington, Nich. knt. | 7 Hen. VIII. | 147 |
| Barkhamsted 'Dominus Leprosorum de' | 31 Hen. VIII. | 42 |
| Barle, Thos. | 16 Hen. VIII. | 101 |
| Barlee, Henry | 22 Hen. VIII. | 5 |
| Barlee, Wm. | 14 Hen. VIII. | 24 |
| Barley, Robt. esq. | 26 Hen. VIII. | 42 |
| Baryngton, Nich. knt. | Hen. VIII. v. o. 2nd bund. | 13 |
| Bashe, Nich. | 43 Eliz. pt. 2 | 104 |
| Basshe, Edw. | 29 Eliz. | 269 |
| Bassingborne, John | 32 Hen. VIII. | 64 |
| Baylye, John | 10 Jas. I. pt. 1 | 196 |

| | | |
|---|---|---|
| Baylye, John | 18 Jas. I. pt. 2 | 65 |
| Baynton, Andrew esq. | 13 Eliz. pt. 1 | 81 |
| Bedell, Cecily | Hen. VIII. v.o. 2nd bund. | 11 |
| Bedford, John, earl of | 1 & 2 Ph. & M. pt. 1 | 80 |
| Belfeild, Wm. | 1 Eliz. pt. 3 | 90 |
| Belfeild, Wm. | 3 Jas. I. pt. 1 | 122 |
| Bellfielde, John | 32 Eliz. | 13 |
| Bellamye, Henry | 26 Eliz. | 19 |
| Bellamye, Wm. | 7 Eliz. | 149 |
| Bennett, Eliz. | 8 Jas. I. pt. 2 | 19 |
| Bennyng, Robt. | 5 Eliz. pt. 1 | 78 |
| Bensted, Wm. esq. | Ric. III. & Hen. VII. v.o. | 83 |
| Benstede, Edw. knt. | 11 Hen. VIII. | 35 |
| Benstede, Wm. esq. | 1 Hen. VII. | 67 |
| Beomounde, Wm. viscount | 1 Hen. VIII. | 62 |
| Berisford, Rowland | 5 Jas. 1 pt. 2 | 8 |
| Besouth, John, gent. (21 Car.) | Eliz. Jas. Car. pt. 26 | 29 |
| Bibbesworth, Thos. esq. | 1 Hen. VII. | 75 |
| Bigges, Thos. | 3 Car. I. pt. 2 | 18 |
| Blackwell, Geo. | 7 Car. I. pt. 3 | 7 |
| Blackwell, Rich. esq. (21 Car.) | Eliz. Jas. Car. pt. 32 | 46 |
| Blackwell, Robt. | 22 Eliz. pt. 1 | 89 |
| Blossam, Thos. | 45 Eliz. | 76 |
| Blunt, Arthur, gent. (3 Car.) | Eliz. Jas. Car. pt. 24 | 186 |
| Blunt, Tho. Pope knt. | 15 Car. I. pt. 3 | 90 |
| Borough, Thos. lord | 5 Edw. VI. pt. 1 | 105 |
| Bostocke, Peter | 16 Jas. I. pt. | 49 |
| Boteler, John (see Leventhorpe) | Hen. VIII. v.o. 1st bund. | 37 |
| Boteler, John | 18 Eliz. pt. 1 | 72 |
| Boteler, Rich. esq. (12 Jas.) | Eliz. Jas. Car. pt. 2 | 49 |
| Boteler, Robt. knt. | 21 Jas. I. pt. 2 | 144 |
| Boteler, Wm. lord (17 Car. II.) | Eliz. Jas. Car. pt. 24 | 56 |
| Botiller, Wm. lord 'fatuus' | 13 Car. I. pt. 1 | 150 |
| Botteler, Philip | 5 Jas. I. pt. 1 | 149 |
| Boughton, John, esq. | 5 Hen. VII. | 131 |
| Bourcher, Anne lady, marchioness of Northampton | 13 Eliz. | 82 |
| Bourgchier, Tho. | 7 Hen. VII. | 3 |
| Bowlde, John | 1 Eliz. pt. 1 | 63 |
| Bowles, John | 35 Hen. VIII. | 14 |
| Bowles, John | 15 Car. I. pt. 3 | 84 |
| Bowles, Thos. | 39 Eliz. pt. 2 | 101 |
| Bowles, Thos. | 9 Car I. pt. 1 | 14 |
| Bowles, Thos. esq. | 14 Car. I. pt. 3 | 111 |
| Bownest, John | 13 Jas. I. pt. 1 | 77 |
| Bownest, Wm. | 11 Jas. I. pt. 3 | 157 |
| Bowyer, Thos. (5 Jas.) | Eliz. Jas. Car. pt. 2 | 50 |
| Bradbury, Thos. | 2 Hen. VIII. | 96 |
| Bradbury, Wm. | 4 Edw. VI. pt. 1 | 123 |
| Brakenfeild, John | 39 Eliz. pt. 2 | 82 |
| Brand, Geo. | Eliz. v.o. 3rd bund. | 127 |
| Brand, Thos. | 3 Car. I. pt. 2 | 95 |
| Brand, Tho. (20 Car.) | Eliz. Jas. Car. pt. 24 | 73 |
| Braughyn, Thos. | 6 Hen. VII. | 78 |
| Braughyng, Rich. | Hen. VIII. v.o. 1st bund. | 254 |

| | | |
|---|---|---|
| Breame, Edw. 'under age' | 10 Eliz. | 125 |
| Brewster, Margt. | 6 Jas. I. pt. 2 | 83 |
| Brisco, Edw. | 6 Jas. I. pt. 2 | 94 |
| Briscoe, Edw. | 13 Car. I. pt. 1 | 14 |
| Bristo, Robt. | 14 Jas. I. pt. 3 | 133 |
| Bristow, Nich. | 15 Jas. I. pt. 1 | 204 |
| Bristowe, Nich. | 27 Eliz. | 12 |
| Bristowe, Nich. | 5 Car. I. pt. 2 | 66 |
| Bristowe, Nich. esq. | 10 Car. I. pt. 3 | 6 |
| Brocket, John, knt. | 41 Eliz. pt. 1 | 42 |
| Brockett, Edw. esq. (43 Eliz.) | Eliz. Jas. Car. pt. 2 | 48 |
| Brockett, Helen, lady | 41 Eliz. pt. 2 | 76 |
| Brockett, John, knt. | 5 & 6 Ph. & M. pt. 2 | 83 |
| Brockett, Wm. | 8 Jas. I. pt. 2 | 29 |
| Brograve, John, knt. | 11 Jas. I. pt. 2 | 8 |
| Brograve, Simon | 15 Car. I. pt. 4 | 18 |
| Broket, Edw. esq. | 4 Hen. VII. | 30 |
| Brokett, John, esq. | 24 Hen. VIII. | 29 |
| Broughton, John | 11 Hen. VIII. | 110 |
| Broughton, Robt. knt. | 23 Hen. VII. | 67 |
| Broughton, Thos. | 11 Hen. VII. | 94 |
| Browne, Humph. knt. | 5 Eliz. pt. 1 | 75 |
| Browne *alias* Broun, John | 5 Edw. VI. pt. 1 | 80 |
| Bruce, Edw. knt. baron of Kinglosse | 11 Jas. I. pt. 2 | 25 |
| Bull, Rich. | 28 Eliz. | 188 |
| Burche, Thos. | 4 Edw. VI. pt. 1 | 124 |
| Burgoyne, Geo. | 31 Eliz. pt. 2 | 85 |
| Burrell, Henry | 14 Eliz. | 81 |
| Burwell, Henry | 11 Eliz. | 59 |
| Butler, Chas. | 7 Jas. I. pt. 1 | 97 |
| Butler, Henry knt. | 7 Jas. I. pt. 1 | 113 |
| Butler, John | 18 Hen. VIII. | 96 |
| Butler, Philip knt. | 37 Hen. VIII. | 109 |
| Butt, Chas. | 31 Hen. VIII. | 79 |
| Cæsar. *See Adelmare.* | | |
| Cage, Anthony | 25 Eliz. | 63 |
| Cage, Daniel esq. | 10 Car. I. pt. 3 | 77 |
| Calton, Henry | 35 Eliz. pt. 2 | 45 |
| Cambridge, Trinity College, 'ad quod dampnum' | 19 Hen. VIII. | 111 |
| Capell, Henry, knt. | 20 Jas. I. pt. 2 | 148 |
| Capell, Arthur, knt. | 8 Car. I. pt. 1 | 54 |
| Capell, Wm. knt. | 7 Henry VIII. | 25 |
| Cardye, John | 11 Car. I. pt. 2 | 129 |
| Carey, Edw. knt. | 17 Jas. I. pt. 1 | 104 |
| Carter, Rich. | 5 & 6 Ph. & M. pt. 2 | 86 |
| Carter, Robt. | 8 Car. I. pt. 3 | 75 |
| Carter, Wm. | 9 Eliz. | 130 |
| Cary, Henry, lord | 11 Car. I. pt. 2 | 30 |
| Carye, Adolphus knt. | 7 Jas. I. pt. 1 | 107 |
| Carye, Henry lord visc. Falkland | 12 Car. I. pt. 3 | 20 |
| Cason, Edw. esq. (2 Car.) | Eliz. Jas. Car. pt. 27 | 4 |
| Chamber, Rich. | 3 Edw. VI. | 75 |
| Chambers, Edw. (9 Car.) | Eliz. Jas. Car. pt. 21 | 141a |

| | | |
|---|---|---|
| Chambers *alias* Halsey, Wm. | 38 Eliz. pt. 1 | 7 |
| Chauncey, Henry | 29 Eliz. | 159 |
| Chaworth, Eliz., who was the wife of Wm. Chaworth knt. and late wife of John Dunham | 18 Hen. VII. | 33 |
| Cheney, John | 37 Eliz. pt. 2 | 65 |
| Cheney, John | 38 Eliz. pt. 2 | 58 |
| Chester, Edw. | 21 Eliz. pt. 2 | 8 |
| Chester, Magdalen, lady | 29 Eliz. | 231 |
| Chester, Robt. knt. | 17 Eliz. | 51 |
| Chester, Robt. | 16 Car. I. pt. 3 | 65 |
| Chester, Wm. | 26 Eliz. | 162 |
| Cheyne, John | 33 Eliz. pt. 1 | 93 |
| Cheyney, John | 14 Jas. I. pt. 3 | 58 |
| Child, Mathew | 11 Jas. I. pt. 3 | 131 |
| Child, Mathew | 11 Jas. I. pt. 3 | 134 |
| Child, Tho. gent. (20 Car.) | Eliz. Jas. Car. pt. 26 | 20 |
| Christian, John, gent. (14 Car.) | Eliz. Jas. Car. pt. 30 | 63 |
| Clanricard, Rich. earl | 13 Car. I. pt. 1 | 60 |
| Clare, Nich. | 5 & 6 Ph. & M. pt. 2 | 88 |
| Clarke, John | 3 & 4 Jas. I. v. o. | 32 |
| Clarke, John | 22 Jas. I. pt. 2 | 102 |
| Clarke, Thos. | 39 Eliz. pt. 2 | 60 |
| Clowes, Anth. (3 Car.) | Eliz. Jas. Car. pt. 24 | 156 |
| Cobham, Thos. knt. | 20 Hen. VII. | 56 |
| Cock, Henry, knt. | 8 Jas. I. pt. 2 | 200 |
| Cock, John | 4 & 5 Ph. & M. pt. 1 | 82 |
| Cock, Wm. | 9 Jas. I. pt. 1 | 160 |
| Cocks, John | 5 & 6 Ph. & M. pt. 2 | 84 |
| Coke, John, 'idiot' | 6 Edw. VI. pt. 1 | 96 |
| Coleman, Christr. | 8 Jas. I. pt. 2 | 38 |
| Colet, John, mercer of London 'ad quod dampnum' | 5 Hen. VIII. | 69 |
| Colet, John, clerk | 14 Hen. VIII. | 25 |
| Collett, Henry | 21 Hen. VII. | 31 |
| Colley, Rich. gent. (9 Jas.) | Eliz. Jas. Car. pt. 2 | 53 |
| Combes, Fras. esq. (20 Car.) | Eliz. Jas. Car. pt. 21 | 114 |
| Combes, Fras. | 2 Car. I. pt. 3 | 56 |
| Combes, Rich. | 37 Eliz. pt. 2 | 63 |
| Coningesbie, Fras. knt. (7 Car.) | Eliz. Jas. Car. pt. 30 | 35 |
| Connyngsby, Henry knt. | 34 Eliz. pt. 2 | 51 |
| Conyers, Thos. | 18 Jas. I. pt. 2 | 109 |
| Conyngesbie, Ralph, knt. (15 Jas.) | Eliz. Jas. Car. pt. 30 | 34 |
| Coop *alias* Godfrey, Fras. | 7 Car. I. pt. 3 | 50 |
| Copwood, John | 34 Hen. VIII. | 85 |
| Corbett, Robt. knt. | 5 Hen. VIII. | 70 |
| Corbett, Roger esq. | 30 Hen. VIII. | 120 |
| Corbett, Rowland | 11 Car. I. pt. 2 | 108 |
| Courtney, Gartrud | 37 Hen. VIII. | 93 |
| Cowper *alias* Godfrey, John | 11 Eliz. | 57 |
| Cox, Thos. | 16 Jas. I. pt. 1 | 46 |
| Coxe, John | 6 Car. I. pt. 3 | 41 |
| Coxe, Rich. knt. | 22 Jas. I. pt. 2 | 34 |
| Coxe, Thomas | 31 Eliz. pt. 1 | 62 |
| Crawley, Wm. | 7 Jas. I. pt. 1 | 92 |

| | | |
|---|---|---|
| Cressey, Constance, widow | Ric. III. & Hen. VII. v.o. | 51 |
| Crouche, John | 16 Jas. I. pt. 1 | 35 |
| Crowche, John gent. | 4 Jas. I. pt. 2 | 86 |
| Crowche, John 'melius inquirend' | 5 Jas. I. pt. 2 | 1 |
| Crowche, John | 14 Jas. I. pt. 3 | 50 |
| Crowche, Thos. | 15 Jas. I. pt. 1 | 147 |
| Cutte, John knt. | 17 Hen. VIII. | 169 |
| | | |
| Dacre, Geo. | 23 Eliz. pt. 2 | 56 |
| Dacres, Robt. | 37 Hen. VIII. | 89 |
| Dacres, Thos. knt. | 14 Jas. I. pt. 3 | 119 |
| Darcy, Robt. | 6 Hen. VIII. | 94 |
| Darvall, Henry (v.o. 1st pt. 6) | 6 Jas. I. pt. 2 | 11 |
| Daye, Ralph | 10 Car. I. pt. 3 | 43 |
| Delabere, Geo. | 15 Eliz. | 68 |
| Delawood, Fras. | 14 Jas. I. pt. 3 | 5 |
| Delawood, Fras. | 17 Jas. I. pt. 3 | 36 |
| Denny, Edw. | 12 Hen. VIII. | 49 |
| Dennye, Anth. | 4 Edw. VI. pt. 1 | 115 |
| Dennye, Edw. knt. | 43 Eliz. pt. 2 | 69 |
| Dennye, Hen. | 16 Eliz. pt. 2 | 85 |
| Derby, Edw. earl of | 15 Eliz. | 67 |
| Derby, Thos. earl of | 13 Hen. VIII. | 77 |
| Dockwra, Periam esq. (19 Car.) | Eliz. Jas. Car. pt. 32 | 97 |
| Dockwra, Thos. | 3 Jas. I. pt. 1 | 144 |
| Dockwraye, Thos. | 19 Jas. I. pt. 1 | 122 |
| Dodyngton, John | 38 Hen. VIII. | 102 |
| Dodynsell, Alice, widow | 8 Hen. VII. | 62 |
| Drewell, Rich. | 18 Hen. VII. | 119 |
| Drewell, Wm. | 1 Hen. VII. | 134 |
| Druell, John | 11 & 12 Hen. VII. | 12 |
| Druell, Rich. | 18 Hen. VIII. | 23 |
| Duke, John | 5 Jas. I. pt. 2 | 131 |
| Duncombe, Rich. | 3 & 4 Ph. & M. pt. 2 | 79 |
| Dune, Griffin knt. | 35 Hen. VIII. | 79 |
| Dunstable, Margt. | Ric. III. & Hen. VII. v.o. | 65 |
| Dysney, John | Ric. III. & Hen. VII. v.o. | 105 |
| Dysney, Wm. | 33 Hen. VIII. | 120 |
| | | |
| Edlyn, John | 18 Car. I. v.o. | 6 |
| Edmondes, John | 45 Eliz. | 34 |
| Edmonds, Henry, gent. (8 Car.) | Eliz. Jas. Car. pt. 21 | 118 |
| Ellys, Tho. gent. (12 Jas.) | Eliz. Jas. Car. pt. 2 | 54 |
| Elveden, Henry | 7 Hen. VIII. | 47 |
| Elveden, Henry jun. | 9 Hen. VII. | 24 |
| Emerson, Rich. | 5 Eliz. pt. 1 | 76 |
| Emerson, Wm. | 1 Mary | 49 |
| Eton, College of, 'ad quod dampnum' | 8 Hen. VIII. | 101 |
| Ewer, David | 8 Car. I. pt. 1 | 15 |
| Ewer, Thos. gent | 8 Car. I. pt. 1 | 27 |
| Exelbie, Wm. | 8 Car. I. pt. 1 | 26 |
| | | |
| Fairefax, Humph. | 21 Eliz. pt. 2 | 5 |
| Faldoe, Robt. | 21 Jas. I. pt. 2 | 53 |
| Falkland, Henry Lord Cary, visc. | 11 Car. I. pt. 2 | 30 |

| | | |
|---|---|---|
| Falkland, Henry Lord Cary, Visc. | 12 Car. I. pt. 3 | 20 |
| Fanshawe, Henry, knt. | 14 Jas. I. pt. 3 | 111 |
| Fanshawe, Thos. | 45 Eliz. | 104 |
| Feild, John | 11 Car. I. pt. 2 | 106 |
| Feilde, Wm. | 8 Jas. I. v.o. pt. 2 | 137 |
| Fenrother, Robt. | 16 Hen. VIII. | 99 |
| Ferrers, Geo. | 21 Eliz. pt. 2 | 2 |
| Ferrers, John, knt. | 16 Car. I. pt. 3 | 61 |
| Ferrers, Julius | 38 Eliz. pt. I. | 135 |
| Ferrers, Knighton | 16 Car. I. pt. 3 | 39 |
| Finch, Thos. | 8 Car. I. pt. 1 | 23 |
| Fish, Leonard | 15 Car. I. pt. 4 | 31 |
| Fishe, Thos. | 16 Car. I. pt. 3 | 38 |
| Fishe, Wm. | Hen. VIII. v.o. 3rd bund. | 15 |
| Fisher, Rich. | 41 Eliz. pt. 2 | 53 |
| Fisher, Rich. | 6 Jas. I. pt. 2 | 78 |
| Fitzherbert, Robt. | 7 Hen. VIII. | 95 |
| FitzJohn, Edw. (12 Jas.) | Eliz. Jas. Car. pt. 2 | 51 |
| Fitzwilliam, Thos. | 6 Hen. VIII. | 53 |
| Fitzwilliam, Wm. | 18 Hen. VIII. | 87 |
| Fitzwilliam, Wm. knt. | 27 Hen. VIII. | 21 |
| Fortescue, John | 10 Hen. VIII. | 126 |
| Fortescue, John, knt. | 16 Hen. VII. | 3 |
| Foster, Humph. | 4 Eliz. | 101 |
| Foster, John | 1 Eliz. pt. 1 | 64 |
| Fox, Wm. | 36 Hen. VIII. | 130 |
| Francklyn, John | 38 Eliz. pt. 1 | 96 |
| Francklyn, John | 39 Eliz. pt. 1 | 36 |
| Fraunces, Ralph | 27 Hen. VIII. | 4 |
| Freeman, John | 7 Jas. I. pt. 2 | 108 |
| Frowick, Tho. knt. | 22 Hen. VII. | 125 |
| Fyshe, John | Ric. III. & Hen. VII. v.o. | 136 |
| Fyshe, Leonard | 14 Car. I. pt. 3 | 79 |
| | | |
| Gale, Wm. | 9 Jas. I. pt. 1 | 164 |
| Gale, Wm. | 12 Jas. I. pt. 1 | 132 |
| Gape, John | 12 Car. I. pt. 3 | 38 |
| Gardener, Henry | 10 Eliz. | 127 |
| Gardener, John | 5 Edw. VI. pt. 1 | 107 |
| Gardner, Henry | 8 Eliz. | 122 |
| Garnett, Wm. | 2 Eliz. pt. 2 | 6 |
| Garrard, John, knt. | 2 Car. I. pt. 2 | 142 |
| Gaseley, John | 9 Jas. I. pt. 2 | 32 |
| Gelgate, Edw. | 14 Hen. VIII. | 27 |
| Gerrard, John, knt. & bart. | 13 Car. I. pt. 4 | 149 |
| Gery, Rich. | 12 Hen. VIII. | 78 |
| Gery, Robt. | 31 Hen. VIII. | 18 |
| Gibbe, Edw. | 5 Jas. I. pt. 1 | 89 |
| Gibbe, John | 4 Jas. I. pt. 2 | 47 |
| Gill, Geo. knt. | 22 Jas. I. pt. 2 | 95 |
| Gill, John | 43 Eliz. pt. 2 | 77 |
| Gille, Geo. esq. | 11 Eliz. | 58 |
| Gille, John | 2 Edw. VI. pt. 1 | 97 |
| Godfrey alias Coop, Fras. | 7 Car. I. pt. 3 | 50 |
| Godfrey alias Cowper, John | 11 Eliz. | 57 |

| | | |
|---|---|---|
| Godley, Blastus | 11 Car. I. pt. 2 | 76 |
| Goldesburgh, Joan, who was the wife of John | 13 Hen. VII. | 70 |
| Goodridg, Thos. | 5 Car. I. pt. 2 | 47 |
| Gostwyck, John, knt. | 37 Hen. VIII. | 95 |
| Grace, Rich. | 2 Eliz. pt. 2 | 8 |
| Graue, Edw. (11 Jas.) | Eliz. Jas. Car. pt. 2 | 45 |
| Grave, Edw. | 11 Jas. I. pt. 2 | 12 |
| Graveley, Fras. | 27 Eliz. | 42 |
| Graveley, Geo. gent. (43 Eliz.) | Eliz. Jas. Car. pt. 2 | 47 |
| Graveley, Rowland | 9 Jas. I. pt. I. | 162 |
| Graveley, Thos. | 26 Eliz. | 192 |
| Graveley, Thos. | 30 Eliz. pt. 1 | 104 |
| Graye, Anne | 3 Car. I. pt. 2 | 83 |
| Greene, Edw. son & heir of Cicely who was the wife of Robt. Greene knt. & late wife of John Acton | 8 Hen. VII. | 20 |
| Greene, Rich. | 9 Jas. I, pt. 1 | 174 |
| Greene, Rich. | 11 Car. I. pt. 2 | 37 |
| Grenehill, Henry | 6 Car. I. pt. 3 | 3 |
| Grey, Andrew | 13 Jas. I. pt. 1 | 75 |

*To be Continued.*

# Church Terriers.

## ALDBURY.

JULY 22 ANNO D'NI 1638.
ALDBURIE RECTORIE.

A TRUE SURVEY OR TERROR of all the landes & possessions belongindg to the Rectory of Aldebury in the County of Herford and in the deanrie of Barkhamsted made and tacken by the veiw and Esteimat of the [*blank*] Churchwardes and other inhabitans their whose names are subscribed as followeth:

Imprimis the Homstall or scite of the parsonage house scituate and lying betweene the kinges highway on both sides and butting theron on the West and the close of Hend Hvdnall on the east and conteinth by estimacion 2 Acres.

Item with in the said bounde is conteinad on garden hedged in containg 4 poles and on orchard plott by estimacon an acre.

Item in the parsonage house consisting of v baies built with timber wherof 2 baies are coverd w^th tyles chamber over and borded the rest are . . . . . . . thatch and are disposed into 8 roomes viz. the hall pls the butterie . . . . . . . the hay house and 3 chambers.

Item one barne consisting of 4 baies built w$^{th}$ timber and thached w$^{th}$ on little stabule and a carthouse of Three little baies.

Itē one close comonlie called Toms close ling betweene the lande one the south and the land of William Glenester one the north and butteth one the high waie one the west and a close called Jack Roberts one the east by estimacion tooe ackers.

Itē in the comonde feilde called above the waie one halfe acre in magis furlong betweene the land of William Johnson on the east and the land of Hend. Hvdnall on the weast and butteth north on Magis lane.

Itē one acre lying betweene the land of S$^r$ Thomas Hyde one the north and Bennet Winch south and butteth upon Bursden east and the high way one the west.

Itē an other acre in the same furlong abutting as before and lying betweene William Johnson on the north and Bennet Winch south.

Itē further in the feillde one halfe acre lying betweene the land of Bennet Winch on both sides and buteth vppon and hed halfe acre of Bennet Winch north and Richerd Youing south.

Itē one acre lying by the waie side and as butting on the land of Bennet Winch on the north and M$^r$ Hendrey Sandes on the south.

Itē in the same furloing one acre lying betweene the land of Bennet Winch on both sides and butting on the land of the said Bennet north.

Itē at the ends of the same acre on the south on acre lying betweene the land of John Barnes on the east and John Doggat on the west and abutteth vppon the land of Richard Youing on the south.

Itē one halfe acre in Wilbore Leshes betweene the land of Bennet on both sides abbutteth one land of Northcot Court on the east.

Itē an other acre lying betwene the land of Bennet Winch one the north and William Johnson on the south and abutteth west vppon an headland of Richerd Youing.

Itē vppon Rattlesbourne hill three Rodes betweene the land of Bennet Winch west and William Johnson est.

Itē further vppon the hill an acre betweene John Doggat on the east and Bennet Winch west and abbutteth vppon Hicke Downe.

Itē in Muckborow on acre Richerd Young on the west and Hendrey Hvdnall east and abbutteth on Peackburifeld south.

Itē by Tring feild side ney the waie one long halfe acre hauing Frainces Hall one the east.

Itē in Norfeilld one acre between the land of Edward Glenester one the south and Frainces Hall on the north and butteth on the high way one the east.

Itē in the same furlong on halfe acre betweene the land of Bennet Winch south and John Pell one the north.

Itē on acre betweene the land of Bennet Winch on the south and John Benning north.

Itē one head halfe acre having S$^r$ Thomas Hyd on the north and butteth on the headland of Bennet Winch on the west.

Itē on head acre having Richard Young on the east and Bennet Winch one the south.

Itē from thence on acre stretching in to Tring feilde betweene the land of John Beinge one the south and William Johnson north.

Itē in great Chiseley one halfe acre betweene the land of John Doggeat on the west and William Pelle on the east and Tymothy Davney north.

Itē in Micklefeild in Comley furlong on acre betwene the land of Bennet Winch on the north and Hendrey Hvdnall on the south.

Itē in the same furlong on acre betweene the land of Mr Sandes north and John Smart south.

Itē further in the feilde one short halfe acre betweene the land of Sr Thomas Hyde on the east and Richard Yonng one the west and buteth on the south vppon the headland.

Itē by Kinges peece on acre betweene the land of Sr Thomas Hide on both sides and one the end on the east.

Itē vnder the hedg one Roode having the land of John Doggeat on the west.

Itē in litle Chiseley vnder the hedg on acre having the land of Robart Dvncombe south.

Itē in great Chiseley one acre betweene the land of John Doggdat on the north and Robart Dvncombe south and butteth on the high way one the west.

Itē on other white acre lying betweene the land of Bennet Winch on the west and William Glenester on the east and abbutteth north on Bursden and south on Northot Cort.

Itē one halfe acre in Hawcroft Deane betweene the land of Hendrey Hvdnall on the east and Bennet Winch west and abbutteth as before.

Itē in Capthorne furlong one acre lying betweene the land of Robart Dvncombe north and of Hendrey Hvdnall south and buteth on the high waye.

Itē on other acre in the same furlong lying betweene the land of William Johnson on the south and the land of Samuell Pattrig north.

Itē one acre in Steane furlong lying betwene Sr Thomas Hyde on the west and Samuell Pattrig on the east and abbutteth north on the head land.

Itē on halfe acre in short Catmur betweene the land of John Doggdat one the East, Hendrey Hvdnall west and butteth south on Doggdates headland.

Itē in Stonie craft an acre and a Rood togither lying bettweene the land of Bennet Winch on the west and Richard Hvdnall east and butteth one the high waie on the south.

Itē one the other side of the waie one acre and three Rodes betweene Bennet Winch on the west and Hendrey one the east.

Itē in the same furlong on head acre abbutting one the high waie one the easte and lying by the land of Samuell Pattrig south.

Itē one the Knole on halfe acre betweene the land of Samuell Pattrig one the north and Sr Thomas Hyde south and buteth one the land of Sr Thomas Hyde west.

Itē in Sharpenedg one acre betweene the land of John Doggeat one both sides and butteth on the land of Mr Hendrey Sandes west.

Itē in the same furlong another acre lying betweene the land of Hendrey Hvdnall south and Sr Thomas Hyde north.

Itē one halfe acre abutting on Pitseyhed one the north and lyeth betweene the lande of Mr Hendrey Sondes on the east and Sr Thomas Hyde one the west.

Itē in Waterforrowes on acre betwene the land of John Smart one both sides.

Itē at Pendley lainende one acre betweene the land of William Johnson south and Bennet Winch north.

Itē in the same field one halfe acre betweene the land of John Doggat on the west and William Pelle on the east and Tymothy Davney north.

Itē in Frainkleden one acre between the land of Bennet Winch one the east and John Doggat one the west and abbuteth south one William Smart and north on John Doggat.

Sm. totalis 41 acres.

[*The rector has here inserted the following note:* 'This terrier of Glebs, gardens, orchards, howses, is answeirables to y<sup>e</sup> former ancient terrier & so farr forth y<sup>e</sup> sett to my hand: Thomas Gilpin rector.']

Itē the tyth hay and herbage of lordes meade belonging to the lorde of Aldebury lying betweene the pishes Northchurch and Wigginton are paible tow the parsson of Aldebri.

Itē all mainor of tythes of twoo closes belonging to Thomas Putnam of Hawridgs conteining six acres more or lesse and lying betweene the pishes of Hawrid and Wiggdinton are paiable by custome to the Rectorie of Aldebury and never detained and yearly paid in money vjs. viijd.

[(*Marginal note.*) 'Abowt 1638 ap<sup>d</sup> Wheth: Bennett Winch & John Daveney came & affirmed . . . since the giving of this Terrier that Thomas Puttnam doeth not intend to maintaine this Custome but yeilds to paye his tythes in kinde for this pticuler. (*Signed*) Bennet Winch, sig. John Daveney.']

Itē w<sup>th</sup>in the pish of Tring the tyth hay of viij ackers on Lowsey Hill belonging to the lord of Alldebury and of one hooke of M<sup>r</sup> Cheyneis lying on the west thereof and another hooke at the ende therof on the south called Hebby Hooke.

Itē of one acre on the east called Madge acre and on the east therof of twoo halfe acres beloing by Custome to the Rectori of Aldeburie and never detained.

Itē of acre in Wingrave mead called Cheiker acre.

Itē of one acre of Goddard<sup>s</sup> lying in Tring pish abbutting one the pastures of my lord willut on the south and short Sebroke one the north.

Itē of on acre in the pish of Dratton Beaucham called Brooke acre.

Itē of three Rodes of M<sup>r</sup> West lying by Hobling slack.

Itē of hed acre of meade by Pegg<sup>s</sup> more late beloinging to Stonell Heddeng Harmans hooke.

Itē of Harmans hooke belonging to M<sup>r</sup> West are payable to the Rectorie of Aldeburi and never detained.

Itē all the tythes of M<sup>r</sup> West house and pasturs in Goblecot are payable by Custome vnto the Rectorie of Aldeburie and all small the small tythes of his Close called Ten akres lying within the pish of Tring.

Itē wich ther hath beinge payed yearley for tythes by the Oners of Trying parsonag at Easter by Custom iij<sup>l</sup>.

Itē ther hath being payed yearley for all the small tythes of the mainor and farme of Pendley by the owners and occupiers vnto the Rectore of Aldebury at Esster payed in money by Cusstome toow poundes.

Itē ther hath being payed yearley by the owners of Penley at Esster in money for all the Corne and great tythes by Custome Three poundes six shillens and Eaight pennces.

[*Signed*]. Bennet Winch }
John Davney } Churchwardens.
Edward Whitman, William Smart his marck.
John Barnes his marke, Fraince Hall his marck.

[*The rector adds*] 'This terrier concerning out tyths & custome y<sup>e</sup> am confident, tends to y<sup>e</sup> damage & detriment of y<sup>e</sup> church & therefor y<sup>e</sup> refuse to set to my hand.'

## ALDENHAM.

APRILL 11TH 1638.  A TERRIER of the Lands Houses & Portions of Tithes & other emoluments belonging to y^e Vicaridge of Alldenham in y^e Countye of Hartford & Diocesse of Lincolne.

Inp. a vicaridge house standing on the east side of the Churchyard now in good repaire containing a kitchen, Hall, Parlor, 5 lodging Roomes, a barne, a stable & other out houses.

Item an orchyard, a garden, a little pikle of ground adjoyning to it.

Item seauen acres of Glebland called Pigmer scituate & being on y^e south east side of y^e Church adjoining next boyonde the Parke.

Item a Rode of ground within the Parke costing all along the Glebland Hedge for w^ch is payed from the Lord to the Vicar xs. p annum.

Item a Rode of medowe ground in le heymead *alias* Ashey meade.

Item all profitts arising from Chancell or Churchyard ground are the Vicars.

Item to y^e vicar is due the tithe of Lambe & Wooll & all other tithes whatsoeuer. saue Corne & Hey.

Item all oblations & mortuaryes.

Beniamin Spencer vicar.

Churchwardens } John Nicoll. Henry Francis.

---

Aldenham: in the County of Hertford 1674 Septem. 14.

There are Seven acres of arable Land belong to the vicaridge.

An Orchard & church yard w^th a Little slip of ground by estimation two acres.

A faire vicaridge house w^th an adjacent barne, very well in repaire & fenced about.

William Finch } Churchwardens.
Thomas Dell

---

# Notes relating to the Family of Penn.

## INQUISITIONES POST MORTEM.

### RALPH PENNE.
[*Inq. p.m. 2 Hen. VII. No.* 16.]

Inquisition taken at Hertford 'die sabbati prox. post festum Omnium Sanctorum,' 2 Hen. VII. [1486], before John Tey, esheator, by the oaths of Roger Strete, John Kyng, Tho. Hill, Tho. Dowde, Wm. Fader, John Bukney, Tho. Stokes, Tho. Cook, Wm. Broude, John Hert, John Reynold & John Ive, who say that Ralph Penne was seised as of fee of the manor of Pygott̃, a messuage called Pennes Place & 70 acres of land in Aldenham, and a messuage & 20 acres of land in the parish of Illestre & so seised, by a certain indenture shewn to the said jurors on the taking of this inquisition, enfeoffed Humph. Conyngesby, Rich. Grotmore, Wm. Skipwith & Thos. Coke to the use & intention of preserving the s^d Humph., Wm. & Thos. & their executors indemnified against John Penbury & Alice his wife etc. etc.

The said Ralph was also seised of the manor or messuage called Charyngys, a messuage called Eydens, a messuage called Wodes, a messuage called Rolues and 40 acres of land & 12 acres of wood in the parishes of Aldenham, Illestrye, Rugge & Shelney & so seised enfeoffed John Verney knt. late esquire & Humph. Conyngesby, to the use of s^d Ralph to fulfil his last will [*fully recited*].

The manor of Pygotts & Penns Place are held of the Abbot of S^t Peter's, Westminster. The manor of Charyngs & messuages called Wodes & Rolues are held of John Foster as of his manor of Welde & are worth 8*l*. per ann. The messuage called Eydens is held of the heirs of Robt. Louth & is worth 4*l*. per ann. The 20 acr. in Illestre & 30 of the s^d 40 acr. of land are held of the Abbot of S^t Albans & are worth 40*s*. per ann. & the remaining 10 of the 40 acr. & the 12 acr. of wood are held of Wm. Stonore as of his manor of Shelney Hall & are worth 5*s*. per ann.

Ralph Penne died 3 Oct. I Hen. VII. [1485] & John Robarth is 'consanguineus' & next heir & aged 16 years & more.

## JOHN PENNE, ESQUIRE.
[*Inq. p.m. 5 & 6 Phil. & Mary. Pt. 2. No. 87.*]

Inquisition taken at West Barnet *alias* West Chepynge Barnet, 18 Oct. 5 & 6 Phil. & Mary [1558] before John Wiseman, escheator, after the death of John Penne esquire, by the oaths of Rich. Grubbe, Rich. Birchemore, Hen. Kentishe, Hen. Rusheley, Wm. Royse, John Feelde, John Wilkoxe, Tho. Marson, Tho. Baldewyn, Robt. Nutkyn, John Redwood, Miles Gallewey, Wm. Shardley, Wm. Rolfe & Wm. Chestre who say that

The late King Henry VIII. was seised as of fee, of the manor of Codycott & so seised by letters patent dat. 7 Nov. 37 Hen. VIII. [1545], granted his said manor to said John Penne & Lucy his wife.

And so seised John Penne died & Lucy his wife survives at Coddycott.

John Penne & Lucy his wife were also seised of the manor of Sissiferns *als*. Syssyfernes & 30 acr. of land & wood in Coddycott late belonging to John Chyld & Edw. Fylyan *als*. Russhelyn, viz: - to him & the heirs of s^d John Penne & so seised John Penne died 21 Aug. last past & the s^d Lucy survives.

The manor of Coddycott is held of the king & queen *in capite* & service of the fortieth part of a knights fee & services & a rent of 3*l*. 15*s*. 10*d*. per ann. & is worth 18*l*. per ann. The manor of Syssifernes is held of the king & queen in free socage & not in chief & is worth 30*s*. per ann.

Thomas Penne gent. is son & next heir & aged 25 years 9 months & 18 days & more.

## ROBERT PENNE, GENTLEMAN.
[*Inq. p.m. 35 Eliz. pt. 2. No. 97.*]

Inquisition taken at Hertford, 8 June, 35 Eliz. [1593] before Richard Glascocke, escheator, after the death of Robert Penne gent. by the oaths of Fras. Symondes, John Smithe, Tho. Hodge, Edm. Asser, Tho. Glascock, John Taylor, John Fynche, Robt. Dawson, Edm. Yonge, Wm. Grave, Geo. Gynne & Tho. Smithe who say that

Robert Penne was seised as of fee in 2 messuages, a cottage, 3 orchards, 3 gardens, a dovecote, 340 acres land, 20 acr. meadow, 30 acr. pasture & 30 acr. wood in Codycott, Wellwynne & Kimpton & so seised said Robert & Dorothy then his wife, by licence of the Queen first obtained, by a fine levied at Westminster in Mich. Term 28 Eliz. granted said messuages & lands to Robt. Graye & Tho. Yonge & the heirs of s^d Robt. Graye for ever. And s^d Robt. Penne & Dorothy by indenture dat. 15 Dec. 28 Eliz. [1585] declared that s^d Graye & Yonge by virtue of s^d fine, should stand seised of certain parcels of land in Codycott called Codycottbury, le Inner yarde, le foreyarde *als.* Greenfeild, le Reckyarde, le Hovell yarde, le hemplande, le Orchyarde, a piece of land lying betweene the Orcheyarde & le Wick, a piece of land called le Wick & the site of the manor aforesaid, le Green, Lowewood, the Launde, le Slipe, Woodesden Valie, Conydell fielde with 2 hedgerowes adjoining, Conydell Springe, Seu'all Thyckney, Thickeney Bottome, Churche Hill, Churchwood, with a close adjoining, Rolses wicke, Lyshott, Churchfielde, le great medowe, 3 acr. land in Common Thickney hill, and 1 acr. land in same field, to the use of Walter Gray & Anne Penne & the heirs of s^d Anne for ever; and of & in other parcels & premises lying in Wellwynne & Codycott, called Hollwarde *als.* Parke, Pond Close, Bottome close, Longe Croft, le farther close, Coksell grove, 7 acr. & a half in Cokreth fielde, Pounsons acre *als.* Coksell close, 3 roods & 10 parts of land lying in same field, half an acre & 5 parts of land in same field, 1 acre meadow in Coksell meade, 2 acr. land in same field called Coksell fielde next Coksell grove, 6 acr. 3 roods in Okeallfielde, 1 acr. & 4 parts of land in Pullforde fielde, 3 roods in Cokrethfielde, half an acre & 6 parts of land in same field, 3 roods land in Pullforde fielde, 1 rood in Coksell feilde, half an acre & 20 parts of land in same field, half an acre & 30 parts of land in same field, one acre in Groundsell feilde, 10 acr. in Okeallfielde, Cokrethfielde close, half an acre & 10 parts land in same field next same close, 7 acres & 3 acres of land in same field, 2 acr. adjoining same in same field, 9 acr. & 1 rood adjoining same, 4 acr. enclosed in same field, 4 acr. & a half enclosed lying between same field & Marcolse feilde, 1 piece of land in Pullfordefielde, 7 acres & a half land in same field, 3 acr. & a half in same field next the gate leading into same field, 3 acres in same field called Pullfordefeilde, Padmeade, Froggmeade, & Cokreth Ryddye, to the use of s^d Robert Penne & Dorothy his wife for life & after the death of the survivor to the use of Susan Penne dau. of s^d Robt. & Dorothy, her heirs & assigns for ever; and of another parcel of land & wood in Codycott called Cokrethwood, to the use of s^d Robt. & Dorothy his wife for life & after the death of the survivor to s^d Susan Penne & her heirs, with remainder to the use of the right heirs of s^d Dorothy for ever; and of other parcels in Codycott viz. a cottage, a rood of meadow in Herringmeade & 2 swathes there, & other parcels called Myllmeade, Willowhedgemeade, 1 acr. meadow in Westmeade, 8 acr. land in Rayfielde, 10 acr. land in Westfielde, 2 acr. & a half land in Hayden, 3 acr. & half land in Marcolsefeilde between Ryddy aforesaid & a close called Whelers & a close & parcel of land called Churchfeilde & Highe heathe, to the use of s^d Robt. & Dorothy for life & after the death of the survivor, to the use of Dorothy Penne dau. of s^d Robt. & Dorothy & her heirs & assigns for ever.

So seised Robt. Penne died 4 Feb. 35 Eliz. [1592-3] at Codicote & Dorothy survived.

The tenements in Codycott limited to the use of Walter Graye & Anne Penne are held of the Queen in chief, by knight's service, by the hundredth part of a knight's fee & are worth 6*l*. 13*s*. 4*d*. per ann. The tenements in Wellwyne & Codycott limited to the use of Robt. & Dor. Penne with remainder to Susan Penne, also the land called Cockrethwoode in Codycott are held of the Queen in chief by knight's service, by the hundred & twentieth part of a knight's fee & are worth 4*l*. 6*s*. 8*d*. per ann. The tenements in Codycott limited to Dorothy Penne the dau. in remainder, are held of the Queen by knight's service by the 140th part of a knight's fee & are worth 3*l*. per ann.

Said Anne, Susan & Dorothy the daughters are of the following ages viz. Anne aged 28, Susan 26 & Dorothy 20.

### THOMAS PEN, GENTLEMAN.
[*Inq. p.m.* 1 *Jas. I. pt.* 1. *No.* 21.]

Inquisition taken at Hertford, 19 Aug. 1 Jas. I. [1603] before Henry Fanshawe knt., Wm. Curll esq. one of the auditors of the Kings Court of Wards & Liveries, John Courtman esq, escheator & Robert Carter gent. feodary, after the death of Thomas Pen gent, by the oaths of Henry Bull gent, John Smith, Wm. Mannistie, Tho. Glascocke, Edw. Asser, Robt. Mann, John Fynche, Tho. Kirbie, Edw. Peede, Wm. Sewarde, Robt. Spencer, Tho. Smith, Robt. Dawson & Wm. Nicholson *als*. Carter who say that

Thomas Pen was seised as of fee of the manor of Codicote *als*. Corricote (except 2 messuages, a cottage, 3 orchards, 3 gardens, 1 dovecote, 340 acres land, 20 acr. meadow, 30 acr. pasture & 30 acr. wood in Codicote, Welwen & Kympton, late parcels of the demesne of the manor of Codicote & formerly granted by s[d] Tho. Pen & Lucy Pen, widow, his mother, to Robt. Pen gent. late deceased, brother of s[d] Thomas), also of 30 acr. land & wood in Codicote formerly belonging to John Childe & Edw. Fyliam *als*. Russhelyn.

The said manor [*not previously mentioned*] of Sissifornes is held of the king in chief, by knight's service & is worth 10*l*. per ann. The manor of Codicote *als*. Corricote (except as aforesaid) is held of the king in chief, by the fortieth part of a knight's fee & a rent of 33*s*. 4*d*. per ann. & is worth 4*l*. per ann. The lands & wood formerly of John Child & Edw. Fyliam *als*. Russhelyn, are held of the king, but by what service the jurors know not, & are worth 30*s*. per ann.

Tho. Pen died 13 July last past & Thos. Pen is next of kin & heir (viz. the son & heir of John Pen, son & heir apparent whilst he lived of s[d] Thos. Pen senior) & was aged 15 years on 24 June last past.

# Subsidy Rolls for Hertfordshire.

### HUNDRED OF DACORUM, 1545.

INDENTURE made the 5th July 37 Hen. VIII. whereby [John Conyngesby, John] Broket, Tho. Skipwythe, Henry Heydon, Rich. Raynshawe & . . . [Heyworthe] esq[rs] commissioners allotted within the hundred of Dacorum, appoint John Jeames of Northmymes, yeoman, high collector.

[N.B.—g. stands for 'goods,' l. for 'lands.']

## DACORUM HUNDRED.

Hertf. **HEMEL HEMPSTED** cum membris videlicet Bouyngdon & Flaunden. Rich. Combes gent. l. xxs. Robt. Emes l. vjs. viijd. John Rolff of Pygott g. iijs. iiijd. Tho. Feld g. xiijs. iiijd. John Parteriggo g. iijs. iiijd. John Pope of Hyllende g. iiijs. Wm. Syster g. iijs. iiijd. John Roger g. xiijs. iiijd. John How of Gadbrige g. vs. iiijd. Rich. Mayne g. xvjs. Tho. Axtell g. xiijs. iiijd. Tho. Golde sen. g. xvs. iiijd. John Golde jun. g. xvjs. Tho. Golde jun. g. xiijs. iiijd. Roger Hunt g. iijs. iiijd. John Southende g. iijs. iiijd. Rich. Prynce g. vs. iiijd.

*Sm.* vijli. xixs.

**BERKHEMPSTED.** John Waterhouse gent. l. xxs. John Long gent. g. xiijs. iiijd. John Alee g. xviijs. viijd. Rich. Monoxe g. xiijs. iiijd. Roger Clerk g. vs. Robt. Grubbe g. xiijs. iiijd. John Phyllip g. xiijs. iiijd. John Penne g. iijs. iiijd. John Halsey g. xiijs. iiijd. Robt. Guye g. xiijs. iiijd. Wm. Fremau g. iijs. iiijd. Eliz. Hewet widow g. iiijs. iiijd. Henry Dauncer g. iijs. iiijd.

*Sm.* vjli. xviijs.

**TRYNG MAGNA.** Tho. Blaket g. xiijs. iiijd. Robt. Sende g. iijs. iiijd. John Colyns g. vs. iiijd. Jas. Wylliams g. iiijs. John Foster g. iijs. iiijd. John Norton g. iiijs.

*Sm.* xxxiijs. iiijd.

**DUNESLEY** cum Grove. John Dagnall g. vjs. John Felde g. xiijs. iiijd. Tho. Bate g. iijs. iiijd. Wm. Grace g. vjs. John Foster g. iijs. iiijd.

*Sm.* xxxijs.

**STUDH'M HAMLETT.** Wm. Bellfeld g. [v? s.] Summa patet.

**GADDESDEN.** Rich. Pare gent. lands & fees . . . . . . Gilbert Pare gent. l. . . . . Wm. Halsey g. . . . . . Geo. Wells g. . . . . . Wm. Young g. . . . . John Knyght . . . . Rich. Knyght . . . . Robt. Halsey . . . . John Ryngsoll . . . . . . . .
   Gaddes . . . . . .
   Wyllester . . . . .

**PUTENH'M.** Thos. Graunge g. iijs. iiijd. John Thornton g. iijs. iiijd.

**LONGMERSTON.** Rich. Duncombe g. xxs. John Godderd g. xxvjs. viijd. Robt. Aleyne g. vs.

*Sm.* ljs. viijd.

**WYGGYNGTON.** *Nil.*
. . . . . . . . Thos. . . . . John Robyns g. . . . . . Rich. Heyward g. xiijs. iiijd. Robt. Albright g. vjs. viijd. Rich. Payse g. xvjs.

*Sm.* lvs.

**CADYNGTON & MERKEYATE.** Tho. Bray l. xxd. Robt. Denner g. iijs. iiijd. Tho. Mershe g. xiijs. iiijd.

*Sm.* xviijs. iiijd.

**LANGLEY REGIS.** Tho. Ketyll gent. g. xxvjs. viijd. Robt. Perle g. xiijs. iiijd. Ralph Ewer g. xiijs. iiijd. Nich Aldwyn g. xiijs. iiijd. Nich. Kyng g. iiijs. iiijd. Tho. Carter g. iijs. iiijd. Robt. Roberts g. iijs. iiijd.

*Sm.* iijli. xvijs. viijd.

ALBURY. Tho. Harmon g. xiijs. iiijd. Barth. Ryppyngton g. iiijs. vd. Rich. Duncombe g. vs.
   Sm. xxijs. ixd.

COLSYLL. Nil.

FLAMSTED. Nich. Drables l. viijs. viijd. Barth. Payse g. iijs. iiijd. Barth. Payne g. iijs. iiijd. Rich. Halsey g. iijs. iiijd. Mich. Lodge g. iijs. iiijd. Rich. Halsey junr. g. iijs. iiijd. Tho. Bradwyn g. iijs. iiijd. Wm. Smyth g. iijs. iiijd. John Smyth g. xiijs. iiijd. Rich. Whytley g. iijs. iiijd. Wm. Grygg g. vs. Tho. Coke *alias* Lee g. xiijs. iiijd. Joan Okyng wid. g. iijs. iiijd. John Blakwen g. iijs. iiijd. Wm. Symonds g. xiijs. iiijd. Hugh Slowe g. iijs. iiijd.
   Sm. iiijli. xs. iiijd.

HARPDEN cum Hamlet de Tytburst. Edm. Bordolf esq l. iijl. Wm. Cressey gent. g. xiijs. iiijd. John Lee g. xiijs. iiijd. Tho. Ivery g. xiijs. iiijd. Wm. Fryth, g. iiijs. vd. John Ryman g. xiijs. iiijd. Wm. Kylby g. iijs. iiijd. Robt. Cutt g. iijs. iiijd.
   Sm. vjli. iiijs. vd.

TYTBURST. Edw. Brystoo g. xxs. Wm. Fletcher g. xiijs. iiijd. Wm. Chalkhyll g. xiijs. iiijd. Alex. Bayly g. iiijs. S. . . . . Cokdall g. iijs. iiijd. Eliz. Warne . . . . . . . s.

WHETH'MSTED. John Brokett esq l. vjl. John Bu . . . . . . gent l. xlvs. . . . . yent g. xls. . . . . g. xxs. . . . . g. iijs. iiijd. . . . . iijs. iiijd. . . . . iijs. iiijd.
[Traces of seven other names remain but the document is sadly mutilated.]
   Sm. xiijli. vs. viijd.

SHENLEY. Lady . . . . Clyfforde wid. l. vjli. Rich. He . . . gent. l. ls. Tho. . . . ys gent. g. vs. Thos. Heywarde g. xiijs. iiijd. Tho. Dyche g. xiijs. iiijd. Nich. Pate g. iijs. iiijd. Wm. Fraunc g. vs.
   Sm. xli. xs.

NORTH MYMS. John Conyngesby esq. l. ixli. Henry Grubb l. ijs. iiijd. Thos. Snowe l. ijs. Agnes Je . . . . s wid. g. xiijs. iiijd. Geoff. Hyll g. iiijs. viijd. John Jeamys g. iijs. iiijd. Henry Rushley g. iijs. iiijd. Henry . . . . esfeld iiijs. vd. Rich. May . . . . g. iijs. iiijd. John Cole g. iijs. iiijd. Tho. Roberts de le Hyll g. iijs. iiijd. Tho. Roberts de Water ende g. iijs. iiijd. John Hode g. vs.
   Sm. xjli. xjs. ixd.

NORTHCHURCH. John Sare g. xiijs. iiijd. Tho. Axstall g. xiijs. iiijd. John Axstall g. vjs. Wm. Wetherhedd g. iiijs. vjd. Rich. Kene g. iijs. Wm. Whytley g. iijs. iiijd. John T . . . . . g. vs. Wm. Typtoo g. iijs. iiijd. Nich. Hutchynson g. iijs. iiijd.
   Sm. lvjs. ijd.

BUSSHEY. Thos. Walker gent. . . . . . . . . . . . . .
   [Rest missing].

# Abstracts of Wills.

## ARCHDEACONRY OF HUNTINGDON (HITCHIN REGISTRY).

### REGISTER III. 1579 to 1614.

f. 1. JOHN GRAUE the elder of Muche Mūdeu, yeoman. (*Dat.* 10 Jan. 1579). Sons John, Geo, Henry, Edwd; Daus. Kath. (under 20), Bridget; Son Wm. (under 24); Sons Tho. & Robt.; Peter Esgae my man; Wife Margt extrix; Cous. Robt. Graue of Newgate in psh of Stansted. W*it*ˢ:—Wm. Curlewis clarcke, Robt. Graue, Thos. Grave. (*Pr.* 11 Oct. 1580).

f. 1ᵇ MARGERY SKARBOROWE widowe of Walcorne. (*Dat.* 20 June 1578). Daus. Sara & Dorothy: Son Thomas Ralfe; Son Wm. Skarborough exor. W*it*ˢ:—Edward Wilson, Edw. Norwood, Rich. Pake & John Wat'man. (*Pr.* 9 Nov. 1580).

f. 2. ALCE CHILT'TON widow of Wm. Chilt'ton late of Aston decᵈ (*Dat.* 14 Sep. 1579). Bur. at Aston; Geo. Reve of Aston: John Mardall of Shephall & Eliz. wife of Henry Lucye of same town my husbands godchⁿ; Goddau. Beatrice Ratchurche; John Cop; Goodman John Kent of Aston; Henry Kent of Aston; John Byncke of Shephall; Sons Robt. & Wm. Pecock; My other five childⁿ had by Wm. Chilt'ton; Symon Browne of Shephall; Son Wm. Pecocke; Husband George Pecocke; Bro. Symon Ginne exor. W*it*ˢ:—John Kent, Wm. White, Symon Browne & Wm. Butler. (*Pr.* 9 Nov. 1580).

✓ f. 2ᵇ THOMAS CHAKELYE of Flamsted, husbandman. (*Dat.* 6 July 22 Eliz.) Dau. Ellin; Son Wm; Dau. Kath; Wife Agnes & eldest son Thos exors. John Astwicke of Flamsted overseer. W*it*ˢ:—Robt. Hasye thelder, Rich Hasey, Thos. Smithe, John Boorne & Firmin Adams, writer. (*Pr.* 11 Oct. 1580).

f. 3. WILLM CLARCKE of Weath'msted, yeoman. (*Dat.* 11 Jan. 21 Eliz.) Son John; Lands & tenements in Bps. Hatfield, in occ. of Thos. Field; To poor of Harpeden xₛ. Poor of Sandridge xₛ. 'To Mʳ Docter Goodman deane of the collegiat churche or colledge of St. Peters in Westminstʳ and to the Masters & Schollers of the same howse the sume of vj*li*. xiij*s*. iiij*d*. of the wᶜʰ sume of vj*li* xiij*s*. iiij*d*. namelye I geue & bequeth vnto Mʳ Deane xl*s*.' etc; Sons Thos. & Edw.; Dau. Johan Svbley & her two daus. viz. Margt. & Anne Sibley. Son John & Thos. Northe of Herons one of the yeomen of her maᵗⁱᵉˢ honarable chamber, exors. Mʳ Docter Goodman deane of Westminster overseer. W*it*ˢ:—Rich. Vause & Rich. Whyte. Codicil 1 June 22 Eliz. names Francis Sibley my daughters son, and Alce & Margery my maid servants. W*it*ˢ:—George Burden gen, Rich. Vale gen, Rich. Thomas Crawley, [*sic*] Wm. Wraste. (*Pr.* 12 Oct. 1580).

f. 3ᵇ WILLM ROLFE of Hemilh'msted, yeoman. (*Dat.* 23 Jan. 22 Eliz.). Son Rich: Dau. Margt. Rolfe; Dau. Issabell Puddifat; Hughe Sowthen: Dau. Eliz. Stone: Dau. Johan Sowthen; Dau. Agnis Shadde; Alexʳ son of Alexʳ Stone; Wm. son of Rich. Rolfe; John Shade; Dor. Shadde; Margery Rolfe dau. of Rich. Rolfe; Rich., Robt. & Thos. sons of Rich. Rolfe; Rich., Thos. & Wm. sons of Hugh Sowthen; Agnis & Helen daus. of Hugh Sowthen; Wm. son of Wm. Martin; My 4 daus; Son Robt. & Alce his wife; Son Robt. exor. *Witˢ* :—Richard Gawton, minister, Rich. Dolte, John Bunne, Robt. Shadde. (*Pr.* 23 Mch. 1579-80).

f. 4ᵇ ELIZABETH BIGGE of Kings Hatfield *alias* Bishops Hatfield, widow. (*Dat.* 10 July 1580). Daus. Agnis & Ellin; The sonne of John Clarcke of the beche wᶜʰ my daughtʳ Elizabeth Bigge bare vnto him (under 12); Cosen Thos. White; Sist. in law Johan Barton of Hartford; Son John Bigge & Son Geo. exors; Wm. Grubbe thelder overseer. *Witˢ* :—John Dunwill, John Hawkes & Geo. Gurley *alias* Griffin. (*Pr.* 20 July 1580).

f. 5. ELIZABETH FIELD of Little Gaddisden, widowe. (*Dat.* 30 Apr. 1580). Son John (under 20); Dau. Eliz; Bro. John Field exor; Bro. John Puddiforde overseer. *Witˢ* :—Tho. Windsor clercke, Wm. Edmundes, John Puddiford & Wm. Field. (*Pr.* 20 July 1580).

f. 5. THOMAS TOODE of Kimpton. (*Dat.* 17 Jan. 1580). Eldest son Tho; House & lands in Kimpton; Lands in the churchefield, millefield & weste field; Son John (minor); House in occ. of Robt. Laine in Kimpton; Lease of ground which Tho. Catlin now holdeth of me; Lease of Mr. Nich. Brocket; Wife Margt. extrix; Tho. Todde of Luton & Gilb. Greine overseers. *Witˢ* :—Jas. Alrede vicar of Kimpton, Tho. Hynde, John Ancell, Nich. Tayler. (*Pr.* 13 Sep. 1580).

f. 5ᵇ WILLM ALLIN of Aston. (*Dat.* 30 June 1579). Rich. Hills of Anstye; Legacy to poor of Anstye & Aston; Sist. Johan Cooke; Sist. Johan Coule; Sist. Margt. Dickᵉ; Eliz. Martin; Agnis Allin; Thos. Cooke; Symon Alberye; John Cobem; Wm. Rofe; Wm. Wood; Bro. John Allin exor. *Witˢ* :—Tho. Chapman, Geo. Refed, John Cobem. (*Pr.* 20 July 1580).

f. 6. JOHN NORTHE thelder of psh of Allhallowes in Harford, yeoman. (*Dat.* 8 July 1580). Daus. Anne & Mary; House in Sᵗ Andrews psh. which Andrew Mande now dwelleth in; Wife Eliz.; Son John; Wm. & Robt. sons of Leonard Gurley my son in law; Son John exor; Son in law John Heathe overseer. *Witˢ* :—Geo. Turner minister, John Heath. (*Pr.* 11 Oct. 1580).

f. 6. AGNIS NORRIS of town of Hartford. (*Dat.* 20 June 1579). Eldest son John; Tho. Norris; Christʳ Norris; Wm. Norris; Daus. Margt. & Jone; Christr Norris & Wm. Norris exors. *Witˢ* :—Wm. Clarcke vicar of Amwell, John Mauldon, Peres Patmare. (*Pr.* 20 July, 1580).

f. 6ᵇ THOMAS MYLES of Flamsted. (*Dat.* 29 July 1580). Son Water; Dau. Isabell (under 18); Goddau. Jane Baselye; Wife Eme extrix; Bro. in law John Fuller & son in law Robt. Stepney overseers. *Witˢ* :—Thos. Norburye, Robt. Stepney, Wm. Alce, Tho. Camfyle. (*Pr.* 12 Oct. 1580).

f. 6b **THOMAS ARCHER** of Baldocke. (*Dat.* 26 July 1580). Son John (minor); House in Hitchin; Son Geo. (under 21); Son Sam; Wife extrix: Bro. John Cullicke overseer. *Wit*s:—Anthony Fage, Edw. Hynde, John Manison, Andr. Pratte & Jas. Wilson. (*Pr.* 11 Oct. 1580).

f. 7. **WILLIAM ANDREWE** of Flamsted, husbandman. (*Dat.* 30 Nov. 1580). Son Robt. (under 23); Son John (under 21); Wm. son of my son in law Rich. Straighte; Wm. & Alice son & dau. of my son Wm. Andrewe; Dau. Johanne wife of Rich. Straighte; Son Tho. Andrewe, exor; Land in Clarks felde; Wife Margt; Neighbour Robt. Brydon supervisor. *Wit*s:—Robt. Boydon [*sic*] Robt. Halsey *alias* Chamber thelder, John Payes, John Munde, Wm. Bigge & John Atwoode. (*Pr.* 18 Jan. 1580-1).

f. 7b **THOMAS NORRIS** of psh of Allhallowes in Hartforde, shomaker. (*Dat.* 19 Dec. 1580). Dau. Eliz. (under 18); Wife Mary extrix; Bro. in law John Springham & John Redington overseers. *Wit*s:—Geo. Turner minister, John Springham & John Redington. (*Pr.* 18 Jan. 1580-1).

f. 8. **GEORGE SEARLE** of Walcorn. (*Dat.* 21 Nov. 1580). Wife Kath. extrix. *Wit*s:—Geo. Norrice, Moyses Wright, Tho. Colbye the wryter. (*Pr.* 18 Jan. 1580-1).

f. 8. **BENNET RUSHELYE** of Northemyms. (*Dat.* 22 April 1576). Son Henry; House called Polecatte; Wife Awedry; Son Wm; House & mill at Hodesdon; Field called Littell hills; Wm. son of Henry Rushelye; Daus. Alice & Eliz.; The 5 chn of son Henry viz. Bennet, Wm., John, Thos. & Eliz; The 3 chn of my son in law Thos. Jeames viz.:—Thos, Awedrye & Johann James; Cysselye dau. of Robt. Horrwoode; Wife & son Wm. exors; Son Henry overseer. (*Pr.* 15 Feb. 1580-1).

f. 8b **RICHARD COCKE** of Great Munden, husbandman. (*Dat.* 1 Mch. 21 Eliz.) Wife Margt.; Sons Robt, John, Rich., & Wm; Wife extrix. *Wit*s:—Wm. Curleawes clarke, & Anth. Daughton. (*Pr.* 15 Feb. 1580-1).

f. 9. **JOHN HALL** of Ashewell. (*Dat.* 16 Jan. 1580). Son John & daus. Johanne, Margt, & Mary (all under 21). (Admon. with will annexed 18 Jan. 1580-1 to Wenifrid Hall relict):

f. 9. **GEORGE LINCOLN** of Therfelde, yeoman. (*Dat.* 18 Oct. 1580). Wife Eliz; Son Geo.; Son Henry exor. *Wit*s:—Wm. Say, Edw. Hassarde & Thos. Smithe clerke the writer herof. (*Pr.* 8 Dec. 1580).

f. 9b **EDWARD ROBINS** of Kennisworth, yeoman. (*Dat.* 16 Nov. 1580). Eliz. Heywarde; The chn of John Capon viz. John the eldest son, Wm, Jane & Margery Capon; The chn of bro. Robt. Cooke viz. Rich. his eldest son, & Thos. Cooke; The chn of bro. Rich. Pedder viz. Henry, Alice & Rich. Pedder; Robt. Barboure & Tho. Heywarde both of Kennisworth; Bro. Robt. Robins; Lands in the feldes of Kennisworth lately bought of Rich. Albrighte of Dunstable; Henry Marshe; Bro. Robt. Robins exor; Robt. Barboure overseer. *Wit*s:—Robt. Barbur, Tho. Heywarde, John Heywarde, Wm. Heywarde & Edw. Heywarde. (*Pr.* 8 Dec. 1580).

f. 10ᵇ FLORENCE WATTSON of Bucklande in psh. of Therfilde, widow. (*Dat.* 12 Mch. 1572). Dau. Johanne Addams: Dau. Margt. Osbostone; Dau. Alice May; Dau. Kath. Tunke: Sons Robt., Henry, John & Wm. Watson; Bridget May dau. to Alice May; Eliz. Watson dau. to John Watson; Kath. May dau. to Alice May; Mary Watson dau. to Henry Watson; Anne Watson dau. to John Watson; Johanne & Jane daus. to my son John Watson; Son Wm. exor; Son John overseer. *Witˢ*:—John Watson, Hen. Watson, John Pitches & Thos. Adams. (*Pr.* 6 June 1580).

f. 10ᵇ JOHN WEST of Litle Barkehamsted, husbandman. (*Dat.* 4 Nov. 23 Eliz.) Son John West: My 3 daus. by my first wife; My 4 sons Robt. Wm. Salamon & Edward; Wife Eliz. extrix. *Witˢ*:—Rich. Wickᵉ, John Penyfather. (*Pr.* 8 Nov. 1581).

f. 11. SIMON BULLYN of Purton, laborer. (Nuncupative. *Dat.* 14 Sep. 1581). Eliz. & Joan Marshall daus. of John Marshall of Purten; Bro. Henry Bullyn; Wido. Carter & 5 of her chⁿ; Wm. Grige; John Marshall; Jeffrey Fraincis; Eliz. Hanscowie; Oliver Laurence; Thos. son of Henry Bullyn; Eliz., Joan & Agnes Marshall; Wife Ellyn extrix. *Witˢ*:—Robt. Hanscome, Tho. Bullyn, & Herie Bullyn. (*Pr.* 7 Oct. 1581).

f. 11ᵇ JOHN HAWGOOD of Hemelhamsted, yeoman. (*Dat.* 7 Sep. 23 Eliz.) Daus. Agnes, Margrit & Alice; My two young sons John & Frauncis; Son in law Tho. Marson; Griseld Flinden sist. of the sᵈ Thomas; My sist. Eliz. Humfrie; My other children; Henry son of Rich. Puddfast of Robinhood; Wife Emme & son Rich. exors; Bro. John Tailor overseer; Godson John Knolton. *Witˢ*:—Rich. Gnoton minister, Nich. Martin, Rich. Puddifast of Robinhod, John Talor. (*Pr.* 6 Oct. 1581).

f. 12. HENRIE TOKEFEELD of Baldocke. (*Dat.* 10 July 1581). Son Thos; Lands in Radwell; Son Henry; Messuage in Welles streat in Baldock wherein John Haydie now dwells & next the messuage of John Manyngson on the south and lands in Norton; Wife Jane; Lands in Bigrave & Clotall; Son Leonard; Son Wm; Messuage in Wells street wherein Leonard Hamant now dwells; Lands in Wiliem; Son Daniel; Daus. Annis, Jone & Allse; Cous. Gorge Larke; Sist. Finche; Tho. Scegge & Wm. Speed; Bro-in-law John Smythe overseer. *Witˢ*:—Wm. Chatburne, Rich. Knight, John Scegge, Geo. Larle & John Smyth. (Date of probate not given. Will badly written & testator's name given as Colfeyld, but at f. 14ᵇ the will is again and more correctly registered. Date of probate 7 Oct. 1581).

f. 12ᵇ WILLIAM CATLYN of Harpeden, yeoman. (*Dat.* 14 Apr. 1581). Willm Brigges curate of Harpeden; Bro. John Catlyn; Sist. Jone Angill; John Dary theldʳ; Myghell Dary; Alice Burton; Ellyn Hunte; Robt. Tomkyn, Rich. Auncill, John Coop, Eliz. Auncill & Eliz. Chamber; Dau. Eliz. Sible; Geo. & Sallomon Sible, Eliz. Sible & John Sible; Dau. Agnes Catlyn; Son Wm. (under 18); Wife Grace; Lands at Harpeden & Wethamstede; Wife extrix; Wm. Hunt overseer. *Witˢ*:—Tho. Nichols, Wm. Hunt, Tho. Cut, Tho. Fynch, John Halse, Rich. Squier, Wm. Bur, John Lewes, Tho. Christian. (*Pr.* 21 June 1587).

## ABSTRACTS OF WILLS.

f. 13. EDWARD HUMBERSTON of Walkhorne. yeoman. (*Dat.* 5 Apr. 1583). Wife Agnes: Eldest son Wm. (under 26); Second son Geo, & youngest son John (both minors); Eldest dau. Agnis (under 18); Second dau. Sislie; Bro. John Humberston; Bro. Wm. Humberston; Alce Hagger my sisters dau; Servants Robt. Clarke, Jeames Sheppte, Blase Nashe, Isbell Rayment & Agnis Gilbert; Mr. John Clarke vicar of Potton; Mr. John Headlam vicar of Graffin [*sic*]; Mr. Broweman vicar of Sandon: Wife extrix; Father in law Wm. Clarke overseer. *Wit*ˢ:—Wm. Middelton, clarke & Wm. Clarke. (*Pr.* 10 July 1583).

f. 13ᵇ WILLIAM SCINER of Wilstorne in psh. of Tring, laborer. (*Dat.* 27 Sep. 1570). Bur. at Tring; Dau. Annis; Tenement in Long Marston; Cottage in Tringe; Dau. Eliz.; Cottage that John Clarke dwelleth in; Wife Annis; John Learey; Wm. Lake & Robt. Sebrooke exors. *Wit*ˢ:—John Lake, Wm. Lake, & Robt. Sebrook. (*Pr.* 21 June 1581).

f. 13ᵇ WILLIAM YEORKE of Harpeden. (*Dat.* 8 Apr. 25 Eliz.) House & land to bro. Geo. Yeorke; Margaret North; Wm. Roo of Redbourne; Nich. Kylbe; Agnis North; Tho. Hayworth; Sist. Alice extrix; Tho. Chressey & Nicholas Kylbe overseers. *Wit*ˢ:—Thomas Chressey, Tho. North, Nich. Kylbe & Wm. Lane. (No date of probate given).

*To be Continued.*

---

# Feet of Fines for Hertfordshire.

### TUDOR PERIOD.

(CONTINUED FROM VOL. I., PAGE 348.)

1567-8. Hilary Term. 10 Eliz. (*Cont.*).

Robt. Mounson esq. & Rich. Loue gent: Giles Lloyd son & heir of Evan Lloyd decᵈ & Nichˢ Chowne cit. & haberdasher of London & Eliz. his wife. Messuage & lands in Aldenham.

Edw. Styward: Wm. Hyde. Lands in Sandon & Layston.

Henry Hickeman: James Pargeter gent & Kath. his wife. Manors of Bornehall & Hartesborne & 20 messuages & lands in Busshee.

Wm. Bawnett: Anthony Prior & Margt. his wife, Robt. Birbuge & Agnes his wife, Edmund Richard & Marion his wife & Eliz. Londines *alias* Jermyn. Four parts of a messuage & lands in Anstey & Great Hormede, into seven parts divided.

Christʳ Marshall: John Brokett esq & Ellen his wife. Messuage & lands in Ipollettᵉ *alias* Pollettᵉ.

Wm. Barlee & Ivo Grey gents: Wm. Bawnett & Hellen his wife & Wm. Warde & Joan his wife. Six parts of a messuage & lands in Anstey & Hornemead *alias* Great Hormeade, into seven parts divided.

### 1568. Easter Term. 10 Eliz.

John Knyghton esq: John Byrcheley gent & Phillippa his wife. Lands in Bayford & Hertford.

Edw. Baeshe esq & Thomasine his wife: Tho. Couldeham gent. Messuage called Jackrobyns & lands in Leyston, Buntyngforde, Affledwyche, Beauchampes & Crogyswylnes.

John Ivery & Robt. Darcknoll: Geo. Rotheram esq & Jane his wife. Messuage & lands in Kings Walden, Kympton, Whethamsted & Marckyate.

Nich⁸ West esq: Roger Harman & Kath. his wife. Manor of Goblecote & eight messuages & lands in Goblecote, Aldeburye *alias* Abery & Tringe.

John Danyell: Peter Rosewell & Dorothy his wife. Messuage in Hertford.

Tho. Kyghtley esq: Humph. Fayrefax, Robt. Savege & Wm. Raynes & Eliz. his wife. A barn & lands in Est Barnett.

Robt. Higbyde: Tho. Whyttymore & Anne his wife. Three messuages in Hitchen.

Matthew Mallett gent: John Fermer & Joan his wife dau. & heir of Andrew Clyfton. Messuage & lands in Bishops Stortforde.

John Parrys: Tho. Parrys & Alice his wife. Two messuages & lands in Stockyng Pelham & Brent Pelham.

Wm. Cecill knt, principal secretary of the Queen: John Parratt & Jane his wife & John Staple & Cecily his wife. Two messuages & lands in Chesthunt.

### 1568. Trinity Term. 10 Eliz.

*Anthony Cage, Edw Hampden esq, Tho. Asshefeld esq & Edm. Wyseman gent: Michael Hampden esq. Manor of Norcothyll *alias* Norcotcourt & 8 messuages & lands in Northchurch, Tryng & Wygynton.

*Nich⁸ Fitzhugh gent: Edw. Bridges gent & Frances his wife. Manor of Grenehall & lands in Sandon.

Rich. Brytnell: John Saunders & Isabel his wife. Messuage & lands in Long Marston.

John Sanders *alias* Burton: John Chappell & Emote his wife. Two messuages & land in Whethampsted.

Tho. Higate esq: Tho. Tyndale esq. Land in East Barnett.

Clement Guñell: Ralph Dixon gent & Ann his wife. Messuage & lands in Aschewell & Henxworth.

Rich. Baker senior: Wm. Ferneley & Bridget his wife. Lands in Great Monden.

Nich⁸ Bacon knt. lord keeper of the Great Seal & Anne his wife: John Machell esq & Frances his wife. A watermill, lands & free fishery in psh. of Sᵗ Michaels near Sᵗ Albans & Redborne.

Rich. Barbour & Agnes his wife: Geo. Bedell, Rich. Bedell & Simon Bedell. Messuage & land in Stondon.

### 1568. Mich. Term. 10 & 11 Eliz.

*Valentine Dale, doctor of laws: John Forth. Six messuages & lands in Baldocke, Wellen, Bigrave & Norton.

Wm. Clerke esq: Tho. Tyndale esq. Lands in Est Barnet.

Wm. Powlter gent: Adam Wylson. Messuage in Hertford.

Tho. Docwra: Tho. Garnons gent & Alice his wife & Wm. Hawkẽ gent. Manor of Puryton *alias* Pyrton & ten messuages & lands in Puryton *alias* Pyrton, Ikleforde & Kympton.

Wm. Nicoll: Alan Nicoll & Petronilla his wife. Messuage & land in Ilestrey.

Wm. Aylwarde: Wm. Huett gent. Messuage & lands in London Colney in psh. of Shenley.

John Mershe gent: Wm. Barlee gent. & Eliz. his wife. Moiety of lands in Bucklond & Barkwey.

Henry Chauncey gent. & Edw. Hubberd gent: John Chauncey gent. & Eliz. his wife. Manor of Overhall in Gedleston.

Wm. Frankelande: Geo. Burrell gent. Messuage & lands in Hoddesden, Broxburne & Hamwell.

### 1568-9. Hilary Term. 11 Eliz.

Wm. Kympton: John Myston & Anne his wife. Two parts of the manor of Roxeforth *alias* Rokesforth & of lands in Hertyngfordbury.

Rich. Holforde & John Hall: Rich. Smyth gent. Two messuages & land in Hertford.

Wm. Bygge & Eliz. his wife: Rich. Hyckman & Eliz. his wife. Messuage & land in Bishops Hatfeild.

Rich. Howe: Wm. Shelley. Lands in St Albans.

Roger Shadd: Hugh Mantell gent. & Eliz. his wife. Two messuages & land in St Albans. Warranty against sd Hugh & Eliz. & the heirs of sd Eliz., also against John Shadd & Margt. his wife & her heirs, Henry Webbe gent. & Alice his wife & her heirs & Stephen Cartelledge, junr, & against the heirs of Stephen Cartelledge senr decd father of the sd Eliz.

### 1569. Easter Term. 11 Eliz.

*Thomas Smalewod: Robt. Staunford esq & Roger Carewe esq & Alice his wife. Lands in Northmymmys.

Nich{s} West esq: Tho. Halsey *alias* Chambers & Margt. his wife. Lands in Northbarkhamsted.

Robt. Grave & Tho. Grave: John Yerlynge. Messuage & land in Hoddesdon & Brokkesbone.

Ralph Sadler knt: Jas. Hennage gent & Margt. his wife. Manor of Dooes *alias* Dowces & messuage & lands in Standon.

John Stubbes & Joan his wife: Robt. Holmes & Alice his wife. Two messuages & land in Watford.

Robt. Pope: Zachary Smyth gent. & Kath. his wife. Messuage and lands in Gosshams Ende in the parishes of Barkhamsted Mary *alias* Northchurche & Barkhamsted St. Peter *alias* Grete Barkhamsted.

Robt. Tomson: John Archer & Alice his wife. Messuage in Amwell.

Andrew Grey gent: Tho. Lambert gent. & Anne his wife. Three messuages & lands in Hinxworthe, Calcott & Asshewell.

Robt. Cage: Tho. Burton & Thomasine his wife, John Ward & Agnes his wife & Edw. Ward son of sd John. Four messuages & lands in Hunsdon & Estwicke.

### 1569. Trinity Term. 11 Eliz.

Robt. Gravenor: Wm. Andelsby. Lands in Stondon.

Wm. Stokes & Lucy his wife: John Derycke & Eliz. his wife. Messuage in Watford.

John Laurence: Rich. Lee knt., Humph. Connyngsbye esq & Mary his wife, Rich. Maydwell & Jas. Rogers. Four messuages in psh. of St. Albans.

Henry Foster: Tho. Docwra esq. & Mildred his wife. Messuage and lands in Kings Walden & Offlaye.

Edw. Skegges gent: Edw. Bray knt & Mary his wife. Manor of Quenehawe *alias* Quenehoo. Twelve messuages & lands in Branfeld *alias* Brantfeld, Tewyng, Watton, Stapulford, & Dacheworthe.

John Purevey esq : Walt. Tooke gent. & Angeleta his wife. Moiety of two messuages & lands in Amwell & Brickenden & common of pasture in Amwell Marshe, Nethinghoe Marshe & Amwell Heathe.

Hugh Moyser : Peter Harman & Joan his wife. Messuage in Hytchyn.

Nich. Bacon knt. lord keeper of the great Seal of England : John Marston & Eliz. his wife. Land in psh. of S$^t$ Michaels near S$^t$ Albans.

Fras. Powre gent. & John Lenthall gent : Edw. Denton gent. & Joyce his wife. Manors of Holwell *alias* Holdwell Greye & Ludwicke & 16 messuages & lands in Holwell Hide, Ludwicke Hide, Digonswell, Welwyn, Kings Hatfeilde *alias* Bps. Hatfeld, Twyng & Hartingfordbury, and free warren in Holwell & Ludwicke.

### 1569. Mich Term. 11 & 12 Eliz.

[Very few of the feet of fines and none of the notes for this term exist.]

Wm. Frankelande : Geo. Burrell gent. Messuage & lands in Hoddesden, Broxburne & Hamwell.

*Valentine Dale doctor of laws : John Forth gent. Six messuages & lands in Baldocke, Wellen, Bygrave & Norton.

### 1569-70. Hilary Term. 12 Eliz.

*Giles Poulett esq als Lord Giles Poulett & Wm. Chyvall : Margt. Caulton wid. & Wm. Caulton. The rectory of the church of Willey als Willyen & an annual rent out of & the advowson of the vicarage of the same church.

*Edw. Wyngate : Rich. Trowghton & Jane his wife. Manor of Keynesworthe & 10 messuages & lands in Keynesworthe.

*Tho. Russell : Tho. Sherley esq & Anne his wife, Christ$^r$ Rythe gent. & Kath. his wife. The 3rd pt. of lands in Ridge.

*Wm. Cecill knt. principal secretary of the Queen : Anne, marchioness of Northampton *alias* Lady Anne Burchier & Lovayne, dau. & heiress of Henry, lord Burchier & Lovayne earl of Essex & Ewe & Marie his wife one of the daus. of Wm. Say knt. dec$^d$. Manors of Baas, Perryers *alias* Perrers, Hoddesdon *alias* Hoddisdonberye, Geddyngs, Langtons, Foxtons, Maryons, Halls, Jerkyns, & Jerkyns Fee & 120 messuages & lands in Broxborne, Hoddesdon, Wormley *alias* Wormesley, Cheston *alias* Chesthunt, Amwell, Langtons, Foxtons, Maryons, Halls, Jerkyns, Sawells, Cockeshutt, Conygarth, and the psh. of All Saints, Hertford.

Rich. Baker : Tho. Myles & Eliz. his wife. Lands in Great Monden.

Edw. Felde : Fras. Mathew & Margery his wife. Messuage in Barkhampsted Peter.

Nich. Baeshe & John Hipworthe gents : Tho. Lovell esq. Messuage & lands in Chesthunte & Waltham Crosse.

Leonard Rogers : Tho. Claxsonne & Margt. his wife. Two messuages in Ware.

Tho. Letcheworthe : Jas. Letcheworthe & Alice his wife. Messuage & land in Asshewell.

Wm. Crawley & Rich. Spicer *alias* Helder : John Spicer *alias* Helder. Manor of Wells *alias* Welberye & lands in Great Offley, Lynley *alias* Lyly & Little Hetchyn.

Wm. Pulter gent. & Kath. his wife : Adam Wylson & Kath. his wife & John Wylson & Isabel his wife. Two messuages in Hertford.

Wm. Ketheringe *alias* Deye & Agnes his wife : Jas. Gryffyn & Alice his wife. Messuage in S$^t$ Albans.

Tho. Foster senior, gent : Edw. Stowell & Joan his wife. Lands in Hunsdon.
John Turuey : Jas Cowper & Joan his wife. Messuage & lands in Keneswourthe.
John Done : Robt. Bestney gent & Ellen his wife. Messuage & land in psh. of S$^t$ Michaels in S$^t$ Albans.
Robt. Grave & Simon Waypole *alias* Nobbes : Tho. Grave. Messuage & lands in Stansted Abbott.
Geo. Ferrers esq & Margt. his wife : Eliz. Bardolphe wid. & Edm. Bardolphe esq. son & heir app. of s$^d$ Eliz. Messuage & lands in Redburne & Flamsted.
Rich. Platt : Rich. Seale gent. & Eliz. his wife, & Robt. Seale. Messuage in S$^t$ Albans.
Wm. Skipwithe esq : Eliz. Barnes wid. one of the daus. & heirs of Margery Maynard & Robt. Cotes & Dorothy his wife another of s$^d$ daus. & heirs. Manors of Westwyke Apsebery & Praye with Kyngesbury & 40 messuages & lands in pshs. of S$^t$ Peters, S$^t$ Michaels & S$^t$ Stephens in S$^t$ Albans, & the advowson of the vicarage of S$^t$ Michaels.
Tho. Johnson : Walt. Myldmaye gent. & Anth. Tunbridge. Lands in Sabridgeworthe.

*To be Continued.*

# Abstracts of Wills.

## ARCHDEACONRY OF MIDDLESEX (ESSEX AND HERTS).

REGISTER "RAYMOND"—Continued from Vol. I. Page 376.

f. 223. THOMAS BATTSFORTH of Buntingford, husbandman. (*Dat.* 2 Feb. 1571). Bur. at Laiston ; Christian now my wife ; Son in law Robt. Roiston & Margt. his wife my dau ; Son in law Nich. Birles & Johane his wife my dau. ; Wife extrix. *Wit$^s$* :—Robt. Ayer, John Harrys & Wm. Clere. (*Pr.* at Stortford 8 Mch. 1575).

f. 223. THOMAS SHORTER of Ware, husbandman. (*Dat.* 25 Mch. 1575). Margt. now my wife ; House in Cripstreet *alias* Crib street in Ware ; Youngest son Tho ; Wife extrix. *Wit$^s$* :— John Laicok, Wm. Bonam, Wm. Wenham & Roger Sayer. (*Pr.* at Stortford 12 Dec. 1575).

f. 224. JOHN BIRDE of Thorlie. (*Dat.* 21 Oct. 1575). John Birde my bro. George's son ; My wifes sisters children ; Son Wm ; Messuage called Mandefelds in which I live in Thorlie & lands in Thorlie & Sabridgworth ; Land called the Hampstalls ; Tenement called Baustrets ; Godson Wm. Birde my son John's son ; John son of son John Birde ; Henry Roche ; Dau. Johane Brette wife of Giles Brett ; Tenement in Hockerell in Stortford ; Lands called Lewes felde, Shortescrofte, Bulfans meade in Gt.

Hallingbury, co. Essex; Dau. Suzan: My 3 daus. Johane, Alice & Grace: Rich. Pounte: Son. Wm. exor; Sons in law Rich. Pount & Giles Brette & Wm. Barnard overseers. *Wit*ᵉ:—John Miller, Wm. Miller & Wm. Barnarde the writer. (*Pr.* at Stortford 12 Dec. 1575).

**f. 226.** WILLM REYNOLDE of Thundriche, joiner. (*Dat.* 28 Aug. 1575). Daus. Johane, Grace & Kath; Wife Isbell extrix; John Laurence overseer. *Wit*ᵉ:—Wm. Dixon minister, Fulke Curlewes, Raffe Carter, Thos. Phillipps, John Lingewode. (*Pr.* at Stortford, 7 Nov. 1575).

**f. 226.** JOHANE EDMUNDE of Harestrete in psh. of Muche Hormed, wid. (*Dat.* 2 Oct. 1575). Sons Thos, John, & Henry; Daus. Margery & Kath. Edmunds; Dau. Agnes Churche; Mother Broke; Son in law Rich. Reignolds; Alice Reignolds of London; Dau. Eliz. Edmunde extrix. *Wit*ᵉ:—John Diason vicar of Much Hormed, Rich. Hawke, Wm. Colles & Henry Edmunde. (*Pr.* at Stortford 7 Nov. 1575).

**f. 227.** HUGHE PRICE of Chesthunt yeoman. (*Dat.* 27 May, 1575). Bro. John Price to have all the portion bequeathed to me by my late father; Dau. Eliz. Pryce; Wife Eliz. extrix; Friends John Cooke, Perse Daie, Tho. Spicer & Symon Will'ms vicar of Chesthunt overseers. *Wit*ᵉ:—John Cooke, Tho. Spicer & Sym. Williams. (*Pr.* at Stortford 4 July 1575).

**f. 228.** JOHN STERE of Chesthunt, husbandman. (*Dat.* 13 June 1575). Bro. Robt. Stere of Braughing; Dau. Alice Stere extrix.; Bro. Roberts childⁿ; Tho. Monedaie & Symon Williams overseers. *Wit*ᵉ:—The said overseers. (*Pr.* at Stortford 4 July 1575).

**f. 228.** JANE WOORTEN. (*Dat.* 8 Mch. ? 1574-5). Bur. at Stondon; Johane Wenham & Robt. Wenham her husband; Robt. Wenham's son; The good wife Wenham; Mʳ Rich. Sadler; Agnes Bridgeman; Alice Wrattynge; Margt. Kinge; Margt. Hoode; Mrs. Porter; Mother Watson; Margt. Atkyns; Margt. Gill; Henry Skingle; Tho. Skingle; Goodwife Dawlton of Barwicke; Dor. Kinge; Goodman Smartfoote; Chas. Wrattinge; Wm. Kinge overseers; Goodman Wenham exor. *Wit*ᵉ:—Robt. Porter minister of Stondon, Robt. Wenham, Margt. Hoode, Wm. Kinge, Chas. Wrattinge, Alice Wrattinge. (*Pr.* at Stortford 4 July 1575).

**f. 228.** JOHN TREDGOLDE of Sabridgeworth, husbandman. (*Dat.* 28 July, 1575). The child my wife now goeth with; Eldest sister Jenetrix Barker; Sist. Margt. Tredgolde; Sist. Johane Tredgolde; Wife Barbarie extrix. Mʳ Wm. Chauncye & Thos. Hutchin my father in law, overseers. *Wit*ᵉ:—Wm. Chauncye gent, Tho. Hutchin, Rich. Pillis, Dennis Cramphorne, Tho. Chramphorne, Robt. Spilman & John Nellson the wrighter hereof. (*Pr.* at Stortford 19 Sep. 1575).

**f. 229.** CHRISTOFER HODGE. (*Dat.* 6 Sep. 1574). Bur. at Stondon; Youngest dau. Sara (under 21); Dau. Isabell; Dau. Kath; Rich. Laurence of Greneende in psh. of Stondon; Land in Thudemashe; Wife Margt. extrix; Sons Thos. & Samuel; Land in Staplefelde & Cornert felde. *Wit*ᵉ:—Robt. Porter minister of Stondon. *Wit*ᵉ:—Rich. Laurence, John Lamkyn. (*Pr.* at Stortford 13 June 1575).

f. 231. JOHN HERDMAN of Chesthunt, tailor. *Dat.* 20 Apr. 17 Eliz.) House in Chesthunte street nexte the Water lane & land in Brokefelde vpon the stones which tenement is called Marybones; Wife Gartered; Son Thos; Dau. Margt. Herdman; Johane Shanbroke dau. of John Shanbroke dec$^d$; John Pynknye exor. *Wit$^s$:*—Simon Williams vicar of Chesthunt, Rich. Chaier, John Pinkenye, Tho. Bumsted. (*Pr.* at Stortford 17 May 1575).

f. 231. JOHANE HEMMINGE of Hunsden. (*Dat.* 11 Oct. 1575). Thos. & Johane Kynge ch$^n$ of John Kinge; Son in law John Kinge; John Howe of Hunsden; Eliz. Kinge dau. of my dau. Eliz. Kinge; Dau. Ellen; Son John Cornishe & Agnes Cornishe his dau; Dau. Eliz. & s$^d$ John Howe exors; John Heming of Amwell overseer. *Wit$^s$:*—Wm. Preston, Wm. Sharpe & Eliz. Qvynowe. (*Pr.* at Gedleston 22 Aug. 1575).

f. 233. ALICE CLARKE of Ware, widow. (*Dat.* 3 Jan. 1575). Johane & Mary Clarke daus. of Tho. Clarke of Braughinge; Eliz$^t$ Siluester; Serv$^t$ Margery Maie; Agnes wife of John Laicocke; Widow Forde; Wm. Sales wife; Dionesse Browne; Eliz. Sale; Serv$^t$ John Hart; Edm., John & Rich. sons of John Chapman of Ware shoemaker; Agnes wife of s$^d$ John Chapman; Wm. son of John Westlie late of London powlter dec$^d$; Radygun Westly dau. of s$^d$ John; Johane Branche; Alice Scotte; Grace Luke; Wm. Russell; Serv$^t$ Alice; Three of the daus. of Wm. Russell; Anne Chapman; Said Tho. Clarke of Braughing exor; John Chapman & Wm. Russell overseers. *Wit$^s$:*—John Laicocke, Henry Wyllan & Wm. Laurence. (*Pr.* at Braughing 7 Mch. 1575).

f. 234. GEORGE CRAMPHORNE thelder of Sabridgeworth. (*Dat.* 7 Dec. 1574). Wife Johane; Tenement called Challon's als. Chandlers; Son Thos; Pasture ground called Forebury; Land in Purchefelde; Croft called Laisonsley; Croft called Cowleies; Longcrofte; Wren parkecroft; Fryers croft w$^{th}$ a hoppett called Thoms. Adams; Ground called Mistell well belonging to Fryers, Gratton Meade, Cobies croft, Litle Blackeley als. Parcke valey, Old parkemeade, Stockeley, one piece of Permenters, meadow in Hallison abutting upon the mill shotte, Lindsells halferoode; Geo. Bull; Birchcroft, Stonecroft *alias* Ston'ds felde; Son George; Daus. Marie & Grace, Eliz. & Kath; Godson Wm. Browne; John son of Richard Wall; Johane Wall dau. of s$^d$ Rich.; Bro. John Cramphorne supervisor; Wife extrix. *Wit$^s$:*—Marke Pearse, Laur. Browne & John Barnarde the wryter. (*Pr.* at Stortford 18 Apr. 1575).

f. 240. ROGER BRIGES. (*Dat.* 10 May 1576). To be bur. in churchyd. of Amwell; Dau. Alice; Tho. Railyng my wifes son; Edw. Walkyr; Wife Agnes. *Wit$^s$:*—Wm. Clarke vicar of Amwell. (*Admon.* 2 July 1576 to Agnes relict).

f. 240. RICHARD WATHE of Tunfordstone in psh. of Chesthunt. (*Dat.* 24 July 1576). Child$^n$ Christr & Johane; Wife Alice extrix. *Wit$^s$:*—Trustram More clearke & pson of Wormely, Wm. Ward. (*Pr.* at Hoddesden 4 Feb. 1576).

f. 240. THOMAS KINGE of Barlie. (*Dat.* 26 Mch. 1576). Wife Johane; Son Robert (under 20); Sons Thos. & John; Lands bought of John Chapman in divers felds of Thissel; Agnes

Holbem; My mother; Legacy to the repair of Pillats Bridge; Wife extrix. *Wit*ˢ:—Mʳ Wm. Stanton. Tho. Grūwell. Hen. Hawke. Wm. Keyford. (*Pr*. at Stortford 10 Sep. 1576).

f. 241. **GEORGE PERMENTER** of Sabrigeworth, yeoman. (*Dat*. 17 Aug. 1576). Eldest son John; Lands & tenements called Jenker Attwodes; Son Thomas; Dau. Agnes; Wife Agnes; Son George (under 20); Dau. Marie; Wife extrix: Wm. Spenser overseer. *Wit*ˢ:—John Nelson the wryter hereof, Peter Lyndsell, John Bayford, Laur. Browne. (*Pr*. at Stortford 10 Sep. 1576).

f. 241. **HENRY WARDE** of Braughinge, maulteman. (*Dat*. 4 Feb. 1576). Dau. Margt. Warde & Dau. Anne (both under 26); Wife Eliz. extrix. *Wit*ˢ:—Wm. Hutchyn, Leon. South, Rich. Pett, per me Johannem Hedlam. (*Pr*. at Stortford 12 Feb. 1576).

f. 242. **RONYON BESOWTH**. (*Dat*. 15 June 1574). Bro-in-law Geo. Lincolne; Alexʳ Lincolne (under age) eldest son of sᵈ Geo; Bro-in-law Geo. Westwode & Joice Westwode his dau; Bro. John Besowth; Bro. Edw. Besowth; Henry son of Edw. Besowth; Tenement called Nycholls in psh. of Rede & lands given me by my father's will; John Besowth junʳ, son of Wm. Besowth; Bro. Wm. Besowth; Bro. John exor. or if he refuse then bro. Edw. *Wit*:—Rich. Turstwell, Tho. Turner, Wm. Anckell, John Warren sen. (*Pr*. at Braughing 4 June 1576 by Edw. Besowth).

f. 246. **THOMAS BOWNES** of Thundrich, weaver. (*Dat*. 18 Mch. 1576). Wife Margt. (probably a second wife); My children's chⁿ; Tho. Reynolde; Wm. Weles & Robt. Dobson exors. *Wit*ˢ:—Wm. Dyxon minister there, Tho. Reynolde. (*Pr*. at Braughing 9 Apr. 1576).

f. 246. **RICHARD CHARE** thelder of Chesthunt, yeoman. (*Dat*. 4 Feb. 1576). Bro. Robt. Chare thelder; Tho. Monday; John Chare thelder; Dau. Anne Chaire; House in Chesthunt strete that John Poor dwelleth in; Land bought of Rich. Chare the yonger my cosen; Daus. Alice Chare, Susan Chare, Kath. Chare & Margt. Chare; Wife Johane; House Wm. Cokᵉ dwelleth in; Son John Chare (under 21); Wife extrix; Thos. Browne of Lucas end overseer. *Wit*ˢ:—Robt. Chare sen, Tho. Monday, Robt. Cordall & John Chare senʳ. (*Pr*. 11 Feb. 1576).

f. 247. **WILLIAM BUSSHEY** of Chesthunt, yeoman. (*Dat*. 4 July 1574). Wife Johane; House in Hamon Strete in Chesthunt; Son Wm. Boushey; Dau. Constance Boshey; Son George; Ground called Meltons field; Son Robt., Wm., Henry & Simon; Servᵗ Agn. Cooke; Wife extrix; Son Wm. overseer. *Wit*ˢ:— Edw. Vicars, Robt. Bosshey, John Addams. (*Pr*. at Hoddesdon 4 Feb. 1576).

f. 247. **JOHN ISAAKE** of Chesthunt, tailor. (*Dat*. 10 Oct. 1576). Dau. Eliz. Isaacke; Son George Isaacke; Wife Kath. extrix; Tho. Hoddesden & Simon Williams vicar of Chesthunt overseers. *Wit*ˢ:—George Redishe, Tho. Hoddesdon & Simon Williams. (*Pr*. at Hoddesden 4 Feb. 1576).

*To be Continued.*

# Marriage Licenses.

## ARCHDEACONRY OF HUNTINGDON (HITCHIN REGISTRY).

[I can find no trace of the existence of any of the Marriage Allegations and Bonds in this Court previous to 1756. Notes of earlier ones are scattered here and there amongst the *Acta* of the Archdeaconry and are here printed. These *Acta*, unfortunately in a fragmentary state, are now preserved at Somerset House and I must record my indebtedness to Mr. E. Cheyne, of the Probate Office, for kind assistance in deciphering several of the very badly-written entries.—ED.]

1610.

Mch. 29   Tho. Grubb of Aldenham yeoman & Hellen Hawkins of same, widow.

Apr. 9   John Luke of Harpeden & Eliz. Reade of same.

,, 9   Wm. Lawrence of St Ippollits & Cath. Addams, maiden, of Wallington, dau. of Tho. Addams of same.

,, 14   Anth. Ashbey de Tring & Rabecca Bates of Albury.

,, 24   Thomas Tewar & Jane Feild of Shenly.

,, 28   John Godfrey of Shenly & Eliz. Deacon of Harpeden.

,, 28   Roger Gibbs of Great Gaddisdon gent. & Sarah Neele, maiden, dau. of George Neele of Harpeden.

May 12   John Gilet of Kimpton husbandman, son of John Gilet of Benfeild co. Northampton, husbandman, & Eliz. Newman, of Kimpton, maiden, dau. of Audrey Gilet [*sic*] of Kimpton, widow.

,, 19   Jas. Royce of Hemelhampsted, blacksmith, son of Rich. Royce of same, blacksmith, & Joan Deeremer of same, maiden, dau. of Agnes Deeremer of Barton de le Claye co. Bedf. widow.

May 10   John Saunders of Harpeden shoemaker & Cath. Cooke of Kings Walden, widow.

,, 22   John [page worn away] [of Watton] at Stone, bricklayer, & Cath. Warren, of same, maiden, orphan.

[Apr. 7 ?]   Lionel Campion of Aldenham, son of George Campion & Agnes Harrys, maiden.

[Apr. 7 ?]   Wm. Grubb of Hartingfordbury & Anne Archer, maiden, of same.

July 21   Roger Partridg of Hemelhampsted, widower & Jane Kentish of Kings Langley, maiden, dau. of Rich. Kentish of Abbots Langley, yeoman.

,, 13   Tho. Hayward of Ayot St Lawrence & Mary Ginns of Harpeden.

,, 27   Wm. Kinge of Ickleford widr & Sarah Chambers of Hitchin, widow.

Aug. 14   Henry Stowe of Aldenham, husbandman, son of Rich. Stowe of Sarrat, & Sarah Hunt of Bovingdon, maiden, orphan, aged about 20.

Sep. 29. Tho. Eliott of Kimpton & Agnes Vnderwood of Hitchin, widow. Marr. at Kimpton.
Oct. 5 John Pryor of Bishops Hatfild & Alice Potter of Hartingfordbury, maiden. Alleged by s^d Pryor & John Potter, brother of s^d Alice. Marr. at Hartingfordbury.
,, 10 John Newman of Sandon & Eliz. Cobb, widow, of same.
,, 20 George Clarke of Knebworth, yeoman & Anne Godfrey *als* Coop of Letchworth, maiden.
Nov. 28 Tho. Welshe of Shephall, son of John Welshe of Kings Walden, yeoman, & Frances Deremer of Great Wimonly, dau. of Robt. Deremer of Shephall.
Dec. 5 Roger Dikes of Clothall, yeoman, aged 39, & Anne A[u?]strey of same, widow.
,, 13 Rich. Freman of Clothall, labourer & Anne Hubbard of Walkerne, dau. of Henry Hubbard of same dec^d.
,, 16 Wm. Palmer wid^r of Aldenham & Ursula Evelinge of same, widow.
,, 29 Griffin Bruer of King's Langley & Agnes Shakemaple of Bovingdon, widow.
,, 29 John Leonard of Easenden & Cath. Burton of same.
Jan. 15 Wm. Edlyn of Northchurch & Judith Nicholl of same, maiden, dau. of Rich. Nicholl of Hendon yeoman. Marr. at Northchurche.
,, 19 Rich. Hudnall of Albury, husbandman, aged 26, & Eliz. White of Barkhempsted S^t Peter, maiden, dau. of Jas. White of Northchurch, husbandman. Marr. at Barkhempsted.
,, 19 John Garrett of Little Gaddisden, wid^r & Sarah Feild of Hemelhampsted, maiden, dau. of John Feild of same, yeoman. Marr. at Gaddisden. Said Garrett & Tho. Deane of Edesborough, co. Bucks make oath that the parents of s^d Sarah consent.
,, 20 Tho. Chappell of Harpeden, husbandman, aged 25, son of Eliz. Chappell of same, widow, & Marrian Nicholls, maiden, dau. of John Nicholls of same, yeoman. Marr. at Harpeden.
,, 22 Robt. Hawkes of Bps. Hatfeild tayler & Eliz. How of same, maiden, orphan. Marr. at Hatfield. Said Hawkes & Michael Baker sworn.
Feb. 6 Peter Hamond of Aldenham & Eliz. Ockeley, dau. of Tho. Okeley of same. Marr. at Aldenham.
,, 7 Francis Jaques of Harpeden & Eliz. Bigg of same. Marr. there.
,, 24 Henry Hudnall of Albury, husbandman, orphan, about 28 & Joan Doggett maiden, dau. of John Doggett of same, yeoman. Marr. at Wigginton.
Mch. 16 Giles Edwards, son of Geo. Edwards of Sandon, gent, & Jane Butterfeild, maiden, dau. of John Butterfeild of same.

1611.
May 23 Wm. Dixe of Hitchin chapman & Anne Frone ? maiden, dau. of [blank] Froe? of same, labourer. Marr. at Hitchin.
,, 4 Thos. Stile of Bps. Hatfield & Eliz. Maskoll of same.
,, 4 Wm. Higbye of Hemelhampsted & Rebecca Pope of same.
,, 4 Daniel Wood of Sandon & Agnes Norris of Cottered.
Apr. 10 Henry Carter & Joan Trott dau. of Henry Trott of Hartford S^t Andrews.

MARRIAGE LICENCES.

May 7    Tho. Bilby of Wigginton & Mary Geery of same.

" 8    Edw. Sibley of Hartingfordbury son of Wm. Sibley of Kings Walden & Prudence Bucke of Hartingfordbury, maiden, orphan, aged 22. Marr. at Hartingfordbury.

" 11    John Webb of Northmims son of John Webb of [blank] Marson, co. Bedf. & Joan Harwood dau. of Eliz. Harwood of Northmims.

" 11    Wm. Hayward of Shenly son of Tho. Hayward of St Stephens near St Albans, husbandman, & Dorothy Jewett, maiden, dau. of Wm. Jewett of Kings Langley, husbandman. Said Wm. sworn that there is no legal impediment on account of a precontract with one Blanch Foldes.

" 18    Rich. Aberry of Hemelhampsted, husbandman, & Agnes Shreve of Great Gaddisden, maiden, aged 40 years. Marr. at Gaddisden.

May 18    Francis Pitkin of Little Gaddisden, widower, & Joyce Norris of Northchurch. Officium contra Jocosam Norris de Northchurch. Quo die comparuit et submisit se &c. Cui dominus obiecit that she hath byn 3 seu'all tymes asked publiqly in the pish Church of Northchurch vnto one Thomas Brigg⌠ and yet she hath deferred to solemnize the said marriadg whereby som scandall and offence is given Cui r'ondendo fassa est that the banns were soe asked but saith she neuer was contracted vnto him but made him only a ρmise so as he ment plainly, but since he is rune awaye and respecteth her not vnde facta fide virtute Juramenti &c. de veritate [responsi?] dominus ad humilem peticionem eiusdem concessit licentiam ad solemnizandam matrimoniam inter eandem et Franciscum Pitkin de Gaddisden parva viduo [sic].

June 5    Robt. Wood & Anne Willett of Aldenham, widow.

Sep. 16    Robt. Hurst, widr, & Eliz. Birde of Kensworth, maiden, orphan. Marr. at Kensworth.

Sep. 25    John Brockitt junior, of Macaryes ende in psh. of Wheth. esq. & Jane Lacon of Willion, maiden, dau. of [blank] Lacon of same esq. Marry there.

Oct. 12    Wm. Rutter of Wigginton & Eliz. Hide of same, widow. Marr. there.

" 15    Robt. Abbott of St Andrew's, Hartf., brickmaker, aged 43, & Mary Deane of Little Munden, maiden, dau. of Jane Clarke *alias* Deane wife of [blank] Clarke of Dunmoe, co. Essex.

[blank]    Ezechiel Halfhide son of Wm. Halfhide of Wallington, yeoman, & Brigitt Thackham, maiden. Marr. at Wallington.

1616-7

Jan. 9    . . . . *alias* Chambers of Flampsted & Susan Alee *alias* . . . . widow.

" 13    Robertus Cheyney gen. de Bramley Hanger infra p . . . Luton in Com. Bedfd. comparuit personaliter et submisit se . . . allegavit quod matrimoniam contraxit cum Leticie Norton filie Lucæ de Offli in Com. Hartff. Ari de et cum consensu expresso dic . . . Norton patris eiusdem et de et cum consensu Francisce Chenie matris dicti Roberti et allegavit quod heres [factus?] est Thome Chenie patris sui defuncti virtute Testamenti sui terrarum et hereditamentorum ad valorem ducentarum annuatim et 50 librarum legalis &c. petiit facultatem sibi concedi pro solemnizacione dicti maritagii in Ecclesia pochiali de Offley vbi dicta Leticia nunc habitatat ac obtulit se promptum et paratum ad prestandum Juramentum ac ad interponendam Cautionem obligatoriam juxta Jura &c: dominus facta fide juxta jura concessit eidem facultatem predictam: obligantur dictus Robertus et Henricus Cheny de eadem generosus.

Jan. 18 Leonard Hawkswell, bruer, & Margery Taverner of Shenly, maiden, dau. of John Taverner of same, husbandman.

,, 21 Christopher Boyfeild of Aldenham, carpenter, & Sarah Hodsden of Shenlye.

Feb. 11 Tho. Cocke of Watton at Stone, husbandman, son of John Cock of Little Munden, husbandman, & Agnes Rudd of Watton afores$^d$, dau. of Rich. Rudd of same, husbandman.

Feb. 12 Tho. Birchmore of Flampsted, son of Wm. Birchmore of same, yeoman, and Grace Underwood, maiden, dau. of Geo. Underwood of Weston, yeoman.

,, 21 John Platt of Aldenham & Hellen Shepheard of same.

,, 28 Robt. Yardly of Weston, clerk, & Susan Leuse of Wallington, maiden.

,, 28 Wm. Marret of Whethampsted & Dorothy Armesbey of same, widow.

1617
May 3 John Brooke, clerk, & Mary Lillingston of Great Gaddesden, maiden, dau. of William Lillingston.

*To be Continued.*

## Abstracts of Herts Wills.

### ARCHDEACONRY OF ST. ALBANS.

REGISTER "STONEHAM."—CONTINUED FROM VOL. I., PAGE 384.

f. 22. JOHANNES HALE senior. (*Dat.* 10 Dec. 1433). Bur. at Norton; Son Walter exor.

f. 22. ALICIA CRECY. (*Dat.* 21 Oct. 1433). Bur. at S$^t$ Helens of Whethamstede; Legacies to Churches of Harpden & S$^t$ Stephens; Sir John Marchall; Son Mathew; Daus. Eliz. & Isabelle; Alice Rose; Serv$^t$ Agnes; Wm. Crecy & Mathew Sepset exors.

f. 22. WILLELMUS SKELE of S$^t$ Albans. (*Dat.* 14 Apr. 1434). Bur. S$^t$ Peters; Joan Boltwelle; Son Thos; Wife Alice & Wm. Crofton exors.

f. 22. JOHANNES BENTON of Slepe in psh. of S$^t$ Peters in S$^t$ Albans. (*Dat.* 'die martis post festum Sancti Marci Euangeliste' 1434). Bur. S$^t$ Peters; John Bernewell; Joan Vogge my sister extrix.

f. 22. JOHANNES COKDELLE. (*Dat.* 24 Mch. 1434). Bur. at Watford; Sir Robt. the chaplain; John Caunche, clerk; Ralph the clerk; Wife Anne extrix; Roger Kettere supervisor.

f. 22. THOMAS MARTIN. (*Dat.* 20 Apr. 1434). Bur. at Watford; Ralph, the parish clerk; Wife Christian & Roger Aldewyn & Laurence Martyn exors.

f. 22. RICARDUS STEVYN. (*Dat.* 10 Apr. 1434). Bur. Watford; Legacy to the Rector of the church of Whitchirch; Wife Matilda extrix.

f. 23. JOHANNES CLERKE. (*Dat.* 13 July 1433). Bur. S$^t$ Peters; Ralph the parish clerk; Wife Margaret extrix; Rich. Fuller supervisor; Legacy to Church of Northmȳmys.

f. 23. WILLELMUS RANDOLF. (*Dat.* 18 May 1434). Bur. in Mon. of S$^t$ Albans; My brother; The wife of my brother; My sister; The dau. of my sist.; Isabelle Randolf; The dau. of s$^d$ Isabelle; 'Unam togam de Mustyrvelerys'*; John Tawerneyr; Adam de Fermer; Elenor Breton; Margaret Corior; Sir John Trylle exor; Roulond Breton.

f. 23 JOHANNES SMYTH of Leuesden. (*Dat.* 16 Feb. 1433). Bur. Watford; Sir Robt. the chaplain; John Cauche; Ralph Smyth clerk; Rich. Baron & wife Alice exors; Thos. Lauenham supervisor.

f. 23. HENRICUS BRABEBON. (*Dat.* 11 Mch. 1433). Bur. Watford; Wife Margaret extrix.

f. 23. JOHANNES SABBE. (*Dat.* 25 May 1434). Bur. St. Stephens; Sir John Marchall chaplain there; Walter Sabbe my father exor.

f. 23. JOHANNES DURDAN. (*Dat.* 30 Apr. 1434). Wife Agnes & Walter Durdan exors.

f. 23. THOMAS ROWHEDE. (*Dat.* 10 July 1434). Legacy to Church of Barnet; Son Wm.; Bro. Henry; John Peris; Wife Alice & Robt. Alwey & Wm. Mulle exors. (*Pr.* in vigil of S$^t$ Laurence 1434).

f. 23. JOHANNA BELCH widow, of Rykmersworth. (*Dat.* 10 May 1434). Bur. at Rykmersworth; Legacy to the Church of Saret; Tho. Godthanke; John Rowe; Roger Belch; Thomas of y$^e$ Felde; John Sansū; Margery Bryan; Tho. Dauy; Henry Holm; Kath. Frowe; Henry Kynge; Tho. Godthanke & John Rowe exors. (*Pr.* 10 Sep. 1434).

f. 23. WALTERUS PODYFATE. (*Dat.* 12 Sep. 1434). Bur. S$^t$ Mary of Redburn; Wife Joan & Edmund Milward exors. (*Pr.* 18 Sep. 1434).

f. 23. THOMAS STRETELE of Little Horwode. (*Dat.* 'die decoll.' S$^t$ John Bapt. 1434). Bur. at Little Horwood; Bro. John; Bro. Rich; Bro. Wm.; My mother; John Smyth & John Geffus exors.

f. 23. JULIANA BROUN of Little Horwode. (*Dat.* 'in crastino decoll.' S$^t$ John Bapt. 1434). Bur. at Little Horwood; Joan wife of John Wareyn; Helen wife of John Geffus; Alice wife of Henry Wareyn de [Swankœne?]; Isabelle wife of Rich. Frankeleyn; John Smyth & John Geffus exors.

f. 23. JOHANNES BURGUN. (*Dat.* 'x° kl. Octobris' 1434). Bur. at Norton; Wife Mary extrix.

* Mustredevilliars. See Halliwell's Dict.

f. 23. JOHANNES SMYTH of S$^t$ Albans. (*Dat.* 25 Sep. 1434). Bur. S$^t$ Peters: Wife Alice extrix: John Smart supervisor.

f. 23. JOHANNES LOWYN of Cuffelygh, senior. (*Dat.* in the feast of S$^t$ James 1434). Bur. Northawe; Wife Margt.; Wm. Pyk[ & Roger Lowyn; John Daueney sen$^r$ & Wm. Whyte exors. *Wit$^s$*:—Tho. Leeys chaplain, Edw. Jordan, Wm. son of s$^d$ John Lowyn & others.

f. 23. ROGERUS BENDYNG. (*Dat.* Aug. 1433). Bur. S$^t$ Laurence of Langley; John Miland & Willm Pratte exors.

f. 23. ISABELLA HILL. (*Dat.* 1433). Bur. S$^t$ Laurence of Langley; Son Robt. Hill exor.

f. 24. RICARDUS SPENSER. (*Dat.* 'die Mercurii in festo Sancti Randulfi Episcopi et confessoris' 1426). Bur. Codicote; John Brode vicar of the church of Codicote; Wife Margery & John Brewere exors.

f. 24. JOHANNES DOGET. (*Dat.* 9 May 1434). Bur. Codicote; Wife Joan & son John exors.

f. 24. JOHANNES DAWNEY now of Northawe. (*Dat.* 18 Sep. 1434). Wife Joan.

f. 24. JOHANNES TYLER, maltman, of Rykmersworth. (*Dat.* 28 Mch. 1434). Bur. at Rykmersworth; John Braunangr clk; Tho. Stretman clk; Simon Croile pauper; Legacy to church of S$^t$ Peter of Chalfonte; Sons Richard & Thos; Dau. Margt; Roger son of John Daye; Henry [Berg?]wasch my vicar & curate; Tho. Botervylde maltman; Wife Sarah & Roger Daye exors.

f. 24. WALTERUS CLERK. (*Dat.* 'in festo Marci et Marcelliani' 1434). Bur. S$^t$ Peters; Wife Justina & John Bradcrofte exors. *Wit$^s$*:—John Bromley, Tho. Tyler.

f. 24. MATILDA ATT MILLE of Bernett. (*Dat.* 7 Apr. 1434). Bur. in chapel of S$^t$ John Baptist; Agnes Hardewyn; Agnes Amye; Legacy for the souls of Tho. Newman & John att Mille; Wm. Hardewyn & Agnes his wife exors.

f. 24. THOMAS BREYKSPEYR of S$^t$ Albans, gent. (*Dat.* in crastino S$^t$ Thomas Apost. 1434). Bur. S$^t$ Peters; Legacies to the vicar of the chapel of S$^t$ Andrew & to Sir William & Sir John, the friars of Dunstable, anchorite of S$^t$ Michaels, Sir John Mason 'capellando de Maudlayns'; Wife Margt. extrix; Wm. Bowre supervisor.

f. 24. JOHANNES GARDENER. (*Dat.* 11 Jan. 1434). Bur. S$^t$ Peters; My son; Robt. Scoun exor.

f. 24. NICHOLAUS BOTLER of Sleype in psh. of S$^t$ Peters. (*Dat.* 24 Jan. 1434). Bur. at Northmimmys; Sir William parish chaplain of S$^t$ Peters; John Tauerner; Son John exor; The vicar of S$^t$ Peters & John Wrattyng supervisors.

f. 24. WILLELMUS WEST. (*Dat.* 9 Mch. 1434). Bur. at Redburne; Legacy for mending the king's highway in Bunnyslane; Kath. Grenehood; Joan Trewe; Wife Julian & son Thos. exors. (*Pr.* before J. Peyton, archdeacon, 20 Apr. 1435).

f. 24. JOHANNES GOLDING of Northawe. (*Dat.* 1432). Bur. Northawe; Wm. Whyte & Tho. Swatthorpe exors; Wife Joan. *Wit$^s$*:—Wm. Pypar, John Lewys, Wm. Haynde. (*Pr.* before Wm. Alnewyk archdeacon, 9 Apr. 1435).

f. 24. RICARDUS CREKE of S⁺ Albans. (*Dat.* Invenciono Sancte Crucis 1435). Bur. S⁺ Peters; Wife Alice extrix; John Turner, baker, supervisor. (*Pr.* 28 May 1435).

f. 24. GILBERTUS CHAPMAN of Cotley. (*Dat.* 20 Dec. 1435). Bur. Northaw; Robt. Dene & his wife; Agnes Herwell; John Pykᵉ & Gilbert Busawe exors. (*Pr.* 18 June 1435).

f. 25. MARGARETA late wife of William BREKESPER of S⁺ Albans. (*Dat.* in vigilia Ascencionis 1435). Bur. S⁺ Peters; Wm. Bower exor. (*Pr.* 6 June 1435).

f. 25. JOHANNA WODEWARD of Watford. (*Dat.* 3 Apr. 1435). Bur. Watford; Legacies to the churches of Abbots Langley & S⁺ Stephens; Sir Robert; Ralph the clerk; 'ad vnam viam circa Potteryscrowche xx*d*.'; Son John Wodeward exor. *Witˢ*:—Wm. Wynche, John Penger & Ralph the clerk. Dated at Levysdene. (*Pr.* 16 June 1435).

f. 25. JANYN FRENSCHMAN of Gadmerend, in psh. of Tyngerst, dioc. of Lincoln, co. Bucks. (*Dat.* S⁺ Alban the Martyr's day 1435). Bur. S⁺ Peters in S⁺ Albans; Legacy to the rector of Tyngerst; 'Lego fabrice vnius pontis vocati Cheslyngton brygge vj*d*.'; John Mercham of Newenton exor. *Witˢ*:— John Adam, skynner, John Sawger, John Cany, Rich. Cony, Hen. Cook. (*Pr.* 16 June 1435?).

f. 25. JOHANNES ADAM of S⁺ Albans. (*Dat.* die dominica prox. post festum S⁺ Thome Martiris 1435). Bur. S⁺ Peters; Wife Margery extrix. *Witˢ*:—Tho. Fauntoner, John Songer, Wm. Schetbolt, John Wrottyng. (*Pr.* 22 July 1435?).

*To be Continued.*

---

# Amphillis Washington.

The following extracts from the parish registers of Tring (which I have recently examined by the kind permission of the Rev. S. W. Tidswell, the present vicar) will serve a double purpose. A small printer's error and an omission in the matter of dates in the extracts given in Mr. Waters' memorable pamphlet on the Washington ancestry, are hereby set right, and I am enabled to make a suggestion as to the family of which Amphillis was a member.

*Extracts from Tring Parish Registers.*

*Baptisms.*

| | | |
|---|---|---|
| 1635. | June 18. | Layaranc sonn of Layarance Washington. |
| 1636. | Aug. 17. | Elizabeth da of Mʳ Larranc Washington. |
| ,, | Oct. 12. | Nickles the sonn of Edmvnd ffidgharbor. |
| 1636-7. | Feb. 21. | Peter sonn of Mʳ John Bovden. |
| 1641. | Oct. 14. | William sonn of Mʳ Larranc Washenton. |

*Marriages.*

| | | |
|---|---|---|
| 1638. | Dec. 14. | Mʳ John Bilin & Mⁱᵗʳˢ Svsand bovdon. |
| 1641. | June 24. | John Dagnall & Elizabeth bovden ware Marred one Midsomer daye. |

### Burials.

1634-5. Mch. 3.   John Dagnall of Grove the elldar.
1635.   May 26.  Ann Dagnall widdo.
1637.   Apr. 25. Ann the wif of Andrw Knowling.

On page 14 of the above-mentioned pamphlet Mr. Waters sets out a grant of the tuition of the two daughters of John and Susan Billing, to John Dagnall of Grove, the husband of Elizabeth Dagnall, she being 'matertera dictarum filiarum.'

Susan Billing and Eliz. Dagnall, therefore, were sisters, and I think I am justified in assuming them to be the Susan Bovdon and Elizabeth Bovdon named in the above register extracts. Andrew Knowling, in his will, calls Susan Billing his daughter-in-law. He also calls Amphillis Washington his daughter-in-law, and I therefore venture to suggest that Ann, the wife of Andrew Knowling, who was buried in 1637, had been previously married to —— Boudon or Bowdon, and that Amphillis was one of her daughters by that marriage.

---

# Transcripts of Parish Registers.

## NORTHAW.

(CONTINUED FROM VOL. I., PAGE 383).

---

In the Parish of Northaw in the County of Hertford from Lady-Day, 1743, to Lady-Day, 1744.

| Baptized. | Buried. |
|---|---|
| Page, William | Samuel Burgall |
| Tiler, Edward | Ann Claxton |
| Head, Peter | William Page |
| Fowkes, John | Hannah Parker |
| Mansfield, John | Thomas Saggers |
| North, Ann | John Butler |
| Newman, Matthew | John Head |
| Stephens, John | Sarah Collyer |
| King, Jane | Ann North |
| Godwin, Susan | James Robey |
| Wacket, Thomas | John Mansfield |
| Field, Samuel | Susannah Parker |
| Jordan, Edward | Susannah Harding |
| Olney, Oshea | Mary Clark |
| Todd, Sarah | John Fowkes |
| Pearce, William | Jane Stringer |
| Poole, Mary | Francis Claxton |
| Hurry, Sarah | Mary Nash |
| *Married.* | Edward Jordan |
| Richard Senton of the Parish of S<sup>t</sup> James Westminster Middlesex & Margaret Dixon of the Parish of Egmondesham in the County of Bucks, bringing a Licēse. | Michael Woodfield |
| | Joseph Prior |
| | Elizabeth Jones |
| | Mary Griffith |

Thomas Preston, Minister.

*To be Continued.*

# The Herts Genealogist and Antiquary.

## Humberstone of Walkern, etc.

### WILLS AND ADMINISTRATIONS FROM THE P.C.C.

(CONTINUED FROM PAGE 4.)

[*P.C.C. Alchin* 182.]

ELIZ. HUMBERSTON widow, of Clothall, co. Hertf. (*Nunc. will dat.* Oct. 1653). To Mary Cannon of Clothall dau. of Tho. Cannon 7s. 6d.; Same to Tho. son of s$^d$ Tho. Cannon; To Thos., Wm. & John three sons of s$^d$ Tho. Cannon 2s. 6d. each; Residue to Robt. Freeman of Clothall whom I make exor. Wit$^s$:—Hellener Heatly, Mary Cannon. (*Adm.* 30 Jan. 1653-4 to Robt. Freeman).

[*P.C.C. Alchin* 316.]

EDWARD HUMMERSTON of Clothall, co. Hertf., husbandman. (*Dat.* 23 Aug. 1652). To wife Eliz. £5 & use of household stuff, but if she remarry or remove out of Clothall then my cozen Susan Webb wife of Edw. Peerman or her dau. Mary wife of Wm. Straton shall enjoy the feather bed etc.; To cous. Jone Hummerston 40s.; To cous$^s$ John & Tho. sons of my bro. Wm. each 40s.; To Mary wife of Wm. Marvell of Kelshall another of bro. Humerston's daus. £3; To cous. Eliz. wife of Tho. Whitley another dau. of s$^d$ bro. Wm. 40s.; To John, Suzan & Mary Webb ch$^n$ of cous. Leonard Webb dec$^d$, each 20s.; To Ann Castle dau. of John Castle of Clothall 20s.; To Ann Peereman wife of John Stratton 3l.; To Eve wife of John Edwards of Yardley 20s.; To so many of the ch$^n$ of s$^d$ John Edwards as shall be living at my decease 20s. apiece; To cous. Jone wife of Rich. Edwards 40s.; To the child$^n$ of s$^d$ Rich. Edwards living at my decease 20s. apiece; To cous. Adam Webb & his child$^n$ 5l.; To the ch$^n$ of cous. Wm. Young living at my decease 20s. apiece; To Eliz. wife of Geo. Sherodd of Braffin 40s.; To Alice Crasbey of Huntington 30s.; To Anne Freeman 20s.; To Anne wife of Wm. Young 12d.; To cous. Edw. Peereman 40s.; To the dau. of my cous. Leonard Humberston 40s.; To Bette Freeman 20s.; To the poor of Clothall 5s.; To John Cannon of Clothall 12d.; Residue to cous. Susan Webb now wife of Edw. Peereman & cous. Wm. Stratton whom I make exors. [*Mark*]. Wit$^s$:—Wm. Bucknall, John Harrison, Eliz. Peacoke. (*Pr.* 20 Jan. 1653-4).

[*P.C.C. Alchin* 437.]

JOHN HUMBARSTON of Stevenedge, co. Herts., gent. (*Dat.* 8 Nov. 1652). To be bur. at Stevenedge in the Chancell there near my late wife; Dau. Anne H. sole extrix; I entreat coz. Henry Chancey of Yardley esq. & my son John Humbarston of Aston gent. to be supervisors & to them 10s. apiece; To son Wm. 10s. 'advisinge my said Executrixe that she should use my said sonne William as I intended if I had lived that is not to suffer him to come within the house either for meat or drinke diet or lodginge but to cause him to provide for himselfe as he can'; I desire my s$^d$ extrix if she die possessed of any of the goods she shall have as extrix, to leave same to Anne Humbarston my grandchild one of the daus. of my s$^d$ son John, if living, and if not then to Mary H. another of s$^d$ daus.; To the poor of Stevenedge 40s. Wit$^s$:— Wm. Humbarston, Joane Woodward, Wm. Marshall ×. (*Pr.* 12 Dec. 1654).

[*P.C.C. Alchin* 451].

WILLIAM HUMMERSTONE of Brantfeild, co. Herts., gent. (*Nunc. will dat.* 11 July 1654). Wife to be extrix.; To dau. Alice Frobisher 10l.; To dau. Anne Storer 5l.; To poor of Walkehorne 40s. 'and if there be any one of his owne name that doe receive collection to haue then a double portion'; To poor of Brattfeild 20s., whereof Goodman Herbert to have a full part; To John Berge, Jane Drapers poore [*blank*] 10s. to help bind him out apprentice; To the poor in the Close of Lincolne & Saint Peters in Eastgate 20s. to be distributed by Master Rich. Wistantly; To the last named & his wife 5s. in gold each; To John Fayrecloth & every serv$^t$ in Master Rich. Ashwood's house in Bratfeild 2s. 6d. each; To serv$^t$ maid Eliz. Cooke 4 marks; To bro. Master Charles Chauncie now in New England 40s. if he come over or anie of his sonnes. Wit$^s$:—Wm. Strayearne, Tho. Owen, Eliz. Cooke ×. (*Pr.* 25 Oct. 1654. The christian name of the extrix is not given).

[*P.C.C. Ruthen* 369].

FRANCIS HUMBERSTON of Weston, co. Herts., yeoman. (*Dat.* 3 May 1656). To wife Sarah all my Tile Kilne in Weston, with the working house & Kilne house & the piece of ground whereon the same stands containing 2 acr. & another piece of ground abutting on same towards the east & on Burnage field towards the west containing 2 acr., also two other closes lately purchased, & lands in the Townefeild, Lannock field, Mill Hill in psh. of Weston, Stoneley dell in Weston etc. for her life & after to Francis son of my son Giles; My wife to dwell in the house wherein I now dwell called Paddocks for six years, and afterwards s$^d$ house to s$^d$ Francis Humberston; To son Giles 12d.; To son Wm. 12d.; To the ch$^n$ of son Giles viz:—Marie, Emme, Dorothie, Eliz. & Anne 10s. each; To Fras. son of my son Wm. 5l. at 23; To the rest of my son William's ch$^n$, viz:—Robt., Marie, Susan, Wm., John & Thos. 10s.

each: To the ch^n of dau. Anne Cutt, viz:—Nich., Marie & Susan Cutt 10s. each; To dau. Anne Cutt 20s.; Residue to wife Sarah whom I make extrix. Wits:—Jo. Fairedough, Giles Wallis. (*Adm.* 24 Dec. 1657 to Giles Humberston the son, the extrix having predeceased testator).

[*P.C.C. Wootton* 110.]

JOHN HUMERSTONE of Bayford, co. Herts., husbandman. (*Dat.* 25 Jan. 1657). To Leonard son of Tho. Feild of Wellin 5l. within one month after my wife Margaret's death, but if s^d Leonard be dutiful & please my s^d wife, he shall have 10l. To Jone Tuker of Bayford 1s.; To Eliz. Birt of Bayford 1s.; To Ellen Denton dau. of John Denton of Munden 20s.; To goddau. Eliz. Humerstone 20s.; To bro. Edw. Humerstone of Hatfeild 20s.; To sist. Anne Feild 20s.; To Edw. son of Wm. Burd of London flaxman one silver spoon & the great skillett; Residue to wife Margt. & she extrix. (*Mark*). Wits:—Edw. Bushe. (*Pr.* 15 Mch. 1657-8).

[*P.C.C. Wootton* 612.]

WILLIAM HUMBERSTONE of Stickney, co. Linc., yeoman. (*Dat.* 18 Mch. 1656). Eldest son John (minor); Second son Wm.; Third son Thos.; Fourth son Edm.; Youngest son Geo.; Sist Anne Knight; Wife Mary extrix; John Craven & Geo. Greswell supervisors. *William Humberstone.* Wits:—John Craven, John Meedlay, Geo. Greswell. (*Pr.* 27 Nov. 1658).

[*P.C.C. Juxon* 14.]

JAMES HUMBERSTONE cit. & grocer of London. (*Dat.* 20 Jan. 1662). My wife's sist. Mary Francis; Sist. Eliz. Hewett; Cous. Nath. Hewett; Cous. Mary Willgrasse; Bro. Woodcocke & his wife; Cous. Anne Rowell of Asfordby in Leicestershire; Maid serv^t Mary Hooton; Houses in Long Lane, London; Sam. Willgrasse; Kinsman Daniel Walton; Wm. Wethered; Edw. Potter; Wife Dorothy; Houses in Swanne Alley in Long Lane in Little Eastcheape & White Chappell & messuages & lands in Tattenam co. Midd; Cous. James son of my bro. Francis Humberstone; Cous. Wm. son of my bro. Wm. Humberstone; Cousins Jas. & Wm. H. exors & Cous. Dan. Walton, Wm. Wethered & Edw. Potter overseers. *James Humberstone.* Wits:—Tho. Greenhill, Wm. Wetherhead, Edw. Potter, Nath. Hewett, Humph. Satterthwaite scr, Wm. Bancks his servant. (*Pr.* 5 Feb. 1662-3 by Wm. Humberstone, reservation to the other exor). *In the margin appears a receipt for the original will, for the use of the exor., signed 'Geo. Gaell' and dated 4 June* 1663.

[*P.C.C. Mico.* 143.]

THOMAS HUMBERSTONES of Alveley, co. Essex. (*Dat.* 5 Apr. 1666). Money due from M^r Tho. Fenton of London, cit. & skinner, Tho. Browne & the r^t hon^ble the Lady Dacres being due for 3 years service; The Hon^ble Rich. Barrett esq & M^r Barretts foure most hopefull children; Bros. Edmund & Edward H. & sist. Anne; Sist-in-law Eliz. Humberstones & her dau; Neph^s Geo. & John H; Cous. Peter H.; Cous. Wm. Bright & his wife; M^r Adler & M^r Potkins & M^rs Higate; M^r Rich. Owen exor. *Thomas Humberstones.* Wits:—Anth. Adlard, Silvester Adams. (*Pr.* 26 Oct. 1666).

[P.C.C. Eure 136.]

JOHN HUMBERSTONE of Walton co. Suff. & now belonging unto his Majesties ship the Revenge under the command of S^r Edward Spragg Admirall. (*Dat.* 21 Nov. 1671). To Edward Finch & Sarah Humberstone his wife all my pay that is due which is about 15 months time. *John Hummerstone.* Wit^s :—John Dalling, Joseph Hall. (*Adm.* 8 Nov. 1672 to Sarah Humberstone *alias* Finch wife of Edw. Finch & sist. of testator).

[P.C.C. Foot 38.]

JOANE HUMMERSTON of psh. of S^t Margarets, Westminster, widow, being aged. (*Dat.* 21 July 1686). To be buried near the corps of my deceased husband Edward H.; Sist. Margt. Taylor of psh. of S^t Saviour's Southwark widow; Susanna Worsencroft of Westminster widow; Mrs. Newton; Mr. Richard Lapley; Grandson John Lapley son of s^d Rich. exor; Friends M^r Wm. Bounty & M^r Tho. Barrell overseers. [*Mark*]. Wit^s :—John Cranfeild, Tho. Bragg serv^t to Jn^o Thompson scr. (*Pr.* 11 Mch. 1686-7).

[P.C.C. Vere 115.]

PETER HUMBERSTON cit. & draper of London. (*Dat.* 6 May 1691). Messuage in Waltham Abbey adjoining to the Sunne Inne there, lately bought of Thos. Morrisbee of Westminster; Messuage called Nether Wells in Stevenedge co. Hertf. & lands thereto belonging; To all & every my cosens or kinsfolks being not above twice removed from mee in blood' 12d. each; To Elianor wife of Richard Taylor 5l. To [*blank*] Wakeland late the wife of George Wakeland dec^d 5l.; Rich. Crew & Edw. Crew his bro. exors; Rich. Taylor of S^t Margarets, Westminster. *Peter Humberstone.* Wit^s :— Mary Richmond, Will. Dowse, Geo. Greene, Fr. Gregory. (*Pr.* 25 July 1691).

[*A.A.* 1572 to 1580. *f.* 111.]

WILLIAM HUMBERSTON of Dunwiche, co. Suff. esq. *Adm.* 21 Nov. 1576 to Robt. Ashefilde of Stowe Langtofte co. Suff. esq.

[*A.A.* 1572 to 1580. *f.* 115.]

LEONARD HUMBERSTONE of Hackney, co. Midd. *Adm.* 25 Jan. 1576-7 to Beatrice Humberstone *alias* Daniell, the sister.

[*A.A.* 1592 to 1598. *f.* 160.]

CICILIA HUMBERSTONE of Walterstone, in psh. of Piddle Towne, co. Dorset. *Adm.* 18 Mch. 1595-6 to Wm. Humberstone of Grayes Inne, co. Midd. gent. the brother.

[*A.A. April* 1605 to 1610. *f.* 63.]

HENRY HUMBERSTON of Dagenham, co. Essex. *Adm.* 31 Jan. 1606-7 to Margerie Humberston, relict.

[*A.A. Aug.* 1625 *to* 1627. *f.* 139.]

LEONARD HUMBERSTON of Walkerne, co. Herts. *Adm.* 22 Mch. 1626-7 to Giles Humberston 'nepoti ex fratre.' *Adm. de bonis* 9 July 1628 to Richard Halfehead, nephew of s<sup>d</sup> Leonard (described as of Walkern Parke.) Another *admon. de bonis* 6 Feb. 1628-9 to Robert Humberston 'nepoti ex fratre,' the grant to Rich. Halfehead having been renounced.

[*A.A. June* 1636 *to* 1638. *f.* 226.]

CHARLES HUMBERSTONE of Eastbergholt, co. Suff. junior. *Adm.* 9 Nov. 1638 to Thomas Goodall, a creditor.

[*A.A.* 1647. *f.* 102.]

HENRY HUMBERSTON of psh. of S<sup>t</sup> Olave's, Hart Street, London. *Adm.* 29 July 1647 to James Humberston & Garnons Humberston brothers of dec<sup>d.</sup>

[*A.A.* 1650. *f.* 75.]

MARY HUMBERSTON of Westham, co. Essex. *Adm.* 17 May 1650 to Mary Pratt, widow, the dau. of dec<sup>d.</sup>

[*A.A.* 1651. *f.* 175.]

JAMES HUMBERSTONE of psh. of Clement Danes, co. Midd. bach<sup>r.</sup> *Adm.* 26 Nov. 1651 to W<sup>m.</sup> Johnson one of the creditors.

[*A.A.* 1653 & 1654. II. *f.* 222.]

MARGARET HUMBERSTON of Walesby, co. Linc., widow. *Adm.* 25 Nov. 1654 to Anne Johnson only child.

[*A.A.* 1657. *f.* 261.]

GEORGE HUMBERSTON of Naseing, co. Essex. *Adm.* 23 Oct. 1657 to Eliz. Humberston, widow, the relict.

[*A.A.* 1660. *f.* 141.]

MILES HUMMERSTON of psh. of S<sup>t</sup> Andrews, Holborn, London. *Adm.* 24 Sep. 1660 to Mary Hummerston, relict.

[*A.A.* 1673. *f.* 43.]

FRANCES REEVE ALIAS HUMBERSTONE of psh. of Stepney *als.* Stebonheath, co. Midd. *Adm.* 14 Apr. 1673 to Samuel Reeve the husband.

[*A.A.* 1681. *f.* 147.]

THOMAS HUMBERSTONE of Newington, co. Midd., bach<sup>r.</sup> *Adm.* 19 Nov. 1681 to W<sup>m.</sup> Humberstone, the brother.

[*A.A.* 1685. *f.* 135.]

EDWARD HUMMERSTON of the psh. of S<sup>t</sup> Margaret's Westminster, co. Midd. *Adm.* 15 Oct. 1685 to Joan Hummerston, widow, the relict.

*To be Continued.*

# A List of Inquisitiones post Mortem.

**HENRY VII. TO CHARLES I.**

(CONTINUED FROM PAGE 19).

| | | |
|---|---|---|
| Grey, Ralph | 13 Hen. VII. | 108 |
| Grubbe, Eustace, gent. (21 Car.) | Eliz. Jas. Car. pt. 18 | 37 |
| Grubbe, Geo. | 19 Eliz. pt. 1 | 110 |
| Grubbe, Henry | 3 & 4 Ph. & M. pt. 2 | 82 |
| Gulston, John esq. (20 Car.) | Eliz. Jas. Car. pt. 26 | 16 |
| Gybbe, John | 7 Jas. I. pt. 1 | 106 |
| Gybbe, Wm. gent. (2 Car.) | Eliz. Jas. Car. pt. 26 | 138 |
| Hale, Rich. | 19 Jas. I. pt. 1 | 110 |
| Hale, Wm. | 11 Car. I. pt. 2 | 148 |
| Hale, Wm. (18 Car.) | Eliz. Jas. Car. pt. 16 | 65 |
| Halfhidde, Edw. | 27 Eliz. | 70 |
| Halsey, Wm. | 14 Car. I. pt. 3 | 46 |
| Halsey *alias* Chambers, Robt. | 17 Jas. I. pt. 1 | 102 |
| Halsey *alias* Chambers, Wm. | 38 Eliz. pt. 1 | 7 |
| Hammond, John (18 Car.) | Eliz. Jas. Car. pt. 16 | 63 |
| Hamond, Edw. | 22 Eliz. pt. 1 | 88 |
| Hamond, Edw. | 16 Car. I. pt. 3 | 46 |
| Hamond, Wm. | 2 Car. I. pt. 3 | 110 |
| Hamonde, Alexr. esq. | 2 Jas. I. pt. 2 | 96 |
| Hampden, Jerome | 33 Hen. VIII. | 188 |
| Hanchett, Wm. | 8 Hen. VIII. | 57 |
| Harmer, Thos. | 6 Car. I. pt. 2 | 33 |
| Harmer, Thos. (7 Car.) | Eliz. Jas. Car. pt. 25 | 171 |
| Harper, John | 40 Eliz. pt. 1 | 65 |
| Harrison, Robt. | 12 Car. I. pt. 3 | 58 |
| Hartwell, John, gent. (21 Car.) | Eliz. Jas. Car. pt. 26 | 78 |
| Harvey, Steph. knt. | 12 Car. I. pt. 3 | 84 |
| Harvey, Wm. (2 Car.) | Eliz. Jas. Car. pt. 26 | 135 |
| Harvye, John | 7 Jas. I. pt. 1 | 82 |
| Haukyns, John | 4 Hen. VII. | 71 |
| Hawese, Wm. | 38 Hen. VIII. | 96 |
| Hawgood, John | 23 Eliz. pt. 2 | 57 |
| Heigham, Henry | 30 Eliz. pt. 1 | 105 |
| Hemyng, Robt. | 3 Car. I. pt. 2 | 27 |
| Hemynge, Sam. gent. (15 Car.) | Eliz. Jas. Car. pt. 31 | 30 |
| Hewett, Henry | 41 Eliz. pt. 2 | 69 |
| Heydon, Wm. | 38 Hen. VIII. | 48 |
| Hickes, Rich. | 3 Jas. I. pt. 1 | 83 |
| Hickes, Rice | 17 Jas. I. pt. 2 | 125 |
| Hickes, Rice | 18 Jas. I. pt. 2 | 146 |
| Hickes, Rice 'melius' | 19 Jas. I. pt. 1 | 17 |
| Hickman, Geo. (11 Car.) | Eliz. Jas. Car. pt. 22 | 64 |

| | | |
|---|---|---|
| Hickman, Henry | 36 Eliz. pt. 2 | 40 |
| Hickman, Henry | 20 Jas. I. pt. 1 | 39 |
| Hide, Nich. | 2 Car. I. pt. 3 | 177 |
| Hide, Robt. | 6 Jas. I. pt. 2 | 128 |
| Hill, Gilbt. | 43 Eliz. pt. 2 | 116 |
| Hoo, Thos. esq. | 2 Hen. VII. | 5 |
| Horsey, Marie, of Dyggeswell | 5 Edw. VI. pt. 1 | 104 |
| Horsey, Jasper | 3 Car. I. pt. 2 | 86 |
| Horsey, Jasper | 13 Car. I. pt. 1 | 119 |
| Hurst, John | 11 Car. I. pt. 1 | 132 |
| Hurste, Robt. | 25 Eliz. | 34 |
| Hutchinson, Rich. lunatic | 9 Eliz. | 129 |
| Hyde, Wm. | 23 Eliz. pt. 1 | 69 |
| | | |
| Ibgrave, Benj. | 2 Jas. I. pt. 2 | 140 |
| Ibgrave, John esq. | 5 Eliz. pt. 2 | 24 |
| Ibgrave, Thos. | 1 Eliz. pt. 1 | 89 |
| Ibgrave, Wm. | 2 & 3 Ph. & M. pt. 1 | 80 |
| | | |
| Jacobb, Jas. | 3 Eliz. | 106 |
| Jennis, Thos. | 37 Eliz. pt. 2 | 94 |
| Jennynges, John, knt. lunatic | 5 Jas. I. pt. 2 | 63 |
| Jennynges, Ralph | 27 Eliz. | 15 |
| Jenyns *alias* Jenynges, John | 8 Jas. I. pt. 2 | 156 |
| Johnson, Thos. | 19 Eliz. pt. 1 | 109 |
| Josselyn, John | 17 Hen. VIII. | 21 |
| | | |
| Kent, John | 34 Eliz. pt. 2 | 137 |
| Kent, John | 16 Jas. I. pt. 2 | 137 |
| Kent, John | 4 Car. I. pt. 4 | 59 |
| Kent, Thos. | 11 Car. I. pt. 2 | 17 |
| Kentish, Rich. (11 Car.) | Eliz. Jas. Car. pt. 22 | 161 |
| Kentish, Thos. | 4 Car. I. pt. 4 | 81 |
| Kentish, Thos. (20 Car.) | Eliz. Jas. Car. pt. 30 | 161 |
| Kentish, Wm. (19 Car.) | Eliz. Jas. Car. pt. 32 | 102 |
| Kindesley, Wm. | 15 Jas. I. pt. 2 | 112 |
| Kinge, Arthur | 6 Car. I. v.o. | 11 |
| Kinge, John | 16 Car. I. pt. 3 | 124 |
| Kirby, Rich. | 7 Jas. I. pt. 1 | 164 |
| Knight, Wm. | 20 Car. I. | 9 |
| Knighton, Geo. knt. | 12 Jas. I. pt. 1 | 143 |
| Knighton, John | 28 Eliz. pt. 2 | 191 |
| Knighton, John | 41 Eliz. pt. 2 | 77 |
| Knighton, John | 11 Car. I. pt. 2 | 129 |
| Knighton, Thos. | 36 Hen. VIII. | 11 |
| Knott, Edw. | 16 Jas. I. pt. 2 | 138 |
| Knyght, John | 9 Car. I. pt. 2 | 56 |
| Kympton, Geo. | 7 Jas. I. pt. 1 | 118 |
| Kympton, Wm. | 26 Eliz. | 127 |
| | | |
| Lane, Wm. | 10 Eliz. | 126 |
| Lane, Wm. | 12 Car. I. pt. 3 | 53 |
| Laurence, Alice lunatic | 3 Jas. I. pt. 1 | 77 |
| Lazenby, Rich. | 7 Car. I. v.o. | 32 |
| Lee, Geo. | 40 Eliz. pt. 1 | 11 |

| | | |
|---|---|---|
| Lee, Rich. knt. | 22 Eliz. pt. 1 | 86 |
| Leigh, Thos. | 5 & 6 Ph. & M. pt. 2 | 85 |
| Leventhorpe, Agnes | 9 Hen. VIII. | 74 |
| Leventhorpe, Edw. | 6 Edw. VI. pt. 1 | 94 |
| Leventhorpe, Edw. | 9 Eliz. | 125 |
| Leventhorpe, John | 4 Hen. VIII. | 11 |
| Leventhorpe, John, proof of age | 9 Hen. VIII. | 137 |
| Leventhorpe, John knt. & bart. | 8 Car. I. pt. 3 | 93 |
| Leventhorpe, Thos. | Ric. III. & Hen. VII. v.o. | 127 |
| Leventhorpe, Thos. | 15 Hen. VII. | 86 |
| Leventhorpe, Thos. | 19 Hen. VIII. | 49 |
| Leventhorpe, Thos. | Hen. VIII. v.o. 1st bund. | 37 |
| Leventhorpe, Thos. bart. | 12 Car. I. pt. 3 | 115 |
| Litton, Rowland | 24 Eliz. pt. 2 | 89 |
| Litton, Roland | 14 Jas. I. pt. 3 | 114 |
| Louth, Robt. | 2 Hen. VII. | 20 |
| Lovell, Fras. late viscount 'de petitione recti' | 8 Hen. VII. | 92 |
| Lovell, Henry, lord Morley | 5 Hen. VII. | 48 |
| Lovell, Joan | 12 Eliz. | 158 |
| Lucie, Edm. knt. | 8 Car. I. pt. 2 | 58 |
| Lucy, Edm. knt. | 13 Car. I. pt. 1 | 186 |
| Lytton, Robt. knt. | 6 Edw. VI. pt. 1 | 99 |
| Lytton, Wm. | 10 Hen. VIII. | 5 |
| Mannyngham, John | 21 Jas. I. pt. 1 | 137 |
| Marsh, John (11 Car.) | Eliz. Jas. Car. pt. 22 | 63 |
| Marshe, Andrew | 4 Car. I. pt. 4 | 41 |
| Marshe, John | 8 Jas. I. pt. 2 | 57 |
| Marston, Fras. | 23 Eliz. pt. 1 | 71 |
| Marston, Geo. | 11 Car. I. v.o. | 23 |
| Marston, Joseph | 14 Car. I. pt. 3 | 26 |
| Marston, Wm. | 1 Jas. I. pt. 1 | 17 |
| Maynard, Henry | 9 Jas. I. pt. 1 | 161 |
| Maynarde, John | 3 & 4 Ph. & M. pt. 1 | 58 |
| Maynerde, John | Eliz. v.o. 1st bund. | 511 |
| Mayne, Henry gent. | 4 Jas. I. pt. 2 | 35 |
| Mayne, Jas. | 1 Car. I. pt. 2 | 102 |
| Mayne, Jas. esq. | 20 Car. I. | 62 |
| Mayne, John (21 Car.) | Eliz. Jas. Car. pt. 32 | 98 |
| Melkisham, John | 3 Hen. VII. | 73 |
| Melton, Geo. gent. (15 Jas.) | Eliz. Jas. Car. pt. 2 | 55 |
| Meperteshale, John (vide Leventhorpe) | Hen. VIII. v.o. pt. bund. | 37 |
| Mercers of London 'ad quod dampnum' | 5 Hen. VIII. | 69 |
| Mershe, Agnes | 22 Hen. VIII. | 29 |
| Michell, John | 38 Eliz. pt. 1 | 9 |
| Michell, Thos. | 10 Jas. I. pt. 1 | 107 |
| Mildmay, Walter knt. | 5 Jas. I. pt. 1 | 85 |
| Milward, Wm. | 37 Hen. VIII. | 85 |
| Milward, Wm. | 38 Hen. VIII. | 97 |
| Milward *alias* Alexander, Wm. | 7 Eliz. | 100 |
| Moore, Tho. esq. | 5 Jas. I. pt. 2 | 150 |
| Moreton, Agnes | 9 Hen. VIII. | 88 |
| Morgan, David Gwillin | 16 Hen. VIII | 105 |
| Morgan, Marg. Gwillin | 4 Hen. VIII. | 54 |

| | | |
|---|---|---|
| Morrison, Chas. knt. & bart. | 9 Car. I. pt. 1 | 17 |
| Morrison, Rich. knt. | 1 Eliz. pt. 1 | 65 |
| Morryson, Chas. knt. | 41 Eliz. pt. 1 | 45 |
| Moseley, John | 20 Jas. I. pt. 2 | 52 |
| Mountford, Tho. | 9 Car. I. pt. 1 | 41 |
| Mussett, Wm. | 7 Jas. I. pt. 1 | 131 |
| | | |
| Nashe, Wm. | 2 Eliz. pt. 1 | 85 |
| Nedeham, Jas. | 36 Hen. VIII. | 112 |
| Nedham, Geo. | 2 Car. I. pt. 3 | 161 |
| Nedham, John | 34 Eliz. pt. 1 | 63 |
| Nele, Geo. (9 Jas.) | Eliz. Jas. Car. pt. 2 | 46 |
| Nevill, Geo. son & heir of Isabelle who was the wife of Wm. Norris & late wife of John Nevill late Marquis Montague | 2 Hen. VII. | 81 |
| Newce, Clement | 22 Eliz. pt. 1 | 92 |
| Newce, Thos. | 2 Car. I. pt. 3 | 131 |
| Newce, Wm. | 10 Jas. I. pt. 1 | 99 |
| Newport, Edw. | 3 Car. I. pt. 2 | 125 |
| Newport, George | Rich. III. & Hen. VII. v.o. | 61 |
| Newport, John | 16 Hen. VIII. | 96 |
| Newport, John | 1 Mary | 48 |
| Newport, Robt. | 11 Henry VIII. | 96 |
| Newport, Robt. | 25 Eliz. | 52 |
| Nicholls, John | 35 Eliz. pt. 1 | 41 |
| Nicholls, Wm. senr. (20 Car.) | Eliz. Jas. Car. pt. 26 | 59 |
| Nodes, Geo. esq. (20 Car.) | Eliz. Jas. Car. pt. 32 | 91 |
| Nobbes, Steph. | 38 Eliz. pt. 1 | 92 |
| Noble, Thos. clerk (7 Car.) | Eliz. Jas. Car. pt. 25 | 159 |
| Nodes, Chas. | 35 Eliz. pt. 2 | 37 |
| Nodes, Geo. | 6 Eliz. | 73 |
| Nodes, Geo. esq. (20 Car.) | Eliz. Jas. Car. pt. 32 | 124 |
| Noreis, Isabell, who was the wife of Wm. Noreis knt. and late wife of John Nevil, Marquis Montague | 2 Hen. VII. | 61 |
| Norfolk, Thos. duke of | 14 Eliz. | 79 |
| Norres, John | 14 Hen. VIII. | 34 |
| North, Edw. | 5 Jas. I. pt. 2 | 80 |
| Northampton. *See Bourcher*. | | |
| | | |
| Ogard, Andrew | 18 Hen. VIII. | 104 |
| Oxford, John, earl of | 5 Hen. VIII. | 68 |
| | | |
| Page, Rich. knt. | 4 & 5 Ph. & M. pt. 1 | 79 |
| Paker, John gent. | 4 Jas. I. pt. 2 | 22 |
| Palmer *alias* Pigotte, Margt. | 23 Eliz. pt. 1 | 54 |
| Palmer, Thos. | 6 Jas. I. pt. 2 | 77 |
| Partridge, John | 27 Eliz. | 117 |
| Patmere, Henry | Hen. VIII. v.o. 1st bund. | 225 |
| Paulett, Lady Eliz. | 36 Eliz. pt. 1 | 66 |
| Paver, Jas. | 21 Eliz. pt. 2 | 9 |
| Payne, Thos. | 26 Eliz. | 114 |
| Peacock, Wm. | 22 Jas. I. pt. 1 | 157 |

| | | |
|---|---|---|
| Pemberton, John esq. (21 Car.) | Eliz. Jas. Car. pt. 26 | 64 |
| Pemberton, Marie | 8 Jas. I. pt. 2 | 101 |
| Pemberton, Ralph gent. (21 Car.) | Eliz. Jas. Car. pt. 26 | 76 |
| Pemberton, Roger | 6 Car. I. pt. 3 | 50 |
| Pen, John | 5 & 6 Ph. & M. pt. 2 | 87 |
| Pen, Thos. gent. | 1 Jas. I. pt. 1 | 21 |
| Penne, Ralph esq. | 2 Hen. VII. | 16 |
| Penne, Robt. | 35 Eliz. pt. 2 | 97 |
| Peryent, Thos. | 33 Hen. VIII. | 61 |
| Peryent, Thos. | 37 Hen. VIII. pt. 2 | 89 |
| Pett, Henry (10 Car.) | Eliz. Jas. Car. pt. 22 | 84 |
| Phillipps, John | Eliz. Jas. Car. pt. 1 | 6 |
| Philpott, — lunatic | 34 Hen. VIII. | 84 |
| Philpott, John knt. | 19 Hen. VII. | 44 |
| Pigotte, John | 20 Eliz. pt. 1 | 115 |
| Pigotte. See Palmer. | | |
| Pindar, Paul esq. (21 Car.) | Eliz. Jas. Car. pt. 26 | 23 |
| Plomer, Wm. | 3 Car. I. pt. 2 | 84 |
| Pope Blunt. See Blunt. | | |
| Poulton, Fras. esq. (18 Car.) | Eliz. Jas. Car. pt. 16 | 72 |
| Powtrell, John idiot | Ric. III. & Hen. VII. v.o. | 38 |
| Pranell, Henry | 12 Jas. I. pt. 1 | 168 |
| Prannell, Henry | 32 Eliz. | 64 |
| Pratt, Augustine | 18 Jas. I. pt. 2 | 123 |
| Pratt, Simon | Hen. VIII. v.o. 2nd bund. | 276 |
| Pratt, Thos. | 9 Car. I. pt. 1 | 49 |
| Preistley, Wm. | 19 Jas. I. pt. 1 | 34 |
| Preston, Wm. | 33 Eliz. pt. 1 | 99 |
| Preston, Wm. gent. (20 Car.) | Eliz. Jas. Car. pt. 26 | 27 |
| Puckeringe, John | 38 Eliz. pt. 1 | 125 |
| Pulteney, Fras. | 2 Edw. VI. pt. 1 | 98 |
| Pulteney, Michael esq. | 9 Eliz. | 128 |
| Pulteney, Thos. | 22 Hen. VII. | 113 |
| Pulter, Edw. | 5 Car. I. pt. 2 | 94 |
| Pulter, John | 3 Hen. VII. | 74 |
| Pulter, Litton | 6 Jas. I. pt. 2 | 111 |
| Pultney, John knt. | 15 Jas. I. pt. 1 | 189 |
| Pultney, Thos. knt. | 32 Hen. VIII. | 87 |
| Purevey, John | 25 Eliz. | 71 |
| Purevey, Wm. | 16 Jas. I. pt. 1 | 165 |
| Purevey, Wm. | 18 Jas. I. pt. 2 | 45 |
| Pygott, Thos. | 8 Jas. I. pt. 2 | 153 |
| Pylkington, Thos. 'attainted' | Ric. III. & Hen. VII. v.o. | 98 |
| | | |
| Radcliffe, Ralph esq. (20 Jas.) | Eliz. Jas. Car. pt. 13 | 25 |
| Ramrige, — lunatic | 35 Hen. VIII. | 42 |
| Ramsey, Thos. | 3 Eliz. | 107 |
| Reade, Innocent | 39 Eliz. pt. 2 | 81 |
| Reade, Rich. knt. | 19 Eliz. pt. 1 | 102 |
| Redinge, Thos. | 2 Eliz. pt. 2 | 12 |
| Redwood, John | 16 Eliz. pt. 2 | 87 |
| Richmond, Margt. countess of | Hen. VIII. v.o. 3rd bund. | 313 |
| Richmond & Somerset, Henry duke of | Hen. VIII. v.o. 3rd bund. | 88 |
| Roberts, Thos. | 28 Hen. VIII. | 41 |
| Robotham, Margt. | 14 Jas. I. pt. 3 | 52 |

| | | |
|---|---|---|
| Rogers, Thos. | 4 Hen. VII. | 29 |
| Rolfe, Jas. | 7 Car. I. pt. 2 | 57 |
| Rolfe, Wm. idiot | 12 Car. I. pt. 3 | 46 |
| Rowce, Thos. | 5 Eliz. pt. 2 | 25 |
| Rowlett, Ralph | 35 Hen. VIII. | 40 |
| Rowlette, Ralph | 27 Eliz. | 3 |
| Rudd, Thos. | 11 Jas. I. v.o. | 45 |
| Rudd, Thos. | 13 Car. I. v.o. | 98 |
| Rushley, Henry idiot | 22 Eliz. pt. 1 | 85 |
| Ryvers, Anth. earl | 1 Hen. VII. | 37 |
| | | |
| Sadler, Lee | 35 Eliz. pt. 2 | 72 |
| Sadler, Ralph knt. | 29 Eliz. | 259 |
| Sadler, Thos. | 5 Jas. I. pt. 1 | 95 |
| Sadlier, Rich. | 1 Car. I. pt. 2 | 118 |
| St. Albans Abbey, 'ad quod dampnum' | 7 Hen. VIII. | 87 |
| Sanbache, Joan, wid. | 4 Jas. I. pt. 2 | 34 |
| Sankey, Edw. | 6 Edw. VI. pt. 1 | 97 |
| Sanson, John | 29 Eliz. | 130 |
| Saunders, John | 11 Jas. I. pt. 3 | 187 |
| Sawyer, John | 17 Hen. VIII. | 44 |
| Say, Wm. knt. | 22 Hen. VIII. | 50 |
| Scrogges, John | 39 Eliz. pt. 2 | 69 |
| Scrogges, John | 14 Jas. I. pt. 3 | 10 |
| Scroggs, Thos. | 30 Hen. VIII. | 147 |
| Scrope, John, de Bolton, knt. | 14 Hen. VII. | 138 |
| Scudamore, Clement, knt. | 11 Car. I. pt. 3 | 12 |
| Seyntmont, Eliz. who was the wife of Roger Tocotes | 6 Hen. VII. | 49 |
| Sharnebrooke, Wm. | 5 Eliz. pt. 1 | 80 |
| Shelley, John, cit. & mercer of London | 2 Hen. VII. | 47 |
| Shelley, John | 19 Hen. VIII. | 40 |
| Shelley, Thos. | 15 Hen. VII. | 127 |
| Sheldon, Rich. | 10 Hen. VII. | 70 |
| Sheldon, Rich. | 14 Hen. VIII. | 88 |
| Sheppard, Thos. | 4 Car. I. pt. 4 | 44 |
| Sibley, John | 29 Eliz. | 61 |
| Skegges, Edw. | 21 Eliz. pt. 2 | 6 |
| Skelton, Robt. (8 Car.) | Eliz. Jas. Car. pt. 21 | 145 |
| Skynner, Augustine | 15 Car. I. pt. 3 | 80 |
| Sleape, Philip | 36 Eliz. pt. 2 | 67 |
| Sleape, Rich. | 10 Jas. I. v.o. pt. 2 | 43 |
| Smartfote, Thos. | 44 Eliz. pt. 2 | 116 |
| Smithe, Anthony | 43 Eliz. pt. 2 | 73 |
| Smithe, Isabell | 39 Eliz. pt. 2 | 92 |
| Smyth, Anth. gent. (12 Car.) | Eliz. Jas. Car. pt. 24 | 168 |
| Smyth, Edw. | 8 Jas. I. pt. 2 | 35 |
| Somerset, Alianore, duchess of, wife of Thos. lord Roose, attainted | 2 Hen. VII. | 89 |
| Sowthend, John | 11 Jas. I. pt. 2 | 54 |
| Spencer, John | 13 Jas. I. pt. 1 | 151 |
| Spencer John, bart. | 10 Car. I. pt. 3 | 4 |
| Spencer, Rich. knt. | 1 Car. I. pt. 1 | 95 |
| Spencer, Robt. | 7 Car. I. pt. 3 | 13 |

| | | |
|---|---|---|
| Spencer, Wm. | 15 Car. I. pt. 4 | 12 |
| Spicer *alias* Helder, Rich. | 9 Jas. I. pt. 1 | 117 |
| Spurlinge, John | 2 Jas. I. pt. 2 | 127 |
| Stafford, Humph. earl of Devon | 5 Hen. VII. | 52 |
| Stafford, Humph. knt. | 18 Eliz. pt. 1 | 74 |
| Stafford, Kath. late wife of Humph. | 2 Hen. VII. | 72 |
| Stanford, Joan, late wife of John | 5 Hen. VII. | 23 |
| Stanford, John | 9 Hen. VII. | 56 |
| Stanford, John (vide Leventhorpe) | Hen. VIII. v.o. 1st bund. | 37 |
| Stanley, Eliz. late wife of Wm. Stanley, knt. | 14 Hen. VII. | 21 |
| Stanley Jas. | 12 Jas. I. pt. 1 | 179 |
| Stepneth, Ralph | 3 Edw. VI. | 72 |
| Stepneth, Ralph | 8 Eliz. | 123 |
| Stepney, John | 21 Hen. VIII. | 13 |
| Steward, John esq. | 12 Car. I. pt. 3 | 114 |
| Stubbing, Mark clerk (14 Car.) | Eliz. Jas. Car. pt. 27 | 194 |
| Sturges, Thos. | 2 Jas. I. pt. 2 | 15 |
| Sturman, John | 3 & 4 Jas. I. v.o. | 59 |
| Sturman, John | 6 Jas. I. pt. 2 | 36 |
| Stuttesbury, John (20 Jas.) | Eliz. Jas. Car. pt. 5 | 98 |
| Sulihart, Edw. | 8 Hen. VIII. | 97 |
| Sulyard, Eustace | 2 Edw. VI. pt. 1 | 99 |
| Sulyard, Wm. knt. | 33 Hen. VIII. | 88 |
| | | |
| Tavener, Peter gent. | Eliz. Jas. Car. pt. 2 | 52 |
| Tayleor, Henry | 25 Eliz. | 31 |
| Tayler, Edw. | 14 Eliz. | 78 |
| Taylor, Thos. | 2 Jas. I. pt. 2 | 92 |
| Taylor, Wm. | 16 Jas. I. pt. 1 | 48 |
| Tebbes, Rich. | 18 Eliz. pt. 1 | 70 |
| Thorougood, Thos. | 5 Eliz. pt. 1 | 77 |
| Thorowgood, John | 12 Eliz. | 156 |
| Thurgood, Tho. | 16 Car. I. pt. 3 | 30 |
| Tocotes, Roger knt. | 8 Hen. VII. | 96 |
| Tooke, John esq. | 10 Car. I. pt. 3 | 83 |
| Tooke, Ralph esq. | 12 Car. I. pt. 3 | 103 |
| Tooke, Thos. | 21 Jas. I. pt. 2 | 65 |
| Tooke, Walter | 8 Jas. I. pt. 2 | 163 |
| Tooke, Walter | 18 Car. I. pt. 1 | 10 |
| Tooke, Wm. auditor | 38 Eliz. pt. 1 | 124 |
| Tooke, Wm. | 16 Jas. I. pt. 1 | 149 |
| Turnor, John | 44 Eliz. pt. 1 | 55 |
| Turnor, Rich. | 3 & 4 Jas. I. v.o. | 4 |
| | | |
| Vaughan, Henry | 17 Jas. I. pt. 3 | 35 |
| Vaughan, Tho. | 2 & 3 Ph. & M. pt. 1 | 79 |
| Vaughan, Tho. | 40 Eliz. pt. 2 | 70 |
| Vaus, Nich. lord | 16 Hen. VIII. | 97 |
| Venables, Tho. attainted | 27 Eliz. | 106 |
| Verney, John knt. | 21 Hen. VII. | 20 |
| Verney, Ralph | 17 Hen. VIII. | 74 |
| Verney, Ralph | 38 Hen. VIII. | 99 |

| | | |
|---|---|---|
| Waferer, Arden | 16 Jas. I. pt. 1 | 44 & 71 |
| Walter, Jeremy gent. (11 Jas.) | Eliz. Jas. Car. pt. 2 | 44 |
| Walwen, Thos. | 23 Eliz. pt. 1 | 64 |
| Warren & Surrey, Edw. earl of | 5 Hen. VIII. | 71 |
| Warren, Geo. | 32 Hen. VIII. | 48 |
| Warren, John | 13 Car. I. pt. 1 | 70*b* |
| Warren, Lawr. | 3 & 4 Ph. & M. pt. 2 | 80 |
| Warren, Simon | 11 Car. I. pt. 2 | 79 |
| Warren, Wm. | 15 Eliz. | 69 |
| Warren, Wm. | 31 Eliz. pt. 1 | 113 |
| Warren, Wm. | 2 Car. I. pt. 2 | 44 |
| Warrenn, John | 18 Car. I. pt. 1 | 5 & 11 |
| Warrenn, John | 19 Car. I. | 14 |
| Warwick, Anne countess of | 2 Jas. I. pt. 2 | 184 |
| Waterman, Eliz. widow (7 Car.) | Eliz. Jas. Car. pt. 22 | 79 |
| Watson, Edw. | 22 Hen. VIII. | 13 |
| Wattes, John alderman of London | 14 Jas. I. pt. 1 | 135 |
| Wattie, Henry | 1 & 2 Jas. I. v.o. | 26 |
| Wattye, Henry (11 Car.) | Eliz. Jas. Car. pt. 22 | 83 |
| Webbe, Wm. knt. | 41 Eliz. pt. 1 | 25 |
| Weld, Humph. knt. | 9 Jas. I. pt. 1 | 173 |
| Weld, John knt. | 21 Jas. I. pt. 2 | 132 |
| Welsh, John (4 Car.) | Eliz. Jas. Car. pt. 24 | 148 |
| Wethered, John | 15 Car. I. pt. 4 | 56 |
| Wight, Thos. | 7 Jas. I. pt. 1 | 95 |
| Wilcocks, Rich. | 6 Eliz. | 74 |
| Wilkinson, Gilb. | Eliz. v.o. 2nd bund. | 41 |
| Willesborne, Anne who was the wife of Giles W. esq. | 10 Hen. VII. | 31 |
| Willett, Andrew | 22 Jas. I. pt. 2 | 51 |
| Willoughby, Robt. lord de Broke | 16 Hen. VIII. | 98 |
| Willis, Rich. | 1 Car. I. pt. 1 | 64 |
| Willshere, John | 12 Car. I. v.o. | 46 |
| Willson, Edw. | 24 Eliz. pt. 2 | 88 |
| Wilshire, Tho. | 12 Eliz. | 157 |
| Wilson, Edw. | 5 Eliz. pt. 1 | 79 |
| Wilson, Edw. | 15 Car. I. pt. 3 | 65 |
| Wilson, Ralph | 13 Car. I. pt. 1 | 199 |
| Wiltshire, Thos. (20 Jas.) | Eliz. Jas. Car. pt. 5 | 97 |
| Wolley, Robt. | 45 Eliz. | 160 |
| Wolley, Tho. | 7 Jas. I. pt. 1 | 114 |
| Woodhall, Edw. | 15 Car. I. pt. 3 | 75 |
| Woodliffe, Wm. | 2 Edw. VI. pt. 1 | 102 |
| Wroth, Robt. | 18 Hen. VII. | 102 |
| Wrothe, Wm. | 37 Eliz. pt. 2 | 64 |
| Wydevill, Rich. attainted | Ric. III. & Hen. VII. v.o. | 9 |
| Wyndout, Barth. | 13 Hen. VIII. | 76 |
| Yonge, Rich. | 36 Eliz. pt. 2 | 89 |

## Abstracts of Wills.

### CONSISTORY COURT OF THE BISHOP OF LONDON.

REGISTER "SPERIN." (CONTINUED FROM PAGE 12).

f. 136. RICHARD PHILLIPS of Much Haddham. (*Dat.* 5 Sep. 1595). Sons Thos, John, Wm. (under 24), Tobias & Richard (under 21); Daus. Kath. Barsfoote, Eliz. Fest; Sist. Margt. Porter; Wife Agnes extrix & bro. Tho. Phillips supervisor. *Wit*<sup>s</sup>:—Tho. Phillips & Allen Howe. (*Pr.* 31 Mch. 1596).

f. 147. THOMAS REEVE of Hoddesdon, butcher. (*Dat.* 24 Nov. 1594). Wife Johane extrix; Three cottages in Hoddesdon bought of Wm. Rusheley; Joane Reeve my bro. Roberts dau; Thos, Nich. & Christ<sup>r</sup> Reeve my brothers sons; Rich. Browne my sist. Joane Brownes son; Friends Robt. Michaell & Robt. Guthre overseers. *Wit*<sup>s</sup>:—The two overseers. (*Pr.* 15 Dec. 1596).

f. 150. WILLIAM LOWIN of Tunforde in psh. of Chesthunte, yeoman. (*Dat.* 31 Oct. 1595). Houses & lands in Tunford; Wife Margery; Son Thos. exor. *Signum Will'mi Lowen.* *Wit*<sup>s</sup>:—Signum Johannis Lowin, Edw. Colt, hujus scriptoris. (*Pr.* 14 [*blank*] 1597).

f. 156. RICHARD HILL of Wormelye, husbandman. (*Dat.* 7 Mch. 1597). Son Edw; Money owing at Barkhamstead & Bayford; My wifes four girls. *Wit*<sup>s</sup>:—Polidore Wardroppe, Wm. Saringe. (*Pr.* 28 June 1598).

f. 157. THOMAS WILLIATT parson of the parishe churche of Barley. (*Dat.* 13 Apr. 40 Eliz). Bur. in churchyard of Barley; Wife Margt. extrix. *Per me Thomā Wylliatt.* *Wit*<sup>s</sup>:—Henry Scott, Signū Johannis Kinge de Foulsmire, Jane Stape. (*Pr.* 1 July 1598).

f. 159* JOHN SKYNNER of the psh. of S<sup>t</sup> Albones in S<sup>t</sup> Albans. (*Dat.* 8 Aug. 1598). Dau. Alice now wife of Walter Cutberd; Isabell Cutthertt dau. of s<sup>d</sup> Alice; Dau. Eliz. wife of Richard Winstanley; House called the Well house abutting upon the Lether markett in Sainct Albons; Wife Joane; Dau. Dorothy wife of Wm. Hill of London gent; Dau. Margery wife of M<sup>r</sup> Cannon Rawlin; Sons in law M<sup>r</sup> Conon Rawlin & Rich. Winstanley exors. *Signu Johannis Skynner.* *Wit*<sup>s</sup>:—Roger Williams minister of Sainct Alb., Wm. Anterbus, Wm. Spencer. (*Pr.* 15 Sep. 1598).

f. 160. JOHN STANNOPE als. SANNATT of Rugg *als.* Ridge, laborer. (*Dat.* 12 June 1598). Son Edw; Wife Joane extrix. John Beamon jun. overseer. *John Stannatt.* *Wit*<sup>s</sup>:—John Browne writer hereof, John Beaman, John Bowman. (*Pr.* 26 Sep. 1598).

* Also registered at f. 213 where the date of probate is given as 25 Sep. 1598.

## ABSTRACTS OF WILLS.

f. 163. JOHN PORTER of S$^t$ Albans. (*Dat.* 24 Nov. 1598). Two houses in S$^t$ Peters Street the one occupied by Symonds & the other by the Collermaker: John Nashe & W$^m$. Nashe (both minors); Michaell Nashe; Gyles Nashe; Anne Saunders (minor); Trustram Nashe exor; Roger Nicholls of Willin and John Saunders of S$^t$ Albans overseers. (*Mark*). *Wit$^s$*:— Thomas Porter clarke, Roger Nicholls. (*Pr.* 18 Jan. 1598-9).

f. 164. ANNE ADDAM widow, late wife of Robert Adam of Brawghinge, yeoman, dec$^d$. (*Dat.* 14 Feb. 1595). Son Henry Johnson; Daus. Alice Johnson, Eliz. Orger, Kath. Colt & Marryon Hamond; My sons & daughters child$^n$; Cous. Robt. Kinge of Aldbury & Joane Kinge of Dunmowe; Edw. son of W$^m$. Maior of Aldbury & Tho. son of Henry Orger of Brawghinge (both under 16); Anne Barrett dau. of Joane Barrett & Ursula Barrett his sister; Dau. Jenings; Joane Orger; Son Tho. Jenings fishmonger of London exor; Sons in law Jas. Orger thelder & Geo. Hamond overseers. *Wit$^s$*:— Henry Orger, Rich. Burton. (*Pr.* 23 Jan. 1598-9).

f. 165. NICHOLAS HAWGOOD of Woddend in psh. of Redburne, yeoman. (*Dat.* 13 Sep. 1593). Sister Amye wife of Tho. Wilson; Kinsman John Hawgood; Son Tho. & son-in-law Henry Strayte exors; Kinsman Nich. Martyn overseer. *Wit$^s$*:— Tho. Carpenter, Tho. Younge, Nich. Martin. (*Pr.* 19 Dec. 1598).

f. 170. HENRY BUMSTEDD of Wormeley, basket maker. (*Dat.* 14 Aug. 1598). Son W$^m$.; Dau. Alice; Dau. Joane; My sister Bumstedd; Wife Kath. extrix. *Wit$^s$*:—Cesar Walpoole, John Johnson, W$^m$. Turner, W$^m$. Parratt & Geo. Clarke. (*Pr.* 9 Dec. 1598).

f. 173. WILLIAM HARVEY of S$^t$ Albans, butcher. (*Dat.* 27 Sep. 1598). Bur. at S$^t$ Peters; Lands in Ware & Amwell; Houses & lands in S$^t$ Albans; Son W$^m$.; Daus. Alice & Margt.; Son Rich.; Wife Joane; Son John; Son W$^m$. exor. (*Mark*). *Wit$^s$*:—Richard Denton, W$^m$. Everett, John Browne, Tho. Harvey & Tho. Wells scr. (*Pr.* 4 Dec. 1598).

f. 190. GEORGE HARDINGE of S$^t$ Albans, shoemaker. (*Dat.* 1 Nov. 1598). Bur. at S$^t$ Andrews in S$^t$ Albans; Wife Joane; Child$^n$ Agnes, Geo. & Marie; Tho. Webster of S$^t$ Albans tanner; Bro-in-law John Trulock of Staple Inn, London, gent. exor. *Wit$^s$*:—J. Trulocke, W$^m$. Pratt, Eliz. Browne. (*Pr.* 12 Oct. 1598).

f. 191. RAPHE DAYE of Puckeridge in psh. of Brawghinge, yeoman. (*Dat.* 29 Aug. 1598). Freehold messuage in Brawghinge streete, land called Swaines; Neph. Francis son of my bro. W$^m$. Day & his bro$^s$ Raphe Daie, Rich. & W$^m$. Daie; The child$^n$ of my sist. Eliz. Bull; Sist. Mereye Stronge; Sist. Ellyn Atridge her children; Child$^n$ of my bro-in-law Thomas Barfoot 'w$^{ch}$ he had by his sister my late wief'; Cous. Margt. wife of Paule Parnell; Andrew Benton & bro. W$^m$. Daie exors; S$^d$ Paule Parnell & friend W$^m$. Hutton overseers. *By me Raphe Daie.* *Wit$^s$*:—Tho. Manynge, Tho. Course & Rich. Rolfe. (*Pr.* 12 Oct. 1598).

f. 193. ALICE WAYNEMAN of Rickmansworthe, widow. (*Dat.* 14 May 1591). Venus Rushley; Anne Robson my son's child: Eliz. & Wm. Robson other children of s^d son; John, George, Marie & Anne Rusheley; John Rusheley the elder; Marie Rusheley the younger; Son Jonas Robson exor; Bro. Charles Spencer overseer. (*Mark*). *Wit^s* :—John Cornewall & Nich. Bedworthe scr. (*Admon. with will annexed* 5 Mch. 1598-9 to Anne Emyn *als* Robson wife of Wm. Emyn & relict & administratrix of the goods of Jonas Robson dec^d.)

f. 194. ROBERT KIFFORD of Barley. (*Dat.* 21 Aug. 1598). Wife Eliz.; Son Thos. exor. *Wit^s* :—Robt. Fordham, John Kefford, Dan. Smithe. (*Admon. with will annexed* 13 Apr. 1599 to Eliz. relict, the exor. having renounced).

f. 197. WILLIAM PARRATT of Wormeley, fisherman. (*Dat.* 14 Nov. 1599). Wife and children; Bro. John Parratt exor. (*Admon with will annexed* 13 Sep. 1599 to Margt. relict, the exor. having renounced).

f. 205. KATHERYN STOCKE of Chesthunt, widow. (*Dat.* 10 Aug. 1598). My maid Marie Royne exor; Neighbour John Chare senior overseer. *Wit^s* :—John Rowe, Xpofer Hardinge. (*Pr.* 16 May 1599).

f. 210. THOMAS BIGGE of psh. of S^t Peter near S^t Albans. (*Nunc. will dat.* 29 Nov. 1598). Wife Agnes extrix; Dau. Agnes. *Wit^s* :—John Sleap, Rich. Lewes & Phillipp Sleap. (*Pr.* 24 Jan. 1598).

f. 212. JOHN LEOWYN of Wormeley. (*Dat.* 18 July 1599). Son John; Wife Eliz.; Son Tristram; Daus. Joan, Eliz. & Kath. Wife extrix; John Collopp; Bro. Tho. Leowyn of Broxborne & Wm. Clarke of Nasinge, co. Essex yeoman, overseers. (*Mark*). *Wit^s* :—Nich Turner, Wm. Turner, Robt. Sawyer. (*Pr.* 26 Sep. 1600).

f. 215. THOMAS EWER of Lewsden in psh. of Abbots Langley, yeoman. (*Dat.* 14 Sep. 1601). Bur. at Langley; Son John; Daus. Jane & Bridgett; Dau. Anne Hogg; John Lewes vicar of Langley; Sons Nich. & Roger; Wife Alice extrix. *Wit^s* :— John Lewes clarke, Wm. Ewer. (*Pr.* 23 Oct. 1601).

f. 215. THOMAS SHEPPERD of Redbourne, husbandman. (*Dat.* 14 Sep. 1601). Wife Joane; Son in law Robert Judd; Son Wm. Sheppard exor. *Wit^s* :—Edw. Mills & Nich. Marten. (*Pr.* 11 Nov. 1601).

f. 216. NICHOLAS GODFREY of Colliers end in psh. of Standon. (*Dat.* 12 Sep. 1601). Wife Ellyn; Son Thomas; Son John; Dau. Marie Godfrey (under 26); Dau. Anne Godfrey; Mother Margt. Graie; Francis Challis my man; Eliz. my maid; Poor people of Colliers end i.e. Wm. Allen, John Butler, John Knight, Widow Beckett, John Skyngell & Edw. Smithe; Father Lucas of High Crosse; Wife extrix; Neighbour John Greene overseer. *Wit^s* :—Tho. Gamble scr., John Gyles, John Greene. (*Pr.* 13 Nov. 1601).

f. 221. JOHN HUSTE of Wormeley, husbandman. (*Dat.* 9 May 1601). Geo. Nashe, Tho. Nashe & Cisley Nashe my wife's child^n; Wife Eliz. extrix. *Wit^s* :—Edw. Giluer, Wm. Nashe. (*Pr.* 16 June 1601).

f. 225. THOMAS ABRAHAM of psh. of S<sup>t</sup> Stephens, near S<sup>t</sup> Albans, husbandman. (*Dat.* 2 Jan. 1599). Bur. at S<sup>t</sup> Stephens; Margt. wife of Rich. Collins of S<sup>t</sup> Stephens & John Basford her cousin; Robt. Tayler; Thos. son of M<sup>r</sup> Thos. Wollie of S<sup>t</sup> Albans; Mary Crosbye; Mary & Martha Lightfoote; John Crosbie; Agnes Bonner extrix; Friend M<sup>r</sup> John Crossebie overseer. *Wit<sup>s</sup>*:—Per me Richardum Lightfoote scriptorem et ecclesie sancti Stephani vicarium, John Crosbee. (*Pr.* 15 Sep. 1601).

f. 232. THOMAS LEWYN of Broxborne, 'servaunt to the Queenes maiestie, being three score and seaven yeares of age and vpwards.' (*Dat.* 12 Aug. 1601). Son Wm.; Daus. Eliz., Agnes & Ledia Lewyn; Wife Alice extrix; Sons in law John Kirby & Thomas Lawrance overseers; Felex Palmer my dau. Kirbyes sonne; John Busbie my dau. Phillipps son. By me Thomas Lewin. *Wit<sup>s</sup>*:—Tho. Lawrence, John Kirbye, Nich. Turner, Henry Archer. (*Pr.* 16 Sep. 1601).

f. 239. JOHN MAULDEN of Broxborne, yeoman. (*Dat.* 21 Oct. 1601). Wife Mary; Cottage called Cresses in Tymford Hamlett in psh. of Chesthunt in occupation of Nich. Smithe; Dau. Mary Malden; Constance & Hellen Buttler; Son-in-law John Clarke; Son-in-law John Greene; Eliz. Smith dau. of Wm. Smithe; Son-in-law Wm. Smithe; Wife extrix; Sons in law John Greene & Wm. Smithe overseers. *Wit<sup>s</sup>*:—Wm. Arther & Robt. Guthree. (*Pr.* 24 Mch. 1601).

f. 251. LETTICE MILLS of Widford, singlewoman. (*Dat.* 22 Oct. 1601). Kinsman Oliver Mills of Widford; Cous. Agnes now wife of Nich. Rea; Child<sup>n</sup> of s<sup>d</sup> Oliver Mills, Agnes Rea, & Thos. Mills the younger, John Mills of Widford; Goddau. Mathy Smithe; Oliver Mills & Nich. Rea exors. *Wit<sup>s</sup>*:—John Payton, parson of Widford, Parkers wife of Widford, [*blank*] Grave. (*Pr.* 10 Nov. 1601).

f. 253. JOHN ADAMS of Bushey, yeoman, 'being aged.' (*Dat.* 28 May 1600). Wife Joane; Son John; Dau. Anne Addams; Son. Tho. Adams exor; Friend John Huddell of Bushey & Tho. Fotherley overseers; kinsman Wm. Barrett. *Wit<sup>s</sup>*:—Tho. Fotherley the writer hereof, John Huddell & Wm. Barrett. (*Pr.* 14 Nov. 1601).

f. 256* ELIZABETH ROBOTHAM dau. of John Robotham of the town of S<sup>t</sup> Albon, gent. (*Dat.* 22 July 1598). My uncles Wm. Levison of London merchant & Robt. Benbridge of Calke co. Darby esq<sup>r</sup> exors; Jas. Rolfe, Wm. Rolfe & Wm. Rockett; John Ketcher late of London alderman & now of same city esq<sup>r</sup>; Tho. Hickman cit. & haberdasher of London. *Elizabeth Robotham*. *Wit<sup>s</sup>*:—Jeffery Bower servaunt to John Mayle scr, Tho. Foxcrofte, Phillipp Younge. (*Pr.* 19 Apr. 1602).

f. 258. WILLIAM ROLFE the elder of the psh. of S<sup>t</sup> Albans, co. Herts. gent. (*Dat.* 8 Aug. 1601). Wife Dorothy; House where Cooper the fuller dwells; Dau. Anne; Lands occupied by Robt. Ellis; Three closes bought of Dewbery; Son Braie Rolfe; Son. Jas.; Farm called Duncrafte; Son John; Five closes called Westfeilds etc; Dau. Anne Jopson; Wm. &

* Registered again at f. 276.

Michael sons of Wm. my late son ; Closes called Oyster hills :
House in Market Place ; 'The house w^ch Smithe the baker
dwelleth in in Spicers streete and the howse where Benton
dwelleth excepte the parlor and my close att the Townesend by a
lane leadinge downe towards Luton lyinge in Bowgate ' ; Land
in Catheryn lane ; Dau. Grace ; Close called Longe acre ; Houses
where John Campion & Peter Coulter dwell ; Dau. Anne to be
cared for by my wife ' because she hath noe helpe of her
husband ' ; Wife extrix.  Wit^s :—Wm. Rockett, Hughe Rolfe,
Wm. Peacocke, Robt. Johnson the writer hereof.  (Pr. 13 Oct.
1601).

f. 260. JOHN SYMONS of Chesthunt, husbandman.  (Dat. 19 Oct.
43 Eliz.)  Wife Margerie ; House called Brancks in Kynfford
co. Kent ; Dau. Suzan Symones ; Wife extrix. John Symones.
Wit^s :—Wm. Turner, M^r William Cooke John Norman. (Pr.
22 Dec. 1601).

f. 281. RICHARD KINGE of Wormeley, yeoman.  (Dat. 4 Jan.
1600).  Land in Cheston Feild ; Wife Margt. ; Son Rich. ;
Tenement called Laie Smallwells & Great Smallwells ;
Son Robt. ; Tenement called Cadmans ; Son Thos. ; Land
bought of Wm. Malden ; Dau. Anne Lowin ; John Lowin my
dau's eldest son ; Cous. Wm. Mauden the younger & Robt.
Becke overseers ; Son-in-law John Lowin ; Land in Milfeild ;
Nich. Lowin my dau's son ; Wife extrix. Wit^s :—John Havers,
Edw. Colts hujus scriptoris, Robt. Becke.  (Pr. 8 July 1602).

f. 291. WILLIAM TURNER of Wormeley, blacksmith. (Dat. 1 May
1604).  Son Edw. ; John, Edward & Joane my child^n ; Son
John exor ; Robt. Becke & Christ^r Collopp overseers. Wit^s :—
Samuell Halingdale, Robt. Becke, Christr. Collopp. (Pr.
29 June 1604).

f. 293. JOHN CHEYNEY of Stortford, yeoman.  (Dat. 15 June
1604).  Wife Agnes ; House at Stortford wherein Robt. Basse
gent. now dwells ; Bro. George Cheanie & Coz. John Cheany
his son exors ; Friends John Sweetinge butcher & John
Mathewe barbor of Stortford overseers ; Cous. Wm. Cheany son
of s^d bro. George.  Wit^s :—Wm. Barnard scr, Thos. Barnard.
By me John Cheany.  (Pr. 8 Oct. 1604).

*To be Continued.*

# Church Terriers.

### ASHWELL.

ASHWELL  A TRUE TARRYE of all the glibe lands houlden of
IN COM. HERTF. the lord Bishope of London high tresurer of
APRIL 12, 1638.  England w^thin the said pishe.
Item one peece of Earrable land called by the name of Winde mill
peece contayninge by estimation                              35 Acres.

Item one peece of Earrable land called Snakes peece contayninge by estimation    35 Acres.

Itt. one peece of Earrable land lyinge one stone hill contayninge by estimation    iij Acres.

Itt. one peece of Earrable land lyinge one Backworthehill conteyninge by estimation    iij Acres.

Itt. one peece of Earrable land called Piked peece conteyninge by estimation    12 Acres.

Itt. one peece of Earrable land lyinge att the Berry gate conteyninge by estimation    viij Acres.

Itt. one peece att Hellbecke by estimacon    viij Acres.

Itt. one peece buttinge on Willm Barlyes hedge conteyninge by estimacon    10 Acres.

Itt. one peece in Prisom of Earrable land by estimacon    viij Acres.

Itt. Lamas Ground called by the name of greate prisom & Little prisom by estimacon    10 Acres.

Itt. a peece of Lamas Ground called by the name of Lordę meadow by estimacon    10 Acres.

Itt. a pasture Close called Foottball Close conteyninge by estimacon    4 Acres.

Itt. Belonging to ye Vicaridge only One Close by Estimation 3 Roodes butting on Mr Wallers Ground on the North & East, & one Mr Clarkes Ground on ye South, & on ye West On ye Vicaridge House & Barnes. All wch, House & Barnes & all Buildings belonging to ye sayd Vicaridge are in very Good & Sufficient Repaire, Except One Barne wch hath beene new Built this Yeare (ye Old One being Ready to fall) & is not yet altogether thatched.

     Herbert Palmer, Vicar.
     Francis Chapman, } Churchwardens.
     Thomas Wright,

---

October the 22th Anno D'ni 1638.

A True Tarre made the daye and yeare aboue written of the Mannor House in Ashwell belongeinge to the Lord Bishoppe of London wth all the glive landę meadowes and Pasture therevnto belonginge by wee the Church wardens whose names are vnderwritten.

Imprimis the Mannor House yardę orcyard & garden Conteyninge by estimacon    two Acres.

Item a Close of pasture called Footeball Close Conteyninge by estimacon    fower Acres.

Item two Closes of Lamas growne Called by the names of great Prisom and little Prisom Conteyninge by estimacon    Tenn Acres.

Item a Meadowe Called by the name of Lordę Meade Conteyninge by estimacon    Tenn Acres.

Item plowed Prisom Conteyninge by estimacon    Eight Acres.

Item in the northe Feilde A pesse of Earrable land the west hed buttinge one William Barlyes Close Conteyninge by estimacon    Tenn Acres.

Item a pesse lyinge by Helbecke lane the south west hed buttinge on John Clarkes Close Conteyninge by estimacon    Eight Acres.

Item a pesse att the Mañor House gate conteyninge by estimacon    Eight Acres.

Item a pesse called by the name of Snakes pesse Conteyninge by estimacon    five & Therty Acres.

Item a pesse called Windmill pesse Conteyninge by estimacon five & Therty Acres.

Item a pesse one Stone hill betwene two balkes Conteyninge by estimacon Three Acres.

Item a pesse one Backeworthe hill betwene two balkes Conteyninge by estimacon Three Acres.

Item the Vicarage House wthe yard orchyard and garden Conteyninge by Estimacon two Acres.

    Thomas Wright,
    Francis Chapman,  Church wardens.

---

A pticuler of the Gleabelands & tyths & other pfitts belonging to the Viccaridge of Ashwell in y<sup>e</sup> County of Hertf.

A dwelling house Garden Orchard two barnes for grayne One hey barne stable & granary.

All small tyths renewing or ariseing w<sup>th</sup>in the said pish & all tyth hey there.

The third pte of y<sup>e</sup> tyths of all corne & grayns ariseing or groweing w<sup>th</sup>in y<sup>e</sup> said pish.

    Ralph Baldwyn
    Church Warden.

---

## ASPENDEN.

ASPEDEN, 1638.   A TERRIER of the personage house, and all glebe Lands there &c : all of them being now in y<sup>e</sup> occupacon of M<sup>r</sup> Richard Tailor, Rector.

Inprimis 3 acres of pasture and Orchards at the homestall butting about y<sup>e</sup> homestall, being in reasonable repayr.

It. in Moone-meade-field 3 roodes of arable land, butting vpon the land of Willm Plumer in the West & upon Willm Plumers on the North.

It. in Peridowne 3 half acres butting vpon M<sup>r</sup> Brands on the West and vpon Henry Randolls on the North.

It. in Windmill field 3 roodes butting on the Kings high waie in the East and on Lewis Crowders on the North.

Item in the same field, one acre butting vpon the Kings high way on the East and vpon Henry Botterells on the North.

It. in the same field, one acre butting vpon the riu' on the West and running vp by John Snow's on the North.

It. in the same field 3 half acres butting upon the Kings high way on the East & vpon John Snow's on the North.

It. in the same field 3 roodes lying by the Kings high waie on the East & butting upon William Burr's on the North.

It. in the same field, one half acre, butting vpon Willm Burr's on the North and lying by John Hamonds on the East.

It. in the same field, one half acre butting vpon Pease-meade on the West and by Abraham Tiplars on y<sup>e</sup> North.

It. in Stonie-field 3 acres butting vpon Ree-meade on y<sup>e</sup> East and by John Snow's on the North.

It. there ; 1 acre butting upon the high waie to Westmill on the East & leading by Abraham Tiplars on y<sup>e</sup> North.

It. there ; 3 acres butting upon the high waie to Westmill on the East & by the land in the occupacon of John Snow on the North.

It. there ; 2 acres & a half butt vpon Sauncell meade on the West & by John Hamonds on the North.

It. there ; 3 half acres butt vpon Harts Croft on the North & leading by Willm Brown's on yᵉ East.

It. there ; One half acre butt upon Sancell on the South & leading by John Snow's on yᵉ West.

It. in Ree-Meade one poell of Meadow containing a pole wide butt upon the river on the East & upon the meadowe of John Snowe on the South & upon the meadow of Samuel Kirby on the North.

It. in Little-field in the pish of Wakely one acre butt upon the land of Michael Jordan on the East and West & lying by the land of the said Michael Jordan on the North.

Henry Randall } Churchwardens.
Henry × Win }
Richard × Cherry   Sidesman.

---

A Terror of the Gleabes belonginge to the psonage of Aspeden in yᵉ County of Hertford.*

In a Certaine feild Called Stony feild is

1. One halfe acre of areable land abutting on a certaine feild belonging to Watbones caled Sanswayes on the south.
2. One acre and a halfe in yᵉ same feilde lying by yᵉ highway leading to Westmill on yᵉ west side and Hartscroft on yᵉ north head.
3. Thre Acres in yᵉ same feild abutting vppon Reamead east.
4. One acre in yᵉ same feild abutting vppon Rifford water east.
5. Thre acres in yᵉ same feild on Rifford hill yᵉ east hed abutting on the high waye.
6. Two acres and a halfe in yᵉ sᵈ feild lying on the North side of yᵉ Balke yᵗ ptes Westmill and Aspeden pishes the west hed toward Sansway nether Corner.

In a certaine feild called Windemill feild is

7. One halfe acre yᵉ west head abutting on Jo. Hamonds Pease Mead.
8. One halfacre in yᵉ sᵈ feild one end abutting on Founcly valley south.
9. Thre roods in the sᵈ feild lying a long by the Roade side east and Fonncly vally south head.
10. One acre and a halfe in yᵉ sᵈ feild abutting on yᵉ roade east called Draggon Bush peice.
11. Thre roodes in ye sᵈ feild abutting on the roade east.
12. One acre in ye sᵈ feild abutting on yᵉ high way on yᵉ west.
13. Three roods in the sᵈ feild abutting on the high way easte.

In a Certaine feild called Perrydon is

14. One acre and a halfe abutting on Pryor lane on the east.

In a Certaine feild called Monemead feild is

15. Thre roodes the east head abutting on Chappell feild.

In a certaine feild Called Littell feild is

One acre the lands of Jeames Snow lying on both sides of it.

In a certaine Meade Called Reameade is

16. One Roode the east head abutting on yᵉ riuer yᵉ west head on Pryor lane.

* No date is given in this terrier. A more modern hand has endorsed it 1638.

The psonage house and homestall conteyning foure acres Lying betwene Aspeden strete on y<sup>e</sup> North and Woodlane on the south the land of Raf Freman Esq<sup>r</sup> west and the land of Willyam Burre east.

Richard [Sea ?]well.

## ASTON.

APRILL 13 1638.   A TRUE & PERFECT TERRIER of al the Glebe lands, Meadowes, Gardens, Orchards, Houses, belonging vnto the Parsonadge of Aston : as followeth

There is a dwelling house w<sup>th</sup> an Orchard, a garden, a Courtyard : And an outyeard w<sup>th</sup> 2 barnes, 2 stables, one hayhouse, a Cart house, a Doue coate, 2 smal garners : a woodhouse, a woodyard, a henhouse, w<sup>th</sup> an old outhouse.

W<sup>ch</sup> containe two acres thirty pooles.

Medowes adioyning to y<sup>e</sup> house, being in three Diuisions containe 4 acres, 3 roodes, 4 poles.

Errable land : The horse close Contayning Eight acres, two rodes, 17 poles.

The Church close, Contayning 9 acres, one rode, 38 poles.

The Comon fyld grounds.

In y<sup>e</sup> wind-mill fyld a peice comonly called y<sup>e</sup> Brade, Containing Eleuen acres, 3 rodes, abutting East & North on y<sup>e</sup> highway.

In Brooke fyld 2 peices : The farthest peice runing downe by Hemlies hedge & abutting east upon y<sup>e</sup> Riuer & west upon y<sup>e</sup> highway Containes 2 acres, 2 roodes 15 poles.

The peice next unto y<sup>e</sup> Church Called y<sup>e</sup> Brade, abutting South & west on y<sup>e</sup> high waies & East on y<sup>e</sup> yard & grounds of Thomas Kent, Contayning 3 acres, One roode 9 poles.

Sum Tot. 42 Acres.  2 roodes.  29 poles.

Ita testor Joh'es Burnapp
Rector.

John × Wallice  
John Risse       } Churchwardens  
Thomas Phippe

## AYOT ST. LAWRENCE.

...... LAUR.
...... HARTF.
........ 1638.   A NOTE OR TERRIER of the Gleabe belonging to the Parsnage.

Imprimis About the parsnage house, One close of two acres ; one litle Pikle, a spot of Ground cald the Orchyarde.

2° The Churchyarde.

3° A close of six acres next the Land of William Carter east called Hyemares.

4° Five acr(e) & a halfe in the Common lyeing in severall peices.

5° A close called Kingsland of 2 acr(e) & a halfe.

6° Halfe an acre vnder S<sup>r</sup> John Garrett(e) warren pale being in the parish of Sandridge.

T. Read, Rector ibid.
John North.
The marke of Thomas Scotbrut.

## CHURCH TERRIERS.

Com. Hertf.  }  Ayot S⁺ Laurence
Dioces. Lincoln  }  1686.

A TRUE & PERFECT TERRIER of the Glebe-lands belonging to the Rectory of Ayot S⁺ Laur. aforesᵈ.

| | ACRE | ROOD |
|---|---|---|
| Impʳmis An Orchyard & one pightell of Pasture adjoyning to yᵉ Rectory | 01 | 01 |
| It. one close adjoyning to yᵉ foresᵈ Pightell | 02 | 00 |
| It. one close conteining by estimacon 2 Acres beyond yᵉ Hill farm between yᵉ lands late of Jonathan Wacket on yᵉ south and Willm Bristow Esq on yᵉ north | 02 | 00 |
| It. one close called six Acree Close nere adjoyning & abutting on a feild lane called yᵉ Green lane on yᵉ north | 06 | 00 |
| It. 5 acres & ½ in a certain Close called yᵉ Comon in four peices whereof One calld yᵉ Gap-peice yᵉ foresᵈ Green lane on yᵉ South, Another three acres bounded by yᵉ land of yᵉ said Willm Bristow Esq on every side Another called yᵉ middle peice leading from yᵉ Gap peice aforesd between yᵉ land of yᵉ foresd Willm Bristow on yᵉ North & South to yᵉ Lowest peice abutting on yᵉ Green lane aforesd conteyning together one Acree & . . . . . . . . . | 05 | 02 |
| It. One Pightell . . . . . . . . . . . . . . Park | 00 | 03 |

---

Ayot Sᵗ Laur. A NOTE OR TERRIER of yᵉ Glebe-land belonging to yᵉ Rectory of Ayot Sᵗ Laurence. [Endorsed with date 1693].

Impʳ. The Parsonage House new built, Gardens & Orchyards lately planted wᵗ a Close of two Acres adjoyning.

It. A six Acre close nere another close called yᵉ Comon yᵉ land of Willm Bristow Esq on yᵉ East & yᵉ land of Ralph Skiñer Gent on yᵉ South.

Item in yᵗ Close called yᵉ Comon five acres & an half in severall pieces whereof One Acre is called yᵉ Gap peice another yᵉ 3 acre peice wᵗʰ two other peices well known & adjoyning to yᵉ land of Willm Bristow Esq only.

Item one Close of two acres nere yᵉ foresd close called yᵉ Common yᵉ land of yᵉ sd Willm Bristow Esq on yᵉ South East abutting Southward on a lane called yᵉ Green-lane.

It. a Close in yᵉ parish of Santridg by Estimacon 3 Roods comonly called or known by yᵉ name of Penly park, yᵉ Hedges therof on both sides belong to yᵉ same.

Hen. Sykes, Rectoʳ
Signū Edri × Nash, Gard.

## Abstracts of Wills.

**ARCHDEACONRY OF HUNTINGDON (HITCHIN REGISTRY).**

REGISTER III.—Continued from Page 33.

f. 14. JOHN HEYWARD of Aston, husbandman (*Dat.* 12 June 1575). My boy Wm. Greene; Wife Sisley; My child w$^{ch}$ my wife is greate w$^{th}$; Tenement called Tymmes; Eldest son John; John Smyth of Watton at Stone; Thos. Ridgedale of Watton; Son John exor; Bro. Heyward$^{s}$ child$^{n}$; Bro. Ridgedales child$^{n}$. *Wit$^{s}$*:—Robte Tattersale, Tho. Bedle, John Lawrence. (*Pr.* 13 Dec. 1581).

f. 14$^{b}$ HENRY TOKEFEELDE. [See before at f. 12].

f. 15. SYMON BULLYN. [Registered before at f. 11].

f. 15. MATHEW KINGE servant w$^{th}$ Jeames Senior of Bushoppes Hatfeeld, beerebrewer. (*Dat.* 29 Mch. 1581). Legacy to Northmimes; My sist. the wife of John West of Litle Barkhamsteed & her child$^{n}$; Sist. Joyce; Widow Longe my aunt & godmother; Widow Bridgman my cousin; Gilbert Basset; Alice Basset; Godch$^{n}$ John Randall & John Jonson; Isabell Senior my min'sters daughter; Agnes Hawkines his dau-in-law; Eliz. & Agnes Senior my M$^{rs}$ daus; John & Wm. Thorowgood; Peter, Tho. & John Hawkines; Geo. & Wm. & Sara Senior; Edw. Webbe, John Atkynes, John Conningford, Wm. Buckmaster, Tho. Ballard, John Shepde, John Grave, John Coop & Eliz. Tompson my fellow servants w$^{th}$ my sayd M$^{r}$ Senior; s$^{d}$ M$^{r}$ Jeames Senior exor. *Wit$^{s}$*:—Tho. Rason, Wm. Cartur, Wm. Bucmest$^{r}$. (*Pr.* 12 Apr. 1586).

f. 15$^{b}$ STEPHEN FOXE of Hitchin, gent. (*Dat.* 2 Aug. 1582). John Foxe of Huffyngham, co. York; Anne Snowe; Marion Lawford; Son-in-law M$^{r}$ S$^{r}$iaunt Boore his child$^{n}$; Son-in-law Robert Carters child$^{n}$ & Mary Carter their mother; John Papworth; Edw. Marshall exor; M$^{r}$ Haylocke clerk, vicar of Pawles Walden overseer. *Wit$^{s}$*:—Tho. Dockeraye esq, Robt. Hatton gent, Wm. Coker, Mich. Long, Wm. Hurst & Robt. Kent. Codicil names the wife of Edw. Gardiner of Hitchin. *Wit$^{s}$*:—John Hutcinson & Tho. Barfoote. (*Pr.* 25 Sep. 1581).

f. 16. WILLIAM ALBRIGHT of Kynsworth. (*Dat.* 31 Mch. 23 Eliz.). Father Tho. Albright; Frances Carpentor; Godson Wm. Robynes; Richard Pratt; Rich. Edwards; Margt. Wilson; Joane Carpenter; [Emma?] Chapman; Robt. Albright; Henrie Lodge; John Wodhouse; Tho. Henchman; Wm. Albright; s$^{d}$ father exor; Robt. Carpenter overseer. *Wit$^{s}$*:—John Wodhouse & Augustine Frith. (*Pr.* 12 Apr. 1581).

f. 16. THOMAS BESOWTH of Hemelhemsted, yeoman. (*Dat.* 1579). Eldest dau. Eliz; Daus. Joane & Rose; Wife Alice exor; Child<sup>n</sup> Christ<sup>r</sup>, Alice & Susan; Bros. Geo. & John Besowth overseers. *Wit<sup>s</sup>*:—Tho. Axstyll, Wm. Coleman, Robt. Grover. (*Pr.* 21 Feb. 1581).

f. 16<sup>b</sup> RICHARD IVORIE the younger of Offley, servant to Thomas Deeremer thelder of Offley. (Undated). Manor of Westburie; Bro. Robt; John Helders land; Bro. Thos; Uncle Thos. Ivorye; Sisters-in-law Annis & Elizabeth Ivorye; Uncle Rich. Ivorye; Bro-in-law Wm. Ivorie; John Homes; Mother Homes; Widow Beane; John Headey; Mother Jordaine; Water Saunder; Uncle John Saunder; Wm. Plumes wife; John Child; Rich. Helder; Mathew Hanscombe & Marie Chaukley; Thos. Deremer senior overseer; Bro. Robt. exor. *Wit<sup>s</sup>*:—Rich. Ivorie, Tho. Ivorie & Tho. Deremer junior. (*Pr.* 20 Sep. 1581).

f. 17. THOMAS FEILD of Kings Hatfield *alias* Bishops Hatfield, yeoman. (*Dat.* 24 Feb. 1581). Sons Wm. & John; Daus. Marie Feild & Alicia Feild; Wife Cath. extrix. *Wit<sup>s</sup>*:— John Astrie, John Chapell, Harrie Parker. (*Pr.* 12 Apr. 1581).

f. 17. THOMAS OCKLEY of Aldenham, taylor. (*Dat.* 30 Nov. 1580). Wife Amye; Son Thos; The now fower children of Agnes my dau.; S<sup>d</sup> wife & son exors. *Wit<sup>s</sup>*:—Thomas Bartillemew vicar of this parish, John Plate the younger & Rich. Greene the younger. (*Pr.* 12 Apr. 1581).

f. 17<sup>b</sup> THOMAS WILLIAMSON of Aldenham, yeoman. (*Dat.* 10 Dec. 1580). Wife Agnes; House at Hedge grove in psh. of Aldenham & lands in the lane between Kemprow & Hedgrove; John Elye; Daus. Cath. & Joane; Sons Wm., John & Robt.; Son Wm. & dau. Joane both under 18; Wife extrix; Rich. Brightwell & Wm. Strett overseers. *Wit<sup>s</sup>*:— Thomas Bartillmew, vicar of this parish, & the overseers. (*Pr.* 12 Apr. 1581).

f. 18. BASILL FLOWER of Harpeden, yeoman. (*Dat.* 10 Feb. 1580). Wife Agnis; Son John; Son Robt; Son Wm.; Wife & son John exors; Tho. North gent supervisor. *Wit<sup>s</sup>*:— Willm Brigg curat, John Style, Wm. Pope, John Sebroke & Rich. Grover. (*Pr.* 3 May 1581).

f. 18. JOHN WEST [Registered before at f. 10<sup>b</sup>].

f. 18. THOMAS GYLNAR of Bengeo, yeoman. (*Dat.* 1 May 1581). Sons Wm., Ralph, Thos, Nich. & Robt.; Son Edmund; Daus. Joane & Eliz.; Wife Lettis & son John exors; Wm. Archell overseer. *Wit<sup>s</sup>*:—Wm. Pernell, Tho. Becksfeld & Rich. Haylye the writer. (*Pr.* 31 May 1581).

f. 18<sup>b</sup> JOHN WHITLOCKE of Wethamsteede, husbandman. (*Dat.* 18 Jan. 1580). Dau. Eliz.; Son John; Dau. Joane; Son Edw.; Geraud Whitlock son of John Whitlocke of Vxbridge; Wife Alice extrix; Tho. North of Hearons overseer. *Wit<sup>s</sup>*:—Tho. North, Rich. Vause. (*Pr.* 30 Apr. 1581).

f. 19. JOHN SPRINGHAM of psh. of Alhallewes, in Hartf., yeoman. (*Dat.* 11 July 1581). Daus. Anne, Judith, Eliz. & Susan, all under 21; Wife Judith; Land bought of Mislen Jury lying in Wrengeo meade; Son John, under 21; Wife extrix; Geo. Turner overseer. *Wit<sup>s</sup>*:—John Hopkins, John North, Harrye Bannester. (*Pr.* 20 Sep. 1581).

f. 19. THOMAS WELCHE of Walden Regis, th'elder. yeoman. (*Dat.* 19 July 1581). Wife Olife; Son Thomas: Daus. Alice, Joane & Agnes; Son John; The house sometime Pockthropes; The lane leading from Brache wood greene unto the church of Walden Regis; Culvers croft butting on the way leading from S$^t$ Albons on the south; Land lying in Bilknall by the lands of John Ivorye; Lands in the middle shott of y$^e$ leye butting on the land of Edward Evered on the north & lying by the land of Thos. Welche the youngest on the east; Lands in Legatts feild &c; Edw. Welch; Land in Hayhanger; Son Wm; House wherein I dwell which sometime was Wm. Welche's dec$^d$; Bocket wicke; Lane end close; Robt. Burr; Oke acre in Legatts feild; Thomas Feild of Legatts; Tho. Wells; Brache hatche laynes end; John Sybley; Son Edw$^d$ (under 24); Three closes called Langmers & Stockings; Tho. Godfray *als*. Coop my daughter's son & John Godfraye, Wm. Godfraye, Alice Godfraye & Eliz. Godfraye *als*. Cooper child$^n$ of my s$^d$ dau; Son Thos. exor; John Sybley of Stopeslye, Tho. Welch & Tho. Ritchardson clarke overseers. *Wit$^s$*:—Tho. Welch, Tho. Welch the younger & Thos. Richardsonne clarke. (*Pr.* 21 Feb. 1581).

f. 21. ROBERT NORTH of Bengeo, yeoman. (*Dat.* 16 June 1578). Wife Joane; Dau. Frauncis; An 'acre of whete abuttinge vpon Thomas Gylnars head pece'; Son John North y$^e$ elder; John North y$^e$ younger; Eliz. Beckesfelds child$^n$; Dau. Joane & her child; Son Wm. North & his 3 child$^n$; Annis Broune; Tymothye North; Son Robt. exor; Bro. John North overseer. Rose Kerbye; John Kerbye. *Wit$^s$*:—Rich. Haylye, wrighter. (*Pr.* 31 May 1581).

f. 21. JOHN HEYDON servant to John Axtell of Cobbley in psh. of Digswell. (*Dat.* 7 May 1577). Bro. Thos. Heydon; Father in law Rafe Heddeson & my mother; Thos. Heddeson & George his bro.; Rafe, John & Wm.; Sist. Dorothe; Father in law exor. *Wit$^s$*:—John Matrevers pson of Digswell, John Axtell & John Celye. (*Pr.* 6 Oct. 1581).

f. 21$^b$ HUGH SOUTHEN of Hemelhemstead, taylor. (*Dat.* 3 Dec. 24 Eliz.). Wife Joane; Son Rich.; Dau. Annis (under 18); Sons Wm, Thos, & John; Eme Partridge; Wife extrix; Wm. Southen, Tho. Southen & Robt. Shadd overseers. *Wit$^s$*:—Rich. Gawton, Robt. Shad, Tho. Howe, Rafe Perte, Robt. Rolfe, John Baker, Rich. Turner. (*Pr.* 21 Feb. 1581).

f. 22. RICHARD BRYTNELL of Longm'ston in psh. of Tringe, yeoman. (*Dat* 8 Feb. 1581). Legacies to the repair of the bells of Tring, poor of Wilstorne &c; Eldest son Robt. Britnell; Land in Tringe dole meade & in Betlowe feild; Son Edw$^d$; Land in Masworthe neither feild; Son Jessper Britnell; Tho. Allen of Betlowe; Wm. Willet of Norchurch; Daus. Eliz. Mary & Annis (under 21); Son Thos; Wife Joane extrix; Wm. Newman, Tho. Allyn & Wm. Wossyter my bro-in-law overseers. Signed 4 Oct. 1582. *Wit$^s$*:—Wm. Woster. (*Pr.* 30 Apr. 1582).

f. 22$^b$ ELIZABETH BELGRAUE of Flamsted, widow. (*Dat.* 13 July 1581). Son Wm.; Marye Belgrave wife to my son Wm; Son Thos. exor.; Dau. Joane; Eliz. wife of Edw. Smyth; Son

Edw.; Son John; Rich. Halsye *als* Chambers overseer. *Wit^s*:—
Rich. Hasye *als* Chambers, John Borne, John Aicon & Frimyne
Addams curat. (*Pr.* 13 Dec. 1581).

f. 23. EDMUND CUCKOWE of Stevenage, husbandman. (*Dat*
4 Aug. 1581). Dau. Alice Thurbie; Alice Thurbie dau. of
Tho Thurbie; Son John Cuckow; Joane, Thos, John & Annis
child^n of Tho. Thurbie; Son in law Tho. Thurbie; Edm.
Cooke, taylor dwelling in Stevenage; Serv^t. Alice Porter; Son
John exor. *Wit^s*:—Tho. Clarke of Stevenage Parsonage, Robt.
Pattinson, Edw. Wylsheyre. (*Pr.* 20 Sep. 1581).

f. 23. WILLIAM KAKIS of Harpeden. (*Dat* 25 Jan. 1580).
Sister Chrystian Yeorke & her son Wm. Yorke my godson &
her child^n Agnis Baye, Geo. Yeorke & Alice Yorke; s^d sister
extrix. *Wit^s*:—John Slocome, Nich. Kilbye, Joue Potter.
(*Pr.* 3 May 1581).

f. 23^b WILLIAM WILLET of Norchurch. (*Dat.* 11 Apr. 1581).
Mother Cathrin; Powle Willet; Wm. Axtells; Wm. Becke;
John Willet thelder; Wm. Cocke of Dudswell; Daus. Alys &
Cath.; Son Wm. (under 21); John Cocke & Rauffe Cocke;
Serv^ts Agnes Moors & Mary Graye; Geo. Cocke, Jas. Priest &
Annis Tatnell; Rich. Birch now dwelling in psh. of Chessam &
John Goolde of Benigdon exors; Jas. Dabeney of Northchurch
*als* Barkomsted Marie & John Dabenye his bro. overseers.
*Wit^s*:—Fras. Hedgekin, clarke, Jeames Dabenye *alys* Cooke.
(*Pr.* 31 May 1581).

f. 24^b THOMAS FORTUNE of Hartingford burye. (*Dat.* 25 Aug.
1581). Dau. Grace; John Whight, yeoman; Sist. Christian
Fortune; John Bredgman; Wife Ellen extrix. *Wit^s*:—
Phillip Lawrence minnest^r, Tho. Ellys gent. & Robt. Heyward.
(*Pr.* 20 Sep. 1581).

f. 24^b WILLIAM KELSEY of Langley Regis. (*Dat.* 12 Jan. 1581).
Son Wm.; Dau. Alice Kelsey; John Hebson; Wife Cecylie
extrix; Neighbours Tho. Ewer & Jeames Mvnne overseers.
*Wit^s*:—Wm. Coe, minester, Jeames Mvnne, John Gregorie &
John Fanche. (*Pr.* 14 Mch. 1581).

f. 25. WILLIAM FORDHAM of Sacombe, husbandman. (*Dat.*
27 Mch. 1581). Wm. Fordham my late father dec^d; Henry
Bole; Edw. Carde servant to M^r Phillip Butler; Geo. Tyler;
Bro. Phillip Fordham; Wife Joane; Daus. Eliz. & Sara (under
21); The ferme called the Seale in Hartford; Bro. Thos.
Fordham; Sisters Joane, Margt. & Agnes Fordham; Father
in law John Skyngle & Nich. Shanbroke exors. *Wit^s*:—
Edmond Bridgman, Nich. Gylman, John Wolm', Wm. Browne,
Wm. Chamber. (*Pr.* 31 May 1581).

f. 25^b ROBERT HOWE of Northbarkhmstede, yeoman. (*Dat.*
6 Jan. 1581). Wife Joane; Tenement at Barkhamstede wherein
Nich. Winckfeld lives; Son Robt; Son in law John Howe;
Dau. Luce; John How my sonne Thomas his sonne & his
bros. Edw. & Rich; Dau-in-law Jane Glenester; Son Roberts
child^n; Son Robt. exor; Son John & cous. Rich. How of
Fraesden overseers. *Wit^s*:—John Whellplye, John [*blank*],
Rich Pope, Roger Whellpley, Nich. Christie, Tho. Hollydaye.
(*Pr.* 2 May 1582).

f. 26. PETER HARMER of Hitchin, yeoman. (*Dat.* 3 Mch. 1581). Eldest son John; Lands purchased of Wm. Kent & lands in the fields of Walseworth; Wife Joane; Son Peter; Son Thos; Dau. Alice Harmer; Wife extrix; Thos. Harmer of Weston overseer. *Wit*ˢ:—Tho. Chapman thelder, Wm. Symson, Robt. Warner, Robt. Papworth. (*Pr.* 2 May 1582).

f. 26 JOHN MONGETT of Flaunden, laboror. (*Dat.* 2 Jan. 1579). Dau. Margt. Monget (under 21); Son Jonas Munget (under 16); Wife Annis extrix; Bro-in-law Xpofer Hardinge & John Same of psh. of Agmondeshm overseers. *Wit*ˢ:—Edmund Grove, Tho. Mvngett, Wm. Twitchell, Rich. Butterfeild, Geo. Pudifoote. (*Pr.* 2 May 1582).

f. 26ᵇ JOHN FORSTER of Bennington, husbandman. (*Dat.* 9 July 24 Eliz.). Sons John, Michael & Edwᵈ; Mary Kent my wifes dau; Wm. Kent my wifes son; Wife Bettryce extrix; Godson John Hyll. *Wit*ˢ:—Willm Midleton, clarke, John Coo, John Hyll, Wm. Walker, Wm. Kent. (*Pr.* 12 Dec. 1582).

f. 27. THOMAS DEACON of Boveingdon, yeoman. (*Dat.* 1 June 1582). My 3 daus. Awdrey, Margt. & Marie; Sons Roger & Thos.; Wm. Ewer & Anne Ewer the son & dau. of John Ewer my son in law; Wm. Parret, Fras. Axtell & John Feilder; Hen. Style; Wife Jone & Rich. Allen her bro. exors; Henry Mayne & John Goold of the lane, overseers. *Wit*ˢ:—Thos. Hallam, Raphe Bullocke, John Deacon & Thos. Fielde. (*Pr.* 20 June 1582).

f. 27. WILLIAM DUNNE of Cottered, husbandman. (*Dat.* 1 Apr. 1582). Dau. Joane Austen; Wife Anne extrix; Son Peter Dunne. *Wit*ˢ:—George Lowyn & Wm. Entwessell. (No date of probate).

*To be Continued.*

# Feet of Fines for Hertfordshire.

### TUDOR PERIOD.

(CONTINUED FROM PAGE 37.)

1570. Easter Term. 12 Eliz.

*John Goodwyn esq & Wm. Walter gent : John Cheyne esq & Fras. Cheyne gent. Manor of Wylesthorne als. Willesthorne & lands in Wylesthorne & Trynge.

Henry Thomson : Mich. Mede. Messuage & lands in Ware & Great Amwell.

Edward Cason : Henry Dighton & Agnes his wife. A barn in Hartford.

Walt. Tooke gent : John Fynche & Margery his wife. Messuage & land in Wormeley.

Rich. Cranfelde & Julian his wife : Roger Byrcheley & Kath. his wife. Messuage & garden in psh. of S<sup>t</sup> Nicholas in the town of Hertford.

John Myller : Robt. Chaundeler & Joan his wife. Messuage in Stortford.

Ralph Rowlett knt : Matthew Davye & Dennis his wife. Two messuages in S<sup>t</sup> Albans.

Philip Melles : Wm. Patmar. Messuage & lands in Much Hadham.

Tho. Whittamore : Dionisius Broune & Eliz. his wife. Messuage in Hytchyn.

John Page : Henry Swayne & Eliz. his wife. Cottage & land in Barnett.

Wm. Cecyll knt. Principal Secretary of the Queen : Geo. Dacres esq & Eliz. his wife. Lands in Cheston *als*. Chesthunt.

John Myller : John Thurgood senior & John Thurgood jun. & Margaret his wife. Messuage & lands in Stortford.

John Crowche : Tho. Pole & Alice his wife. Three messuages in Sabrichesworth.

Gilbert Hyll & Humph. Colly : Tho. Lenard, John Harvy sen. & Tho. Lotton. Two messuages & lands in Ware, & land in Amwell.

Ralph Rowlett knt : Tho. Appowell & Margaret his wife & Grace Johnson widow. Lands in Sandridge.

Joan Laxton widow : Nich. Luddington & Rich. Thornhill. Manor of Roos Hall *als*. Rosehall & 10 messuages & lands in Sarrett.

Geo. Whyte gent & Jas. Gardyner gent : Edm. Huddelston esq & Dorothy his wife. Manor of Stockyng Pelham & 40 messuages & lands in Stockyng Pelham, Forneux Pellham & Brunt Pelham & the advowson of the Church of Stockyng Pelham.

### 1570. Trinity Term. 12 Eliz.

John Brysco : Tho. Brysco & Isabel his wife. Lands in Titteburst & Aldenham.

Wm. Cecyll knt : John Harryngton esq & Isabel his wife. Messuage & lands in Chesthunte.

Tho. Dollwyn *als*. Dollyng : Wm. Aylewarde & Joan his wife. Messuage & land in Aldenham.

Henry Cade : John Parnell & Joan his wife. Messuage & land in Wydforde.

Wm. Newman : Wm. Hyde gent & Geo. Fage & Anne his wife. Lands in Clothall & Weston.

Tho. Besteneye : Wm. Besteneye & Alice his wife. Lands in psh. of S<sup>t</sup> Peters in S<sup>t</sup> Albans.

Tho. Brysco : John Ayleward & Anne his wife. Manor of Pygottes & a messuage & lands in Aldenham.

Wm. Kynce : Edw. Russell gent & Kath. his wife. Messuage & lands in Much Hadham.

John Thurgood : Edw. Payne & John Payne. Messuage & land in Sabridgeworth *als*. Sabridgeford.

John Chawncye gent & Eliz. his wife : Henry Pole esq & Eliz. his wife. Manor of Overhall & 4 messuages & lands in Gedleston, Estwick, Sabridgeworthe & Hunsdon.

Ralph Rowlett knt : Ralph Maynarde gent. Manor of Apsa *als*. Apsaburye & 10 messuages, a mill & lands in pshes of S<sup>t</sup> Peters & S<sup>t</sup> Stephens near S<sup>t</sup> Albans, Colney & Shenley.

Nich. Bacon knt. lord keeper of the Great Seal & Anne his wife : Ralph Maynard gent. Manors of Westwyck & Pray with Kyngesbury & 40 messuages & lands in the pshes of S$^t$ Peter, S$^t$ Mich. & S$^t$ Stephens near S$^t$ Albans, & the advowson of the vicarage of S$^t$ Michaels.

John Hale : Edw. Denton gent & Wm. Denton gent. Three messuages & lands in Welwes als. Welwen & Dygonswell als. Dyggeswell.

John Pery : Augustin Pery. Messuage & lands in Sabridgeworth.

John Spencer & Joan his wife : Jesper Waren & Athoma his wife. Manor of Mawdlynbury & 10 messuages & lands in Welwyn & Thacheworth als. Dacheworth.

Tho. Tyrrell : Wm. Hyde junior. Lands in Weston alias Wesson, Baldock, Clotoll, Yerdley, Wallyngton & Rylesdon.

Benj. Gonson esq, Laur. Grene, Wm. Webbe & Steph. Wooderoff : Christr. Draper knt. & Margt. his wife. Manors of Chambers Bury als. Leeslangley als. Abbotts Langley & Hyde & 15 messuages & land in Lees Langley alias Abbotts Langley & Hyde. Also the rectory of Abbotts Langley.

Rich. Peyton & Tho. Shadbolt gents : Robt. Colte & Roger Colte gents. Manor of Woodwikes & lands in Rickmansworth.

Oliver lord Saint John, Tho. Baryngton, Tho. Sadler, Henry Capell, Wistan Browne, Henry Jooselyn, John Gyll, Oliver Saint John, esquires & Thos. Grymesdyche gent : Tho. Leventhorpe esq & Dorothy his wife. Manors of Aldeburye als. Alburye, Cockehamsted, Darcyes & Actons & 30 messuages & lands in Aldeburye als. Alburye, Cockehamsted, Braughinge, Sabrigeworthe, Estwicke & Wydford & free warren in Aldeburye.

Nich. Bacon knt., lord keeper & Anne his wife : Nath. Bacon esq & Edward Bacon esq. Manors of Westwyck, Goram als. Goreham als. Gorehams als. Gorehambury & Pray with Kyngesbury & 40 mess. & lands in parishes of S$^t$ Peter, S$^t$ Michael, & S$^t$ Stephen in S$^t$ Albans, & the advowson of S$^t$ Michaels.

### 1570. Mich. Term. 12 & 13 Eliz.

*Nich. West esq one of the Six Clerks of the Court of Chancery : Tho. Penyston esq. Land in Masseworth.

Edw. Baeshe esq & Jane his wife : Tho. Grave & Agnes his wife. Land in Stansted Abbott.

Rich. Pecoke : Henry Bellamy & Ellen his wife. Lands in Easte Barnett.

Wm. Sutton : John Eliatt & Julian his wife. Land in Est Reed.

Ellen Weste dau. of Wm. Weste gent : Wm. Atkyns. Messuage & lands in Hatfyld als. Bishops Hatfelde, Essyngdon & Dixwell als. Dydgeswell.

Henry Wattye : Rich. Grene gent. Land in Braughyng.

Stephen Marten : Ralph Layche & Kath. his wife & Tho. Phillippes. Messuage & land in Barkhampsted S$^t$ Peter.

Rich. Wyseman gent : Wm. Salkyns & Jane his wife & Wm. Hyde gent. Lands in Weston, Clothall als. Cloth Hall & Throcking.

Fras. Aldrych & Edw. Vaughan gents : Christr. Smythe esq. & Margt. his wife. Messuage & lands in Harpeden in psh. of Whithamstede.

Geo. Burgoyne esq & Godfry Burgoyne gent : Robt. Awstyn & Eliz. his wife & Wm. Awstyn son of s$^d$ Robt. & Eliz. Messuage & lands in Meesdon als. Meesden.

Christr. Wrey serjeant at law, Peter Osborne, Wm. Clerke esquires : Rich. Lee knt, Humph. Conyngsby esq & Mary his wife, eldest dau. of s$^d$ Richard & Edw. Sadler esq & Anne his wife the other dau. of s$^d$ Richard. Manors of Soppwelle, Soppwelbury, Newe-lande, Lees Langley *alias* Abbots Langley & Breakespeares *als*. Breakespeares Fee & 200 messuages & lands in parishes of St Albans, St Peters in St Albans & St Stephens near St Albans, & Less Langley *als*. Abbots Langley & the rectory of the church of Hexton, tythes etc. & the advowson of the vicarages of Hexton & St Stephens.

Henry Elsynge : Rich. Byrchemore & Alice his wife. Messuage & lands in Aldenham & in the psh. of St Stephens near St Albans.

Wm. Hagar : Tho. Letcheworthe & Suzan his wife. Two messuages in Ashewell.

Augustin Cooper : Wm. Lyncolne & Agnes his wife & John Judde & Kath. his wife. Messuage & land in Barkewaye.

Wm. Franckland esq : Wm. Bottomley & Kath. his wife. Two messuages & lands in Hoddesdon & Broxbourn.

Tho. Halsey *als*. Chambers : Wm. Markham esq & Frances his wife. Messuage & land in Flamsted.

Rich. Blounte : Ralph Layche & Kath. his wife & Tho. Phillippes. Messuage & land in Barkhampsted St Peter & Barkhampsted Marie *alias* Northchurch.

Wm. Warner : Humph. Whytlok & Anne his wife. Lands in Aldenham.

Leonard Stepnyth clk : Walt. Byrchemore. Messuage & lands in Caddyngton.

Jas. Goodacres : John Welles & Joan his wife. Messuage in St Albans.

Wm. Campion gent. Walt. Morgan gent & Jane his wife. Three messuages & lands in Stevenadge, Graveley, & Great Wymondley.

Robt. Payge : Roger Fysshe & Margt. his wife. A third part of a messuage & land in Hartingfourdbery.

## 1570-1. Hilary Term. 13 Eliz.

*Roland Hayward & John Langley alderman of the City of London : Roger Colt gent. Manor of Woodwickes & 6 messuages & lands in Rickmansworthe, Gt. Munden, Little Munden, Aldenham, & Barkehampsted & the advowson of the church of Rickmansworth.

*Wm Lee : Tho. Russell & Anne his wife. A third part of lands in Ridge.

Edw. Fitz John : Edw. Halfhedd gent. & Anne his wife. Messuage & land in Yardeley *alias* Ardeley.

Henry Basse : Tho. Appowell *alias* Lewes gent & Margt. his wife. Lands in Dacheworth & Tuyng.

Rich. Same : Geo. Same. Messuage & land in Pyrton *alias* Piriton.

Tho. Packyngton knt & Rich. Cowper esq : John Shepard gent. & Margery his wife. Messuage & lands in Offley, Hytchyn, Kings Walden & Lylley *alias* Lynley.

John Gunnell : Tho. Warde gent. Three messuages & lands in Asshewell.

Geo. Horsey, Edw. Baesshe, Wm. Doddes & Henry Conyngsby esqrs : Rich. Lee knt. Manor of Hexton & 20 messuages & lands in Hexton.

John Kynge : Wm. Arryngton & Rose his wife & Tho. Earle & Alice his wife. Two parts of a messuage & lands, in six parts divided, in Buntyngforde, Leystone, Aulsewycke, Wydeall, Apseden & Throckynge.

Geo. Horsey, Edw. Baesshe, Wm. Doddes & Henry Coningsby esqrs : Ralph Sadler knt chancellor of the Duchy of Lancaster. Manor of Temple Dionesley & 20 messuages & lands in Temple Dyonesley, Hechen, Kings Walden, Pollett(, Offeley & Gosmer, & the rectory of Kings Walden &c.

Henry Tokfylde : Tho. Leccheworthe & Suzan his wife. Messuage in Baldok.

### 1571. Easter Term. 13 Eliz.

*Geo. Nicolls esq & Robt. Frith : Rich. Fitzhughe & Nich. Fitzhughe. Manor of Grenehall & lands in Sandon.

Edmund Franckland : Robt. Tompson. Two messuages & land in Hoddesdon & Broxbourne.

Robt. Wolley : Humph. Connyngesbye esq & Edw. Grace. Messuage & land in psh. of S$^t$ Andrews in S$^t$ Albans.

Tho. Watt$^e$ clk. archdeacon of Middlesex : Ralph Dyxon & Anne his wife. Three messuages & lands in Ashewell.

John Eames : Leon. Tymperley gent. Messuage & land in Little Gaddesdon.

Jeremy Gray & Henry Adams : Wymond Cary. Messuage & lands in Pelham Arsa.

Tho. Wyseman esq : Wm. Hyde gent. Manor of Throckyng & six messuages & lands in Throckynge, Clothall, Weston, Sondon, Layston & Apesden, and the advowson of the church of Throckynge.

Roger Byrcheley, Mich. Irelande & Rich. Pyper : John Byrcheley & Philippa his wife. Three messuages & lands in Hertford & Bayford.

John Bryscoo & Reginald Aman : Hen. Conyngesbye esq & Eliz. his wife. Four messuages & lands in Aldenham, Tytburste, & the psh. of S$^t$ Stephens near S$^t$ Albans.

Marian Pryce widow : John Dunwell, Wm. Borne & Alice his wife & Margery Slepe senior. Messuage & garden in Bishops Hatfelde *alias* Kings Hatfeld.

Joan Smythe *alias* Clarke widow : Roland Elyott gent & Anne his wife. Messuage in Stortford.

Tho. Norwood sen$^r$ gent : Jasper Smyth & Eliz. his wife. Manors of Cantlowbury & Wattonbury *alias* Henxworthbury & 4 messuages & lands in Henxworth *alias* Hynxworth, Edworth, Calcott & Asshewell.

John Marshe gent & Anne his wife : John Adams gent & Margt. his wife. Moiety of a messuage & lands in Bokelond, Newchyppyng & Barkewey.

### 1571. Trinity Term. 13 Eliz.

*Hen. Halton & Agnes his wife & Constantius Frenche son & heir of Wm. Frenche dec$^d$ : Christr. Cristmas *alias* Wilversey & Joan his wife & Wm. Kympton son & heir apparent of said Joan. Lands in Kennesworthe.

*Tho. Russell & John Brakenfeld : Edw. Taylar esq & Kath. his wife & Henry Taylar gent. & Kath. his wife. Five messuages & lands in Chyppinge Barnett.

*Robt. Hallywell & Wm. Lee gents : Jas. Hales esq & Alice his wife. A third part of lands in Rydge.

John Homarston : John Hogge & Agnes his wife. Messuage in Amwell.

Owen Waller : Roger Tounsend esq. Lands in Furnys Pellham & Storford.

John Somer : Tho. Benette & Eliz. his wife. Messuage & land in Broxbourne & Hoddesden.

Edw. Horne : Margt. Horne widow. Messuage & lands in Kennesworth.

Rich. Pechye & Alice his wife : Hen. Chauncey esq & Rose his wife. Messuage & land in Sabrydgeworthe *alias* Sapsforde & Gedleston *alias* Gelston.

Wm. Franckland & Edm. Franckland : John Cannon. Two messuages & lands in Broxbourn & Amwell.

Geo. Grave : Robt. Hadley & Cecily his wife. Two messuages & lands in Chesthunt.

Rich. Forster : Tho. Appowell *alias* Powell & Margt. his wife & Henry Johnson. Moiety of the Manor of Dacheworthe & of a messuage & lands in Dacheworthe *alias* Datcheworthe *alias* Thatcheworthe.

Robt. Wolley : Rich. Lee knt. & Rich. Chaddisley. Five messuages & gardens in St Albans.

Edw. Clere esq, Rich. Bedyll gent, Andr. Hemerford gent. & John Cowper gent : Tho. Clere esq & Anne his wife, Edw. Lewkenor esq & Suzan his wife. Manor of Sowthall & a messuage & lands in Great Gaddesden & Hempsted.

### 1571. Mich. Term. 13 & 14 Eliz.

*John Goodwyn knt : Wm. Husee esq & Mary his wife. A third part of ten messuages & lands in Agmondesham.

*Nichs Bacon knt. lord keeper of the Great Seal of England : Ralph Maynard gent & Margery his wife. Manor of Abbatts Bury *alias* Rowletts Bury, Mynchynbury, Hores & Apsabury *alias* Napsebury & 12 messuages & lands in Barley, Barkwaye & the parish of St Peters near St Albans.

Henry Hudnall jun : Edm. Verney esq. Messuage & land in Great Tryng.

Thos. Blossom : Rich. Rowe & Eliz. his wife. Land in Braffyng.

John Goodman : Tho. Bowles esq. Lands in Wallington.

Wm. Campion gent : Walter Morgan gent & Jane his wife & Thos. Vaughan gent. Three messuages & lands in Stevenadge, Graveley & Great Wymondley [not in index and apparently belongs to the previous Mich. Term].

John Andrews *alias* Woodroof : Thos. Chandler & Joan his wife. Moiety of a messuage & land in Pokeriche & Braughinge.

John Eames : Rich. Foster & Isott his wife. Messuage & lands in Great Tringe & Little Tryng.

Walter Fynche : Tho. Fynche sen. & Eliz. his wife. Land in Redborn.

Thos. Wright : Edw. Duñe. Two messuages & land in Asshewell.

Thos. Stanley esq : Edw. Wytton. Messuage & land in Standon.

Henry Kynge cit. & brycklayer of London : Thos. Aspynne *alias* James & Eliz his wife. Messuage & land in Hodgeden *alias* Hoddysdon, Broxborne & Amwell.

John Dyer : Geo. Dyer. Two messuages & lands in Albury *alias* Aldebury.

Robt. Bagsha gent & Matilda his wife : John Wygan gent & Joan his wife. Messuage & lands in Northmyms *alias* Northmymes.

Nichs Bacon knt. & Anne his wife : Wm. Atkynes & Wm. Weste & Ellen his wife. Lands in psh. of St Michaels near St Albans.

Augustine Cooper : Wm. Lyncolne & Agnes his wife & John Judde & Kath. his wife. Messuage & lands in Barkewaye [not in index and apparently belongs to the previous Mich. Term].

Robt. Hyrst gent : Thos. Gooday & Dionisia his wife. Manor of Sabrychesworth *alias* Sabrychforde als. Sabrysforde als. Sabbesforde als. Sabrysforth & lands in Sabrychesworth & Much Hadham.

Wm. Brokett gent : Rich. Godfrey *alias* Cooper. Two messuages & lands in Kings Walden & Ipolletts.

Edm. Dardes : Wm. Gardiner & Frances his wife. Messuage & lands in Northemymes *alias* Northmyms.

Henry Mayne & Rich. Shakemaple : Tho. Penyston esq & Eliz. his wife. Lands in Bovyngton *alias* Bovyngdon & Northchurche.

Henry Hyckman & Joan his wife : Rich. Wythe. Messuage & land in Watford. Remainder (after the death of said Richard) to George Wythe his son & heir apparent.

Wm. Cranfyld : John Boxsted & Agnes his wife. Messuage & land in Watton Atstone.

Wm. Kentishe : Francis Heydon esq & Frances his wife. Messuage & land in Watford.

Benedict Averell : Thos. Bayes & Ellen his wife. Lands in Much Hadham & Little Hadham.

Francis Heydon esq : Francis Newdegate esq, John Newdegate esq & Martha his wife & Thos. Newdegate gent. Moiety of manor of Oxeyhall & of a messuage & lands in Watford.

Thos. Cobbe gent & Rich. Mason gent : Lewis Mordaunt knt, lord Mordaunt & Francis Willoughbye gent. Two parts of lands in Kympton.

Thos. Cobbe gent. & Rich. Mason gent : Lewis Mordaunt knt., lord Mordaunt & Francis Willoughbye gent. Two parts of a messuage & lands in Kympton.

John Yonge : Wm. Skypwyth knt & Eliz. his wife, Wm. Marson & Francis Marson. Manor of Woodhalle & messuage & lands in Hemel Hamsted.

John Cade gent : Tho. Conyngesbye esq. Tenement in Aldenham [not in bundle].

### 1571. Hilary Term. 14 Eliz.

*Thos. Howe & Wm. Knyght : Robt. Pett & Eliz. his wife. Lands in Cadyngton.

*Wm. Cecill knt, baron of Burghley : Robt. Savill esq & Anne his wife, John Massingberd esq & Dorothy his wife, Margaret Tharold widow, Mary Hall widow, Thos. Horseman esq & Wm. Clopton esq. Manors of Baas, Perryers, Perrers, Hoddesdon, Hoddisdonberye, Geddyngs, Langtons, Foxtons, Maryons, Halls, Jerkyns & Jerkyns Fee & 120 messuages & lands in the said places & Broxborne, Brokesborne, Wormeley, Wormesley, Cheston, Chesthunt, Amwell, Sawells, Sadrells, Cockeshutt, Conygarth & the psh. of All Saints in Hertford.

John Bayforde : John Carter & Mary his wife. Land in Stortford.

Wm. Brockett gent : Wm. Clarke. Land in Flamsted.

Nich⁸ Dyer & Joan his wife : Walter Hayward. Lands in Aldebury.

Wm. Collyn : Wimond Carye esq. Land in Stortforde.

John Brokett of Brokett Haule esq, Geo. Horsey esq & Thos. Doowra gent : John Brokett of Stowe longa gent & Kath. his wife & Edw. Brokett gent & Ellen his wife. Manor of Bradfield *alias* Brodfield & 10 messuages & lands in Bradfield *alias* Brodfield, Rusheden & Codreth *alias* Cotered & the advowson of the church of Bradfield *alias* Brodfield.

Thos. Bownest : Edw. Howe & Agnes his wife, Edw. Crosse & Margt. his wife & John Kinge & Kath. his wife. Messuage in Baldock & five parts of two messuages & lands, in six parts divided, in Buntyngforde, Leyston, Alleswyke, Wydyall, Apseden & Throckynge.

Walter, viscount Hereford : Robt. Savill esq & Anne his wife, John Massingberd & Dorothy his wife, Margt. Tharold, widow, Mary Hall widow, Thos. Horseman esq & Wm. Clopton esq. Manor of Benington & 60 messuages & lands in Benington, Watton At Stone, Walkehorne & Mondon.

*To be Continued.*

# Transcripts of Parish Registers.

## NORTHAW.

(Continued from Page 48).

In the Parish of Northaw in the County of Hertford from Lady-Day, 1744, to Lady-Day, 1745.

*Baptised.*
- Day, Martha-Mary
- Page, Elizabeth
- Aynsel, Martha
- Pope, Sarah
- Pryor, William
- Grace, Thomas
- Coral, Sarah
- Morris, James
- Porter, Joseph
- Parsons, Joseph
- Fensom, Henry
- Olney, Martha
- Jordan, Thomas
- Roby, Sarah
- Langley, Frances
- Field, Elizabeth

*Buried.*
- William Harris
- Richard [Inshco?]
- John Lever
- Edward Creacy
- Elizabeth Pryor
- Martha Brown
- Susannah Wood
- Elizabeth Chapple
- Susannah Davison
- William Jennens
- John Overman
- Ann Brettand
- Simon Barnet
- Sarah Walters

*Married.*
- Thomas-Frewen Moor & Mary Brown.
- Thomas Skinner & Esther Morrell.

Thomas Preston, Minister.

---

In the Parish of Northaw in the County of Hertford from Lady-Day, 1745, to Lady-Day, 1746.

*Baptized.*
- Mansfield, Mary
- Warner, Susannah
- Griffin, Mary
- Flindal, William
- Tyler, Ann
- Godwin, Abednego
- Newman, Ann
- Howe James
- Wacket, Amy
- Chappel, Hannah
- Todd, Ann
- Lane, John
- King, Ann
- Heald, Ann

*Buried.*
- Martha Aynsell
- Samuel Campion
- Martha Olney
- Mary King
- Mrs. Lucy Leman
- Jane Adams
- Thomas Jordan
- Hannah Chappel
- Ann Bailey
- Lady Leman
- John Cutts
- Joseph Porter
- Thomas Roker
- Ann Hurry
- Frances Utterridge
- Sarah Vass

*Married.*
[None]

Thomas Preston, Minister.

In the Parish of Northaw in the County of Hertford from Lady-Day, 1747, to Lady-Day, 1748.

| Baptized. | Buried. |
|---|---|
| Page, Ann | Mary Poole, Inf<sup>t.</sup> |
| Lane, Charles | Sarah Aynsel, Inf<sup>t.</sup> |
| Godwin, Adednego | Sarah Sage, Inf<sup>t.</sup> |
| Parsons, Thomas | Thomas Hammond, Esq<sup>r.</sup> |
| Wacket, James | Bird Adams |
| Clark, Mary | William Specer |
| Todd, Edward | Mary Aynsel |
| Hide, Richard | Thomas Wacket, Inf<sup>t.</sup> |
| Manfield, Ann | Susan Godwin, Inf<sup>t.</sup> |
| Maple, James | Benjamin Shaw |
| Claxton, William | Elizabeth Cockford |
| Stevens, Richard | Richard Aynsel |
| Field, John | Ann Robinson |
| Griffin, John | Thomas Parsons, Inf<sup>t.</sup> |
| Fowkes, Francis | Mary Claxton |
|  | Eleanor Philips |
| *Married.* | Abednego Godwin, Inf<sup>t.</sup> |
| Henry Smith & | Charles Lane, Inf<sup>t.</sup> |
| Jane Newlin | Daniel Jordan |
|  | Christopher Peel, Inf<sup>t.</sup> |
|  | Richard Stevens |

Thomas Preston, Minister.

[*About a dozen Northaw Transcripts exist for later years, but I do not propose to continue the series further in this Magazine.*—ED.]

# Abstracts of Wills.

### ARCHDEACONRY OF MIDDLESEX (ESSEX AND HERTS).

REGISTER "RAYMOND"—CONTINUED FROM PAGE 40.

f. 247. JOHN GRIGS the elder of Waltham Cross in psh. of Chesthunt. (*Dat.* 6 Oct. 1576). Bro-in-law Hugh More; Thos. Hawse my wifes bro-in-law & Thos. Hawse his son; Serv<sup>t</sup> W<sup>m</sup>. Cauldon; Sister More; My sons wife; Wife Mary extrix; Son John; Geo. Preston & Symon Williams overseers. *Wit<sup>s</sup>*:—Simon Williams vicar of Chesthunt. (*Pr.* at Hoddesden 4 Feb. 1576-7).

f. 248. JOHN SMITH of Stansted Abbot, smith. (*Dat.* 15 Jan. 1576). Wife Margery; Son John Smith; Daus. Jane, Eliz. & Grace; Bro. Thos. Smithe; Land in Horse homes in Riemeade; Raffe Lewes my daughters son; My youngest dau. Grace; Wife extrix. *Wit<sup>s</sup>*:—John Lewes clk., John Bevys, Simon Nobbys, Henry Grave, John Forsett vicarius. (*Pr.* at Hoddesden 4 Feb. 1576-7).

f. 249. JOHN LEE of Stondon, yeoman. (*Dat.* 28 Apr. 1516 *sic*). Alice my maid; Wife Eliz.: Son-in-law Henry Miles & Anne now his wife: Ursula Miles dau. of s$^d$ Henry & Anne (under 12); Wife & s$^d$ son in law exors; Tho. Lamkyn of Collyersende & Wm. Tailer of Stondon overseers. *Wit$^s$*:—Robt. Bate & John Daniell. (*Pr.* at Braughing 2 July 1576).

f. 249. JOHN MORGAN of Ware, innholder. (*Dat.* 14 July 1576 nuncupative). M$^r$ Keye, vicar of Ware; All to my wife 'for I broughte nothinge to her and therfore will geve nothinge from her'; Wife extrix. (*Pr.* at Stortford 29 July 1576).

f. 251. ROBERT DOBSON of Thundriche, barbor. (*Dat.* 31 Mch. 1576). Wm. Dixon o$^r$ minister; Wife Johane & Nich. Lavender my wife's daughter's son exors; John Allyn overseer; To Johane Maples my shaving bason. *Wit$^s$*:—Wm. Dixon minister ther, Wm. Wells. (*Pr.* at Ware 3 May 1576).

f. 254. ALICE WATHE of Tunfordestone in psh. of Chestunt. (*Dat.* 14 July 1577). Daus. Sara, Kath. & Faythe (all under 16); Dau. Agnes extrix; Jane Wette; John Dawlton & Wm. Warde overseers. *Wit$^s$*:—Wm. Warde & Geo. Fuller.

f. 255. HUMFREY PAGE of Ware, husbandman. (*Dat.* 2 Jan. 1578 [*sic*]). Sons Humph., Henry & Geo. Page (under 21); Daus. Anne & Mary; House & land at Bakers ende called Gymmes; Wife Mary & Son Francis exors; John Barnes & John Throuhgood overseers. *Wit$^s$*:—John Thouhgood & John Barnes. (*Pr.* 8 Feb. 1577-8).

f. 256. JOHN SPENCER of Ware, wheelwright. (*Dat.* 19 May 1577). Wife Eliz; House called the White Horse in Ware; Son Humph.; Daus. Joane & Eliz; Wife extrix; Friend Thos. Cramphorne overseer. *Wit$^s$*:—Nich. Thurgood, Tho. Claxon, Wm. Pike & Edw. Nicolson. (*Pr.* at Stortford 18 Nov. 1577).

f. 256. ELIZABETH WARDE late wife of Henry Warde late of Brawghin. (*Dat.* 30 Sep. 1577). Eldest dau. Margt. Warde; Dau. Anne Warde; Agnes, Margt. & Joane Meritowne my sisters; Father Thomas Meritownge exor. *Wit$^s$*:—John Wood, Leonard Southe, Jeffrey Wrenne, John Hedlam vicar of Brawghn. (*Pr.* at Ware 23 Oct. 1577).

f. 257. SIMON LOWEN of Cheston. (*Dat.* 29 May 1577). Son Wm. Lowen; Copyhold lands in Ferle & house on same ground; Wife Agnes; Son John; Land at Tunforde; Son Nich.; Wife extrix. *Wit$^s$*:—Henry Cordle, Tho. Lowen & Symon Cordle. (*Pr.* at Ware 23 Oct. 1577).

f. 257. THOMAS RAYMONDE of Sabridgworthe, gent. (*Dat.* 13 June 1579). Bro. Wm.; Sist. Bridget & her child$^n$; Bro. Alex$^r$ Chancy & Bridget my sister & Geo. her son; Bro. Wm. Chaney dec$^d$ & Alexander; Sisters Bridget & Marie Chancye; Frances Collier; Thos. Pillie; Joane Whale; Jas. Towler; Bro. Alex$^r$ Chancye & sist. Bridget Chancie exors. (*Pr.* at Sabridgworthe 23 July 1577).

f. 258. HENRYE CURTYS of Chesthunt, yeoman. (*Dat.* 13 May 1577). Wife Margt.; Tenements in Chesthunte Streate; My two daus. Dorothy & Eliz.; Lands in Frethey, the Leese or crofte at Marshe gate in occupation of widow Isacke, Blackdole grove. land in tenure of widow Warthe, land in Bullwelfeilde: Tenement in Chesthunt Street w^th the yard through to Bullwelldiche; Land at Marshgate in tenure of widow Pynkanie; Turners hill occupied by John Cordell; M^r Dakers; Henry Cañon my sisters son; Sist. Staynes; Henrie of London; John Chare sen^r; Land in Brockefeilde of the manor of Androwes; Abm. Symous; M^r Courle; Wife extrix; Symon Williams vicar & John Chare sen^r overseers. *Wit^s*:—Thomas Mondie & Geo. Redich. (*Pr.* 23 May 1577).

f. 260. THOMAS CLERKE of Chesthunt, yeoman. (*Dat.* 22 Mch. 1576). Bro. Christ^r Clerke; Dau. Alice; John Shambrocke, Rich. Shambrock, Marye Shambrock & Margt. Lowdam the child^n of my sister Lowdam; John, Thomas & Agnes Barnes child^n of my uncle John Barnes; Kath. Seely my mother; The child^n of Reynold Wyberde of Enfeilde; Child^n of Widow Chaire of Chesthunt late wife of John Chaire; Servants Eliz. Shambrocke, John Hoorewood & Cicillie Fesaunte; Bro. Edw. Northe exor; Bro.-in-law W^m. Lowdam & neighbours John Picking, Cutberd Angel, John Shambrock & Symon Williams overseers. *Wit^s*:—W^m. Lowdam, Henry Cockerel, John Picker, Symon Williams. (*Pr.* 20 May 1577).

f. 261. HENRY VICCAS of Harestrete in psh. of Leiston. (*Dat.* 24 Apr. 1577). Son John; My 5 daus. Agnes, Prudence, Mary, Jone & Susan; Thos. Brand the elder; Wife Kath. extrix. *Wit^s*:—John Diason, Michael Meritowne & Titus Chapman. (*Pr.* at Ware 20 May 1577).

f. 261. JOHN SYMMS of Stansted Abbot. (*Dat.* 6 May 1577). Son Thomas; John Chalice; W^m. & Nich. Sweete; W^m. Rowe my m^rs servant; W^m. Sweete 'the dum Boye'; Wife Joane extrix. *Wit^s*:—Tho. Grave, Henry Bayforde, John Bevys & Symon Nobbs. (*Pr.* at Ware 20 May 1577).

f. 261. THOMAS BUCKE of Leyston, tanner. (*Dat.* 22 Mch. 1576). Dau. Susan (under 23); Wife Margt.; Bro. Geo. Bucke; Bros. John Bucke & W^m. Hubberde exors; John Hubberd my father & W^m. Hawes my uncle overseers. *Wit^s*:—Lewys Reynold vicar of Leyston, Tho. Watts, John Etridge. (*Pr.* 20 May 1576 [*sic*]).

f. 263. WILLIAM WOMWELL of Barley. (*Dat.* 23 June 1577. Wife Alice; Sons W^m. & Felix; Lands called Little grene strete, bird pightle meade & the little close at Well ende, close next the mylle lane, bakers pightle, hey thorne hylle, land purchased of John Dowell, the pece at the Sallowes; House called the Bull purchased of Henry Hagar; Land at Settcopp hille; The child^n of sons W^m. & Felix & dau. Kath. Stalibras & of dau. Margt. Crowche dec^d; John Goodchild; Lands held of manor of Hadleys & land lying at Harson pathe; Son Felix exor. *Wit^s*:—John Grenell, W^m. Womwell & Rich. Stalibras. (*Pr.* at Gedleston 23 Apr. 1577).

f. 264. WILLIAM LOWEN of Hamonde strete, in psh. of Chesthunte, yeoman. (*Dat.* 12 Mch. 1576). Sons Thos. & Rich. exors; Dau. Agnes Lowen; Thomas Lowyn's wife. *Wit^s*:—John Cocke elder & Symon Lowen & W^m. Lowen my sons & Simon Williams. (*Pr.* at Ware 17 Apr. 1577).

ABSTRACTS OF WILLS.

f. 264. JOHN HALYWELL of Chesthunte, smith. (*Dat.* 24 Mch. 1576). Daus. Kath. Halliwell & Marie Halliwell: Robert 'my servante & brother': Bro-in-law John Nottingham: Wife Eliz. extrix. *Wit*ˢ:—John Notingham & Simon Williams vicar. (*Pr.* at Ware 17 April 1577).

f. 264. JOHN CARTER *alias* YPGRAVE of Barkway. (*Dat.* 12 Mch. 1576). Wife Eliz.; Son Wm.; House lately purchased of John Mapleton; Son Geo. (under 21); Wife extrix. *Wit*ˢ:—Rich. Turner, Nich. Fowler, Tho. Ipgrave *als* Carter, Wm. Raymonde & Felix Womwell. (*Pr.* at Ware 17 Apr. 1577).

265. BARTHOLOMEW BROCKE of Broughin yeoman. (*Dat.* 19 Mch. 1577). Wife Joane; Son John; Houses which Thos. Beñet & Tho. Jackest now dwell in with a pightle at Roydon Hille & land in Spackwel feilde, Erlsey feilde; Son Robt; One pightle at Fordebridge; Lands at Cockyn, Mounecrofte; Son Michael; Dau. Mercie Castel; Dau. Joane Brocke; John Hedlam, vicar of Browghin; Henry Wattie & John Isacke my wife's bro. overseers; Wife extrix. *Wit*ˢ:—Ralphe Brocke & John Brocke. (*Pr.* at Ware 17 Apr. 1577).

*To be Continued.*

# Inquisitiones Post Mortem.

### RALPH ROWLETT.

[*Inq. p.m.* 35 *Hen.* VIII. *No.* 40].

Inquisition taken at Stevenage, co. Herts. 14 April 34 Hen. VIII. [1543] before Edward Bury esq, escheator, after the death of Ralph Rowlett, senior esqʳ, by the oaths of George Clerk, Leonard Humerston, Edward Wilson, Wm. Eyer, Wm. Hinone, Rich. Glandvile, Wm. Smythe, Wm. Chapman, John Hobyll, Wm. Hide, Thos. Hethe, Walter Ward, Wm. Iverye & Henry Curteys who say that

The said Ralph was seised as of fee in the manor or lordship of Mynchenbury etc. in the parish of Barley, the manor of Horys in Barley, the manor of Newneham & the rectory & advowson of the vicarage of Newneham, the manor of Caldecot, & the advowson of the church or rectory of Caldecot, the manor of Radwell near Baldok & the advowson of the church or rectory of Radwell, the advowson or patronage of the vicarage of Redborn, two closes lying in Stillinglane in Sᵗ Albans, a close lying in Halywell 'ultra rivulam' in Sᵗ Albans, four messuages in Sopwellane in Sᵗ Albans, a messuage in Halywell strete in Sᵗ Albans, a messuage called Everards in Halywell strete, twenty acres of meadow next the capital house or messuage in which the sᵈ Ralph was living, a messuage in Fisshepolestrett in Sᵗ Albans, a close in the psh. of Sᵗ Stephens, the manor of Sandrige *alias* Sanderugge & all lands whatever & Brydell tythe etc., in the parish of Sandrigge which were formerly parcel of the Monastery of Sᵗ Albans, the manor of Appesbury *alias* Apsabury & all & every views of frankpledg etc. appurtenant to the manors of Sandrige, Newneham, Caldecot. Radwell, & the manors of Praye, Whestewyk, Goram Bury & Apsobury in as full a manner as Richard Bowreman abbot of the monastery of S^t Albans held the same as by letters patent of the King to the s^d Ralph appears, also s^d Ralph was seised of the messuage in which he was living in S^t Albans, a tenement in which Wm. Harrys dwells in the psh. of S^t Stephens . . . . . . . . . & a tenement in which Rich. Bradbury dwells in S^t Albans.

The s^d Ralph made his last will in form as follows [*will recited**].

The manor of Minchenbury is worth xij*l*. per ann. The manor of Horys in Barley is worth v*l*. vj*s*. viij*d*. per ann. & is held of the king in chief by service of the 20th part of a knights fee. The manor of Newneham & the advowson of the church are worth xix*l*. xs. vj*d*. per ann. The manor of Caldecott & advowson etc. are worth viij*l*. xviij*s*. per ann. The manor of Radwell & the advowson etc. are worth xiij*l*. vj*s*. viij*d*. per ann. The manor of Sandryge with the brydell tythe, etc, are worth lxx*l*. per ann. The manor of Appesbury etc. are worth x*l*. per ann. All s^d manors etc (except the manor of Horys) are held of the King in chief by knight's service. All the messuages & closes in S^t Albans & S^t Stephens are held of the King in socage but at what rent the jurors are ignorant & are worth x*l*. per ann.

Said Ralph died 4th March last & Ralph Rowlett is his son & next heir & aged 30 years & more at the taking of this inquisition.

## SIR RALPH ROWLETT, KNIGHT.
### [*Inq. p.m.* 27 *Eliz.* No. 3].

Inquisition taken at S^t Albans, co. Herts., 26 Mch. 27 Eliz. [1585], before John Brockett knt. & Walter Tooke gent., feodaries, commissioners of the Queen in s^d county, by virtue of a commission to Geo. Horsey esq., Rich. Francks esq., escheator, & Wm. Tooke esq. auditor general of the Court of Wards & Liveries, after the death of Ralph Rowlett knt. by the oaths of John Astwick gent., Rich. Adkyns, Henry Feilde, Rich. Gronwynne, Wm. Cutt, Tho. Nicholles, Nich. Syblye, Roger Nicholles, Wm. Robyns, Tho. Gronwynne, Geo. Carpenter, Geo. Besowthe & Wm. Turner, who say that

Ralph Rowlett, knight, was seised, as of fee, of a meadow called Hallywell Meadowe near S^t Albans & a close in Sandridge called Lytle Halheath & of the manor & rectory of Sandridge & 7 acres & 10 virgates of wood in a field called Potterswicke in Sandridge & 2 closes in Sandridge called Walmondes Close & Jennings Feildes containing 30 acres & of certain parcels of land called Bewberries *alias* Bowberies in Sandridge & 20 messuages, 12 cottages, a dovecote & 4000 acres of land, 300 acres of meadow, 2000 acres pasture, 800 acres wood, 600 acres of furze & heath & xxx*l*. rent in Sandridge, Whethamsted, Bishops Hatfeilde & S^t Peter's near S^t Albans.

So seised, on the last day of June 8 Eliz. [1566], by indenture tripartite, made between s^d Ralph Rowlett by the name of Ralph Rowlett of Hallywell near S^t Albans, knight, of the one part & Robt. Catlyn knt. chief justice of the Court of Queen's Bench, John Southcote esq. one of the justices of the s^d court, Gilbert Gerrarde esq. attorney general, Wm. Lovelace esq. & Thos. Rolf gent. of the other

---

* The Editor intends printing this will, and those of Sir Ralph and Affable Rowlett, in the next number.

part, the s^d Ralph agreed that he, by good assurance, would convey to the s^d Robt., John, Gilbert, Wm., & Thos. or the survivors of them, the afores^d manor & premises by the name of the manor of Sandrige *alias* Sandruge & the rectory of Sandridge & all that annual pension of 26s. 8d. issuing from the vicarage of Sandridge, & the advowson of s^d vicarage to hold the same to the use of Jas. Bacon, Thos. Andrewes & Barth. Kempe for a term of four years, then to the use of s^d Ralph for life & after s^d Ralph's death, as he should by will appoint, with remainder to the heirs of the body of s^d Ralph & in default of such heirs then to the use of Ralph Genuyns esq. & his heirs etc. And the s^d Ralph afterwards by indenture dated 1 July 8 Eliz. [1566] conveyed s^d premises to s^d Robt. Catlyn & others accordingly.

Ralph Rowlett was also seised of a capital messuage called Hallywell in S^t Albans & divers lands adjoining, called the Parke, lying on the east side of s^d messuage, with lands in S^t Albans called Bradfords or Bradfords Close, an acre of meadow in same parish now in tenure of Thos. Bradforde, land called Pondewicke in the psh. of S^t Albans, a close in Hallywell in the psh. of S^t Michaels in tenure of Geo. Bunne, [*blank*] acres in S^t Michaels parish on the eastern side of the common way leading from the psh. of S^t Albans to the psh. of S^t Stephens, & three messuages & lands in S^t Michaels & S^t Albans.

So seised, on 25 July 8 Eliz. by deed between s^d Ralph of the one part & Thos. Colbye esq., Wm. Phillips & Thos. Rolfe gents of the other part, s^d Ralph agreed, before the Michaelmas following to convey all s^d last mentioned premises to s^d Colbye & others to the use of Jas. Bacon, Tho. Andrewes & Barth. Kempe for a term of four years, to uses similar to those previously mentioned. Said Ralph by deed dated 27 July 8 Eliz. conveyed s^d premises accordingly.

Ralph was also seised of the manors of Newneham & Radwell & the rectory & advowson of Newneham, which, with hereditaments in Newneham, Radwell, Caldecote, Hixworthe, Bigrave & Baldock, he conveyed in trust to s^d Robt. Catlyn, John Southcotte & others with ultimate remainder to Wm. Skipwith esq. & his heirs.

Ralph was also seised of the manor of Thedingworthe in the counties of Leicester & Northampton etc., which he settled in similar manner as before on trust for Henry Goodier esq. & his heirs.

The said Ralph made his will dated 28 July 8 Eliz. [*fully recited*].

The meadow called Hallywell meade is held of the Queen in chief by knights service & is worth 20s. per ann. The close in Sandridge called Little Hall Heathe (how held the jurors do not know) is worth 33s. 4d. per ann. The manor & rectory of Sandridge etc. are held of the Queen in chief by the service of the 40th part of a knights fee & rent of 8l. 6s. 1½d. & are worth 67l. 8s. 4½d. per ann. Messuage called Hallywell with the Park, Bradfords, Pondwick & closes etc. are held of the Queen in chief by knights service & are worth 13l. 6s. 8d. per ann. The manors of Newneham & Radwell are held of the Queen by knights service & worth 32l. per ann. The manor of Thedingworth etc. are held of the Queen in chief by knights service & worth 30l. per ann.

Said Ralph died 20 Apr. 23 Eliz. [1581] & at the time of his death, Ralph Jennings esq., Henry Goodiere esq., Ralph Maynarde gent., Wm. Skipwith esq., [*blank*] wife of Geo. Herde & [*blank*] wife of Wm. Sheather were next of kin & next heirs of s^d Ralph, viz. Ralph Jennings esq. (aged 42 & more) son & heir of Dorothy late wife of Barnard Jennings esq. dec^d one of the five sisters of s^d Ralph

Rowlett; Henry Goodiere esq. (aged 35 & more) son & heir of Ursula late wife of Francis Goodiere esq. dec^d another of s^d sisters; Ralph Maynard gent. (aged 34 & more) son & heir of Margery late wife of John Maynarde esq. dec^d another of s^d sisters; W^m. Skipwith esq. (aged 40 & more) son & heir of Joan late wife of Thos. Skipwith esq. dec^d another of s^d sisters; & — Herde (aged 26) one of the two daus. & coheirs of Margaret late wife of Thos. Latham gent. dec^d another of s^d five sisters, & — Sheather (aged 24 & now wife of W^m. Sheather) the other dau. of s^d Margt. Lathom.

## Abstracts of Herts Wills.

### ARCHDEACONRY OF ST. ALBANS.

REGISTER "STONEHAM."—CONTINUED FROM PAGE 47.

f. 25. JOHANNES FORTHO vicar of the church of S^t Stephens near S^t Albans. (*Dat.* 1 Aug. 1435). Bur. in chancel of S^t Stephens, before S^t Stephens' altar; To the fabric of s^d church 6s. 8d.; To the convent of the monastery of S^t Albans 26s. 8d. 'ad orandum etc.'; To John Hilton for his good service a bed & two sheep; To be distributed to the poor & for my burial cs.; John Fortho my bro. & John Vessy sen^r to pay 13s. 4d. 'cuidam pictori ad pingendum ymaginem sancti Stephani supradicti'; Residue to s^d bro. John Fortho & s^d John Vessy sen^r; Dated at S^t Julians. (*Pr.* 18 Aug. 1435).

f. 25. RICARDUS ELDEBURY of Sarette. (*Dat.* 1 Oct. 1435). My two daus; Three other daus; Wife Rose & son John exors.

f. 25. THOMAS FAUNTONER of S^t Albans. (*Dat.* 'die lune prox. ante festum' S^t Barth. apostle 1435). Bur. S^t Peters; John Tanner clerk of s^d church; My mother; Alice late wife of John Smyth, skinner; Rich. Cony; John Strynger; John Mannyng; Wife Agnes extrix; Rich. Wermyngton overseer.

f. 25. WALTERUS HALE of Hexton. (*Dat.* 'die Sancti Edwardi Regis et martiris' 1435). Bur. at S^t Faith the Virgin's in Hexton; Legacy to the friars of Huchyn, Dunstabul, Bedforde & Cantebrig; Thos. son of Thos. Hale & W^m. Hale 'confilijs meis'; Marion Taylor; John & John Hale my sons exors. Willm. Basse, clerk, perpetual vicar of s^d church supervisor.

f. 25. MARTINUS NORTHEY of Hexton. (*Dat.* S^t Giles the Abbot's day 1435). Bur. at S^t Faith's in Hexton; Legacy to the mending of a road called Lyrchefflayne; The Carmelite Friars of Hychyn; Serv^t Alice Wodewarde; Dau. Alice; John Crowch & W^m. Crowch.

f. 25. WILLIELMUS ATTEWYNCHE of S^t Albans. (*Dat.* in the vigil of S^t Matth. the apostle 1435). Bur. at S^t Peters; Legacy to the vicar of S^t Andrews; Wife Alice & John Hoggekyn exors.

f. 25. JOHANNES PENY barbor of S<sup>t</sup> Albans. (*Dat.* in vigil of S<sup>t</sup> Andrew the apostle 1435). Bur. S<sup>t</sup> Peters; Wife Matilda extrix; Tho. Bordale supervisor.

f. 25. THOMAS RUSSELL of Watforde. (*Dat.* 2 Nov. 1435). Bur. at S<sup>t</sup> Mary's; John Wellis of Watforde; Dionis my wife; Dau. Kath. (*Pr.* 3 Dec. 1435).

f. 25. JOHANNES ELE of Northhawe. (*Dat.* S<sup>t</sup> Stephen's day 1434). Bur. Northawe; John Lowyn son of my wife; Wife Thomasine extrix.

f. 25. JOHANNES SPANNER of S<sup>t</sup> Albans. (*Dat.* in the feast of S<sup>t</sup> Benedict the abbot & confessor 1435). Bur. at S<sup>t</sup> Peters; Wife Matilda extrix; John Alkeburn & Robt. Bradley supervisors.

f. 26. THOMAS WEYBYN clerk & rector of Lawrenc Ayott. (*Dat.* 15 Jan. 1435). Bur. at S<sup>t</sup> Giles', Codicote 'ubi clausi extrema'; Legacies to churches of Codicote, Ayot & Abbots Waldeyn; Agnes North; Evace Trewbody; John Northe; Henry Wynt<sup>r</sup>forde vicar of Abbots Walden supervisor & John Skegge of Wadysmyle exor.

f. 26. THOMAS DAYE of Rykem'sworth. (*Dat.* 8 Jan. 'ultimo elapso'). John Brannanttr clerk of the parish; Tho. Stretman parish clerk; To the kings highway between the tenement of Wm. Flete & the garden of Elen Bayly vjs. viijd.; Agnes wife of John Cartere; Alice my mother; Alice wife of Simon at y<sup>e</sup> verne & Margt. her dau; Kath. & Agnes her sisters; Margt. wife of Wm. Wymond; John son of John Cartere & Rich. his bro. & Eliz. his sister; Wm. son of Rich. Slyngere & Margerie his sist.; Matilda Kyng widow & Kath. her sist.; Anice Rot<sup>r</sup> widow; John Kepe; Simon Croile; Isabel Colle; Tho. Dauy; John Rowe; Kath. Frowe; Walter Pauper; John Batte; Rich. Godfrey; Sim. Webbe; William Pauper; Walt. Daye; John Cartere & Rich. Slyngere exors. (*Pr.* before John Peyton archdeacon of S<sup>t</sup> Albans 12 Feb. 1435-6).

f. 26. JOHANNES MARTIN of Newnham, junior. (*Dat.* S<sup>t</sup> Thomas the Martyr's day 1434). Bur. at Newnam; Dau. Alice; Wife Agnes, Thos. Rocheforde & Rich. Martin exors. (*Pr.* 13 Mch. 1435-6).

f. 26. JOAN WALSCH of S<sup>t</sup> Stephens without S<sup>t</sup> Albans. (*Dat.* 10 Mch. 1435). Bur. at S<sup>t</sup> Stephens; Legacy to the friars of Ware & 'duobus clericis sancti Stephani'; John Wrygte & Christian his wife; Said John Wrigte. (*Pr.* 14 Mch. 1435-6).

f. 26. THOMAS LUNDON of S<sup>t</sup> Albans. (*Dat.* 1 June 1433). Bur. at S<sup>t</sup> Peters; Legacies to the friars minors of Ware, the preaching friars of Dunstaple, Katherine the anchoress of S<sup>t</sup> Michaels in S<sup>t</sup> Albans, Philip Gerarde servant of s<sup>d</sup> Katherine; Wife Elen extrix. Wit<sup>s</sup>:—Roger Selle chaplain, Tho. Heyne of S<sup>t</sup> Albans. (*Pr.* 30 Mch. 1436).

f. 26. CHRISTIAN MARYON. (*Dat.* 10 Jan. 1435). Bur. at Watford; Sir Robt. Bryton chaplain of that church; John Cauche clerk of s<sup>d</sup> church & Ralph Smyth clerk of s<sup>d</sup> church; Son. Rich. Maryon exor. (*Pr.* 3 Apr. 1436).

f. 26. JOAN CHAPMAN of Northehawe. (Dat. 16 Mch. 1435). Bur. at Northhaw: Sir Robert chaplain of s<sup>d</sup> church: Dau. Joan Flexmere exor.

f. 26. JOHANNES FYNELL of Little Horwode. (Dat. 4 June 1436). Bur. at Horwode afores<sup>d</sup>; Thos. Wynterton perpetual vicare of s<sup>d</sup> church & wife Joan exors.

f. 26. WILLELMUS BARNABE of Barnet. (Dat. in the feast of S<sup>t</sup> Barnabus the apostle 1435). Bur at S<sup>t</sup> John the Baptist's, Barnet; Legacies to churches of Sowthmymys & Monkynchyrche & the chapel of Barnet; My wife; Dau. Agnes; Philip Barnabe & Rich. Barnabe exors.

f. 26. JOHANNES FREND of Chepyng Barnet. (Dat. 5 May 1435). Bur. at S<sup>t</sup> John Baptist's; Wife Isabell & Wm. Nycoll exors. Wit<sup>s</sup>:—Walter Forster, John Prior, Edmund Elyse, John Bechamp.

f. 26. JOHANNES BYSCHOP of S<sup>t</sup> Albans. (Dat. in the feast of saints Fabian & Sabastian the martyrs 1435). Bur. at S<sup>t</sup> Peters; Laurence Cros; Alice servant of John Holond; John Holond & Helen his wife exors. (Pr. 16 July 1436).

*To be Continued.*

# Marriage Licences.
## Archdeaconry of St. Albans.
### By A. E. GIBBS.

(Continued from Page 8).

October 31. William Rawlins of Carrington, tailor, bachelor, and Elizabeth Stone of St. Albans, maiden. Edward Stephens of St. Albans, cowper, a surety.

November 25. Thomas Hutchinson of St. Albans, gent., bachelor, and Elizabeth Lightes, maiden. William Chappell of Berkhamsted, miller, a surety.

November 25. Samuell Turner junr., bachelor, and Anne Chambers *alias* Halsey, daughter of Edward Halsey of Flamstedd, maiden; at Flamstedd, Samuel Turner of St. Albans, gent., his father, a surety.

December 24. John Kilbey of St. Albans, weaver, bachelor, and Mary Pooley of Harpenden, maiden. John Mathews of St. Albans, weaver, a surety.

December 28. Thomas Sabisford of Watford, gent., and Mrs. Sarah Edlyn of Watford, maiden. John Burton of St. Albans, innholder, a surety.

1670-1

January 30. John Monke of Greenwich, co. Kent, gardener, bachelor, and Sara Halsey now of St. Albans, maiden. William Lawton of Luton, co. Bedford, keeper, a surety.

February 11. John Preist of Abbots Langley, bachelor, and Sarah Neale of the same. John How of the same, a surety.
February 21. Emanuel Kentish of St. Albans and Sarah Capon of the same. Solomon Smyth of the same, a surety.
February 25. Jonathan Edmonds of Watford, yeoman, bachelor, and Elizabeth Hill of the same, widow. Joseph Bailey of St. Stephen's, yeoman, a surety.
March 19. John Sibley of Kimpton Street, gent., bachelor, and Susan Nash, daughter of William Nash of Kimpton. Seth Gladman of the same, yeoman, a surety.

1671

March 25. William Neale of Harpenden, yeoman, widower, and Anne Knight of Broughton, co. Buckingham, widow. Thomas Royston of Harpenden 'scriba' a surety.
March 25. Thomas Thebridge of Sandridge, husbandman, bachelor, and Mary Hawkes, maiden. Francis Chappell [*signed* Chappill] of Sandridge, blacksmith, a surety.
April 15. Thomas Carter of St. Albans, bachelor, and Sara Dunne of the same, maiden. Thomas Carter of Harpenden, husbandman, a surety.
May 30. Nicholas Hunt of St. Albans, husbandman, bachelor, and Elizabeth Weedon of the same, maiden.
[*Undated*]. Henry Beech of Northaw, yeoman, widower, and Ruth Bareleggs, the daughter of Jo. Bareleggs, maiden. [*Unsigned and no surety*].
June 10. Robert Smith of Ridge, husbandman, bachelor, and Mary Robins, maiden, daughter of Joseph Robins of South Mims. Edward Ffowke of St. Albans, gent., a surety.
June 19. Thomas Slow of St. Albans, bodymaker, bachelor, and Anne Johnson of Hatfeild, maiden. Edward Ffowke of St. Albans, a surety.
June 28. Robert Ivory of Luton, co. Bedford, husbandman, widower, and Elizabeth Hill of the same, widow. Edward Ffowke of St. Albans, a surety.
September 23. John Bunby of Bushey, yeoman, bachelor, and Elizabeth Dell of the same, maiden. Edward Dell of St. Stephens, yeoman, a surety.
September 27. Isaack Freeman of Biscott in the parish of Luton, co. Bedford, yeoman, bachelor, and Vertue Rotheram of Caddington. Thomas Hall of St. Albans, yeoman, a surety.
September 29. William Stephens [*signed* Steevens] of St. Albans, cooper, bachelor, and Dorothy Robinson of Aldenham, maiden. William Milward [*signed* Millard] of St. Albans, butcher, a surety.
September 29. Richard Grover of Gaddesden but now of St. Albans, yeoman, bachelor, and Margaret Potten, daughter of Thomas Potton of Gaddesden. Thomas Hall of Gadsden, yeoman, a surety.
October 7. Francis Catlyn 'tempore licentie obtente de Sco Albano' bachelor, and Hannah Darnell, maiden, daughter of Edward Darnell. Richard Lloyd, a surety.
October 7. John Cooke of St. Albans, tailor, bachelor, and Mary Cannon of the same, maiden. John Barnett [*signed* John Barnard junr.] of the same, gent., a surety.
October 12. Thomas Wright of Whethamsted, bachelor, and Ellen Bockett of St. Albans, widow. Thomas Fensham [*signed* Fensam] of St. Albans, husbandman, a surety.

October 28. Isaack Scott of St. Albans, cutler, bachelor, and Mary Crawley, maiden. William Crawley of St. Albans, her father, a surety.

November 8. William North of Codicott, husbandman, bachelor, and Elizabeth Blindell, maiden, daughter of William Blindle of Wellen. Thomas Rotheram [*signed* Rotherham] of St. Albans, innholder, a surety.

November 15. Thomas Jones of Harpenden, gardener, widower, and Mary Dixon of St. Albans, maiden. Edmund Camfeild of St. Albans, chandler, a surety.

December 2. John Lever of Hatfeild, brewer, bachelor, and Anne Baker of the same, maiden. George Barnes of St. Albans, innholder, a surety.

December 11. Thomas Hodierne of Titenhanger, gent., bachelor, and Mary Gray of Coney, maiden. Thomas Spooner of Titenhanger, gent., a surety.

December 25. John Blake [*signed* Black] of St. Albans, bachelor, and Mary Matthews, daughter of John Matthews of St. Peters. John Matthews [*signed* Mathew] of St. Albans, a surety.

[*Undated*]. John Baldwin of Abbots Langley, yeoman, bachelor, and Mary Taylor, maiden, daughter of John Taylor of Pynner, co. Middlesex.

1671-2

January 2. Thomas Bulmer of Little Gadsden, yeoman, and Mary Mun, maiden. George Barnes of St. Albans, a surety.

January 6. John Sheppard of Abbots Langley, husbandman, bachelor, and Elizabeth Heggs of Rickmersworth, maiden. George Barnes of St. Albans, plumber, a surety.

January 31. Benjamin Robinson of Southmims, gent., bachelor, and Mary Manfeild, maiden. Thomas Pursey of South Mims, yeoman, a surety.

February 3. Thomas Roberts of Whethamstedd, yeoman, widower, and Anne Coles, widow. George Barnes of St. Albans, a surety.

February 12. Henry Holford, of Watford, widower, and Sarah Dossett, maiden. John Dossett, her father, of St. Albans, tailor, and Richard Beech of the same, glover, sureties.

February 15. William Slowe of Flamsted but now of St. Albans, bachelor, and Elizabeth Smith, maiden, daughter of Thomas Smith of Flamsted. Michael Slowe of the same, yeoman, a surety.

February 17. Richard Foxon of Abbots Langley, tanner, and Mary Walcupp of the same, maiden. George Barnes of St. Albans, plumber, a surety.

March 2. Benjamin Tilyard of Bushey, husbandman, bachelor, and Sara Grubb of the same, maiden. George Barnes of St. Albans, plumber, a surety.

[*Undated*]. Robert Arrowsmith of St. Albans, husbandman, bachelor, and Margaret Heyward, maiden. George Barnes, a surety.

March 3. George East of Harpenden but now of St. Albans, husbandman, widower, and Anne Chambers *alias* Halsey of St. Albans, widow. Joseph Ewer of St. Albans, cooper, a surety.

March 23. George Williams of Sandridge, husbandman, and Elizabeth Hinde of Great Ayte, widow. George Barnes of St. Albans, a surety.

1672

April 1. John Sparkes of Redborne, husbandman, bachelor, and Anne Kelsey, maiden, daughter of Daniell Kelsey of the same. Walter Beech, a surety.

April 20. Joseph Robins [*signed* Robbins] of South Mims, co. Middlesex, husbandman, bachelor, and Mary Thrale of Sandridge, maiden. Solomon Smith of St. Albans, a surety.

April 20. Edward Randall of Tuddington, co. Bedford, and Mary Hooker, maiden. John Hudson of St. Stephens, a surety.

May 15. John Spenser of St. Albans, blacksmith, bachelor, and Martha Harford of St. Peters, maiden. John Mathews of St. Albans, a surety.

May 15. Ralph Claxstone [*signed* Claxson] of Bushey, miller, bachelor, and Sara Taylor of Harrow-on-the-Hill, co. Middlesex. Thomas Smith of Abbots Langley, milwright, a surety.

June 8. William Kentish of Watford, tailor, widower, and Agnes Greene of St. Peters, maiden. John Hall of St. Albans, a surety.

June 15. John Nash of St. Albans, husbandman, bachelor, and Dorothy Blaker of Luton, maiden. Belknap Tibbalts of St. Albans, plumber, a surety.

June 15. William Clements of St. Albans, husbandman, bachelor, and Elizabeth Shakespeare, maiden, daughter of William Shakespeare of Whethamsted. Bellknap Tibbalts of St. Albans, plumber, a surety.

June 17. Nathaniel Myles of Redborne, weaver, bachelor, and Anne Clerke of St. Albans, maiden. Francis Sleape of St. Albans, tailor, a surety.

June 30. Richard Ticheler and Elizabeth Shelton, widow. Robert Lemmon of St. Albans, a surety.

July 20. William Neale of Sandridge, tailor, widower, and Elizabeth Kilby of Harding, maiden. John Leonard of St. Albans, tailor, a surety.

July 25. Joseph Bayley [*signed* Bailey] of St. Stephens, and Susanna Smith of the same, maiden. Edward Ffowke of St. Albans, a surety.

August 3. Thomas Horseman of Watford, and Elizabeth Halsey of Great Gadsden. John Hall of St. Peters, a surety.

August 5. Hugh Michell of St. Stephens, and Elizabeth Preston of St. Albans. John Wingfeild of St. Albans, a surety.

August 9. John Twydy of St. Andrew, Holborn, London, bachelor and Ableing Walcope. John Tilby of St. Stephens, a surety.

September 16. James Barber of Harrow-on-the-Hill, co. Middlesex, mealman, bachelor, and Martha Downer of St. Albans, maiden. William Steevens of St. Albans, cooper, a surety.

September 17. John Gurney of Luton, co. Hertfordshire [*sic*] and Rose Nicolls of the same. Richard Baker of St. Peters, a surety.

September 19. John Shepheard of St. Stephens, bachelor, and Sarah Grunwind of the same, maiden, spinster. William Nicholls of St. Peters, a surety.

September 23. Thomas Turner of Abbots Langley, bricklayer, widower, and Elizabeth Lightwood of the same, widow. John Mathew of St. Albans, weaver, a surety.

September 24. William Field of Hexton, yeoman, widower, and Rebecca Hales of the same, maiden. Thomas Reynolds [*signed* Rennolds] of St. Albans, dyer, a surety.

September 30. Edward Perrott of Market Streete, bachelor, and Anne White of St. Albans, maiden. Stephen Huggens of Harpenden, a surety.

September 30. James Penn of Hatfeild but now of St. Albans, husbandman, bachelor, and Jone Cox maiden. John Richardson of Hatfeild, husbandman, a surety.

September 30. Edward Seabrooke of Redborne, husbandman, bachelor, and Mary Reddinge of same, maiden. George Barnes of St. Albans, a surety.

[*Undated*]. Richard Allen of Hempsted, but now of St. Albans, husbandman, bachelor, and Joane Hutt of St. Albans, maiden. John Mathew of St. Albans, weaver, a surety.

October 3. William Chalkley of Codicot, widower, and Mary Adams of the same, maiden. Jo. Adams of the same, a surety.

October 22. John Chapman of Ridge, husbandman, bachelor, and Mary Kentish of the same, maiden. John Spencer of Southmims, gardener, a surety.

November 9. Edward Grunwyn [*signed* Grunwin] of St. Albans, widower, and Sarah Burre of the same. William Richmond of St. Peters, a surety.

November 15. Joshua Carpenter of St. Albans, innholder, widower, and Anne Chamberlaine of the same, widow. Richard Neale of the same, innholder, a surety.

November 23. Roger Harris of St. Albans, yeoman, bachelor, and Anne Wilson of St. Peters. Thomas Goodspeede of St. Albans, husbandman, a surety.

December 11. Thomas Catlyn [*signed* Catlin] of Flamstedd, husbandman, bachelor, and Mary Walker, maiden, daughter of Nathaniell Walker of Redborne. William Seabrooke [*signed* Seabroke] of St. Albans, gent., a surety.

December 16. Thomas Scott of St. Albans and Anne Baldwin of Abbotts Langly, maiden. Thomas Cowley junior of St. Albans, a surety.

December 20. John Eedes of Hempstedd, husbandman, bachelor, and Susan Hancocke of St. Albans, maiden. George Barnes of St. Albans, plumber, a surety.

December 24. Thomas Corneford of Northaw and Mary Westwood of Cheshunt. John Hall of St. Peters, a surety.

December 28. Henry Turpin of Redborne, butcher, bachelor, and Susan Sturgis of the same, maiden, daughter of John Sturgis. James Hulme of St. Albans, shoemaker, a surety.

1672-3

January 15. John Crawley of Kimpton, yeoman, bachelor, and Elizabeth Mashall, widow. Thomas Oxenford of Luton, co. Bedford, tailor, a surety.

[*Undated*]. Thomas Stevenson of Harpenden, yeoman, bachelor, and Martha Sturley, maiden. Francis Neves of St. Albans, brewer, a surety.

January 21. Anthony Paulkkinghoorne [*signed* Polkinghorne] of St. Albans, glover, and Katharine Drew of the Abbey parish, maiden. Richard White of St. Albans, glover, a surety.

January 31. Thomas Leach of Harding and Anne Man. Jeremiah Whethered [*signed* Jeremy Wethered], a surety.

February 3. Henry Kentish of St. Stephens gent., bachelor, and Sarah Kentish of same, widow. John Leigh of St. Albans, gent., a surety.

February 8. William Dearmer of Cadington but now of St. Albans, yeoman, and Mary Smith, maiden, daughter of Richard Smith of Whethamsted, gent. Joseph Ewer of St. Albans, cooper, a surety.

February 10. John Lawrence of St. Albans, gardener, bachelor, and Penelope Jackson, maiden. Thomas Towersend of St. Albans, gardener, a surety.

*To be Continued.*

# The Herts Genealogist and Antiquary.

## Humberstone of Walkern, etc.

(Continued from Page 53.)

**WILLS AND ADMINISTRATIONS FROM THE ARCHDEACONRY COURT OF HUNTINGDON (HITCHIN REGISTRY).**

[*Register* 3. 13].

EDWARD HUMBERSTON of Walkorne, yeoman. (*Dat.* 5 Apr. 1583). Bur. in psh. church of W.; To wife Agnes all leases of all the demeanes of Walkerne for 15 years after my decease for the bringing up of my child$^n$ & she to have the occupation of all my copy lands for life; To eldest son Wm. 100*l.* at 26; To second son Geo. 100 marks at 21; To youngest son John the like; To eldest dau. Agnis 40*l.* at 18; To second dau. Sislie 40*l.*; After wifes interest expires all s$^d$ leases to s$^d$ Wm., with remainders to sons Geo. & John; Money owing me by bro. Wm. Humberston, I give to bro. John H. & Alce Hagger my sisters dau. equally; To servant Robt. Clarke x*s.*; To servants Jeames Sheppte, Blase Nashe, Isboll Rayment & Agnis Gilbert iij*s.* iiij*d.* each; To poor of Walkern xx*s.*; To M$^r$ John Clarke vicar of Potton for preaching of one sermon at my burial x*s.*; To M$^r$ John Headlam vicar of Braffiu for preaching one sermon within one month after my decease vj*s.* viij*d.*; To M$^r$ Broweman vicar of Sandon the like; To the repair of Walkern church x*s.*; Residue to wife & she extrix; Father in law Wm. Clarke overseer. Wit$^s$:—Willm. Middelton, clarke, & Willm. Clarke. (*Pr.* 10 July 1583).

[*Register* 3. 31$^b$].

RICHARD HUMBERSTON of Walkorne in dioc. of Lincoln. (*Dat.* 3 July 1576). Bur. in psh. church of W.; To the poor mens box xx*d.*; To eldest son John the messuage called Holmes wherein I now dwell & all my lands etc. in W. to him & his heirs male, with successive remainders to sons Leonard, Edw., Wm., Henry, & Gyles, remainder to my right heirs for ever; Wife Agnes to dwell in s[d] messuage called Holmes; To sons Edw., Wm., Henry & Gyles 53s. 4d.; To dau. Alice Humberston 40s.; To dau. Grace Humberston 7l.; Residue to wife Agnes & she extrix. Wit[s]:—Tho. Weddell, John Philer, Wm. Clere & others. (Pr. 2 May 1582).

[*Register* 4. 400].

WILLIAM HUMMERSTONE of Wellwin. (*Undated*). 'To my vij children to every on of them j cawe and a pugge'; To dau. Cath. a pair of sheets 'on of the an open seme sheete which was her granmothers'; To 'my iij other' sons Wm., Lewis & John to either of them one sheet; Residue to wife An. Wit[s]:—Robart Barret, Nycolas Siggines, Jeames Penyfather, Eliz. Penrye, Tho. Fryth. (Pr. at Whethamsted 9 Apr. 1606).

[*Register* 5. 32].

JOHN HUMBERSTONE of Bramfeild. (*Dat.* 17 May 1610). Bur. in churchy[d] of B.; To wife a cowe, bed etc. & 'all the stuffe that shee did bringe to me when I married her first'; To my 4 daus. 10s. each; To grandch. Edw. H. 30s.; To son John 5s.; Son Robt. exor. Wit[s]:—Alice Butler, Robt. Bird, John Hill, Tho. Butler, Wm. Bazill ×. (Pr. at S[t] Albans 9 June 1610).

[*Register* 5. 119[b]].

LEWIS HUMMERSTONE (*Undated*). To bro. John all such things as are in his house of mine as also my cloak my best suit of apparel with a table cloth; To bro. Wm. second suit of clothes; To my two sisters Kath. & Anne two chests 'each of them one my payre of sheetes one of them to winde mee in the other to Martha Kinge'; Residue to bro. John; My sheep I give to Thomas, my brother John his son. (Pr. 1613).

[*Filed Wills.* 1625].

THOMAS HUMBARSTON of Stevenage, yeoman. (*Dat.* 25 Oct. 1625). To sons Edward, George & Robert 30l. at 26 by even portions, the portion of any son dying before that age to be equally divided between my two daus. at 26; To son Thos. 20s. at 26; To my two daus. Agnes & Ellin Humbarston 10l. at 26 by even portions; To wife Eliz. all lands & tenements in Stevenage for term of 17 years & all moveable goods, she to bring up my child[n] etc.; To son John & his heirs all lands & tenements in Stevenage with remainder to my son Thos. conditionally on them paying to my said wife after the end of 17 years, for her life 6l. yearly; Wife extrix; Wm. Greene sen[r] & Rich. Adams overseers. [*Mark*]. Wit[s]:—Wm. Wilshere, Francis Homberston, Robt. Andrew ×, Rich. Kimpton, John Kent ×. (Pr. at Whethampsted 16 Nov. 1625).

[*Acta* 1626-7. *f.* 34].

LEONARD HUMBERSTON. Note of admon. 19 Apr. 1627.

[*Act Book* "No. 5." *f.* 14].

ELIZABETH HUMBERSTON of Walkern, maiden. Admon. 23 June 1636 to Thomas Humberston, gent. 'nepoti ejusdem.'

[*Filed Bonds.* 1638].

THOMAS HUMBERSTON of Walkerne, gent. 'A decree against Mr Humberston to exhibite a true and full certificate of his due frequentinge of his parishe church of Walkerne & divine service there had vnder the hands of the Ministers & Churchwardens there from the daye of the monicon judicially given him in this behalfe.' Dated 25 Oct. 1638.

[*Filed Wills.* 1639.]

JOHN HOMERSTONE of Stevenage. (*Dat.* 1 Jan. 1639). To wife Cicely all lands & tenements, freehold & copyhold, during minority of Thos. my eldest son, for the education of sd Thos. also of Robt. my other son; On Thos. attaining 21 then sd lands and tenements to him & his heirs he paying to my son Robt. 30*l.* at 21 & in default of payment I devise to sd Robt. a close of land in Lucefeild called the three acre close abutting on a lane leading to Hertf[ord] on the north; After sd Thos. attain 21, he to pay to my sd wife 6*l.* yearly: To sd wife all moveables & I make her extrix. [*Mark*]. Wit{s}:— Edw. Fisshe, John Greene, John Harvey ×. (*Pr.* at Wellwin 27 Jan. 1639).

[*Filed Bonds.* 1650].

WILLIAM HUMBERSTONE of Bishops Hatfield. Bond dated 22 Feb. 1650 in 40*l.* by Thos. Humberston, taylor, brother of deceased & Richard Wilkinson, clerk, both of same place. Wit{s}:—Wm. Rolfe, notary public.

[*Register* 6. 75].

ROBERT HUMBERSTON of Hatfeild. (*Dat.* 16 Sep. 1661). To dau. Eliz. wife of John Turner 20*s.* & to John & Mary her child{n} 10*s.* each; To son Edw. 5*l.*; To dau. Anne 10*l.*; To dau. Alice 10*l.*; To wife Alice 5*l.*; Working tools to my two sons; My house to wife Alice for life & after to son John & he exor. [*Mark*]. Wit{s}:— Fras. Hare, Tho. Wilkinson. (*Pr.* 27 Nov. 1661).

[*Filed Wills.* 1662].

MARGARET HUMMERSTON of Little Barkhamsteed, widow. (*Dat.* 28 Aug. 1662). To Edw. Bird son of Wm. Bird living in Aldersgate Street in London, hempman 10*l.*; To Eliz. Humerston dau. of Edw. H. of Hatfield my best featherbed etc; To Wm. Field of Welwyn 20*s.* & to Mary Field of same 20*s.* & to her sist. Eliz. Field 20*s.*; To Anne Write wife of Samuel Write of Hartingfordbury 20*s.* & to Margt. wife of Rich. Okely of Hartford 20*s.*; To poor of Little Barkhamsteed 10*s.*; Residue to bro. Edw. Hummerston of Hatfield & he exor. [*Mark*]. Wit{s}:—Nath. Matthew, Francis Barton ×. (*Pr.* 3 Feb. 1662).

[*Register* 8. 98{b}].

WILLIAM HUMBERSTON of Weston, co. Herts, yeoman. (*Dat.* 27 Sep. 1667). To wife Suzan the house wherein I now live & the pightle over against ye doore etc; To son Robt. my mansion house wherein Thos. Shadboult lives etc.; also my tile kill etc.; To son Wm. tenement wherein I dwell after my wife's decease, he paying to my son John 10*l.*; To son Fras. ye kill closes in Stoonley etc.; To son Thos. messuage where John Titmous liveth; To my two daus. Mary & Susan 15*l.* apiece; Wife Susan & eldest son Robt. & son-in-law Thos. Shadboult exors. *Wm. Humberston*. Wit{s}:—John Harmer, Barbury Humberston ×, Dorothy Humberston ×. (*Pr.* 14 Oct. 1667).

*[Filed Bonds. 1669].*

EDWARD HUMBERSTON of parish of Hertford All Saints. Bond dated 8 Jan. 21 Chas. II. in 200*l.* by Mary Humbarston of Hertford All Saints widow & relict & Thos. Hawkins of Bennington, husbandman. Wit[s]:—T. Burges, Edw. Spranger.

*[Filed Wills. 1670].*

JOHN HUMBARSTONE of Aston, gent. (*Dat.* 13 Aug. 22 Chas. II.) To son Wm. full two parts of all my goods, chattells & moneys; To dau. Frances & dau. Mary all residue of my goods etc. equally; Son Wm. exor. *John Humbarstone.* [Seal of arms. Three bars & in chief as many roundels, a crescent for difference]. Wit[s]:—Mary Ballett, Ni. Clerke, John Burnapp.

Codicil dat. 13 Aug. 1670, appointing kinsman Nich. Clerke of Barnards Inn, London, gent. exor during minority of son Wm. My child[n] to allow to my exor the yearly payments to my Aunt Humbarstone, her daughter & my sister Ann Humbarstone for their lives. (*Pr.* at Welwin 14 Dec. 1670). Inventory of goods appraised 19 Aug. 1670 by Thos. Kent gent. & John Burnapp gent. Total 614*l.* 8*s.* 7*d.*

*[Filed Wills. 1675].*

THOMAS HUMBERSTONE of Clayend in psh. of Walkerne, 'vman' [? yeoman]. (*Dat.* 17 June 1675). To wife Catheren house I now live in & three pasture closes belonging to it, with orchard & other premises, for her life & after to son John & his heirs for ever; Residue to wife & son together & they to be exors. [*Mark*]. Wit[s]: —Giles Olliuer. (*Pr.* at Bennington 19 July 1675).

*[Filed Wills. 1677].*

JOHN HUMBERSTONE of Diggeswell, miller. (*Dat.* 14 Dec. 1676). To bros. Robt., Henry & Thos. Humberstone 5*s.* each; To sist. Eliz. Withers 5*s.*; Residue to wife Anne whom I make extrix. *John Huemberston.* [Seal of arms*:—a fess between three plates: crest:— an arm holding in the hand a lions gamb.] Wit[s]:—Will. Minors, Dauid Day. (*Jurat* dated 6 Feb. 1676-7).

*[Filed Wills. 1684].*

WILLIAM HUMBERSTON of Weston, labourer. (*Dat.* 7 July 1683). To wife Mary all my goods & chattels & the house I now dwell in with the two pightells of pasture adjoining for her life or widowhood & after her decease or marriage then to dau. Mary; Said wife extrix. [*Mark*]. Wit[s]:—Giles Wallis, Mary Shottbolt ×, Mary Humberston ×. (*Jurat* dated 2 May 1684).

*[Filed Wills. 1684].*

MARY HUMBERSTON of Hertford, spinster. (*Dat.* 5 Mch. 1683). To sist. Anne Humberston all rights & title to the house wherein I now live, also all goods etc. in s[d] house & elsewhere; Said sist. extrix. [*Mark*]. Wit[s]:—Elizabeth Wren, John Greeninge, Charles Fox. (*Jurat* dated 13 Sep. 1684).

* These are the armorial bearings of the Minors family.

[*Filed Bonds.* 1686].

EDWARD HUMBERSTON of Bishops Hattield. Bond dated 7 Dec. 1686 in 100*l*. by Margaret Humberston, John Thredder & Hen. Bole all of same. Wit$^s$:—Wm. Goodwin, Sam$^l$ Fox, Reg$^{rius}$ Assumpt. [Endorsed with Jurat dated same day of Mary [*sic*] H. widow & relict of Edw. Humberston. In the body of the bond the name is given once as *Mary*].

[*Filed Bonds.* 1687].

JOHN HUMMERSTON of Flamsted. Bond dated 23 June 1687 in 100*l*. by Elizabeth Hummerston of Flamsted, widow & relict, Tho. Smith of Flamsted, yeoman, & John Selles of Hemel Hempsted. Wit$^s$:—Robt. Whitehead & Joseph Hackney.

[*Register* 12. 3$^b$].

TIMOTHY HUMBERSTON of Walkern, lathrender. (*Nunc. will dat.* 22 Apr. 1702). To dau. Anne 40*s*. at 21 to be paid by her bro. Edw. out of money the testator lately gave s$^d$ Edw. 'to sett up with'; To dau. Anne 40*l*. to be paid by her mother at 21; To son Timothy 10*l*. to be paid by his mother at 23; Residue to wife Ann & she to divide the goods testator had left him by his former wife equally between his two sons Edw. & Tim.; Wife extrix. Wit$^s$:—John Oliver, Peter Haword, Susanna Martin. (*Pr.* 24 Apr. 1702).

[*Filed Wills.* 1705].

THOMAS HUMBERSTONE the Elder of Knebworth, yeoman. (*Dat.* 11 Jan. 1701). To grandson Joseph Dixon 50*l*. at 21; To grandson Thos. Dixon 20*s*. to buy him a ring; To granddau. Susan Dixon 10*l*. at 21 or marriage; To sist. Ellen Mathew 20*s*. a year for life; Residue to wife Mary & son Thomas Humberstone whom I make exors. [*Mark*]. Seal of arms*:—On a pile three trefoils slipped. Wit$^s$:—Geo. Nodes, Sam. Sale, Jn$^o$ Nodes. (*Jurat* dated 9 Oct. 1705).

[*Admon. Act Book.* 1706–1727].

JOHN HUMBERSTON of Hertford. Admon. 24 June 1713 to Grace Humberston the relict.

[*Admon. Act Book.* 1706–1727].

SARAH HUMMERSTON of Bengeo. Admon. 3 Apr. 1721 to Francis Hummerston the brother.

[*Register* 15. 7].

JOHN HUMBERSTONE of Walkerne. (*Dat.* 4 Feb. 1720-1). To son Thos. all parcels of land being copyhold in Walkern viz. two closes called Smarts, one close called Tonecrofts, close called Wellfield Mead & close called Wellfield; Son Thos. exor & he to board my wife Mary for life & pay her 30*s*. a year. [*Mark*]. Wit$^s$:—Geo. Kimpton, Sam. Munt, Sarah Sell ×. (*Date of probate not given*).

[*Admon. Act Book* 1727–1754.]

GEORGE HUMBERSTON of Bishops Hatfield. Admon. 15 Sep. 1729 to Mary, relict.

* The arms of the Nodes family.

f. 371. JOHN WALKER of Wormeley. (Dat. 27 Apr. 1591). Eliz. Walker my sons dau.; My sister; Kinsman Robert Kinge; W<sup>m</sup>. Walker my sons son, and his sister Eliz.; Tho. Burgin; John Chaundler, W<sup>m</sup>. Swansom of Hodesdon; Tho. Lowin of Wormeley; Thos. Johnson of Wormeley; M<sup>r</sup> Walpoole parson; Dau. in law Kath. Turner; John Walker my sons son; Harry Maunder of Pimbridge; John, W<sup>m</sup>. & Eliz. ch<sup>n</sup> of my son Rob<sup>t</sup>. Walker; Isabell Bird; Grandson John Walker exor; John Chaundler & W<sup>m</sup>. Swanson overseers; John Walker son of Rob<sup>t</sup>. Walker & his mother Kath. wife of John Turner. Wit<sup>s</sup>:—Cesar Walpoole, Nich. Turner, W<sup>m</sup>. Turner ×. (Pr. 6 May, 1605\*).

f. 376. WILLIAM BROCKE of Sandridge, husbandman. (Dat. 1 Aug. 1604). Son George & my 4 daus; Edw. Smithe; S<sup>r</sup> John Jenings knt; Rich. Wilsheire of Towerhill farm; W<sup>m</sup>. Gunttynne. *William Brocke*. Wit<sup>s</sup>:—John Clarke, Michael Barefoote. (Pr. 4 Mch. 1604-5).

f. 385. WILLIAM JINGOULD of Stondon, husbandman. (Dat. 14 June 1605). Son Thos.; House where W<sup>m</sup>. Mans now dwelleth; Wife Agnes & son W<sup>m</sup>. exors. (Mark). Wit<sup>s</sup>:— John Turner & W<sup>m</sup>. Witham. (Pr. 25 Oct. 1605).

f. 390. JOHN HAUKINS of Wormeley, basket maker. (Dat. 18 Feb. 44 Eliz.) Bur<sup>d</sup> at Wormeley near my wife; Dau. Jone wife of John Glascocke; Son Nich<sup>s</sup>; Dau. Ellen; Dau. Joane extrix. (Mark). Wit<sup>s</sup>:—W<sup>m</sup>. Malden, Water Clarke ×. (Pr. 26 Jan. 1603-4).

f. 394. PHILLIPP DIXON of psh. of S<sup>t</sup> Peters in S<sup>t</sup> Albans. (Dat. 31 Aug. 1604). Wife Anne; My two boys Raphe & Phillipp; Hugh Smithe; John Morris; Bro. John Dixon his son John; Bro. John Redall; My wifes mother; Wife's sist. Joane Hall her three children; Child<sup>n</sup> of bro. John Dixon & bro. John Redall; Hugh Smithe & John Morris overseers; Wife extrix (Mark). Wit<sup>s</sup>:—Edm. Estwood ×, W<sup>m</sup>. Forrest. (Pr. 5 Mch. 1604-5).

f. 395. WILLIAM PARANT of Little Hadham, tayler. (Dat. 3 Dec. 1592). My house situate at the church end in Little Hadham; Youngest son James; Son Thos; Neph. & godson Rich. Parrant; Son James exor. *William Parrant*. Wit<sup>s</sup>:—Richard Rolfe writer hereof. (Pr. 9 Apr. 1605).

f. 401. TYMOTHIE SHARNBROOKE of Hoddesdon, yeoman. (Dat. 18 Sep. 1607). Wife Eliz.; Tenement in the Valey in tenure of Sam. Walkyn; Lands in Broxborne & Amwell; Son W<sup>m</sup>.; Daus. Rose, Eliz. & Suzan; Jane Cotton dau. of Eliz. Hide; Son in law Thos. Hide; 'Rie nowe growinge in Strickendon'; John Hide. Wit<sup>s</sup>:—Rob<sup>t</sup>. Micheley, John Saringe. (Pr. 11 Mch. 1607-8).

f. 401. ANDREW CROXON of Stondon, butcher. (Dat. 14 Sep. 1 Jas.) Sons John & George; My two daus. Eliz. & Marg<sup>t</sup>. Croxen (All ch<sup>n</sup> under 21); Wife Joane extrix. (Mark). Wit<sup>s</sup>:—Thos. Watson scr, Rich. Withroll. (Pr. 11 Mch. 1607).

f. 401. ROBERT GIPPES of Puckeridge in psh. of Stondon, tayler, (Dat. 13 Sep. 1607). Wife Christian; My 4 ch<sup>n</sup> Thos, Henry. W<sup>m</sup>. & Eliz. Gippes; Son Nich<sup>s</sup> Gippes exor. (Mark). Wit<sup>s</sup>:—W<sup>m</sup>. Northadge, John Burie & Henry Bayford. (Pr. 11 Mch. 1607).

\* This will is registered again at f. 375.

f. 410. **WILLIAM WARD** of Wormeley. (*Dat.* 15 Apr. 1608). Son Wm.; My stoole in Leaden Hall: Son Josias: Sons Nichs & Edward: Wife Joane: Wm. Fynche son of John Fynche my son-in-law; Alice Fynche & Eliz. Fynche the daus. of my dau.; Wife & son Josias exors; Robt. Becke & John Turner overseers. (*Mark*). Wits:—John Turner, Robt. Becke ×. (*Pr.* 29 Apr. 1614\*).

# Church Terriers.

### AYOT ST. PETER.

A Terrier of all ye glebe lands belonging to ye Rectory of Ayott St Peter wthin ye Archdeaconry of Huntingdon Año dom. 1638.

Inp. a pcell of land lying in ye feild called Wellwin feild hauing on ye East side a litle piece of ground belonging to Nicholas Wellinghā, on ye West a piece belonging to Jo. Beamond, x acres.

Itē a piece of land in ye same feild hauing on ye East a rood of ground belonging to Jo. Irland and on ye West a close of pasture ground belonging to Nath. Manisty, an halfe acre.

Itē a pcell lying in ye feild calld Churchfeild butting vpō a piece of Nich. Wellinghā on ye North side and vpō a piece of Will. Conny on ye South and vpō ground of Mr Hale at each end, an acre.

Itē a pcell in ye same feild hauing on ye East an acre of Nich. Wellinghā, on ye West an acre of Nich. Hind, an halfe acre.

Itē a pcell in ye same feild butting vpō an acre of Mr Hale on ye South, and an acre of Nich. Hind on ye North, by estimacō 4 acres.

Itē a pcell in ye same feild hauing an acre of Mr Hale on ye North, and an enclosed feild of his on ye South, one acre.

Itē a pcell in ye same feild hauing on ye North side an acre of Nich. Hind, on ye South a piece of enclosed ground belonging to ye Parsonage, 4 acres and an halfe.

Itē a pcell in ye same feild butting Northward vpō an acre belonging to Rich. [Will. *erased*] Woodfine, Southward vpō a piece of ground of Will. Conny and another of Jo. Beamond and other, being an halfe acre.

Itē a pcell enclosed hauing on ye South a close of Jo. Moate, on ye North butting vpō ye highway which leads frō Ayott to Wellwin, on ye East a close of Rich. Woodfine, on ye West a wood ground, 4 acres.

Itē a pcell enclosed hauing on ye South a close of Jo. Dance, on ye North ye Parsonage house or orchard, 4 acres.

Itē an enclosure hauing on ye North ye comōn feild calld Churchfeild, on ye South Parsonage house or homstall, xj acres and an halfe.

\* Marginal note in pencil. 'This will is dated Apl. 1608. It was proved before Dr. Edwards V.G. He became V. G. 6 Feb. 1608-9 The month of proof being in Apl. cannot have been earlier than Apr. 1609. It cannot either have been later than 1609, for Tho. (Ravis) the Bp. died in Dec. 1609. No origl. nor P.A. in V.G. book.'

Itē a peell enclosed hauing on yᵉ West side therof an enclosure of Mʳ Hale, on yᵉ East yᵉ Parsonage dwelling house, 2 acres.

Itē of pasture grounds, yᵉ enclosure adioyning to yᵉ Mansion house wᵗʰ yᵉ orchard and gardē, 2 acres et dimid.

Itē a medow ground lying by yᵉ riuer on yᵉ North and butting vpō yᵉ highway on yᵉ South, one acre.

Itē yᵉ Churchyard an halfe acre.

Itē of wood grounds a wood hauing an enclosure of Rich. Woodfine on yᵉ East, an enclosure of Good. Waterman on yᵉ South being by estimaciō 6 acres.

*Sum. tot.* lij acres et dimid.
Jo. Iuory Rect. ibid.
Nich. Wellinghā Churchward.

---

## BALDOCK.

BALDOCK. 1638. A TERRIER OR NOTE of yᵉ house and land belongeinge to yᵉ rectorie of Baldocke in the yeere 1638.

The house ioyneth to yᵉ Churchyard against yᵉ west end theare off It hath 5 lower roomes a bakeing or brewhouse a hall 2 little buteries and a parlour It hath a loft ouer yᵉ bake house a chamber ouer the parlour a studdie and a little loft at yᵉ staires head theare is a barne and a woodhouse in yᵉ yard yᵉ barne hath 2 bayes or mowsteads besides yᵗ cominge in yᵉ woodhouse ioyneth to it and will houlde some 4 or 5 loades of wood, they are both thatched and soe is yᵉ one side of yᵉ bakehouse yᵉ rest is tyled.

The Churchyard containeth by estymation an aker. The slade a roode. The orchyard halfe a roode. The yard halfe a roode.

Gleabe lande 6 akers and an halfe.

One aker lyeth in Clathall betweene yᵉ lande of yᵉ Earle of Salisburie on yᵉ south and the lande of yᵉ same Earle and John Cock of Baldock on yᵉ north and butteth on yᵉ lande of yᵉ sayde Earle north east and of yᵉ same land south west. Item one aker lyeth in yᵉ pish of Wesson betweene yᵉ landes of Mʳ George Kimpton on yᵉ south west and of yᵉ same lande north east and butteth on yᵉ land of George Cooke bishop of Hereford on yᵉ north & yᵉ lande of Doctor Newell on the south. Item one aker lyeth in Wesson aforesaide by the lande of Mʳ George Kimpton on yᵉ north east and the lande of John Cock of Baldock on yᵉ south west and butteth on yᵉ wood called by yᵉ name of Wesson wood on yᵉ south and yᵉ lande of Mʳ Kimpton north. Item 2 akers lye in Willian yᵉ west ende buts vpon yᵉ lande of John Pitches yᵉ East and vpon yᵉ high way yᵗ leadeth to London yᵉ north lies against yᵉ way they call Lingens way yᵉ south lyes by yᵉ lande of Mʳ Way. Item theare is one aker more theare and buts vpon Hitchen highway with the south ende, Edward Willsons lande lyeth on the north ende, Edward Willsons lande lyeth on the east side & on yᵉ west side. Item theare is a halfe aker & it buts yᵉ south ende on yᵉ way yᵗ leades to Hitchin yᵉ north ende on yᵉ lande of George Mills. Edward Willsons lande lyeth on yᵉ east side & on yᵉ west side.

Josias Byrd
Thomas Baldock }
John Plummer } Church Wardens.

A Terrier of the house and land belonging to the Rectory
of Baldock in the County of Hertf. May 5, 1671.

The Rectory house and barn
The Church yard — an acre.
The slade — a rood.
The hortyard — half a rood.
The yard — half a rood.

Glebe
in Clothal-field
glebe — one acre.
in Weston-field
glebe — two acres.
in Willian-field
glebe — three acres & half.
in tot. by estimatiō six acres & half

Ri. Wortley Rect<sup>r</sup>
Thomas Matthews } Church
Richard Wilson } Wardens.

---

### BENGEO.

1638. A Terrier of the Glebe lands, orchard & house belonging to the Parish of Bengeo.

Imprimis The Parsonage is valued to be yeerly worth sixscore pounds & It is farmed at this present by John Allis.

2. The vicarage is valued to be yeerely forty pounds a yeare.

Ther belongs to the vicarage foure acres & an halfe.

One acre & an halfe lies in Barondan feild & it butts on Bengeo feild on the East & on Temple land on the west.

Also ther is of it five roodes lying in Bengeo feild w<sup>ch</sup> buts on Ricknes land in the East & on Revells hall land on the west.

Moreover ther is of thes four acres & an halfe, three roods lying in Crouch feild w<sup>ch</sup> butts on the highway leading to Hartford on the west & butting on Bengeo hall land on the east.

There is likewise of it one acree lying in Church feild & butting on the high way leading to Hartford on the west and on Revells hall land on the East.

2. The vicarage orchard bounds vpon the river southward & on the churchyard Northward & on a close called Jack Hobbs his on the East & on Gennings hill on the west.

John Bewick vicarius de Bengeo.
Gorge Tyler ×
Thomas Boxer } Churchwardens.
John Scot }

---

### BENNINGTON.

April, 13°, A Terrier of all the Glebe belonging to the Rectorie
1638.     of Bennington in Hertfordshire.

|  | acr. | roode | pole |
|---|---|---|---|
| The Parsonage house with yard Barnes stables with other outhouses Garden & close called the orchard | 4 | 1 | 5 |
| A close of arrable called Barne close | 8 | 0 | 36 |
| A close of arrable called y<sup>e</sup> Stable Croft | 6 | 2 | 21 |
| A close of arrable called Kitchen close lying on y<sup>e</sup> west side of y<sup>e</sup> house & stable croft | 7 | 0 | 13 |

|  | acr. | roode | pole |
|---|---|---|---|
| A field of Pasture called Dockcroft | 5 | 3 | 16 |
| The Woode | 3 | 3 | 39 |
| The litle Spring | 0 | 0 | 36 |

### In the Common Feilds.

|  | acr. | roode | pole |
|---|---|---|---|
| A meaddow called Badd-meads by y<sup>e</sup> river side | 5 | 0 | 18 |

### In Dane Feild.

|  | acr. | roode | pole |
|---|---|---|---|
| A Parcell of arrable lying betweene High-wood & y<sup>e</sup> Kings high-waie | 7 | 0 | 0 |
| A Peice vnd<sup>r</sup> Bad-meade hedge | 1 | 2 | 0 |
| A Parcell abutting the east & west ends on y<sup>e</sup> high-waies | 1 | 2 | 0 |
| A Peice abutting east side on S<sup>r</sup> Charles Cæsars land & west side on John Chapmans land | 1 | 0 | 0 |
| A Peice on Walkerne Hill | 1 | 2 | 0 |
| Another Parcell thereabouts north side on M<sup>r</sup> Treswells south side on M<sup>r</sup> Scriveners | 0 | 3 | 0 |

### In Peate croft.

|  | acr. | roode | pole |
|---|---|---|---|
| A little Peice abutting east end on Gores west end on Hartford high-waie | 0 | 2 | 0 |

### In Puckells hedge feild.

|  | acr. | roode | pole |
|---|---|---|---|
| A litle Parcell lying east side on M<sup>r</sup> Treswells west side on M<sup>r</sup> Humberstone wales | 0 | 2 | 0 |
| The fifth Peice from Langden hedge | 0 | 2 | 0 |
| A litle Peice joyning to a Peice of M<sup>r</sup> Treswells being the fourth peice from Puckells hedge Gapp, the east end lying in a place called Paddocks Penn & the west end on Tho. Kent of y<sup>e</sup> Church end | 0 | 1 | 0 |
| A Parcell east end on Jo. Chapman, west on Poulters high waie | 0 | 2 | 0 |
| A small Peice east end on M<sup>r</sup> Hugh Dods land going crosse, west end on Poulters high waie | 0 | 1 | 0 |

### In Great brooke feild.

|  | acr. | roode | pole |
|---|---|---|---|
| A Parcell lying east on Hartford high waie, west on Winters meade | 2 | 0 | 0 |
| Ox shott Hill | 2 | 0 | 0 |
| A Parcell west end on Hartford high waie | 0 | 3 | 0 |
| A nother Parcell, east side on M<sup>r</sup> Humberstone wales, west side Jo. Betts | 0 | 2 | 0 |
| A Peice lying between M<sup>r</sup> Nobles land & divers head lands turning east & west | 2 | 0 | 0 |
| A Peice by y<sup>e</sup> River at y<sup>e</sup> west End | 1 | 2 | 0 |
| Another Parcell neere adjoyning | 0 | 1 | 0 |
| Another Peice by y<sup>e</sup> River | 1 | 0 | 0 |
| Another Peice there { north side Jo. Betts / south side Jo. Chapmā } | 1 | 0 | 0 |
| A Peice east & west Hartford highway & y<sup>e</sup> river | 0 | 1 | 0 |
| Another Peice soe abutting | 0 | 3 | 0 |
| A Parcell { East End M<sup>r</sup> Treswell / West End Hartford high waie } | 0 | 2 | 0 |
| A Parcell { East side Tho. Kent of Church end / West side Will. Cranwell } | 0 | 3 | 0 |
| A Peice { East end Tho. Kent / West end Poulters high waie } | 1 | 0 | 0 |
| A Peice { East side S<sup>r</sup> Charles Cæsar / West side Moyses Rowley } | 0 | 2 | 0 |
| A Peice vnd<sup>r</sup> Levetts hedge | 0 | 2 | 0 |

## CHURCH TERRIERS.

| | acr. | roode | pole |
|---|---|---|---|
| In litle Brooke-feild. | | | |
| A Peice next Sawcombe hedge | 1 | 0 | 0 |
| A parcell.—East end River—west Jo. Lawrence | 0 | 2 | 0 |
| A nother Parcell abutting east & west on y⁰ former.— North side Ambrose Chandler, South s. Mʳ Noble | 0 | 2 | 0 |
| In Lether-feild. | | | |
| A litle Peice abutting east side on Tho. Croutchs land, west side on Sʳ Charles Cæsar | 0 | 2 | 0 |
| In Popp-hill-feild | | | |
| A Peice of Arrable in Chisill hill shott | 1 | 2 | 0 |
| A Peice more there | 0 | 2 | 0 |
| Another Parcell in a shott of 4 Peices on Chisill hill | 0 | 2 | 0 |
| A Peice in a shott shooting north east & south west on Chisill hill | 0 | 3 | 0 |
| A Peice in Stocking Corner shott | 0 | 2 | 0 |
| A Peice in Levetts hedge | 0 | 2 | 0 |
| More there | 0 | 2 | 0 |
| A Peice abutting on Windmill hillway | 0 | 2 | 0 |
| More in yᵉ same shott | 0 | 2 | 0 |
| A Peice abutting east on Betts croft | 0 | 2 | 0 |
| At Beaddales Bush | 0 | 1 | 0 |
| More there abutting on Mill-way | 0 | 2 | 0 |
| More in yᵉ same shott | 0 | 3 | 0 |
| A Peice abutting on Stocking hedge south-east | 0 | 2 | 0 |
| More there | 0 | 1 | 0 |
| A Peice in Langdale shott | 0 | 2 | 0 |
| A Peice of Arrable in yᵉ same shott | 1 | 2 | 0 |
| A Parcell in Stowdale | 0 | 1 | 0 |
| More in Stowdale | 0 | 2 | 0 |
| A Piece in yᵉ Leading shoote quite through | 1 | 0 | 0 |
| Another Peice there | 1 | 2 | 0 |
| In litle feild shott | 0 | 1 | 0 |
| More there | 0 | 3 | 0 |
| In a shott of 3 landes | 0 | 3 | 0 |
| In Row dale shott | 0 | 1 | 0 |
| More in yᵉ same shott | 0 | 2 | 0 |
| In Popp hill furlong | 0 | 1 | 0 |
| An headland pt of Rowdale shott | 1 | 0 | 0 |

There are divers Parcells of land lying in the Parish of Apesden wᶜʰ did pay Tith to the Rectorie of Bennington: but in yᵉ time of Thomas Coo, Rector of Bennington, 1558, in recompence thereof, there was a composition made betweene yᵉ Rectors yᵗ then were of 3s. 4d. to be payd annuatim for yᵉ sayd Tithes to yᵉ Rector of Beñington, wᶜʰ summe was often received by Mʳ William Middleton Parson of this Parrish.

    Ita testor Nathanael Dod
        Rector ibidem.
           John Hill, Churchwarden.

### BERKHAMSTED ST. PETER.

A TRUE TERRYER of the glebe landes belonging to the Churche & parson of Barkamsted S Peter.

Imprimis two litle closes lyeinge neere to the parsonage house conteyninge two acres abuttinge East and West vpon the landes of the free schole there southe vpon a Common feilde called Sᵗ Edmondes & northe vpon a lane called the parsonage lane.

Itm 13 acres more in Northchurche parishe whereof one acre lyethe in closed by the highe waye leadinge from Barkamsted to Tringe and the other xij acres lye in a Common feilde there called Lagleye adjoyninge to the close aforesd northe & extendeth it selfe in contynued lenght vnto the lande of Thomas Salter on the southe.

      Tho. Newman Rector.
      Robart Renold  } Churchwardins.
      Michael Young
      Thomas House  } Sidemen.
      John Climson

---

Another Terrier endorsed with the date 1674 is almost word for word the same as the last except that Edward Salters name takes the place of Thomas Salters in the last line. It is signed by

      Joh: Napier Rector.
      Ed. Seymir  } Church-
      Fra. Pitkin  } wardens.

---

### LITTLE BERKHAMSTED.

BARKHAMSTEED PARVA.   A Terrier of the gleabe lands house & Tythes taken & deliu$^r$d into this courte by vs whose names are vnd$^r$ written, May 18. 1638.

#### Gleabe Lands, houses.

Imp$^r$: a dwelling house containing below staires seauen roomes, a hall, a plo$^r$, kitchin, two butteries, milkhouse, tubhouse: Aboue staires fiue lodging chamb$^{rs}$, a studie, a malte loft, a cheese loft.

Itm a Wheat barne w$^{th}$ a thrashing floore, plancked, & a barne for lent graine: a stable & hayhouse in 3 bayes, a Carthouse, all thatched.

Itm on the south side of the house a garden & oarchard wherin is a pond & a priuie and a litle garden on the north side of Roses, a Churchyeard att the West end of the house to be fenced by pish round about by the order of M$^r$ Do$^r$ Morrison.

#### Closes.

Itm a pitle of halfe an aker on the southside of the churchyeard a field on the eastside of the barnes two akers & dimid., one close called Church field 6 akers abutting on the high way east, on the Comon field called churchfield west, haueing a pcell of gleabe of 4 pole w$^{th}$ a ponde in it on the north & on Richard Mayhoe his orchard south: diuied [sic] into two akers & foure.

Itm a close called the brach diuided into 2 pcells, 12 akers abutting on the high way south, on M$^r$ Fost$^r$ north, on Wm. Wetherd west: on the Com̄o Sproatsfield east, all my fence.

Itm a close inclosed out of pondfield called Sheepcoatewicke two akers w$^{ch}$ may appeare by a courte roule to be hadd in exchange for a pcell of land in ashfield leading downe to the brooke when the warren was pte of the said ashfield but afterwards taken into Bedwell warren.

Itm a close of 4 akers called Woollands diuied abutting on Nicholas Phillips land east, on M$^r$ Fost$^r$s west, on Wm. How south, on M$^r$ Humphrey Wellds north: a pcell in the Com̄on called Sproats field called long aker compassed w$^{th}$ M$^r$ Fosters ground, one aker in the same Com̄on called idle mans shott compassed w$^{th}$ M$^r$ Fosters ground, one pcell in Millfield abutting on M$^r$ Pendreds land east &

west, on Phillipps south. on M^r Fosters north: another pcell in Fellhedges abutting on Cullu^rt groune north: another in peesefield compassed w^th M^r Knighton Ferrers his land.

Itm 3 akers in the comon mead in six pcells call the Hose, Stoannes aker, path rodd, washing block rodd, psonage aker and the ash rodd.

### Tithes.

For herbiddg out of Bedwell Parke hath beene vsually payed ii*s*. 8*d*: & vj*s*. viij*d*. out of Water Meads.

All the tythes of the parke are due but o^r pson being not able to wage law w^th such potent adu^rsaries sitteth still.

The rest of tythes are all taken in kinde.

Tho. Falthropp     John Vsher, Robt. Ruskin. guard.
Rector ibd.     John Foster, sidgman.

---

### Rectory of Berkhamstead Parva
### in the County of Hertford
### and
### Diocese of Lincoln.

Terrier of the Glebe Lands belonging thereto.

| Inclosed Lands. | | A. | R. | P. |
|---|---|---|---|---|
| Rectory House, Garden Offices, &c. | | 1 | 1 | 37 |
| Barn Field | Pasture | 2 | 2 | 32 |
| Church Yard | Do. | - | 3 | 25 |
| Church Yard Pightle | Do. | - | 2 | 1 |
| Breeches Clover | Arable | 4 | 3 | 2 |
| Newgate Field | Pasture | 2 | - | 12 |
| Pond Field | Do. | 3 | 3 | 5 |
| Upper Breach Field | Do. | 5 | - | 2 |
| Lower Breach Field | Do. | 4 | 3 | 37 |
| Woollands | Do. | 4 | 3 | 35 |
| Long Acre or Bassel's | Do. | 1 | 1 | 27 |
| Roger Baker's Field | Arable | 2 | - | 30 |
| Common Field Lands. | | | | |
| In Great Sprouse Field | Arable | 1 | - | 11 |
| In Mill Field | Do. | - | 2 | 7 |
| In Fell Hedges | Do. | - | 2 | 35 |
| In Pierce Field | Do. | 1 | - | 3 |
| In Turner's Common | Do. | - | - | 11 |
| Six Pieces in Berkhamstead Common Mead | Do. | 2 | 3 | 18 |
| | | 41 | - | 10 |

The Rector is entitled to the Great and small tithes of about 1100 acres of land. One Farm of about 240 acres pays a modus of 6s. 8d. per annum: and another of about 150 acres pays a modus of 11s. 8d. per ann.

We, whose names are hereunder signed being the Rector, Churchwarden and certain Inhabitants of the Parish of Little Berkhamstead do hereby certify the above to be a correct terrier and statement, as witness our hands this [*blank*] Jan. 1829.

R. G. Baker, Rector     Tho^s Cheek     } Inhabitants.
Tho^s Daniell, Churchwarden     Thomas Dewey
William Stratton.

# Transcripts of Wigginton Parish Registers.

[*The existing Registers commence in 1674.*]

### 1601.*
#### Marriages.
Oct. 10 Georg Reeve maried to Elizabeth Dawes.
#### Christ.
Nov.  5 John Bigges sonn of Elixander Bigges.
Apr.  8 Alies Moris Daughter of Richard Moris.
,,   13 Thomas Davie sonn of William Davie.
,,   18 Vssalye Roodes Daughter of John Roods.
June  3 Henery Peacke sonn of Frauncis Peack.
Aug. 19 William Reeve sonn of George Reeve.
,,   26 William Cooles sonn of John Cooles.
Mch. 10 Mathew Dell Daughter of William Dell.
Apr. 10 John Haris sonn of John Haris.
#### Bur.
May   5 Jonas Edmonce sonn of William Edmonce.
,,   17 William Edmonce.

Church Wardens { John Wetherede.
{ William Nickholes.

---

### Mich. 1614 to Mich. 1615.
#### Bapt.
Apr. 10 Johanes Bilbie filius Thome Bilbie et Elizabethe Bilbie.
,,   25 Anna Russell filia Joh'is Russell.
July 16 Johanes Spiggins filius Willm. Spigins.
Aug. 20 Willims Reve filius Joh'is Reve.
,,   24 Sussana Nashe filia Gwalteri Nashe.
#### Marr.
July 17 Thomas Burder et Susana Wood.
#### Bur.
Dec. 11 Richardus Blaked.
Sep. 16 Alicia Pratt filia Willimi Pratt.
Jan. 16 Willims Surmar.
,,   25 Arthir Bins.
Apr. 10 Elizabetha Bilbie et Johanes Bilbie.
Aug. 20 Elleana Reve vxor Joh'is Reve.

p me Rowlandū Heblethwet Curat. de Wigginton
predict.
Willm Partridge senior.
et Willm. Partrige Ju. Gard. de Wigginton in
Anno D'ni 1615.

* This transcript is undoubtedly dated as above, but the endorsement in a later hand is 'Michas. 1609 to Michas. 1610.'

TRANSCRIPTS OF WIGGINTON PARISH REGISTERS. 113

### Mich. 1616 to Mich. 1617.
#### Bapt.
Apr. 14 Enock filius Willmi Partridge.
" 14 Elizabetha filia Willmi Partridge.
June 1 Michaell Holyman filius Edwardi Holiman.
" 19 Arnet Pratt filius Willm. Pratt.
Oct. 29 Henricus Moris filius Richardi Moris.

#### Marr.
Sep. [blank] Johanes Reve et Rebecka [blank].

#### Bur.
Feb. 14 Elizabetha Partridg.
Mch. 22 Willmus Partridge.
July 7 Thomas . . . ard.
Oct. 10 Richard F . . . .

Per me Rowland Heblethwett Curat ibm.
Walter Stock<sup>e</sup> } gard.
Franciscū Burch

---

### Mich. 1620 to Mich. 1621.
#### Bapt.
Dec. 24 Charles y<sup>e</sup> sonne of Charles Hill & Lettis his wife.
Jan. 1 Jude y<sup>e</sup> daught<sup>r</sup> of Edward Hollyman & Elizabeth his wife.
Mch. 11 Raph y<sup>e</sup> soñe of Raph Munne & Joane his wife.
May 27 John y<sup>e</sup> sonne of Thomas Bilbe & Margarett his wife.
June 3 John y<sup>e</sup> soñe of John Russell & Annis his wife.
July 1 Christian y<sup>e</sup> daught<sup>r</sup> of Robert Harrison & Christian his wife.
" 23 John y<sup>e</sup> son of John Dinton & Elizabeth his wife.
Aug. 5 Mary y<sup>e</sup> daught<sup>r</sup> of John Boorder & Mary his wife.

#### Marr.
Oct. 2 Richard Douer widdower of this parrish & Elizabeth Sere of y<sup>e</sup> parrish of Masseworth in the county of Buck.
Jan. 18 Simon Durrant & Alse Patridge both of this parrish.
Apr. 10 Roger Deacon of the parrish of Norchurch widdower & Elizabeth Bayley widow of this parrish.
" 30 Henry Hudnoll widdower & Alice Quarrington widdow both of them of y<sup>e</sup> parrish of Aldbury, obtained a licence.
June 3 Edmund Burt of this parrish & Ellen Edmunds of Pendley in y<sup>e</sup> parrish of Albury.

#### Bur.
Feb. 3 Joane Goddard widdow.
June 4 William Spiggins.
July 23 John Dinton, a little infant.

Thomas Tangley, minister.
George Mussell } Ch. wardens.
. . . . . .

---

### Mich. 1621 to Mich. 1622.
#### Christ.
Dec. 26 Thomas the sonne of Thomas Wigginton & Mary his wife.
Feb. 3 Mary y<sup>e</sup> daught<sup>r</sup> of Francis Burgen & Anne his wife.
" 17 Susan y<sup>e</sup> daught<sup>r</sup> of Simon Durrant & Alse his wiff.

H

Mch. 12 John y e soñe of Thomas Tangley Minist r & Elizabeth his wiff.
,, 25 Joyce y e daught r of Edward Durrant & Ursly his wiff.
Aug. 4 Robert y e soñe of Thomas Sheppard & Clare his wiffe.
Oct. 5 Elizabeth y e daught r of Richard Douer & Elizabeth his wiffe.

### Marr.

Oct. 31 James Heydon & Marth Hall both of them of the parrish of little Gaddesden hauing a licen.
Nov. 29 Thomas Rutland of y e parrish of Tringe, widdower, & Elizabeth Tredway of this parrish, widdow.
Mch. 22 Robert Redman of Tringe widdower & Jane [Ouiatt?] of the same parish.
June 11 George Dauy & Ellen Pierce both of this parrish hauing a licence.
,, 27 John Luke of Rockson & in y e county of Bedford gentleman & Mary Tokefield of this parrish, hauinge a licence.

### Bur.

Dec. 20 Isabell Pierce, widdow.
Jan. 11 Margaret Bayley of Champnes.
,, 17 Richard Arnett.
Apr. 12 Joane Peake, widdow.
Aug. 4 Robert the sonne of Thomas Sheppard.

        Thomas Tangley Minister.
        John Pratt       } Churchwardens.
        George Mussell }

---

## Mich. 1622 to Mich. 1623.

### Christ.

Oct. 6 Elizabeth y e daughter of Richard Douer and Elizabeth his wiffe.
Nov. 17 Priscilla the daughter of Alse Spiggins, widdow.
Dec. 8 Francis the soñe of Edward Hollyman & Elizabeth his wiffe.
,, 15 Anne Phillis the daughter of Edmund Burt & Ellen his wiffe.
Jan. 26 William the soñe of William Axtell & Joane his wiffe.
Feb. 9 Mary the daughter of John Dinton & Elizabeth his wiffe.
Mch. 2 Martha the daught r of John Foster & Joane his wiffe.
Apr. 13 John y e soñe of George Dauy and Ellen his wife.
June 11 Mary the daughter of Richard Grouer & Rebecca his wife.
Aug. 24 John y e soñe & Martha y e daughter of John Reeue & Rebecca his wife.

### Marr.

Feb. 25 Edward Glennester of the parrish of Albury & Joane Doggett of this parrish.
Aug. 10 Marke Cleuer widdower & Annes Weedon of the parrish of .. addesden, having a licence.

### Bur.

Nov. 12 Elizabeth Douer, a little infant.
Jan. 15 Isabell Russell, widdow.

        Thomas Tangley Minister.
        Richard Grover } Churchwardens.
        Richard Tredway }

### From. Mich. 1623 to Mich. 1624.

#### Bapt.

Nov. 5 John yͤ soñe of John Boorder & Mary his wiffe.
Feb. 10 John yͤ sonne of John Spiggins & Elizabeth his wiffe.
 ,, 15 John yͤ sonne of Charles Hill & Lettis his wiffe.
 ,, 17 John yͤ sonne of John Bayley & Christian his wiffe.
Mch. 25 Richard yͤ sonne of Mary Harrod base borne.
Apr. 25 James yͤ sonne of John Russell & Annis his wiffe.
Aug. 1 John yͤ sonne of William Axtell and Joane his wiffe.
Sep. 26 Richard the sonne of Francis Burgen & Anne his wiffe.
 ,, 26 Abraham yͤ sonne of Thomas Wigginton & Mary his wife.

#### Marr.

Jan. 22 John Geery of this parrish & Hester Gate of yͤ parrish of Chessam in the county of Buck.
Mch. 18 William Brian of Aylessbury in the county of Buck, widdower, & Margarett Biggs of the parrish of Tringe obtayned a licence.
 ,, 25 John Smith of the parrish of Tringe & Anne Brouton of yͤ same parrish, obtained a licence.
Apr. 29 George Foster of Barckamstedde Saint Peters husbandman & Bridgett Purratt of the same parrish obtained a licence.
May 3 Thomas Dwight of Prince Risborow in the county of Buck, shooemaker, & Miriam Tangley of this parrish, by vertue of a licence.

#### Bur.

May 11 Samuell Dagnall a nurse child.
Sep. 23 James Russell a little infant.

Thomas Tangley, Minister.
Richard Grover } Churchwardens.
William Axtell }

---

### From Mch. 23 to Sep. 29 [endorsed 1624].

May 21 Alice the wife of John Woode. Buried the 21 of May.

John Gery.  William Axtell.
Churchwardens.

---

### From Mich. 1625 to Mich. 1626.

#### Bapt.

Aug. 24 Jeane Kimpton.

#### Bur.

Sep. 21 Meary Tit.
Oct. 5 Frances Bvrgine.

Thomas Fuller, Curate.
John Gearye } Churchwardens.
Mathew Kimton }

---

### 'For this whole yeare 1626.'

#### Bur.

Apr. 26 Ezeckell the sonne of John Spidgens.
Aug. 24 Jane the daughter of Matthew Kempton 'baptised.'
Sep. 21 Mayrie the daughter of Daniell Tidd.
Oct. [blank] Francis Burgaine.

*Bapt.*

Dec. 10   Jane the Dafter of William Axtill.
Jan.  1   Ezekell the sonne of John Russell.
Feb.  3   Hester the Daughter of Richard Douer.
„  15   Widdow Durrant 'buried.'
Mch. 4   John Wood & Marie Martin maried by vertue of a licence.
„  13   Widdow Arnot buried.
„  20   Ann the daughter of Widdow Burgain baptised.

            Thomas Fuller, Curat.
            John Gearye        } Churchwardens.
            Mathew . . . ton

*To be Continued.*

---

# List of Rentals and Surveys in the Public Record Office.

*[The Official reference is placed at the beginning of each entry.]*

Portf. 1/15.   Aldbury. Portion of a detailed rental. [? Hen. VI.] 4 ms.

Portf. 1/16.   Aldbury. Detailed rental of the manor. 34 Hen. VIII. 2 ms.

Portf. 1/17.   Aldbury. Detailed rental of the manor. [? Eliz.] 2 ms.

Roll 268.   Anstey (Austii ad Castrum). Detailed rental of the manor. 18 Edw. IV. 6 ms.

Portf. 2/50.   Barnet. Terrier of demesne lands. [Hen. VIII.] 1 m.

Roll 269.   Bedwell, Little Berkhampstead, Harmebenegate & Blountes. Detailed rental or extent of the possessions of John Say, knt. 7 Edw. IV. 6 ms.

Roll 270.   Berkhampstead. Rental of John Godrych. [Edw. II.] 1 m.

Roll 271.   Berkhampstead. Extent or survey of the manor. 30 Edw. III. 5 ms.

Roll 272.   Berkhampstead. Duplicate of the last.

Portf. 8/19.   Berkhampstead. Schedule of rents due to the honor. 31 Eliz. 2 ms.

Portf. 8/20.   Berkhampstead. Part of a rental of the honor. [Jas. I.] 2 ms.

Roll 273.   Berkhampstead, Albury, Wingrave (Bucks) & Swanbourne. Survey of rents & duties appertaining to the honor of Berkhampstead taken by Special Commission of the Court of Exchequer. 5 Jas. I 1 m.

Roll 274.   Breton in Essendon & Hatfield. Detailed rental. [? Ric. II.] 2 ms.

Portf. 8/21.   Brookman's in North Mimms. Detailed rental of the manor. 20 Hen. VIII. 1 m.

LIST OF RENTALS AND SURVEYS. 117

Portf. 8/22. Bush Hall. Valor of the manor. [2 Hen. VIII.] 2 ms.
Portf. 22/71. Cheshunt & Halstead (Essex). Part of a valor. [Hen. VIII.] 1 m.
Roll 275. Cheshunt etc. Rentals (a packet of documents much decayed & almost entirely illegible). [? Edw. III.—Hen. VI.] 6 ms.
Portf. 2/57. Divers land. Part of a detailed rental for what manor does not appear [? Hen. VI.] 2 ms.
Portf. 8/23. Divers lands. Valor (very imperfect). [Hen. VIII.] 2 ms.
Portf. 8/24. Divers lands. Fragment of a survey of lands, the name of which does not appear. [? Eliz.] 1 m.
Portf. 8/25. Eastwick. Survey of part of the demesnes of the manor. [Jas. I.] 2 ms.
Portf. 8/26. Flamstead. Valor of Warwicks lands. 18 Hen. VIII. 3 ms.
Portf. 8/27. Halle. Portion of a detailed rental. [Hen. VI.] 4 ms.
Roll 276. Hatfield. Valor of the manor. [Hen. VIII.] 3 ms.
Roll 277. Hertford, Priory of. Demonstration of the state of the Priory before a general chapter of the Monastery of S$^t$ Albans. 13, 14 Hen. VII. 1 m.
Portf. 8/28. Hertingfordbury. Summarised valor of the manor. 37 Edw. III. 1 m.
Portf. 8/29. Hitchin. Survey of the priory. 37 Hen. VIII. 8 ms.
Roll 278. Hoddesden. Survey of the 'Key of Hoddesden.' [? Eliz.] 1 m.
Portf. 8/30. Hunsdon, Eastwick & Stanstead. Survey of the possessions of Vincent Randall. [Eliz.] 4 ms.
Portf. 8/31. Hyde in Sawbridgeworth. Extent or survey of the manor. 12 Edw. [I]. 1 m.
Roll 279. Langley & Shenley. Extent or survey of the manors late belonging to Queen Eleanor. 19 Edw. I. 1 m.
Portf. 8/32. Langley. Detailed rental. 10 Hen. IV. 1 m.
Portf. 8/33. Meesden. Detailed rental. [Edw. III.] 2 ms.
Portf. 8/34. Mulssey. Rental or rent roll. 4 Hen. VIII. 2 ms.
Roll 280. Munden [Furnivall]. Rental or rent roll of the manor. 20 Edw. III. 1 m.
Roll 281. Munden, Great. Detailed rental of the manor. 31 Edw. III. 1 m.
Roll 282. Munden. Custumal of the manor. 14 Ric. II. 1 m.
Roll 283. Munden Furnivall. Rental or rent roll of the manor. [Ric. II.] 2 ms.
Roll 284. Munden. Rental or rent roll of possessions of John Duram. [Ric. II.] 1 m.
Roll 285. Munden, Great. Detailed rental of possessions of Margaret late wife of Robt. Dykeswelle. 5 Hen. IV. 2 ms.
Roll 286. Munden & Churchfield. Part of a detailed rental of possessions of John Fray. [circa 36 Hen. VI.] 1 m.
Roll 287. Munden, Great & Munden Little. Detailed rental of possessions of Lady Agnes Fray. 2 Edw. IV. 3 ms.
Roll 288. Munden. Detailed rental of possessions of Dame Agnes Fray. 13 Edw. IV. 1 m.
Roll 289. Munden. Part of a terrier of the manor. [Hen. VII. ?] 1 m.
Roll 290. Munden, Great. Detailed rental of the manor. [Hen. VII. ?]. 3 ms.

| | |
|---|---|
| Roll 291. | Munden, Great. Detailed rental of the manor. 3 ms. |
| Portf. 3/42. | Munden, Great. Part of a return or survey relating to the manor. [Edw. IV. ?.] 2 ms. |
| Roll 292. | Parkbury & Marden. Part of a survey of possessions belonging to the Mon. of S$^t$ Albans. [Hen. VIII]. 1 m. |
| Portf. 8/35. | Pisho. Valor of the manor. [Hen. VIII.] 1 m. |
| Portf. 8/36. | Radwell. Rental. 32 Hen. VIII. 1 m. |
| Portf. 8/37. | [Royal lands]. Schedule of rents due in co. Hertford (fragmentary), 1652. 1 m. |
| Roll 293. | Rownay priory. Rental or survey of possessions of the priory. [Edw. III.] 6 ms. |
| Portf. 8/38. | S$^t$ Albans. Rental or rent roll of S$^t$ Mary de Pratis. Circa 12 Edw. II. 1 m. |
| Roll 294. | S$^t$ Albans, Town of. Rental of S$^t$ Mary's Sopwell. 25 Hen. VI. 1 m. |
| Portf. 8/39. | S$^t$ Albans. Survey of the monastery taken by special commission. 2 Edw. VI. 4 ms. |
| Portf. 8/40. | S$^t$ Albans. Note of the value of rents. [? Hen. VIII.] 2 ms. |
| Portf. 8/41. | S$^t$ Giles in the Wood, Priory of. Valor of possessions. [? Hen. VIII.] 4 ms. |
| Portf. 8/42. | Sawbridgeworth. Pedigree of natives on the manor taken by inquisition [? Edw. I.] 1 m. (Printed in 'Villainage in England' by Vinogradoff 1892). |
| Portf. 8/43. | Sawbridgeworth. Extent or survey of the manor. 32 Edw. I. 1 m. |
| Roll 295. | Sawbridgeworth. Detailed rental of possessions of John Heron. [? Edw. IV.] 1 m. |
| Roll 296. | Shenley, Titeburste, Edgware & Stanmore. Extent or survey of the said manors. 2 ms. |
| Roll 297. | Shenley & Holmes. Detailed rental. 9 Ric. II. 2 ms. |
| Portf. 5/12. | Stagenhoe, Meppershall, Hextoneston & Walden. Fragment of a rental or rent roll. [Edw. I.] 1 m. |
| Roll 298. | Stortford. Rental or rent roll of possessions of the Bishop of London. [? Hen. III. or Edw. I.] 3 ms. |
| Roll 299. | Stortford. Detailed rental of possessions of the Bishop of London. 37 Hen. VIII. 11 ms. |
| Portf. 8/44. | Waltham Cross. Rental of lands probably belonging to the manor. [? Eliz.] 2 ms. |
| Portf. 8/45. | Ware. Rental & custumal of possessions late of Gilbert Hill. 36 Eliz. 3 ms. |
| Portf. 8/46. | Watford. Terrier of possessions of John Watford. 18 Edw. IV. 1 m. |
| Portf. 8/47. | Watford. Detailed survey of the manor. 3 Jas. I. 8 ms. |
| Portf. 8/48. | Wedon Pinkney. Memorandum as to the possessions of Wm. de Weston. [Edw. III.] 1 m. |
| Roll 300. | Wormley, Baas, Gedding, Langton, Foxton & Marions. Roll of Assize & other rents. 14 Ric. II. 4 ms. |
| Portf. 8/49. | [ ? ] Fragment of a rental or rent roll. [Edw. III.] 1 m. |

[*N.B.—In addition to the above there are numerous & important rentals & surveys classed under 'Divers Counties' & 'Counties Unknown.'*]

# Abstracts of Wills.

## ARCHDEACONRY OF MIDDLESEX (ESSEX AND HERTS).

REGISTER "RAYMOND"—Continued from Page 87.

f. 266. JOANE CROWCHE of Stondon, widow (*Dat.* 10 Apr. 1577). Child$^n$ of dau. Agnes Barboure ; Child$^n$ of dau. Joane Curlesse ; Child$^n$ of son Geo. Crouche; John son of my son John Crowche & Emanuel his bro.; Child$^n$ of dau. Ellyn Jordyne; Bro-in-law Geo. Crowche late of London skinner dec$^d$ ; Rich. Crowche my late husb$^d$ ; Jaques Jurdeine husband of s$^d$ Ellen; Eliz. Finche my son George Crowche's wife's dau. ; Agnes my maid ; Sara Worland ; Marie Fawkener ; Son Geo. exor ; Cous. M$^r$ Hen. Gardner & son-in-law Fulke Curlewes overseers. Wit$^s$ :—Tho. Crowche the elder, Tho. Crowche the yong$^r$, Tho. Skiugle, Henry Skingle. ('This wille was not pved for that he had daye gyven hym tell Ester followinge 1578').

f. 267. THOMAS BRANCHE of Ware. (*Dat.* 22 Feb. 1578). Son Gylbert (under 18); Tenement in Orybbe streate wherein I dwell; Son Thos; Wife Kath. exor; Wm. Larrence & Thos. Forde overseers. *Thomas Braunche.* Wit$^s$ :—Vessey Symon Appryce (*sic*) Thomas Watt$^e$ Thomas Wynchester. (*Pr.* at Ware 9 Mch. 1578).

f. 268. JOHN CORDELL of Podingspitts in psh. of Chesthunte, collier. (*Dat.* 28 Jan. 1578). Eldest son Wm.; Son Robt.; Roger Jackson; Son Thos; John Lucas of Burbus ende; Son John; Son Edmund; Youngest son Henry; Wm. Cordell of Podingspits; Dau. Joan; Bro. John Lucas; Marie wife of Wm. Cordell; Robt. Bulle exor; Wm. M'kyn overseer. Wit$^s$ :—John Lucas, Roger Jackson, Nich. Dryver. (*Pr.* at Sabridgworth 17 Feb. 1578).

f. 268. RICHARD LAWRENCE of Grene ende, in psh. of Standon. (*Dat.* 7 June 1578). Tenement at Green end in tenure of Wm. Browne; Dau. Wynnefrythe Lawrence; Dau. Anne Lawrence; Eliz. More; Wife Agnes; Son Edw. exor. Wit$^s$ :—Tho. Lambky, Tho. Smithe, Wm. Chalice. (*Pr.* at Sabridgworthe 17 Feb. 1578).

f. 269. JOHN KYLFORDE of Chesthunte, singleman. (*Dat.* 17 Jan. 1578). Bro. Wm. Kylforde; Kath. Kylforde my bro. Thos. his dau.; Geo. Jackson, my bro. Roger Jacksons son; Ralphe Wrighte; John Chauntrell; John Wolf; Mystres Hawkyns; Bro. Thos. exor; Friends Rich. Page glasier & Simon Williams vicar of Chesthunt overseers. (*Pr.* at Sabridgworthe 17 Feb. 1578).

f. 269. RICHARD FLETCHER of Woode greene in psh. of Chesthunt, tyler. (*Dat.* 26 Feb. 1571). Wife Mawdelyne; Son Roger;

Dau. Anne Fletcher; Wm. Hodges my sisters son; Wife extrix; Neighbour Robt. Petite overseer. Wit$^s$:—Simon Lowen, Robt. Petit & Symon Williams vicar of Chesthunte. (*Pr.* at Sabridgforde 9 Jan. 1578).

f. 272. **JOHN FOOTE** of Sabridgworth. (*Dat.* 15 June 1578). Son John; The child my wife now goeth with; Bro. Anthony Foot's child$^n$; Aunt Frances child$^n$; Godson Wm. Argente; John Trotte; John & Eliz. Cocke; John & Jaine Browne; My father; Wife Margt. extrix; Tho. Browne overseer. Wit$^s$:—John Foote my father & Thomas Frances. (*Pr.* at Storforde 1 Sep. 1578.)

f. 274. **JOHN ETHERIDGE** of Buntingforde, glover. (*Dat.* 11 Apr. 1577). Bur. at Leyston; Wife Isabell; Margt. Bucke; Eldest son John; Son Thos.; Son Wm.; Lands in Wyndemylefeilde in Leyston, copyholds of manor of Cornyeburie; Wm. Sprigge; Daus. Agnes, Johan & Margt; Wife extrix; Thos. Northup & Robt. Hattley overseers. Wit$^s$:—Lewys Reynolds minister & Wm. Hitche. (*Pr.* at Stortforde 28 July 1578).

f. 275. **RALPH PERRYE** of Sabridgworthe, yeoman. (*Dat.* 28 June 1578). Youngest son Christ$^r$; Messuage called Jeffes where I now dwell; Wife Margerie; Lands called Greate Bustards, Hetche Crofte, Hookefeilde *alias* Okefeilde, Mynnams, Grete highe feilde, Little highe feilde, Great Hallison; Son Robt; Eldest son John; Lands in Clerke feilde, Wolle Crofte, Purthfeilde, Bullbrokes croft; Son George; Messuage called Keales & lands called Keales croft; Lands in Greate Manfeilde; Son Christ$^r$ exor; Peter Lyndsell of Sabridgworth overseer. Wit$^s$:—John Nellson the writer. Thos. Hutchyn thelder, Peter Lyndsell. (*Pr.* at Stortford 28 July 1578).

f. 277. **JOHN ADAM** of Nownes ferme in psh. of Sabridgforde, husbandman. (*Dat.* 22 Mch. 20 Eliz.) Son Jerome Adam; Daus. Agnes Flayle & Alice Burle; Serv John Herde; Son Wm. Adam; Land called Whittengers; Serv$^t$ Johan Kinge; Sons Thos. & Wm. Adam exors; Peter Lyndsell of Sabridgforde & Rich. Fanne of same yeomen overseers. Wit$^s$:—Peter Lyndsell, Rich. Fanne & Nich. Compton clerke the writer herof. (*Pr.* at Stortford 23 June 1578).

f. 278. **JOHN BANESTER** of Standen. (*Dat.* 8 Dec. 1577). Wife Alice; Son Henry & John his youngest bro. Wife extrix. Wit$^s$:—Hen. Osbaston, Richard Courtney, Nich. Osbaston, John Clerke. (*Pr.* at Braughin 17 May 1578).

f. 279. **JOHN HOLLAM** of Braughin. (*Dat.* 26 Mch. 1575). Wife Dorothy exor.; Son Wm. Hollam overseer. Wit$^s$:—John Hedlam, Wm. Daye, John Wright, Margt. Allderiche. (*Pr.* at Braughin 17 May 1578).

f. 280. **ROGER BYLFYLD** of Chesthuntt. (*Nunc. will dat.* 2 Apr. 1578). Son Wm.; Dau. Alice. Wit$^s$:—Rich. Flecher & Wm. Whitehed of Chesthunt. [No date of probate].

f. 280. **JEAMES PORTER** of Barley. (*Dat.* 13 Feb. 1577). Wife Ellen; Son John; Daus. Grace, Agnes, Sybell, Alice & Marie (all under 20); Wife extrix. Wit$^s$:—John Grenell, Wm. Kefforde. (*Pr.* at Braughin 16 May 1578).

## ABSTRACTS OF WILLS.

f. 281. GYLES COXE of Ware, laborer. (*Dat.* 28 Feb. 1579). Son Mathew; Dau. Margrie Coxe; Dau. Alyce Coxe; Dau. Eliz.: Wife Agnes extrix: Bros. Thos. & Peter Coxe overseers. Wits:—Goodman Veseye & Hughe Holder, Rich. Cortneye & Tho. Swynsed. (*Pr.* at Braughinge 18 Mch. 1579).

f. 282. THOMAS COOKE of Chesthunte singleman. (*Dat.* 4 Jan. 1579). Robt. Cooke my brothers son; Wm. Cooke my brothers son (under 21); Henrie bro. of s^d Robt. & Wm.; Margt. sister of s^d brethren (under 16); John Cotteis my sisters son (under 21); Robert & William Cooke my elder brother John's sons; Henrie Cooke; Alice Vales dau. of Thos. Vales & Thos. Vales her bro.; John Cooke my bro. John's son dec^d; Eliz. & Marie sisters of s^d John; Kinswoman Agnes Fletcher; Bro. John & Simon Williams vicar of Chesthunt overseers; Thomas Cooke my elder bro. Johns son exor. Wits:—Wm. Lowdam & Simon Williams. (*Pr.* at Sabridgworth 5 Feb. 1579).

f. 282. THOMAS JORDAN of Anstie. (*Dat.* 19 Dec. 1579). Wife Kath.; Child my wife goeth with; Dau. Kath.; Son Richard; Son Thos. exor. Wits:—John Allen, John Oaker, Geo. Thorgood & Anthony Crede. (*Pr.* at Sabridgworth 5 Feb. 1579).

f. 285. WILLIAM WREN of Thundriche, husbandman. (*Dat.* 28 Aug. 1579). Rich. Bachilers child^n which he had by Eliz. my dau.; Marie Bigges, Johan Bigg^e eldest dau.; Wife Kath: Son Robt. Wren's wife; Eldest son Robt. exor.; John Hutchyn overseer. Wits:—Wm. Dixon vicar there. (*Pr.* at Sabridgforde 14 Dec. 1579).

f. 286. WILLIAM ROGERSON of Standon, milner. (*Dat.* 27 Sept. 1579). Wife Agnes; Sons Robert & Wm.; Dau. Eden wife of John Daniele; Dau. Mary wife of Antoine Eive; Dau. Kath. wife of Wm. Sigrave gent.; Kath. Daniele dau. of s^d son-in-law John Daniell; Wife extrix; M^r Romayne vicar of Standon supervisor. Wits:—Hughe Bowman, Robt. Bate & Roger Thomson. (*Pr.* 19 Nov. 1579).

f. 288. AUGUSTINE COWPER of Barkewaye, in the Countie of Essex [*sic*] malster. (*Dat.* 19 Aug. 1579). Henrie Peppercorne; M^r Johns; Land between Thorpes close now Richard Roystons on the south & Grayes meade on the north, the east end abutting on Willowes meade; Brother's son Mathewe Cowper; Child^n of Henrie Chapman of Barley & of John Kinge of Barrington; My brothers daus.; Said Matt. Cowper exor. Wits:—Rich. Royston, Philip Womwell, Wm. Warde, Nich^s Powell. (*Pr.* at Sabridgforde 11 Sep. 1579).

f. 291. JOHN LAMBERDE of Sabridgworthe, joiner. (*Dat.* 7 Mch. 1578). Eldest son Edward (under 21); Youngest son Richard; Dau. Grace Lamberde; Wife Alice extrix; Gabriel Lenthrope gent. and Wm. Spencer yeoman overseers. Wits:—Wm. Perrie, Tho. Curtys and Rich. Spencer. (*Pr.* at Sabridgworth 1 Apr. 1579).

*To be Continued.*

# Inquisitiones Post Mortem.

## HENRY GRUBBE.
[*Inq. p.m. 3 & 4 Phil. & Mary. 2nd part. No 82.*]

Inquisition taken at Bysshoppe Hatfelde, co. Herts. 13 July 2 & 4 Philip & Mary [1556] before Robert Harrys esq, escheator, after the death of Henry Grubbe, by the oaths of John James, Geo. Marston, Thos. Roberds, Rich. Birchemore, John Tompson, John Barnarde, Robt. Norres, John Cutt, John Foster, John Mosse, John Howe, John Whitfelde, Robt. Sene & Roger Nodes who say that

The said Henry Grubbe was seised as of fee in the Rectory and Church of Northmymes with the appurtenances, also three messuages & 200 acres of land, pasture meadow & wood in Northmymes & all tithes belonging to the said Rectory & the advowson & right of patronage of the vicarage of Northmymes.

So seised said Henry by deed dated [*blank*] 36 Hen. VIII sold to one Richard Grubbe two messuages, 60 acres of land & 20 acres of pasture in Northmymes, parcel of said Rectory then in tenure of Geo. Slepe & said Richard is now in possession thereof.

Said Henry died 8th May last.

The said Rectory & other premises are held of the King & Queen in chief, by service of the twentieth part of a knights fee & a rent of 8s. 8d. per annum & are worth 4l. 5s. 4d. per ann.

George Grubbe is son & heir & aged 30 years & more.

## GEORGE GRUBBE.
[*Inq. p.m. 19 Eliz. 1st part. No. 110.*]

Inquisition taken at Busshoppes Hatfield *alias* Kingshatfield, co. Herts. 5 June 19 Eliz. [1577] before John Brockett knt, Wm. Tooke esq, auditor of the Court of Wards & Liveries, Henry Connysbye esq & Walter Tooke gent. etc. after the death of George Grubbe, yeoman, by the oaths of Edw. Brisco, John Brisco, John Thompson, John Haddon, Thos. Adam, Clement Manustie, John Clerke de le Beche, Tho. Nicholl, Thos. Samonde, Edw. Smythe, John Astrey, Rich. [? Cr]ofte, Humph. Haywarde, John Clerke de Harpesfieldhall, Philip Sleape & Wm. Smith of Threehowses who say that

Long before the death of sd George, one Henry Grubbe his father was seised as of fee in the Rectory & Church of North Myms & in 3 messuages, 200 acres of land & all tithes belonging to sd Rectory & the advowson of the vicarage & sd Henry so seised by indenture dated 36 Hen. VIII. & by the royal licence sold to one Rich. Grubbe, two messuages & 60 acres of land in North Myms, parcel of sd Rectory, then in tenure of Geo. Slepe. Thus seised sd Henry died 8 May 2 & 3 Phil. & Mary, after whose death sd Rectory etc descended to sd George as son & next heir which Geo. on the 13 July 2 & 3 Phil. & Mary was 30 years old & more.

Said George thus seised of all sd Rectory & lands except as above mentioned on 26 Mch. 1577 (Eliz. 19) at North Mymes made his will [*recited*] by virtue of which Dorothy his wife now holds one third part of s^d Rectory & lands.

Said Rectory & premises are held of the Queen in chief by service of the twentieth part of a knights fee & rent of 8s. 8d. per ann. & are worth (deducting 10l. for salary of the vicar there) 5l. per ann. clear.

George Grubbe died ——— March last past & Eustace Grubb is son & next heir & aged 26 years 11 months & 29 days & more at the time of taking this inquisition.

## EUSTACE GRUBB.

[*Inq. p.m.* 21 *Car. I. part* 18 *Miscel.* No 37].

Inquisition taken at S^t Albans, co. Herts 11 July 20 Car. I. [1644] before John Tooke esq, escheator, after the death of Eustace Grubb gent, by the oaths of Wm. Smith, Rich. Mitchell, Wm. Marston, Jas. Arnold, John Dell, Solomon Trott, Rich. Sheppard, Rich. Feild, Robt. Newe, John Beldon. Joshua Bayley, Wm. Hinksman, John Cooper & Edw. Paupett who say that

Said Eustace was seised in fee of the Rectory & Church of Northmyms & all & every the tithes annually arising therefrom & of 3 messuages, 200 acres of land, meadow, pasture & wood in Northmyms belonging to s^d Rectory & the advowson of the vicarage. Said Eustace was also seised of a messuage called Redhall & 80 acres of arrable & pasture land & a cottage with a pightell of land, parcel of s^d Rectory, lying in Northmyms & a messuage called Densham & 2 acres belonging thereto in Northmyms.

So seised s^d Eustace & John Grubb his son & heir apparent by indenture dated 19 May 10 Jas. I [1612] & a fine levied in court, conveyed to one Robt. Hattley & Giles Blofeild gent, the s^d Rectory of Northmyms & all belonging thereto in Northmyms to the intent that Mary Preston dau. of Wm. Preston of Chilwicke in s^d county, gent. whom s^d John Grubb then intended to marry & afterwards did marry, should have to her & her asigns an annual rent of 100l out of s^d Rectory etc. during her life if she should survive s^d John Grubb & further that s^d Robert Hattley & Giles Blofeild should stand seised of s^d Rectory etc. to the use of s^d Eustace for life with remainder to the use of s^d John Grubb & his heirs male by s^d Mary Preston & in default to the use of the heirs of the body of s^d John etc.

So seised s^d Eustace died at Northmyms on 28 May 18 Chas. I [1642] & s^d John is son & next heir of s^d Eustace & was at the time of s^d Eustace's death aged 21 years & more.

The Rectory of Northmyms & the advowson of the vicarage are held of the King in chief by knights service viz. by the service of the 20th part of a knights fee & annual rent of 8s. 8d. & worth, clear, (deducting 10l. per annum for the salary of the vicar there) 5l. per ann.

The messuage called Redhall & lands are held of the king in chief by knights service, but by what part of a knights fee the jurors are ignorant, & are worth per ann. clear 13s. 4d.

The message called Densham etc. the jurors are ignorant how or of whom held.

# Rowlett Wills.

### RALPH ROWLETT.
[*P.C.C. Spert* 17.]

In the name of god amen, The xvj<sup>th</sup> day of February In the xxxiiij<sup>th</sup> yere of the Reigne of our soueraigne Lord King Henry the Eight, I Raufe Rowlett thelder Esquier marchaunt of the Staple of Caleys, being of god and parfite remembraunce, lawde and prayse be vnto almighty god, make and declare this my p'nt will and testament in maner and fo<sup>r</sup>me folowyng that is to saye First I bequethe my soule vnto almighty god, my saviour maker and Redemer and to his glorious and most blissid mother our lady saint mary ever virgyn and to all the holy Company of heaven and my body to be buried yf it chaunse to be a place convenient for buriall in our lady chapell within the late monastery of saint Albons where my wife lyeth and my sonne And yf the same shalbe noo suche place mete for buriall Than I will my body to be buried within the Chapell of saint Andrewe, by the discrecion of my executors. Item. I bequeth to the highe awter of the said Chapell of saint Andrewe xiijs. iiijd. Item. I bequeth to the highe awter of saint Mighells xiijs. iiijd. Item. I will geve and bequethe every weke wekely In the Wensday and Friday Twenty shilling*f* sterling*f* egally to be devided to and among*f* the poure people within the said Albons where most nede shalbe to pray for my soule and all xpen soules and to saye fyve tymes the holy prayour of the pater noster, fyve tymes the Salutacion of our lady called Ave maria &c. and oon tyme Tharticles of our faithe callid Credo in Deum &c. in hono<sup>r</sup> of the fyve woundes of our lord Jhu Criste, vntill the sume of fourscore pound*f* sterling*f* be gevyn distributed and delte of in and abowte the same. And further I will that the said fourscore pound*f* sterling*f* be deliuered to the handes of Sir Richard Stondon priest to distribute and geve it in maner and fourme aforesaid. Item I will that there be distributed at my buriall and at my monethis mynde and for blak clothe for my wife my doughters the mourners and for my seruant*f* fourscore pound*f*. Item I will and bequethe to an honest prest to say diuine seruice and to pray for my soule my frend*f* soules and all xpen soules at suche place where my body shalbe buried yerely during the space of Tenne yeres next ensuyng after my decesse Six pound*f* xiijs. iiijd. Sm. threscore six pound*f* xijs. iiijd. Item I will that myn Executours do yerely distribute and dispose during the space of Tenne yeres next and Immediatly folowing after my decesse for and aboute oon Anniu'sary or obite yerely, at suche place, where it shall fortune me to be buried to pray for my soule and all xpen soules xxs. Sm. x<sup>li</sup>. Item I bequethe and geve to my welbeloued wife these parcell*f* folowing that is to say all Jewell*f* as do belonge to hir for hir wearyng and asmoche of my plate suche as she will choese as shall amounte to the sume of xxx<sup>li</sup>. deliuered w<sup>t</sup> his owne handes and Twenty poundes deliuered w<sup>t</sup> his owne hand*f* xl<sup>i</sup>. in redy money, she to do therw<sup>t</sup> her hole will and pleasure as with hir own propre goodes and Catall*f*. And that my said wife shalhaue thuse and occupying of all suche housholdestuffe as shall remayn and be in my dwelling howse at saint Albons at the tyme of my decesse. And that my said wife leave the same at the tyme of her decesse to my sonne Rauf Rowlet w'out embeselyng spoyling or wasting thereof, by her or any other in her name. The reasonable wearyng therof always exceptid vpon condicion that she clayme or take noo dower or any other estate, for terme of lyfe in any other my landes and tenementℓ, than suche londs and ten'tℓ as I haue gevyn hir by my wille. Item I bequethe to sir John Baker knyght a Cupp of siluer and gilt price v*li*. Item I bequethe to Martyn Bowes knyght a Cup of siluer and gilt price v*li*. Item I bequeth to Barnard Jennyn, skynner of London, a Cup of siluer and gilt price v*li*. Item I bequeth to Thomas Skipwith Esquier a Cup of siluer and gilt price v*li*. Item I bequeth to Franceℓ Goodyere Esquier a Cup of siluer and gilt price v*li*. Item I bequeth to John Maynard gent a Cup of siluer and gilt price v*li*. Item I bequeth to sir Richard Stondon clerk a Cup of siluer and gilt price v*li*. Item I bequeth to my sonne Affabell goddℓ blessing and myn and the lease and terme of yeres whiche I haue to come of and in the parsonage of Redborne in the countie of Hertford. Item I bequeth to the said Affabell my sonne the Tythe of Henry Bechys ferme wherin he nowe dwellith. Item I bequeth to the said Affabell all the Store of Gorhambury that is to say, Shepe, Beestℓ, Kyne, Horsse, Carte and all the Tymbr and selyng bourde and pale, hooly as it standith at the houre of my dethe. Item I will and geve him the Implementℓ of the house of Gorh'mbury aforsaid as shall appere by an Inuentory theeof to be made, by my sonne Jennyns and my sonne Skipwith. Item I geve and bequethe to the said Affabell a Cupp of siluer gilted, a gilt Salt and xij Spones of siluer. Item I geve and bequeth to Rauf Rowlett my sonne and heire apparaunte goddeℓ blessing and myn and oon hundrethe poundℓ in redy money. Item I geve and bequeth to Dorathe Rowlett his wife a gilt Cupp w$^t$ flowres, to the value of x*li*. and in Redy money fourty markℓ. Item I geve to the said Dorathe a Ryng of golde with an Emerawde in it. Item I will that all my apparell be devided bitwene my said twoo sonnes indifferently. Item I geve and bequethe to John Maynard my sonne in lawe in recompence of his marriage fourty and fyve poundℓ. Item I geve and bequethe egally to be devided bitwene Rauf Jennyn my godsonne, the Childern of Thomas Latham, the Childern of Thomas Skipwithe, the Childern of John Maynard, the Childern of Fraunces Goodyere my sonnes in lawe, that they haue or shalhave by my doughters twoo Thousande markℓ egally to be devided as euery of theym shall attayne to their mariages or full agis. And further I will that if any of them dye before they be maried or come to their full age, that then I will that that parte so to them gyven be devided gevyn and deliuered to them that over lyvith in fourme aforsaid. Provided always that my sonne Skipwith and his executours shall haue and receyve of myn Exeutours the sume of oon hundreth markℓ vpon the premisses before gevyn vnto his Childern and vpon the payment of the same he to deliuer vnto Raufe Rowlett my sonne oon obligacon for the payment of oon hnndreth m'kℓ wherin I stande bounde to be discharged and cancelled. Item I give and bequeth to my sonne Thomas Latham oon Cupp of siluer to the value of v*li*. Item I will that my wife haue twoo of my geldyngℓ such as she will chose, And the Residue of my horsses I geve and bequethe to my sonne Rauf Rowlett and Affabell indifferently to be devided. Item I geve to my seruantℓ William

Harres, William Ambler, Richard Padbery and Robert Baker, euery of them xxs. and to Robert Holland, Rowlande, Thomas Saunders, Nicholas Horskeper, Thomas Tyler and William Cook euery of them xs. and to Alice Shelton xls. and to Mawe my seruant xxs. and to mother Roose xs. and to the Rest of all my seruantƟ I will there be gevyn xls. at the ditcrecion of myn executors. Item I will that my sonne Rauf Rowlett shalhaue the housholde stuffe in my Chamber at London. Item I will that myn Executours shalbe accountant for all suche sumes of money as they shall Receyve. Item I will that my wife shalhaue the Custodye and occupacion of a Chalesse, a pair of CruettƟ a paire of CandelstickƟ of siluer, one pax of Ivery garnysshed with siluer during hir lyfe. And after hir decesse I geve them to my sonne Affabell Rowlett wt all other my ornaments belonging to my aulter at my house in saint Albons. Item I will that my Executors shalhaue all suche reasonable costƟ as they and eu'y of them shall dispende in and aboute the pfourmaunce and mayntenance of my last will. Item I will all suche goodes as shall happen to be at Gorh'mbury that were ordeyned vsed and appoynted to be at my howse at saint Albons for the apparylinge of the same shalbe deliuered by my Executours maynten'nt after my deathe, at the said house of saint Albons, there to remayne according to my will. Item I geve and bequeth to Alice Calowaye and her husbande either of them a blak gowne. Item I will and geve to Maister Kyng vicar of saint MighellƟ in saint Albons oon blak gowne of iiij yardƟ and a hoode. The Residue of all my goodes not bequethed my dettƟ paid my funerall expencƟ borne and doon And the legacies in this my p'nt testament conteyned performed and fulfilled I geve and bequethe to Sir Martyn Bowes knyght, Barnard Jenyns Skynner of London and Thomas Skipwithe Esquier whom I ordeyn and make my Executours they to ordre and dispoase the same as by their discrecions shalbe thought conuenient for my soule helthe. And I make Sir Richard Stondon priest my supuisour to whom I geve for their labours [blank]. Also I do Renounce and vtterly forsake all other willƟ made before the day and date of these presentƟ and they to be adnychillate and voide. In witnesse wherof etc. Wits:—Rauf Rowlett the yonger, Sir Richard Stondon Clerk, Thomas Kyng vicar of saint MighellƟ, Hugh Hardyng vicar at Sandryche, Robert Holland, Rowland Griffith and John Brumbrogh.

Ultima voluntas ejusdem Radulphi.

This is the last will of me Raufe Rowlett thelder Esquier made the xvjth day of February In the xxxiiijti yere of the Reigne of our soueraigne lord King Henry the Eight concernyng the order and disposicion of all my Manours landes TenementƟ and hereditamentƟ hereafter named expressid and declared First I will geve assigne bequeth and devise vnto Elizabeth my wife all that my Manor of Sandryge *alias* Sandruge with all other my landƟ and tenementƟ within the parishe of Sandryge *alias* Sandruge wt the appurten'ncƟ in the Countie of Hertford And all my landƟ tenementƟ and hereditamentƟ whiche haue ben knowen letten to ferme reputed or taken as parte parcell or membre of the said Manour or of any parte or parcell of it All the woddes stewardship and profitƟ of the CourtƟ of the same oonly except To haue and to holde all the said Manor londes tenementƟ and other the premisses wt their appurten'ncƟ except before excepted vnto the said Elizabeth my wife and hir assignes during and by the holo terme of her naturall lyfe vpon condicion that she clayme or take no dower or any other estate for terme of lyfe in any other londᵉ or tenementᵉ than suche londᵉ and tenementᵉ as I haue gevyn her by my will And I will and ordeyn that Immediately after the deceas of my wife the said Manour londes tenrmentᵉ and other the premisses wᵗ their appurten'ncᵉ shall goo bee and Remayn vnto myn Executours To haue and to holde to them during and by the hole terme of xxjᵗʰ yeres next after the decesse of my said wife my said executors to pᵉeyve receyve and take the Issues Reuenues and profiᵉ comyng and growyng of the said Manoʳ and other the premisses for and towardᵉ the payment of my dettᵉ and to and for the payment of twoo Thousande markᵉ in my testament mencioned and to the perfourmaunce and fulfillyng of my legacᵉ and bequestᵉ as well in my foresaid Testament of this my last will as otherwise expressed and declared And further I will the Manoʳ of Appysbury *alias* Apsabury & all other the londes ten'tᵉ and hereditaments which haue ben knowen letten to ferme reputed or taken as parte pᵉell or membre of the said Manoʳ or any parte or parcell therof with all the woddes groves hedgerowes and spryngᵉ whiche are growyng or hereafter shall growe of in and vpon the said Manoʳ of Sandryge *al.* Sandruge & vpon all other my londes and fermes within the parishe of Sandryge aforsaid my said Executors to fell and cutt downe the same at their will and pleasure wᵗ all the fynes Issues perquysitᵉ & all other profitᵉ of Courtᵉ (the Tymber vpon the premisses oonly except) shall goo be & remayn vnto myn Executoʳs To haue & to holde to them Immediately after my decesse to thende and terme of Twenty and oon yeres to pᵉeyve receyve and take the Issues Revenues and profitᵉ comyng & growyng of the said manoʳ and other the premises for & towardᵉ the payment of my dettᵉ & to & for the paymᵗ of twoo Thousand merkᵉ in my testament mencyoned & to the pᵉourmaunce and fulfilling of my last wille And after my dettᵉ legacies and bequestᵉ well and truely contentid and paid than I will that all & singuler the said Manours londes & tenementᵉ & other the premisses wᵗ their appurten'ncᵉ shall holy and fully go be and remayn in fourme folowing that is to sey The Manoʳ of Sandryge *alias* Sandruge and all other my londᵉ and tenementᵉ within the parishe of Sandruge aforsaid with the premisses concernyng the same vnto Raufe Rowlett the yonger my sonne and heire apparaunte & to the Issue of his body laufully begotten foreuer And the Manoʳ of Appysbury *al.* Apsabury & all other the premisses concernyng the same shall remayn and come to Dorathe Rowlett my doughter for terme of hir life To remayne after that to Raufe Rowlett my sonne and to the Issue of his body laufully begotten And for defawte of suche Issue to remayn to Affabell Rowlett & to the Issue of his body lawfully begotten And for defawte of suche Issue all the said landᵉ & tenementᵉ & other the premisses wᵗ the appurten'ncᵉ to Remayn to my doughters & doughters Childern & their heires for euer Provided alwayes I will & ordeyn that Elizabeth my wife shalhaue sufficient fuell for her expencᵉ of in & vpon the Manoʳ of Sandryge *alias* Sandruge during her lyfe to be appoynted and assigned vnto her by the discrecions of myn Executors or by the Executours of the overlyuer of them Also I will assigne bequethe and geve vnto Elizabethe my wife my dwelling howse in saint Albons To haue and to holde to her for terme of hir naturall lyfe And also I geve and bequethe all my Copyholde londᵉ and tenementᵉ in the parishe of Redborne and all my Copylondᵉ that I bought of Mʳ Berney of Langley late Marstons and a howse at Bednam ponde with all the londᵉ that apperteyn to them and euery of them to my sonne Affabell

Rowlett and his heires foreuer. Item I will that William Ambler my seru'nt shalhaue the howse he dwellithe in freely during his lyfe. Item I will that the said Wilfm shalhaue ffourty shillingȝ by the yere to be paid to him by thandȝ of myn Executours during his lyfe to be levyed and taken out of the premisses. Item I will that William Harres my seru'nt shalhaue the howse he dwellithe in freely during his lyfe. Item I will that my wife shalhaue during her lyfe the howse wherein oon Palmer dwellith yf she do so longe dwell and contynue at Gorhambury. Item I will that Padbery my seru'nt shalhaue the howse he dwellith in freely during his lyfe. Item I will that if my sonne Raufe Rowlett or his heires or assignes by his comaundement or procurement doo trouble molest or sue in the lawe or otherwise myn Executours for the Receyte and taking of the profitȝ of the Manor of Sondryge *alias* Sandruge and Apsbury *alias* Apsabury and other the premisses or any parte therof with the appurten'ncȝ gevyn and sett forth by this my will That then I will that after my will pfourmed and hoolly fulfilled myn executours that shall happen to lyve shall Receyve and take the moytie of the profitȝ of the said Manors of Sandryge *alias* Sandruge and Apsbury *alias* Apsabury during their lyves and the longer lyver of them to their owne vse and profite. Also I do Renounce and vtterly forsake all other willȝ concernyng my londȝ and ten'tȝ made before the day and date of these presentȝ and they to be adnychillate and voyde. In witness whereof etc. Per me Rauf Rowlatt thelder. [Witnesses as before]. *Proved* 12 March 1542 by Thos. Skipwith; reservation to Sir Martin Bowes & Bernard Jenyns.

## AMPHABELL ROWLETT.

[*P.C.C. Alen 22.*]

In the name of God amen the xviij<sup>th</sup> day of Aprill in the xxxvij<sup>th</sup> yere of the Raign of owr soveraign Lord King Henry theight, I Amphabell Rowlett Esquyer being of good and perfitt remembrance, laud and prayse be to almighty god make ordeyn and declare this my present will and testament in manner and forme folowing that is to say first I bequeathe my soule vnto almighty god my maker sauiour and Redemer and to his gloryous and most blessed mother our lady sainct Mary ever virgyn and all the hole company of hevyn my body to be buryed where my brother Rowlett shall think good. Item I gyve to the high aulter of Digonswell for my tythes negligently forgoten iijs. iiijd. Item I will there be bestowed in and vpon my funerallȝ five markȝ at the discrecion of my said brother. Item I give to my dere and welbeloued wif thies parcellȝ folowing that is to say all such Juellȝ as doo belong to her for her wering and xvj<sup>li</sup> in redy money, she to doo therwith her hole will and pleas<sup>r</sup> as wyth her proper goodes and cattellȝ and that my said wif shalhaue the houshold stuff and store at the house of Digonswell which were of the goodes of Thomas Peryent Esquyer deceased after such rate and rates as they be praysed in his Inuentary, corne lyme tymber and lath alweys except. And further shall haue x q<sup>r</sup>ters of malt vij acres of otes in the personage grounde and all my wheate at Digonswell and two ambling geldingȝ one white thother gray yong vpon condicion that she clayme or take no dower or any other estate for terme of liff in any of my copy hold landes. And then suche goodes as are before remembred being the goodes of my late father Peryent I will my brother shall answere vnto the heires of my foresayd father Peryent as I shuld haue don in all cases according to the true purporte and tenor of his sayd last will and testament and my sayd wif to have them without any thing paing for them. Item I give to my loving suster Dorothee Peryent a black gowne and foure mrkℯ for her diligent payne taken in my sickenes. Item I give my vncle Willyam Peryent a gowne faced with satten. Item to Robert Battell my best cote. Item to Willyam Battell my chamlett Jackett. Item to John Lockey my tawny satten dublett. Item to Wymbushe my secound cote. Item to my brother Skypwyth a dublett cloth of satten. Item to my welbeloued suster Rowlett a ryng of fyne gold weing ls. Item I give my dere beloved and most faythfull brother Rowlett my leases of Redborne tythe To haue and enjoy the same during the yeres yet to come. Item I gyve my said brother Rowlett all my goodes stock and store belonging to my house of Gorhambury and also I gyve him my velvett Jackett my best gowne my gowne of wursted and a furr of soynes and all other my apparell not before bequethed. Item I give to my sayd brother Rowlett two hundreth poundes of money whiche I haue payde vnto the executours of my father Rowlett for the leases of Redborne and the stock and store at Gorhambury whiche was bequethed me by my father's last will and testament. Item I gyve my sayd brother xj/i. vijs. whiche I payd for certen apparell likewise. Also I gyve him all suche plate as is bequethed me in the same my father's last will and testament. Item I gyve to Deix and Edward my serunt besides their wages eche of them xxs. Item to Chrophor Sympson, Mergery and Cicely my seru'ntℯ besides their wages eche of them xs. The Resedue of all my goodes not bequethed my dettℯ payd my funerall expenses borne and don and the legacyes in this my present testament performed I gyve and bequethe to my brother Rowlett whom I ordeyne and make my soule executor he to order and dispose the same as by his discrecion shalbe thought convenyent for my soules health. In witness etc. Per me Amphabell Rowlett. Witˢ:—Robert Battell, Willyam Battell, Edward Squyer. *Proved* 23 Oct. 1546 by Ralph Rowlett esq. the exor.

*To be Continued.*

# Feet of Fines for Hertfordshire.

**TUDOR PERIOD.**

(Continued from Page 82.)

1572. Easter Term. 14 Eliz.

*John Goodwyn knt : Thos. Sandes gent & Robt. Sandes gent & Anne his wife. A third part of 10 messuages & lands in Agmondesham.

*Rich. Warde esq : Daniel Snowe esq. Manor of Pychelesthorne & 3 messuages & lands in Pychelesthorne, Chedington & Eldesborowghe.

*Innocent Rede esq & Francis Sills gent : John Robyns. Three messuages & lands in Cadington & Kensworth.

*Wm. Cooper sen$^r$ : Wm. Cooper jun$^r$ & Alice his wife. Lands in Caddington & Kensworthe.

John Rumbold : Wm. Clopton esq, Tho. Horseman esq, Margt. Tharolde widow, Robt Savill esq & Anne his wife, John Massingberd & Dorothy his wife. Manor of Tolmer *als* Tollmer in Newgett Strete *als* Newgatt strete & messuage & lands in Bishops Hatfield & Newgett Strete.

Nich$^s$ Bristowe sen esq : Wm. Clopton esq, Thos. Horseman esq, Margt. Tharold widow, Robt. Savill esq & Anne his wife & John Massingberd & Dorothy his wife. Manor of Laurence Ayot *alias* Great Ayot & lands in Laurence Ayot *als* Great Ayot, Kimpton, Sandridge, Codicote, Whetehamsted, Welwyn, Wymley, Willyon, Radwell, Ashwell, Newnham, Stevenage, Knebworthe, Huchyn, Walden, Hatfield, S$^t$ Albans & Ayot Mountphichet & the advowson of the psh. church of Laurence Ayot.

John Wakeman gent : Rich. Lee knt, Humph. Conningesbye esq & Mary his wife. Manor of Newlande *alias* Nova terra & 30 messuages & lands in the parishes of S$^t$ Albans, S$^t$ Andrews, S$^t$ Michaels, S$^t$ Stephens & Idlestre.

Rich. Lee knt, Humph. Coningesbye esq & Mary his wife & Edw. Sadler esq & Anne his wife : Henry Butler esq & Alice his wife. The Rectory of the church of Hexton & advowson of same.

Robt. Stepneth esq : John Stepneth gent & Anne his wife. Manor of Aldenham & messuages & lands in Aldenham & the rectory of Aldenham.

Wm. Barlee & John Bell gents : John Bosgrave gent & Jane his wife & Henry Giles & Agnes his wife. Lands in Ashewell.

Wm. Browne : Tho. Grave & Agnes his wife. Lands in Hadham *alias* Hadam.

Robt. Watson : Rich. Philpott gent. & Eliz. his wife. Messuage & lands in Buntingford, Apsten and Laiston.

Wm. Cecill knt. baron of Burghley : Edw. Baesshe esq & Jane his wife. Messuage & lands in Waltham Crosse in psh. of Chesthunt.

Tho. Weeden : John Woodroffe *alias* Andrewes & Alice his wife. Messuage & land in Stondon.

Michael Meade & Eliz. his wife: Francis Roberts gent. Two messuages & lands in Ware, Great Amwell & Little Amwell.

John Cranfeld & Alice his wife: John Byrchley gent. & Phillippa his wife. Messuage in psh. of St Nichs in Hertford.

Francis Alley gent: Roger Grubbe & Eliz. his wife. A toft & land in Barkhamsted St Peter.

Thos. Hanchett esq & Rich. Chare: Tho. Bumpsted & Eliz. his wife. Lands in Great Munden.

Thos. Warden: Rich. Worland & Joan his wife. Land in Standen.

Wm. Chalkley: Valentine Knyghte alias Brother. Messuage & land in Crechemere, Offley & Kings Walden.

### 1572. Trinity Term. 14 Eliz.

Ralph Cadwell: Thos. Rocheford & Ellen his wife. Messuage in Baldock.

Edw. Baeshe esq & Jane his wife: Walter earl of Essex & Wm. Garnett gent. Manor of Cosyns & two messuages & lands in Ware, Wadesmyll, Great Amwell & Stanstede Abbots.

Geo. Clarke: Rich. Whyttyngstall alias Whittenstall & Eliz. his wife. Messuage & lands in Walcorne.

John Wykes & Kath. his wife: Wm. Penton & Eliz. his wife. Messuage in Hatfield.

Michael Meade: Wm. Geldener & Anne his wife & Wm. James gent & Joan his wife. Messuage & lands in Great Amwell, Little Amwell, & Alhallowes & common of pasture for seven cows in Nethenhowe marshe in Great Amwell.

Fulk Onslowe & Mary his wife: John Wykes & Kath. his wife & Wm. Penton & Eliz. his wife. Messuage in Hatfield.

Wm. Garnett gent: Walter earl of Essex. Manor of Watersplace & 6 messuages & lands in Ware, Wadesmyll, Great Amwell & Stanstede Abbots.

Rich. Ferrers & Anthony Stibbyng gents: Francis Ferrers gent & John Vyneyarde gent & Kath. his wife. Manor of Hallys & 6 messuages & lands in the town of St Albans, Sandryge & 'infra Socam de Parke' in psh. of St Peters.

Charles Moryson: Francis Haydon esq. & Frances his wife. Land in Watford.

Geo. Golde & Joan his wife: Rich. Longe & Eliz. his wife. Messuage in Watford.

Henry Dighton: Rich. Draper & Agnes his wife. Messuage in psh. of All Saints in Hertford.

Leonard Jebson son & heir of Clement Jebson decd: Joan Chambers widow. Messuage in Little Gaddesden.

Geo. Burgoyne esq: Henry Barkley knt, lord Berkley of Mowbray, Segrave & Bruce. Manor of Weston alias Weston juxta Baldock, & 40 messuages & lands in Weston.

### 1572. Mich Term. 14 & 15 Eliz.

*Henry lord Norrys of Rycott & John Goodwyn knt: Rich. Wenman knt. & Isabel his wife. Manor of Beckonsfeild & 120 messuages & lands in Beckonsfeild.

Leonard Chaundeler: Edm. Twynyho esq & Eliz. his wife. Lands in Benington.

John Cade gent: Thos. Conygesbye esq. Messuage & lands in Aldenham.

Jasper Wryghte: Thos. Gladwyn & Jane his wife. Messuage in Pelham Furnax.

Clement Manestee: John Harmar & Alice his wife. A third part of a messuage in Welwyn.
Robt. Wolley: John Shadd & Margt. his wife. Messuage in St Albans.
Nichs. Johnson: Thos. Sympson & Margt. his wife. Moiety of a messuage & land in St Albans.
John Kympton: Simon Warren. Six messuages & lands in Hytchyn.
Thos. Blocke: Rich. Adam & Alice his wife. Messuage & land in Tuyeng.
Alexr. Chauncy gent: Robt. Brooke. Two messuages & lands in Sabrydgeworth.
Geo. Santon *alias* Mathewe: Henry Sommersham & Eliz. his wife, & John Jerdfelde. Two messuages in Stortford.
Edw. Hyckeman & Agnes his wyfe: Wm. Barley gent. Messuage & land in Gustedwood & Whethamstede.
Rich. Bovyngdon & Kath. his wife: Robt. Nasshe & Margt. his wife. Messuage & lands in Agmondesham.
Nichs. Brokett & Edw. Bowghton esqrs: Thos. Hoo esq. Manor of Hooburye *alias* Hoo & 8 messuages & lands in Powles Walden *alias* Abbots Walden & Kympton *alias* Kempton.
Wm. Parker sen.r: John Chauncye & Eliz. his wife. Manor of Overhall & 10 messuages & lands in Geddleston, Estwick, Hunsdon & Sabridgeworth.
John Williams & Kath. his wife: Henry Baldewyne & Anne his wife. Messuage & land in St Albans.
Simon Ewer gent.: Thos. Bellamy gent. & Kath. his wife. Moiety of a messuage & land in Great Munden.
Rich. Barnett: Wm. Morynge & Christian his wyfe. Messuage & land in Barkhampstead Peter.
Nichs. Johnson: Ranulph Spyggyns. Moiety of messuage & land in St Albans.
John Adam: Rich. Adam & Alice his wife. Messuage & land in Datchworth.
Thos. Allen: Wm. Allen & Agnes his wife. Messuage & lands in Tryng, Betlowe, Marson & Tyscote.
Roger Stokes: Roger Stoughton & Mary his wife, & Henry Dowman & Margt. his wife. Messuage & lands in parishes of St Michaels & St Stephens near St Albans.
John Alley gent.: Wm. Bacheler & Joan his wife. Lands in Barkhamsted.
John Cawley: John Horton gent. & Mary his wife. Messuage & lands in Estbrokehaye & Hemelhamstede.
Roger Farthinge & Mary his wife: Rich. Worland & Joan his wife. Messuage & land in Stondon.
[*This fine is tied up in mistake with the bundle for the following Mich. term*].

### 1572-3. Hilary Term. 15 Eliz.

*Francis Hinde esq, Thos. Hinde & Robt. Shutte gents: Nichs West esq & Joan his wife & Wm. West son & heir apparent of sd Nich. Two messuages & lands in Ashwell.
*Christr. Cowper: Wimond Cary esq. Lands in Bishops Stortford.
Nichs Barfoote: Henry Ednam & Eliz. his wife & John Barfoote & Joan his wife. Cottage in Hitchyn.
Jeremy Gray: Wimond Cary. Three messuages in Stortford.
Edm. Knott: Edw. Brokett esq & Etheldreda his wife. Messuage & lands in Hichin, Ickleford & Walsworth.

Rich. Marshe : Thos. Marshe. Manor of Sowches *alias* Caddington Sowches & messuage & lands in Cadington.

Wm. Cecil. K.G., baron of Burghley, High Treasurer of England : Geo. Penruddocke knt & Anne his wife, Thos. Wrothe knt & Mary his wife & Henry Cocke esq. Manor of Beamonthall & 2 messuages & lands in Beamonthall, Wormeley & Cheston.

John Spurlyng & John Graveley gents : Geo. Nycolls & Hamond Nycolls. Moiety of two messuages & lands in Asshewell *alias* Ashewell & Henxworthe.

Andrew Byll & Eliz. his wife : Ivo Gray gent. Messuage & lands in Asshewell.

Hugh Mantell gent : Rich. Lee knt., Humph. Connyngsbye gent & Mary his wife & Robt. Lee gent. Three messuages & lands in S<sup>t</sup> Albans.

### 1573. Easter Term. 15 Eliz..

*Rich. Rede knt : Fras. Sill & Wm. Cocke. Manor of Pepshull *alias* Pepshall & the site of the late Priory of Redborne & 20 messuages & lands in Redborne, Flamsted, Harpenden & the psh. of S<sup>t</sup> Michaels.

*Wm. Cecill, K.G. baron of Burghley etc. : Edw. Baeshe esq & Jane his wife. Manor of Cullings & 12 messuages & lands in Chesehunt & Walthamcrosse.

Rich. Foster : John Shawarden esq. Moiety of manor of Datcheworthe & of 20 messuages & lands in Dacheworthe *alias* Datcheworthe *alias* Thatcheworthe.

Wm. Snowe : John Dowsette & Joan his wife. Two messuages in Stortford.

Edw. Beash esq & Jane his wife : Wm. Garnett gent & Margery his wife. Manor of Cosens & 8 messuages & lands in Ware, Wadesmyll, Great Amwell, Stansted Abbott & Thunderich.

James Whitlom *alias* Barbor : Barnabas Sparrowe. Five messuages & five gardens in Stortford.

Wm. Napton & John Sare : John Done [? Doue] & Joan his wife. Two messuages and land in the borough of S<sup>t</sup> Albans & in the psh. of S<sup>t</sup> Michaels.

Wm. Thorowgood : Geo. Bennett & Ellen his wife. Land in Amwell.

Robt. Warner & Christr. Thurgood : Rich. Wathe & Alice his wife, Thos. Wett & Joan his wife. Two messuages in Cheshunt.

Robt. Awsopp & Margt. his wife : Wm. Swynowe clerk & Eliz. his wife *alias* Eliz. Turner one of the daus. & coheirs of John Turner dec<sup>d</sup>. Moiety of a messuage & land in Storteford.

Geo. Dell : John Clarke & Alice his wife & Humph. Taverner & Ellen his wife. Two messuages & land in Bishops Hatfeld *alias* Kings Hatfield.

Thos. Sadlier esq & Ralph Baesh gent : Wm. Garnett gent. & Margery his wife. Manor of Waters place & 4 messuages & lands in Ware.

Paul Pope : Rich. Skipwith esq son & heir apparent of Wm. Skipwith knt. Manor of Beachewood *alias* Seynt Gyles in the Wood & 3 messuages & lands in Beachewood.

Wm. Revett : Steph. Creke gent & Olave his wife & Rich. Overton gent. & Guthlac Cordall clerk. Manor of Myckelfeild *alias* Mychelfeild *alias* Myckelfeild Hall & 3 messuages & lands in Ryckm'sworth *alias* Rickmansworth.

### 1573. Trinity Term. 15 Eliz.

Henry Martyn gent : Geo. Jacob jun. & Ellen his wife. Land in Stortford.

Wm. Note esq & Alex. Glover gent: Nich. Brystowe esq. Messuage & land in Ayatt S<sup>t</sup> Lawrence.

Thos. Hoye *alias* Odye: Timothy Sturman. Moiety of two messuages & land in Benington.

Margt. Hodge widow: Wm. Norice. Messuage & land in Wadesmyll & Standon.

Edw. Hubbert gent one of the cursitors of the Court of Chancery: Oliver Adam & Joan his wife & Geo. Adam. Messuage & lands in Sabricheworth.

Ralph Haydon: Roger Ovyatt & Joan his wife. Messuage and lands in Sarrett.

Robt. Shadde: John Shadde & Margt. his wife. Lands in East Barnett & Chippyng Barnett.

Dionisius Hynde & Edw. Fage gents: Edm. Hynde. Lands in Staplefforde, Bengeho & Watton & the advowson of church of Staplefforde.

John Graveley gent & John Glandfyld *alias* Nevell: John Wynne & Jane his wife. Lands in Wyllyen & Clothall.

John Godfree *alias* Cowper: Wm. Godfree *alias* Cowper gent & Joyce his wife. A barn & lands in Hitchen, Stevenache *alias* Stevenage, Ipolletts & Langeley.

Thos. Webbe & Humph. Hooper: Thos. Bayes & Ellen his wife, Benj. Potkyn gent & Susan Robynson. Messuage & lands in Much Hadham & Little Hadham.

### 1573. Mich. Term. 15 & 16 Eliz.

*Rich. Wyllye: Wm. Pylston & Joan his wife. Three messuages & land in Stortford.

*Anthony Crane esq: John Massingberd gent & Dorothy his wife. A twentieth part of the manor of Wikehamehall & 20 messuages & lands in Bisshoppe Storford, Little Hadham & Abrey.

John Browne: John Kilbyfe and Dorothy his wife. Messuage in S<sup>t</sup> Albans.

Robt. Forrest & Christr. Olyver: Edm. Salmon. Moiety of a messuage & lands in Tewing & Brantfeld *alias* Bramfeld.

Edm. Nodes gent: Henry Gynne & Joan his wife. Messuage & land in Stevenage *alias* Stevenache.

Wm. Adam: John Byllingham & Isabel his wife. Messuage in Sabridgworth.

Christr. Robynson & Owen Robynson: Robt. Kynwelmershe gent & Anne his wife. Two messuages & lands in Wormeley Chestunt & Broxburne & common of pasture for eight cows in Tunford Marsh in Chestunt.

Thos. Crabbe: Wm. Pilston & Joan his wife & Rich. Willye. Cottage in Stortford.

Geo. Davy, Wm. Taylour & Nich. Segrave: Rich. Farnefold gent. Manor of Rennesley & 16 messuages & lands in Standen *alias* Stonden, Bengeo, Ware, Westmyll, Sacombe and Hornemede.

Rich. Robson gent: James Thomasyn & Joan his wife. Messuage etc in S<sup>t</sup> Albans.

Edm. Hale: Rich. Hale & Agnes his wife. Messuage & land in the town of Hertford.

Sam. Clinton: Edw. Halfhide gent. Messuage & lands in Wimondley *alias* Little Wimley.

John Goodyere: Edm. Bardolffe esq. Three messuages & lands in Redburne & Whethamsted.

Robt. Blackewell: Andrew Jenoure & Grezagon his wife. Manor of Busshey & 100 messuages & lands in Busshey Watforde & Awdenham.

Robt. Shrympton & Robt. Lee gents: Wm. Kendall & Margt. his wife & Brian Chapman & Alice his wife. Three messuages & land in S<sup>t</sup> Albans.

Wm. Parker & Agnes his wife: Wm. Dymoke & Joan his wife. Messuage in Little Hadham.

John Gosnolde & Edm. Kynwelmershe gents: Robt. Kynwelmershe gent & Anne his wife dau. & heir of Jas. Howghton son & heir of Rich. Howghton of Wormeley. Two messuages & lands in Wormeley, Cheshunt & Broxburne & common of pasture for 8 cows in Tunforde Marshe.

William Francklande & others: Jas. Johnson & others. Tenement in Hoddysdon. [*Not in bundle.*]

*To be Continued.*

---

# Marriage Licences.
# Archdeaconry of St. Albans.

### By A. E. GIBBS.

(CONTINUED FROM PAGE 96).

**1672-3**

February 19. John Ewington of Ayte Parva, husbandman, widower, and Anne Camfeild of St. Albans, maiden. Edward Camfeild of St. Albans, grocer, a surety.

March 17. Edward Newill of Whethamsted, husbandman, bachelor, and Mary Holland of St. Albans, maiden. Belknap Tibbalts of St. Albans, plumber, a surety.

March 22. Robert Monke of Chafford St. Peter, co. Buckingham, husbandman, bachelor, and Anne Dell of St. Albans, maiden. John Hall of St. Albans, weaver, a surety.

**1673**

March 26. Thomas Pedder of Luton, co. Bedford, carpenter, widower, and Hester Hewitt, maiden. Nathaniel Pryor of St. Michaels, tailor, a surety.

April 1. John Church of Harding *alias* Harpenden, husbandman, bachelor, and Rebecca Stredder of Redborne, maiden. Ralph Darmer [*signed* Darmar] of St. Albans, yeoman, a surety.

April 5. Thomas Halsey of Flamsted, yeoman, bachelor, and Jane Smith, maiden, daughter of Thomas Smith of the same. John How of Abbots Langley, yeoman, a surety.

April 8. Hugh Sparling of St. Albans, husbandman, bachelor, and Margaret Deane of the same, maiden. Nicholas Sparling of St. Albans, haberdasher, a surety.

April 18. Robert Scott of St. Albans, glover, bachelor, and Mary Tanner of the same, maiden. John Taylor of St. Albans, chandler, a surety.

[*Undated*]. Richard Bibee [or Bibbee, *signed* Beby], of the city of London, butcher, bachelor, and Elizabeth Barnes, maiden, daughter of George Barnes of St. Albans. George Barnes of St. Albans, plumber, a surety.

April 19. William Rolfe [*signed* Rollfe] of St. Stephens, joiner, bachelor, and Mary Meddowes of St. Albans, maiden. Thomas Scott of St. Albans, cutler, a surety.

April 26. Walter Kent of St. Albans, glazier, bachelor, and Christian Dorsett, maiden, daughter of John Dorsett of the same. John Dorsett [*signed* Dossit] of the same, yeoman, a surety.

May 16. Thomas Bigge of Redborne, bachelor, and Margaret Purbart of the same, maiden. William Moore [*signed* More] of St. Albans, glover, and Isaack Stepney [*signed* Isack Stagney] of Redborne, glover, sureties.

June 21. Ralph Long of Colney, widower, and Sara Taylor of the same, maiden. Griffith Jones of the same, yeoman, and George Barnes of St. Albans, plumber, sureties.

June 23. John Yoward of St. Albans, yeoman, bachelor, and Mary Sparkes of the same, maiden. George Barnes of St. Albans, a surety.

July 2. Thomas Browne, citizen, silkedyer, of London, bachelor, and Elizabeth Howse of Whethamsted, maiden. Joseph Marshall of St. Albans, coachman, a surety.

July 5. Thomas Hogg of St. Albans, bachelor, and Sara Pecocke of the same, maiden. William Day of Luton, co. Bedford, yeoman, and Thomas Carpenter of St. Albans, yeoman, sureties.

July 12. William Knight of King's Langley, widower, and Mary Clarke of Bubbingdon in the parish of Hempstead. William Erbury [*signed* Earbury] of Bubbington, tailor, and William Knight of St. Albans, tailor, sureties.

August 2. William Bradwyn of St. Albans, victualler, bachelor, and Elizabeth Speares of the same, maiden. Joseph Tarbox of St. Albans, tailor, a surety.

August 2. Thomas Hall of St. Albans, bachelor, and Elizabeth Finch, widow. George Barnes of St. Albans, a surety.

August 20. John Higgs of Harrow-on-the-Hill, co. Middlesex, bachelor, and Judith East of Bushey, maiden. Nathaniel Newman of Harrow-on-the-Hill, gent., and George Barnes of St. Albans, plumber, sureties.

August 23. Charles Rowell and Mary Finch of St. Stephens. John Catlin of the same, a surety.

August 30. Thomas Chalkley of Watford, cooper, bachelor, and Mary Field, maiden. George Barnes of St. Albans, a surety.

Last day of [*blank*. Attached to the preceding obligation]. William Grigg junr. of St. Peters, bachelor, and Elizabeth Child, maiden. William Grigg senr. of St. Peters, yeoman, and John Mathew of St. Albans, sureties.

September 19. George Lawrence of Kimpton, husbandman, widower, and Sara Chalkley, widow. George Barnes of St. Albans, plumber, a surety.

September 27. John Richardson of St. Albans, glover, bachelor, and Elizabeth Heyward, maiden. Richard Richardson of the same, glover, a surety.

October 13. Benjamin Bunne of Langley, parish of Hitchin, and Mary Seabrook of Harpenden. Edward Berry of Harpenden, a surety.

October 21. John Leonard of Harpendine and Martha Cooke of St. Albans. John Burton of St. Albans, a surety.
October 22. Zachary Price of Idlestree, husbandman, bachelor, and Mary Hatch of the same, maiden. Joseph Ewer of St. Albans, joiner, a surety.
November 1. Sylas Palmer of Aldenham, wheelwright, bachelor, and Mary Perry of Idlestree, maiden. George Barnes of St. Albans, a surety.
November 1. Thomas Mitchell of Codicot, and Margaret [? Shenton]. Joshua Carpenter of St. Albans, a surety.
November 23. William Weedon of Edgborough, co. Buckingham, yeoman, bachelor, and Frances Morris. Henry Morris of the same, her father, a surety.
November 27. John Broadley of Hallifax, co. York, stapeler, bachelor, and Frances Yoward of St. Albans, maiden. James Tattenham of St. Albans, tailor, a surety.
November 29. John Cooper of Harpenden, husbandman, bachelor, and Mary Birch, maiden, daughter of John Birch of Redborne. John Chaworth of Harpenden, husbandman, a surety.
December 4. Henry Puddyfatt of Watford, bachelor, and Sara Bigge daughter of Thomas Bigg of the same. George Barnes of St. Albans, plumber, a surety.
December 6. Thomas Kentish of St.Stephens, gent., and Elizabeth Bradshaw of Watford. Edward Ffowkes of St. Albans, gent., a surety.
December 13. Francis Maylin of St. Albans, tobaccopipe maker, bachelor, and Elizabeth Bournham, maiden, daughter of Richard Bournham of the same. Isaac Scott of the same, cutler, a surety.
December 18. Salomon Smith of Harpenden, but now of St. Albans, mason, bachelor, and Anne Steppinge, widow. William Smith of Harpenden, blacksmith, a surety.
December 27. William Wilson of St. Albans, butcher, bachelor, and Elizabeth Hart of the same, widow. John Casselden of the same, sawyer, a surety.

1673-4

January 10. William Winfeild of Watford and Jane Russell of Whipswell. John Russell of Whipswell, a surety.
January 10. James Gibson of Aston and Sarah Dell of St. Albans. Belnapp Tiballs of St. Peters, a surety.
February 14. Henry Towensend of St. Albans, gardener, widower, and Abigall Davies of St. Michaels, maiden. William Pembroke of St. Albans, gent., a surety.
February 21. John Arnett of St. Michaels, yeoman, widower, and Elizabeth Speares of St. Albans, widow. Joseph Carter of St. Michaels, yeoman, a surety.
February 21. John Marham of Flamsted, husbandman, bachelor, and Elizabeth Gittings, maiden. Nathaniel Pryor of St. Michaels, tailor, a surety.
March 5. John Godman of St. Albans, glover, widower, and Rebecca Berry of the same, maiden. Richard Richardson of St. Albans, glover, a surety.
March 13. William Barr of St. Albans, cordwainer, bachelor, and Elizabeth Campion of the same, maiden.
March 15. William Smith of Redborne, bachelor, and Sara Hawgood of the same. Walter Hawgood of the same, joiner, her father, and James Hawgood of the same, joiner, sureties.

1674

April 7. Hugh Smyth of Stretley, co. Bedford, yeoman, bachelor, and Alice Coleman, maiden, the daughter of Wm. Coleman of Shephall. Thomas Hall of St. Albans, innholder, a surety.

April 16. Joseph Tockfield of London, bachelor, and Esther Cotton, daughter of Josias Cotton of Watford, gent. Josias Cotton and William Cuthbert of St. Albans, butcher, sureties.

April 20. Thomas Kentish of St. Peters, gent., bachelor, and Mary Pudefatt of Abbotts Langley, maiden. George Barnes of St. Albans, plumber, a surety.

April 21. Edward Waterton of Marketstreete, co. Bedford, husbandman, bachelor, and Anne Seare of the same, maiden. Robert Eves of Redborne, cordwainer, bachelor, a surety.

May 14. Francis Butler [*signed* Boottler] of Watford, mealman, bachelor, and Mary Hodsden of the same, maiden. Henry Wilson of St. Albans, tapster, a surety.

May 27. Thomas Ellis of Redborne, mealman, bachelor, and Ann Meadowes of the same, maiden. Nicholas Sparlin of St. Albans, hatter, a surety.

May 31. John Elisha of St. Albans, farrier, and Mary Woodards of Watford, maiden. Clement Snug [*signed* Snuggs] of St. Albans, victualler, a surety.

June 15. John Gregory of Chipping Barnett and Susannah Sturgis of Redburne. John Burton senr. of St. Albans, a surety.

June 22. William Thorp of St. Albans, and Judith Blitheman of the same. John Canfield of St. Peters, a surety.

July 25. Robert Coles of Gadsden, bachelor, and Mary Meadowis of Redburne. William Bush of St. Albans, brewer, and Robert Siggins of St. Peters, blacksmith, sureties.

July 25. William Abbatt of Flamsted, husbandman, and Damorose Goulding of Redbourne, maiden. John Jackson of Redbourne, husbandman, a surety.

July 27. John Taylor of St. Albans, butcher, bachelor, and Mary Rugsby of the same, maiden. George Barnes of the same, innholder, a surety.

August 1. Edward Hayward of Harpenden, husbandman, bachelor, and Mary How of Sandridge. George Barnes of St. Albans, innholder, a surety.

September 19. William Harvey of St. Stephens, yeoman, bachelor, and Joane Deacon of the same, maiden. Richard Fearnesly [*signed* Farnsly] of St. Albans, yeoman, a surety.

September 29. Timothy Seares of Sandridge and Susannah Shepherd of the same. Gregory Heath of St. Michaels, a surety.

October 1. William Evans of Studham, co. Bedford, and Mary Cater of Hemsted. Edward Stephens of St. Albans, a surety.

October 18. John White of Flamstead, bachelor, and Abigail Etheridge of the same. Edward Rogers of Great Gadsden, a surety.

November 11. George Collett of Markett Streete, bachelor, and Sarah Seaman of Redburne, maiden. John Burton of St. Albans, innholder, a surety.

December 12. Alexander Trott of St. Albans, butcher, bachelor, and Issabell Turner, maiden, daughter of William Turner of the same. George Barnes of the same, plumber, a surety.

December 20. Wm. Marston of St. Michaels, bachelor, and Anne Darvell, maiden, daughter of John Darvell of the same. Jeremiah Coleman [*signed* Coman] of the same, yeoman, and John Pollin [*signed* Pallen] of the same, blacksmith, sureties.

December 28. William Eelinge of Bushey, yeoman, widower, and Mary Rogers of the same, maiden. John Streete of the same, cordwainer, a surety.

[*Undated*]. Isaack Freeman, widower, and Awdry Laurence of Paulswalden, widow. Richard Freeman of Biscote, co. Bedford, husbandman, and Thomas Hall of St. Albans, innholder, sureties.

1674-5

January 6. William Deacon of Redborne, husbandman, bachelor, and Elizabeth Lane of the same, maiden. James Barnes of St. Albans, plumber, a surety.

February 22. Daniel Smith of Shenley and Elizabeth Millar of Ridge, widow. James Barnes of St. Albans, a surety.

March 6. Richard Williams of the City of London, grocer, bachelor, and Sarah Fitch of St. Albans, maiden. Matthew Iremonger of St. Albans, grocer, a surety.

1675

April 9. Richard Finch of St. Albans, widower, and Anne Leach of the same, maiden.

[*Undated*]. Joseph Tarbox of Gaddesden, husbandman, bachelor, and Rebecca Pheasant of St. Albans, maiden. James Barnes of St. Albans, a surety.

April [? 2]. William Babb of Abbotts Langley, husbandman, and Mary Sheppard of the same, maiden. James Barnes of St. Albans, a surety.

April 20. John Mooreton of Flamstedd, husbandman, bachelor, and Anne Peacocke of St. Albans, maiden. John Mathewes of St. Albans, weaver, a surety.

May 2. Thomas Baldwin of Little Heath, husbandman, bachelor, and Rebecca Field of St. Albans, maiden. James Barnes of St. Albans, husbandman, a surety.

June 2. Richard Hawkins of Paulswalden, bachelor, and Elizabeth Hill of the same, maiden. Thomas Hill of the same, yeoman, and James Barnes of St. Albans, husbandman, sureties.

June 16. John Morse of Watford, widower, and Sarah Turner of the same, maiden. Edward Horsell of St. Albans, "pharmacopola," and James Barnes of St. Albans, husbandman, sureties.

July 5. Thomas Robinson of St. Albans, butcher, bachelor, and Ellen Snugg of the same, widow. Thomas Belcher of the same, gent., a surety.

July 6. William Gibson of St. Albans, cordwainer, bachelor, and Anne Gladman of the same, maiden. Edward Ffowke of St. Albans, gent., a surety.

July 31. Samuel Cock, bachelor, and Katherine Pecocke, maiden. John Cock of Luton co. Bedford, husbandman, and Henry Morton of the same, husbandman, sureties.

August 23. John Parker of Watford, tanner, bachelor, and Mary Twichett, maiden, daughter of Roger Twichett of the same. William Nicholls of St. Peters, joiner, a surety.

September 1. John Sanders of Abbots Langley, husbandman, bachelor, and Mary Rolfe of the same, maiden. Joseph Sanders of Hempstedd, brickmaker, a surety.

September 11. Thomas Hanell of Abbots Langley, blacksmith, bachelor, and Mary Newman, maiden, daughter of Richard Newman of Watford. George Barnes of St. Albans, plumber, a surety.

September 18. William Harpur of Paulswalden, husbandman, widower, and Elizabeth Woodnoth of St. Albans, maiden. George Barnes of St. Albans, plumber, a surety.

September 21. Mathew Blithman of St. Albans, carpenter, bachelor, and Ellen Wilkinson, maiden. William Wilkinson of St. Albans, yeoman, her father, a surety.

September 28. John Mathews of Carrington, co. Bedford, grocer, bachelor, and Ann Turpin, maiden. Matthew Iremonger of St. Albans, grocer, a surety.

September 29. William Hill of St. Albans, bachelor, and Mary Chappell, maiden; and Thomas Puddefatt of Redborne, bachelor, and Elizabeth Field, maiden.

October 8. Thomas Coston of Rickmersworth, bachelor, and Alice Shrimpton of the same, maiden. William Jackson of St. Albans, laceman, and George Barnes of St. Albans, plumber, sureties.

October 11. Richard Rogers of St. Albans, cordwainer, bachelor, and Joane Neale of the same, maiden. John Godman of the same, glover, a surety.

October 18. Robert Thrustle of Norton, husbandman, widower, and Mary Dickens of the same, widow. William Beasley of St. Albans, a surety.

October 18. Thomas Hickford of Sandridge, bachelor, and Anne Barloe, maiden. George Barnes of St. Albans, plumber, a surety.

October 19. James Carter now of St. Albans, bachelor, and Joane Doe of the same, maiden. John Garrell [*signed* Garill] of Cadington, husbandman, and George Barnes of St. Albans, innholder, sureties.

November 6. Joseph Mutchett of Redborne, yeoman, bachelor, and Elizabeth Chandler of the same, maiden. John Sheerer of St. Albans, innholder, a surety.

November 16. Robert Robinson of St. Albans, butcher, bachelor, and Mary Canfeild, maiden. John Canfield of the same, grocer, a surety.

November 23. Thomas Grover of Chesham, co. Buckingham, bachelor, and Ann Darrell of St. Peters, maiden. Robert Swinston of St. Peters, a surety.

November 24. William Kentish of St. Albans, grocer, bachelor, and Mary Richards, maiden, daughter of Thomas Richards of St. Albans. Thomas Richards junior of St. Albans, gent., a surety.

December 13. Henry Whitcroft [*signed* Whetcroft] of East Barnet, gent., widower, and Mary Gazley, maiden. Samuel Gazely of Cadington, co. Bedford, gent., a surety.

December 13. John Mun of Ivingo, co. Buckingham, yeoman, bachelor, and Mary Wright, maiden, daughter of John Wright of the same. Daniel Roberts of Edgborough, co. Buckingham, yeoman, a surety.

December 20. Daniel Treacher of Sarratt, bachelor, and Sara Loddington, maiden, daughter of William Toddington of the same, gent. William Jole of the same, clerk, and George Barnes of St. Albans, plumber, sureties.

1675-6

January 1. Robert Kentish of Wheathamsted, gent., bachelor, and Mary Hill, maiden, daughter of Edward Hill. Edward Taylor of Carrington, yeoman, a surety.

January 12. Nathaniel Nuttinge of Harding, yeoman, bachelor, and Elizabeth Uncle, maiden, daughter of John Uncle. John Whitlocke of Whethamsted, yeoman, a surety.

January 15. Henry Sawell of Abbotts Langley, carpenter, bachelor, and Mary Aldin, maiden. William Stevens of St. Albans, cooper, a surety.

January 17. William Stepney of Redborne, yeoman, bachelor, and Mary Burton of St. Albans, widow. George Barnes of St. Albans, plumber, a surety.

January 29. Nathan Gladman of Abbotts Langley, bachelor, and Hester Ley of the same.

February 19. William Goodwin of Lilly, widower, and Mary Kilby of the same, maiden. John Kilby of Harpenden, a surety.

March 18. James Lawrence of Codicote, carpenter, widower, and Anne Hill of the same, widow. Richard Preston of St. Albans, carpenter, a surety.

1676

March 31. Henry Andrewes of St. Albans, weaver, bachelor, and Joane Rose of the same, maiden. William Andrewes of the same, hosier, a surety.

April 1. John Sparling of St. Albans, brazier, bachelor, and Anne Nash of the same, maiden. Nicholas Sparling of St. Albans, haberdasher, a surety.

*To be Continued.*

---

# Marriage Licenses.

### ARCHDEACONRY OF HUNTINGDON (HITCHIN REGISTRY).

(Continued from Page 44.)

1627.
Oct. 10    Smyth & Chakeley. Note of license.
,, 10    Febridge & Mitchell. Note of license.

1631-2.
Feb. 16    Edward Fairclough of Weston, esq., & Mary Coleman of Letchworth, widow. At Letchworth.
,, 21    Thos. Warren of Tharfeild & Cath. Kimpton, maiden. At Aston or Caldecott.
,, 25    George Farmer of Kimpton bach$^r$ & Eliz. Payton of same, maiden, orphan. At Whethampsted or Harpeden.
Mch. 23    George Bibsworth of Bps. Hatfeild, bach$^r$ & Dorothy Stevens of same, maiden, orphan. At Bps. Hatfeild.

1632.
Mch. 29    Edw. Wabie of Stevenage, bach$^r$, & Martha Smyth of Hatfeild maiden, dau. of Henry Smyth of Hatfeild. At Hatfeild.

| | | |
|---|---|---|
| Apr. | 3 | John Dagnall of Trvnge, bach<sup>r</sup> & Helen Baylie of Wigginton, maiden. At Kings Langley or Wigginton. |
| ,, | 12 | Edw. Covill of Kings Hatfield, co. Essex & Anne Farand of same, maiden. At S<sup>t</sup> Andrew's, Hertford. |
| ,, | 11 | Jas. Harrison, bach<sup>r</sup>, & Joan Bragg maiden, dau. of Thos. Bragg of Whethampstead, gent. At Kimpton or Ayott S<sup>t</sup> Laurence. |
| ,, | 24 | John Lilley of Stapleford, bach<sup>r</sup> & Rebecca Tomson of Watton, maiden. At Watton or Stapleford. |
| ,, | 30 | Daniel Burte of Cranfeild, co. Bedf. bach<sup>r</sup> & Sarah Gaseley of Gt. Gaddesden, maiden, dau. of Anne Gaseley wid. At Gt. Gaddesden. |
| May | 9 | John Hawkins of Codicote, bach<sup>r</sup> & [blank] Clarke of Ayott S<sup>t</sup> Peter, maiden, orphan. At Ayott S<sup>t</sup> Peter. |
| ,, | 9 | Thos. Graves of Baldocke, bach<sup>r</sup> & Agnes Clarke of same, maiden, dau. of Nich. Clarke of Amwell, gent. |
| ,, | 9 | Thos. Cost of Yardley, bach<sup>r</sup> & Eliz. Thorogood of Yardley, wid. At Aston or Bennington. |
| ,, | 9 | Thos. Loyde of Hemelhempsted & Sarah Heydon of same. At Hemelhempsted. |
| ,, | 9 | Henry Sheppard & Anne Turner. At Hemelhempsted or Bovingdon chapel. |
| ,, | 14 | Wm. Plumer of Aston, bach & yeoman & Mary Walker, of Watton, wid. At Whethampsted. |
| ,, | 21 | Robt. Tapp of Watton, bach<sup>r</sup> & Anne Nashe of same, maiden. At Graveley or S<sup>t</sup> Ippollits. |
| ,, | 24 | Geo. Ballard of Bps Hatfeild wid<sup>r</sup> & Mary Ive alias Munne of same, widow. At Bps. Hatfeild. |
| June | 16 | Wm. Woster, of Tryng, bach<sup>r</sup> & Cath. Pratt of Wigginton, maiden. At Albury or Wigginton. |
| ,, | 13 | Edw. Kiffett of Esendon, bach<sup>r</sup>, & Anne Deane of same, maiden, orphan. At Esendon. |
| ,, | 22 | Thos. Carter of Purton, bach<sup>r</sup>, & Sarah Hurst of Hitchin, maiden, dau. of Jane Huckle alias Hurst. At Hitchin or S<sup>t</sup> Ippollits. |
| ,, | 28 | Geo. Bruton of Offley, bach<sup>r</sup>, & Susan Rotherham of same, maiden, orphan. At Offley or Lilley. |
| ,, | 29 | Geo. Slowe of Ayott S<sup>t</sup> Laurence, wid<sup>r</sup>, & Anne Wells of Gt. Gaddesden, widow. At Gt. Gaddesden or Hemelhempsted. |
| July | 2 | Geo. Grub of Hartingfordbury, bach<sup>r</sup>, & Anne Carter of Gt. Wymondlie, maiden, orphan. At Gt. Wymondlie or S<sup>t</sup> Ippollits. |
| ,, | 8 | Thos. Freeman, bach<sup>r</sup>, & Sarah Oxley of Bark[hampstead], maiden, dau. of Wm. Oxley of same. At Tryng, Wigginton or Long Marston. |
| ,, | 9 | Wm. Randoll of Esendon, bach<sup>r</sup>, & Rebecca Harris of Shenly, widow. At Shenly. |
| ,, | 21 | Thos. Halle, wid , & Alice Wells of Gt. Gaddesden, widow. At Whethampsted, Hatfeild or Harpeden. |
| ,, | 31 | Robt. Wynch of Wellwin, bach<sup>r</sup>, & Eliz. Gabriel of same, maiden. At Ayott S<sup>t</sup> Peter or Digswell. |
| Aug. | 2 | John Collins, wid<sup>r</sup> & yeoman, & Agnes Hill of [Offley?], maiden, dau. of John Hill of same, yeoman. At Offley. |
| ,, | 2 | Wm. Archer of Hartingfordbury & Cicily Thorne of Hatfeild, maiden. At Bps. Hatfeild. |

| | | |
|---|---|---|
| Aug. | 8 | Amphibolus Bibsworth of S<sup>t</sup> Ippollits, wid<sup>r</sup>. & Grace Chambers of same, widow. At S<sup>t</sup> Ippollits. |
| ,, | 28 | Stephen Hawkins of Whethampsted, wid<sup>r</sup>, & Emma Lodge of same, maiden, dau. of Thos. Lodge. At Whethampsted or Kimpton. |
| Sep. | 7 | Symon Burtweesle, bach<sup>r</sup>, & Izabel Cobb, maiden, dau. of Peter Cobb of London, gent. At Bps. Hatfeild. |
| ,, | 19 | John Phipp & Grizild Kimpton. At Datchworth. |
| Oct. | 1 | Josias Feild of Hemelhempsted, wid<sup>r</sup>, & Alice Bunne of same, maiden, dau. of W<sup>m</sup>. Bunne of same, yeoman. At Gt. Gaddesden. |
| ,, | 1 | W<sup>m</sup>. Hurst of Albury, wid<sup>r</sup>, & Eliz. Pope of same, maiden. At Albury, Gt. Gaddesden or Little Gaddesden. |
| ,, | 12 | John Roberts, bach<sup>r</sup>, & Agnes Foster, maiden, of [Bennington?]. At Bennington. |
| ,, | 12 | John Crouch of Hartf. S<sup>t</sup> Andrew, bach<sup>r</sup>, & Joan Thorne of Little Barkhampsted, maiden. At Little Barkhampsted. |
| ,, | 24 | John Dawson of Standon, bach<sup>r</sup> & clerk, & Sarah Benn of Weston, maiden. At Weston. |
| ,, | 26 | Thos. Whittamor wid<sup>r</sup>, & Hannah Chawkley, maiden, of Hitchin. At S<sup>t</sup> Ippollits. |
| ,, | 29 | John Edmonds of S<sup>t</sup> Stephens & Priscilla Gosbell of Little Gaddesden, maiden. At Little Gaddesden, Gt. Gaddesden, or Hemelhempsted. |
| Nov. | 8 | Thos. Browne & Agnes Heath of Stevenage, maiden. At Stevenage or Hitchin. |
| ,, | 20 | Thos. Willson of Royston, yeoman, wid<sup>r</sup>, & Emma Battell of Tewinge, maiden, dau. of Ralph Battle of Tewinge, yeoman. At Tewinge. |
| ,, | 13 | Thos. Watts of Hitchin & Eliz. Rugmore of same, maiden. At Hitchin. |
| ,, | 22 | John Child of Rickm'sworth, bach<sup>r</sup> & wheeler, & Cath. Aman of Barkhampsted S<sup>t</sup> Peter, maiden, dau. of Robt. Aman of same. At Barkhampsted. |
| ,, | 22 | Robt. Halsey of Willion, wid<sup>r</sup> & Joan Retchford of Baldock, wid. At Baldock or Willion. |
| ,, | 28 | Geo. West of Luton, wid<sup>r</sup> & Agnes *alias* Anne Rotheram of Harpeden, maiden, orphan. At Harpeden. |
| Dec. | 5 | John Feild, bach<sup>r</sup> & yeoman & Jane Norton of Lilley, late of Sundon, maiden, dau. of Eliz. Norton of Sundon widow. At Lilley. |
| ,, | 6 | Jas. Munn of Ivingo wid<sup>r</sup> & Abigal Hill of Trynge, maiden. At Hemelhempsted. |
| ,, | 10 | Jas. Hoppie of Hertford All Saints, bach<sup>r</sup>, gent. & Joan Barleggs of Bps Hatfeild, maiden. At Whethampsted. |
| ,, | 20 | Samuel Curteyn of Luton, bach<sup>r</sup> & husbandman & Sarah Dixon of Whethampsted, maiden, dau. of Agnes Dixon of same widow. At Harpeden. |

1632-3.

| | | |
|---|---|---|
| Jan. | 4 | Ralph Game & Eliz. Enderbie of Baldock, maiden, dau. of Edw. Enderbie of same. At Baldock. |
| Feb. | 2 | W<sup>m</sup> Hobson of Watton, bach<sup>r</sup> & Mary Rowley of same, maiden, orphan. At Datchworth. |

*To be Continued.*

# Notices of Books, etc.

SEARCHES INTO THE HISTORY OF THE GILLMAN OR GILMAN FAMILY. *By Alex. W. Gillman. London : Elliot Stock.*

A portion of this work entitled *The Gillmans of Highgate and Samuel Taylor Coleridge*, has been published separately, and received many favourable reviews. The complete work, now in our hands, proves to be all that lovers of family histories could desire. Mr. Gillman is entitled, in no small measure, to the gratitude of all who bear his name for the exhaustive way in which he has treated his subject. The chapter relating to the Gilmans of St. Albans will be of especial interest to Hertfordshire genealogists, and enables us to put an end to the confusion which has hitherto existed betwixt the Gilmans and a family of Gilmett resident in St. Albans about the same period. The latter family produced two Mayors of the town, and there are entries in the parish registers undoubtedly relating to them, in which the superior social position of the Gilman family probably caused the scribe to erroneously insert the surname of Gilman.

All well-known sources of genealogical information appear to have been drawn from in the compilation of this work, and handsomely bound, beautifully printed, and profusely illustrated, it will rank as one of the most valuable contributions to genealogical literature ever published. The edition is limited to 300 copies, at 25s.

---

A HISTORY OF THE PUTNAM FAMILY IN ENGLAND AND AMERICA. *By Eben Putnam. Salem [Mass.] ; The Knickerbocker Press, New York.*

Our American cousins are far ahead of us in genealogical enterprise, and the number of family histories compiled by them during the last few years is legion. What is more important, they are printed and published so that all interested may, at small cost, see what has been done. Large collections of genealogical matter are constantly being made in England, but their usual fate is to remain in a manuscript form inaccessible to all but a favoured few, and any stranger wishing to study the genealogy has to work out the whole thing afresh.

In the introductory portion of the above history which now lies before us, Mr. Putnam has put together in a concise form a large mass of material—the result of careful investigation—and has traced, so far as he was able, the various families of his name resident in England, commencing, of course, with the original stock who derived their surname from Puttenham in Herts. The actual home of the John Putnam, who founded the American branch, was at Wingrave, co. Bucks, into which county the family spread at a very early date.

---

### ELY MARRIAGE LICENSES.

In that excellent publication *The Northern Genealogist*, so ably edited by Mr. A. Gibbons, of York, a series of these Licenses has been appearing. Several of the entries relate to this county, and we propose, when Mr. Gibbons' series is completed, to make an alphabetical list of such and publish it in this magazine. We notice two small errors :—

P. 73, line 22. *Cousselie* should be *Couffelie*. P. 76, line 4. *Barbye* should be *Barlye*.

# The Herts Genealogist and Antiquary.

## Rental of Sir John Say, 1468.*

BEDWELL. Rental of John Say, knight, lord there, made the 13th day of January, 7 Edw. IV., before John Luthyngton, auditor, & John Knyghton, steward, by the oaths of John Credy, John Coke, Hen. Luddeford, John Taverner, Thos. At Hille, Nich$^s$ Sonder jun$^r$, Wm. Wright, John North, Walter Webbe, John Morewell, John Toky & Robt. Batell, twelve jurors who say upon oath that

John Credy holds of the lord there by charter in right of Joan his wife a messuage called Eldebury late in tenure of Wm. Budder, before of John Budder his father & pays rent therefor yearly at Easter & Michaelmas by equal portions.—xij$d$.

The same John holds half an acre of land, freely by charter, lying in the Chirchefeld in right of his said wife, late in the tenure of s$^d$ Wm. Budder & before of John Budder his father & pays rent therefor yearly at the aforesaid terms equally.—ij$d$.

The same John holds, at the will of the lord, a croft called Branescrofte, late in tenure of Wm. Budder & before that of John Budder his father & pays rent etc.—ij$s$. & suit of court & ij 'precariæ.'

John Budder of the Chirchende holds an acre of land freely, lying in the Chirchefeld late in tenure of John Budder his father and pays rent etc.—iiij$d$.

John Coke holds of the lord freely an acre of wood called Estgrove near Hangyngrove late in tenure of Thos. Budder & before of Wm. Budder his father & pays rent etc.—iiij$d$.

The same John holds two acres of land at the will of the lord, lying in the Northfeld, late in tenure of Wm. Budder & before of John at Hille & pays rent etc.—viij$d$.

The same John holds at the will of the lord a tenement with two crofts belonging thereto, late in tenure of Edm. Burton & before of Wm. Smyth & pays rent etc.—x$s$.

Henry Luddeford holds by charter a croft called Catelyncrofte late in tenure of Margery Luddeford & before of Nich. Sonder & pays rent etc.—x$d$. & suit of court & one cock & one hen.

* The original, of which this is a translation, is preserved in the Public Record Office. The official reference is 'Rentals & Surveys. Roll 269.'

The same Henry holds freely a messuage late of Robert Elderbek's & before of Roger Hethe's & pays rent etc.—iijd.

The same Henry holds freely half an acre of land lying in the Estfeld, late in tenure of Robt. Elderbek & before of Roger Hethe & pays rent etc.—iijd.

The same Henry holds freely another acre of land late in tenure of sd Robt. & before of sd Roger at Hethe & pays rent etc.—ijd.

The same Henry holds freely a plot with iij. acres of land late of John Luddeford his father's & before of John Sexteyn & pays rent etc.—xd.

The same Henry holds freely an acre of land lying in the Haythorne late in tenure of John Luddeford his father & pays rent etc *—iiijd.

The same Henry holds an acre of land lying in the Hammez in three parcels, at the will of the lord. late in tenure of [blank] & pays rent etc.—iijd.

The same Henry holds at the will of the lord a tenement with certain lands & crofts belonging thereto, late in tenure of John Luddeford his father & before of Thos. Couper & pays rent etc.—ijs.

John Taverner holds a messuage at the will of the lord. late in tenure of John at Hille senr & formerly of John Maundevyle & pays rent etc.—viijd.

The same John holds a messuage, at the will of the lord, late in tenure of sd John Hille & before of Wm. Arnolde & pays rent etc.—vjd.

The same John holds two crofts called Gobones-crofte at the will of the lord, late in tenure of John Hille & pays rent etc.—iiijs.

Thomas at Hille holds freely a parcel of meadow in Challedell late in tenure of Robert at Hille his father & before of Wm. at Hille father of the sd Robt. & pays rent etc.—jd. ob.

John FitzJohn holds freely an acre of land & half an acre of meadow lying in the Northfeld late in tenure of John Huntewade & before of Wm. Elyot & pays rent etc.†—xiiijd. & suit of court.

The same John holds freely a tenement late of sd John Huntwade's & before of the sd Wm. Elyot's & pays rent etc.—vjd. & suit of court.

Nicholas Sonder junr holds freely a tenement late of Nich. Sonder his father's & before of John Sonder's & pays rent etc.—iiijd.

The same Nichs holds freely a garden late in tenure of sd Nichs Sonder his father &.before of John Soke & pays rent etc.—jd.

The same Nichs holds freely a tenement late of Nichs Sonder his father's & before of Wm. Barely & pays rent etc.—ijd.

The same Nichs holds freely a curtilage with certain lands & meadows belonging to it lying at Postelbarre. late in tenure of sd Nichs Sonder his father & before of John Ludeford & pays rent etc.—vjd. & j precaria.

Wm. Wright holds freely a croft called Hokefeld late in tenure of John Wright his father & before of Nichs Tonbrigge & pays rent etc.—ijs.

The same Wm. holds freely an acre of land lying in Chalkedell late in tenure of sd John Wright & before of [blank] Waldonnes & pays rent etc.—iiijd.

Richard Britte alias Webbe holds freely a messuage with garden lying in Hatfeld near the kings highway. late in tenure of John Wright & pays rent etc.—ijd.

John North holds freely an acre of land lying at the Hammegate, late in tenure of Thos. Trotte & before of Nichs Sonder & pays rent etc.—iiijd.

Roger Sparke holds freely half an acre of meadow land lying in Stanford mede late in tenure of Emma Ayliff & pays rent etc.—ijd.

Walter Webbe alias Cheyne holds freely 5 acres of land called Lemmanscrofte late in tenure of Geo. Meppesale & before of Waremans & pays rent etc.—ixd.

The same Walter holds at the will of the lord an acre of land in Bradewell late in tenure of sd Geo. Meppesale & pays rent etc.—vjd.

Thomas Idonbrace holds freely a messuage late in tenure of sd Geo. Meppesale & before of Rich. Gobet & pays rent etc.—jd.

Edmund Burton lately held an acre of land lying in the Northfelde at the will of the lord, lately in tenure of Robert Cokerell & before of Wm. Barbor & paid rent etc.—iiijd.

* In the margin opposite this paragraph is written 'inquiratur.'
† In the margin is written 'in manum domini eo quod perquisivit.'

The same Edmund lately held freely a tenement with certain lands belonging to it lately in tenure of sd Robt. Cokerell & before of Wm. Barbor & paid rent etc. —iiijs. iiijd.

John Holstok holds freely an acre of land in the Chalkedell late in tenure of John Phelip & pays rent etc.—iijd.

John Stalworth holds freely half an acre of meadow lying in Highmede late [in tenure] of Wm. Stalworth his father & before of Thos. Pope & pays rent, etc.—ob.

John Morewell holds freely a tenement called Tilles late in tenure of Peter Forster & before of John Couper & pays rent, etc. - xiijd. & suit of court.

The same John holds at the will of the lord a tenement with certain lands adjoining called Sokkes & Redynges late in tenure of Stephen Roder & pays rent. etc.—xxs.

The same John holds at the will of the lord a croft called Frydayfelde & a meadow called Bolleborne late in tenure of John Node & pays rent, etc. —viijs.

The same John holds at the will a tenement with certain lands adjoining called Maister Andrewes & pays rent, etc.—iiijs.

The same John holds at the will a parcel of land called Hoppettes & pays rent, etc.—vjd.

Robert Batell holds freely a croft called Hariettes late in tenure of Robt. Forster & before of Tho. Tyler & pays rent. etc.—xxd.

The same Robert holds freely a croft of land called Calcote lying at the Wyldehill late in tenure of Stephen Rutter & pays rent, etc.—iijs.

Concerning xxijd. lately received from Thomas Grene & before in the tenure of Rich. Louthe for the farm of a field called Millewardfeld, which rent should be paid annually at the terms aforesaid, equally, now in the hands of the lord. —Nil.*

John Toky holds at the will of the lord a tenement with certain lands & meadows late in tenure of John Dey & before of Wm. Laneham & pays rent, etc.—xxiijs.

John Budder 'sexteyn' holds at the will of the lord a parcel of land called Fareley near Nappultons late in tenure of Wm. Budder his father & pays rent etc.—iijs. & j capon.

The same John holds at the will, two acres of land lying in Northfeld late in tenure of Wm. Budder his father & before of Margerie Parker & pays rent etc.—viijd.

Thomas Smyth holds at the will of the lord a tenement with certain crofts adjoining in North Mymmes late in tenure of Henry Dedyleston & before of Thos. Legate & pays rent etc. beyond the vs. viijd. of rent reserved to the lord of Wenlok for the Manor of Brokemans.—iijs. iiijd.

Concerning vs. lately received of John North for the farm of a certain croft called Phelippesfelde, now in the hands of the lord.—Nil.

Philip at Felde holds at the will of the lord certain lands & a meadow called Margetmedowe late in tenure of Thomas Idonbrace & pays rent, etc.—xvs.

Concerning iiijd. lately received of John at Hille for an acre of land in Smytheshamme now in the hands of the lord for want of a tenant.—Nil.

Thomas Broke holds at the will a curtilage with certain lands & crofts belonging to it late in tenure of Thomas Idonbrace & before of John Idonbrace & pays rent etc.—xs.

The same Thomas holds at the will a close called Litelwodecrofte late in tenure of Robt. Hill & pays rent etc. ['modo Edelyn' in margin]. - ixd.

John Sonder holds at the will of the lord a curtilage with certain lands adjoining it called Sybottes late in tenure of Nichs Sonder his father & pays rent etc.—xvs.

Concerning xiijs. iiijd. of rent [for the land] called Pountesbornesmede lately reserved to the manor of Pountesborne for certain lands lying within the park of Bedwell purchased by the lord there, from the lord of Wenlok there is no rent paid to the lord of said manor of Pountesbornes, because it is included within Bedwell park.—Nil.

Sum total, beyond certain lands & meadows being in the hands of the lord.—vijl. vs. ixd.

* In the margin is noted 'Modo in manus domini eo quod perquisivit.'

**Meadows.** Six acres of meadow lying in divers places in the meadow called Highmede at ijs. iiijd. an acre now in the hands of the lord because it is mown & 'hospitatur' within the manor of Bedwell for the expenses of the horses of the lord.—*Nil.*

Two & a half acres in the meadow called Stanfordmede at ijs. iiijd. an acre now in the hands of the lord because it is mown & 'hospitatur' within the said manor for this expense.—*Nil.*

Half an acre of meadow lying in the meadow called Millemede at the price of xiiijd. now in hand for the cause above named.—*Nil.*

**LITTLE BERKHAMSTED.** Rental of John Say knight, lord there, made the 13th day of January 7 Edw. IV. before John Luthyngton, auditor, & John Knyghton steward by the oaths of Hen. Hardy, Wm. Kevyll, Robt. Pygot, Thos. at Hoo, Nich. Wightman, John Node, Robt. Forster, Wm. at Hoo, Hen. Hugh, John Boure jun. & Wm. Burley, twelve jurors who say upon oath that

John Wenlok knt. lord Wenlok holds freely a tenement with certain lands & meadows belonging to it late in tenure of John Fortescu knt. late Justice of the King & before in tenure of Wm. Toky & pays rent etc.—iiijs. xd.

The same John Wenlok knt. holds freely a tenement with certain lands & meadows belonging to it late in tenure of said John Fortescu knt. & before of John Boker & formerly of John Passemonteyn & pays rent etc.—ijs. vd.

The same John Wenlok knt. holds freely a croft called Blares lately in tenure of said John Fortescu knt & before John Kirkeby & pays rent etc.—viijd. & a red rose at the feast of the Nativity of St John Bapt.

The same John Wenlok knt. holds freely certain lands called Danelond lately in tenure of John Fortescu knt. & before of Alexr Drable & pays rent etc.—xs. xjd.

The same John Wenlok knt. holds freely a meadow called Scropesmede, parcel of that land called Danelond late in tenure of said John Fortescu & before of sd Alexr Drable & pays rent etc.—jd.

Thomas at Hoo holds freely a tenement in which he dwells called Shepes with a garden & croft adjoining late in tenure of John Toky senr & pays rent etc.—xijd.

The same Thomas holds by the rod a tenement with certain lands & meadow called Jurdans late in tenure of sd John Toky & pays rent etc.—vjs. ijd. & suit of court & heriot when it happens.

The same Thomas holds by the rod a parcel of land called Feldehegge, parcel of the demesne lands & pays rent, etc.—ijs. & suit of court.

The same Thomas holds iiijor acres of land in Sprollesfeld, parcel of the demesne lands & pays rent etc.—xijd.

The same Thomas holds by the rod xx acres of land by estimation in the field called Asshefeld parcel of the demesne lands & pays rent etc.—vs. & suit of court.

The same Thomas holds the fishery of the separate water towards the meadow of Berkhamsted & pays rent etc.—ijs.

Wm. Pynke holds by the rod vj acres of land lying in ij crofts, one called Smythfeld & the other Trepynescrofte late in tenure of John Boure & before of John Fortescu knt. & pays rent etc.—ijs. vijd. & suit of court & heriot when it happens.

The same William holds by the rod a tenement called Shusshes *alias* Goldeles with the appurtenances late of John Sonder & before of John Hille & pays rent etc. —viijs. jd.

The same William pays for one days work in the lords meadow & one 'precaria' in autumn annually.—vjd.

The same William holds by the rod xx acres of land by estimation in the field called Peryfeld, parcel of the demesne lands, late in tenure of John Hille & pays rent etc.—iijs. iiijd. & suit of court.

The same William holds a tenement with the appurtenances called Gace Adyham late in tenure of John Hoo junr & before of Wm. Adam & pays rent etc. —xs. & suit of court & heriot when it happens.

*To be Continued.*

# Marriage Licenses.

### ARCHDEACONRY OF HUNTINGDON (HITCHIN REGISTRY).

(Continued from Page 143.)

**1632-3**

Feb. 14. John Boothe & Frances Burgoyne 'celebes' both of Ashwell. At Ashwell or Caldecott.

,, 15. Thos. Smyth of Slapton & Abigail Howe of Hemelhempsted, widow. At Hemelhempsted.

,, 15. Thos. Cocke of Bovingdon, bach$^r$ and Rebecca Wethered of same, maiden. At Bovingdon.

,, 15. Walter Higden of Flampsted, wid$^r$, & Anne [Amy?] Greenwood of Gt. Gaddesden, maiden. At Flampsted.

,, 16. Wm. Younge, bach$^r$, & Dorothy Chawkley of [Kimpton?], maiden, dau. of Thos. Chawkley. At Kimpton.

,, 17. Thos. Middleton of Bps. Hatfeild, wid$^r$, & Agnes Grubb of same, widow. At Bps. Hatfeild.

,, 25. John Hardinge of Tryng, bach$^r$, & Susan Babb of Barkhampsted S$^t$ Peter. At Barkhampsted S$^t$ Peter.

,, 26. Henry Windsor of Kings Langley, bach$^r$, son of Henry Windsor & Eliz. Sowthen of same, maiden, dau. of Ralph Sowthen. At K. Langley.

,, 28. Rich. Moore of Hitchin, bach$^r$, & Anne Layton of Offley, dau. of Thos. Layton of Slapton, co. Bucks. At Offley.

,, 28. John Saywell of Watford, wid$^r$, & Angel Bennett of Aldenham, widow. At Aldenham.

,, 28. Ralph Kimpton of Tewinge & Barbara Gowin, now his wife. Proceeding against them. Ralph Kimpton appeared & swore that their marriage had been solemnized at the psh. church of St. Gregory, London. (Acta 1632-3, fo. 39).

Mch. 13. Rich. Hale of Graveley & Eliz. Hanscombe, maiden, dau. of Thos. Hanscombe of Purton. At Graveley or Purton.

,, 13. John Warkup, bach$^r$, & Dorothy Longe, maiden, orphan. At Hemelhempsted.

,, 18. Robt. Tittmouse of Stevenadge, bach$^r$, & Eliz. Pratt of same, maiden. At Stevenadge.

**1633**

Apr. 18. John Fownell of Hertford All Saints & Mary Browne of Bengeo, maiden. At Hertford All Sts., S$^t$ Andrews or S$^t$ Johns.

,, 25. Wm. Turner of Willion & Grace Dickins of Hartingfordbury, maiden. At Whethampsted.

,, 27. Thos. Kent of Aston, bach$^r$, & Mary Tyler of same, maiden, dau. of Thos. Tyler of Datchworth. At Datchworth or Graveley.

May 3. John Foster of Kimpton, bach$^r$, & Sarah Kinge of same, maiden, dau. of Alice Kinge of Pauls Walden, wid. At Kimpton or Ayott St. Laurence.

May   4   Thos. Siggin of Watton, bach[r], & Joan Hitchin of Stevenadge, widow. At Whethampsted.

 ,,  11   Wm. Androwe of Stevenage, wid[r], & Eliz. Smyth of same, widow. At Stevenage.

 ,,  18   James Webb & his wife, both of Bark. S[t] Peters. Proceeding against them for having been married at Grove Chapel without any lawful license. (See Acta 1632-3, fo. 65).

 ,,  20   Rich. Sparkes of Tewinge, bach[r] & Emma Thredder, dau. of Christian Thredder of same, widow. At Ayott S[t] Peter.

 ,,  24   Lewis Cornellus of Bengeo, bach[r] & Ann Whittakers of Hertford All Saints, maiden, orphan.

 ,,  26   John Feild of Digswell, bach[r], & Eliz. Hand of All Saints, Hertford, widow. At All Saints.

June  3   Nich. French, wid[r], & Anne Dawes *alias* Davis, maiden, of Hertingfordbury. At same.

 ,,   6   Nich. Kynge [of Little Barkhampsted?] & Susan Rodes of same. At Little Barkhampsted.

 ,,   6   Wm. Andrew of Stevenage & Alice Basill, maiden, dau. of Wm. Basill of Bramfeild, yeoman. At Bramfeild.

 ,,   8   Robt. Rogers of Bps. Hatfeild, bach[r], & Agnes Broughton, 'vx' [daughter?] of Richard Broughton of same. At Bps. Hatfeild.

 ,,  22   John Willett of Northchurch, bach[r], & Eliz. Varney, maiden, dau. of Greveil Varney of Barkhampsted S[t] Peter, shoemaker. At Hemelhempsted, Albury, or Wigginton.

 ,,  23   Edw. Nuttinge of Whethampsted, bach[r], & Anne Lawrence maiden, dau. of Tho. Lawrence of same. At same.

 ,,  24   Wm. Nicholls, bach[r], of Whethampsted, & Eliz. Sibley of same, maiden, orphan. At Kimpton.

July 13   Samuel Harvey of Gt. Gaddesden, wid[r], & Agnes Smyth of same, widow. At Gt. Gaddesden.

 ,,  15   Wm. Parsell of Ashwell & Ann Barley *alias* Parsell now his wife. Proceedings against them. (Acta 1632-3, fo. 96).

1634

Oct.  8   Geo. North of Offley, bach[r], & husbandman, & Eliz. Tiler of same, maiden, dau. of John Tiler of Offley. At Whethampsted.

 ,,  10   John Hely of Watton, bach[r], & Grace Joyner of same, maiden, dau. of [*blank*] Joyner of Stevenage. At Watton.

 ,,  12   Edw. Bradley of Northmyms, bach[r], & Dorothy White of same, maiden. At S[t] Andrew's, Hartford.

 ,,  16   Michael Jorden, wid[r], & Rose Newton of Aspeden, maiden, orphan. At Aspeden.

 ,,  17   Edmund Cannon, bach[r] & Eliz. Nashe, maiden, of Datchworth, dau. of Thos. Nashe of same, yeoman. At Datchworth.

 ,,  27   Wm. Haynes of Ayott S[t] Peter, bach[r], & Abigal Haskins of Digswell, maiden. At Hatfeild or Hartingfordbury.

 ,,  28   Wm. Barber of Kensworth, gent., & Mary Thewer of Digswell, maiden, dau. of John Thewer, gent. At S[t] Andrews or All Saints, Hertford.

 ,,  30   Thos. Issard of Weston, bach[r], & Sarah Cooper of same, widow. At Weston or Graveley.

Nov.  5   Jas. Davies of psh. of S[t] Catherine, London, bach[r], & Martha Ellis of Watton at Stone, maiden, dau. of [*blank*] Ellis *alias* Wayte of same. At Watton.

## MARRIAGE LICENCES.

Nov. 8 Thos. Bassett of Wellwin, wid$^r$. & husbandman & Lettice Willshire of same, maiden, dau. of Lettice Willshire of same, widow. At Wellwin or Ayott S$^t$ Peter.

,, 10 W$^m$. Clarke of Hartford All Saints, bach$^r$ & husbandman, & Jane Jursie of same, maiden. At Ayott S$^t$ Peter.

,, 12 Edw. Peele of Hartford, S$^t$ Andrew's, bach$^r$, & Etheldreda Morlie of same, widow. At Hartingfordbury.

,, 17 W$^m$. Farr of Stapleford, bach$^r$ & husbandman, & Prudence Coste, maiden, of same, dau. of John Coste of Bramfeild, husbandman. At Stapleford.

,, 19 John Cornishe of S$^t$ Andrew's, Hartford, wid$^r$ & glover, & Elizabeth Kirbie, late of Thundridge, maiden, aged about 23, now of Bengeo, dau. of [blank] Kirbie of Thundridge. At Bengeo.

,, 20 George Gynne of Datchworth, bach$^r$, & Eliz. Meridithe of same, maiden, dau. of [blank] Meridithe of Luton, widow. At Datchworth.

,, 20 Rich. Stonnell of Longmarston, bach$^r$, & Joyce Jeffes of same, widow. At Hemelhempsted or Barkhampsted S$^t$ Peter.

,, 23 Thos. Jewett of Kings Langley, bach$^r$, aged 31, & Sarah Cater of same, maiden, aged 28 & more, dau. of John Cater of same, wheelwright. At Kings Langley or the chapel of Flaunden.

,, 25 John Eason of Little Wymondlie, husbandman & bach$^r$, & Eliz. Butt, dau. of Cath. Butt of same, widow. At Hitchin or Little Wymondlie.

Dec. 1 Nathaniel Suerties, wid$^r$ & Eliz. Hardinge, maiden, dau. of Michael Hardinge of Hitchin. At Hitchin.

,, 5 Henry Chapman of Hartingfordbury, bach$^r$ & husbandman, & Anne Garroll of same, maiden. At Harpeden.

,, 11 Thos. Woodward of Hitchin, bach$^r$, & Alice Montford of Caldecott, maiden. At Caldecott.

,, 13 Thos. Nicoll of Hempsted, jun$^r$, bach$^r$, & Eliz. Beech of Harpeden, dau. of Walter Beech of Luton, yeoman. At Harpeden.

,, 22 Thos. Croute of Hitchin, bach$^r$, & Judith Hurst, maiden, dau. of Graveley Hurst of same, yeoman. At Hitchin.

1634-5

Jan. 5 John Deacon of S$^t$ Peters, bach$^r$ & yeoman & Sarah Impey of Bishops Hatfield, maiden, dau. of Geo. Impey of Hemelhempsted, yeoman. At Bps. Hatfield.

,, 24 John Willbraham of Ridge, bach$^r$, & Cath. Robertes of Bps. Hatfield, widow. At Bps. Hatfield.

,, 27 Daniel Halsey of Flampsted, bach$^r$, & Agnes Buckmaster, of same, maiden, orphan. At Flampsted.

,, 28 Henry Halfehide of Bennington, bach$^r$, & Sarah Skelton of same, maiden, orphan. At Bennington.

,, 31 Rob$^t$. Seybrooke, wid$^r$, of Hartford All Saints, & Joan Mosse of Esendon, maiden. At Esendon.

Feb. 3 John Dards of Datchworth & Rose Shepheard of Stevenage, maiden. At Knebworth.

,, 6 Daniel Cushie of Hatfeild, bach$^r$, & Mary Harrod, maiden, dau. of W$^m$. Harrod of same. At Hatfeild.

,, 10 Goddard Scourfeild, clerk, bach$^r$, & Frances Brokett, maiden, dau. of Edmund Brokett of Graveley, clerk. At Graveley.

Feb. 17  Wm. Barford of Tewinge, wid[r]. & Margt. Turner of All Saints, Hartford, widow. At Tewinge.

,, 20  Rich. Cannon jun[r], bach[r], of Gt. Munden, & Susan Bryan of same, maiden, dau. of [blank] Bryan of Ware, widow. At Gt. Munden.

,, 26  George Smyth of Weston, wid[r], & Frances Wright of same, maiden, orphan. At Weston or Graveley.

Mch. 2  Roger Ballard of Knebworth, bach[r], & husbandman, & Joan Hill of Hartingfordbury, widow. At Whethampsted.

,, 10  George Joyner of Bruntfeild, bach[r] & husbandman, & Mary Manfeild of same, maiden, dau. of Francis Manfeild, husbandman, of same. At Whethampsted.

,, 21  James Holte, bach[r], & Helen Bannester of Hemelhempsted, maiden, dau. of Grace Bannester of same, wid. At Bovingdon.

,, 24  Wm. Pratt & Anne Addison of Bps. Hatfield, maiden. At Whethampsted, Ayott or Digswell.

1635

Apr. 1  John Clarke of Hemelhempsted, wid[r] & tanner, & Eliz. Feild of same, widow. At same.

,, 10  John Moorton of Hemelhempsted, wid[r], & Cath. Hatch of Kings Langley, maiden. At Hemelhempsted.

May 13  John Fassett of Bps. Hatfield, wid[r], & Eliz. Pursey of Datchworth, maiden, dau. of Mary Pursey of Wellwin, widow. At Bps. Hatfield.

,, 14  Edw. White, wid[r], & Mary Androwe, maiden, dau. of Geo. Androw of Stevenage, wheelwright. At Stevenage.

,, 15  Matthew Readinge, bach[r], of Kings Walden, & Anne Chawkley of Offley, dau. of Wm. Chawkley of same. At Whethampsted.

,, 18  Gregory Wenham of Ashwell, wid[r], & Agnes Wenham of same, widow. At Caldecott.

,, 23  John Clinton, wid[r] & yeoman, & Eliz. Honor of Weston, widow. At Weston or Rushden.

1639

Mch. 27  Thos. Goldsmith of Hitchin, bach[r], & Lettice Hutchinson of same, maiden. At Stevenage or the chapel of Minsden.

1638-9

Mch. 20  Wm. Fellowe of Wigginton, bach[r] & brickmaker, & Susan Nashe of same, maiden, dau. of [blank] Nashe of same, widow, aged about 30; with her mother's consent. At Great or Little Gaddesden. Alleged by Daniel Fellowe.

,, 24  Geo. Saunder of Luton, co. Bedf., husbandman & bach[r], aged about 24, & Eliz. Sibley of Harpeden, maiden, aged about 25 & dau. of Mary Sibley of Luton, widow, who consents. At Whethampsted or Harpenden.

1639

Apr. 3  Rich. Grover & Eliz. Rowe of Barkhampsted S[t] Peter. At same.

,, 11  Michael Baldock of Baldock, bach[r], & Joan Reynolds of same, maiden, dau. of Margt. Lorrymer *alias* Renolds widow. At Baldock or Clothall.

,, 11  John Barnes of Whethampsted, bach[r] & husbandman, & Grace Feild of Ayott S[t] Lawrence, maiden, dau. of John Feild of same, who consents. At Ayott S[t] Lawrence or Whethampsted.

| | | |
|---|---|---|
| Apr. | 10 | Samuel Kingsley of Hitchin, bach<sup>r</sup>, & Eliz. Tristram of same, widow. At Hitchin or Minsden chapel. |
| ,, | 10 | W<sup>m</sup>. Dodkin of Hippollits, bach<sup>r</sup>, & Marg<sup>t</sup>. Clinton of Weston, maiden. At Hitchin or Letchworth. |
| ,, | 23 | John Besowth of Barkhampsted, bach<sup>r</sup>, & Marg<sup>t</sup>. Trowell of same, maiden. At Barkhampsted S<sup>t</sup> Peter. |
| ,, | 23 | John Hawkins of Baldock, wid<sup>r</sup>, & Eliz. Gillman of Ashwell, widow. At Ashwell. |
| ,, | 30 | Thos. Nashe of Stevenage, bach<sup>r</sup> & weaver, & Marg<sup>t</sup>. Hill of same, maiden, orphan. At Stevenage. |
| May | 8 | Rich. Hale, gent., of Codicote, & Agnes Linden of Offley, maiden, orphan. At Kimpton, Wellwin or Minsden. |
| ,, | 8 | Rich Carter of Ridge, bach<sup>r</sup>, & Joan Taverner of Shenly, widow. At Shenly or Northmyms. |
| ,, | 24 | Robert Chambers of Baldock, bach<sup>r</sup>, aged 24, & Jane Maple *alias* Hadie of Baldock, maiden, orphan, aged about 21. At Baldock or Radwell. |
| ,, | 24 | John Cawdell, bach<sup>r</sup>, of Baldock, aged 33 years, & Ellen Brace of same, widow. At Essendon or Bayford. |
| ,, | 24 | John Hurst of Hitchin, bach<sup>r</sup> & yeoman, & Susan Monk of same, widow. At Offley. |
| June | 1 | John Shorte of Little Barkhampsted, bach<sup>r</sup>, & Dionisia Usher, maiden, dau. of John Usher of same. At Little Barkhampsted. |
| ,, | 1 | Edw. Akers of Wormeley, husbandman, & Anne Willett of Datchworth, maiden, dau. of Anne Willett *alias* Tapps of same. At Datchworth. |
| ,, | 1 | Jas. Fraye of Baldock, bach<sup>r</sup> & butcher, & Agnes Stamer of Weston, maiden, dau. of Rob<sup>t</sup>. Stamer of same. At Weston or Clothall. |
| ,, | 1 | Rob<sup>t</sup>. Edwards of Baldock, wid<sup>r</sup>, & Mary Preist of Norton, maiden, dau. of Thos. Preist of same. At Radwell. |
| ,, | 1 | Jasper Lapadge of Wellwin, bach<sup>r</sup>, aged about 22, & Eliz. Batttell of Hatfeild, maiden, dau. of Eliz. Battell of same, widow, aged 19, with her mother's consent. At Ayott S<sup>t</sup> Peter or Whethampsted. |
| ,, | 4 | Robert Killinglie of Hemelhempsted, bach<sup>r</sup>, & Marg<sup>t</sup>. Turney of same, spinster. At same. |
| ,, | 13 | John Hamond of Pirton, bach<sup>r</sup> & yeoman, & Joan Chawkley of S<sup>t</sup> Ippolits, maiden, dau. of Agnes Chawkley of same, widow. At Pirton or S<sup>t</sup> Hippollits. |
| July | 11 | W<sup>m</sup>. Cockinge of Cople, co. Bedf., gent., bach<sup>r</sup>, & Sarah Goodrick of Aspenden, orphan. At Sandon. |
| ,, | 13 | Thos. Arnold of Purton, bach<sup>r</sup> & weaver, & Helen Aunsell, maiden, dau. of Matthew Aunsell of same, weaver. At Whethampsted. |
| ,, | 14 | John Grave of Hatfeild, bach<sup>r</sup>, & Grace Waters of same, spinster, dau. of Eliz. Waters *alias* Sturman of Graveley. At Bps. Hatfield or Northmyms. |
| ,, | 17 | W<sup>m</sup>. Wethered of S<sup>t</sup> Michaels near S<sup>t</sup> Albans, wid<sup>r</sup> & yeoman, & Jane Beamont late of Studham, co. Beds, but now of Whethampsted, maiden, orphan. At Whethampsted, Hemelhempsted or Harpenden. |

| | | |
|---|---|---|
| July | 30 | John Owen, clerk, & Eliz. Hucksley of Throckinge, maiden. At Throckinge. |
| „ | 27 | Symon Gould of Bovingdon, widr, & Judith Gould of Kings Langley, widow. At Kings Langley or Flaunden. |
| Aug. | 24 | Robt. Farr of Gt. Wymondlie & Anne Slowe of same, widow. At Hitchin or Minsden. |
| Sep. | 5 | Wm. Battell & Sarah Huckle of [Hitchin?]. At Hitchin or Minsden. |
| „ | 17 | John Sheppard of Purton, bachr, & Eliz. Same of same, maiden. At Purton. |
| „ | 21 | Wm. Birchmore of Harpeden, bachr & husbandman, & Eliz. Nicholls of same, maiden, dau. of Anne Nicholls of same, widow. At Kimpton or Harpenden. |
| Sep. | 28 | Timothy Taylor of Flamsted, widr & yeoman, & Emma Saunders of Barkhampsted, widow. At Barkhampsted St Peter. |
| Oct. | 14 | Robt. Cocke of Aston, bachr, & Joan Gynne of same, maiden, dau. of Thos. Gynne of same. At Aston. |
| „ | 21 | John Payne of Newnham, bachr, & Mary Mowse of Baldock, maiden. At Sandon. |
| „ | 23 | Jas. Bardolfe of Rushden, husbandman, & Susan Bonoe, maiden. At Sandon. |
| „ | 31 | Robt. Richardson of Sandon, bachr, & Hester Knight of same, maiden. At Sandon. |
| Nov. | 19 | John Peede of Bengeo, widr, & Eliz. Hynde of Hippollits, widow. At Hippollitts. |
| „ | 12 | Daniel Hurst, junr, of Hitchin, & Eliz. Potter of same, maiden. At Hitchin or Minsden. |
| „ | 29 | Nathaniel Grubb of Bps. Hatfield, bachr, & yeoman, aged about 24, & Susan Oxton *alias* Foxe, dau. of Philip Oxton *alias* Foxe of St Peters, in the diocese of London, maiden, aged 22, with her father's consent. At Northmyms. |
| Dec. | 1 | John Simpson of Wellwin, widr, & Eliz. Tatam of same, maiden. At Whethampsted. |
| „ | 4 | Wm. Martin of Hatfeild, bachr, & Eliz. Childer of Northmyms, maiden, dau. of Anne Childer of same, widow. At Northmyms or Shenly. |
| „ | 4 | Henry Price of Northmyms, bachr & yeoman, aged about 28, & Anne Catlin, dau. of Wm. Catlin of Harpeden, brewer, maiden, aged about 22, with her father's consent. At Northmyms. |
| „ | 10 | Wm. Hudson of Bps. Hatfield, bachr, & Mary Lawrence of same, maiden, orphan. At Bps. Hatfield. |
| „ | 20 | Nathaniel Lowe of Hemelhempsted, gent. & bachr, & Margery Chipp of same, maiden, dau. of Wm. Chipp of Wattleton, co. Oxon., husbandman. At Whethampsted. |
| 1639-40 | | |
| Jan. | 2 | Edw. Nuttinge of Codicote, widr, & Martha Wraste of Whethampsted, maiden, dau. of Edw. Wraste of Wades Mill. At Whethampsted. |
| „ | 15 | Ralph Wilshire of Sowthmyms, co. Midd., widr, & Agnes Chambers of Northmyms, widow. At Northmyms. |

*To be Continued.*

# Abstracts of Wills.

**ARCHDEACONRY OF HUNTINGDON (HITCHIN REGISTRY).**

REGISTER III.—CONTINUED FROM PAGE 76.

f. 27ᵇ JOHN WARMAN thelder of Aspden, husbandman. (*Dat.* 12 Apr. 1582). Bur. at Aspeden: Wife Margt.: House & land in Aspeden, copyhold of the manor of Barksden: Land in Laiston, copyhold of the manor of Corney: Land in Pereden & in Movemeadfeilde, Vowsley Valley, Long meade etc; Sons Edw. & Wm.; Youngest son John: John my eldest son; Agnes Warman dau. of my son John; The four daus. of son-in-law John Burdit viz. Cicelye, Agnes, Margt. & [*blank*]: Wife extrix. *Witˢ*:—Ralphe Tomlyn, Wm. Slowe junʳ & Wm. Scowell. (*Pr.* 20 June 1582).

f. 28. EDMOND SHELFOURTHE of Weston, ploughwright. (*Dat.* 22 Apr. 1579). Bur. in Weston church; Wife Eliz.; Freehold & copyhold lands in Weston; Daus. Eliz. & Margt. (unmarr.); Wife extrix. *Witˢ*:—John Beesbroune vicar there, Wm. Izard & John Hall. (*Pr.* 18 July 1582).

f. 28. JOHN BARKEMAKER of Knebworth, yeoman. (*Dat.* 1 May 24 Eliz.). Bur. at Knebworth; Ann Barkmaker my bro. William's wife; Eldest dau. Jone Barkemaker; Second dau. Eliz.; Son John (under 21); House at Hartingefordburie; Bro. Wm. Barkemaker exor; Bros. John Sole, Geo. Feild & Tho. Feild overseers; Son-in-law Fras. Bigge. *Witˢ*:—Robt. Hodgekins, minister, Robt. Dards & Edw. Parker. (*Pr.* 7 Nov. 1582).

f. 28ᵇ WILLIAM HURST of Purton, laboror. (*Dat.* 26 Sep. 1582). Wm. Barbor my master & Thos., Wm. & Beterice Barbor his children; Mathew Carter of Aspley end; Edw. Holmes; John Borough; Anth. Wheatlye; Michael son of John Chapman; Thos. Sparke; Alice Watson; Mary Howson; John Hall, Thos. Peacocke, John Deere & John Webb; Legacy to Shitlington; Thos. Parrat thelder; Said Wm. Barbor exor; Mathew Carter overseer. *Witˢ*:—John Caynhoo, Tho. Peacocke & John Deere. (*Pr.* 10 Oct. 1582).

f. 29. JOHN LYNCOLNE of Westmill, husbandman. (*Dat.* 20 Dec. 1581). Son Geo. (under 24); Sons Ralphe & Wm.; Dau. Anne Lyncolne (under 24); Daus. Mary & Margt.; Son Robt.; Wife Agnes; Lands in Noblay feild; Wife & son Robt. exors; John Hamond of Gaylers overseer. *Witˢ*:—John Jurdane, John Byrde, Wm. Ancell, James Crofte. (*Pr.* 2 May 1582).

f. 29. WILLIAM WHELPLEY of Borne ende in psh. of Bovington, yeoman. (*Dat.* 1 Aug. 1582). Bur. at Bovington; Wife Briget; Land in Northchurch; Borne Feild; My mother; Little meade in Northchurch: Kinswom. Frauncis Higbit and her mother now the wife of Edmonte Cooper of Wendover: Bro. Thos. Whelpley; Rich. Whelpley my brothers son: Nich. Harrys (under 21); Emme Higbit my sisters dau.: Eliz. Whelpley dau. of Thos.; Wife extrix; Bro. Thos. Whelpley & cous. Wm. Southen overseers. *Wit*<sup>s</sup>:—Michael Howe, John Mores, Bennet Cocke & Edw. Sybsey. (*Pr.* 10 Oct. 1582).

f. 30. ROBERT BARFOOT of Hitchin, draper. (*Dat.* 20 Oct. 24 Eliz.). Bro. John Barfoote: Bro. Thos. Barfoot; Father Nicholas Barfoote exor. *Wit*<sup>s</sup>:—Robt. Warner, Wm. Monke, Thos. Barfoote. (*Pr.* 28 Nov. 1582).

f. 30. ROBERT ALDEN of Kings Langley. (*Dat.* 13 Aug. 1581). Dau. Agnes Este; Son Robt. Alden the elder; Dau. Eliz. Alden; Sons Edw. & John the younger; Wife Eliz. extrix; Son Rich. Alden supervisor. *Wit*<sup>s</sup>:—Thos. Ewer, John Buckmaster the elder, Thos. Rotgers thelder, John Alden, John Carter of Jefferyes, Thos. Carter of the Milne. (*Pr.* 10 Oct. 1582).

f. 30<sup>b</sup> WILLIAM BISHOPE parson of the church & rectory of Aldeburye, clarke. (*Dat.* 11 Mch. 1581). Bur. in the high chancel of Aldebury; Cousin Thos. Isacke; Wife Margt. extrix & Wm. Cocke her bro. overseer. *Wit*<sup>s</sup>:—Ed. Pepwell gent., Nich. Cleiton, clarke, parson of Barkamsted Peter, Wm. Tu, Wm. Cocke. (*Pr.* 17 July 1582).

f. 30<sup>b</sup> LAWRENCE WODWARD of Shenley. (*Dat.* 10 June 1582). Bur. at Shenley; Son Thos.; Dau. Margerie; Dau. Angell Chappell; Son Hawes; John Carter my wife's brother, overseer; Wife & son Thos. exors; Richard Carter. *Wit*<sup>s</sup>:—John Howe, Thos. Harris, George [blank] curate of [blank]. (*Pr.* 25 Sep. 1582).

f. 31. THOMAS PODYFAT of Flaunden, yeoman. (*Dat.* 16 Feb. 1581). Bur. in Flaunden Church; Son Thos.; House & land in Sarret; Son Rich<sup>d</sup>; Land in Sarret called Great Mezloe & Little Mezloe; Sons Nich. & Ralfe; Beche grove, Cockes grove & meedowes crofte in Sarret; Son Edw.; Daus. Amye Podyfat & Scislye Podyfat; Dau. Alice wife of Rich. Lovet; Dau. Agnes; Godson Ralphe Southe; Wife Syscelye extrix; Thos. Daye of Rickmansworth yeoman, overseer. *Wit*<sup>s</sup>:—Thos. Hallam, Robt. Podyfat, Richard Lovet of Mynthous. (*Pr.* 12 Dec. 1582).

f. 31<sup>b</sup> RICHARD HUMBERSTON of Walkern. [An abstract of this will has been given before. See page 97 of the present volume of this magazine].

f. 32. WILLIAM HAMMOND of Westmyll. (*Dat.* 6 June 1582). Son John (under 21); My tenement late Scottes & lands belonging except lands in Ridgeway feild; Son Wm.; Land in Row now called Bushlay & land in same field abutting on Segors; Land in Cautes Croft, Nuttings field; Dau. Agnes (under 21); Thos. Warner; Dau. Margaret; Dau. Joane; Child<sup>n</sup> of my son in law Roger Hamond; Child<sup>n</sup> of my son in law Geo. Broune; Wife Agnes extrix; Geo. Newman. *Wit*<sup>s</sup>:— Wm. Broune, Henry Hamond, Geo. Broune the younger, Edm. Goodman & Wm. Hamond the younger. (*Pr.* 10 Oct. 1582).

ABSTRACTS OF WILLS. 157

f. 32ᵇ RICHARD BULL of Muche Wimboly. (*Dat.* 18 Apr. 1582). Son Edw.: Mʳ Edw. Poulter my master: Dau. Alice: Hew & Henrie my two younger sons (under 18): Mʳ Bushe vicar of Wimbolye; Wife Agnes extrix. *Witˢ*:—Edw. Pulter, Ralfe Dell, Rich. Witsey, Thos. Bushe. (*Pr.* 18 June 1582).

f. 32ᵇ WILLIAM LONGE of Hemelhemsted, husbandman. (*Dat.* 2 Mch. 1582). Sons Edm., Thos., & Raphe Longe; John Longe servant to Robert Longe; Edmund & Wm. sons of Edm. Longe; Agnes dau. of Edm. Longe; Son Robt. exor; Thos. Longe overseer. *Witˢ*:—Thos. Grave, Edm. Partridge & Thos. How. (*Pr.* 2 May 1582).

f. 33. JOHN PRATT thelder of Kings Hatfeild *alias* Bushoppes Hatfeild, paylmaker. (*Dat.* 24 Dec. 25 Eliz.) Dau. Eliz. Pratt; Son-in-law Wm. Marche; Son-in-law Wm. Potter; Nicholas son of John Pratt my son; John Marche son of Margt. my dau.; John Potter son of my dau. Kath.; Helden Beale one of the childⁿ of Agnes my dau., late wife of Wm. Beale of Hadley, co. Midd.; Valentine Beale & Johan Beale two other of sᵈ dau. Agnes' childⁿ; John North of Euisden; Said Wm. Marche exor. *Witˢ*:—Wm. Curll, Mathew Parget, Wm. Wayte. (*Pr.* 23 Jan. 1582).

f. 33ᵇ CLEMENS HAMONDE of Westmill, widow. (*Dat.* 15 June 1582). Dau. Agnes; Son George; Daus. Ellyn & Margt.; Dau. Alice & her childⁿ; Alice Newman my daughter's dau.; George Newman my dau. Ellens son; Goddau. Margery Hamond; Son Wm.; Geo. Kynge; Judith Kinge; Thos. Scott & his father; Wm. Browne; Litle John Kinge; Son Wm. exor. *Witˢ*:—John Hamond thelder & Henrie Hammond wrighter. (*Pr.* 10 Oct. 1582).

f. 34. RICHARD OLIVER of Baldocke, yeoman. (*Dat.* 30 Jan. 1579). Thos. & Edw. Oliver sons of Edw. Oliver my late bro.; Fras. Oliver my godson, my cousyn Edw. Olivers son; Wife Johsan; John Oliver & Agnes now wife of Rouland Hartelye, childⁿ of sᵈ Edw. Oliver my bro.; Said Edw. Oliver exor. *Witˢ*:—Wm. Goodriche, cordwayner, London, Geo. Kinge. (*Pr.* 6 Feb. 1583-4).

f. 34. THOMAS NOADES of Northmimes, singleman. (*Dat.* 16 Dec. 1583). My moieties of tenements in Potton, co. Bedf., Godson Thos. Noades son of my bro. John (under 18); Sist. Alice Pegrum; Cous. Thos. Roberts; My mother; Thos. Neale; My brother & sister's childⁿ; Father-in-law Thos. Addam, yeoman, exor. *Witˢ*:—Hen. Peacham mynester of gods word, Jeames Russell, John Carringeton, Edw. Norrise thelder, Wm. Lowin, Audrie Rushlye, Kateryn Tompson, Julian Higden. (*Pr.* 23 Jan. 1583-4).

f. 34ᵇ THOMAS FISHER of Boveingdon, carpenter. (*Dat.* 20 Sep. 1583). Son John; Dau. Anne; 'Unto my brother the somme of iiijˡⁱ yᵗ is to say Edward Fisher the younger and Edmunde Fisher yᵉ wᶜʰ is in the handℓ or custodie of Edward Fisher thelder'; My bro. Edw. Fisher thelder & his two sons; My sister; Rebecka Palmer; My sisters sone yᵗ is the glouer; Thos. Axtell & Edw. Fisher thelder overseers. *Witˢ*:—John Goold of Fuanyans, Wm. Palmar, Wm. Este, Thos. Axtell of

Shantoxe & Edw. Fisher thelder. (*Adm.* 5 Dec. 1583 to Edw. Fisher senior of Chessant, co. Bucks, & Thos. Axtell of Bovington. Will also registered at f. 35ᵇ).

f. 35. JOHN HOYE of Hitchin, 'vittuler.' (*Dat.* 16 Nov. 26 Eliz.). Son Edw. Hoye; Rich. Godlington of Ickleford; Mr. Hatton; Thos. Barfoote of Hitchin, shoemaker; Wife Eliz. & son Edw. exors. *Witˢ*:—Robt. Hatton, yeoman usher of the Queens Chamber, Thos. Barfote, Robt. Lyon. (*Pr.* 19 Mch. 1583-4).

f. 35. ROBERT ROCHE of Hatfeild. (*Dat.* 12 Mch. 23 Eliz.). Son Wm. exor. (*Pr.* 20 Mch. 1583-4).

f. 35. MARION DEACON servant with John Lynd of Barkhamsted. (*Nunc. will dat.* 4 Nov. 24 Eliz.). My master & my godmother; Marion Shanbroke; My brother his son; My sister her son; Agnes Howe; Wm. Shanbroke; Mr John Lynd exor. *Witˢ*:—Eliz. Grubb & Jane Mosse, per me Rouland Hughes clericū. (*Pr.* 30 Oct. 1583).

f. 35ᵇ HUMFRYE BUSHE of Barkhmsted Petri. (*Nunc. will dat.* 8 Aug. 1583). Wife Alice. *Witˢ*:—John Whelpley, John Turner & the goodwif Dagnole. (*Adm.* 13 Aug. 1583 to Alice the relict).

f. 35ᵇ ROBERT HARVEY of psh. of All Saints, Hertford. (*Dat.* 1 Apr. 1583). Eldest son Gyles Harvey; Son Ralph; Sons Robt. & Thos.; Daus. Joan & Agnes; Wife Agnes extrix; Hen. Dighton & John Furrar overseers. *Witˢ*:—The overseers & John Jonson. (*Pr.* 30 Oct. 1583).

f. 36. JOHN HUMFRIE of Hitchin, wheelwright. (*Dat.* 28 July 1583). Bro. Danyell Humfrye (under 30); Sist. Luce Humfrye; Sist. Jane Lancaster; Thos. & Annis Lancaster childⁿ of sᵈ sister; Alice Chamber; John Law my ounckle; Goddau. Jone Deremer; My father Wm. Humfrye exor. *Witˢ*:—Robt. Warner, John Lawe, Henry Warner. (*Pr.* 25 Sep. 1583).

f. 36ᵇ RICHARD BLOW of Wallington, husbandman. (*Dat.* 1 Feb. 1583). The 7 childⁿ of John Hunt of Baldock; Henry Redhead's vj childⁿ of Baldock; The wife of sᵈ John Hunt; Mary Bacheler of Wallington & Edw. Bacheler; The son of Thos. Man of Baldocke; Sist. Joan Blow; Bro. Wm. Blow; Wm. Squier of Baldock; My master Bowles; John Handlye of Wallington; Geo. Handkyn of Wallington otherwise called Cornelius; Cous. John Blow of Wallington; The 2 childⁿ of one Thos. Blow of Lonsnayle; John Bemores *alias* Chapman; Wm. Chatburne parson of Baldock; Bro. Wm. Blow exor. *Witˢ*:—Wm. Chatburne cleric, Rich. Glanfeeld *alias* Nevill, Wm. Squier. (*Pr.* 26 Feb. 1583).

f. 37. BARTHOLOMEW WEDON of Barckmsted Peter, bachʳ. (*Nunc. will dat.* 5 Aug. 1583). Sist. Anne Pope of Hillingdon by Uxbridge, co. Midd.; Uncle Rich. Wellor of Markett; Uncle Wm. Wedon of Ashley greene; John Blunt of Barckhmsted; Kath. Abower; Laur. Balloon; Mʳ Raffe Bullocke; Wm. Hearne. *Witˢ*:—Wm. Hearne, Laur. Ballam, Kath. Abower & Dor. Bramley. (*Adm.* 18 Sep. 1583 to Agnes Poope wife of John Poope of Uxbridge).

## ABSTRACTS OF WILLS.

f. 37. THOMAS ADOCKE of psh. of All Saints in Hertford, blacksmith. (*Dat.* 6 Dec. 1583). Agnes Sawyer my wifes sisters dau.: Wife Jone extrix. $Wit^s$:—Thos. Noblers clericū. (*Pr.* 23 Jan. 1583-4).

f. 37. ROBERT SMYTH of Flamsted, husbandman. (*Dat.* 12 July 1583). Dau. Elizabeth's child$^n$; Son Wm. Smyth; Lands in a field called xx$^{ti}$ acres in Flamsted; Rich. Whitley; Son William's dau. Isabel; Son Robt.; Wife Isabel; Bay horse called Ball; Wife & son Wm. exors. $Wit^s$:—Robt. Bradwyn, Thos. Martyn, Robt. Halsey & Edw. Smyth. (*Pr.* 10 Oct. 1583).

*To be Continued.*

# Transcripts of Wigginton Parish Registers.

(CONTINUED FROM PAGE 116).

### Ano Domeney 1631.
#### Marr.

| | | |
|---|---|---|
| Oct. | 2 | Gillburd Hocheson and Ann Winche. |
| ,, | 6 | John Donton, Jane Mysell. |
| Apr. | 9 | John Dagnall & Ellenor Bayley. |
| ,, | 30 | Robord Dogatt and Ellisabath Tredway. |
| Aug. | 23 | Willam Wosetor of the parsh of Tring and Catorne Pratt of this Parsh. |

#### Christ.

| | | |
|---|---|---|
| June | 3 | Bengamey Bordor sonne of Thomas Bordordor [*sic*]. |
| ,, | 29 | Marey dafter of Gorge Daves. |
| July | 22 | Frances the sonne of Thomas Wigginton. |

#### Bur.

| | | |
|---|---|---|
| Oct. | 9 | Thomas Daves sone of Willm Daves. |

Joseph Gearey } Churchwardens.
John Wood × }

### Mich. 1632 to Mich. 1633.
#### Christ.

| | | |
|---|---|---|
| Nov. | 6 | Mary daughter of John Baylie. |
| Jan. | 20 | Jane daughter of John Dunton |
| ,, | 20 | Richard son of James Wigginton. |
| May | 8 | Annes daughter of Richard Benes. |
| Sep. | 21 | Mary daughter of Tho. Biggs. |
| ,, | 29 | John sonne of Francis Peake. |

*Marr.*

Nov. 24 Thos. Cuttler & Faith Musell.
June 27 John Willet of Norchurch and Elizabeth Varney of Barkehampsted obtayning a licence.

*Bur.*

Nov. 16 John Russell.
Mch. 22 Benjamin sonne of Tho. Border.
Apr. 22 Mary daughter of John Baylie.
May 13 Annes daughter of Richard Bennes.

Eub. Richardson minist.
Edward Holyman } Churchwardens.
Francis Byrche }

---

## Mich. 1633 to Mich. 1634.

*Bapt.*

Jan. 23 Joseph son of Joseph Gearey.
Mch. 4 Tho. son of John Bayley.
Apr. 13 Alse daughter of John Spiggins.

*Marr.*

Jan. 16 Mathew Bishop of Tringe and Elizabeth Mosell of this pish.

*Bur.*

Apr. 4 Richard Morris.
June 26 Amy Wigginton widdow.
July 29 John Clarke.

Eub. Richardson, curat.
Ed. Hollyman } Churchwardens.
Edward Durrant }

---

## Mich. 1634 to Mich. 1635.

*Bapt.*

Apr. 26 William sonne of Thomas Wigginton.
May 27 William sonne of Richard Binns.

*Marr.*

Oct. 28 Thomas Cocks & Marie Perce.

*Bur.*

May 27 Roger Haris *alies* Clarke.
June 10 Sarah the Daughter of Radulphus Douer.

John Baylie } Churchwardens.
John Dunton }

---

## Mich. 1635 to Mich. 1636.

*Bapt.*

Dec. 3 Susan Daughter of Nathanell Nash of London.
Jan. 10 Robert sonne of James Wigginton.
„ 10 Marie Daughter of John Spigins.
Mch. 27 Marie the daughter of Thomas Rutland.
Apr. 24 Francis sonne of Francis Peake.
May 11 Barbarie Daughter of Henry Groue.

May 19 Henrie sonne of Joseph Gearie.
July 31 Radulphus sonne of Thomas Border.
" 31 Elisabeth Daughter of Thomas Warr.
Aug. 7 John Crips sonne of John Crips of London.
" 14 William sonne of Will. Rugmor.
" 14 William sonne of Thomas [blank].
Sep. 4 Marie the daughter of Radulphus Douer.

### Marr.
Oct. 28 Thomas Cocks & Marie Perce.
Nov. 26 James Carter & Martha Baldwin.
Jan. 14 Richard Treadway & Margerie Pope.
June 30 Lenard Bachelder & Elisabeth [Eustes ?].
July 13 John Wood & Anis Clarke.
Sep. 22 John [Guet ?] & Amie Wells w<sup>th</sup> a lisence.

### Bur.
Dec. 6 Marie the wife of John Wood.
" 17 Elesabeth the dafter of Edward Holliman.
May 5 John Pratt.
June 18 Judeth the Daughter of Edward Holliman.
Aug. 6 Barbarie Daughter of Henrie Groue.
" 6 Thomas the sonne of Roger Wiff.
" 14 Richard sonn of Richard Foster.
Dec. 16 Frances the wife of John Crips of London.

John Baylie  } Churchwardens.
Henrie Stonhill

---

## Mich. 1636 to Mich. 1637.
### Bapt.
Nov. 13 William son of Richard Tredway.
Dec. 13 George y<sup>e</sup> son of George Dauis.
May 29 John y<sup>e</sup> son of John Foster.
July 9 Sarah Daughter of Henry Groue.
Aug. 29 Richard son of Richard Binnes.

### Marr.
Oct. 14 Roger Pope and Elisabeth Oviatt both of Tring Parish.

### Bur.
Oct. 21 Mary Daughter of Rodulphus Douer.
June 16 William Rutter.
Sep. 27 Clement son of William Bennet of Tring.

Ric. Robinson, Min.

Henry Stonell } Churchwarden.
John Tofeild

---

## Mich. 1637 to Mich. 1638.
### Christ.
Nov. 1 John son of Rodulphus Douer.
May 3 Susan Daughter of James Wigginton.
" 14 Henry son of Richard Grover.
July 1 George son of William Reeue.
Sep. 9 Alice Daughter of Tho. Rutland.

### Bur.

Nov. 3 John son of Rodulphus Douer.
" 22 Jane Dolton.
" 25 Richard Pearse.
Mch. 18 Bettres Pratt.
" 30 Edward Burte.
Apr. 18 Walter Nash.
" 22 Elizabeth Warre.
May 1 John Baldwin.
" 8 Anne Grouer widdow.

Ri. Robinson, Cler.
Will. Pratt } Churchwardens.
John Tofeild

---

### Mich. 1638 to Mich. 1639.
### Bapt.

Sep. 9 Alce daughter of Thomas Rutland.
Oct. 28 Williā sonne of Arnot Pratt.
Dec. 4 Thomas sonne of Thomas Whyte.
" 24 Sara daughter of Joseph Geary.
Mch. 5 Hannah daughter of Radulphus Douer.
July 14 Edward sonn of Henry Groue [& Barbora his wife. *See Transcript from Lady Day* 1639 *to Lady Day* 1640.]

### Bur.

Nov. 14 Williā Dauis.
" 17 Mary Dauis wife of Williā Dauis.
" 17 Anfillis Adames widowe.
Jan. 4 Anna Munn Widowe.
Feb. 7 Robert Marsh Gent.
Mch. 25 Annah Daughter of John Redman of London.
Apr. 4 Charles Hill.
May 24 Sara Daughter of Williā Dauis.
" 28 Margret Hitchcocke widowe.
June 1 John sonn of John Bodger.
" 22 George sonn of George Dauis.
July 2 Priscilla daughter of John Sprigginee.
Aug. 5 Richard sonne of George Dauis.
" 30 Elizabeth wife of Williā Rugmore [Gugmore *in second transcript*].

### Marr.

Dec. 15 Rich. Moythen & Susan Morris.
July 18 Charles Day of the pish of Saret & Susan Wood of the pish of Norchurch, by licence.

Ri. Robinson, Cler.
William Pratt } Churchwardens.
Robert Calcott

---

### Mich. 1639 to Mich. 1640.
### Christ.

Nov. 1 Elizabeth d. of Rich. Bate & Katharine his wife.
Dec. 8 Sarah d. of Isaac Bunnion & Margaret his wife.
Jan. 12 Susan d. of William Fellow & Susan his wife.

Mch. 25 Harry s. of Francis Peake & Dorothy his wife.
Apr. 7 Esdras s. of John Bayly & Keturah his wife.
„ 12 Elisabeth d. of Rich. Tredway & Margary his wife.
May 14 Susan d. of William Reeue & Susan his wife.
„ 13 Sarah d. of George Dauy & Ellen his wife.
June 7 Jane d. of Thomas Coxe & Mary his wife.
Aug. 9 Mary d. of Henry Dell & Mary his wife.
Sep. 16 William s. of John Tofeild & Martha his wife.

*Marr.*

Oct. 15 Henry Dell & Mary Wheeler.

*Bur.*

Apr. 3 John Hale.
May 3 Joyce wife of Francis Peake.
„ 22 Susan d. of James Wigginton.
Aug. 28 Alice d. of John Spiggins.

Ri. Robinson, Cler.
Robert Calcott } Churchwardens.
......... }

---

### Mich. 1640 to Mich. 1641.

*Christ.*

Jan. 10 Josuah s. of Thomas Rutland & Phillis his wife.
„ 19 Hester d. of Richard Grover & Rebecca his wife.
Mch. 2 Mary d. of Joseph Geery & Susan his wife.
„ 14 James s. of Henry Groue & Barbara his wife.
„ 25 Susan d. of James Wigginton & Susan his wife.

*Marr.*

June 3 Henry Wen Stanley and Susan Moython.

*Bur.*

Oct. 31 Richard Moython.
Nov. 27 Mary wife of Thomas Wigginton.
Mch. 11 Mary d. of Joseph Geery.

Ri. Robinson, Cler.
Rodulphus Dover } Churchwardens.
Samel Munne }

---

### Lady Day 1641 to Lady Day 1642.

*Christ.*

Nov. 23 John & Daniell, Twins, sons of Rodulphus Dover.
Feb. 10 Mary d. of Andrew Bradway & Mary his wife.
Apr. 11 Richard s. of Samuell Grace & Agnes his wife.

*Marr.*

June 3 Henry Wenstanley & Susan Moython.
Feb. 7 Edward Hollyman & Jane Burch.

*Bur.*

Dec. 5 John son of Rodulphus Dover.
„ 7 Daniell son of Rodulphus Douer.
Jan. 8 Elisabeth Binnes widdow.

Ri. Robinson, Cler.
Radulphus Douer } Churchwardens.
Samuell Mone }

[*The following transcript turned up in the bundle for Tring. Although endorsed 'Tring' by a later hand, it undoubtedly belongs to Wigginton. Unfortunately the parchment has been much eaten away.*]

### 1667.
#### Christ.
Dec. 15 Wiłłm sonne of Wiłłm Smyth.
#### Marr.
Oct. 7 Henry Geary & Hannah Grover.
#### Bur.
Apr. 8 Edward Hollyman.
Sep. 11 Francys Humphrey.
Mch. 20 John Reeve.
„ 24 Isaack Bynyon.

### 1668.
#### Christ.
June 6 Wiłłm sonne of Henry Grover.
Oct. 9 Henry sonne of Richard Grover.
„ 9 Susanna daughter of Edward Durrant.
„ 30 Henry sonne of Henry Geary.
#### Marr. None.
#### Bur.
Mch. 30 . . . . n Dinton.
June 20 Susanna wife of Joseph Geary.

### 1669.
#### Christ.
Apr. 4 Daniell sonne of John Webb.
„ 4 John sonne of Wiłłm. Durrant.
Mch. 28 Wiłłm. son of Wiłłm. Johnson.
Sep. 4 Joseph sonne of Joseph Avis.
Feb. 2 . . . . daughter of Henry Geary.
„ 20 [P]eter sonne of John Besonn.
#### Marr. None.
#### Bur.
Apr. 15 Hannah daughter of Edmond Clarke.
„ 16 Hannah daughter of Henry Dell.
May 4 Mary daughter of Wiłłm. Durrant.
June 13 Elianor wife of George Davis.
Nov. 12 [John ?] sonne of Wiłłm Durrant.
„ 15 [Thomas ?] sonne of Wiłłm Gray.
Dec. 24 Sarah daughter of John Webb.

### 1670.
#### Christ.
Sep. 28 Elizabeth daughter of Wiłłm. Ward.
Oct. 18 John sonne of John Dagnall.
May 4 Mary daughter of Abraham Sturton.
June 30 Joseph sonne of Henry Geary.
July 15 John sonne of Richard Grover y$^e$ younger.
Sep. 10 Thomas sonne of Henry Grover.
#### Marr.
Dec. 26 John Reeve & Mary Parkins.
May 23 Edward Egleton & Elizabeth Pegsworth.

*Bur.*

May 28 M[ary ?] daughter of Josias Wiggington.
Sep. 14 Rich[ard] Bynns.
 „  18 Agnes wife of Wiltm Border.
Oct. 16 Elizabeth Dover, widdow.
Apr. 18 John Clarke.

1671.
*Marr.*

Nov. 5 . . . . kin & Alice Feild.
Dec. 26 John Treadway & Rebecca Allen.
Jan. 28 John Harding & Grace Whitchurch.
Feb. 12 John M . . lier & Mary Broadway.

*Bur.*

Nov. 18 . . . . sonne of Wiltm. Reeve.
 „  1[9?]. . . . rman.

[*Memorandum at foot of Transcript*]

'. . . . nt y<sup>t</sup> the Church of W . . . . ton is very much . . . . of Repayre. . . . . . .'

# Hitchin Parish Registers.

Annexed to the Transcript of these Registers for the years 1665 to 1667 is a strip of parchment containing the following note:

"These are to certifie all persons whom it dothe or may concerne, That the regestry for Christnings Marriages and Burialls in the Parish of Hitchin, Countie of Hertford diocese of Lincolne and Archdeaconry of Huntingdon through the carelessnesse and neglect of former Regesters is wholly lost for the space of seventeene yeares & vpwards last past (that is) from the first day of February one thousand six hundred fowerty & eight to the first day of August one thousand six hundred sixtie & fiue. Wittnesse our hands this 8 day of Nouember 1667."

[*Signed*] J. SKYNNER      WILL: GIBBS Vic. of Hitchin.
R. PAPWORTH   THOMAS LUCAS
Jo. PAPWORTH  HAMLET AUDLEY
FRA. AUDLEY   CHARLES RAYNER.
LAW. TRISTRAM
ROBERT LUCAS.

# Marriage Licences.
## Archdeaconry of St. Albans.
### By A. E. GIBBS.
(Continued from Page 141.)

1676

April 3. John Branch of St. Albans, carpenter, bachelor, and Alice Field, daughter of William Field of Chilwick. James Branch of St. Albans, carpenter, a surety.

April 18. Richard Timmins of St. Albans, yeoman, bachelor, and Jane Graves of the same, maiden. John Munt of the same, baker, a surety.

May 8. Richard Johnson of Broughton, co. Northampton, but now of St. Albans, bachelor, and Elizabeth Mabbotts, widow. George Barnes of St. Albans, a surety.

May 19. Timothy Cocke of Hempstedd, yeoman, widower, and Sarah Somes of Watford, maiden. George Barnes of St. Albans, plumber, a surety.

May 27. Thomas Newman of Meynell Hempstedd [sic], yeoman, widower, and Elizabeth Meager, maiden, daughter of [blank] Meager of Abbotts Langley. Edward Ffowke of St. Albans, gent., a surety.

May 31. Joseph Doubtley [or Dowtley] of Sandridge, yeoman, and Mary Hall, maiden. Belknap Tibballs of St. Albans, plumber, a surety.

June 7. Robert Rumford of St. Albans, barber, bachelor, and Elizabeth Coppocke, maiden, daughter of Richard Coppocke of the the same. John Bolton of the same, tailor, a surety.

June 17. Samuel Ewer of Redborne, yeoman, bachelor, and Sara Field, maiden, daughter of Robert Field of Redborne. George Barnes of St. Albans, innholder, a surety.

June 20. Henry Brigginshaw of Kensworth, bachelor, and Sarah Eames of Flamsted, maiden. John Burton, senior, of St. Albans, a surety.

September 3. Roger Brewer of Rickmersworth, gent., and Sara Skidamore. James Ramridge, gent., a surety.

September 6. Luke Pryor of Marketstreete, tailor, bachelor, and Anne Evans, maiden. William Evans of the same, a surety.

September 12. William Guise of Hertford, bachelor, and Mary Lea, maiden. John Mott of St. Albans, yeoman, a surety.

September 13. Robert Heyward of the City of London, tailor, bachelor, and Mary Munt, maiden. John Hall of St. Albans, a surety.

September 21. William Hinde of Sandridge, husbandman, bachelor, and Hannah Hill, maiden. John Hinde of Esington, husbandman, a surety.

September 30. Thomas Sturges and Mary Martyn, maiden. Nathaniel Martyn of Redbourne, tailor, and William Watts of St. Albans, sureties.

October 7. Jeremiah Smith of Watford, weaver, and Anne Hill, maiden. Jeremiah Smith of Abbotts Langley, yeoman, a surety.

October 7. Daniel King of Bushey, husbandman, bachelor, and Elizabeth Page, maiden. Walter Cooke of Bushey, gent., a surety.

October 11. Edward Northcote of St. Albans, miller, bachelor, and Mary Ford, maiden. Samuel Turner of the same, miller, a surety.

October 17. Samuel Wheeler of Wigginton, husbandman, bachelor, and Sara Davies, maiden. John Davies of the same, yeoman, a surety.

October 25. Joseph Hitchcock of Barkhamsted, yeoman, bachelor, and Bethia Scudamore, maiden. William Hitchcock of Barkhampsted, a surety.

October 26. John Dell of Abbotts Langley, mealman, bachelor, and Mary Sheppard, maiden. John Guyse of St. Albans, a surety.

October 28. Abraham Chalkley of St. Pauls Walden, bachelor, and Sarah Jackeson of Harpendine. Richard Crouch of Harpenden, a surety.

November 1. Thomas Mitchell of Codicot, and Margaret Sturton. Joshua Carpenter of St. Albans, a surety.

December 1. Edward Sparkes of Redborne, yeoman, bachelor, and Mary Chandler of the same, maiden. John Sheerer of St. Albans, innholder, a surety.

December 4. Thomas Bunby of Idlestree, yeoman, bachelor, and Frances Perry of the same, maiden. John Twitchett of Watford, mercer, a surety.

December 9. John Grigg of Redborne, gent., bachelor, and Susan Hoare, of the same, maiden. John Burton of St. Albans, innholder, a surety.

[*Undated*]. Edward Long of St. Michaels, husbandman, bachelor, and Margaret Stoevens, maiden. John Longe of the same, a surety.

1676-7

January 1. Joseph Nicolls of Walden, and Abigail Whethered, maiden. Samuel Waterton of St. Peters, a surety.

January 13. Jeremiah Cowley of St. Albans, grocer, bachelor, and Mary Field of the same, maiden. George Barnes of the same, plumber, a surety.

January 16. William Smith of Sandridge and Alice Taylor of St. Albans, maiden. William Christmas of St. Albans, butcher, and William Tryant of the same, tobacco pipe maker, sureties.

February 5. Thomas Windsor of Sage Hill, St. Stephens, yeoman, bachelor, and Damaris Kentish, maiden. William Kentish of St. Albans, grocer, a surety.

February 12. Francis Halsey, bachelor, and Mary Sam, maiden. John Whittlocke of Markett Streete, yeoman, and John Sheerer of St. Albans, sureties.

February 22. John Weedon of Flamstedd, husbandman, widower, and Anne Longe of St. Michaels widow. John Mott of St. Albans, glover, a surety.

March 17. Samuel Mountague of Sandridge, husbandman, and Mary Adnut of St. Peters, maiden. Thomas Stiles of St. Peters, a surety.

March 24. William Hartin of St. Michaels, victualler, widower, and Sarah Pratt of Abbotts Langley, maiden. John Thorneton of St. Stephens, husbandman, a surety.

1677

March 27. James Rolfe of Hempstead, but now of St. Albans, blacksmith, bachelor, and Mary Cooke late of Hempstead but now of St. Albans, maiden. John Trustrum of Hempstead, carpenter, a surety.

March 31. Abraham Feild of St. Albans, cutler, bachelor, and Elizabeth Heyward of St. Peters, maiden. Joseph Tarbox of St. Albans, tailor, a surety.

April 5. Robert Browne of Abusley [? Abbotsley] co. Huntingdon, husbandman, bachelor, aged 20 or upwards, and Alice White of Redbourne, maiden; at Redbourne. Robert White and Thomas Deacon, both of Redbourne, husbandmen, sureties. He alleges that his father is dead but that his mother Bridgett Browne is living.

April 7. James Bradbury of St. Albans, grocer, bachelor, and Rose Ealing of St. Albans, maiden. Samuel Waterton of St. Albans, ironmonger, a surety.

April 13. Thomas Lee of Aldenham, husbandman, widower, and Sarah Hix of Abbotts Langley, maiden. George Barnes of St. Albans, plumber, a surety.

April 13. Thomas Brock of St. Peters, husbandman, bachelor, and Mary Eaton, maiden. John Matthews of St. Albans, weaver, a surety.

April 30. George Neele of London, and Susannah Grover of Harpenden, maiden. Matthew Iremonger of St. Albans, a surety.

May 4. Ralph Doggett of Leighton Beaudesert, co. Bedford, and Mary Seayre of Winslow. Richard Doggett of Leighton, gent., and Thomas Dogget of the same, innholder, sureties.

May 12. Jeremiah Coleman [*signed* Coman] of St. Michaels, husbandman, bachelor, and Mary Longe of the same, maiden. Nathaniel Pryor of the same, tailor, a surety.

[*Undated, attached to previous allegation*]. William Mun of Flamsted, yeoman, and Joane Knight of St. Albans, maiden. John Mun of . . . . gsate, co. Buckingham, yeoman, a surety.

June 5. Joshua Baker of Ridge, yeoman, and Ann Harris, maiden. John Mathewes of St. Albans, weaver, a surety.

June 21. Amos Angles of Dunstable, co. Bedford, tailor, bachelor, and Frances Fawson of St. Albans. Nathaniel Prior of St. Michaels, tailor, a surety.

June 27. Thomas Johnson of Baldocke, bachelor, and Mary Dearemore of Shephall, maiden.

July 24. Michael Selioke of St. Albans, bachelor, and Mary Beaumount of Greenfield, parish of Flitton, co. Bedford. Nicholas Robson of St. Albans, a surety.

September 1. James Baudin of St. Albans, bachelor, and Mary Renne of the same, maiden, at St. Albans. William Tharpe of the same, a surety.

September 8. William Martyn of St. Albans, bachelor, and Elizabeth Marshall of the same, maiden, at St. Albans. Robert Gregory of St. Albans, a surety.

September 17. Nathaniel Reeve of Bovington, husbandman, bachelor, aged 21 years, and Anne Nuton of Sarrat, maiden, aged 20 years. Henry Seare of Barkhamsted St. Peters a surety.

October 5. Henry Chalkley of Kimpton and Anne Skeele (?) of Harpenden, but now of St. Albans; at St. Peters. Edward Berry of Harpendine, a surety.

October 9. William Pendered of Sandridge, bachelor, and Mary Jaques of the same, maiden ; at St. Peters. Jeremiah Lyons of Sandridge, a surety.

October 27. Jeremiah Lattemore of St. Peters, bachelor, and Mary Neaves. Robert Neaves of the same, a surety.

December 1. Samuel Waterton of St. Albans, grocer, bachelor, and Mary Turner of the same, maiden ; at St. Peters.

December 1. Thomas Halsey, bachelor, and Dorcas Pacey of Studham, maiden; at Redbourne or St. Peters. Edward Halsey of Studham, yeoman, his father, and Robert Swinston of St. Peters, sureties. [There is another copy of this dated July 17th, 1678].

December 31. William Huss of Cripplegate, London, and Mary Darvel of St. Peters ; at St. Peters. James Bradbury of St. Albans, a surety.

1677-8

January 26. Samuel Hundsdon of Wheathamsteed, bachelor, and Joane Capon of St. Albans, maiden ; at St. Peters. Francis Halford of St. Albans, a surety.

March 3. William Joyner of Paulswalden, yeoman, aged 27 years, bachelor, and Rebecca Ivory of the same, aged about 25 years, spinster ; at Paulswalden. [*Allegation only.*]

1678

April 4. John Rolfe of Hemel Hempsted and Mary Frankelin of St. Michaels; at St. Michaels. Nathaniel Pryor of St. Michaels, a surety.

May 4. William Henman of Abbats Langley, bachelor, and Rebecca Hawkins of King's Langley ; at Abbots Langley or Rickmersworth. William Osmond of Abbots Langley, a surety.

May 18. Richard Hawkins of Harpenden, bachelor, and Lucy Halsey, now of St. Albans, daughter of Richard Halsey, late of Redbourne, deceased; at St. Peters. John Halsey of Redbourne, a surety.

May 20. Robert Jeffes of Aston Abbots, co. Bucks, maltster, and Sarah Parrott of the same, maiden ; at St. Peters. John Robinson of St. Peters, a surety.

May 29. Thomas Eaton of St. Peters and Frances Chudsdon of Misenden, co. Buckingham ; at Rickmersworth. Belnap Tiballs of St. Peters, a surety.

June 1. George Carpenter of Redbourne, and Katherine Hurst of the same ; at Redbourne. James Hannell of the same, a surety.

June 8. Michael Parratt of St. Albans, tallow chandler, bachelor, and Sarah Darvall of St. Michaels, maiden; at St. Albans or St. Michaels. Joseph Burr of St. Albans, a surety.

July 20. Stephen Roe, junr., of St. Stephens, and Sarah Woodans of St. Michaels, maiden ; at St. Stephens. Stephen Roe, sen., of the same, a surety.

July 31. Thomas Nash of St. Albans, and Sarah Richards of the same. Thomas Oxton of St. Albans, and John Clerke of the same, sureties.

August 3. John Tyler of Redbourne, bachelor, and Anne Rhodes ; at Redbourne or St. Michaels. Joseph Carpenter of St. Michaels, a surety.

September 14. Edward Bigrave of St. Michaels, and Gatheriche Grover of the same; at St. Michaels. Zachariah Reeve of St. Peters, a surety.

September 20. Hugh Glenister of Winslow, co. Bucks, and Mary Greene of the same; at Winslow or Harwood Parva. Joseph Burr of St. Albans, a surety.

October 3. John Norris of Wigginton and Katherine Broune of the same; at St. Peters. James Martin of St. Albans a surety.

October 12. John Clackeson [*signed* Claxson] of Watford, and Elizabeth Chandelour of the same; at Rickmansworth. Bellnap Tiballs of St. Peters, a surety.

October 15. John Clarke of Redbourne, and Mary Hawkins of Harpenden, maiden; at St. Peters. John Deacon of St. Peters, a surety.

November 16. Richard Birchmore of Redbourne, bachelor, and Sarah Fowler of Hexton, co. Hertford, maiden; at Hexton. Thomas Stepney of Redbourne, a surety.

December 6. John Tacker of St. Albans and Mary Gouldin of the same; at St. Albans. John Sheerer of the same, a surety.

December 17. Richard Camfeild of Codicott and Rose Woodwards of the same; at Codicott or St. Pauls Walden. Frances Feild of the same, a surety.

December 20. Henry Francis of Watford and Katherine Cockens of Kings Langley; at Watford. William Christmas of St. Albans, butcher, a surety.

December 24. Joseph Carter of St. Michaels, bachelor, and Ailce Smith of the same; at Abbots Langley or St. Michaels. Henry Smith of the same, a surety.

1678-9

January 23. Isaac Lane of Misenden, co. Buckingham, and Anne Aldrige of St. Michaels; at St. Michaels. Zachariah Aldrige of St. Michaels, a surety.

February 17. Thomas Babbs [*signed* Bab] of St. Stephens, and Mary Smith of the same maiden; at St. Stephens. Henry Wilson of St. Albans, a surety.

February 22. Thomas Brock of St. Stephens, husbandman, widower, and Martha Harris of the same, widow; at St. Stephens. Henry Field of the same, a surety.

1679

April 20. Thomas Warde of Addington, co. Buckingham, mason, and Susan Edden of Winslow, spinster; at Winslow. William Edden junr of Winslow, yeoman, and Robert Eddon of the same, carpenter, sureties.

1679-80.

March 22. Nathaniell Saunders of St. Stephens, brickmaker, and Elizabeth Peacocke, of St. Michaels, spinster; at St. Michaels or St. Albans. Alice Peacocke of St. Michaels, spinster, a surety.

1680 [?]

May 13. Thomas Nichols of Harding, widower, and Elizabeth Law of the same. John Malin of the same, yeoman, and William Morris of St. Albans, sureties.

*To be Continued.*

# Ministers' Accounts, Henry VII.

## RELATING TO THE COUNTY OF HERTFORD.

[*These documents are preserved in the Public Record Office. The numbers indicate the official reference*].

| Number. | | | | |
|---|---|---|---|---|
| 247 | Possessions of the Queen. Berkhampstead & Kings Langley. 16-17 Hen. VII. Collector's accounts. | | | |
| 248 | The like. | 18-19 Hen. VII. | Accounts of the King's Collectors. | |
| 249 | ,, | 20-21 ,, | Collector's Accounts. | |
| 250 | ,, | 22-23 ,, | Account of Receiver & Collector. | |
| 251 | ,, | 11-12 ,, | Receiver's Account. | |
| 252 | ,, | 16-17 ,, | ,, | |
| 253 | ,, | 17-18 ,, | Account of Queen's receiver. | |
| 254 | ,, | 18-19 ,, | ,, | |
| 255 | ,, | 19-20 ,, | ,, | |
| 256 | ,, | 21-22 ,, | ,, | |
| 257 | ,, | 22-23 ,, | Account of King's receiver. | |
| 258 | Hitchin, Standon & Anstey. | 11-12 Hen. VII. | Accounts of bailiffs. | |
| 259 | ,, ,, ,, | 12-13 ,, | ,, | |
| 260 | ,, ,, ,, | 14-16 ,, | ,, | |
| 261 | ,, ,, ,, | 16-17 ,, | ,, | |
| 262 | ,, ,, ,, | 17-18 ,, | ,, | |
| 263 | ,, ,, ,, | 19-20 ,, | ,, | |
| 264 | ,, ,, ,, | 20-21 ,, | ,, | |
| 265 | ,, ,, ,, | 21-22 ,, | ,, | |
| 266 | Stevenage. 1-2 Hen. VII. | Collector's Account. | | |
| 267 | ,, 2-3 ,, | Account of Farmer & Collector. | | |
| 268 | ,, 3-4 ,, | ,, ,, ,, | | |
| 269 | ,, 5-6 ,, | ,, ,, ,, | | |
| 270 | ,, 9-10 ,, | Collector's Account. | | |
| 271 | ,, 10-11 ,, | Account of Farmer & Collector. | | |
| 272 | ,, 11-12 ,, | ,, ,, ,, | | |
| 273 | ,, 14-15 ,, | ,, ,, ,, | | |
| 274 | The Pré (St. Albans). | 2-4 Hen. VII. | Account of the prioress. | |
| 275 | ,, ,, | 6-9 ,, | ,, | |
| 276 | Asswell. | 13-14 ,, | Collector's Account. | |
| 277 | Cheshunt. | 22-23 ,, | Reeve's Account. | |
| 278 | Weston juxta Baldock | 23-24 ,, | Bailiff's Account. | |
| 1107 | Possessions of Richard Hill, late bp. of London. Hadham, Stortford, Eastwick (& divers places in Essex). 11-12 Hen. VII. Onera of accounts of reeves and others. | | | |
| 1125 | Morley's lands. Barley (& other places in divers counties). 16-17 Hen. VII. Receiver's account. | | | |
| 1126 | The like. 18-19 Hen. VII. | | | |
| 1238 | Possessions of Margaret countess of Richmond & Derby. Ware lordship (& divers places in other counties). 23-24 Hen. VII. Accounts of bailiffs and others. | | | |

1241 Poss. of Edward. late lord Roos. Herts (& other counties). 1-3 Hen. VII. Receiver General's account.
1323 Warwick, Salisbury, & Spencer lands held by the King during the minority & after the attainder of Edw. earl of Warwick son & heir of George duke of Clarence. Flamstead (& places in other counties). 21-22 Hen. VII. Accounts of bailiffs & others.
1370 The like. Herts. 3-4 Hen. VII. Receiver-General's Account (imperfect).
1371 The like. 4-5 Hen. VII.
1372 ,, 5-6 ,,
1373 ,, 7-8 ,,
1374 ,, temp. ,,
1696 Monastic. Hertford. 3-4 Hen. VII. View of all the receipts and expenses.

# Feet of Fines for Hertfordshire.

### TUDOR PERIOD.

(CONTINUED FROM PAGE 135).

#### 1573-4. Hilary Term. 16 Eliz.

*Henry Cocke & Jas. Moryce esq$^s$: Anne Newman widow. Two messuages & lands in Bishops Stortford & Thorley.

John Moyer: John Rumbold & Joan his wife. A third part of a messuage & lands in Harpeden & Whethamsted.

Thos. Meade serjeant at law: Ralph Dyxon gent & Anne his wife. Manors of Souwell & Otweys & 8 messuages & lands in Asshewell Hynxworth & Edworth.

Rich. Adam: Thos. Walgrave *alias* Waldegrave gent. Messuage & lands in Brent Pelham.

Rich. Wythe: John Langhton & Alice his wife & Rich. Stanes & Joan his wife. Two parts of a mill & lands, in three parts divided, in Aldenham.

Hugh Spencer & Geo. Craicall: Thos. Vaughan gent & John Clerke. Lands in Sandriche & psh. of S$^t$ Michaels in S$^t$ Albans.

Geo. Beovys: John Bole & Joan his wife & Robt. Smyth *alias* Clarke & Joan his wife. Messuage & land in Hertford.

Tho. Butterfyeld: Rich. Lovet & Ursula his wife. Messuage & land in Flaunden.

Thos. Woodnet & Geo. Basford gent: Roger Colte gent & Mary his wife. Two messuages & lands in Aldenham.

Thos. Andrewes esq & Barth. Kempe gent: Nich. Bacon knt. lord keeper of the Great Seal & Anne his wife. Manors of Gorehams *alias* Gorehambury, Westwick, Praye, Wyndryche, Burston, Butlers, & Apsabury *alias* Napsebury & 80 messuages & lands in the parishes of St Michaels, St Stephens, & St Peters near St Albans & Redborne & the advowsons of St Michaels & Redborne.

Thos. Gascoign: Wm. Aldred & Sibil his wife & Robt. Broune. Land in Ware & Amwell.

Nich. Bacon knt. Lord Keeper: Henry Cocke esq & Ursula his wife. Manor of Wyndriche *alias* Wyndrige & 24 messuages & lands in parish of St Michaels near St Albans.

Thos. Brygham gent: Jonas Awdery. Messuage & garden in Watford.

Wm. Mallowes gent & Geo. Hagarthe gent: Rich. Skipwith esq. Manor of Bechewood *alias* Saynt Gyles in le Wood & 10 messuages & lands in Flamsteade.

Rich. Tredwey gent & Edw. Walrond: Tho. Saunders gent & Jane his wife & Joan Smyth widow. Messuage & garden in Stortford & the moiety of the manor of Pygotts & of two messuages & lands in Stortford & Thorley.

Nich. Wall: Benj. Potkyn & Suzan his wife. Lands in Little Hadham.

Thos. Seye & Rich. Dunham: Thos. Copcott & Cecily his wife. Messuage & land in Pyrton.

Gilbert Gerrard esq, attorney general: John Cutt knt. & Anne his wife. Manor of Shenley *alias* Salesburye & 40 messuages & lands in Shenley, Rudge *alias* Ridge, Hatfeilde, St Peters, St Albons, Northemymes, Southemymes, Shenley Berye, Barnet, Colney & Bishops Hatfielde.

Robt. Barbour: Henry Butler gent & Alice his wife. The impropriate rectory of Hexton & tithes thereto belonging.

Ralph Skypwyth gent: Rich. Lee knt., Humph. Conyngesbye esq & Mary his wife & Robt. Lee gent. Messuage & lands in St Albans.

Thos. Webbe & Humph. Hooper: Nich. Wall & Mary his wife & Henry Averell. Two messuages & lands in Stondon, Little Hadham, [Much Had]ham, Puckeridge, Braffinge & Sabridgworthe.

1574. Easter Term. 16 Eliz.

*Roger Alford & Wm. Clerke esqs: Francis earl of Bedford & Bridget his wife & Chas. Moryson esq. Manor of Caysho *alias* Caysobury & 20 messuages & lands in Caysho *alias* Cayshobury, Watford & Abbots Langley.

*Geo. Bromley esq, Thos. Bromley esq. Thos. Huyck esq, Rich. Bagott esq, Ralph Edgerton esq, Wm. Barnes esq, Thurstan Woodcock esq, Thos. Woodcock gent. & Wm. Tylston gent: Robt Huyck esq. Two messuages & lands in Waltham.

Henry Kynge: Roger Grubbe & Eliz. his wife. Three messuages & lands in Great Barkhampsted *alias* Barkhampsted Peter.

Wm. Querryngton: Michael Manne & Alice his wife & John Cressett gent. Messuage & lands in Northchurch.

Thos. Shotebolte gent & Philip Downes: Rich. Halfehide & Margery his wife. Two messuages & lands in Yerdeley.

Wm. Thorowgood: Geo. Bennett & Ellen his wife. Messuage & lands in Moche Amwell.

Thos. Axtill: Ralph Perte & Joan his wife. Moiety of land in Hemelhemsted.

Wm. Merston : Wm. Skipwyth knt. & Rich. Skipwith esq, & Mary his wife. Manor of Woodhall in Hempstede *alias* Hemelhempstede & 2 messuages & lands in Hempsted.

Rich. Bedell : Christr. Hochynson & Kath. his wife. Messuage & lands in Stondon.

Agnes Bagshae widow : Edm. Nodes & Eliz. his wife. Land in Stevenache.

Leonard Fysshe gent : Geo. Fysshe esq. Messuage & land in Bishops *alias* Kings Hatfeld.

Thos. Cocks sen<sup>r</sup> gent, & Thos. Ellys gent : Fulk Onslowe gent & Mary his wife. Advowson of the Church of Bishops *alias* Kings Hatfeld & of the Chapel of Tatryche.

Jas. Jeve & Nevell Hasylwood gent : John Graveley gent. Messuage & lands in Kings Walden, Offley & Lyllye.

John Saunders : Henry Langley & Eliz. his wife. Land in Puttenham.

Edw. Bardolf gent : Eliz. Bardolf widow. Messuage & lands in Harpden in the psh. of Whetamsted.

Robt. Marryott : Kath. countess of Huntington & Henry earl of Huntington. Messuage & lands in Ware.

Jas. Campe : Nich. Grave & Joan his wife. Messuage in Standon.

Robt. Grave & Thos. Grave : Robt. Luyck & Margery his wife. Two messuages & lands in Cheshunt.

Geo. Leventhorpe gent : Rich. West gent & Elizabeth his wife. Manor of Mepsall *alias* Meptyshall *alias* Mepsall & 20 messuages & lands in Mempsall & Overstondon.

John Seyman : John Catelyen & Eliz. his wife & Thos. Catelyen. Messuage & lands in Stevenage *alias* Stavenage.

Nich. Reade & Wm. Barnard : John Sprygge & Eliz. his wife, Thos. Nayler & John Nayler. Two messuages in Stortford.

Thos. Mowffett : Thos. Hawlsey *alias* Halsey & Margt. his wife. Three messuages & lands in Barkhampsted S<sup>t</sup> Peter & Northechurche.

Walter Myldmay knt, Wm. Cordell knt, Anth. Cooke knt, Gilbert Gerrard esq, Robt. Wingfelde esq, John Purevey esq, Anth. Browne esq, Edm. Halle esq, Wm. Cooke esq, John Conyers esq, Anth. Cooke son of Rich. Cooke esq, John Harrington esq, Roger Alforde esq, Fras. Harrington esq, & Barnard Dewhurst : Wm. Cecill K.G. etc. Manors of Thebaldes *alias* Tongs, Cresbrooks, Darcies, Thom Willms, Clarks, Cullings, Baas, Periers, Hoddesdonburye, Geddings & Beamounthalle & 300 messuages & lands & free fishery in the water of Lee & the Hundreds of Hertford & Braughing in Chesthunte, Walthamcrosse, Tunforde, Wormeley, Broxburne, Hoddesdon, Amwell, Hertford, Braughing, Westmyll, Chelelsey, Gaddesburie, Pansanger *alias* Passanger, Bengeo, Cockmersted, Estwike, Seale, Tewing, Stapleforde, Hunsdon, Blackemere, Wickham & Saye. Also the free warrens of Baas, Hoddesdon, Hoddesdonbury & Geddings & the fair & market of Hoddesdon.

1574. Trinity Term. 16 Eliz.

*Cuthbert Buckell : Thos. Bryckett. Lands in Kennesworthe.

*Thos. Knolles gent : Thos. Sydney gent & Barbara his wife. Manor of Honyland & Pentriches & 20 messuages & lands in Honyland, Pentriches, Enfyeld & Chesthunt.

Robt. Gravenor & Wm. Gravenor : John Smythe & Joan his wife. Lands in Stondon.

Robt. Gravenor gent: John Whitbread *alias* More. Messuage & lands in Standon *alias* Stondon & Sacombe.

Robt. Asheworthe & Margery his wife: Edw. Cope & Joan his wife & Ralph Cope son & heir app. of s⁴ Edw. & Joan. Messuage & land in S⁺ Albans.

Barth. Wrenne: John Archer & Alice his wife. Messuage & land in Cothered.

Francis Marshe: Thos. Somerton & Anne his wife, John Somerton & Agnes his wife & Thos. Bernarde & Ellen his wife. Messuage & lands in Taterudge.

Robt. Newport esq: Humph. Stafford knt. Manor of Russheden *alias* Rusden and lands in Russheden *alias* Rusden & Sandon.

John Harmer: Robt. Swallowe & Jane his wife. Messuage & lands in Rushden.

John Persmythe *alias* Cheyney sen$^r$: Thos. Adam & Eliz. his wife. Lands in Stortford.

Thos. Foster gent: Rich. Foster & Wm. Foster. Two messuages & lands in Hunesdon.

John Harmer: Matth. Edwards & Agnes his wife. Lands in Rushden *alias* Rusden.

John Ingram & Eliz. his wife: Nich. Busshe & Agnes his wife. Messuage & lands in Hoddesdon.

Peter Osbourne esq, Robt. Wrothe esq, Wm. Wrothe & Thos. Wrothe gents: Geo. Mynne esq. Two messuages & lands in Hartingfordburye & in the psh. of S⁺ Andrew in Hartford.

Wm. North: Robt. Pygott & Agnes his wife. Messuage & land in Stevenage.

Ralph Pope & John Bexffeild: Wm. Barley gent. Three messuages & land in Kympton.

1574. Mich. Term. 16 & 17 Eliz.

*Nich. Bacon knt. Lord keeper of the Great Seal: Henry Gooddere esq. & Frances his wife. Manors of Abbatts Burye *alias* Rowletts Burye, Minchinburye, Hoores & Apsaburye *alias* Napsaburye & 12 messuages & lands in Barley, Barckwaye & the psh. of S⁺ Peters in S⁺ Albans.

*Robt. Staunford esq: Edw. Osborne cit. & alderman of London & Anne his wife. Land in Shenley.

Wm. Francklande & Hugh Francklande: Jas. Johnson & Petronilla his wife. Messuage in Hoddesdon. [*This fine belongs to the Mich. term of the preceding year.*]

Wm. Parker cit. & linendraper of London: Geo. Ellyott & Joan his wife. Manor of Upwyckehall & 5 messuages & lands in Aldebury *alias* Albery, Little Hadham & Stortford.

Thomas Meade serjeant at law: James Lecheworth. Lands in Asshewell & Hinxworthe.

Robt. Wolley: Rich. Stepnethe gent. Two messuages & land in S⁺ Albans.

John Bibbye gent: Jas. Gryffythe & Alice his wife. Messuage & land in the psh. of S⁺ Albans in S⁺ Albans.

Thos. Grymsditch & John Spurlinge: Wm. Goodman gent. Manor of Cumberlowe Grene & 3 messuages & lands in Russheden, Clothalle, Codered & Walington.

Edw. Skypwyth gent: Ralph Skypwyth gent. & Alice his wife. Land in S⁺ Albans.

Fulk Heathe: Thos. Smythe & Rose his wife. Messuage in Pokeridge in psh. of Stondon.

John Kent: Robt. Hoye *alias* Odye & Joan his wife. Messuage & land in Benyngton.

Thos. Holden gent. & Joan his wife: Ralph Maynard & Thos. Hudson gents. Land in psh. of St Peters in St Albans.

Robt. Boram: Thos. Bennett & Eliz. his wife. Land in Broxbourne & Hoddesden.

John Mylles: Edm. Grave & Agnes his wife. Two messuages & land in Baldocke & Willien.

Humph. Heywarde: Wm. Bouthe & Joan his wife. Messuage & land in parishes of St Peter & St Stephen in St Albans.

Wm. Sell: Barth. Lane gent. Messuage & lands in Gt. Munden & Westmyll.

Geo. Grave & Nich. Grace: Henry Dighton & Agnes his wife. Messuage in Hertford.

Stephen Woodruffe gent., Edw. Smyth & Robt. Stepnyth: Geo. Ferrers esq & Margt. his wife. Messuage & 8 cottages in St Albans.

Wm. Fletcher: John Fletcher & Eliz. his wife. Two messuages & lands in Chesthunt.

John Mabbe senr: John Clarke & Kath. his wife. Two messuages & lands in Tatteridge & Bisshops Hatfeld.

Geo. Jennyns: Barth. Lane gent. Manor of Gyffords & 4 messuages & lands in Gt. Munden & Little Munden.

John Stone: John Marshe & Eliz. his wife. Messuage in Chepinge Barnett.

Robt. Shrimpton & Rich. Anderson: Humph. Coningesbie & Mary his wife. The site of the late Monastery of St Albans & 10 messuages & lands in St Albans, also the moiety of two mills in psh. of St Stephens.

Wm. Ayloff gent: John Felton gent & Kath. his wife. Messuage & lands in Layston, Auswyck, Westmyll & Buntingforde.

Wm. Thorowgood & Thos. Bennett: Wm. Smythe & Joan his wife. Messuage & lands in Great Amwell & Stansted Thele.

Charles Calthorp gent & John Stubbe gent: Drugo Drury esq & Eliz. his wife & Philip Parker esq. Messuage & lands in Little Hadham.

1574-5. Hilary Term. 17 Eliz.

*John Butler knt., Geo. Rotheram, Phil. Butler, Edm. Anderson, Gabriel Fowler esq{rs} & Thos. Shotbolte gent: Geo. Ferrers esq. Manors of Flamstede & Makeyate & 30 messuages & lands in Flamstede, Redbourne, Kennesworthe & Cadyngton & a certain portion of tithes in Flamstede, & the advowson & right of patronage of the parish church of Flamstede.

Christr. Aleyn gent: Robt. Ayscough gent & Mary his wife. Manor of Brekendonberie.

Rich. Starr: Geo. Starr & Margt. his wife. Messuage & lands in Cotrid.

Edw. Randyll gent. & Geo. Hall: Simon Harvye. Messuage & lands in Sandan.

Fras. Pomforthe & John Pollard: John Yardley. Two messuages & lands in Westone, Yardley & Clothall.

John Smythe: John Wyse & Agnes his wife. Messuage & land in S Albans.

Geo. Elyotte: Thos. Elyotte & Clement Dawes & Margery his wife. Four messuages & land in Wydford & Ware.

Sampson Wolferston gent: Thos. Apowell & Margt. his wife. Three messuages & lands in St Peters, St Andrewes, St Albanes & Harpeden *alias* Hardyn.

Edw. Fyssher: Roger Farthynge & Mary his wife. Messuage & lands in Stondon.
John Laurens: Ralph Lockey & Rich. Lockey. Messuage & land in the psh. of S*t* Albans in S*t* Albans.
John Gyll esq: Henry Chawncy esq. & Jane his wife. Messuage & lands in Wydyall, Leyston, Buntyngford, Aspyden, Buckland, Barkway & Allsladwicke.
Anth. Radclyff: John Davies & Mary his wife. Ten messuages & lands in S*t* Albans.
Thos. Grymesdyche gent. & Hugh Morgan: Gabriel Leventhorpe gent. Two messuages & lands in Sabrydgeworthe.
Rich. Thorneton gent. & Geo. Wylson: Hen. Chauncye esq. & Jane his wife. Manor of Gifford *alias* Gafford & 3 messuages & lands in Gedleston & Sabrisford.
Thos. Hedge: Thos. Dryver & Ellen his wife. Messuage & lands in Chyldewycke in the psh. of S*t* Michaels near S*t* Albans.
Edw. Bashe esq: Edw. Halfehide & Amy his wife. Manor of Wakeley *alias* Wakely & four messuages & lands in Wakeley, Aspeden, Gt. Munden, Westemill & Leiston & the rectory or chapel of Wakeley *alias* Wakely.
Robt. Heathe: Wm. Aldred & Sibil his wife & Robt. Broune. Three messuages &c. in Ware.

### 1575. Easter Term. 17 Eliz.

*John Peter & Frus. Wyndam esq*rs*: Hen. Chauncy esq. The site of the manor of Netherhall & 2 messuages & lands in Gedleston *alias* Gelston & Estwick.
*Robt. Baspole & Thos. Bartlett: Thos. Jernegan gent & Eliz. his wife. Two messuages & lands in Starford & Thurley *alias* Thorley.
John Oxston *alias* Foxe: Wm. Nycholl & Ellen his wife. Messuage & land in Idelstre *alias* Elstree.
Robt. Woodroffe gent & Dionis his wife: Valentine Browne knt & Thomasine his wife. Seven acres of wood in Barnett.
Francis Saunton *alias* Mathewe: John Abbotte & Susan his wife. Messuage in Stortford.
John Colt: Roger Colt esq. Two messuages & lands in Gt. Monden & Little Monden.
John Sommer: Wm. Bellamy & Alice his wife. Messuage in Hoddesdon.
John Androwe: Robt. Parrys gent & Eliz. his wife. Three messuages & lands in Hytchyn & Offley.

### 1575. Trinity Term. 17 Eliz.

*Wm. Francklyn of Kyngesbery & Wm. Page of Wemley: John Lyon of Preston. Seven messuages & lands in Northmyms, Southemyms, Barnet & Chepinge Barnet.
*Robt. Staunforde esq: Wm. Doddes esq & Kath. his wife. Manor of Wyllyottes in Northe mymes.
Henry Bowman: Henry Palmer esq & Jane his wife. Messuage & lands in Northmymmes & Ridge.
Geo. Mede & Eliz. his wife: Mich Mede & Eliz. his wife: Messuage & land in Ware.
John Dyer: Nich. Dyer & Joan his wife. Lands in Alburie *alias* Aldeburie.
John Haynes: James Quarles gent & Joan his wife. Lands in Gt. Hadham.
Roger Barfotte: John Darlyng & Joan his wife. Messuage & land in Codereth *alias* Codred.

Wm. Chauncy gent: Robt. Chauncy gent & Philippa his wife. Messuage & lands in Sabrydgeworthe *alias* Sabrydgesworthe.
Jas. Birche & Thos. Birche: Rich. Birde. Five messuages & lands in Ware, Thunderitche, Wadesmyll & Amwell.
Thos. Fanshawe esq: Henry earl of Huntingdon & Kath. his wife. Messuage & lands in Ware.
Roger Brycheley: John Byrcheley gent & Philippa his wife. Messuage & garden in psh. of All Saints, Hertford.
John Strampro & Eliz. Strampro: Walter Gynne & Jane his wife. Two messuages in Hitchyn.
Edw. Baeshe esq & Jane his wife: Thos. Grave & Agnes his wife & Wm. Grave. Messuage called Phillittes *alias* Fillettes & lands in Hunsdon, Ware, Stansted Abbott & Estwicke.
Wm. Barfoote: Thos. Dyxe. Messuage & land in Stonden *alias* Stondon.
Rich. Fauner & Andrew Wood: Edw. Stowell & Joan his wife. Land in Honnesdon.
Edm. Nodes gent: Francis Markham gent & Mary his wife. Lands in Stevenache *alias* Stevenage.

### 1575. Mich. Term. 17 & 18 Eliz.

*Nich. Bacon knt. lord keeper of the Great Seal: Wm. Skypwyth esq. Manors of Gorehamburye, Westwycke, Pray cum Kyngsbury, Abbatts Bury *alias* Rowlettes Bury, Mynchynbury, Hores & Apsebury *alias* Napsebury & 50 messuages & lands in the parishes of S$^t$ Peters, S$^t$ Michaels, & S$^t$ Stephens, Barley & Barkwaye, also the advowson of the vicarage of S$^t$ Michaels.
Edw. Powter esq: Leonard Halfehyde & Lettice his wife. Messuage in Hitchyn.
Rich. Peachye: Hen. Chauncye esq. & Jane his wife. Messuage & lands in Sabridgworthe & Gedleston.
Thos. Gooddaye: Thos. Payne & Margt. his wife. Messuage in Sabrydgworth.
Geo. Knyghton gent. & John Knyghton son of s$^d$ Geo.; John Byrcheley gent. & Philippa his wife. Lands in Hertford & Bayford.
Rich. Barnet: John Hunt. Messuage & lands in Shenley.
John Puckeringe esq. & Jane his wife: Thos. Kere gent. & Joan his wife. A fourth part of the manor of Chyldwycke *alias* Chylwycke & 3 messuages & lands in Childwycke *alias* Chilwycke in the psh. of S$^t$ Michaels near S$^t$ Albans.
Wm. Necton gent. & Eliz. his wife: Wm. Smythe & Isabel his wife. Land in Rydge.
Simon Rowe & Anne his wife: John Somerton & Agnes his wife & Thos. Barnard & Ellen his wife. Lands in Tatteridge.
Gilbert Hill gent: Edw. Baesh esq. & Jane his wife. Cottage & land in Ware.
Tho. Sadler, Wistan Browne, John Gyll, Edw. Lewkenor & Thos. Grymesdyche esq$^{rs}$ & Mich. Chamber gent: Tho. Leventhorpe esq. Manor of Cockhamstede & 6 messuages & lands in Brawghinge.
John Gybb & Joan his wife: John Roberds & Anne his wife & John Hemyng & Joan his wife. Messuage in Stortford.
Roland Hawarde knt. & John Langley: Roger Colte esq. & Mary his wife. Two messuages & lands in Gt. Munden & Little Munden.
John Godfree *alias* Cowper: Wm. Godfree *alias* Cowper & Josanna his wife. Messuage & land in Hitchyn, Preston, Pollitte *alias* Ipollette & Kings Walden.

Clement Newce esq : John Massyngberd gent & Dorothy his wife. A twentioth part of the Manors of Byggynnes & Barwyckᵉ & 10 messuages & lands in Gt. Hadham & Standon.

Clement Newce esq : Wm. Clopton & Thos. Horseman esqʳˢ. Six parts of the manors of Byggynes & Barwicks & 10 messuages & lands (in 20 parts divided) in Gt. Hadham & Standon.

Robt. Brett : Valentine Browne knt & Thomasine his wife & Wm. Rolf gent & Frances his wife. Lands in Chippinge Barnet.

John Lacye : Edw. Denton gent & Joyce his wife. Manors of Holwell *alias* Holdwell Grey & Ludwick & 16 messuages & lands in Holwell Hide, Ludwick Hide, Digonswell, Kings Hatfeld *alias* Bishops Hatfeld, Twynge & Hartingford Bury and free warren in Holwell & Ludwick.

Wm. Cocke gent & Simon Wyllimot : Ralph Radcliffe gent & Thos. Webbe. The site of the late Priory of the Carmelite Friars of Hutchen & 6 messuages & lands in Hutchen.

Roland Lytton esq & John Mychell gent : John Nedham. Manor of Wymondeley & 10 messuages & lands in Wymondeley, Ikelford, Polletts, Graveley & Great Wymondelye & the site of the late priory of Wymondelye, & the advowson of the church of Wymondelye.

*To be Continued.*

# Abstracts of Wills.

**ARCHDEACONRY OF MIDDLESEX (ESSEX AND HERTS).**

REGISTER "RAYMOND."—CONTINUED FROM PAGE 121.

f. 292ᵇ KATHERINE HOWE, wydowe, of Ware. (*Dat.* 22 Jan. 1573). Son Roger Howe; Tenement in Crispe Streate called Disneis & stable in Garner lane; Son Henry; Dau. Parnelle Cutterwoode; The childⁿ of my son Henry Howe; Henry son of sᵈ Henry Howe; Wm. Howe; Leonard Howe; The childⁿ of Parnell Cutterwood; Peter Smithe; Robt. Smithe; Alice Smithe; Eliz. Smithe; Thos. son of Roger Howe; Joan Claye; Son Roger exor. Witˢ :—Robt. Kaye, Thos. Hallewell & Wm. Davie. (*Pr.* at Ware 9 Mch. 1580-1).

f. 295ᵇ WILLIAM BARNER of Harestrete of [*sic*] Leyston, husbandman. (*Dat.* 13 Nov. 1580). Bur. at Leyston; Son Thos.; Eldest son Wm.; Henry Barner eldest son of my son Wm.; Dau. Marie Shaldon; Wife Kath.; Dau. Kath. Bygrave; Dau. Bridget; Kath. Barner dau. of my son Wm.; Alexʳ & Thos. Barner sons of my son Thos.; John son of Thos. Haldon & his 3 daus.; Wife extrix, & son Thos. overseer. Witˢ :— Thos. Brande, Thos. Warner & Thos. Webbe. (*Pr.* at Sabridgforde 9 Jan. 1580-1).

f. 296ᵇ CHRISTOPHER WRIGHTE of Ware, yeoman. (*Dat.* 11 Jan. 1579). Dau. Marie wife of Thos. Harroden of Baddoe parva, co. Essex; Thos. Pegrome; Geo. Pengrome; Frances Pegrome; Alice Pegrom; Eliz. Pegrome; Diones *alias* Dionee Pegrome; Eliz. Wright dau. of my son Robt. of Cotgrave, co. Nott.; Wife Margerie; Messuage at the Churchgate of Ware; Wife & son-in-law Thos. Harroden exors; John Brett of Little Baddoe overseer. Witˢ:—Christr. Pickeringe, Simon Aprice, Rich. Sybburne. (*Pr.* 11 Jan. 1580-1).

f. 297. RICHARD LOWEN of Chesthunte, husbandman. (*Dat.* 22 Nov. 1580). Daus. Joan Lowen, Lucie Lowen, Agnes Lowen & Alice Lowen; The child my wife is withall; Wife Alice extrix. Witˢ:—John Bushewe & John Lowen. (*Pr.* 9 Jan. 1580-1).

f. 297ᵇ MARGERY PERRIE of Chesthunte, widow. (*Dat.* 6 Dec. 1580). Son Robt. Perrie; Son John Perrie at Sabridgeworthe; 'The howse that I late came forthe of in Sabridgworthe'; Son Geo. Perrie; Son. Christr. Perrie; John Goodwyne sometimes my servant; Son Robt. exor. Symon Williams vicar of Chesthunt overseer. Witˢ:—Simon Williams & Thos. Spencer. (*Pr.* at Sabridgforde 16 Dec. 1580).

f. 298. RICHARD HALLE of Estwicke, blacksmith. (*Dat.* 17 Nov. 1580). Nuncupative will; Wife Eliz.; Sons Robt. & John; Wife extrix. Witˢ:—Anth. Tunbridge, Wm. Birchley & Joan Cramphorne. (*Pr.* at Sabridgworthe 16 Dec. 1580).

f. 299. ISABEL KINGE of Meseden, widow. (*Dat.* 23 Oct. 1580). Son John; House & lands called Bawtons; Andrew son of sᵈ son John; Dau. Agnes Warner; Eliz. Kinge; Eliz. Kinge dau. of John Kinge; Joane & Agnes Totnam; Mother Madle; The wife of Ralph Madle; Servᵗ Andrew Brande; Large; Thos. son of John Kinge; John son of John Kinge; Joan dau. of Henry Totnam; Andrew son of John Kinge; Frances son of Thos. Warner; Thos. Warner's childn; Anthonie Crede; Dau. Marget; Grace wife of John Kinge; Dau. Joane; The rest of the daus. of John Kinge & Henry Totnam; The childn of Henry Hamonde; The childn of Wm. Stallibrasse by my dau. Kath.; Son in law Hen. Totnam; Lawrence Waker; Kath. Pegrome; Son John Kinge exor; Grace & Suzan Kinge daus. of John Kinge; Andrew Kinge my husband (decᵈ). Witˢ:—Wm. Cowell thelder, John Smothe. (*Pr.* at Sabridgforde 22 Nov. 1580).

f. 300ᵇ JOHN COCKE of Hamonde Streete in psh. of Chesthunt, yeoman. (*Dat.* 24 Sep. 1580). Godson Fras. Lowen & Thos. Lowen his father; Wm. bro. of sᵈ Fras. Lowen; Dau. Alice Lowen; Son in law Thos. Lowen; Neither Crofte in occ. of Nich. Lowen; Johan wife of Henry Cordell my kinswoman; John son of Nich. Lowen; Alice wife of Nich. Lowen; Eliz. Cockerell my kinswoman & servant (under 21); Son George Cocke exor; Wife Johan; Symon Williams vicar of Chesthunt overseer. Witˢ:—'Sayde George & Symon.' (*Pr.* at Sabridgforde 5 Nov. 1580).

f. 301. JOHN COXE of Cressbroke Strete in psh. of Chesthunte. (*Dat.* 28 Jan. 1579). Thos. Coxe my younger son; Robt.

Petite of Chesthunte; Father Leate; Anne Beaff; John Hove; Son Wm. Coxe exor; Wm. Thorogood, Antonye Lambert & Robt. Petitt overseers. Wits:—Wm. Thorogood, Anth. Lambert, Leonard Tod & Symon Williams vicar of Chesthunt. (*Pr.* at Sabridgeworth 17 May 1580). List of debts owing from Wm. Fletcher, John Leake & Leonard Tod, & debts owing to Levett of Walthm Holly Crosse, Horevol's wife & Goodwife Wilson.

f. 302. JOHN FYNCHE of Chesthunt, husbandman. (*Dat.* 2 Sep. 1579). Son Wm.; Daus.-in-law Eliz. & Marie; Son-in-law John; Sisters Johan & Eliz.; Cosyn Geo. Cressie his four child<sup>n</sup>; Wife Isbell extrix; Leonard Todd, Giles Harlwen & Geo. Cressie sen<sup>r</sup> overseers. (*Pr.* at Sabridgeworth 17 May 1580).

f. 303. JOHN DAULTON of Standon, husbandman. (*Dat.* 11 Dec. 20 Eliz.). Son Wm.; Agnes Langham my dau.; A cow, colour black, called Ould Crowe & others called Younge Crowe & Wisherd; Daus. Marye & Frances; Sons Anthony & Thos.; Dau. Eliz.; Mary Kente my daughter's dau.; Barnnabas Daulton & John Daulton my servants & kinsmen; Son Robt. exor. Wits:—Rich. Barbor, Wm. Godffrey, Robt. Crouch & Wm. Daultonne. (*Pr.* at Braughin 15 Apr. 1580).

f. 307<sup>b</sup> WILLIAM LYTTELL of Hornsdon. (*Dat.* 2 Feb. 23 Eliz.). John Addams of Royden, co. Essex; Robt. Cramphorne, Rich. Englishe, John Warde, Smyth, Robt. Grave, John Taylor, John Helhm, Margt. Burr; Bro. Richard; Thos. Crosier; Ground in Whelers lye; M<sup>r</sup> Faunces; Bro. Gyles; John Addams exor; M<sup>r</sup> Rich. Fanner overseer. (Exor renounced & admon. granted to Thos. Wakefield 30 June 1581).

*To be Continued.*

# Church Terriers.

### BOVINGDON.

A Particular Account of the Bounds about the Church Yard as they were measured and staked out to be maintain'd and kept up according to an Ancient Custom with us used.

|  | Poles. | Ft. |
|---|---|---|
| Imp<sup>r</sup>: Mary Fisher, Mary Dell, Jos. Astin Jun<sup>r</sup> | 1 | 16 |
| Sam<sup>l</sup> Littlepeaig for Pinks | 0 | 22 |
| John Feild, John Puttnam, Sen<sup>r</sup>, William Batchlour, Sam. Shepard, John Shepard & Sam<sup>l</sup> Littlepeaig | 3 | 12 |
| M<sup>r</sup> Pitkin, John Davey, Joseph Astin | 3 | 0 |
| William Batchlour | 0 | 10 |
| John Axtell, Tho. Astin, Tho. Cason, W<sup>m</sup> Buttler | 0 | 20 |

| | | |
|---|---:|---:|
| John Neale | 2 | 2 |
| John Puttnam Sen^r for Marchants. John Edwards | 0 | 30 |
| Francis King | 2 | 10 |
| Tho. Reeve for late Cottens | 0 | 10 |
| Sam^l Littlepeaig for the Street house | 2 | 8 |
| John Smith for great Shantock | 0 | 24 |
| James Boddy | 0 | 23 |
| Thomas Newman, Jos. Astin Sen^r, Richard Harris | 0 | 28 |
| Daniel Pratt, John Cogdele, William Puttnam | 2 | 10 |
| John Puttnam Jun^r, John Budd | 2 | 0 |
| William Smith for Humphry's Land, Tho. Pearce | 1 | 0 |
| John Clark for the Mare farm | 0 | 25 |
| Stephen Shepard | 1 | 0 |
| Thomas Bunn for late Shakemaples | 0 | 30 |
| John Bunn Sen^r, Jeremiah Feild | 3 | 8 |
| William Arnott for the Hay | 2 | 9 |
| James Clark for New Hall | 0 | 20 |
| John King for Green End, John Mills, Tho. Burch, John Fisher for Becks & Colemans, John Edwards | 3 | 10 |
| Richard Clark Jun^r, Tho. Bavinn, Tho. Bunn, & Richard Clark Sen^r for M^r Knowltons | 4 | 9 |
| Jos. Astin Jun^r for his own, Tho. Clark, John Bunn Jun^r & Thomas Reeve for late Bunkers | 0 | 22 |
| Sam^l Littlepeaig for Whelply Ash | 1 | 0 |
| William Smith for Moldwins | 1 | 0 |
| M^r Crowfoot for Reeves Hills & Hogpitts | 1 | 9 |
| John King, Francis Thorne for the Moore farm | 3 | 4 |
| Richard Gale, Tho. Reeve for Cooks, Daniel Aldwin | 0 | 28 |
| Isaac Pratt | 2 | 7 |

The Gate to be maintained at the Common Charge. The Raile to be kept up by the Cross farm. John Stacey 8 feet, Richard Clark Sen^r & Hudson 8 feet, Henry Baker & M^r Thomas Bunn for Hollimans 8 feet between Will Colemans Hedge & the Vicaridge Pale.

Examined ag^t an Ancient Copy<br>p Sam. Slade

Hertf. We whose names are under written Parrishioners of Bovingdon do allow of the within account of the Bounds of our Church Yard to be according to an ancient Custom with us used. Wittness our hands this 4^th Day of November Anno Domini 1726. [*Signed*]. John King, John Neale, Sam. Slade, Will Smith, Francis King, John Putnam, Sen^r, Tho. Peirce, Zachary King, John Bunn, James Boddy, William Batchelder, Thomas Numan, Joseph Austin, Richard Hares, Humprey Pudephat, John Sheppard, Tho. Bunn, Jonathan King, Isaac Prat, Henry Putnam, John Smith.

## BRAMFIELD.

A TERRIER of all y^e Gleabe lands belonging to y^e Rectory of Branfeild in y^e County of Hartford & Diocess of Lincolne & Archdeaconry of Huntingdon, exhibited this 28^th of June 1638.

Imprimis y^e Rectory howse & outhowses together w^th y^e yards, gardens, orchards and a close adioyning calld Butt close conteyning alltogether by estimation six Acres abutting upon y<sup>e</sup> streete on y<sup>e</sup> west & vpon my lord Buttl<sup>rs</sup> land calld Place feild on y<sup>e</sup> East & vpon Swellings lane on y<sup>e</sup> North & vpon y<sup>e</sup> Kings highway to Hartford on y<sup>e</sup> South.

- Item one close calld Church Close & one other close adioyning calld y<sup>e</sup> slipe conteyning by estimation five acres & one half acre & abutting vpon y<sup>e</sup> churchyard & vpon Edward Bessills land & a howse & orchard calld Smythes on y<sup>e</sup> North & vpon two closes of my lord Buttlers land calld Witherly & Beamonts on y<sup>e</sup> west & vpon a lane on y<sup>e</sup> South.

- Item five pcells of Gleabeland in a Comon feild calld Bukkle Hill conteyning by estimacon five acres vz: one peece at y<sup>e</sup> gate conteyning by estimacon one acre & one half acre abutting vpon a lane on y<sup>e</sup> west & vpon a peece of Edward Hinds land on y<sup>e</sup> North & vpon a feild of my lord Butl<sup>rs</sup> called y<sup>e</sup> Lies on y<sup>e</sup> East & vpon my lord Butlers land lying in y<sup>e</sup> s<sup>d</sup> Bukkle Hill on y<sup>e</sup> south. And one other peece by estimation one Roode abutting vpō y<sup>e</sup> said lane on y<sup>e</sup> west & vpō y<sup>e</sup> fores<sup>d</sup> feild calld y<sup>e</sup> lies on y<sup>e</sup> east & vpon land of y<sup>e</sup> s<sup>d</sup> L<sup>d</sup> Buttl<sup>rs</sup> lying in y<sup>e</sup> s<sup>d</sup> Bukkle Hill vpon y<sup>e</sup> North & South. And one other peece by estimacon one Acre & one Roode abutting vpon y<sup>e</sup> s<sup>d</sup> lane on y<sup>e</sup> west & vpon y<sup>e</sup> fores<sup>d</sup> feild calld y<sup>e</sup> lies on y<sup>e</sup> East & vpon y<sup>e</sup> land of y<sup>e</sup> s<sup>d</sup> L<sup>d</sup> Buttl<sup>rs</sup> lying in y<sup>e</sup> s<sup>d</sup> Bukkle Hill on y<sup>e</sup> North & South. And one other peece by estimacon three Roodes abutting vpon y<sup>e</sup> s<sup>d</sup> lane on y<sup>e</sup> west & vpon y<sup>e</sup> fores<sup>d</sup> feild calld y<sup>e</sup> lies on y<sup>e</sup> East & vpon y<sup>e</sup> s<sup>d</sup> lord Buttl<sup>rs</sup> land lying in y<sup>e</sup> s<sup>d</sup> Bukkle Hill on y<sup>e</sup> North & partly vpon y<sup>e</sup> s<sup>d</sup> lord Butlers land & partly vpon a peece of Gleabland calld a siding peece lying in y<sup>e</sup> said Buckkle Hill on y<sup>e</sup> South. And one other peece calld a siding peece by estimacon one Acre & one Roode abutting vpon y<sup>e</sup> s<sup>d</sup> lane on y<sup>e</sup> West & vpon land of my L<sup>d</sup> Butl<sup>rs</sup> lying in y<sup>e</sup> s<sup>d</sup> Bukkle Hill on y<sup>e</sup> East & vpon a pcell of Gleabeland calld y<sup>e</sup> Heading peece & lying in y<sup>e</sup> s<sup>d</sup> Bukkle Hill on y<sup>e</sup> North & vpon a Comon feild calld Highfeild on y<sup>e</sup> south.

- Item fower pcells of Gleabe land in a Comon feild calld High feild conteyning by estimacon fower acres vz: one peece at y<sup>e</sup> gate at y<sup>e</sup> west end conteyning by estimacon one acre abutting vpon a lane on y<sup>e</sup> west & vpon a comon feild calld Bukkle Hill on y<sup>e</sup> North & vpon lands of my L<sup>d</sup> Buttl<sup>rs</sup> lying in y<sup>e</sup> s<sup>d</sup> High feild on y<sup>e</sup> East & y<sup>e</sup> south. And one oth<sup>r</sup> peece conteyning by estimate one acre abutting vpon y<sup>e</sup> s<sup>d</sup> lane on y<sup>e</sup> west & vpon lands of my L<sup>d</sup> Butl<sup>rs</sup> lying in y<sup>e</sup> s<sup>d</sup> comon feilde on y<sup>e</sup> East North & South. And one other peece by estimacon one acre abutting vpō y<sup>e</sup> s<sup>d</sup> lane on y<sup>e</sup> west & vpon lands of my lord Buttl<sup>rs</sup> in y<sup>e</sup> said feild on y<sup>e</sup> North & East & vpon Edward Hynds land on y<sup>e</sup> South. And one other peece conteyning by estimacon one Acre abutting vpon y<sup>e</sup> fors<sup>d</sup> Buckkle Hill on y<sup>e</sup> North & vpon lands of my l<sup>d</sup> Buttl<sup>rs</sup> lying in y<sup>e</sup> s<sup>d</sup> High feild on y<sup>e</sup> East West & South.

- Item in a Comon feild calld Turnam feild a pcell of Gleabe land by estimacon three acres abutting vpon a lane on y<sup>e</sup> East & vpō a lane on y<sup>e</sup> South & vpon lands of my L<sup>d</sup> Buttl<sup>rs</sup> on y<sup>e</sup> North & vpon lands of George Hills on y<sup>e</sup> West lying in y<sup>e</sup> s<sup>d</sup> Comon feild.

- Item in a Comon feild calld Broome land one pcell of Gleabe land by estimation five Acres abutting vpon a pcell of Gleabe land calld Broome land close on y<sup>e</sup> East & vpon my L<sup>d</sup> Buttl<sup>rs</sup> land & Georg

Hylls land lying in y^e s^d comōn feild on y^e West & vpō land of my lord Buttl^rs in y^e s^d feild on y^e North & vpon a lane called Broome land lane on y^e south.

Item a pcell of Gleabe land calld Broome land Close by estimation five Acres abutting vpō land of my lord Buttl^rs calld Vpper Chater feild on y^e South or vpon land of y^e s^d L^d Buttl^rs calld Middle Chater Hill on y^e East & vpon a Comōn feild called Broome land & land of my L^d Buttl^rs calld Sheedd feild on y^e West & vpon y^e s^d shedd feild on y^e North.

Item a pcell of Gleabeland calld Luce Wants by estimation five Acres abutting vpō a lane on y^e West & vpon a feild of my L^d Buttl^rs calld Grezells on y^e East & vpon a lane on y^e North & vpon certaine woodlands of one M^r Wilds lying in y^e pish of S^t Andrewes in Hertford.

All w^ch pcells of Gleabeland lie w^thin y^e s^d pish of Branfeild.

      Edwarde Boughton Rector.
      Edward Bigge Churchwarden.
      Thomas Chappell × Sideman
        his marke.

# Rowlett Wills.

### SIR RALPH ROWLETT.
[*P.C.C. Holney* 33.]

S^r Rauffe Rowlett late of Halywell nere the towne of Seint Albons, in the countie of Herteford, knight. (*Dated* 28 July 1566). Concerning my manors lands etc. in counties of Hertford, Cambridge, Leiceter, Northampton & Essex, my feoffees to stand seised to such uses as are set out by several indentures tripartite leading the uses & dated 30 June 8 Eliz. & as by an indenture dat. 24 July 8 Eliz. made between me of the one part & Sir Nicholas Bacon, lord keeper, of the other part concerning the manors of Mynchenbury Rowlett(?) bury *als*. Abbott(?) bury & Hores in Barlye & as by another indenture dat. 25 July 8 Eliz. touching the disposition of my capital messuage in the psh. of S^t Albans & all that the parke there, my messuages lands etc. in Hallywell strete Sopwell lane in S^t Albans & S^t Michaels and as by an indenture dat. 27 June 8 Eliz. made unto Jas. Bacon, Thos. Androwes & Barth. Kempe for 4 years & as by this my last will shall be appointed. To Anne Goodere my niece 100*l*. in satisfaction of all she can claim of me as exor to Francis Goodere esq. her father dec^d. To Eliz. Bowles niece to Dorothie my first wife 100 marks. To nephew Rauffe Maynard 100*l*. To Sir Nich. Bacon knt. lord keeper my lease of my mansion house in London. Nephew Rauffe Jennyns to have all my household stuff etc. now in my mansion house called Hallywell. All household stuff in my house in London to s^d Sir Nich. Bacon. To Thos. Ploughe 10*l*. To Thos. Pullforde 10*l*. To Rob^t.

Seale 6l. 13s. 4d. To Anthony Midleton 6l. 13s. 4d. 'To the Maior and bretheren of Seint Albons towards the ereccou of their free scole' 100l. To Nich. Judd towards his education in virtue & learning 100l. Sir Nich. Bacon, the honble Sr Robert Catlyn knt. lord chief justice, John Southcote esq. one of the Justices of the Queens Bench & Gilbert Gerrard esq. attorney general, exors. & to each exor 20 marks. The rt. honble Sir Wm. Cycill knt. overseer & to him 20 marks.

To Rauffe Jennyns esq. & the heirs of his body my manor of Sandridge *alias* Sandruge & the parsonage & rectory of Sandridge & the yearly pension of xxvjs. viijd. going out of the vicarage of Sandridge & the advowson of the vicarage & all messuages etc. in Sandridge, Whethamstede, Bushops Hatfelde & in psh. of St Peter near St Albans. My manor of Thedingworth & the rectory & parsonage of Thedingworth & messuages & lands belonging in counties of Leicester or Northampton to my neph. Henry Goodere for life, remr to the heirs of his body, remr to Thos. Goodere, remr to Wm. Goodere, remr to my niece Anne Goodere etc. My manors of Newneham & Radwell, rectory & parsonage of Newneham, advowsons of Radwell & of the vicarage of Newneham & all messuages etc. appertaining in Newneham, Radwell, Caldecote, Hynxworth, Bygrave & Baldock to neph. Wm. Skipwith esq. for life & to the heirs of his body, remr to Rauffe Skipwith, remr to Edw. Skipwith, remr to Henry Skipwith etc. My capital messuage called Halywell & garden & park adjoining & lands called Bradfords & Poudwick in psh. of St Albans 'that now is' & a close in tenure of Geo. Bun in psh. of St Michaels on the west side of the highway from St Albans to St Stephens & lands & tenements in Hallywell Streate & Sopwell lane unto sd Sr Robt. Catlyn for life paying to my neph. Rauff Jennyns & his heirs one red rose at feast of St John Bapt., remr to sd neph. Rauffe & the heirs of his body. Sr Robt. Catlyn to have all profit of all the Abbye meadowes in Seint Albons for life, remr to sd neph. Rauffe. Provision for securing annuity of 30l. to sd Wm. Skipwith out of manor of Sandridge until a lease for years made by me of parcel of sd manor to Thos. Thrale shall expire. An annuity of 30l. to sd Henry Goodere out of sd manor & lands until the terms for years of parcels of sd manor occupied by Wm. Sherwood & Ranulphe Done shall expire. Annuity of 6l. 13s. 4d. to Thos. Pulfforde until lease of Thos. Norrys expires & annuity of 3l. 6s. 8d. to Anthony Midelton. Wm. Goodere to have annuity of 6l. 13s. 4d. out of manor of Thedingworth until lease of Sr Edward Saunders knt. expires. Edwd Skipwith to have annuity of 10l. out of manor of Newnam until Jas. Dowman's lease expires. Robt. Seale to have annuity of 3l. 6s. 8d. out of messuage called Halywell according to an annuity indented by me made to him dated 26 June 8 Eliz. etc. The parsonage & vicarage of Weston etc. & a yearly rent of 6s. 8d. issuing out of a tenement called Palmers in Weston to neph. Thos. Goodere & the heirs of his body. To sd Sr Nich. Bacon my manors of Mynchynbury, Rowletts bury *alias* Abbotts bury & Hores in Barlye in co. of Hertf. Essex & Cambridge, also the manor of Apsaburye als. Apsburye in psh. of St Peters near St Albans. My exors 'wtin one yere after my decease remove the covered bodies of my deare father and mother deceased wch now lie buried in the pishe churche of Seint Albons and also my deare and welbeloued wyves Dorothie and Margaret wch are and lie buried in the pishe churche of Seint Mary Stayning( in London and to bury the same bodies in the quire of the pishe churche of Sandridge in decent and seamelie manner bestowing suche charigẽ aboute the said funeralle and in other almes and charitable deades as to my said executors shall seame mete and most necessary.' Dated 29 July 1566. Witˢ:—Thomas Colby, Robert Burgoyne, Thomas Rolf, Adrian Thorpe, Rich. Kynwelmershe mercer, Wm. Phillippes. (*Admon.* 8 July 1571 to Henry Goodere of Pollesworth, co. Warw., esq., the exors having renounced).

## Inquisitiones post Mortem.

### CONSTANCE CRESSY.
[*Inq. p.m. Ric. III. & Hen. VII. r.o. No.* 51.]

Inquisition taken at Hertford 'die Sabbati' next after the feast of Sᵗ Faith the Virgin, 2 Hen. VII. [6 Oct. 1486] before John Teye, escheator, by the oaths of John Aldere, Rich. Mone, Nich. Shergott, Wm. Fitzraff, Wm. Plowewryt, Rich. Pycard, John D . . . sy, Rich. Prat, Henry Thurgoode, Rich. Mytt, Gilb. Roos, Geoff. Fox & Wm. Smyth who say that

Constance Cressy, widow, late wife of John Cressy, knight, held the manors of Rothamsted and Sauncij with the appurtenances in Whethamsted, co. Herts., for the term of her life, by the assignment of sᵈ John, her late husband, in the name of her jointure, which manors are held of the abbot of Sᵗ Peter's, Westminster, by socage & are worth, per annum, clear xxl.

Said Constance died 20th June last past and Matthew Cressy is next of kin & heir of sᵈ John Cressy knt. viz. son of Nicholas, son of Edmund, father of John, father of sᵈ John Cressy knt. & at the time of taking this inquisition was aged 40 years & more.

### JOHN GAPE.
[*Inq. p.m.* 11 *Car. I. part* 3 *No.* 38. *(Indexed* 12 *Car. I.)*]

Inquisition taken at Sᵗ Albans, co. Herts. 19 Mch. 11 Chas. [1636] before Ralph Briscoe esq., escheator, after the death of John Gape, by the oaths of John Marston gent., Edw. Neele, Edw. Smith, Robt. Smith, Mordecay Halsey, John Halsey, John Pope, Robt. Putnam, Wm. Herne, Daniel Howe, Joseph Ewer, Mich. Younge & Tho. Lawrence who say that

John Gape was seised as of fee in a messuage lying in Sullypath Street in the parish of Sᵗ Michaels & a close of pasture & meadow containing 4 acr. called Pitwicks in sᵈ parish & so seised by indenture dated 18 March 17 Jas. [1620] conveyed the premises to Giles Marston & John Estridge & their heirs to the use of said John Gape for life & afterwards to the use of Joan his wife for life & the heirs of the body of sᵈ John by sᵈ Joan, with remainder to the right heirs of sᵈ John.

Said John was also seised as of fee, in reversion after the death of Anne Gape widow of 40 acres of land, meadow & pasture in the psh. of Sᵗ Michaels.

So seised s^d John died 19 Nov. 1625 & John Gape is son & next heir & was aged at time of his fathers death 1 year 11 months & 14 days.

The messuage in Sullypathstreete is held of the king now in socage by fealty & is worth, per annum, clear, v*s*. Pitwicke Close is held of the king now in chief by knights service & is worth, per annum, clear v*s*. The 40 acres in St. Michaels are held of the lord of the manor of Gorhambury in free socage & are worth, per annum, clear, xiij*s*. iiij*d*.

Anne Gape mother of s^d John Gape dec^d & Joan Gape his wife now survive, in the psh. of S^t Michaels.

## THOMAS EWER.

[*Inq. p.m.* 4 *Car. I.* (*indexed* 8 *Car. I.*) *pt.* 1, *No.* 27.]

Inquisition taken at S^t Albans 28 Apr. 4 Car. I. [1628] before Wm. Lambe esq. escheator after death of Thomas Ewer gent. by the oaths of Thos. Greenhill gent., Wm. Bayly, John Marston sen^r, John Marsh, Robt. Laysby, John Wethered, John Marston, jun^r, Thos. Sleape, Thos. Knowlton, Wm. Longe, Wm. Hale, Christr. Arland, Anth. Jackson, & Tim. Gould, who say that

Long before death of s^d Thomas Ewer, Henry Hickman & John Scott being seised in fee of all that farm, capital messuage, warren & tenement called Bushy Warren & lands thereto belonging in Watford & Bushey, by indenture dat. 1 Mch. 1 Jas. declaring the uses of a certain fine levied & a recovery &c granted s^d premises to s^d Thos. Ewer & Henry Ewer his son & heir apparent to hold to use of s^d Thos. & Henry & their heirs & assigns for ever; in virtue whereof etc s^d Thos. & Henry were seised as of fee.

Jurors also say that Edward lord Denny, now Earl of Norwich being seised in fee of the site of the manor of Meriden *alias* Mournden & land, meadow, pasture &c thereto belonging in Watford, Aldenham & S^t Stephens & a certain portion of tithes of hay in same places, by indenture dated 1 May 5 Jas. sold s^d premises to s^d Thos. Ewer to hold for life with remainder to John Warner sen^r for life, remainder to David Ewer son of s^d Thos. & the heirs of his body & in default to the right heirs of s^d Thos. for ever. Afterwards for better assurance s^d Edw. Lord Denny & Mary his wife levied a fine etc.; in virtue whereof s^d Thos. Ewer was seised of the premises so conveyed & limited. John Warner died during lifetime of s^d Thomas & Anne late wife of s^d Thomas survives.

Thos. Ewer was also seised in fee of 9 acr. meadow in Bushey meade in the parishes of Bushey & Watford & a water mill called Atterspole mill & 6 acr. meadow belonging in Aldenham & so seised made his last will dat. 31 Aug. 3 Car. & left s^d premises last mentioned to Mary Ewer his grandchild, dau. of s^d Henry Ewer.

Thomas Ewer died 29 Sept. last past & Henry Ewer is his son & heir apparent & at the death of s^d Thomas was aged 30 years & more.

The messuage &c called Bushy Warren is held of the king in chief by knights service & is worth per ann. clear 6*l*. The site of the manor of Meriden is held of the king in chief by knights service & worth per ann. clear 6*l*. The 9 acr. in Bushey meade are held of the lords of the manor of Bushy in free socage by fealty & suit of court & worth per ann. clear 6*s*. 8*d*. Atterspole Mill is held of Henry lord Carye viscount Fawkland as of his manor of Aldenham, in free socage by fealty suit of court & is worth per ann. clear 10*s*.

## DAVID EWER.

*[Inq. p.m. 6 Car. I. (indexed 8 Car. I.) pt. 1. No. 15.]*

Inquisition taken at S<sup>t</sup> Albans 1 Nov. 6 Car. I. [1630] before Wm. Lingwood esq. escheator, after the death of David Ewer gent. by the oaths of John Apowell gent., Rich. Silverlocke, Thos. Gunstone, John Smith, Wm. Bayley, Robt. Marshall, Rich. Sheppard, Wm. Wynche, Steph. Axtell, Jas. Carter, Freeman Nicolls, Thos. Knowlton of S<sup>t</sup> Peters, Roger Marshe, John Nicholls & Thos. Sharpe, who say that

Long before the death of David Ewer, one Edw. lord Denny, now earl of Norwich, was seised in fee of the site of the manor of Meriden *alias* Mourden & a messuage, dovecote, garden, orchard, 80 acr. land, 60 acr. meadow, 40 acr. pasture & 30 acr. wood in Watford, Aldenham, & the psh. of S<sup>t</sup> Stephens & a certain portion of the tithes of hay in Watford & S<sup>t</sup> Stephens, & so seised, by indenture & fine levied, conveyed s<sup>d</sup> premises to one Thos. Ewer, father of s<sup>d</sup> David, for life, with remainder to John Warner sen<sup>r</sup> for life, remainder to Anne wife of s<sup>d</sup> Thos. Ewer for life, remainder to s<sup>d</sup> David & the heirs of his body & in default of such issue to the right heirs of s<sup>d</sup> Thomas; by virtue whereof s<sup>d</sup> Thomas the father was seised in demesne as of free tenement for life, with remainder to s<sup>d</sup> John Warner for life, which John Warner died in the lifetime of s<sup>d</sup> Thomas.

And so seised, s<sup>d</sup> Thomas & Anne his wife by indenture dat. 7 Nov. 9 Jas. & by fine levied, granted s<sup>d</sup> premises to one James Rolfe esq. to hold after the decease of s<sup>d</sup> Thomas for a term of 80 years if s<sup>d</sup> Anne his wife should so long live & s<sup>d</sup> Thomas & David being so seised by indenture dated 6 May 15 Jas. & fine levied, conveyed to Wm. Pecock esq. & Fras. Townley esq. & their heirs 20 acr. meadow & 2 acr. pasture in Aldenham & the psh. of S<sup>t</sup> Stephens, parcel of the s<sup>d</sup> site of the manor of Meriden to the use of Mary wife of s<sup>d</sup> David for her life & afterwards to the use of s<sup>d</sup> Thos. Ewer for his life & afterwards to use of s<sup>d</sup> David & the heirs of his body & in default of such heirs to the use of the right heirs of s<sup>d</sup> Thomas for ever; in virtue whereof s<sup>d</sup> Mary Ewer was seised of s<sup>d</sup> premises in demesne as of free tenement for life, with remainder as last aforesaid.

Thomas Ewer, father of s<sup>d</sup> David, was also seised in fee of 30 acr. in S<sup>t</sup> Stephens & Watford, formerly bought of John Harvy esq. by Wm. Ewer dec<sup>d</sup> & of 33 acr. land called Hunts in Watford & psh. of S<sup>t</sup> Stephens & so seised by indenture dat. 18 Oct. 9 Jas. & fine levied, conveyed s<sup>d</sup> premises last mentioned to s<sup>d</sup> Jas. Rolfe & John Clarke gent. & their heirs to the use of s<sup>d</sup> Thos. Ewer for life & after his decease to the use of s<sup>d</sup> David & his heirs for ever; in virtue whereof s<sup>d</sup> Thos. was seised in demesne as of free tenement for life with remainder to s<sup>d</sup> David & his heirs for ever & s<sup>d</sup> Thos. & David so seised, on 28 Apr. 10 Jas. by indenture of that date, enfeoffed s<sup>d</sup> Jas. Rolfe & John Clarke & their heirs in the last mentioned premises bought of John Harvy & the land called Hunts, to the use of s<sup>d</sup> David for life & after his decease to the use of s<sup>d</sup> Mary his wife for life & after her decease to the use of s<sup>d</sup> David & his heirs for ever; in virtue whereof s<sup>d</sup> David was seised as of free tenement during his life with remainder as aforesaid.

So seised, s<sup>d</sup> David on 2 Apr. last past made his last will & by same willed s<sup>d</sup> premises last mentioned to Mary his wife & her heirs for ever [*short extract from will naming s<sup>d</sup> lands as held of the manor of Croxley Hall*].

And so seised s^d Thos. Ewer died 29 Sep. 1627 during the lifetime of s^d David & Anne wife of s^d Thos. survives & afterwards on 16 Apr. last past said David died thus seised without issue of his body lawfully begotten. And Henry Ewer is bro. & next heir of s^d David & next heir of s^d Thos. & at the death of s^d David was aged 40 years & more.

The site of the manor of Meriden & other premises in Aldenham & S^t Stephens late bought of Edw. earl of Norwich are held of the king in chief by knights service & worth per annum (except s^d 22 acres conveyed to s^d Mary for life), clear 5*l*. The s^d 22 acres are worth per ann., clear, 20*s*. The s^d 30 acr. land bought of John Harvy are held of John Cowper bart. & Mary his wife as of their manor of Parke in free socage by fealty & rent [*blank*] & worth per ann. clear 20*s*. The s^d 33 acres called Hunts are held of Robt. Carter gent. as of the manor of Garston by fealty & rent [*blank*] & worth per ann. clear 20*s*.

# Abstracts of Herts Wills.

## ARCHDEACONRY OF ST. ALBANS.

REGISTER "STONEHAM."—(Continued from Page 92).

f. 27. JOHANNES REYNOLD of S^t Albans, brewer. (*Dat.* 20 Apr. 1436). Bur. at S^t Peters; Legacies to the chapel of S^t Andrew & of the Charnell; Wife Joan & Wm. Baker exor. (*Pr.* 25 Aug. 1436).

f. 27. JOHANNES ALKEBAROW of S^t Audrews in S^t Albans. (*Dat.* 6 June 1436). Bur. at S^t Peters; My father; Sons John & Mathew; Dau. Alice; Henry Maiot, John Bledlow, John Mordon & Thos. Clotheman exors. (*Pr.* 25 Aug. 1436).

f. 27. ROBERTUS NEWMAN of S^t Albans. (*Dat.* 'die Decollacionis Sci. Joh'is Bapt.' 1436). Bur. at S^t Peters; Robt. Boteler; Thos. Martyn; Dau. Helen; Wife Alice & s^d Robt. Boteler & Thos. Martyn exors. (*Pr.* 8 Sep. 1436).

f. 27. JOHANNES POLEY of Norton juxta Baldok. (*Dat.* 28 Aug. 1436). Rich. Abell carpenter; Wife Joan; Bro. Laurence Poley; Wm. Lawman son of s^d Joan my wife; Margaret my mother; Hugh Dunne; Serv^t John Andrew; Wm. Freharn my heir & his wife; Walter Albrede jun^r & Cecilia his dau.; Simon Hale; John Hale; Thos. Rasshe; Joan dau. of Alice Cowell; Marion dau. of John Edwarde of Baldock; Each of my sons & daus. in Norton & Baldok; Alice Rownale; Mabel Friour; Agnes Spenser; Agnes Hale; Kath. dau. of Thos. Poley; John Edward & my bro. Laurence exors; John Hubhull of Caldekote & John Nicoll of Newnam overseers.

*Ultima voluntas.* Lands & tenements in Baldok, Byggreve & Willien; Bro. Thos. Poley; Lands & tenements in Waleton which I inherited after the decease of Richard Poley my father; John Hale & Joan his wife; Land lately bought in the psh. of Weston. (*Pr.* 8 Sep. 1436).

f. 27ᵇ JOHANNES KYTEWELDE of Rugge. (*Dat.* 14 Nov. 1435). Bur. at Sᵗ Margaret's, Ridge: Legacies to the church there & Sᵗ Peters in Sᵗ Albans, the Charnell, Shenle, Aldenham, & Idustre; Legacy for mending the highway between Shenle & Holines; Son Walter exor; John Atkyn & Henry Bysshop of Sᵗ Albans supervisors. Witˢ:—Wm. Stanet, Thos. Newman. (*Pr.* 20 Oct. 1436).

f. 27ᵇ JOHANNES NOD of Redburne. (*Dat.* 'in die Sancti Michaelis in monte tumbu'). Bur. at Redburne; Son Thomas; Dau. Kath.; Wife Agnes & son John exors. (*Pr.* 20 Oct. 1436).

f. 27ᵇ JOHANNES CALDECOTE perpetual vicar of Saret. (*Undated*). Bur. in the choir of the church; Roger Edmund & Henry Baker exors. (*Pr.* 28 Oct. 1436).

f. 27ᵇ JOHANNES WRENNE of Codicote. (*Dat.* 14 Dec. 1436). Bur. at Sᵗ Giles', Codicote; Sir Richard the vicar there; Son Reginald; Dau. Joan; Dau. Helen de Welwys: Wife Christian & sons Reginald & Henry exors. (*Pr.* 7 Jan. 1436-7).

f. 27ᵇ WILLELMUS WYNCHE of Sᵗ Stephens near Sᵗ Albans. (*Dat.* 22 Jan. 1436). Bur. at Sᵗ Stephens; Son Richard; Wife Anne & Wm. Kentysch exors. (*Pr.* 1 Feb. 1436-7 by Wm. Kentisch).

f. 28. WILLELMUS LEYCETRE of Sᵗ Albans. (*Dat.* 'die Sabbati prox post festum Sanctorum Fabiani & Sebastiani' 1436). Bur. at Sᵗ Peters; Wife Joan extrix; Wm. Schotbolt & Wm. Cokke 'wever' supervisors. (*Pr.* 4 Feb. 1436-7).

f. 28. JOHANNES DEYE of Rykemersworth. (*Dat.* 27 Nov. 1436). Bur. at Rykemersworth; Symon Croyle; Wife Isabelle, son Roger & Richard Roberd exors. (*Pr.* 5 Feb. 1436-7).

f. 28. JOHANNES CLOBBE of Sᵗ Albans. (*Dat.* in feast of Sᵗ Agatha virgin & martyr 1435). Bur. in Mon. of Sᵗ Albans; Legacies to Sᵗ Peters, Rykysmansworthe, the friars of Eylysburi & Hechyn; Wife Agnes & John Fereys & Geo. Warde exors. (*Pr.* 6 Feb. 1436-7 by Agnes the extrix).

f. 28. JOHANNES SAWYER of Sᵗ Albans. (*Dat.* 2 Apr. 1436). Bur. at Sᵗ Peters; Wife Felice extrix. (*Pr.* 8 Apr. 1437).

f. 28. HUGO JONES. (*Dat.* 'in die Merc.' 1436). Bur. at Wynselowe; Robert Roper; Robt. Loksmyth; Richard Mawndevile clerk; Kinsman Wm. Jones exor. (*Pr.* 8 May 1437).

f. 28. JOHANNES HYLLE of Sᵗ Michaels. (*Dat.* 23 May 1436). Bur. at Sᵗ Michaels; To the nuns of the Prê 6s. 8d.; Sir John Mason; Wife Issabelle, John Govle, Wm. Bonne exors. (*Pr.* 14 June 1437).

f. 28. ROBERTUS ALWEY of Chepyng Barnet. (*Dat.* 16 May 1437). Bur. at Sᵗ John Bapt. Barnet; Wife Joan extrix. (*Pr.* 16 June 1437).

f. 28ᵇ JOHANNES WYNKEBURN. (*Dat.* 8 May 1437). Bur. at Rykemersworth; 'Lego Braumange' iijs. iiijd.; Thos. Stretman; Symon Croile; Wife Joan extrix & John my elder son overseer. (*Pr.* 4 July 1437).

f. 28ᵇ WILLELMUS FYLYS. (*Dat.* 'in die Sancti Leonis pape' 1437). Bur. at Redburne; Dau. Agnes; Thos. son of Wm. Pecok; John son of Robt. Heyward; Wife Anice & Robt. Heyward exors. (*Pr.* 8 July 1437).

f. 28ᵇ WALTERUS SMYTH of Sandrugg. (*Dat.* 'die Veneris in festo Sancti Basilii confessoris' 1436). Son John Smyth: Roger Petyte; Wife Rose. (*Pr.* 8 July 1437).

f. 28ᵇ WILLELMUS FLOURE. (*Dat.* Sᵗ George the Martyr's day 1437). Bur. at Redburne: Laurence Pegot & wife Margaret exors. (*Pr.* 8 July 1437).

f. 28ᵇ JOHANNES BERNWELLE of Sᵗ Peters of Sᵗ Albans. (*Dat.* 13 May 1437). Bur. at Sᵗ Peters 'coram alta cruce': Legacies to the convent of the monastery of Sᵗ Albans, the monks of the infirmary, the high altar, the charnel, the fabric of Sᵗ Peter's Church, the mending of the road which leads to the town called Harpeden, & the road which leads from Sᵗ Albans to Sandrige, the convent of the Abbey of Waltham, the priory of Bisseter etc: Dau. Custance & John her brother: John son of Katherine my godson; To my wife a croft called Dofhovscroft & a croft 'ante edem domini Abbatis' called Newlane 'exoposito ex altera pte uie' & my house which I bought of John Adam & the house I bought of John Angiltyltille; To dau. Custance a house which I bought of John Adam cook, after my wife's decease; The house I bought of John Angyltille [*sic*] to be sold for the good of my soul etc: My wife to have from the Inn called Keye ten marks a year for life also 40 shillings in Cogyssale; Servants John & Elisabet: John Bernwell; Margt. Grene & her sister; Wife Margaret, Wm. Baker of Coggissale, Sir Robt. Wyte of same town & John Bocher of Sᵗ Albans exors. (*Pr.* 18 July 1437).

f. 29. JOHANNES ALEYN, 'coke' of Sᵗ Albans. (*Dat.* 3 Apr. 1436). Bur. at Sᵗ Peters; Wife Sibill extrix. (*Pr.* 24 July 1437).

f. 29. THOMAS EDWARD of Sᵗ Albans. (*Dat.* 14 July 1437). Bur. at Sᵗ Peters; My sons & daughters; Richard & Agnes my servants; Wife Clemence extrix. (*Pr.* 7 Aug. 1437).

f. 29. WALTERUS ALBREY senior. (*Dat.* 4 Mch. 1436). Bur. at St. Nich. of Norton; Son Walter; Marion wife of sᵈ Walter; Son John exor. Witˢ:—Thos. Colwell vicar of said church, John Colwell, Walter Albrey.

f. 29. JOHANNES MARTIN of Newnam. (*Dat.* 'die veneris prox. ante festum Translacionis sancti Thome martiris' 1436). Wife Alice & son Richard exors. Witˢ:—The vicar of said town & John Nicol.

f. 29. THOMAS CHILDMERE of Sᵗ Stephens 'nativus mon. Sci Albani.' (*Dat.* 5 Oct. 1437). Bur. at Sᵗ Stephens; Rich. atte Watir; Sir Robert the Chaplain of the parish; John Kentysh, Rose dau. of my wife; Emma dau. of my wife; Wife Joan & son Andrew exors.

f. 29ᵇ ADAM CALOWE of Sᵗ Albans. (*Dat.* 16 Nov. 1433). Bur. at Sᵗ Peters; Legacies to churches of Sᵗ Stephens, Sᵗ Michaels & Abbots Langley, the friars of Huchen, vicar of Sᵗ Andrews &c.; Sir Robert, vicar of Sᵗ Michaels; Sir John Masen; Robert de Sewer & John Masen of Scololden exors.

f. 29ᵇ WILLELMUS COUPER of Wynslowe. (*Dat.* 'die lune in festo sancti Edmundi Archiep.' 1437). Bur. at Sᵗ Laurence of Wynslowe; John Cotou & his wife; Wm. son of John Cowper; Son John Coup; Rich. Mandevile clerk; Rich. Stokeshille & my wife Joan & son John exors.

f. 29b ALICIA WHELER of Barnet. (Dat. 8 Feb. 1437). Bur. at S* John Bapt., Barnet ; John. son of my dau. ; Edith atte Hale : Wm. Nicoll exor. Wit*:—John Nicoll, Wm. Hale, Rich. Forster.

f. 29b CLEMENCIA OSNARD. (Dat. 2 Feb. 1437). Bur. at Busshey ; Joan Calf : Margaret sister of s'd Joan ; Joan Colyn : John Gerneys clerk ; Son Nich. Osnard, Thos. Calfe & the priest of the parish of S* Stephens of S* Albans exors.

f. 29b JOHANNES ATTE WYK of Abbots Walden. (Dat. 'die martis in crastino sancti Martini Ep'i, 1437). Thos. Laman : Thos. Whyt.

f. 29b JOHANNES PORTER of Ydelystr. Note of admon. of goods granted to John Bisshop & Joan Portere of the same.

f. 29b ALICIA BROUN of Horwood parva. (Dat. 15 Mch. 1437). Rich. Thomelyn of Horwood ; Alice wife of Robert Gretham of same ; Joan wife of Hugh Thwychyn ; To Cotton & his wife 'duobus clinicis de Wynsloue' xijd. ; Wm. Terry & John Hankyn of Horwood exors.

f. 29b JOHANNES ATTE WELLE of Rikmersworth, died intestate 20 Mch. 1437. Admon. granted to Robt. Gybbe of same.

f. 29b THOMAS SOON of S* Albans. (Dat. 19 May 1437). Bur. S* Peters : Sir John Spicer ; The anchorites of S* Peters & S* Michaels ; Rich. Feelde & Alice his wife exors.

f. 29b ROBERTUS BEDGROUE of Watford. Note of probate.

f. 29b RICHARDUS SMYTH of Watford. Note of probate.

f. 30. PETRONILLA DIER of Rikmersworth. (Dat. 20 Mch. 1437). Bur at Rikmersworth; Son John Dyere; Dau. Agnes; Margaret Diere ; John Diere ; Nich. Clerk & Agnes his wife ; Alice wife of Roger Lucas ; John & Richard sons of John Dier ; Petronilla dau. of Agnes Clerk ; Cicily dau. of John Diere ; Sir Thomas the chaplain ; John Brauvang ; Thos. Streteman ; John Dyere & Nich. Clerk exors. Wit*:—John Brauvang our vicar, Thos. Stretman, Roger Lucas.

f. 30. JOHANNES CAUCHE senior. (Dat. 11 June 1438). Bur. at Watford ; Sir Robert the chaplain ; Ralph Smyth clerk : Son John ; Wife Joan extrix.

f. 30. ROGERUS LOWYN of S* Albans. (Dat. 3 June 1438). Bur. at S* Peters ; Simon my bro. & his wife ; Thomas my bro.; Son Wm.; The wife of Stephen Morcocke ; Legacy to the Church of Northhawe ; Walter Erberd ; Margery Bateman : John Deye ; Legacy to the monks of the monastery of S* Albans ; John Mordon & Alice his wife ; John Taylour ; Agnes [dau. of ?] Stephen Morcok ; Matilda servant of Alice Hecheman ; Bro. Simon & John Moorden exors.

f. 30. RICARDUS ATTE WYKIS of Abbots Walden. (Dat. 25 [blank] 1438). Son John & wife Katherine exors.

f. 30 THOMAS GODTHANK of Rykmersworth. (Dat. 28 Apr. 1437). Sir Thomas the chaplain ; John Brauvangr ; Thos. Stretman ; Son Wm. ; Bro. Richard ; John Rowe ; Margaret my niece ; Thos. son of Thos. Wynkefeld ; Thos. son of John Randulf ; Wife Margery, John Rowe exors & bro. Rich. overseer.

*To be Continued.*

# The Herts Genealogist and Antiquary.

## Rental of Sir John Say, 1463.

(CONTINUED FROM PAGE 148.)

John Boure junior holds v acres of land lying in Sprollesfeld, parcel of the demesne lands & pays rent etc.—xvd. & suit of court.

The same John holds by the rod a tenement called Blasseafter & certain lands & meadows belonging, late in tenure of Wm. Adam & before of Agnes Passemonteyn & pays rent etc.—vs. & suit of court & heriot when it happens.

The same John holds by the rod a tenement called Agnes at Dane with certain lands & meadows adjoining late in tenure of Robt. Pygot & before of John at Hoo junior & pays rent etc.—iijs. & suit of court & heriot when it happens.

William Burley holds by the rod certain crofts of land called Leycrofte (xd.), Chonecrofte (vd.), Somereshawe (jd.) & Berystetyll (xxd.), late in tenure of John Fortescu knt & pays rent etc.—iijs. & suit of court & heriot when it happens.

The same William holds divers parcels of land in Sprollesfeld & Asshefeld & ij acres of land opposite the park of Bedwell, parcel of the demesne lands & pays rent etc.—iijs. iijd. & suit of court.

William Kevyll holds freely a tenement with appurtenances, late in tenure of John at Hille & pays rent etc.—vjd. & suit of court.

The same William holds by the rod a toft with certain lands & meadows adjoining called Robertes late in tenure of John at Hille & pays rent etc.—xjs. viijd. & suit of court & heriot when it happens.

The same William holds a croft called Beryredyn lying in the Longeredyn late in tenure of said John at Hille & pays rent etc.—xiijs. iiijd. & suit of court & heriot when it happens.

The same William holds by the rod a piece of land in Ponfeld, late in tenure of John at Hille & pays rent etc.—xijd.

Thomas Keron holds by the rod a tenement with appurtenances called William at Hilles, late in tenure of William Kevyll & before of Roger Kevyll his father & pays rent etc.—xixs. iiijd. & suit of court & heriot when it happens.

The same Thomas holds by the rod an acre of meadow in Berkhamstedmede & pays rent etc.—iijs.

The same Thomas holds a piece of land called Bradelond containing iij acres & pays rent etc.—vjd.

Robt. Pygot holds freely a tenement in which he lately dwelt called Edyns Scalderowe, late of [blank] Pygot & pays rent etc.—viijd.

The same Robert holds freely xiiijor acres of land lying in the Threfeldes viz:—Millefeld, Grauntpitell & Bradelond, called Scropeslond, and pays rent etc.—jd.

The same Robert holds by the rod a tenement with certain lands & meadows adjoining called Houndeslond late in tenure of [blank] Lurchyns & pays rent etc.—vijs. & suit of court & heriot when it happens.

The same Robert holds a tenement called Parkers, late in tenure of Rich. Pygot his father, & pays rent etc.—iiijs. & suit of court & heriot when it happens.

The same Robert holds by the rod a parcel of land called Milleshotte & Galodelshotte & pays rent etc.—xviijd. & suit of court.

The same Robert holds by the rod viij acres of land lying in the field called Sprolleafeld, parcel of the demesne lands, & pays rent etc.—ijs. & suit of court.

Robert Gamelyn *alias* Forster junior holds a tenement with certain lands & meadows adjoining called Idlyns, late in tenure of John Burton & before of Robert Forster, and pays rent etc.—vs. & suit of court & heriot when it happens.

John at Hoo holds by the rod a tenement with ij acres of land & a half, in severalty, & vj acres of land in common, late of Thomas at Hoo senior & before of Richard at Hoo, & half an acre of meadow in one parcel near the gate of Berkhumsted & a tenement with certain lands & meadows appertaining, late in the tenure of John at Hoo, & pays rent etc.—xs. vjd.

William at Hoo holds by the rod a tenement called Fyppes at Hilles *alias* Clovyars, late in the tenure of [blank], and pays rent etc.—vjs. viijd. & suit of court & heriot when it happens.

The same William pays for a day's work in the lord's meadow & one "precaria" in autumn for the same, vjd.

Robert Gedney holds by the rod a tenement with certain lands & meadows adjoining, called Loklese, late in tenure of John Lokley & before of [blank] Hoo, & pays rent etc.—vijs. ijd. & suit of court & heriot when it happens.

The same Robert pays for j capon (iiijd.) & ij hens (iiijd.) for the same yearly at Christmas, viijd.

The same Robert holds by the rod iiij$^{or}$ acres of land lying in the Asshefeld, late in tenure of John Lokley & pays rent etc. - xijd. & suit of court.

Nicholas Wightman holds by the rod a tenement with appurtenances, called Gardyuers, & a croft called Travelcrofte, containing j acre, late in tenure of Peter Valaunce, & pays rent etc.—vjs. iijd. & suit of court & heriot when it happens.

Robert Forster senior holds by the rod a tenement with appurtenances called Saunders, late in tenure of Nich. Wightman, & pays rent etc.—vjs. viijd. & suit of court & heriot when it happens.

The same Robert holds by the rod a tenement called Bokars, late in tenure of Wm. Moredon, & pays rent etc.—iiijs. & suit of court & heriot when it happens.

John Wightman holds by the rod a tenement with certain lands & meadows adjoining, called Popes, late in tenure of John at Hoo, & pays rent etc.—ixs. iiijd. & suit of court & heriot when it happens.

The same John pays for ij days work in the lords meadows at the time of hay making yearly iiijd.

Henry Hugh holds by the rod a tenement with certain lands & meadows adjoining, called Styles *alias* Willyes at Well, late in tenure of John Turne & afterwards of Wm. Danyell, & pays rent etc.—xiiijs. & suit of court & heriot when it happens.

Richard Prentyce holds by the rod a tenement with a croft called Crouches, late in tenure of John West & before of Thomas Pygot, & pays rent etc.—xiijs. iiijd. & suit of court & heriot when it happens.

Henry Hardy holds a tenement with certain lands & meadows appertaining, called Haywardes, late in tenure of Thos. at Hoo junior & before of John Gibbes, & pays rent etc.—xxiiijs. & suit of court & heriot when it happens.

John Node holds a tenement called Quynelles with certain lands adjoining, late in the tenure of [blank] Prounce, & pays rent etc.—vjs. iiijd. & suit of court & heriot when it happens.

John Lurchyn holds by the rod a grove called Shredshaselles, late in tenure of Robert Pygot, as parcel of the tenement called Parkers, & pays rent etc.—iijs. & suit of court.

Wm. Southwode holds by the rod certain parcels of land & meadow lying in the field called the Stanford, late in tenure of John Langley & before of John Southwode (which used to be rented at vijs. per annum), now pays rent etc.—vs.

Concerning xxxiijs. iiijd. lately received from John Node for certain crofts & meadows called Waterfeldes. Watermede & Foxwelmede, lately in the tenure of Rich. Pygot. which used to be rented at xls. per annum. now in the hands of the lord. nil, which are occupied with the beasts of the lord.

Sum, xiijli. iiijs. vd.

Meadows.  xx acres of meadow lying in divers places in the meadow called Berkhamstedmede at ijs. iiijd. each acre. now in the lord's hands, & mown & "hospitatur" within the manor of Bedwell for the expenses of the horses of the lord.—Nil.

Lyndhawes.  John Seward holds freely a tenement with certain lands, meadows & wood, parcel of Lyndhawes, late in the tenure of Robert Louthe, & pays rent etc.—viijs.

The same John holds a pasture called Russhell, late in tenure of said Robert Louthe, & pays rent etc.—ijd.

John Lurchyn holds freely a tenement, with certain lands & meadows appertaining, called Lyndehawes, & pays rent etc.—xiijs. vd.

John Grubbe holds freely, in right of his wife Joan, certain lands & meadows called Lyndehawes *alias* Bukberdes, late in tenure of Wm. Lyster, before of Wm. Lurchyn, & pays rent etc.—vs. id. ob.

Sum, xxvjs. viijd. ob.

Sum total, besides certain lands in the hands of the lord & certain demesne lands lying in divers fields within the lordship of Berkhamstede, at present unlet.—xiiijli. xjs. jd. ob.

---

LANDS AND TENEMENTS which were ROBERT LOUTHE'S of the MANORS OF HARMEBEMEGATE* AND BLOUNTES.

Rental of John Say, knight, lord there, made the 13th day of January 7 Edw. IV. before John Luthyngton, auditor, and John Knyghton, steward, by the oaths of John Toky, John Martyn, Wm. Basset, John Morewell, John Budder, John at Hille, Robt. Batell, John Laneham, Wm. Wright, Wm. Milton, Wm. at Felde, and Nich. Sonder, twelve jurors, who say upon oath that

Wm. Basset holds freely a tenement called Camvyle, late in tenure of John Camvyle, & pays rent etc.—vjd.

The same Wm. holds freely a tenement with a croft, late in tenure of Peter Cheyne & before of [*blank*] Berkeley, & pays rent etc.—xiijd. & ij "precariæ."†

John Morewell holds freely a tenement, late in tenure of Wm. Dodde & before of Alice Paulyn, & pays rent etc.—viijd.

The same John holds at the will of the lord a field called Wyldefelde & a grove called Wyncestregrove, late in tenure of Wm. Dodde & before of sd Peter Cheyne, & pays rent etc.—vs. viijd.

The same John holds at the will two crofts & a parcel of meadow called Wyncstrafeld, late in tenure of John Laneham & before of John Dey, & pays rent etc.—viijs.

The same John holds at the will a meadow called Deynemedowe, late in tenure of Stephen Potter & before of Robt. Cokerell, & pays rent etc.—ijs. vjd.

The same John holds at the will a croft called the Legh, late in tenure of John Node, & pays rent etc.—ijs.

Robt. Batell holds freely a tenement at Wyldehull, late in tenure of John Forster & before of John Tyler, & pays rent etc.—viijd. & ij boonworks & relief & heriot when it happens.

The same Robert holds at the will of the lord a tenement & certain parcels of land adjoining at Wyldehill, late in tenure of Stephen Rutter & before of John Sonder, & pays rent etc.—xs.

---

* This name is written "Hornebemegate" in the endorsement of this membrane.
† This and the previous paragraph are bracketed together and marked in the margin as being in the hands of the lord by purchase.

The same Robert holds at the will a field called Millewardesfeld, late in tenure of Wm. Basset & before of John Camvyle & pays rent etc.—vs. iiijd. & relief & heriot when it happens.

The same Robert holds at the will a croft called Nyne acres, late in tenure of Wm. Basset & before of Rich. Croucher, & pays rent etc.—vs.

John Edlyn holds freely a croft, late in tenure of John Alcy & before of Thos. Edelyn, & pays rent etc.—ijd.

The same John holds a garden, late in tenure of said John Alcy & before of Thos. Edelyn, & pays rent etc.—ij capons.

John Budder junior holds freely a croft called Pleystowe (ijs. vjd. & ij capons), a grove called Moresgrove (viijd.), iiij acres of lands lying in Stonyfelde called Gelywell (xijd. & ij capons), late in tenure of Wm. Budder, & pays rent etc.—iiijs. ijd. & ij capons.

The same John holds at the will a croft called Kyvescrofte, with other parcels of land lying in Hokefeld & Depedell, Bradwell & Northfelde, late in tenure of Thos. Idonbrace & before of John Idonbrace, & pays rent etc.—vijs.

John Budder, sexton, holds at the will a messuage called Chownehay, late in tenure of Wm. Budder, & pays rent etc.—vjd

John at Hille holds at the will a curtilage & ij crofts called Moresfeld & Hallefeld & j grove called Bretonshawe, lately in tenure of John at Hille senior & before of John Alcy, and pays rent etc.—xiiijs. & ij capons.

The same John holds freely j acre of land next Hallefeld called Smytheshawe, late in tenure of John Hille his father, & pays rent etc.—j capon.

John Toky holds a field called Wodefelde, at the will of the lord, late in tenure of John Luddeford, which used to be rented at xls. yearly, now let at xxvjs. viijd.

Concerning iiijs. lately received from John Martyn for a tenement lying at Wyldehill, now in the hands of the lord for lack of a tenant. *Nil.* [*In the margin,* "modo per Th. Wyngfeld pro iijs. iiijd."]

Nor do they [*i.e.*, the jurors] answer concerning ijs. lately received from John Morewell for certain lands lying in the Hamme, now in the hands of the lord & grazed by the lord's sheep.—*Nil.*

Nor do they answer concerning xiijs. iiijd. lately received from meadows & pastures lying within the park of Bedwell now in the hands of the lord, being included within the same park.—*Nil.*

Alice at Felde holds a croft called Forstercrofte, late in tenure of Richard at Felde *alias* Porter, & pays rent etc.—iiijd. & relief & heriot when it happens.

The same Alice holds a field called Busshefeld, late in tenure of Richard at Felde & before of Richard Porter, & pays rent etc.—vjs. viijd.

John North holds a field called Hamscales, late in tenure of John at Felde & before of John Luddeford, & pays rent etc.—vs.

John Wightman holds freely a tenement late in tenure of John Martyn, & pays rent etc.—xijd.

The same John holds j hawe at Newgatestrete, late in tenure of said John Martyn, & pays rent etc.—viijd.

The same John holds divers lands, meadows & pastures, at the will of the lord, late in tenure of said John Martyn, & pays rent etc.—xvs.

Thomas Mery holds a tenement with garden adjoining at the Newgatestrete, lately in tenure of John Martyn, & pays rent etc.—xijd.

Thomas Archer holds a tenement with garden lying in the Newgatestrete, late in tenure of Simon Walter, & pays rent etc.—xijd.

Simon Lowen holds freely a tenement, late in tenure of John Martyn, & pays rent etc.—xijd.

John Martyn holds at the will of the lord certain lands lying at the Condytehed in Bishops Hatfelde, late in tenure of John Lok, & pays rent etc.—iiijs.

## BLOUNTES.

William at Felde holds at the will of the lord a croft called Bonstelfeld & a meadow called Bonstelmede, late in tenure of Richard Milton, & pays rent etc.—xxjs.

Wm. Milton holds at the will a field called Cookesfeld, late in tenure of Rich. Milton, & pays rent etc.—xs.

Wm. Wright holds at the will ij closes called Mannynges, late in tenure of John Forster, & pays rent etc.—iijs.

Nicholas Sonder holds at the will of the lord j acre of land lying in Todelfeld beneath Bymerhegge, called Forked acre, & a field called Lotefeld, another field called Longefeld, half an acre of land in Willymyllefelde at Bradlyngesbusshe, late in tenure of Nich. Sonder his father, & pays rent etc. - xix*s*.

Agnes Laneham holds j grove called Andrewesleese, late in tenure of Wm. Laneham, & pays rent etc., beyond the rent of xvj*d*. reserved to the Manor of Pountesbornes, viij*d*.

Concerning xij*d*. lately received from the same Agnes for j grove within Popes, called Constablegrove, containing ij acres by estimation, now in the hands of the lord.—*Nil.*

John Newman holds at the will j curtilage called Blounteslonde, j close annexed to it called Culverhouseclose containing at least ij acres, & another grove near said Curtilage containing by estimation j acre, & another croft containing j acre lying between a croft of the Bishop of Ely & the high way, also another close called Wollecrofte containing vj acres by estimation, & a close called Stokkyng containing by estimation x acres of land, & x acres by estimation lying in the field called Todelfelde, & xvj acres by estimation lying in the field called Bymerfeld, & iij acres of land containing by estimation lying in Pytagefelde in exchange from the lord bishop of Ely for certain lands late Robert Louthe's lying within the park of the said Bishop called Innyngesparke, & iiij*or* acres lying in the said field called Pytagefeld next the pale of the said park, also j acre lying in the same field by the road leading from Wynegate, late in the tenure of Thos. Boone, & pays rent etc., besides iij*s*., iiij boonworks & ij capons rent reserved to the same bishop of Ely,—xxiij*s*. iiij*d*.

Wm. Denys holds ij closes called Maggescrofte containing by estimation vij acres viz:—j containing v acres (iij*s*. iiij*d*.) & another ij acres (ij*s*.) lying in Maggesgrene & Bymerfeld, & another croft (ij*s*.) called Huntescrofte lying between the land of Combes & land called Fissheslonde, containing ij acres, & pays rent etc. —which said iij crofts were lately occupied by John Bigge, formerly bailiff & farmer of the lord of Hatfelde, by consent & agreement of John Payntor, farmer of Robert Louthe in the same town, for which the said bailiff & farmer of the Bishop, by consent & agreement of said John Payntor, for their conveniences permitted [him] to hold & occupy a certain croft of the said Bishops, called Brokes, & another croft containing ij acres, the head of which abutted upon Blountesgrene towards the east & upon Harowcrofte towards the west, late Robert Louthe's.—vij*s*. iiij*d*.

John Toky holds a garden next the Cross, called Gracyes, late in tenure of Alice Luddeford, & pays rent etc.—vj*d*.

The heirs of Wm. at Hille hold j acre of land, late in tenure of said Wm. at Hill, & pay rent etc.—iiij*d*.

Sum total, besides certain lands & meadows, being in the hands of the lord.—x*li*. xiiij*s*. ix*d*.

# Transcripts of Parish Registers.

## CHIPPING BARNET.

*[The existing Register commences as to Baptisms in 1708 and as to Marriages and Burials in 1678.]*

### BARNET.

The names of all them that hath byn Marryed, Christenid & Buryed w*t*in the pishe of Chipinge Barnet in y*e* Jurysdiction of S*t* Albons from the feast of S*t* Michaell tharchangell anno D'ni 1569 vnto the same feast 1570.

### *Chrystenyngs.*

Vallantyne Isme was chrystenyd y*e* 9 day of October.
John Greene was chrystenyd y*e* 6 day of Nove͞.

Elsabethe Everyngame was christenyd y&deg; 20 day Novē.
John Wyan was chrystenyd y&deg; 30 day of Novē.
Thomas Hunt was chrystenyd y&deg; 11 day of desem.
Isbell Edlyn was chrystenyd y&deg; 18 day of desem.
Alles goodsonne was chrystenyd y&deg; 26 day of desem.
Thomas Moret was chrystenyd y&deg; same day.
Wyllm Norton was chrystenyd y&deg; 15 day Janu.
Thomas Wyllyams was chrystenyd y&deg; 22 day of Janu.
Jone Coll was chrystenyd y&deg; 5 day of febru.
Elsabeth Cooper was chrystenyd y&deg; 5 day of March.
John Gardner was chrystenyd y&deg; 9 day of Apryll.
Anys Waker } was chrystenyd y&deg; 23 day of Apryll.
Ane Ghy }
Elsabeth Sampsonne was chrystenyd y&deg; 30 day of Apryl.
Valantyne Pemartonne was chrystenyd y&deg; 7 day.o May.
James Cranfyld was chrystenyd y&deg; 28 day of May.
Wyllm Nycoll was chrystenyd y&deg; 2 day of July.
Wyllm Elat was chrystenyd y&deg; 25 day of July.
Margrett Morys was chrystenyd y&deg; 30 day of July.
James foster was chrystenyd y&deg; 13 day of Agust.

### *Buryalls.*

James Wrenche was buryed y&deg; 26 day of october.
Lawrance Wylshere was buryed y&deg; 23 day of Novē.
Anys Kellat was buryed y&deg; 22 day of desem.
Wyllm Croxall was buryed y&deg; 8 day of Janu.
Alles Peeter was buryed y&deg; 17 day of Janu.
Maryan bowman was buryed y&deg; 18 day of Janu.
Anys Allyn was buryed y&deg; 9 day of Marche.
The wyfe of Robert Norman was buryed y&deg; 15 day of Apryl.
Symont Maynard was buryed y&deg; 19 day of Apryll.
Hugh Wealsheman was buryed y&deg; 23 day of Apryll.
John Bell was buryed y&deg; 8 day of May.
Margrett franklyn was buryed y&deg; 27 day of May.
Elsabeth Everyngame was buryed y&deg; 16 day of Sept.

### *Maryges.*

Edmont Morys } were maryed y&deg; 30 day of octobre.
Katren West }

Robert Nycoll } were maryed y&deg; 26 of Novē.
Elsabeth Wetheryngame }

Mychaell fulkember } were maryed y&deg; 21 day of Janu.
Tomysonne fayrfaxe }

Davyd Coker } were maryed y&deg; 29 day of Janu.
Jone Darawaye }

Thomas fyllyan } were maryed y&deg; 23 day of July.
Jone Nele }

Robert Norman } were maryed y&deg; 7 day of Sept.
Anys burton }

Hermon Peeter } were maryed y&deg; 10 day of Sept.
Alles Rytchemont }

        Edward Vnder  Parson.
     Church W. John Brakenfyld.
         James Kellett.
        Ex$^{tum}$ p . . . Vnder . .
       iij&deg; Octobris 1570.

The names of all them that hathe hynne maryed Christened & buryed w'in the prishe of Chepinge Barnett in the Jurisdiction of S' Albones from the feast of S' Mychaell tharchaungell año dō 1581 vnto the same feast 1582.

### Maryges.

John Bancks / Alice Hounte } were maryed the xv day of October.

Andrewe thornle / Elen benson } were maryed y⁰ xxij day of October.

Roger Gyner / Jone Durren } were maryed y⁰ seconde day of December.

Hugh Parker / Margrete Lyonell } were maryed y⁰ seconde of Sept.

### Christenyngs.

Katren Kynge was christened y⁰ viij day of October.
Wyllm Hounte was christened y⁰ xij daye of November.
ffreman Locke was christened y⁰ x$^{th}$ day of December.
James Hounte was christened y⁰ xxiiij day of December.
Alice White was christened y⁰ xxvj day of December.
John Stacye was christened y⁰ xxviij daye of Januarye.

Wyllm Curtys / Roberte Muffett / Susan Saverye } were christened y⁰ iiij day of ffebruarye.

Agnes Royse was christened y⁰ xj daye of ffebruarye.

Susan Marshe / Jone Brekenfyeld } were christened y⁰ xxv day of ffebruarie.

Phillipe Bagerd / Rychard Hackman } were christened y⁰ iiij day of Marche.

Thomas ffrancklyn / Hary Owen } were christened y⁰ xj day of Marche.

John Wryght was christened y⁰ xviij day of Marche.
Alice Cocker was christened y⁰ viij day of Apryll.
Elyzabeth Pemerton was christened y⁰ xxix day of Aprill.
Jone Barton was christened y⁰ x$^{th}$ day of June.
Anne Basse was christened y⁰ xxiiij day of June.
Alice Brysco was christened y⁰ ffyrst day of July.
Sara Oytes was christened y⁰ v$^{th}$ day of August.

Thomas Thornele / Phillip Hardye } were christened y⁰ xvj day of Sept.

Jone White was christened y⁰ xxiij day of September.

### Buryalls.

Thomas Chylderbye was buryed y⁰ ix day of October.
Wyllm Nashe was buryed y⁰ xxiiij day of October.
Wyllm Bradlye y⁰ yonger was buryed xxxj day of October.
Rychard sharparowe was buryed y⁰ xx day of November.
Rose ffrancklyn was buryed y⁰ xxvj day of November.
Thomas chevelye was buryed y⁰ ix daye of December.
Prudence Lambe was buryed y⁰ x$^{th}$ day of December.
Wyllm Bradlye y⁰ elder was buried y⁰ xvij of Dcer.
Margerye Bradlye was buryed y⁰ ffyrst daye of Januarye.
Maryan Tayler was buryed y⁰ vj daye of ffebruarye.
Thomas Turner was buryed y⁰ xij daye of ffebruarie.
Katren Warner was buryed y⁰ xxvj day of ffebruarie.

Daratye Pollerd was buryed yᵉ viij day of Marche.
Thomas ffrancklyn was buryed yᵉ xiiij day of Marche.
Agnes Jacson was buryed yᵉ xxij day of Marche.
Jone Brekenfyeld was buryed yᵉ xxvj day of Marche.
Thomas Thresher was buryed yᵉ xxv day of Apryll.
Elyzabeth Pemerton was buryed yᵉ ffyrst day of Maye.
Nycholas shuttleworth was buryed yᵉ xxviij day of June.
Mary Fyeld was buryed yᵉ xxix day of July.

    Churche Wardens
     Thomas Bycton ×
    larrances coton.

         Exhibit 9 Octobris
           1582.

---

The names of all them that hathe bynne Maryed, Christened & Buryedd in Chepinge Barnett in the Jurisdyction of Sᵗ Albones from the feast of Sᵗ Mychaell tharchangell 1592 vnto the same ffeast 1593.

### *Maryges.*

Henry Daruall } were maryed the last day of Maye.
Mary Tooke

Wyllm Waryner } were maryed the seconde day of July.
Jone Smythe

Wyllm Myllyan } were maryed the xxx day of July.
Jone Large

### *Christenyngs.*

Agnes Barrick was christened yᵉ ffyrst day of October.
Wyllm ffullwood } were christened yᵉ viij of October.
Sybbell Cotton
John gryffyn was christened yᵉ xv day of October.
Elsabeth turvere was christened yᵉ xxix day of October.
Roger Marshe was christened yᵉ xᵗʰ day of December.
John tharpe was christened yᵉ xxiiij day December.
Roberte Brisco was christened yᵉ xxvij day of December.
Susan tynderslye was christened yᵉ vij day Januarie.
Margrett Hyll } were christened yᵉ xiiij day of Januarie.
Edwarde Darvell
Isbell Sampson was christened yᵉ xxj day of Januarie.
Henry Spencer was christened yᵉ xj day of ffebru.
George Hyll was christened yᵉ xviij day of Marche.
Phillip Mason } were christened yᵉ xiij day of Maye.
Thomas gyles
Clemente Homes was christened yᵉ xx day of Maye.
John younge was christened yᵉ xxiiij day of June.
Margrett Kypple was christened yᵉ xv day of July.
Robert Burryge was christened yᵉ xxix day of July.
Wyllm Tynslye was christened yᵉ xij day of August.
Alice Carlell } were christened yᵉ xix day of August.
ffreeman conaway
John Hoodsone } were christened yᵉ seconde day of Septm.
Elsabethe cater
Jone stacye was christened yᵉ xvi day of Septm.

*Buryalls.*

Wyllm Heale was buryed yᵉ vj day of October.
Wyllm Bell was buryed yᵉ xxix day of October.
Roberte ffellowe was buryed yᵉ xxvij day of November.
Roberte cotton was buryed yᵉ xxv day of December.
Vxor Tynderslye was buryed yᵉ ix day of Januarie.
Margrett Hyll was buryed yᵉ xv day of Januarie.
John Hounte was buryed yᵉ xvij day of Januarie.
Agnes Curtys was buryed yᵉ xix day of Januarie.
John Symkyns a stranger was buryed yᵉ xxix day of Janua.
Henry Spencer was buryed yᵉ xiij day of ffebruarie.
Margrett Myller was buryed yᵉ xxvj day of ffebruarie.
Wyllm Pake was buryed yᵉ xxj day of Marche.
Elsabeth Pollerd was buryed yᵉ xxix day of Marche.
John Slacforde was buryed yᵉ xviij day of Aprill.
John Baldyn was buryed yᵉ xxij day of Aprill.
Rychard Shefyeld a stranger was buryed yᵉ xxv of Aprill.
John Stacye of london was buryed yᵉ xxviij day of Aprill.
Wyllm ffullwood was buryed yᵉ iij day of May.
Margerye Warryner was buryed yᵉ xiij day of Maye.
Henry Skaldwell was buryed yᵉ xxviij day of May.
Jone brooke was buryed yᵉ vj day of June.
Jane Kellett was buryed yᵉ xviij day of June.
John Marshe was buryed yᵉ ffyrst day of July.
Chare Ransome was buryed yᵉ seconde of July.
Elsabeth Eydon ⎫
Thomas gyles  ⎭ were buryed yᵉ xviij day of July.
John Palmer was buryed yᵉ iij day of August.
Margerye Roomford was buryed yᵉ vij day of August.
Rycharde Hethe was buryed yᵉ xiij day of August.
Margrett Bottamlye was buryed yᵉ xxv day of August.
Philledellphe Heale was buryed yᵉ iiij day of Septm.
Thomas Sampsone was buryed yᵉ vᵗʰ day of Septm.
Wyllm Potter was buryed yᵉ ix day of Septm.
Anne Dawlyn was buryed yᵉ xᵗʰ day of Septm.
John Sampsone was buryed yᵉ xvij day of Septm.
Wedo Potter ⎫
Agnes Welles ⎬ were buryed yᵉ xxij day of Septm.
Jonne Stacye ⎭
Anne sampsone was buryed yᵉ xxiij day of Septm.
Wyllm Roomforde was buryed yᵉ xxiiij day of Septm.
Elsabeth Whitlocke ⎫
Thomas Burryge    ⎭ were buryed yᵉ xxv day of Septm.
Wyllm Bugberd was buryed yᵉ xxvij day of Septm.

By me Thomas Bigland
Mynister of Chepinge Barnet.

Churche Wardens
   Thomas turvere
   crystover
   botomlaye   ×

Exhibit 3 Octob. 159..
Tho. Rokitt.

The names of all them that hathe bynne Maryed Christened & Buryed in the Parishe of Chipynge Barnett in the Jurisdiction of S$^t$ Albones ffrom the ffeaste of S$^t$ Mychaell tharchaungell año dõ 1598 vnto the same ffeast of S$^t$ Mythaell tharchaungell 1599.

### *Maryges*.

#### October.
Goerge Prestwoode & Jane barber were maryed y$^e$ 9.

#### November.
John Cryke & Ma$^r$gerett Halle were maryed the 16.
Xp$^r$ Stauton & Agnes Buryge were maryed the 19.
Nycholas Astood & Kateren Searle were maryed the 28.

#### Januarie.
Odes Purslack & Cassanderer Daves were maryed y$^e$ 21.

#### June.
John greene & Mary eves were maryed the 12.

#### July.
John Searle & Grace Elton were maryed the 1.
John Holbydge & Kateren Clenton were maryed the 16.

#### Septm.
Abraham Waddell & Anne Browne were Maryed by a lycense 25.

### *Christenyngs*.

#### October.
Percyvale the sone of Gabryell Crofte bapt. y$^e$ 1.
Wyllm the sonn of Rowlande Ince bapt. y$^e$ 1.

#### November.
Symon the sone of Roberte Cryspe bapt. y$^e$ 1.

#### December.
Laurance y$^e$ son of Laurance Shuttlewoorth bapt. y$^e$ 17.

#### Januarie.
Em y$^e$ daughter of Augustyne Pratt bapt. y$^e$ 21.
Thomas y$^e$ sone of Roberte bryan bapt. y$^e$ 21.

#### ffebruarie.
Sara y$^e$ daughter of Ric. Ansell bapt. y$^e$ 18.

#### Marche.
Edwarde y$^e$ sone of John Wynter bapt. y$^e$ 11.
Thomas y$^e$ sone of Rc. Sylverlock bapt. y$^e$ 18.

#### Apryll.
James y$^e$ sone of Edwarde Harrys bapt. y$^e$ 1.

#### Maye.
Susanna y$^e$ daughter of John Stanforde bapt. y$^e$ 13.
Bevis y$^e$ sone of Roger Noble bapt. y 20.
Roberte y$^e$ sone of Phillip Brysco bapt. y$^e$ 20.
Susan y$^e$ daughter of Edmonde bryttyn bapt. y$^e$ 28.

#### June.
Rc. y$^e$ sone of Roberte Brangwen bapt. y$^e$ 17.

#### July.
James y$^e$ sone of John Cryck bapt. y$^e$ 1.
Nycholas y$^e$ sone of Luke Heale bapt. y$^e$ 1.
Isbell y$^e$ daughter of Edwarde Hartwell bapt. y$^e$ 1.
Joan y$^e$ daughter of John y$^e$ colyer bapt. y$^e$ 1.

July (*continued*).

ffraunces ye sone of Goerge Heynes bapt. ye 8.
Agnes ye daughter of John Cotton bapt. ye 25.
Brygett ye daughter of Wyllm Harlowe bapt. ye 29.

August.

Susana ye daughter of John Cade bapt. ye 19.

Septm.

Moses ye sone of Roger Dayntye bapt. ye 2.

*Buryalls.*

October.

The wyfe of Wyllm Norton buryed ye 1.
The wyfe of Odes Purslack buryed ye 10.
Martyn Caple a poore howseholder buryed ye 26.

November.

John Tafte a prentys buryed ye 12.
Thomas Dawson a poore man buryed ye 19.

December.

Rc. Turner a chapman buryed the 29.

ffebruarie.

Thomas Woode a nurse chylde buryed ye 25.

Marche.

Margerett Ismye a poore mayde buryed ye 26.
Edwarde Smewyn a prentis buryed ye 28.

Aprill.

John Jyngkynson a nurse chylde buryed ye 22.

Maye.

Ellen sherlye a nurse chylde buryed ye 24.

June.

Anne Dorman a nurse chylde buryed ye 4.
Wedo Norton buryed ye 6.
John the sone of Wyllm Norton buryed ye 8.
Thomas Leper howseholder buryed ye 11.
Edwarde ye sone of Phillip Brysco buryed ye 11.
John ye sone of Roger buthered buryed ye 13.
Rc. Halle a prentys buryed ye 19.

July.

Mary browne a nurse chylde buryed ye 2.
Em ye daughter of Augustyne Pratt buryed ye 14.
Bevis ye sone of Roger Noble buryed ye 20.

August.

Cleemente browne wedoar buryed ye 6.

Septem.

Roberte ye sone of Wyllm Jacson buried ye 14.

The Church ×
Wardens mark ( ×

Per me Gabrielem Price Barnettæ ministr.

Exhibit 9 Octobris 1599.

The names of all them that hathe bynn Maryed Christened & Buryed in Chepinge Barnett In the Jurisdiction of S<sup>t</sup> Albones from the ffeast of S<sup>t</sup> Mychaell tharchaungell in Anno dom'i 1599 vnto the same feast of S<sup>t</sup> Mychaell tharchaungell 1600.

### *Marages.*
#### October.
Gabryell Price & Israell Bowtell were maryed y<sup>e</sup> 9.
Roberte Elynge & Joan Bennett were maryed y<sup>e</sup> 14.
Hary Henrye & Katheryn Stockam were maryed by a Lycence y<sup>e</sup> 26.
#### July [*sic*].
Ezechiell Couchman & Mary Colborne were maried by a Lycence y<sup>e</sup> 3
#### August.
Rychard Sweane & Elsabeth Grygg were maryed y<sup>e</sup> 2.

### *Christenyngs.*
#### October.
John y<sup>e</sup> sone of Rycharde Bedforde bapt. y<sup>e</sup> 7.
Thomas y<sup>e</sup> sonne of John Cheevelye bapt. y<sup>e</sup> 7.
Susan y<sup>e</sup> daughter of George Prestwoode bapt. y<sup>e</sup> 28.
#### November.
Edwarde y<sup>e</sup> sonne of John Holebydgs bapt. y<sup>e</sup> 11.
Katheryn y<sup>e</sup> daughter of Henry Robynson bapt. y<sup>e</sup> 30.
#### Januarie.
John y<sup>e</sup> sonne of John Owyn bapt. y<sup>e</sup> 20.
Anthony y<sup>e</sup> sonne of Wyllm Jacson bapt. 27.
#### ffebruarie.
Hugh y<sup>e</sup> sone of Hugh Evyn bapt. y<sup>e</sup> 3.
Andrewe y<sup>e</sup> sone of Xp<sup>r</sup> Stanton bapt. y<sup>e</sup> 24.
#### Marche.
John y<sup>e</sup> sone of John Stacforde bapt. y<sup>e</sup> 2.
Oades y<sup>e</sup> sone of John Presson bapt. y<sup>e</sup> 2.
Joan y<sup>e</sup> daughter of Rycharde Whylye bapt. y<sup>e</sup> 9.
#### Aprill.
Katheryn y<sup>e</sup> daughter of Lauraunce Shuttlewoorth bapt. y<sup>e</sup> 27.
#### Maye.
Thomas y<sup>e</sup> sone of Thomas Pratt bapt. y<sup>e</sup> 4.
John y<sup>e</sup> sone of Valantyne Archar bapt. y<sup>e</sup> 18.
Agnes y<sup>e</sup> daughter of Hugh Palynge bapt. y<sup>e</sup> 25.
#### June.
Thomas y<sup>e</sup> sone of Augustyne Pratt bapt. y<sup>e</sup> 1.
John y<sup>e</sup> sone of John Joellye bapt. y<sup>e</sup> 1.
Elyzabeth y<sup>e</sup> daughter of Oades Purslack bapt. y<sup>e</sup> 15.
#### August.
Doratie y<sup>e</sup> daughter of Rycharde Joyllye bapt. y<sup>e</sup> 3.
ffraunces y<sup>e</sup> sonne of Edwarde Hoodson bapt. y<sup>e</sup> 24.
Wyllm y<sup>e</sup> sone of John Cooper bapt. y<sup>e</sup> 24.
Roberte y<sup>e</sup> sonne of Rycharde Bradhurste bapt. y<sup>e</sup> 31.
#### Septm.
Alice y<sup>e</sup> daughter of Wyllm Barton bapt. y<sup>e</sup> 7.

### *Buryalls.*
#### October.
Henry Peele y<sup>e</sup> sone of Henry Peele buryed y<sup>e</sup> 19.

November.

Even Denevett a poore man buryed y&deg; 1.
Hugh Dyckynson a poore man buryed 25.
The wyfe of Jefferie Hethe buryed y&deg; 29.

December.

Rycharde y&deg; sone of Docter Hucchynsone buryed y&deg; 25.

ffebruarie.

Mary y&deg; daughter of Xp<sup>r</sup> Harwarde buryed y&deg; 6.

Apryll.

The wyfe of Roberte Bryan buryed y&deg; 9.
The wyfe of Goerge Thrope buryed y&deg; 20.

Maye.

The wyfe of Myghyll Vnderwood buryed y&deg; 8.
Alice Exsoll Xp<sup>r</sup> Bottamlyes wyfes daughter buryed y&deg; 21.
Thomas Townsende a straunger buryed y&deg; 26.

June.

The wyfe of John Stacye buryed y&deg; 22.
Wyllm the sone of Rycharde Curtys buryed y&deg; 26.

July.

Robert Hopwoode a nurse chylde buryed y&deg; 15.
John y&deg; sone of Rychard Bedforde buryed y&deg; 31.

August.

Myles y&deg; sone of Rycharde Bedforde buryed y&deg; 1.
John Clypsone a prentys buryed y&deg; 8.
The wyfe of Wyllm Waryner buryed y&deg; 12.
Thomas Whitten a nurse chylde buryed y&deg; 21.
Hugh y&deg; sone of Hugh Evyn buryed y&deg; 22.
Thomas Robynson a servaunte buryed the 28.

Septm.

Jhon y&deg; son of Laurance Shuttlewoorth buryed y&deg; 5.
Wedo Cheevelye a poore woman buryed y&deg; 10.
Thomas Pratt howse holder buryed y&deg; 20.

Richardus Boyle minister.

Richerd Sillverlock.
John Crabtree his × marke.

Exhibit 9 Octobris 1600.

*To be Continued.*

---

# Inquisitiones post Mortem.

### THOMAS WOLLEY.

[*Inq.p.m. Series II. Vol.* 308. *7 Jas. I. No.* 114.]

Inquisition taken at Ware 15 Aug. 7 Jas. I. [1609] before John Williams esq., deputy of Rich. Langley esq., escheator, after the death of Thomas Wolley gent., by the oaths of Wm. Cater, John Rowley,

John Wood, John Nodes, John Westwood, Geo. Underwood, John Crowch, Robt. Miles, John Halfehide, Edw. Shepherd, John Bedell, John Miles, Geo. Porter, Robt. Rumbold, Wm. Chandelor, Henry Walker, Robt. Spencer, Wm. Hale & Rich. Rudd, who say that

Thos. Wolley was seised in fee of the Manor of Harpesfeilde Hall, formerly called Harpesfeild, & a messuage lying in the Vyntree in the town of St Albans & a messuage in psh. of St Stephens & a messuage in the Malt Markett in St Albans called the Bores Heade & a messuage in the Malt Market in tenure of John Jewell, & so seised by deed dated 1 Feb. 35 Eliz. [1593] enfeoffed one Ellen West widow & one Robert Woiley of the Clockhouse in St Albans, to such uses as were declared in an indenture dated 1 Jan. 35 Eliz. between sd Thos. on the one part & sd Ellen & Robert on the other part viz:—that sd Manor & messuages etc. belonging situate in the Vyntree in St Albans should be to the use of Robt. Wolley eldest son of sd Thos. for the life of sd Thos. his father & after the death of sd Thos. then to the use of sd Ellen Wolley wife of sd Thomas for her jointure & after sd Ellen's decease then to sd Robert Wolley his heirs & assigns for ever. The sd messuage in the Vyntree to the use of Thomas one of the sons of sd Thos. Wolley the father & the heirs of his body, remainder to Richard Wolley another son of sd Thomas the father & his heirs for ever. The messuage in the Malt Market in occupation of John Jewell, to the use of John Wolley another son of sd Thos. the father & his heirs & assigns for ever. Messuage called the Bores head now in occupation of Thos. Cooley, to the use of Benjamin Wolley another son of sd Thos. the father & his heirs & assigns for ever. [And two messuages to the use of Joane Wolley sole dau. of sd Thos. the father & her heirs & assigns for ever. *Erased.*]

The Manor of Harpesfeild etc. is held of Chas. Morrison knt. as of his manor of Parkbury, in free socage, & is worth, per annum, clear, lxvj*s*. viij*d*. Messuage in the Vyntree is held of the King in free & common socage by fealty & not in chief & is worth per annum, clear, 10*s*. The messuage in psh. of St Stephens is worth per annum 10*s*. & held of Raphael Pemberton & Mary his wife as of the manor of Sopwell in free & common socage. The two messuages in Maltmarket are held of the King in free & common socage & are worth, per annum, clear, 13*s*. 4*d*.

Thomas Wolley died, so seised, about 9 June 6 Jas. [1608] & Robert Wolley gent. is his son & next heir & at his father's death was aged 30 years & more.

## ROBERT WOLLEY.

[*Inq.p.m. Series II. Vol.* 369. 16 *Jas. I. No.* 160.]

Inquisition* taken at Chipping Barnett 15 Sep. 16 Jas. [1618] before . . . . . . . . . escheator, after the death of Robert Wolley gent., by the oaths of . . . . . . . . Grobbe, Hen. Sharpe, Edw. Harris, Wm. Barnard, Rich. Mayne, John Rusley, Wm. Sherewood, Geo. Clerke, Ralph Pollard, Simon Cooper, Rich. Silverlock, . . . . . . . . . . . . . Oxton *alias* Foxe, Thos. Redwood & Thos. Warner, who say that

---

* This document is unfortunately in bad condition and in many places illegible. There appears to be no duplicate amongst the inquisitions returned into the Court of Wards and Liveries.

Robert Wolley was seised in fee of the Manor of Harpsfeild hall in S$^t$ Albans & so seised by deed dated 4 Oct. 25 Eliz. [1583] enfeoffed Thos. Wolley his son of said premises. Said Robert was also seised in fee of a messuage in S$^t$ Albans in a street called the Malt Markett, lying between a tenement called the Crossekeys on the south and a tenement called the Spreadeagle on the north and [another tenement] in said street between the Spreadeagle & a tenement called the Exchecker, also a messuage in the psh. of S$^t$ Stephens now in tenure of Wm. Branche & . . . . . . in the psh. of Sandridge containing by estimation 3 [acres]; And so seised by deed dated 6 June 28 Eliz. [1586] gave . . . . . messuage & close last mentioned to s$^d$ Thomas Wolley his son to hold unto & to the use of s$^d$ Thos. his heirs & assigns for ever.

Said Robert was also seised of a messuage called the Horsehead in the borough of S$^t$ Albans in Halliwell Street . . . . . . . . now in tenure of Christr. Whelpley, & another messuage now called the Checquer & formerly the Crane now in the tenure of William Warner & another messuage in Sopwell lane formerly in occupation of John . . . . . . [& now of . . . . ] Dewberie, widow, & a messuage in Halliwell Street formerly in tenure of Thos. Kell & now of John Berrie shoemaker & another messuage formerly in tenure of [blank] Coxe, widow, & now of Robert Wolley [& another messuage] formerly in tenure of Thos. Welles & now of [blank] Cooley & another messuage in s$^d$ street formerly in tenure of Wm. Towe & nowe of [blank] Colles & a messuage [formerly in tenure of . . . . . . ] Woorton & now of Jas. Ashton, & another messuage in s$^d$ street formerly in tenure of John Taylor & now of [blank] Streete, & another messuage called the Corner Taverne now in tenure of Robert . . . . . . & another messuage in the street called the Vintree formerly in tenure of Robt. Wolley & now of Daniel Peterson & another messuage in the street called the Wheat Markett now in tenure of John Clerke & a messuage in S$^t$ Michael Street formerly in tenure of Robt. Pye & now of Rich. Turner & another messuage in S$^t$ Peters Street in occupation of Rich. Evans; & so seised by deed of feoffment dated 6 Mch. 28 Eliz. [1586] said Robt. Wolley gave & granted all s$^d$ premises last mentioned to Robert Wolley another of his sons.

Said Robert was also seised of a messuage in Hitchin lately bought of Henry Cranwell, late in the tenure of John Wolleys, & so seised, by his last will dated 26 May 33 Eliz. [1591], left s$^d$ messuage to his s$^d$ son Robert.

Said Robert was also seised of a messuage called the Halfe Moon in S$^t$ Albans, in the street called the Malt Markett, & another messuage called the signe of the Exchequer in s$^d$ town & all that the manor of Plentyes in Soppesley within the soke of Luton, & so seised, by indenture dated 27 Jan. 28 Eliz. [1586] made between s$^d$ Robert of the one part & Thos. Coxe & Thos. Hickman of the other part & in consideration of an intended marriage between Richard Wolley one of the sons of s$^d$ Robert & one Mary Coxe one of the daus. of s$^d$ Thos. s$^d$ Robt. agreed to assure the manor & messuage aforesaid to use of him s$^d$ Robt. & his heirs untill s$^d$ marriage should be solemnized & after solemnization thereof would assure the s$^d$ manor to the use of s$^d$ Robt. for life without impeachment of waste, then to the use of s$^d$ Rich. Wolley for his life & after his decease to the use of s$^d$ Mary until the hoir of the body of s$^d$ Richard should attain the full age of

21 years & afterwards to the use of the heirs of s^d Richard . . . .
. . . . & in default of issue to the use of s^d Rich. & his heirs for ever & [also agreed to assure] the s^d messuages to the use of s^d Robt. until s^d marriage take place & then to the use of s^d Rich. & Mary & the heirs of s^d Richard . . . . . . . . . . & in default of such issue to the use of s^d Rich. & his heirs for ever.

The s^d marriage was afterwards solemnized & s^d Robt. in performance of agreement, by deed dated 28 Jan. 28 Eliz. [1586] enfeoffed Thos. Coxe & Thos. Hickman & their heirs to the uses above set forth.

The Manor of Harpsfield Hall is held of Chas. Morrison knt. as of the Manor of Parkburie by fealty & is worth per annum, clear, [xiij ?]*l.* vj*s.* viij*d.* The messuage called the Halfe Moon is held of the king in chief by service of the 20th part of a knight's fee & is worth per ann. clear 10*s.* The rest of the premises in S^t Albans are together worth, per ann. clear xx*s.* viz. the messuage conveyed as abovesaid to Thos. Wolley vj*s.* viij*d.*, the messuage . . . . . . . . . . . . . . . . . . . . . [vj*s.* viij*d.*] & the messuages conveyed to Robt. Wolley vj*s.* viij*d.* The premises in Sandridge are held of . . . . . . . . . . . [as of the Manor] of Sandridge by fealty & are worth per ann. clear, iij*s.* iiij*d.* The messuage in Hitchin (tenure unknown) is worth per ann. clear ij*s.* The manor of Plenties is held of Wm. Markham as of his manor of Flamstead by fealty & rent of xxvij*s.* per ann. & is worth per ann. clear xx*s.*

Said Robt. Wolley died [9 ?] Jan. 45 Eliz. [1603] & Thos. Wolley was his son & next heir & aged 30 years & more at his father's death. Said Thomas son of Robert died 9 June 6 Jas. [1608].

## Marriage Licences.

### ARCHDEACONRY OF HUNTINGDON (HITCHIN REGISTRY).

(Continued from Page 154).

1641
July 8  Symon Faireclough of Bps. Hatfield, 'sutor vestium,' bach^r, & Christian Reynolds of same, maiden, orphan. At Whethampsted or Bps. Hatfield.

,, 16  Thos. Halsey of Throckinge, wid^r, yeoman, & Mary Gutteridge of Kings Walden, maiden, dau. of John Gutteridge of same. At Ayot S^t Laurence or Whethampsted.

,, 17  Geo. Rugmore of Hitchin, bach^r, baker, & Bridget Goard late of Islington, now of Hitchin, maiden, orphan. At Hitchin, Hippollits or Kings Walden.

,, 18  Wm. Phillips of Kings Langley, husbandman, wid^r, & Joan Roache of same, widow. At Kings Langley.

,, 30  John Hilton of Yardley, bach^r, husbandman, & Grace Greene of same, widow. At Yardley, Cottered or Rushden.

| | | |
|---|---|---|
| Aug. | 18 | Henry Gibb of Bps. Hatfield, yeoman, & Eliz. Baker of same, maiden, dau. of Christr Baker. At Hartingfordbury. |
| Sep. | 10 | Richard Clarke of Digswell, bachr, yeoman, & Alice Hale of Datchworth, maiden, orphan. At Whethampsted or Ayot St Laurence. |

1641-2

| | | |
|---|---|---|
| Jan. | 15 | Thos. Hurst of Kimpson, co. Beds., bachr, yeoman, & Judith Crawley of Hitchin, widow. At Offley or Lilley. |
| ,, | 15 | John Burrage of Baldock, widr, & Helen Kinge of same, widow. At Baldock or Clothall. |
| ,, | 27 | Thos. Rattin of Clothall, bachr, yeoman, & Eliz. Plomer of Baldock, widow. At Whethampsted. |
| ,, | 27 | John Roberts of Bps. Hatfield, bachr, yeoman, & Mary Bigge of Sacombe, dau. of Wm. Bigge of same, yeoman. At Sacombe or Watton at Stone. |
| ,, | 31 | Nicholas Williamson of Bps. Hatfield, bachr, tailor, & Margt. Warrenner of same, maiden, orphan. At Bps. Hatfield or Hartingfordbury. |
| Feb. | 5 | Edward Squire of Offley, bachr, blacksmith, & Anne Chawkley, maiden, dau. of Henry Chawkley of Offley, yeoman, aged about 20. Alleged by Edw. Squire. At Kimpton or Whethampsted. |
| ,, | 14 | John Hamond, bachr, yeoman, of Westmill, & Mary Kirbie of Little Munden, widow. At Sacombe or Wellwin. |
| Mch. | 21 | Roland Parker of Knebworth, bachr, carpenter, & Eliz. Wells of Kings Walden, maiden, dau. of [blank] Wells of same, wid. At Offley or Hippollits. |
| ,, | 24 | Thos. Orgar of Stevenage, bachr, 'sutor,' & Eliz. Stamer of same, maiden, dau. of Edw. Stamer of same. At Stevenage or Graveley. |

1642

| | | |
|---|---|---|
| Mch. | 31 | Robt. Cocks of Watton at Stone, bachr, yeoman, & Joan Knott of same, maiden, orphan. At Watton at Stone or Little Munden. |
| Apr. | 14 | Rich. Waterman of Wellwin, yeoman, & Helen Chapman of Digswell, maiden. At Ayot St Laurence, Ayot St Peter or Kimpton. |
| ,, | 21 | Robt. Newman of Hinxworth, yeoman, & Sarah Bowlesse of same, maiden. At Hinxworth. |
| ,, | 23 | Geo. Awdley of Hitchin, bachr, grocer, & Susan Hurst of Hitchin, maiden, dau. of Eliz. Hurst of same, widow. At Letchworth or Willion. |
| ,, | 27 | Christr Knight of Hartford St Andrews, widr, & Helen Graye of same, widow. At Hartford All Saints or Bengeo. |
| May | 11 | Wm. Bockett of Hitchin, widr, & Mary Draper of same, maiden, orphan. At Hitchin, Ickleford, or Letchworth. |
| ,, | 14 | John Tarboxe of Bps. Hatfield, widr, & Winifred Pewterer of same, maiden, orphan. At Bps. Hatfield. |
| ,, | 16 | Wm. Skanmer of St Pauls Walden, bachr, & Grace Welche of Kings Walden, maiden, dau. of Robt. Welche of same. At Kings Walden. |
| June | 3 | John Welche of Great Wymondly, widr, & Joan Swansey of same, widow. At Gt. Wymondly or Hippollit. |
| ,, | 6 | Edw. Manfeild, aged 29, of Hatfield, bachr & yeoman, & Eliz. Waterton of same, maiden, dau. of [blank] Waterton of Digswell. At Bps. Hatfield or Shenley. |

June 15 John Reddall jun^r of Northmyms, bach^r, & Grace Todd, maiden, dau. of John Todd of Sowthmyms, co. Midd. At Northmyms.
,, 16 Thos. Hill of Northmyms, bach^r, & Sarah Norris of same, maiden, dau. of Thos. Norris of same. At Northmyms.
,, 16 Thos. Child of Shenley, wid^r, & Eliz. Crawley of same, widow. At Whethamsted.
,, 28 Bernard Bowlnest of Hinxworth, wid^r, & Eliz. Knowlewater of Ashwell, maiden, orphan. At Hinxworth or Clothall.
July 6 Graveley Hurst jun^r of Hitchin, wid^r, & Frances Trustram of same, maiden, dau. of Laurence Trustram of same, maultster. At Hitchin, Ickleford or Willion.
,, 12 James Nicolls of Wellwin, bach^r, tanner, & Anne Miles of Watton at Stone, maiden, dau. of John Miles jun^r of same. At Watton at Stone or Aston.
,, 14 W^m. Chappell of Harpeden, wid^r, & Agnes Bennett of same, maiden, orphan. At Wellwin.
,, 18 Matthew Hanscombe of Hitchin, bach^r, & Anne Marshall of same, maiden, orphan. At Lilley, Ickleford or Hippollit.
,, 20 W^m. Bayford of Tewinge, wid^r, & Eliz. Sawell late of Chesthunte now of Tewinge, widow. At Tewinge, Weston or Graveley.
,, 26 Josias Hobbs of Hitchin, bach^r, & Mary Izard of same, maiden, dau. of Hannah Izard *alias* Draper of same. At Lilley or Stevenage.
,, 26 W^m. Catlin of Harpeden, wid^r, & Sarah Whitlocke of same, widow. At Whethamsted.
Aug. 10 John Beeche of Flamsted, wid^r, yeoman, & Frances Helder *alias* Spicer of Lilley, maiden, dau. of Rob^t. Helder *alias* Spicer of same, gent. At Harpeden.
,, 20 W^m. Thurston of Easton, co. Hunt., & Anne Seuter of Hartford S^t Andrews, widow.
,, 27 Edw. Lucas of Ickleford, bach^r, miller, & Eliz. Knott of Essenden, widow. At Essenden or Bayford.
Sep. 7 John Williamson of Bps. Hatfield, wid^r, & Dionisia Deacon of same, maiden, orphan. At Bps. Hatfield.
,, 16 Henry Edwards of Wellwin, bach^r, & Anne Pryor of same, maiden, dau. of Anthony Pryor of Little Wymondly. At Ayot S^t Lawrence or Ayot S^t Peter.
,, 29 John Saule of Bps. Hatfield, bach^r, & Eliz. Ivorie of same, maiden, dau. of Nich. Ivorie of same. At Ayot S^t Laurence.
Oct. 1 Thos. Catlin of Harpeden, bach^r, & Eliz. Nicolls of same, maiden, dau. of Joan Nicolls, widow. At Whethampsted or Harpeden.
,, 16 Rich. Harper of Barkhampsted S^t Peter, bach^r, & Grace Halsey of same, maiden. At Whethampsted.
,, 22 Edw. Thorold of Bayford, bach^r, gent., & Anne Walsall of Sandye, co. Beds, maiden. At Bayford.
,, 22 John Darlinge of Hitchin, wid^r, & Eliz. Johnson of same, widow. At Hitchin or Ickleford.
,, 23 Geo. Kilbie of Luton, bach^r, & Eliz. George late of Luton now of Ayot S^t Laurence, maiden. At Ayot S^t Laurence or Kimpton.
, 29 Rob^t. Browne of Luton, wid^r, & Mary Smithe of Hitchin, maiden, dau. of Philip Smithe of Luton. At Whethampsted.

Oct. 31  Rich. Kimpton of Aston, bach^r, & Joan Dodkin of Datchworth, maiden, dau. of [blank] Dodkin *alias* Saunders of Hippollits, widow. At Datchworth.

Nov. 1  Thos. Ablett of Aldenham, wid^r, & Joan Spencer of same, maiden, orphan. At Aldenham.

„ 4  Geo. Renolds of Sowthmyms, co. Midd., wid^r, & Frances Younge of Northmyms, maiden, dau. of Thos. Younge clerk. At Whethamsted.

„ 8  Edw. Bawcocke of Little Barkhampsted, bach^r, & Alice Vsher of same, maiden, dau. of Jo. Vsher. At same.

„ 26  Leonard Wrenn of Codicote, bach^r, & Agnes Tuffnaile of Hitchin, maiden, dau. of [blank] Tuffnaile, widow. At Hitchin or Hippollits.

1642

May 20  Thos. Hills of Hartford All Saints, bach^r & Mary Claye of same, maiden, dau. of Joan Claye of same, widow. At Hartford All Sts.

„ 23  Robt. Salter of Northmyms, bach^r, & Anne Lowen of same, widow. At Northmyms.

„ 30  Robt. Purrye of Little Barkhampsted, bach^r, & Eliz. Michell of same, maiden, dau. of [blank] Michell of Little Munden, husbandman. At Little Barkhampsted.

June 1  Robt. Harper of Wellwin, bach^r, & Alice Wilkinson of same, maiden, orphan. At Great Wymondly or Ayot S^t Peter.

„ 7  Jas. Pryor of Ickleford, bach^r, bricklayer, & Joan Bradwell, maiden. At Letchworth or Ickleford.

Oct. 3  Thos. Greeninge of Wilsthampsted, co. Beds., clerk, & Amy Suttell late of same now of Whethampsted, maiden, dau. of Wm. Suttell of Wiltshamsted, yeoman. At Whethampsted.

Nov. 2  Nich. Rugg of Ille Abbotts, co. Somerset, bach^r, yeoman, & Anne Sellwood of Hatfield, maiden, dau. of Eliz. Sellwood of same, widow. At Hatfeild.

„ 15  Francis Mansfeild of Bramfeild, wid^r, & Alice Catlin of Tewinge, widow. At Ayot S^t Peter or Stapleford.

„ 25  Henry Inskip of Hitchin, bach^r, & Judith Bradwell of same, maiden, dau. of Wm. Bradwell of Ickleford. At Hitchin, Ickleford or Letchworth.

Dec. 11  Wm. Izard of Weston, bach^r, & Ursula Fenney of Clothall, maiden, dau. of Tho. Fenney of same, husbandman. At Clothall.

„ 16  John Clinton of Cottered, yeoman, wid^r, & Anne Kimpton of Weston, maiden, dau. of [blank] Kimpton of same, widow. At Weston or Graveley.

„ 24  John Farr of Hitchin, bach^r, & Eliz. Clinton of Letchworth, maiden, dau. of John Clinton of same, yeoman. At Letchworth or Hippollit.

„ 31  John Holmes of Lilley, bach^r, & Dionisia Bowstred late of Luton, now of Lilley, dau. of [blank] Bowstred of Luton, yeoman. At Lilley.

1642-3

Jan. 3  Jonas Daniell of Hartford All Saints, wid^r, & Eliz. Kinge of same, widow. At Hartford All Sts.

„ 20  Samuel Hale of Codicote, yeoman, & Beatrice Wilshere of same, maiden, dau. of Wm. Wilshere of same. At Wellwin.

Jan. 31  Thos. White of Hitchin. bach^r, & Susan Peirce of same, maiden, dau. of Arthur Peirce of same, tailor. At Hitchin.

Feb. 1  Tho. Campkin of Pirton, bach^r, & Mary Man of same, maiden, dau. of Thos. Man of same, 'fabricator.' At Whethamsted.

„ 6  Tho. Dicenson of Harpeden, bach^r, esq., & Eliz. Rudston of same, gentlewoman, widow. At Whethamsted or Ayot S^t Laurence.

Mch. 3  Robt. Darlin of Gt. Munden, bach^r, & Anne Corbye of Bennington, maiden, dau. of Anne Corbye of same, widow. At Bennington.

„ 24  Salomon Waterman, bach^r, of Gt. Parndon, co. Essex, wheelwright, & Emma Rickett, late of Little Parndon, co. Essex, maiden, dau. of Thos. Rickett of same, yeoman. At Hartford S^t Andrews, Hartford All Sts. or Bengeo.

1643

Mch. 25  John Darlinge of Hitchin, wid^r, & Anne Waterman of Ickleford, widow. At Ickleford.

„ 29  Geo. Hawkins of Watton at Stone, bach^r, & Mary Gilberd of same, maiden, dau. of [blank] Gilberd of Graveley. At Watton.

Apr. 25  Thos. Rayment of Bengeo, bach^r, & Sarah Greene of Willion, maiden, dau. of [blank] Greene of same, widow. At Willion.

May 3  John Warren *alias* Wood of Hitchin, bach^r, & Agnes Hurst of Hitchin, maiden, dau. of Geo. Hurste of same. At Hitchin or Pirton.

„ 10  Henry Warner of Hitchin, bach^r, & Isabel Hitchin of same, maiden, dau. of Edw. Hitchin of same, tanner. At Pirton or Little Wymondly.

„ 29  John Spoure of Whethamsted, wid^r, & Susan Brand of Essendon, widow. At Essendon.

„ 31  Edw. Carte of Ayott S^t Peter, bach^r, & Judith Warde of Kings Walden, maiden, dau. of John Warde of same. At either place.

June 7  Moses Pearpointe of Hitchin, wid^r, & Agnes Gouldsmith of same, maiden, dau. of Samuel Goldsmith of same, brewer. At Hitchin or Gt. Wymondly.

„ 21  Henry Docklee of Bps. Hatfeild, bach^r, & Eliz. Smith of same, maiden, orphan. At Whethamsted.

„ 21  Nathaniel Russell of Datchworth, wid^r, & Susan Kimpton of same, maiden, dau. of Rich. Kimpton of same, yeoman. At Datchworth, Aston or Stapleford.

„ 28  Edw. Feild of Ayott S^t Peter, bach^r, & Dorothy Snell of same, maiden. At same.

„ 29  Rich. Hatton of Bayford, bach^r, & Judith Turner of same, maiden. At Essendon, Little Barkhampsted or Bayford.

July 3  Thos. Wabye of Whethamsted, bach^r, & Mary Wright of Kimpton, maiden, dau. of Alice Wright *alias* George of same. At Bps. Hatfeild, Wellwin or Harpeden.

„ 19  Edw. Roberts of Aston, wid^r, & Dorothy Jordan of S^t Andrews, Hartford, widow. At Aston, Datchworth or Digswell.

MARRIAGE LICENCES. 213

July 23 Thos. Watkins, bach<sup>r</sup>, & Mary Rawlins, maiden, dau. of Joseph Rawlins of same. At Ayott S<sup>t</sup> Lawrence or S<sup>t</sup> Hippollits.

„ 24 Thos. Plumbe of Offley, bach<sup>r</sup>, & Alice Deermer of Walkerne, maiden, dau. of Thos. Deermer of same, yeoman. At Walkerne, Weston or Baldock.

„ 27 Wm. Foster of Wellwin, husbandman, bach<sup>r</sup>, & Eliz. Chappell of same, widow. At Whethamsted.

Aug. 5 John Gootheridge of Kings Walden, bach<sup>r</sup>, & Sarah Godfrey of same, maiden, orphan. At Offley or Whethamsted.

„ 7 Robt. Rudd of Datchworth, bach<sup>r</sup>, & Sarah Welche of Tewinge, maiden, dau. of [blank] Welche of same, yeoman. At Willion or Bayford.

Sep. 14 John Goode of Knebworth, bach<sup>r</sup>, & Eliz. Mondell of same, maiden, orphan. At Ayott S<sup>t</sup> Laurence.

„ 28 John Lucas of Hitchin, bach<sup>r</sup>, & Eliz. Watts of same, maiden, dau. of Thos. Watts of same, maultster. At Hitchin or Gt. Wymondly.

„ 30 John Sheppard of Pirton, wid<sup>r</sup>, & Mary Feild late of Shitlington, co. Beds, maiden, now of Pirton, dau. of John Feild of Shitlington, yeoman. At Lilley, Offley or Kings Walden.

„ 30 Rich. Dellowe of Hitchin & Mary Fawcett *alias* Artur, maiden, of Hippollitts, dau. of Judith Fawcett *alias* Artur. At Hitchin or Hippollits.

Oct. 1 John Randolphe of Willion, bach<sup>r</sup>, & Grace Knight of Weston, maiden, dau. of Geo. Knight of same, yeoman. At Weston or Letchworth.

„ 7 Nich. Shittleton of Bps. Hatfeild, bach<sup>r</sup>, & Olive Marshall of same, widow. At Northmyms or Ayott S<sup>t</sup> Peter.

„ 18 Robt. Hale of Knebworth, bach<sup>r</sup>, & Grace Hale of Codicote, maiden, dau. of Robt. Hale of same, yeoman. At Knebworth.

„ 20 John Warde of Sandridge, wid<sup>r</sup>, & Eliz. Wethered of Bps. Hatfield, maiden, dau. of Wm. Wethered of same. At Essendon.

„ 23 John Carter of Gt. Munden, bach<sup>r</sup>, & Eliz. Earle of same, maiden. At Little Munden, Sacombe or Bennington.

„ 26 Thos. Sheffeild of Hitchin, wid<sup>r</sup>, & Mary Campion of same, widow. At Hitchin or Gt. Wymondly.

Nov. 8 Geo. Beadle of Watton at Stone, wid<sup>r</sup>, & Eliz. Tilcocke of same, widow. At Sacombe or Stapleford.

„ 14 Edw. Spicer of Flamsted, tailor, & Anne Monke of Hitchin, maiden, dau. of Susan Monke *alias* Hurst, wife of John Hurst. At Hitchin, Hippollits or Gt. Wymondly.

1643-4
Jan. 1 John Jorden of Watton at Stone, wid<sup>r</sup>, & Eliz. Hollingworth of same, widow. At Sacombe or Little Munden.

„ 19 John Hawkins of Wellwin, bach<sup>r</sup>, & Frances Gouldsmith of same, maiden, dau. of [blank] Gouldsmith of Hexton. At Ayott S<sup>t</sup> Peter or Datchworth.

„ 20 Wm. Cosen of Baldock, bach<sup>r</sup>, & Mary Laundey of same, maiden, dau. of Edw. Laundey of same, yeoman. At Baldock.

„ 26 Cadwallader Riddell of Bps. Hatfield, wid<sup>r</sup>, & Louria Tiddar of same, maiden. At same.

f. 314. MARGARET MARSHALLE of Braughinge, widow. (*Dat.* 6 Aug. 23 Eliz.) Bur^d at Farnam in Essex next unto my late husband; Margt. my dau. Finton's child & the rest of dau. Finton's child^n, viz., Alice, Marie, Margerie & Martha; Grace Awtriche; My dau. Gardner's child^n, viz., John, Wm., Thos., Margt., Eliz., Jane, Anne & Susan; My loving son-in-law exor. Wit^s:—Rich. Barber & John Brooke. (*Pr.* at Braughinge 6 Feb. 1581).

f. 318. ROBERT CHAMBERLEN of Much Hormede, laborer. (*Dat.* 1 Sep. 1581). Sons Fras. & Walter exors; Dau-in-law Joane Rumbolde; Bro. Thos. Chamberlen; Son William: Fras. Delawood gent. overseer. Wit^s:—John Diason vicar of Hormede afores^d, Anth. Bawcocke & Rich. Jurden the younger. (*Pr.* 14 Nov. 1581).

f. 319. WILLIAM BRYGGES of Laiston, gent. (*Dat.* 15 Sep. 1582). Bur^d at Laiston; Son Wm. (under 21); Lands in Aspeden & Throckinge; Son Arthur (under 21); Daus. Joone, Margt., Brygett & Anne (under 21 & unmarr^d); Bro. Chareles; Godchild^n Wm. Feild & Adame Hemyngwaye; Wife Margt. & John Wattes the elder my bro-in-law exors; Thos. Wattes my father-in-law & Jas. Bulton supervisors. Wit^s:—Lewys Raynoldes, vicar of Laiston, Jas. Boulton, Thos. Wattes & Thos. Northappe. (*Pr.* at Braughing 6 Oct. 1582).

f. 320. JOHN CHAYRE junior of Chesthunt, syngleman. (*Dat.* 16 Feb. 1582). Bur^d at Chesthunt; Sisters Alice, Susanne, Cath. & Margt.; Mary Podmer; Uncle Wm. Cocke; Sist. Anne Tydye; John & Robt. sons of Robt. Chayre my uncle; Thos. Price the late husband of Eliz. Pryce my awnt late dec^d & his poore children; Sist. Anne Tydye extrix; Symon Williams & kinsman Wm. Chayre overseers; James Steyinges wife; Ground in Brokefild. Wit^s:—John Sterman, Wm. Cocke. (*Pr.* at Ware 29 Mch. 1582).

f. 321^b JOHN GRAVE of Standon. (*Dat.* 8 Jan. 25 Eliz.). Wife Agnes; Son Edward; Wm. Hampton & Robt. his bro.; Said wife & son exors. Wit^s:—Rice Barber, Robt. Batte & John Huntman. (*Pr.* at Stansted Abbot 14 Feb. 1582).

f. 322^b WILLIAM FOSTER of Ware, chaundler. (*Dat.* 8 June 24 Eliz.). Bur^d at Ware; Emme Foster; Eliz. Foster; Jane Foster; Jas. Foster (under 21); Agnes Foster; Wife extrix; Rich^d Vessey overseer. Wit^s:—Rich^d Vessey, John Thrikelt & Oliver Herne. (*Pr.* at Stansted Abbott 25 Jan. 1582).

f. 323^b THOMAS CROWCHE thelder of Lotceforde in psh. of Stondon. (*Dat.* 13 Mch. 23 Eliz.). M^r Bowman, curate of Stondon; Wife Alice; Sons Thomas, John & Michael; Wm. Taylor; Dau. Joane; Marie Hoye my daughters child & the rest of my daughters child^n; Sist. Margt. Bonde; Son Thomas' child^n; Son Thos. exor; Rich^d Barbor & Geo. Crowche overseers. Wit^s:—George Crowche, John Bonde, Wm. Ponde & Henry Beche. (*Admon.* 25 Jan. 1582 at Stansted Abbot, to Thos. Crowche the exor he having first renounced probate).

f. 325^b ANNIS SKINGEGELL of Ware. (*Dat.* 1579). Bur^d at Ware; Dau. Joane Skinggell; Son Thos. Skingells child^n of Mattocks place 'which is in number six'; Son Robt. Skingell exor; Joan Miles dau. of John Miles the younger 'w^ch was y^e child of Alice Miles y^e wife of y^e said John Miles.' Wit^s:—John Wotsone, Rich. Benyt, Rich^d Butler y^e writer. (*Pr.* at Ware 29 Mch. 1582).

*To be Continued.*

# Feet of Fines for Hertfordshire.

## TUDOR PERIOD.

(CONTINUED FROM PAGE 179).

### 1575-6. Hilary Term. 18 Eliz.

*Joan Feeld widow : Rich. Kympton & Grace his wife. Messuage in Studdeham, co. Herts.

*Nich. Bacon knt, lord keeper: Geo. Herde & Eliz. his wife. Manors of Gorhamburye, Westwicke, Praye cum Kingsburye, Abbotts Burye *alias* Rowletts Burye, Mynchinburye, Hores & Apseburye *alias* Napseburye & 50 messuages & lands in parishes of St Albans, St Peters, St Michaels, & St Stephens in St Albans, Barley & Barkwaye & the advowson of the vicarage of St Michaels.

Edward Cason: John Bolle & Joan his wife. Messuage & land in the town of Hertford.

Rich. Kyrbie senior: Wm. Plompton esq. Lands in Sacombe *alias* Sacomppe.

Wm. Wabie : John Darlyng & Joan his wife. Messuage & land in Codereth *alias* Cottred.

Rich. Cranefield : John Bolle & Joan his wife. Messuage & land in the town of Hertford.

Rich. Awncell: Thos. Copcot & Cecily his wife. Messuage & land in Pyrton.

Wm. Crane: Thos. Clarke & Beatrice his wife. Messuage & lands in Yardley & Coddred *alias* Cottred.

Mark Pearce & Rich. Turner: Geo. Bayford & Eliz. his wife. Orchard & land in Sabridgworth.

Rich. Platt: Thos. Brande & Constance his wife, Agnes Bradshawe wid. & Margt. Boraston. Lands in Awdenham.

Bastian Grace & Edw. Hardynge: Thos. Seare & Agnes his wife, Wm. Fountayne & Joan his wife, Wm. Syewell & Mary his wife, John Dagnall & Eliz. his wife, John Seare & Jane his wife & Alice Seare. A toft & lands in Northbarkamsteade, Aberye, Alberye & Trynge.

Edmund Bardolfe esq: Thos. Appowell & Margt. his wife. Two messuages & lands in Wethampsted *alias* Wethamsted & Herpden *alias* Herpenden.

Gilbert Stoughton: Hugh Mantell gent. & Eliz. his wife, Henry Webbe gent. & Alice his wife, & Rich. Swyfte. Six messuages & land in St Albans. Warranty against sd Hugh & Eliz. & against the heirs of Stephen Carteledge decd.

### 1576. Easter Term. 18 Eliz.

[*The feet of fines for this term are missing.*]

John Brockett esq : Robt. Bagsha gent & Matilda his wife. Messuage & lands in North Mymmys.

Nich. Hoo gent: John Pope gent. & Wm. Handforte. Lands in Whethamsted.

Wm. Barfoote: Wm. Genyn & Anne his wife. Messuage & lands in Thundryche.
Wm. Marshall esq: Thos. Pygram *alias* Peygrem *alias* Pygryme & Eliz. his wife. Three messuages & land in Ware.
Wm. Hytch: Arthur Breame esq. Nine messuages & orchards in Layston, Aspiden & Throckynge.
John Hamon: Arthur Breame esq. Messuage & lands in Westmyll.
John Wright gent & Wm. Samwayes: Thos. Coke. Messuage & land in Barley.
Wm. Perles: John Cooe & Kath. his wife & John Hubberd & Joan his wife. Two messuages & land in Hytchyn.
Edw. Kympton: John Phippes & Eliz. his wife. Lands in Weston.
John Laurence: John Seward & Cecily his wife. Messuage in S$^t$ Albans.
Wm. Joyse: Wm. Baron. Messuage & lands in Leyston, Alswyck, Great Hormead & Little Hormead.
John Clarke: Wm. Copwood. Messuage & lands in Tateridge.
John Cock: Edw. Brockett esq & Etheldreda his wife. Three messuages & lands in Watton & Wemsted.
Rich. Gunne: Fras. Roberts gent. Messuage & land in Ware.
Thos. Gaskyn: Fras. Roberts gent. Land in Ware.
John Harvey: Fras. Roberts gent. Messuage & land in Ware.
John Gadsden: Edw. Saunder & Eliz. his wife. Messuage in Hitchyn.
Edm. Bardolf esq: Thos. Doggett & Alice his wife. The fourth part of a messuage & lands in Harpeden & Whethamsted.
Rich. Hale: Wm. Burgh knt. lord Burgh & Kath his wife. Manor of Kinges Walden & 12 messuages & lands in Kings Walden, Powles Walden & Polletts.

1576. Trinity Term. 18 Eliz.

*Andrew Corbett knt, Geo. Bromley esq. & Thos. Trentham esq: Sampson Meverell esq. Manor of Inges & 12 messuages & lands in Inges.
Henry Edmonds & Rich. Longe: Rich Carter. Messuage & land in Watforde.
Robt. Norrys: Wm. Norrys & Mary his wife. Two messuages & lands in Harpeden.
Wm. Davies: Thos. Chare. Messuage in Chesthunte.
Geo. Robson: John Boole & Joan his wife. Land in Little Brickendon.
Rich. Clerke: Edw. Cattelyn, Rich. Byworthe & Agnes his wife & John Mongke & Eliz. his wife. Messuage & lands in Kympton.
Christr. Bales: Henry Cooke & Matilda his wife. Messuage in Hoddesdon in psh. of Broxborne.
Wm. Androwe gent. & Thos. Emery: Edw. Pulter esq. & Mary his wife & Julian Hanchett widow. Twenty messuages & land in Hitchin.
Anthony Throkmorton esq: Wm. Whitacres gent. & Joan his wife. Moiety of a messuage in Ware.
Thos. Strayte: Bernard Brocas esq. Four tofts & lands in Kenneswourth *alias* Caneswourth.
Wm. Skipwith esq: Ralph Skipwith gent, Edw. Skipwith gent. & Henry Skipwith gent. Manor of Newneham & 20 messuages & lands in Newneham, Caldecott, Radwell, Hinckesworth & Asshewell, & the rectory of Newneham & the advowson of the vicarage.

Jas. Dowman gent. & Joan his wife: Wm. Skipwith esq. Manor of Newneham, etc. [*as in previous fine.*]

Wm. Skipwith esq: Geo. Herde & Eliz. his wife. Manor of Newneham etc. [*as before*].

Wm. Aylewarde & Joan his wife: Wm. Hewett. Messuage & lands in Shenley.

Rich. Alexander & Thos. Webbe: Thos. Lane & Alice his wife. Messuage & lands in Ryckmersworth & Watforde. A settlement; names John Lane one of the sons of s^d Thos. & Alice.

### 1576. Mich Term. 18 & 19 Eliz.

*Christr. Ventam: Edw. Harman & Isabel his wife. Land in Tryng.

*Gerard Cosyn gent: Rich. Veale. Messuage & land in Watford.

Philip Wingefilde: Robt. Warren & Isabel his wife. Messuage in Aldenham.

John Broke & Joan his wife: Thos. Lawghton & Ellen his wife & Henry Gryme & Dorothy his wife. Messuage & land in St Albans.

Rich. Wryght & Thos. Bayland: Innocent Rede esq. Messuage & land in Redborne.

John Parmyter: Rich. Turner & Eliz. his wife. Messuage & land in Sabrydgewourth *alias* Sapysworth.

John Dowsett: John Dyer & Joan his wife. Messuage in Stortforde.

John Redewood: Henry Bellamye & Joan his wife. Messuage & land in Watford.

Robt. Dey gent. & John Plomer gent: John Brokett esq. Manor of Lee and two messuages & lands in Kympton & S^t Pauls Walden.

Wm. Tooke esq. & Alice his wife & Walter Tooke gent: Daniel Perrey. Messuage & lands in Esendon *alias* Esingdon & Bps. Hatfeld *alias* Kings Hatfeld. A warranty against Anne Fyssher mother of s^d Daniel.

John Jones: John Warren & Joan his wife. Cottage & land in Shenley.

Wm. Dodds esq: Edmund Dardes. Messuage & lands in Northemymes *alias* Northmyms.

John Jardfeild: John Whippull & Wm. Whippull. Two messuages & lands in Stortford.

Clement Newce esq: John Mounson esq. and Margt. Thoralde widow. The 20th part of the manors of Byggynnes and Barwicks and of 10 messuages & lands in Great Hadham & Stondon.

Wm. Dune, Wm. Antwissell, John Thorneton, Wm. Hunte, Joan Swallowe, Humph. Swallowe, Edm. Swallowe, Philip Antwissell, Wm. Palmer, Edw. Woodshawe, John Austen, Wm. Walleys, Thos. Smythe sen^r, Robt. Duxford & Thos. Smyth jun^r: Thos. Clerke & Beatrice his wife. Eight messuages & lands in Cothered.

Robt. Bell esq. & Steph. Thymylbye esq: John Tufton esq. & Christian his wife & Thos. Wylforde esq. & Mary his wife. Two parts of a third part of the manor of Hockenhanger & Kympton (into three parts divided) & of six messuages & lands in Hockenhanger, Kympton, Drakelowe & Redborne.

Philip Butler esq: Thos. Bradberye gent. & Dorothy his wife & Wm. Bradberye gent, brother of s^d Thos. Manor of Bardoles & 30 messuages & lands in Bardoles, Watton Astone, Benyngton, Mundin, Sacon & Stableforde.

### 1576-7. Hilary Term. 19 Eliz.

*Rich. Smyth & Thos. Smyth: Fitzralph Chamberleyne esq. & Dorothy his wife, Rich. Skypwith esq, Wm. Mallowes gent, Geo. Ager gent. & Paul Pope & Kath. his wife. Manor of Bechewood *alias* Becheswood *alias* Saynt Gyles in le Wood & 5 messuages & lands in Flampstede, Stodham & Gaddesden.

Wm. Russell *alias* Pearse: Anth. Throckmarton esq. & Kath. his wife. Messuage in Ware.

Rich. Fanner: Thos. Smyth & Joan his wife. Lands in Hounsden.

Valentine Browne knt: Wm. Blytheman. Messuage & lands in Totterage.

Francis Godfrey *alias* Cowper: Wm. Godfrey *alias* Cowper & Josanna his wife. A third part of a messuage & lands in Lecheworth, Langley & Hitchen & of all tithes in Brok(?) Chappell *alias* Burleys Chappell in Lecheworth.

John Gaselye: Robt. Seibroke & Geo. Waters & Eliz. his wife. Messuage in Hitchin.

Henry Butler esq: Philip Butler esq. & Grisel Butler widow. Messuage & lands in Harpeden & Kenesbourne.

Wm. Thorowgood: Wm. Phillipps & Frances his wife & Robt. Gryffyn clerk. Two messuages in psh. of Broxborne.

John Barowe: Henry Bowghe & Philippa his wife. Moiety of a messuage & lands in Ryckmansworthe.

Edw. Cason: John Bole & Joan his wife. Messuage in psh. of All Saints in Hertford.

John Ewer: Thos. Bollamy gent. & Kath. his wife. Moiety of a messuage & lands in Shelney *alias* Shenley, Rydge & Chipping Barnett.

Thos. Clackson & Margt. his wife: Rich. Wright. Messuage in Ware.

### 1577. Easter Term. 19 Eliz.

*George Blythe gent. & Fras. Blythe gent: Henry Cheney knt. lord Cheney of Tuddyngton & Jane his wife. Three messuages & lands in Assheridge *alias* Assherudge, Frethesden, Barkempstead *alias* Barkhamstead & Gaddesden.

*Thomas Bromley esq. solicitor-general & Edmund Anderson esq: John Fortescue esq. & Alice his wife & John Warrener & Kath. his wife. Ten messuages & lands in St. Albans.

Wm. How: Edmund Payne. Messuage & lands in Kensworth.

Andrew Grey esq: Rich. Bedell & Anne his wife. Messuage & lands in Bennyngton.

John Cogdell: Robt. Woodwarde & Frances his wife. Messuage & lands in Watford.

Edw. Bardolf: John Annesley & Letice his wife. Messuage & lands in Rudge *alias* Rygge.

Edw. Baeshe esq: Wm. Wakeham & Eliz. his wife. Messuage & lands in Ware & Newhall.

John Skyngell: Thos. Jurnyman & Kath. his wife. Messuage in Stortford.

Rich. Clerke: Edw. Hubbard gent. & Jane his wife. Two messuages & lands in Sabridgworth.

Rich. Peachie & John Howe: Henry Chauncy esq. & Jane his wife. Messuage & lands in Gedleston and Sapsford.

John Brockett esq: Barth. Lane gent. Two messuages & lands in Hytchin, Langley, Mynseden & Walden.

Robt. Grave & Frances his wife: Wm. Whitmore & Joan his wife. Two messuages & lands in Kennesworth.

Edw. Betham: Henry Rusley. Lands in Northmymes.

Rich. Symons: Ralph Whytnall & Anne his wife. Messuage in Sabrydgeworth.

Nich. Whytle & Anne his wife: Rich. Whytle. Messuage & lands in Stodham.

Edw. Halfehide gent: Edw. Baeshe esq. & Jane his wife. Manor of Wakeley *alias* Wakely & 4 messuages & lands in Wakeley, Aspeden, Great Munden, Westmilles & Leyston, & the rectory or chapel of Wakeley.

Wimond Carye esq: Rich. Monke & Philippa his wife. Messuage & lands in Brent Pellham, Stockings Pellham & Furnys Pellham.

Thos. Whyttamore: Rich. Chamber *alias* Chambers & Eliz. his wife & Thos. Foster gent. & Joan his wife. Nine messuages & land in Hitchin.

Robt. Hall senior, Rich. Tredwaye, Wm. Lee & Robt. Dawbeney: Robt. Hall jun. gent. & Anne his wife & Thos. Saunders gent. & Jane his wife. Manor of Pygotts & 10 messuages & lands in Stortford & Thorley.

## 1577. Trinity Term. 19 Eliz.

Fras. Wetheryd: Thos. Partridge & Mary his wife. Messuage in Barkhamstede Peter.

Rich. Blysedale: Nich. Eylat & Margery his wife & Thos. Wedowes. Messuage in Broxborne & Hoddesden.

Robt. Grygg: Julian Horne. Two messuages & land in Kennesworth.

Clement Newce esq. & Mary his wife & Wm. Newce gent: Thos. Grymesdiche esq. & Eliz. his wife. Lands in Much Hadham.

John Comodall: Henry Marshall & Kath. his wife. Messuage & land in Buntyngford in the psh. of Absten [*sic*].

Francis Wynche: Robt. Stevyns & Kath. his wife. Land in Albury.

Joan Smyth widow: Thos. Newman & Bridget his wife. Two messuages in Stortford.

Henry Standysshe: Robt. Kynwelmershe gent. & Anne his wife. Messuage & lands in Hoddesdon.

John Skynner & Thos. Skynner: Edw. Denny esq. Rectory of Amwell & the advowson of the vicarage of Amwell.

Wm. Cecill K.G. baron of Burghley &c: John Harington esq. & Isabel his wife. Messuage & lands in Chesthunte.

Margaret Forster: John Moorecock. Messuage in London Colney.

Thos. Warde: Thos. Parkyns & Cecily his wife. Messuage in Barkhamsted.

John Mabbe sen: Rich. Kynaston & Margery his wife & Thos. Eyms. Messuage & land in Tatturidge.

Humph. Colly gent: John Cannon & Dorothy his wife. Land in Ware.

## 1577. Mich. Term. 19 & 20 Eliz.

[*The feet of fines for this term are missing.*]

*Thos. Forster gent: Robt. Newys & Scolastica his wife. Messuage & lands in Aldenham & Busshie.

Edw. Potton: Wm. Skypwith esq, Edw. Skypwith gent. & Henry Skypwith gent. Manor of Radwell & 14 messuages & lands in Radwell & Norton, view of frankpledge &c. & the advowson of the church of Radwell.

John Goodman gent: Fras. Fortescue esq. Manor of Cumberlowe Grene & a messuage & lands in Russheden, Clothalle, Coterede & Wallington.

Wm. Burdall: John Morley. Two messuages & land in Royston.

Ezechiel Rithe: Fras. Hayden esq. & Frances his wife. Six hundred acres of wood in Watford.

Robt. Hare: Nich. Marshall & Adria his wife. Messuage in psh. of All Saints in Hertford.

Rich. Yonge gent: Urias Verney esq. & Letice his wife. Nine messuages & lands in Barkhamsted, Northchurche & Hammelhamsted.

John Nicoll & Wm. Nicoll: Robt. Nycoll & Eliz. his wife. Messuage & land in Ilestrey.

John Gladman: Wm. Edlyn & Cecily his wife. Messuage & land in Watford.

### 1577-8. Hilary Term. 20 Eliz.

John Brockett knt: Thos. Burton & Alice his wife. Messuage & lands in North Mymmes.

Thos. Iverie: John Iverie. Lands in Kynges Walden & Offeley.

Wm. Brett: Thos. Saunders & Jane his wife. Messuage & lands in Stortford.

Rich. Cornewell: Gabriel Colston & Alice his wife. Messuage & lands in Chesthunt.

Wm. Brotherton: John Helye & Agnes his wife. Messuage in Watford.

Rich. Birchemore: Walter Birchemore. Two messuages & lands in Cadyngton.

Rich. Peagrem: Wm. Fernesley gent. & Bridget his wife, John Brett & Thos. Brett. Messuage & lands in Stondon.

Rich. Pecock: Edm. Bardolphe esq. & Eliz. his wife & Eliz. Bardolphe widow. Manor of Laurans & 6 messuages & lands in Redborne. A warranty against the heirs of Matthew Cressey of Harpeden esq. dec[d].

Henry Conyngesbye esq. & Eliz. his wife. Barth. Dodes gent. & Charity his wife. Messuage & lands in Northemymes *alias* Northmyns.

Thos. Golston *alias* Bartelmewe & Anne his wife: Wm. Carter & Bridget his wife. Lands in Kyngeslangley.

Geo. Burgoine jun. gent: Geo. Burgoine sen. esq. & Dorothy his wife. Manor of Lannock & 20 messuages & lands in Lannock, Weston & Graveley & the rectory of Weston & the advowson of the vicarage of Weston.

Edw. Hyde: Edw. Halfehide gent. & Anne his wife. Manor of Wakeley *alias* Wakely & 4 messuages & lands in Wakeley, Aspeden, Cottered, Great Munden, Westmyll & Leyston & the rectory or free chapel of Wakeley.

Nich. Brokett esq: Thos. Appowell & Margt. his wife. Lands in Harpenden & Whethampsted.

Martha Heigham widow: Thos. Clere esq. & Anne his wife & Edw. Lewkenor esq. & Suzan his wife. Manor of Southall & messuage & lands in Great Gaddesden & Hempsted.

## FEET OF FINES.

### 1578. Easter Term. 20 Eliz.

*Rich. Smyth & Thos. Smyth: Rich. Skypwyth esq. & Mary his wife. Manor of Bechewood *alias* Becheswood *alias* Saynt Gyles in le Wood & 5 messuages & lands in Flampstede, Stodham & Gaddesden.

Edw. Woodshawe: Wm. Antwyssell. Messuage & land in Cothered.

Wm. Pomford: John Blowe & Joan his wife. Messuage & land in Baldocke.

John Somer: John Graye & Alice his wife. Two messuages & land in Hodesdon in the psh. of Broxborne.

Thos. Goddard: Thos. Smythe & Ellen his wife. Lands in Longemarston & Trynge.

Ralph Perrye: Geo. Waller. Land in Sabridgeworthe.

Henry Cocke knt: Robt. Kynwelm'she gent. & Anne his wife. Lands in Broxborne & Wormley.

Mark Pearce: Geo. Bayford & Eliz. his wife. Messuage & land in Sabridgworth.

John Westwood: John Hyll & Anne his wife. Messuage & lands in Standon.

Wm. Sherewood: Thos. Fynche & Eliz. his wife, & Edw. Fynce & Margaret his wife. Two messuages & lands in the town of St. Albans.

Humph. Corbett gent. & Anne his wife: Wm. Parker. Manors of Overhall & Vpwickhall & 20 messuages & lands in Gelston, Overhall, Vpwickhall, Aldbury, Stretford, & Little Haddam.

Wm. Grace senior: Thos. Smyth & Ellen his wife. Lands in Willesthorn, Longmarston, & Tryng.

Wm. Curle gent. & Frances his wife: Thos. Pygott gent. Four messuages & lands in Busshopps Hatfyld *alias* Hatfyld Regis & Essenden.

Wm. Snowe: Thos. Saunders gent. & Jane his wife. Lands in Thorley.

Humph. Meade & Anne his wife: Michael Meade & Eliz. his wife. Two messuages & lands in Ware.

John Arnold: Wm. Skypwyth esq. & Frances his wife, Edw. Potton, Edw. Goodes & John Kent. Five messuages in St. Albans.

Rouland Hayward knt: Wm. Skypwyth esq. & Frances his wife. Manor of Radwell & 14 messuages & lands in Radwell & Norton & the advowson of the church of Radwell.

John Sybthorp & Samuel Perry: Francis Porter & Love his wife. Three messuages in Sabridworth.

Thos. Moryson esq.: Wm. Hyde esq. & Eliz. his wife, Leonard Hyde gent. & George Hyde gent. Manor of Danyells & 20 messuages & lands in Sandon, Russheden & Wallyngton.

Edw. Peede jun. & Thos. Peede son of said Edw.: John Tufton esq. & Christian his wife. The third part of the manor of Hokenhanger *alias* Kympton & of 4 messuages & lands in Kympton, Barklowe & Redborne.

*To be Continued.*

# Church Terriers.

**CALDECOTT.**

A true & pfect Terrier of all the glebe Landes w^th the tythes rentes & emoluments belonging to the Rectorie of Caldecott in y^e Countie of Hertford & Diocess of Lincolne made the 12^th of April An^o D^ni 1638 by vs whose names are here vnder written.

Inp'mis the psonage howse & yearde w^th a barne a stable a hayhowse & another outhowse at the end of that w^th a garden before y^e howse & a backside behinde the barne & y^e other outhowses, the plott of ground being in all by estimation about the Quantitie of three roodes of grounde lying on the north side of the Church & compassed about on every side w^th high wayes save only on the west side lyeth the Cottage ground now in y^e Tenure of Willm Starre.

Itē a pightell called the long pightell lying betwixt Slattes grove in y^e Tenure of Oliver Rush on the west & the farme yeard in y^e Tenure of John Paine on the East. Also another called the little pightell at the South end of that haveing the Saffron ground in the Tenure of Oliv Rush on y^e East & compassed on y^e other sides w^th high wayes, both of them being by estimation a roode of ground.

Item in the Fieldes Betwixt the Middfield Way or Maybush balk & the way to Newnham in the red field In the Shott next Newnham an half acre lying betwixt y^e land belonging to Newnham Berrie on the East & the middle Farme land in y^e Tenure of John Paine on the West. In the Shott at the North end of that An half acre betwixt Newnham Berrie land on the East & the Middle Farme land in y^e Tenure of John Pain on y^e West. Another half acre betwixt the middle farme land on the West & the Little Farme and also in y^e Tenure of John Paine on the East. And another half acre betwixt the middle Farme land on the West & the Newnham Berrie land in Tenure of Oliv. Rush on the East.

Itē in the Willow Furlong at y^e North end of that A roode & half betwixt the Middle Farme land on the East And the Little Farme land both in y^e Tenure of John Paine on the West. Also an half acre there betwixt y^e middle Farme on the West & Newnham Berrie land in the Tenure of Oliv. Rush on y^e East. An another half acre there betwixt Newnham Berrie land on the East & the Little Farme land in y^e Tenure of John Paine on the West.

Itē in Shott at y^e North End of that An half acre by the balk betwixt Newnham Berrie land on the West & Caldecott Berrie land in y^e Tenure of Oliv. Rush on the East. An another half acre in the same Shott the middle farme land in the Tenure of John Paine lying on both sides.

Itē in y^e Shott at y^e North end of that & butting vppon the Maybush balk a roode & half lying betwixt Newnhā Berrie land in y^e Tenure of Oliv. Rush on the West & the middle Farme land in y^e Tenure of John Paine on the East.

Item a long roode goeing through both these Shotts downe to the Maybush balk betwixt the middle Farme land on the West & the Little Farme land on the East.

It. in the Marsh corner an half acre betwixt the Middle Farme land on the South & the little Farme land on the North both in y⁺ Tenure of John Paine. Also an half acre of Swarde lying vnder the hedge on the North & the Middle Farme land on the South.

It. in the Claye. A roode & half at y⁰ Townes end the middle Farme land in y⁰ Tenure of John Paine lyeing on both sides.

It. a roode in y⁰ Shott at end of that betwixt the middle Farme land on the west & the little Farme land on the East in y⁰ occupatiõ of Joh. Paine.

It. an half acre butting vppon the headland lying along by the Fitch close side betwixt Newnham berrie land in the Tenure of Oliv. Rush on the North & the little Farme land in y⁰ Tenure of Joh. Paine on the South.

It. a roode & half being a pickt headland to some part of the 8 acres piece of Caldecott Berrie land in y⁰ Tenure of Oliv. Rush on the South & the little Farme land in y⁰ Tenure of Joh. Paine on the North.

Item in the White Field betwixt the Middfield way & Ashwell field on Backworth hill side. A roode & half lying betwixt Caldecott Berrie land on the East & the Little Farme land on the West. An half acre in the same shott lying betwixt y⁰ Middle Farme land on the west & the little Farme land on y⁰ east. An half acre more in y⁰ same Shott betwixt the Middle Farme land on y⁰ East in the Tenure of Joh. Paine & Newnham Berrie land on y⁰ west in y⁰ Tenure of Oliv. Rush.

It. in the Short Furlong that lyes along by Ashwell field side. An half acre, the Middle Farm land on both sides.

It. in y⁰ Furlong below that butting vppõ Ashwell field. An half acre lying betwixt Newnham Berrie land on the North & the middle Farm land on the South.

It. in the Furlong below that Butteth vppon Newnham waye an half acre lying betwixt Newnham Berrie land on the East & the middle Farme land on the West.

It. in y⁰ Furlong vppõ the White hill an half acre betwixt Newnhã berrie land on the South & on the North.

It. in y⁰ Furlong wᶜʰ lyes on the west side of that an half acre betwixt Newnham Berrie land on the west & the middle Farme land on the East.

It. in the Furlong wᶜʰ lyes at the South end of that. An acre butting on y⁰ west against the Bush standing on the Middfield way & lying betwixt the middle Farme in y⁰ Tenure of Joh. Paine on the North & Newnham berrie land in y⁰ Tenure of Oliv. Rush on the South. Also another half acre in the same shott below lying betwixt the Newnham berrie land on the South & the middle Farme land on the North.

All the land on both sides these foresayd parcells is the Inheritance of Rich. Hale of Tewin in y⁰ Countie of Hertford Gentleman. The landes of Caldecott Berrie & Newnham Berrie mentioned in this schedule are all in the tenure at this time of Oliv. Rush of Caldecott & the landes belonging to both the other two farmes in the handes of John Paine of the same pish.

Moreover there is belonging to the sayd Rectorie a rent of sixteene shillinges p annũ issueing out of the psonage of Hinxorth & hath bin payd time out of minde by the psons of Hinxworth & their deputies or Tennants in liew of the tyth of a certaine coppie hold of y⁰ number of thirtie acres or thereaboutes belonging to the Lordshipp of Caldecott though lying dispsed among the fieldes of Hinxworth.

P

Lastly all the tythes ariseing of grass & graine in the sayd pish excepting those landes belonging to Newnham Berrie w^ch formerly were alienated & given to y^e Abbie of S^t Albanes. All small tythes as of pigges calves egges hempe fruite &c. The Custome for milch cowes is fourepence a piece for ghest cowes twopence for lambes whose number amountes not to a tyth fourepence a piece & for weaneling calves but half pence.

There belongeth also to the sayd psonage the goring of two calves in the Common & the custome of paying twopence for every plowe.

And for testimonie of the trueth of all this wee have subscribed our Names.

      Tho. Marshall rector.
      Oliver Rush
      John Paine
      William Starre churchwarden.
        his × marke.

## CLOTHALL.

A terryer of the glebe-land belongeinge to the parsonadge of Clothall [1638].

Inprimis one Close of pasture on the South side of the house beeing 8 acres more or less one pytell on the East side of the house beeinge one rood more or less.

Before the parsonadge gate 12 acres land by the way goeinge to Baldocke.

Vnder the Church yard hedge 2 acres land.

Vpon the Church hill 2 acres land buttinge vpon Quixswood Church path.

Ashanger Feild. In Ashanger feild 2 acres by the hollow way goeing frō the farme to Baldocke.

In the same feild 3 half acres butting on the sayd 2 acres from the top of the hill.

At the East end of the other, 3 halfe acres on the top of the hill.

In the bottom 5 acres buttinge into Maultmans waye.

Item 3 acres buttinge on the way goeinge from Weston to Royston.

Birds hill. Item 2 acres butting vpon the warren hedge.

2 halfe acres buttinge into the way from the Burysteed to Baldocke.

3 halfe acres buttinge on the Northend of Hawthorne bake.

6 acres on the Sowtheast side of Steepington hill butting on the top of the hill.

Beyond Butlers way 9 acres buttinge into the way goinge into Clothall end.

Item 2 acres buttinge into the way at Baldocke Townsend.

In Quixswood feild 1 acre butting vpon the long walke hedge.

Item 3 halfe acres in the next shott, Quixwood land on every side of it.

1 acre buttinge into Wallington way to Baldocke.

3 halfe acres lyeinge vnder the East end of the penns.

In Wildgoose feild 3 acres in the bottom Quixswood land on every side.

2 acres butting vpon the way frō Baldocke to Royston.

2 acres in Bigsdell bottom butting vpon Poulters way.

      James Graue, Curat.
      Thomas Searle, Churchwarden.
      Signum
      Hen. × Pollard.

# Abstracts of Wills.

**ARCHDEACONRY OF HUNTINGDON (HITCHIN REGISTRY).**

REGISTER III.- Continued from Page 159.

f. 37ᵇ ALICE BUSHE of Barchamstede Peter, widow. (*Dat.* 15 Aug. 1583). Bro. Thomas; Bro. Francis Prior; My mother; Sist. Margeret of London; Cous. Eliz. Catlyn; Bro. Francis' wife; Bro. Francis' dau. Dorathye; Rich. Catlyn; Frauncis Catlyn a mayde; Thos. son of Wm. Prior; Bro. Wm.; Sist. Dorathye; Margt. Nicholes; Rich. Bushe; Legacy to poor of Flamsted; Bro. Francis exor; Bro. Thos. Prior overseer. *Witˢ*:—John Michaell Allexaunder curat, John Whelpley, John Turner, Goodwif Dagnall & Thos. Chappell. (*Pr.* 10 Oct. 1583).

f. 37ᵇ JOHN WREN of Tharfield. (*Dat.* 10 Sep. 1582). Bur. at Tharfield; Wife Agnis; Dau. Alice now wife to John Hollye; Geo. Hollye son of sᵈ Alice (under 21); Rachaell & Marye Hollye daus. of sᵈ Alice; Dau. Rachaell now wife to Rich. Trundeye & her two childⁿ; George my youngest son; Eldest son Thos. Wren; Wm. Wren grandfather to a Thos.; Lands in Old hill in psh. of Tharfield; Robt. Glawdin & Daniel Rayner; Son Geo. exor. *Witˢ*:—Thos. Wynn, Rich. Rysleye, John Ankell & Jeames Bramfield. (*Pr.* 23 Jan. 1583-4).

f. 38ᵇ WILLIAM HAWSE of Liffnahell in psh. of Yardlye, yeoman. (*Dat.* 3 Aug. 1583). Bur. in Yardley Church 'neere vnto thende of the seate wher I vsed most comonlye to syt'; Legacy to poor of Walcon; My daughters childⁿ viz. Edw. Hamond, Wm. Norton, Eliz. Norton, Anne Norton & Marye Norton; Bro. Thos. Hawse; Thos. Blowse & Alce his wife; Henry Hubberd & Anne his wife; Wm. Baker; Robt. Watson my shepard; Servants John Campion, Marke Warren, Margt. Thurlye & Jane Preston; Sist. Eliz. Lane & her daus. Eliz. & Jone Lane; Thos. Austen my sisters son; Ellen Halfhyde my sisters dau.; Mary Shotbolt dau. of Jeames Shotbolt of Luffyn Hall decᵈ; Wm. Norton gent. & Jeames Shotbolt of Munnes exors; Thos. Shotbolt of Yardlye esq. & Robt. Tattersole clerk, vicar of Yardley, overseers. *Witˢ*:—Thos. Shotbolte esq., John Lane, Thos. Blowse & Robt. Tatterson [*sic*] vicar of Yardley. (*Pr.* 23 Jan. 1583-4).

f. 39. JOHN COWDON of Boorne in psh. of Boveingdon, laborer. (*Dat.* 13 Aug. 1583). Bur. at Bovingdon; Thos. Byggins of Hemelhemsted, labʳ; My wife. *Witˢ*:—Henry Mayne gent., Wm. Coop, Wm. Southen & Rich. Grover. (*Pr.* 9 Oct. 1583).

f. 39. HARRYE PAYNE of Hemelhemsted, husbandman. (*Dat.* 6 Sep. 1583). Wm., Robt., Thos. & John my 4 sons; John Stone & John Godfrye overseers; Daus. Anys & Elizabeth; (All above-named childⁿ under 15); Son Francis; Wife Agnes extrix. *Witˢ*:—Thos. Howe, John Pope, John Stone, John Godfrey & Wm. Dolte. (*Pr.* 18 Nov. 1583).

f. 39ᵇ ROBERT LOSTRIGE of the town of Hertford, locksmith. (*Dat*. 18 Sep. 1583). Bur. at All Saints, Hertford; Son Wm.: Daus. Joane & Anne; Wife Joan extrix. *Witˢ*:—Henry Dighton, Thos. Lawrence, Edw. Eason, Cutbert Stevenson, Edmund Gravener. Item my lord of Hunsdon oweth to me for worcke yᵗ was done to the vallue of xljs. jd. ob. (*Pr*. 30 Oct. 1583).

f. 39ᵇ WILLIAM BRUSTER of Essendon. (*Dat*. 1583). Bur. at Essendon; Wife Joan; Dau. Annis; Sons John, Francis, Ralfe, Thos. & Wm.; Dards my sister; Son John exor; John Bunchleye overseer. *Witˢ*:—John Bunchleye, Thos. Gyles, Edw. Bruster & Rich. Butler. (*Pr*. 19 Mch. 1583).

f. 40. JOHN HUDNOLE of Northbarckhmsted, Mary *alias* North church, yeoman. (*Dat*. 22 Apr. 1581). Bur. at Northchurch; Sons Wm. & John; Dau. Mary Blacknell; Susan Hardinge; Son John's 3 childⁿ; Dau. Alice Dover's childⁿ; Thos. Doggats childⁿ; Geo. & Joane Hardynge; Legacies to Barkhmsted Peter & Alburye; Wife Sybbell; My two sons Henry the elder & Henry the younger exors; Wm. Cocke & Henry Heare the younger overssers. *Witˢ*:—John Whellple, Thos. Hicman, Henry Erle. (*Pr*. 8 May 1583).

f. 40. AWDRYE RUSHLIE of Northmymes 'beinge sicke one her death bedd 24 December 1583 sent for the minister there to come to her but her death drew one so fast that when he saw there was not tyme enough to wright her will he exhorted her first to prepare her selfe towardℓ god and next he sayd thus vnto her, Mother Rushley to whom will yo geue yoʳ goodℓ, she mode hym aunswer sayinge, to Harrye, hauinge thus sayd she spake no more & so died wᵗʰin two howers after.' (*Pr*. 23 Jan. 1583-4.

f. 40ᵇ WILLIAM BYSHOPP of Great Tringe, yeoman. (*Dat*. 23 July 25 Eliz.). Rich. Cooke; John Feild my sisters son; Rich. Beason my sisters son; Rich. Atkynsonne; Godson Wm. Grigorie; Goddau. Anne Byshopp; Godson Wm. Feild; Rich. Baldwin my wife's son; Godson Poole Tokefeild; Godson Wm. Garrett; Jane Baldwyne; John Norton my wife's son; Elsabeth Norton; Daniel Feild; Geo. Feild; Margt. Byshopp & Joane Garret my daus.; Thos. Garrett & dau. Margt. Byshopp exors; John Blachead overseer. *Witˢ*:—John Blachead & Wm. Blacheade. (*Pr*. 23 Jan. 1583-4).

f. 41. EDWARD HUDDLE thelder of Aldenham, yeoman. (*Dat*. 27 Feb. 1583). Wife Eliz.; Son Thos.; Lands in Great Busshey; Son Edward; Dau. Constaunce; Eliz. & Joane daus. of Rich. Grubb late decᵈ (under 21); Son Wm. exor; Robt. Wickℓ and Thos. Briskoe overseers. *Witˢ*:—Thos. Golston *als*. Bartylmew vicar of this pishe, Robt. Wickℓ, Thos. Briskoo, Humph. Lucke & Thos. Briskoe. (*Pr*. 30 Oct. 1583).

f. 41ᵇ RICHARD PIGGOT of Hatfild esq. one of her maᵗⁱᵉˢ Jentlemen vshers. (*Dat*. 14 Apr. 1583). Bur. in Hatfild church 'before the place I doe sitt in the same church'; Mr. Mountford preacher; Cous. Wm. Humferstone of Rafford co. Nott. gent.; Cous. Robt. Coop; Sons-in-law Peter Boron & Paule Boron; Cous. Thos. Pigott gent.; My seale of armes; Cous. Rich. Pigotte son of sᵈ neph. Thos. Piggott; Servᵗ Thos. Greene;

John Piggot 'now in my house who I haue brought vp'; Cous. Fulke Onslowe esq.; A grant of certain of her ma^ties lands in the counties of York, Bedf. & other places; Said Fulke exor; Friend Wm. Curle gent. overseer; Mistress Martha Scott; My dau-in-law the wife of Peter Boron; Susan Bacon; The wife of s^d Wm. Curle; Wm. Tooke esq. & his wife; John Hakes; Geo. Bigge; Wife Eliz. *Wit^s* :—Paule Boron, Robt. Coop, Wm. Streate, Caddwalader Tyders, Wm. Waight. (*Pr.* 27 Feb. 1583-4).

f. 42^b JOANE AUDLYE of Hitchin, widow. (*Dat.* 14 Mch. 1581). Bur. at Hitchin; Dau. Joane Audlye; Sons Wm. & John; The signe of the Cocke in Hitchin; Dau. Agnes Williams & her child^n James & Joane; Dau. Eliz. Coop & her child^n; Son Robt. Papworth & his child^n & Wm. his son; Wm. Audlye my last husband; Jeames Tydye of Dunstable; The Water Close at Cholton in psh. of Hitchin & Busshey leases; Kings pownd close & the tenement Rich. Blocke dwelleth in; Son Wm. Audlye exor; Son Robt. Papworth & friend Mr. Thos. Parrys overseers. *Wit^s* :—Thos. Parrys, Mich. Longe, Thos. Saye notary publique, Rich. Coop, Wm. Audlye, John Audlye, Robt. Venables. (*Pr.* 6 Feb. 1583-4).

f. 43. JOHN NEWMAN of Westmyll, maltman. (*Dat.* 14 June 1583). M^r Bowman vicar of Stondon; Alce wife of Thos. Lewes, Margerye wife of John Dellow my daus.; Margt. Newman, Kath. Newman & Jane Newman daus. to Geo. Newman my late son dec^d; Alice late wife of s^d Geo. my son & John Newman her son & Geo. & Wm. his bro^s; House & lands called Betones; John Reanolds, Danyell Reanolds, Joane Dellow & Mary Dellow child^n of s^d dau. Margery; Sist. Joane Turner; Alice Newman extrix; John Bird supervisor. *Wit^s* :—John Byrd, Jeames Crofte. (*Pr.* 18 June 1583).

f. 44. EDWARD NORTH th^elder of Tuinge, yeoman. (*Dat.* 4 Nov. 1582). Bur. at Tuinge; Wife Eliz.; Son Edw.; My farm called Mereden; Sons Oliver, Hugh & Wm.; Dau. Eliz.; Wm. Michell; Serv^t Edw. Nashe; John Fesante; Joane Fesant; Thos. Mounford; Lease of Tuinge burye; House at Church end where John Battell now inhabiteth; Lease of such woods as I have of Eliz. Bardolfe & Edmund Bardolfe in Dacheworth, Wellwen, Watton Atstone, Brentfild & Tuinge; Tenement in tenure of Lewes Treherne on the south side of Over green; Lytle Otymer; Tenement called Makynes; Sons Edw. & Wm. exors; Wife Eliz. overseer. *Wit^s* :—Edw. North sen^r, John Thorogood, Oliver Chanbroke, Thos. Dighton. (*Pr.* 10 Apr. 1583).

f. 45. JOHN TYTMOS of Wallingeton, bach^r. (*Dat.* 14 Jan. 1583-4). Bur. at Wallington; 'To the Common Well xx*d*.'; My father & mother; Bro. Wm. Tytmos; Bro. Lawrence Tytmos & his son Edw.; Bro. Rich.; Bro-in-law Anthony Buckhouse & my sister Annis his wife & their dau. Luce; Sisters Joyce & Margt.; Sist. Aice Rayment & her 3 child^n; [*blank*] Mylles of Baldocke; John Ballawbye of Clothall & his child^n; Two poor men of Newnam viz :—Robt. Sive & Humph. Frost; John Glaunfield *alias* Neuell exor. *Wit^s* :—John Piches, Wm. Glover *als*. Tomson & Henry Howe, clerk. (*Pr.* 9 Apr. 1584).

f. 45ᵇ JOHN SEBROCKE of Harpden. (*Dat.* 5 Apr. 26 Eliz.) Bur. at Harpeden; Wife Eliz.; Son Edw.; Daus. Alice, Eliz., Kath. & Joane; Son Rich.; Dau. Amye; Item I owe at the White Hart vjs. viijd.; Bro. Law. Heyward of Redborne; Wife & son Edw. exors; Bro. Wm. Michell overseer. *Witˢ*:—Wm. Michell, John Flower & Marke Stubbinge script. (*Pr.* 30 Apr. 1584).

f. 45ᵇ JERRAM WELLS of Great Gadsdon, yeoman. (*Dat.* 3 Jan. 1583). Dau. Avys Wells (under 16); Wife Joane extrix. *Witˢ*:—Thos. Wells, Geo. Rooste & Wm. Baylie. (*Pr.* 30 Apr. 1584).

f. 46. JOHN WHITE of Hitchin, collermaker. (*Dat.* 2 Nov. 1584). Bur. at Hitchin; Sons John & Edward; Wife Ellyn; Friend Edw. Marshall overseer; Kath. Oncle my daughters dau.; Annys Vncle; Edw. Dyer. *Witˢ*:—Edw. Audlye, Edm. Symes, John Dermer, Edw. Hall & Wm. Abbott. (*Pr.* 14 Jan. 1584-5).

f. 46. WILLIAM COOPER of Borneend in psh. of Bovenden. (*Dat.* 11 Oct. 25 Eliz.). Dau. Lewes Cooper; Annis Webe my wife's dau. extrix; Abraham Horslye; George Rosse of Great Gadesden my wifes bro. & uncle to my extrix to be overseer. *Witˢ*:—Abr. Horslye & Wm. Palmer. (*Pr.* 9 Apr. 1584).

f. 46ᵇ AGNES BROWNE of Great Monden, widow. (*Dat.* 7 Apr. 22 Eliz.). Thos. Dellow my dau. Elizabeth's son; Basell Huckle my dau.; Dau. Alice Foster; Son Rich. Broune; Everyone of my children's childⁿ; Son-in-law Thos. Dellow exor. *Witˢ*:—Hugh Graue, John Warner, John Hamonde & Wm. Chamber. (*Pr.* 15 Oct. 1584).

f. 46ᵇ HENRY MAHO of Northmymes, yeoman. (*Dat.* 15 July 1584). My four childⁿ Robt., Lawrence, Dorothy & Eliz. (under 21); Wife Jane extrix; Friend John Langdale of Rowgreene in psh. of Hatfild overseer. *Witˢ*:—Wm. Chappell, John Langdale, Roger Goddard. (*Pr.* 10 Dec. 1584).

f. 47. JOHN HALFHIDE of Watton at Stone, tanner. (*Dat.* 25 Jan. 1582). Wife Denisse; Son John; My three daus. Joane, Kath. & Eliz.; My daughters' childⁿ; The childⁿ of my son John; Dennise dau. of sᵈ son John; Elizabeth dau. of my son; Son John exor. (*Pr.* 9 Apr. 1584).

f. 47. GEORGE CARPENTER of Whethamsteed, yeoman. (*Dat.* 3 Sep. 1584). 'My tythe corne neare wᵗʰin the tythe barne of Harpeden'; Wife Alice; Son Geo. (under 21). Lease of the tithe of Harpeden; Close called the Church Close in Whethamsted; Dau. Annas (under 18); Eliz. wife of John Weedon; Thos. son of Thos. Carpenter; Geo. son of Christʳ Carpenter; Wife extrix; Thos. North & John Christian overseers. *Witˢ*:—Stephen Cocken, Thos. North, John Christian, Rich. Vausse, Rich. Crumwyne, Wm. Cutt. (*Pr.* 15 Oct. 1584).

*To be Continued.*

# A Rental of St. Mary's, Sopwell, 1446.

RENTALE redditus assisi et firme tam infra villam Sancti Albani quam extra pertinentis domui beate Marie de Sopwell Renovatum per dominum Robertum Crofton Custodem ibidem in festo Sancti Michaelis Archangeli Anno regni regis Henrici sexti post conquestum Angliæ vicessimo quinto.

### SALIPATH.

De Monialibus de pratis pro terris quondam Alicie Bonde de redditu assiso per annum ijs.

De Thoma Westbury pro uno tofto quondam edificato de redditu firme per annum xxd.

### FYSSHPOLESTRET.

De Thoma Ayle pro duobus tenementis nuper Willielmi Baker de redditu assiso per annum xxd.

De Stephano Dychefeld pro uno tenemento ibidem nuper Ricardi Kw de redditu assiso per annum ijs. iiijd.

De Johanne Mordon pro uno tenemento quondam Thome Wolvey de redditu assiso per annum ijs. iiijd.

De Johanne Stodeley pro uno tenemento quondam Johannis Roys de redditu assiso per annum xijd.

De eodem pro uno tenemento ibidem de redditu firme per annum ijs.

### SCOLANE.

De Matheo Bepset pro uno tenemento quondam Thome Mylle de redditu assiso per annum xvjd.

De Magistro Johanne Whethamsted pro tenemento vocato le Squylers de redditu assiso per annum xijd.

### DAGENHALE.

De ixs. unius vacue placee ibidem quondam Johannis Gyssyng per annum nil quia solum ignoratur.

De ixd. unius selionis ibidem quondam Johannis Pounfreyt per annum nil quia solum ignoratur.

De xviijd. unius tenementi quondam vocati Petytes ibidem per annum nil quia solum ignoratur.

### CHIRCHESTRET.

De Johanne Grove, smyth, pro uno tenemento ibidem de redditu assiso per annum vjs.

De Johanne Duce Excestr pro Hospicio vocato le George in quo Johannes Vessy junior inhabitat de redditu assiso per annum vjs.

De Willielmo Dogelas pro hospicio vocato le Swan de redditu assiso per annum partis sacriste iiijs.

De Johanne Ingham pro hospicio vocato le Bere sive le Belle pertinente officio sacriste quondam Willielmi Burges de redditu assiso per annum xiiijs.

De Johanne Felow, Barbour, pro uno tenemento ibidem de redditu firme per annum xjs.

De Thoma Jonys pro uno tenemento ibidem de redditu firme per annum xxvjs. viijd.

De Johanne Vessy seniore pro hospicio vocato le Corn'halle de redditu assiso per annum xiiijs. iiijd. unde officio sacriste viijs.

### FRENSSHROWE.

De Johanne Barbour pro uno tenemento quod tenet ad firmam de coquinario Sancti Albani de redditu assiso per annum xviijd.

### HEYROWE.

De Johanna Farnecombe pro uno tenemento ibidem de redditu assiso per annum iijs.

De Johanne Holand pro ij tenementis simul situatis ibidem de redditu firme per annum xxs. iiijd.

De eodem pro uno tenemento in le Lethershamell de redditu firme per annum xvijd.

### MALTCHEPYNG.

De Roberto Clopton pro uno tenemento ibidem de redditu assiso pertinente officio sacriste per annum iijs. iiijd.

De Matheo Bepset pro uno tenemento quondam Thome Mylle de redditu assiso per annum ijs.

### FYSSHAMELL AND SHOPROWE.

De iiijs. unius vacue placee ibidem quondam Thome Shank nil quia solum ignoratur.

De Edmundo Westby pro una vacua placea nuper combusta de redditu firme per annum xviijd.

De vd. unius selionis terre quondam Ade Lanchestr nil quia solum ignoratur.

De Johanne Bocher pro una shopa de redditu firme per annum ijs. iiijd.

De Roberto Oscroft pro uno tenemento novo edificato de redditu firme per annum vijs.

### VICUS SANCTI PETRI.

De Johanne Ferys seniore pro uno tenemento quondam Johannis Bryght de redditu assiso per annum iiijs.

De Roberto Boteler pro uno tenemento vocato le Wolsak de redditu assiso per annum xijd. Et pertinet officio Sacriste.

De Johanne Cowper, Tyler, pro uno tenemento de redditu assiso per annum iijs.

De Willielmo Cok pro uno tenemento de redditu assiso per annum xijd.

De eodem pro tenemento nuper Ricardi Wylyot de redditu assiso per annum iijs.

De Henrico Bysshop pro uno tenemento de redditu assiso per annum iijs.

De Ricardo Grenehode pro uno tenemento ibidem de redditu assiso per annum ijd.

De eodem pro uno tenemento quondam Johannis Hawden de redditu assiso per annum vjs.

De Willielmo Clerk pro uno tenemento nuper Walteri Clerk de redditu assiso per annum xijd.

De Johanne Smyth pro uno tofto de redditu firme per annum xiiijd.

De Henrico Sawyer pro uno tenemento de redditu firme per annum vjs.

De Johanne Slynger pro uno tenemento de redditu firme per annum vs.

### BOWGATE.

De Johanne Vessy seniore pro vacua placea quam Ricardus Stonham quondam tenuit de redditu firme per annum iiijd.

De viijd. unius crofti ibidem nil quia in manu subcellarii.

### HALYWELSTRET.

De Relicta Reginaldi Glasyer pro tenemento quondam Henrici Sawtry de redditu assiso per annum ijs.

De Roberto Bredcroft pro ij tenementis juxta portam le Orcheyard de redditu assiso per annum xxjd.

De Johanne Smyth, Skynner pro uno tenemento de redditu firme per annum xs.

### Vicus ultra Pontem de Halywell.

De Thesaurario Conventus sancti Albani pro uno prato ibidem de redditu assiso per annum iiij*d*.

De Relicta Thome Gefray pro j tenemento de redditu assiso per annum vj*d*.

De Johanne Spendloue pro uno crofto quondam vocato Coppeshall de redditu assiso per annum vj*d*. Et pertinet officio Sacriste.

De eodem pro uno crofto juxta Grovettum de Sopwell & uno prato vocato Crasleymede de redditu firme per annum xvj*s*. viij*d*.

De Terra quondam Thome Shank & nuper Willielmi Dod de redditu assiso per annum xij*d*.

De Subcellario Monasterii pro terris quondam Ade Bolom de redditu assiso per annum ij*s*.

De Thoma Podyfat pro uno tenemento quondam Thome Punchon de redditu assiso per annum xij*d*.

De Georgeo Barbour pro j tofto de redditu assiso per annum vj*d*.

De Thoma Adam pro j crofto quondam Johannis Adam juxta vicariam Sancti Stephani & gravam coquinarii de redditu assiso per annum ij*s*.

De uno crofto quondam Alicie Fote & nuper Willielmi Dyxy juxta Gylbodelane de redditu assiso per annum xiiij*d*.*

---

# Penn Wills.

[*P.C.C. Rous* 12.]

JOHANNES PENNE cives et mercerus civitatis London. (*Dat.* 18 July 1450). To be buried in the church of S*t* Alban of Wodestrete, London; To the high altar of Aldenham, co. Hertf. xx*s*.; Legacy for the repair of Aldenham church & the bells; To sister Joan c*s*.; John Awmer; Sister Margerie; John Kytfeld her son; Tho. Kytfeld my apprentice; Elen Witborn of Aldenham; Each of the daus. of said Elen; Uxor Haynes of Aldenham & each of her child[n]; The dau of John Atte Pennes & each of her child[n]; Apprentice John Elys; Alexander my apprentice; Wm. Chamber & Wm. Trace my apprentices; John Gardyner; Servants Wilkyn, Peter & Isabel Baker; Matilda Burford of Barnet & her dau.; Wife Alice; Son John; Son Thomas; Son Ralph; Dau. Alice; Dau. Margt.; John Lok & Wm. Grand citizens & mercers of London exors; John Spanby; Thos. Fereby bro. of my wife; John Olney cit. & alderman of London overseer. (*Pr.* 7 Sep. 1450).

[*P.C.C. Logge* 27.]

RAUFE PENNE of the Countie of Hertf. gentilman. (*Dat.* 11 Mch. 1483). To be buried in he church of Aldenh'm betwene Edmūde Broke & the Chauncell vnder the Arch and if I do dye so nyghe But wheresoeu' that I dye I wull that myn executors doo make a Tombe in that forseid Rome for the Remembrance of my soule; All my goods & lands in the counties of Hertf. Midd. &

---

* In the margin appears "xviij*li*. xvij*s*. xj*d*. *ob*.," but to what it refers I cannot say. The sum total of the rents above enumerated amounts to a little over ten pounds. The document is endorsed with a long list of names of persons owing debts (to the priory presumably) in the time of Dom. Robert Croft, also a list of debts paid.

Surrey; I will that all the profits of all my lands go to the ordennce of a chapell on Coppidthorn hill till it be fynyshed for the ease of the neyghbours that hath fer to y'e church. Also I wull that they purchase a licence from Rome for all maner of eases to the same chapell. Also I wull that myn executours doo prouide and ordeyne a chauntry of xj marc. a yer yerely of my lond for eu' to fiend a p'st to pray for me foreu' mor. Itm of the foreseid sume I will that xiijs. iiijd. be for a yerely obite to be had yerely in Aldenh'm church. Alsoo I wull that myn executors prouide such lond for the forseid Chauntry that shall not hereaft' dekey And that it be no howsyng. Alsoo I wull that myn executors doo ordeyne & make sure for eu'more as moche londe to the yerely value of xxs. for to kepe and repayre the church wey betwene Illestre and Rylond gate. And when the wey is well repaired Then I woll that the rent of the same lond doo make and amende such weys as is most nede in the pish of Aldenh'm. Also I wull that the churchwardens haue the ou'sight and the expenses of that londe for the welefare of the pish. Alsoo I will that Richard Howell shall haue the grete Whitt for euyr mor to hym and hys heyres. Also I wull that myn executors sell my lond in London and Lamehith. And that they geve euerich of my cosyns Ferbeis xli. I will that John Peke haue to hym, t'me of hys liefe v marke a yer and all hys cost[ that he doth abought me. The like to Rich. Grotemore; To every godchild xs. John Verney, John Peke, Humfrey Conyngesby & Rich. Grotemore exors. (*The will ratified* 30 Sep. 1485, *but date of probate not given*).

[*P.C.C. Chaynay* 16.]

JOHN PENNE esquyre. (*Dat.* 15 Aug. 5 & 6 Phil. & Mary). To be buried in the church of Codyute [*sic*]; To the high altar of Codyute xxd.; The like to Welwyn; To eu'y of my daus. Elen, Elizabeth & Dorothye 40l. at marriage or 16; Said legacies to be levied out of the manor of Syceforns; To Robert Penne his wif two kyne; To son Robert Peñ & his heirs my myll of Codyute, paying yerely to Will'm my sonne 20s. for life; Residue to wife whom I make extrix. *By me John Peñ.* Wits:—By me Michaell Hogkyn. (*Pr.* 6 May 1559 by Lucy the relict).

[*P.C.C. Aylett* 28.]

THOMAS PENN of Sessavernes in the parish of Dodecote [*sic*] co. Herts. gent. (*Dat.* 28 July 1654). To be buried in my chapel at Dodicott by my grandfather Mr Tho. Penn decd at the discretion of my wife Alce whom I make extrix; To eldest son John the reversion of all my houses at Sissavernes &c.; To my two younger sons Fras. & Simon each a standing bed &c.; To my three sons Robt., Jonathan & Fras. all the trees growing in the psh. of Dodecote upon Rably Heath to remain solely to the three houses these which I have assured to my said sons; To my two daus. Ellen & Alice £100 each to be paid by son Wm. out of the land he holds called the Noads in psh. of Dodecoate; To each of son John's childn 10s. & to the residue of my grandchildn 5s. each; To son Thos. 5l.; To grandch. Thos. Kirke 5l.; To wife Alice a close called Thomas Croft in Wellwin; Son Robt. overseer. *Thomas Penn.* Wits:—John Ford writer, John Rookes. (*Pr.* 29 Jan. 1654-5).

[*P.C.C. Aylett* 32.]

SYMON PENN of Clements Lane, London, chirurgion. (*Dat.* 3 Jan. 1654). To my mother Mistress Alice Penne £10; To sister Mistris Elianor Ambrose £5, & my bed & bedding which I have remaining in the country; To bro. Francis Penn 40s. which he now oweth me: To bro. Thos. Penn 30s. & 30s. more due to me from Master John Clarke; Clothing to four bros. John, Wm., Robt. & Chevall Penne: To sist. Alice Kirke 5s.; To nieces Alice, Dorothy & Frances Ambrose 20s. each; To nephs. John & Thos. Kirke 10s. each; To my nursewoman & to Abigaile Mayden servant to my Master & Mistris Bullock 20s. each; To the poor of Curricott where I was born 20s. Gloves & ribbons to my master Robert Bullock & his wife & their son Christopher & dau. Katherine, also to Thos. & Elizabeth their servants, Thomas servant to Master Pennaut, apothecary, Master Warren's two men servants, Master Glover's two men servants, Master Allen's two men servants, the Scrivenor's man servant dwelling at the Crosse in Thames [*sic*], Master Alsworth's man serv$^t$, Master Leigh's man serv$^t$, Master Stretter's man serv$^t$ dwelling at the Lambe in Thames Street & the Grocer's man serv$^t$ dwelling at the end of Clements Lane; My messuage &c. & lands thereto belonging containing 20 acres in the parishes of Welling & Curring [*sic*] co. Hartford, now or late in tenure of Wm. Penn, to my s$^d$ sist. Elianor Ambrose & my bros. Jonathan & Francis Penn equally divided amongst them; Residue to s$^d$ sister & bros. & s$^d$ two bros. exors. *The marks of the said Symon Penn.* Wit$^s$:—Jane Lloyd ×, Abigaile Bullock & Robt. Richardson, scr. *Codicil* of same date, giving gloves & ribbons to friend Master Norway & to Mary who formerly dwelt with my father & now dwells in S$^t$ Martins. (*Pr.* 9 Jan. 1654-5).

[*P.C.C. Hene* 8.]

CHEVALL PENN of Wellwyn, co. Herts., gent. (*Dat.* 7 Dec. 1667). To daus. Mary & Sarah Penn £100 each at 21 or marriage, to be paid by my son Thos. Penn, the s$^d$ £200 being layed out by me for the building of the mills in the parish of Coddicott now in the possession of John Chalkley & in other repairs of tenements descending from me to him; To wife Eliz. a close of land in Wellwyn called Thomas Croft to hold to her after the decease of my mother Alice Penn who holds for life; Bro. Jonathan Penn exor; My son Thomas to be a dutiful son to his mother-in-law. *Chevall Penn.* Wit$^s$:—Ro. Vaughan, Nath. Manestey, Wm. Hill. (*Pr.* 21 Jan. 1667-8).

[*P.C.C. Leeds* 167.]

JONATHAN PENN of the Town of S$^t$ Albans, gent. (*Dat.* 24 May 1710). To dau. Eliz. Penn 400*l.* & also the 14*l.* yearly payable to her out of her Majesties Exchequer which I purchased in my said daughters name; To wife Charity the lease made to me & my s$^d$ wife by Humph. Hackshaw cit. & vintner of London dated 29 Oct. 1708 & the messuages & lands therein ment$^d$ for the residue of the term therein ment$^d$ etc. Residue of s$^d$ wife whom I make extrix. *Jonathan Penn.* Wit$^s$: — Thomas Motte, Eliz. Mott, J$^n$ Perrott. (*Pr.* 22 July 1713).

[*P.C.C. Whitfield* 102.]

CHARRETY PENN of Wethamstead, widow. (*Dat.* 24 Aug. 1716). To dau. Eliz. wife of M$^r$ Richard Crouch of Weathamstead 100*l.*; To granddau. Eliz. Crouch 50*l.* at 15, a silver tankard, two gold rings etc.; Residue to son-in-law M$^r$ Richard Crouch who I make exor. *Charity Penn.* Wit$^s$:—Eliz. Carter ×, Sarah Curbey ×, Wm. Burton. (*Pr.* 9 May 1717).

## Abstracts of Herts Wills.

### ARCHDEACONRY OF ST. ALBANS.

REGISTER "STONEHAM."—(Continued from Page 192).

f. 30. **RICARDUS WYNTIR** of S$^t$ Albans. (*Dat.* 1438). Wife Margaret sale extrix.

f. 30. **THOMAS HOLMES** of Cheypngbarnet. (*Dat.* 'in festo sancte Anne matris Marie' 1438). Bur. at Chepyngbarnet; Legacies to the high altar & the fabric 'novi operis'; John Sale; Wife Alice; John Gladwyn of Wheston in psh. of Fynchelee & wife Alice exors. *Wit*$^s$:—John Bechampe, Thos. Nicoll, Rich. Bate, Thos. Janyn, Rich. Foster.

f. 30$^b$ **NICHOLAUS MUNDE** of Newnam. (*Dat.* All Saints day 1438) Bro. Thomas; Sister Matilda; Wife Anne extrix.

f. 30$^b$ **AGNES BURGEYS** wife of Thos. Burgeys of Hexton. (*Dat.* 'die Jovis prox. ante festum Assumpcionis' B.M.V. 1438). John Turnour son of Thos. Turnour of same; Every son or dau. of the sons & daus. of Walter my son & Agnes my dau.; Wm. Hale; Thos. my husband exor.

f. 30$^b$ **MARGARETA HALE** wife of Walter Hale of Hexton. (*Dat.* the feast of the invention of the holy Cross, 1438). The wife of John my son; The wife of John my elder son; Son John exor.

f. 30$^b$ **WILLELMUS LYNDE** of S$^t$ Albans. (*Dat.* 1 May 1438). Son Thomas; Wife Joan extrix & Thos. Bordal & Geo. Barbour supervisors.

f. 30$^b$ **WILLELMUS MORE** of Chepyngbarnet. (*Dat.* 1 Oct. 1438). My father; my mother; Wife Agnes extrix & Hugh Langford supervisor.

f. 30$^b$ **THOMAS ROYSE** of S$^t$ Stephens. (*Dat.* 12 Aug. 1437). Note of Probate granted to Richard Roys son & exor.

f. 30$^b$ **JOHANNES BIRCHEMOR** of S$^t$ Albans. (*Dat.* 1438) Wife Ellen extrix & Henry Horwood supervisor.

f. 30$^b$ **THOMAS BAKER** alias Machell of S$^t$ Albans. (*Dat.* 11 Sep. 1438). Matthew Baker my father & Isabell my wife exors.

f. 30$^b$ **RICARDUS TRENTHAM** sadeler, of S$^t$ Albans. (*Dat.* 6 Nov. 1438). Sons Robert & Christopher; Apprentice John Warde; Wife Petronilla; Geo. Barbour, Wm. Crofton & Robt. Crosse of S$^t$ Albans exors.

f. 30$^b$ **THOMAS PALMER** of Busshey. Legacies to church of Watford & Robt. Baron clerk of said church; Wm. Dyche & my wife Agnes exors; Thos. Laneham supervisor.

f. 31. **JOHANNES SABBE** of S$^t$ Albans. (*Dat.* 29 Oct. 1438). Wife Agnes executrix.

f. 31. **WILLELMUS COWPER** of Abbots Langley. (*Dat.* S$^t$ Edmund the Confessor's day 1438). My wife & son John the elder exors.

f. 31. JOHANNES CLOPTON of S$^t$ Albans, baker. (*Dat*. 15 Nov. 1438). Son Henry; Wife Felice extrix.

f. 31. JOHANNES ADAM of Sandrug. (*Dat*. 'die Martis in Annunciatione Beate Marie' 1438). William att y$^e$ Naysh, Robt. Belamy, Adam my son & Anabile my wife exors.

f. 31. WILLELMUS JOHNSON of S$^t$ Albans, tailor. (*Dat*. 1 Jan. 1438). Bur. at S$^t$ Peters; Benedict Edrych chaplain, 'custodi dicte capelle' [*i.e.* S$^t$ Andrews]; Son Thomas; Thomas Rychardisson 'in Com Carelyll de Corkeby magno'; John Makeholme, fuller, of Carelyll; Wm. Hardewyk; Marion my sister wife of Robert Patyngmaker of York dwelling at Girdelergate; John wife of my brother; John Lane tailor & Reginald Clare dyer of S$^t$ Albans exors. (*Pr*. 8 Jan. 1438-9).

f. 31. THOMAS MYSE of Watford. (*Dat*. 6 Dec. 1438). Robt. Bryton priest of the church of Watford; Rich. Baron clerk of s$^d$ church; Wm Newman, Roger Mapulton & Isabell my wife exors.

f. 31. EDWARDUS ATTE HOO of Abbots Walden. (*Dat*. 22 Oct. 1438). John Shakevyle; Agnes Hoo; The high altar of Ayote; John Jordan; Church of Kympton; John Smyth; Godson Edward; Stephen Hoo to have full estate in all the tenements & lands in Hycchin, Pyrton & Ikilford, from John Hoo & John Cowper; John Hoo to have full estate in all lands & tenements in Offley, a messuage called Halfacre & 40 acres of land there only excepted which John Legat & Margery his wife by deed gave to Wm. Hoo & Petronilla his wife; I will that s$^d$ John have full estate in all my lands & tenements in Lyton to him & his heirs from the s$^d$ Stephen & John Cowpere &c. Thomas, John & Stephen 'nepotes meos' to be exors.

f. 31. JOHANNES SNAW of Chepyngbarnet. (*Dat*. 14 May 1438). Wm. Bechaunt; Hugh Langford supervisor.

f. 31$^b$ KATERINA DYTTON anachorita juxta ecclesiam sancti michaelis in villa sancti Albani. (*Dat*. 11 June 1437). Joan Gerard & Agnes Verdesans exors; John Ditton 'nepotis mei.'

f. 31$^b$ JOHANNA LEPER of Sandrugg. (*Dat*. Thursday in the feast of S$^t$ Maurice the Abbot 1438). John Clerk; Thos. Palmer of Sandrug.

f. 31$^b$ WILLELMUS HUNTE of Potteriscrowche. (*Dat*. 'die cinerum' 1438). Legacies to the vicar of S$^t$ Michaels, to John Mason, Wm. Fuller clerk; Wife Ellen & Wm. Douer my son exors; John Robyns supervisor.

f. 31$^b$ WILLELMUS BLUNDELL of Colney in psh. of S$^t$ Peters. (*Dat*. 4 May 1438). To Shenle Church 'pro campanis de novo emendis vj$^s$. viij$d$. & si nullas campanas emerunt tunc lego ad opus dicte ecclesie vj$^s$. viij$d$. pro una vacca emenda ad supportandum lumen coram crucifixo'; Legacies to the Charnell & the Anchoress of S$^t$ Peters; Wife Alice & son John exors.

f. 31$^b$ EGIDIUS CALAMOCHE of Watford. Note of probate of will 26 Mch. 1439 granted to Wm. Newman 'per concensum executorum quia ipsi non possunt laborare &c.'

f. 31$^b$ JOHANNES HYLLE of Watford. Note of probate of will 26 Mch. 1439 granted to Wm. Cardinall.

f. 31b THOMAS HALE of St Albans. (*Dat.* Thursday in the feast of St Gregory the pope 1438). Legacies to St Stephens & St Peters churches, the Charnell chapel, the nuns of Sopwell: Bro. Henry Hale; The friars minors of Ware; Sist. Margery Hale; Sist. Grace; Bro. Richard; Roger Whyte & Thos. his son; John Rose & Agnes his wife; John Ely; John Hale & Rich. Hale exors.

f. 31b RICARDUS REFHAM of St Albans, tanner. (*Dat.* 20 Mch. 1438). Benedict Edrych 'custos' of the chapel of St Andrew; John my servant; Margery Westwode 'custodi mee'; John Studley 'straylwever' exor; Benedict Edrych supervisor.

f. 31b JOHANNES EUERESDONE of Wynslowe. (*Dat.* St Dionisius' day 1438). Bur. at Wynslowe; Legacy to the Friars of Alesburie &c.; Agnes Cotum; John Broun; Sister Agnes; Alice Jenkyn; John Davy; Wm. Eueresdone & my wife Matilda exors.

*To be Continued.*

---

## Marriage Licences.
## Archdeaconry of St. Albans.
### By A. E. GIBBS.

(CONTINUED FROM PAGE 170.)

**1680-1**

January 8. Jonathan Evans of Markett Street, co. Hertford, bachelor, and Ann Feild of Shedlington, co. Bedford, spinster; at Shedlington or St. Albans. Luke Pryor of Markett Street, tailor, a surety.

February 12. Daniel Young of Pauls Walden, yeoman, and Rachell Uncle of Kempton, spinster; at St. Albans Abbey. Robert Scott of St. Albans, haberdasher, a surety.

February 12. John Adams of Sandridge, yeoman, and Elizabeth Sibley of the same; at Sandridge. George Barnes of St. Albans, innholder, a surety.

**1681**

March 31. Robert Pierce of Highgate, co. Middlesex, and Prudence Lovell of East Barnet. Gregory Lovell of East Barnet, a surety.

May 14. Walter Herbert, aged about 24 years, and Eliz. Smallbones of Winslow, spinster, aged about 22 years; at Little Harwood.

[*Undated, but attached to preceeding*]. Richard Wootton, aged about 28 years, and Avis Hopkins of Winslow, spinster, aged about 30 years; at Little Harwood.

**1681-2**

February 4. Joseph Finch of Wethamstead, bachelor, aged about 40 years, and Mary Warby of the same, spinster, aged about 22 years; at Wethamstead or Kenesworth. Joseph Mitchell of Wethamstead, gent., and John Lord of Kenesworth, clerk, sureties.

1682
May 13. John Hawkins [*signed* "junr"] of Hoaton Regis, co. Bedford, yeoman, and Judith Halsey of Flamsted, spinster; at St. Albans.
May 23. Joseph Marshall of St. Albans, innholder, widower, aged about 51 [?] years, and Elizabeth Long of St. Michaels, widow, aged about 45 years; at St. Michaels. "John Doe," a surety.

1683
April 7. John Nicholl of Little Bushey, gent., and Margaret Marsh; at East Barnet. Joseph Martin of Clifford's Inn, London, gent., a surety.
April 9. Nicholas Bradwin *alias* Evans of St. Albans, cordwinder, bachelor, and Susan Feild of the same, maiden; at St. Albans. John Bradwin [*signed* Bradwyn] *alias* Evans of St. Albans, bricklayer, a surety.
April 10. Thomas Barnes of St. Peters, and Joane Jee of the Abbey parish, widow; at St. Albans. John Seares of St. Peters, a surety.
April 19. John Oxton of Aldenham, yeoman, and Sarah Eve, daughter of Richard Eve of Rickmersworth, spinster; at Rickmersworth, Sarret, Abbots Langley, or Watford. John Barnes of St. Peters, plumber, a surety.
June 2. William Tofeild of Sarret, bachelor, and Mary Fardean of the same, spinster; at Sarret. Thomas Rogers of Sarret, tailor, and Robert Siggins of St. Peters, blacksmith, sureties.
September 22. James Weedon of Redborn, widower, and Mary Gladman of Abbots Langley; at Abbots Langley. Samuel Heaward of St. Albans, a surety.
September 29. Joseph Ewer of Watford and Elizabeth Cogdell of St. Albans; at Saundridge. Thomas Grubb of St. Albans, a surety.
November 23. Henry Dollinge of Redborn and Sarah Redding of the same; at Redborn. James Dolling a surety.
November 25. Thomas Hiccox of St. Albans and Elizabeth Wethered of the same; at St. Albans or St. Stephens.
December 18. William Collins of Chiddenden, co. Buckingham, and Catherine Burdon of St. Michaels; at St. Stephens. James Richardson of St. Michaels, a surety.

1684
March 27. Henry Dell of St. Michaels, widower, and Mary Greenhil of St. Stephens; at St. Stephens. John Long of St. Albans, a surety.
March 29. Richard Kempster of Watford, mealman, and Sarah Beck of the same; at Watford. Michael Tomkins of Pinnar, co. Middlesex, mealman, a surety.
April 30. Thomas Young of Pauls Walden, bachelor, and Mary Goldsmith of the same; at St. Peters. Thomas Oney of Kings Walden, a surety.
June 17. James Arnold of St. Albans, and Mary Cowley of the same, widow; at St. Albans or Sandridge. Nicholas Robinson of St. Albans, innholder, a surety.
July 9. Joseph Coles or Cole of Cadington, co. Hertford, husbandman, bachelor, aged about 28 years, and Mary Bennet of Kings Walden, spinster, aged about 27 years, with the consent of her father, John Bennet, of Kings Walden; at Kings Walden or St. Albans. Joseph Osman of Flamstead, husbandman, a surety.
July 30. Matthew Heyword of St. Stephens, and Anne Wingfeild of the same, widow; at St. Stephens. Jonas Heyward [*signed* Haward] of the same, stationer, a surety.

September 29. James Halsey of Great Gaddesden, gent., bachelor, aged about 22 years, and Elizabeth Mace of Abbots Laugley, spinster. having neither father nor mother; at St. Michaels or Abbots Langley. Ephraim Babb of Abbots Langley, yeoman, a surety.

September 29. Thomas Welsh of St. Peters, husbandman, and Judith Johnson of Hatfeild, widow; at St. Peters. Ralph Howard of St. Peters, mealman, a surety.

October 29. Nicholas Ewington of St. Michaels, husbandman, and Elizabeth Palmer of St. Peters, maiden; at St. Peters. Ralph Howard of St. Peters, mealman, a surety.

November 1. Andrew Peacock of Redburn, bachelor, and Esther Manfield of Sandridge, maiden; at Redburn. William Morris of St. Albans, a surety.

1684-5

January 31. Richard Reading of St. Michaels, labourer, and Joane Simonds of Luton, co. Bedford; at St. Michaels, St. Albans, or Redbourn. Thomas Simonds of Luton, labourer, a surety.

1685

April 6. Stephen Huggins of Harding, bachelor, and Rachel Scott of St. Albans, spinster; at St. Michaels. Robert Scott [junior *inserted above the line and then erased*] of St. Albans, haberdasher, and Robert Scott senior of the same, glover, sureties.

April 18. John Smith of Watford, apothecary, bachelor, aged about 23 years, and Hannah Plummer of the same, spinster, aged about 21 years and some months, daughter of Samuel Plummer and Hannah Plummer his wife, with their consent; at Watford, Rickmersworth, Bushey, or Abbotts Langley. Thomas Hayes of Watford, innkeeper, a surety.

April 24. Richard How of Foresoe, co. Northampton, grasier, bachelor, aged about 27 years, and Elizabeth Oyle, spinster, aged about 24 years, daughter of George Oyle of Watford, butcher, aged about 59 years; at Watford. Richard Oyle of Watford, butcher, and Bellnap Tibballs of St. Peters, plumber, sureties.

July 27. James Freeman, bachelor, aged about 23 years, son of James Freeman of Luton, co. Bedford, and Anne Browne of the same, maiden, aged about 22 years, with consent of mother, her father dead; at Luton or St. Peters. William How of Luton, yeoman, and Edmund How of St. Peters, carpenter, sureties.

July 29. Thomas Serrey of Flamstead, yeoman, bachelor, aged about 25 years, and Mary Meadwees of the same, spinster, aged about 22 years; with her parents' consent; at Flamstead or St. Peters. Peter Meadwees of St. Michaels, miller, her brother, a surety.

August 8. John Taylor of Stanmore, co. Middlesex, widower, and Sarah Hudding of St. Stephens, widow; at St. Albans, St. Michaels, or St. Stephens. John Barnard of St. Albans, schoolmaster, and Francis Taylor of the same, sureties.

August 28. William Boorks of Whethamstead, yeoman, bachelor, and Anne Marshall of the same, spinster; at Whethamstead or St. Peters.

September 29. George Philips of Heamsted, bachelor, and Sara Cutler of Hearding, maiden; at St. Stephens. Thomas Lawrance [*signed* Laranc] of St. Michaels, tailor, a surety.

September 29. John Andrews of Carinton co. Hertford, bachelor, and Ann Preston of the same, maiden; at Carinton or St. Peters. Richard Baker of St. Peters, sexton, a surety.

*To be Continued.*

# The Herts Genealogist and Antiquary.

## Funeral Certificates.

### SIR RICHARD ANDERSON. 1632.

The right worshipfull Sir Richard Anderson of Pendley, co. Hartford, knight. Died at his house called Pendley Parke 3 Aug. 1632. Married Mary eldest dau. of Robert, Barron Spencer of Wormleighton & sister to William Lord Spencer now living by whom he had issue 5 sons & 10 daus. viz:—Henry eldest son & heir (who married Jacomina dau. of Sir Charles Cæsar knt. of Bennington co. Hartford, M$^r$ of the Chauncery, Judge of y$^e$ Audience & Comisary of y$^e$ Faculties), Robert 2$^{nd}$ son, student of y$^e$ Comon lawe & of Lincolns Inne, John 3$^d$ son, Wm. 4$^{th}$ son & Rich$^d$ 5$^{th}$ son died young, Elizabeth eldest dau. married Robert Peyton Esq. son & heir of Sir John Peyton of Doddington in Isle of Ely knight, Mary 2$^{nd}$ dau., Francis 3$^{rd}$ dau., Margaret 4$^{th}$ dau., died young, Margaret 5$^{th}$ dau., Katherin 6$^{th}$ dau., Dorothy 7$^{th}$ dau., died young, Penelope 8$^{th}$ dau., Anne 9$^{th}$ dau. & Bridget 10$^{th}$ dau. He was buried in the chancel of the church of Tring, co. Hartford. Sole executor of his will, Henry Anderson son.& heir. Certificate by Thos. Thompson, Rouge Dragon & testified by Robt. Anderson 2$^{nd}$ son of defunct. [Signed] Ro. Anderson.

Arms:—Quarterly 1 & 4 Argent a chevron between three crosses patonce sable [Anderson] 2 & 3 Sable three water-bougets argent [Anderton] *impaling*, Quarterly of eight, 1 Quarterly argent and gules in the second & third quarters a fret or, over all a bend sable charged with three escallops or [Spencer of Althorpe], 2 Azure, a fess ermine between six sea mews heads erased argent [Spencer of Warwickshire], 3 Gules, three stirrups with leathers in pale or [Deverell]. 4 Or, on a cross gules five estoiles argent [Lincolne]. 5 Argent, a chevron between three cinque-foils gules [Warsted]. 6 Ermine, on a chevron gules three bezants, in chief a crescent for difference [? Grant]. 7 Argent, on a bend between two lions rampant sable a wyvern volant of the field [? Rudings]. 8 Per chevron azure and or three lions passant guardant in pale counter changed. [Catlin].

# Transcripts of Parish Registers.

## CHIPPING BARNET.

(Continued from Page 205.)

| | | |
|---|---|---|
| Cheping Barnet. | A Register bill from the ffeast of S<sup>t</sup> Michaell Tharchangell 1629 to the same feast 1630. | |

*Christninges.*

| | | |
|---|---|---|
| Octobr. | ffrancis the daugh<sup>r</sup> of Henrie Owen & Sarah | 7 |
| | Richard Sonne of Edward Turner and Margret his wief | 20 |
| | Katherine the daugh<sup>r</sup> of Thomas Androwes & Elizabeth | 25 |
| Novembr. | Susanna daugh<sup>r</sup> of William Hunt & Bathshuah | 1 |
| | Elizabeth daugh<sup>r</sup> of Edward Emerton & Joan his wief | 19 |
| | John Sonne of John Bradshawe & Anne [Joan *erased*] his wief | 24 |
| | Charles Sonne of Charles Millington & Joan his wief | 25 |
| | Margret daugh<sup>r</sup> of Edward Townk(?) & Philadelphia & Hanna daugh<sup>r</sup> of Edward Scarbrough & Susan | 29 |
| Decembr | Richard Sonne of George Deere & Margret his wief | 11 |
| | Griffith Sonne of Marreddeth Jones & Anne his wief | 27 |
| Januarie | Steven Sonne of John Stanford & Christian his wief | 3 |
| | Ellin Daugh<sup>r</sup> of William Lancaster & Marie his wief | 12 |
| | Peter Sonne of John Haynes & Philis | 24 |
| ffebruarie | Richard Sonne of Daniell Nicoll & Joan | 2 |
| | Thomas Sonne of Thomas Oleney & Marie | 3 |
| | John Sonne of John Layton & Joan & John the Sonne Richard Bedford & Alice | 14 |
| | Anthony the Sonne of Jacob ffisher & Isabell | 21 |
| | Elizabeth the daugh<sup>r</sup> of Richard North & Susan | 26 |
| March | Henrie Sonne of Nathanaeel Dowdale & Marie & Richard Sonne of Stephen Jones & Katherine | 25 |
| | Marie Daugh<sup>r</sup> of William ffinch & Marie | 21 |
| Aprill | Thomas Sonne of Thomas Barber & Elizabeth | 6 |
| | Richard Sonne of Robert Beechernole & Mercie & Steven the Sonne Thomas Hade & Alice | 25 |
| May | Anne Daughter of Thomas Stevens & Elizabeth | 2 |
| | Joseph Sonne of Thomas Marsh & Alice | 4 |
| | Elizabeth the daugh<sup>r</sup> of Richard Bacheller & Elizabeth | 9 |
| | William Sonne of William Shettleworth & Anne | 16 |
| June | Thomas Sonne of Thomas Holbidge & Amey | 1 |
| | Jane Daugh<sup>r</sup> of Thomas Parson & ffrancis | 13 |
| | Susanna daugh<sup>r</sup> of John Norris & Elizabeth | 15 |
| | Sarah daugh<sup>r</sup> of Steven Axtell & Sarah | 27 |
| July | Austen the Sonne of Thomas Ellis & Joan | 25 |
| August | Valentine Sonne of Henrie Greene & Marie | 5 |
| | Thomas Sonne of John Baldwen & Susan | 17 |

| | | |
|---|---|---|
| August | Marie Daughr of Thomas Sutton & Anne | 22 |
| Septmbr | John the Sonne of John Darby & Pernell | 7 |
| | John the Sonne of Thomas Childersbee & Anne | 16 |

### Marriages.

| | | |
|---|---|---|
| Octobr | Henrie Waler and Katherine Allan maried with a Licence | 20 |
| Novembr | Thomas Barber & Elizabeth Kentsham | 5 |
| Decembr | Thomas Godfry & Alice Seely wth a Licence | 24 |
| March | John Grange & Joan Poole with a Licence | 29 |
| | Richard Tratman & Anne Warcop with a Licence | 30 |
| Aprill | Henri Warner & Abigaile Marsh | .. |
| May | Richard Wilde & Joan Norton | 12 |
| | Henrie Cash & ffrancis Richmond | 31 |

### Burialls.

| | | |
|---|---|---|
| Septembr | Marie ffinche a Childe | 23 |
| Decembr | Marie Dell a Childe | 17 |
| | the wief of Thomas Sibley | 19 |
| | John Carter a Childe | 22 |
| | an Infant Sonne of Alice Collier widdow stranger | 24 |
| | the wief of Thomas Gyll | 26 |
| Januarie | widdow Holbidge a poore woman | 4 |
| | Marie Ambler a Nurschild | 18 |
| ffebruarie | Edmond Morley a poore man & Ellin Lancaster a Childe | 2 |
| | Richard Shepheard a Child | 8 |
| | William Lancaster a poore man of Mims side | 18 |
| | [blank] Cowper a Childe of Mims side | 27 |
| March | ffrancis Bletso a youth Apprentice of London | 4 |
| | John Bryriehurst a Nurschild | 9 |
| | [blank] Hudson a Childe | 10 |
| | Philipi Wright a Childe | 13 |
| | Adonia ffox a Nurschilde <br> & an Infant Daughter of Thomas Howells } | 26 |
| April | Anne Sanders a Nurschilde | 23 |
| May | William Winter a housholder | 4 |
| June | the wief of John Tratman | 2 |
| | the wief of John Bun | 7 |
| | widdow Anthony a poore old woman | 8 |
| | widdow ffowlk a poore woman of Mims side | 19 |
| | Nicholas Simon a housholder of Mims side | ·25 |
| July | Richard Bedford a poore housholder   Buried | 3 |
| | the wief of Henrie Cash | 15 |
| | John Tratman a poore housholder | 15 |
| | Peter Simon a housholder | 29 |
| August | Robert Page a Housholder | 1 |
| | the wief of the said Robert & Hanna Lawrence a childe | 6 |
| | William King a Housholder <br> and Thomas [blank] an apprentice } | 15 |
| | Thomas Gregorie a childe | 18 |
| | ffrancis Meacock a wench | 28 |
| | Alice Lishman & Grace Gregorie Children | 30 |
| Septmbr | The wief of Daniell Gregorie | 11 |
| | Anne Lytherland a wench | 20 |

Matthias Milward Rector
de Barnett.

## CHIPPING BARNET.

1687 *Christnings.*

Ap. 3 Jeremy Son of Richard & Anne Seers baptized.
,, 17 John Son of John & Susanna Field baptized.
,, 24 Charles Son of Humphery & Anne Cooper baptized.
,, 24 Katherine daught' of Jn° & Eliz. Webb baptized.
May 5 Jasper son of John & Eliz. Clark baptized.
,, 8 Christian daught' of James & Margaret Burges baptized.
June 5 Michaell son of Richard & Mary Allison baptized.
,, 6 Sarah daughter of Tho. & Sarah Dogget baptized.
,, 7 Tho. son of Tho. & Katherine Godfry baptized.
July 21 Eliz. daught' of M' Wm. Marsh & Elizabeth his wife baptized
Aug. 7 John son of Peter & Anne Harris baptized.
,, 19 Nathaniell son of Jn° & Anne Stevens baptized.
,, 21 Sarah daughter of Jn° & Martha Bell baptized.
Octo' 4 Andrew son of Rob' & Mary Brior baptized.
,, 23 Mary daught' of Jn° & Sarah Hickman baptized.
Nov' 20 Anne daugh' of Wm. & Anne Woodley baptized.
,, 27 Sarah daugh' of Charles & Anne Hollingworth bap.
,, 27 Sarah daught' of Tho. & Sarah Woley baptized.
Jan. 12 Mary daug' of John & Mary Mascall baptized.
,, 17 Eliz. daug' of John & Katherine Sawell baptizd.
,, 23 Wm. son of James & Hannah Burrus baptized.
Jan. 31 Anne daugh' of Jn° & Mary Hart baptized.
Feb. 1 Wm. son of Wm. & Ellen Sharp baptized.
,, 7 Sarah daug' of Jeremy & Mary Husted baptized.
,, 19 Sarah daugh' of Jn° & Mary Eates baptized.
,, 19 Honner daugh' of George & Eliz. Kempe baptizd.

1687 *Burialls.*

Ap. 19 William Coxall buryed.
May 9 John Smith buryed.
,, 15 Margaret Wood buryed.
,, 31 Richard Palmer buryed.
June 17 Sybilla Grimes buryed.
July 6 Mary Windsor buryed.
,, 25 Charlton Webb buryed.
Aug' 27 Rose Beachingal buryed.
Sep' 6 M'' Susannah Ellaby buryed.
,, 8 Anne Bell buryed.
,, 8 Deborah Prior buryed.
Oct' 13 Anthony Gurney buryed.
,, 25 Ralph Mascall buryed.
Nov' 4 Eliz. Hunt Buryed.
,, 6 Katherine Farrine buryed.
,, 13 James Duck buryed.
,, 26 M' William Buryed [*sic*]
,, 29 Jn° Field buryed.
Dec. 2 William Hyde buryed.
,, 19 M' William Master buryed.
,, 27 Henry Harrup Buryed.
,, 6 Eliz. Burges buryed.
Janu. 22 Priscilla Goodall buryed.
,, 25 Mary Barnet buryed.

Janu. 25  Lucy Wable buryed.
Feb.  1   Walter Smith buryed.
 ,,  25   Honer Kempton buryed.
 1688
Mch  14   M$^r$ Wm. Marsh sen$^r$ buryed.
 ,,  15   Susannah Wright buryed.
 ,,  21   Elizabeth Marsh buryed.
Mar. 29   Sarah Dorrington buried.
Ap.   1   Francis Smith buryed.

---

A Transcript of y$^e$ burials Christnings & Weddings in High Barnett in y$^e$ County of Hertford from March 25. 1688 to March 25. 1689.

1688
Frances Raper buryed April 18$^{th}$.
Elizabeth Burgess buryed Ap. 29$^{th}$.
Edward Hollingsworth buryed May 3$^d$.
Georg Snow buryed May 4$^{th}$.
Mary Flexmore buryed May 11$^{th}$.
M$^{rs}$ Anne Smith buryed Octob$^r$ 18$^{th}$.
Mary Duck buryed Novemb$^r$ 5$^{th}$.
Susanna Saggs buryed Novemb$^r$ 8$^{th}$.
Mary Hunt buryed Novemb$^r$ 16$^{th}$.
Catharine Sparks buryed Decemb$^r$ 19$^{th}$.
John Kemp buryed Jan. 2$^d$.
M$^{rs}$ Elizabeth Molloy buryed Feb. 6$^{th}$.
Sarah Hollingsworth buryed Feb. 9$^{th}$.
Peter Cook buryed Feb. 14$^{th}$.

---

A Transcript of y$^e$ burialls & marriages & Christnings in y$^e$ Parish of Chipping Barnett in y$^e$ County of Hertford from Lady day 1689 to Lady day 1690.

May       14$^{th}$ John Clark buryed.
 ,,       15   Wm. Wicks buryed.
 ,,       19   Thomas Seers buryed.
June      2$^d$  Mary Highland buryed.
 ,,       15   Wm. Hunt buryed.
 ,,       26   Elizabeth Smith buryed.
August    11   Anne Lucas buryed.
 ,,       20   Peter Kingsbury buryed.
 ,,       29   John Huddlestone buryed.
Septemb$^r$ 5$^{th}$ John Smith buryed.
 ,,        6   Elizabeth Betts buryed.
 ,,       13   Anne Geery buryed.
 ,,       23   John Archer buryed.
Octob$^r$   4   Anne Hollingsworth buryed.
Novemb$^r$ 20   Elizabeth Cooper buryed.
 ,,       27   M$^{rs}$ Ravenscroft buryed.
Decemb$^r$  5   William Howard buryed.
 ,,       17   Elizabeth Duck buryed.
 ,,       20   Wm. Barcock buryed.
Feb.      20   John Hanscome buryed.
March     10   M$^{rs}$ Mary Maid buryed.
 ,,       19   W$^m$ Kingman buryed.

### Christnings.

| | | |
|---|---|---|
| March | 20 | Elizabeth daughter of John & Elizabeth Whitaker baptisd. |
| April | 3d | Henry son of Thomas & Elizabeth Harrip baptisd. |
| ,, | 21 | Mary daughter of Francis & Anne Dorrington baptisd. |
| May | 1st | Elizabeth daughter of Tho. & Elizabeth Crew baptisd. |
| June | 2d | William son of Thomas & Susanna Bechonal baptisd. |
| ,, | 9 | Anne daughter of Peter & Anne Harris baptisd. |
| ,, | 19 | Elizabeth daughter of Richard & Elizabeth Hodson bapt. |
| ,, | 23 | Joseph son of Wm & Elizabeth Smith baptisd. |
| Aug. | 9 | Elizabeth daug. of Thomas & Elizabeth Crowchly baptsd. |
| ,, | 10 | Sarah daughter of Wm. & Anne Gardiner baptisd. |
| ,, | 18 | John son of John & Anne Archer baptisd. |
| ,, | 24 | Anne daug. of Charles & Anne Hollingsworth baptisd. |
| ,, | 26 | John son of John & Mary Huddlestone baptisd. |
| Sept. | 8 | James son of James & Mary Barcock baptisd. |
| Octobr | 13 | Anne daughter of Richard & Anne Slacher baptised. |
| ,, | 18 | Richard son of John & Mary Mascal baptisd. |
| Novemb. | 21 | Wm. son of John & Mary Howard baptisd. |
| Decembr | 4 | Thomas son of John & Sarah Hickman baptisd. |
| ,, | 6 | Wm. son of Benjamin & Mary Kingman bapt. |
| ,, | 8 | John son of John & Mary Palmer baptisd. |
| ,, | 15 | Wm. son of Samuell & Ellen Barcock baptisd. |
| ,, | 29 | John son of John & Elizabeth Clark baptisd. |
| Jan. | 12th | Mary daug. of Wm. & Mary Laurence baptisd. |
| ,, | 19 | Elizabeth daughter of Peter & Elizabeth Veranderfeild baptisd. |
| Feb. | 9 | Elizabeth daughter of Wm. & Elizabeth Stiles baptisd. |
| ,, | 13 | John son of John & Susanna Hanscome baptisd. |

### Weddings.

April 4th Thomas Palmer & Ellenor Cuddington marryed

---

A Copy of the Christnings in the Parish of Chipping Barnet in ye County of Hertford for ye year 1692.

Susanna Feild of John & Susanna March 27th.
John Hall of Mordecai & Rebecca April 25th.
Mary Saywell of John & Catharine June 17th.
William & John Styles twins of William & Elizabeth July 3d.
Sarah Harris of Peter & Ann July 17th.
Mary Cooper of Richard & Susanna July 19th.
Mary Stamford of Thomas & Ann July 30th.
William Briars of Robert & Mary August 10th.
Mary Heel of John & Mary Augt 14th.
Mary Heel of Henry & Katharine August 15th.
Ann Smith of William & Mary Septr 13th.
John Hart of John & Martha Octobr 7th.
Elizabeth Smith of William & Mary Octobr 14th.
William Gunnel of William & Mary Octobr 16th.
Luke Brickland of Luke & Martha Octobr 20th.
Edward Wright of John & Susanna Octr 27th.
Jeremiah Croutchly of Thomas & Elizabeth Novr 6th.
Ann Yates of John & Mary Novr 22d.
Peregrine Barcock of James & Margaret Novr 23d.
Ann Thompson of John & Alice Novr 30th.

William Flexmore of William & Anne January 2ᵗ.
Thomas Cole of Thomas & Mary } Jan. 15ᵗʰ.
Elizabeth Crew of Thomas & Elizabeth
Ann Buckle of Humphrey & Sarah February 12ᵗʰ.
Jasper Clark of John & Elizabeth Febr. 17ᵗʰ.
Maria of John & Elizabeth Wittaker Febr. 19ᵗʰ.
Mary Hanscomb of John & Susanna March 12ᵗʰ.
John Lawrence of William & Mary March 19ᵗʰ.

          Willᵐ Bisset, Curate.

---

A Copy of the Burials in the parish of Chipping-Barnet in yᵉ County
  of Hertford, for yᵉ year 1692.

Thomas Allinson buryed March 31.
William Turney April 10ᵗʰ.
Sarah Barcock May 26ᵗʰ.
John Gleave June 25ᵗʰ.
Robert Allingsby July 1ᵗ.
William & John Styles July 9ᵗʰ.
Mary Whitehead July 22ᵈ.
William Smyth August 24ᵗʰ.
William Humfreystone Septembʳ 7ᵗʰ.
William Hollingsworth Septʳ 30ᵗʰ.
Grace Maynard Octobʳ 21ᵗ.
Martha Hollingsworth Octʳ 30ᵗʰ.
Joseph Thorp Novʳ 9ᵗʰ.
Ann Harrup Novʳ 15ᵗʰ.
Ann Thompson Decemʳ 16ᵗʰ.
Thomas Palmer Decʳ 27ᵗʰ.
Susanna Stephens Jan. 18ᵗʰ.
Mary Stamford January 22ᵈ.
William Meek January 30ᵗʰ.
Mary Dorrington February 10ᵗʰ.
William Flexmore March 8ᵗʰ.
Grace Draper March 15ᵗʰ.

          Willᵐ Bisset, Curate.

---

# Church Terriers.

## COTTERED.

COTTRED IN COM HERTF AND DIOC. OF LINCOLNE.

A TEROR of the psonidge and Gleebe Land their vnto belongeinge as followeth by the pticulars.

 The ground about the Homsted and that neere adioninge
A dwellinge house, with two barnes and a hogge coate. The grownd aboute the house in all by estimacon foure acars. A little arrable feild neere vnto the psonidge knowne by the name of Brixbury, the highway lyinge north and East, the grownd of the Lord of Cottred South and Franc(e) Wright west by estim. six acr.

The land lyinge in Churchfeild in there seuerall pcells.

Itm in a Comonfeild called Churchfeild one acar neere the Towne lyinge at the Backside of a Tenement late John Bedles south, the land of George Parkinson north, Willm Austin East & West.

Itm half an acar in the same feild pt meadow, the Towneland at the south end, Cheynes land west & Wm. Austin East.

Three Roods their one the Middle shott, buttinge north & south one the Lordshipp land, the saide Lord one the West, y^e towne land East.

One Rood their Lyinge neere to Coles greene buttinge North & south vppon the Lordshipp land and one Samuell Plumer East & West.

One Rood more their lyinge beneath Roodole, buttinge south vppō Richard Crouch, North vppon John Wedun, Robert Clinton lying one the West side and the Land belongeinge to Cheynes one the East.

### The Land lying in little Northfeild.

Itm in Little Northfeild two acars neere the mill hill, the Lordshipp land north and south & East and the Highway one the West side.

Half an acar more their the land of the Lord lyinge East West & south and the Land of Richard Crouch vppon the North.

Three Roods more their lyinge neere Stocking-hill buttinge West vppon Willm Duñ and East one Cheynes land the Lord^pp land south and the Land late Richard Crampornes North.

One Headen rood their lyinge one Haresdenhill, buttinge East one Richard Crouch and West one the highway.

One rood more their in the bottome buttinge north one Cheynes land & south vppō Christ: Knight, the Lord^pp land East, Samuell Plum' west.

One other Rood in the same bottom, buttinge north vppon Rushden feild, south vppon the highway Cheynes land East & Richard Crouch West.

### The Land as it lyeth in Great North feild.

In Great Northfeild half an acar lyinge by Rushen feild side sided north and south w^th S^r Thoms Standleys land, The West end vppon the highway and the land late Willm Elbornes one the East.

Three Roods more in the same feild pte arrable & pte meadow, neere the valey the Lord^pp land lyinge West & North the land of Christopher Knight East and Cheynes Land South.

Halfe an acare more in the same feild lyinge one Quamstey hill the land belongeinge to the Lordshipp lyinge West and South Samuell Plumer East and Cheynes land North.

One half acare more their lyinge neere the Mill hill buttinge West vppon Christopher Knight, one Samuell Plumer East Richard Crouch one the North side and the towne land one the South.

One Rood more their, buttinge south and North one Richard Crouch the towne land East and the land late John Starrs West.

One other Rood their, buttinge south and North one the saide Richard Crouch, sided West vppon Richard Crouch and the Towne land one the East.

### The land lyinge in Holbrooke.

In Great Holbrooke Two acars buttinge North ward vppon Bradfeild grownd, and vppon Cheynes land south the Land belonginge to the Lord of Cottered west, And the Land belonging to the Mannor of Cheynes East.

Three Roodes more their in the same feild lyinge neere to Coles-greene buttinge North vppon the Lordshipp land and South vppon Jo: Wallis, The Land late Wiltm Plumers East and the Lordshipp land West.

Sum. 22 acars 1 rood.

This Terror made the xvj^th of Aprill Anno Dom. 1638 vnder the hands of those whose names are heere vnto prescribed.

Thomas Gardiner Rector
Wiltm × Dun  ⎫
Thoms × Sadler ⎬ Churchward.
John × Wren Sidesman
Wilham Austin
George Bardollfe.
× Christopher Knight
Edward Symons scr. aged 34 y.

---

COTTERED IN
COM. HARTFORD.

A true and perfect Terrier of all the houses and Glebs pertaining to the Rectory of Cottered aforesaid, exhibited at Mr. Archdeacons visitation holden at Hitchin May the 12^th Annoque Dom'i 1709 as followeth.

The Parsonage house coucred with Tiles, The roomes in the said house, one Hall, one parlor floored with deal, one Kitchin floored with Bricks with Chambers ouer the said hall parlor and Kitchin seeled, one Cellar and buttery.

One Barn with Six bays of building, one Barne of Three bays of building with a Stable, Coats for Swine and Cow house.

One orchard at the east end of the said house, one garden, one yard in parte paled in.

One Close of pasture, on the North side of the said Parsonage house of foure acres, more or less, lyeing between the Common feild called Church feild east and north And a lane, out of that feild into the Street, And a tenem^t. of Charles Hankin west.

One Close of arable land, ouer against the said parsonage house, on the other side of the Street, called Bricksbury, of Six acres more or less abutting east and north vpon the highway, South vpon the pasture of Madam Forester, called Matsford, And west, in parte vpon a Close of arable land belonging to John Sadler, and part vpon his house, the lane between the hedge and the house, belonging to the Rectory.

In a Common field called Churchfield.

One acre lyeing between the land of George Astin east and west, abutting south vpon an orchard of John Chapman, north vpon the land of John Exton.

One Rood of arable and meadow, in the next Shott towards the valley between the land of George Austin east and the land of the Lord of Chaineys west, abutting vpon the Lords swarth north And the land belonging to the Towne of Cottered South.

Three Roods vpon that Shott lyeing vp by that path that leads to Bradfield next the land of the town of Cottered east: and land of Madam Forester west north and south.

One Rood in the Shott, comeing down from Clarks Pen to the Valley: between the land of John Exton east and Edward Webb west, abutting vpon the way through the valley, South, And the land of Madam Forester north.

One Rood vpon the shott, in which the foot path leadeth from Cottered to Coles green: between the land of the Lord of Chaineys east and the land of Madam Forester west abutting vpon the way through the valley north and the head land of Richard Crouch, south.

### In Rushden field.

One halfe acre lyeing between the land of Joseph Edmunds Esq$^r$ South and north, abutting vpon the highway leading from Walkerne to Cumberlow green west and the land of Edward Feild esq$^r$ east.

### In a Common field called Holbrooke.

Two acres of arable land lyeing between the way leading to Foxholes, next the land of Madam Forester west and the land of the Lord of Chaineys east, abutting vpon the pasture belonging to Foxholes north and the land of John Tompson south.

One acre lyeing between the land of the said John Thompson east and the way leading to Foxholes aforesaid west, abutting vpon the land of Madam Forester north, and the pasture of Robert Crane south within the hedges of the said pasture, there is a peice of ground belonging to the said Glebe for which is paid foure pence.

### In a Common field called little north field.

Two acres lyeing vpon Mill hill between the way leading from Cottered to Cumberlow green west, and the land of Madam Forester east, abutting vpon the way which lyeth through Church field valley south, and the land of Madam Forester and John Beal north.

One half acre in the same shott, between the land of Madam Forester east and west, abutting as the former.

Three Roods below Stockin hill between the land of Madam Forester, south and the land of John Chapman north abutting vpon the land of the Lord of Chaineys east and the land of Robert Frost west.

One headland Rood by Haresden hill between the land of Madam Forester south and the lands of diuers men north, abutting vpon the way leading to Rushden west and the land of Edward Webb east.

One Rood in the Shott next Rushden field abutting vpon that field north and the highway through the valley south, between the land of the Lord of Chaineys east and the land of Richard Crouch west.

One Rood in the same shott between the land of John Exton east and west abutting vpon the land of Edmund Knight south and the land of the Lord of Chaineys north.

### In a Common field called Great North field.

One Rood in the Shott, northward, below Mill hill, not far from the high way between the land belonging to the Town east and the land of Edward Webb west abutting vpon the land of Richard Crouch south and north.

One Rood near adioyning, between the land belonging to the Town of Cottered east and the land of Richard Crouch west, north and south.

One halfe acre, between the land of Richard Crouch north and the Towne land south, abutting vpon the land of Madam Forester east and Edmund Knight, west.

Three Roods of arable land and meadow, between the land of the Lord of Chaineys south, and the land of Madam Forester north and west, abutting vpon the land of Edmund Knight east.

One half acre vpon the vpper Shott westward, between the land of the Lord of Chaineys north, and the land of Madam Forester south and east, abutting vpon the land of Madam Forester west.

The incumbent is a Rector, all manner of Tithes are due to him in kind and noe land w<sup>th</sup>in the parish is Exempted, noe offerings are paid, piges are tithed att seuen and lambes at ten, 4 pence for euery single lamb; for Cows that calue 6 pence p Cow, And for farrow milshed 4 pence halfe peny, wooll paid by the pound.

Surplice fees, for Churching 6 pence, for burialls 12 pence, for marriages w<sup>th</sup> Licence 8s. 2d, w<sup>th</sup>out Licence 4s; Furniture in the Church 5 bells, necesarie bookes and Surplice; with a Small old Communion Cupp Siluer. The Clarks wages is 4 p house.

       John Sykes Rector
       Robt. Wright Churchwarden.

[Endorsed] The small old comunion Cup mentioned on y<sup>e</sup> other side is now made into a very fair Chalice & Patten at y<sup>e</sup> Charge of Pulter Forester Esq<sup>r</sup> the Patron of y<sup>e</sup> Living. The weight of both is 13 oz. 17 p.w.

       John Sykes R<sup>r</sup>.
       Rob<sup>t</sup> Wright Churchwarden.
       Edw. Webb.

---

## DATCHWORTH.

A SURVEYE OR TERRIER of all the possessions belongeing to the Rectory of Datchworth *alias* Thatchworth in the County of Hertford & Diocesse of Lincolne made and taken by the veiw pambulation & estimate of the minister Churchwardens & sidesmen & other the Inhabitants nominated & appointed for that purpose.

Imp<sup>r</sup> There is belongeing vnto the saide Rectory one dwelling house couered with tiles scituate vpon part of the gleabe land belonging to the saide Rectory, the cheifest part of the building whereof is 62 foote longe North & south & is 18 foote broade East & West, w<sup>ch</sup> is deuided into two stories conteyning 10 roomes whereof 5 are vpon the ground viz. one little lodgeing chamber one seller one hall, one parlor one buttery And fiue roomes ouer these viz:— one chamber ouer the seller & little chamber, one chamber ouer the hall with a closett or studye belongeing to it & one chamber ouer the parlor, with a studye ouer it ouer y<sup>e</sup> buttery.

Item. One other part or parcell of the said dwellinge house adjoyning vnto the forenamed part and is 35 foote longe East and West and 14 foote broad which containeth 4 Roomes viz. one kitchin and a brewhouse on the ground and 2 chambers & boarded over the kitchin.

Item. There is neere adjoyninge vnto the foresaid dwellinge house one other parcell of buildinge covered with straw or Thatch and is 44 foote longe East and west and 15 foote broad devided into 3 severall roomes vpon the ground and one roome at the west end hath a chamber boarded over it.

Item. Not far from the foresaid parcell of buildinge there is an other parcell of buildinge covered with straw or Thatch and is 19 foote longe East and West and 16 foote broad which is devided into 2 roomes vpon the ground and y<sup>t</sup> roome which is on the west end of this buildinge hath a chamber boarded over it.

Item   There is one longe barne covered with straw or Thatch which is 94 foote longe North and South and 24 foote broad and is devided into 6 bayes.

Item   There is one other little barne covered with straw or Thatch which is 34 foote longe East and west and 15 foote broad and is devided into 2 bayes.

Item   There is lyinge about the foresaid buildinges belongeinge to The foresaid Rectory 10 acres of land more or lesse which is devided into severall parts viz. one garden, one orchard, one yard called the barne yard lyinge betweene the great barne and the mansion house and other yardes for wood &c alsoe 2 closes of arable land, and one close of pasture called the springe all w$^{ch}$ beinge conjoyned together abut vpon a lane leadinge from Thatchworth green towards Knebworth on the North, on the lands of S$^r$ Rowland Litton knight belongeinge to Marly Berry, on the South on the land of Richard Rudd East and a lane leadinge from Thatchworth church toward Wolmer greene west.

Item   There belonge to the said Rectory 6 acres of arable land more or lesse lyinge in a common field there called Candell whereof one acre and an halfe more or lesse lyeth, betweene the lands of George Shotboult south and the lands of Thomas Kimpton north and abbutteth vpon the lane which leadeth from Brackberrie end to Thatchworth Church East and the lands of Richard Kimpton west. And one other peice in the said feild conteyninge one acre more or lesse lyeth betweene the landes of Thomas Kimpton South and the lands of Thomas Foster North and abutteth vpon the fore sayd lane leadinge from Brackberrie end to Thachworth church East and y$^e$ lands of Thomas Foster west.

And one other peice in the foresaid common feild conteyninge one acre and an halfe more or lesse lyeth betweene the forenamed lane which leadeth from Brackberrie end to Thatchworth church East and the lands of Richard Rudd on the West and abutteth vpon the said lane North and vpon the lands of Francis Bigge South.

And one other peice in the foresaid common field contayninge by estimation one acre more or less lyeth betweene the lands of Thomas Foster west and the lands of William Rudd East, and abutt vpon the lands of John Man north and of Frauncis Bigge south.

And one other peece in the foresaid common feild contayninge one acre more or lesse lyeth betweene the lands of John Man East and West and abutteth vpon a parcell of medow of y$^e$ sayd John Man and others &c north, and vpon the lands of Thomas Kimpton south.

And one other parcell of land in the foresaid feild contayninge halfe an acre more or lesse lyeth between the lands of John Man north and of John Deards south and abutteth vpon the lands of the foresaid John Man East and West.

Item   There belonge vnto the said Rectory 4 acres of arable land lyinge in a common feild of the foresaid parish called Chibden whereof 3 acres more or lesse by betweene the lands of Thomas Mitchell on the south, and the lands of the said Thomas Mitchell and Thomas Kimpton North and abutt vpon the lands of the sayd Thomas Mitchell west and of the sayd Thomas Kimpton east.

And one other peice in the foresaid common feild contayning halfe an acre more or less lyeth betweene the lands of George Kimpton East and the lands of Charles North, west and abutteth vpon the lands of the said George Kimpton south and of Richard Kimpton North.

And one other peice in the foresaid common feild contayninge halfe an acre more or lesse lyeth betweene the land of Richard Kimpton on the South and the lands of Thomas Mitchell and Thomas Foster North and abutteth vpon the lands of the foresaid Thomas Mitchell West and the lands of Richard Kimpton East.

Stockes, Implements, Tenements or any other thinge inquireable by the Canon and not herein before intimated and expressed there is nothinge belongeing to this Rectory as far as wee know or can learn.

      Richard Newman Rector de Datchworth
      Arthur Feild } Churchward.
      Geo. Lewis  }
      Tho. × Lucy Sidsman.

# Feet of Fines for Hertfordshire.

## TUDOR PERIOD.

(CONTINUED FROM PAGE 223).

### 1578. Trinity Term. 20 Eliz.

John Foull : John Broke & Margt. his wife. Two messuages & lands in Little Munden & Great Munden.

Ralph Radcliff esq : John Tristram & Cecily his wife. Lands in Hitchen.

Wm. Beadle : Wm. Antwissell. Messuage & land in Cothered.

Ralph Grunell : John Grunell. Messuage & land in Barley.

John Spurlynge gent. : Robt. Hyde gent. Two messuages & lands in Hynkesworth, Edworth, Asshewell, Caldcotte & Astwicke. A warranty against the heirs of Leonard Hyde esq dec$^d$.

Wm. Wedon : Wm. Warren & Joan his wife. Messuage and garden in Watford.

Tabell Ailmer : Wm. Rustat & Mary his wife. Messuage and lands in Ashewell.

Thos. Holden : John Vaughan gent & Anne his wife. Two messuages and land in S$^t$ Albans.

Roger Byrcheley : John Byrcheley gent & Philippa his wife. Messuage, shop and garden in psh. of All Saints, Hertford.

Wm. Newman : John Smyth junior & Eliz. his wife. Messuage and garden in Baldocke.

Thomas Crabbe & John Skyngle : Thos. Saunders gent & Jane his wife. Manor of Pygotts & 3 messuages & lands in Storteford.

Thos. Salysbury gent : Henry Chauncy esq & Jane his wife. Messuage & lands in Gedleston, Estwicke & Sabrygeford.

John Brockette knt : Miles Pendreth gent & Francis Pendreth gent & Ursula his wife. Five messuages & lands in Bishops Hatfield.

Geo. Rotheram esq & Wm Toocke esq: Edw. Smyth & Dorothy his
wife, Humph. Meade & Anne his wife & Wm. Preston & Frances
his wife. Three parts of the Manor of Chylwycke (in four parts
divided) & of 10 messuages & land in Chylwicke, Seynt Michells,
Harpeden, Sandrige & Redborne.

### 1578. Mich. Term. 20 & 21 Eliz.

Paul Pope: Wm. Skipwith esq & Frances his wife. Four messuages
& lands in the psh. of S<sup>t</sup> Peters, in S<sup>t</sup> Albans.

Wm. Saunders: Edw. Bardolf & Kath. his wife. Messuage & lands
in Rudge *alias* Rygge.

Thos. Shodbolte esq & Wm. Shodbolte gent: John Connyes. Four
messuages & lands in Layston, Buntingeforth & Walkehorne.

Henry Sadleyer esq & Rich. Bankes gent: Thos. Grymesdyche esq.
Manor of Jewcys & 20 messuages & lands in Gt. Hadham & Little
Hadham.

Wm. Wrothe gent: Rich. Pegrim, Thos. Brett & Wm. Brett. Lands
in Stondon.

John Lacye & John Swetinge: Edw. Parker lord Morley & Eliz. his
wife. Manor of Johns de Pellam & 10 messuages & lands in Furnix
Pellam & Brent Pellam.

### 1578-9. Hilary Term. 21 Eliz.

*Thos. Style: Rich. Davye & Alice his wife, & Nich. Parratt & Joan
his wife. Lands in Flampstede & Cadington.

*John Scott gent & Rich. Scott gent: Thos. Bysshop esq & Anne his
wife. A third part of lands in Rudge *alias* Rydge.

*Roger Warfeilde & Wm. Brockbancke: Thos. Cogger & Joan his
wife. Two messuages & lands in Barnett *alias* Est Barnett &
Asshewell.

Wm. Wabie: Edw. Wilson gent & Marion his wife. Messuage and
land in Walkorn *alias* Walkern.

Thos. Fynche: Edm. Bardolphe esq & Rich. Bardolphe son & heir
apparent of s<sup>d</sup> Edm. Lands in Whethamsted.

Henry Sadleir esq: John Philpott & Eliz. his wife. Lands in Aspiden
*alias* Aspden.

Wm. Snowe: Thos. Jernegan gent & Eliz. his wife. Garden &
orchard in Stortford.

Jas. Whytlome *alias* Barbor: Thos. Jernegan gent & Eliz. his wife.
Messuage & gardens in Stortford.

John Pope gent & Wm. Handforte: Edm. Bardolphe esq & Rich.
Bardolphe son & heir apparent of s<sup>d</sup> Edm. Lands in Whethamsted.

Thomas Mowffytt: John Barley & Eliz. his wife. Lands in Asshewell.

Nich. Bacon knt lord keeper of the great seal & Barth. Kempe gent:
Thos. Drurye gent, Thos. Pullyson, Wm. Curtys & John Payne.
Moiety of three messuages & lands in Shenley.

Geo. Foster *alias* Cooke & Scolastica his wife: John Sole & Joan his
wife. Messuage & land in Hartingfordburye.

John Daye *alias* Palmer & Margt. his wife: Rich. Graynger. Four
messuages & lands in Tewynge.

### 1579. Easter Term. 21 Eliz.

*Rich. Tredwey gent. & Geo. Calfehild gent: Rich. Huddilston esq &
Isabel his wife. Lands in Beconsfild *alias* Beckensfelde, Pen,
Burneham, Farnam *alias* Farneham Royall, Chalfount S<sup>t</sup> Peter,
Chalfount S<sup>t</sup> Giles Agmondesham *alias* Amersham.

Geo. Ellyott gent: Henry Jernygan gent & Anne his wife. Lands in Farneham.
John Porter: John Sanders. Messuage & land in S<sup>t</sup> Albans.
Thos. Whyte: Thos. Smyth & Ellen his wife. Messuage & lands in Tryng & Cubblecote.
Wm. Ewyer: John Harvye esq & Margery his wife. Messuage & lands in Watford & Saynt Stephens.
Henry Heigham gent: Nich. Morgan gent & Jane his wife. Two messuages & land in Sabridgeworth. A warranty against Henry Johnson senior, John Mathewe & Wm. Mathewe.
John Goore: Richard Pecock & Joan his wife. Messuage & garden in Stortford *alias* Bysshoppes Stortforde.
Wm. Byrchemore: Francis Sabbe gent & Eliz. his wife. Two messuages in Seynt Albons.
Henry Pranell cit. & vintner of London: Edw. earl of Oxford, high chamberlain of England. Manor of Newsyll *alias* Newsells & 40 messuages & lands in Barkewaye, Barley, Reade & Royston & liberty of free faldage in same places.
Geo. Moreland: Edw. Goodwyn & Eliz. his wife. Messuage & lands in Barkwaye & Reade.
Nich. Potts gent: Ralph Bullocke gent & Mary his wife & Wm. Buñe. Messuage & lands in Estbrokehaye & Hemelhamstede.

### 1579. Trinity Term. 21 Eliz.

*John Webbe gent: Rich. Warde esq & Mary his wife. Manor of Pychelesthorne & 3 messuages & lands in Pychelesthorne, Chedington & Eldesboroughe.
Christ<sup>r</sup> Hudson: Wm. Marshall gent & Alice his wife. Messuage & garden in Ware.
Thos. Holland: Rich. Vessey & Eliz. his wife. Land in Amwell.
Oliver Crosse: Wm. Marshall gent & Alice his wife. Messuage in Ware.
Simon Harvye senior: John Harvye & Cecily his wife. Messuage & land in Sandon.
Wm. Tooke gent & Mary his wife: Christ<sup>r</sup> Bulle gent & Agnes his wife. Two messuages & lands in parishes of All Saints & S<sup>t</sup> Andrews in Hertford.
Nich. Badger: Christr Wyllyamson & Agnes his wife. Messuage & land in Kings Hatfeild *alias* Bysshoppes Hatfeild.
Rich. Wylcock & Anne his wife: Wm. Wylkinson & Eliz. his wife. Messuage & gardens in Hoddesdon.
John Mason & Thos. Porter clk: John Porter & Geo. Porter. Messuage & lands in Graveley & Chisefeld.
Henry Carey, knight of the bath, lord Hunsden: Henry Chauncye esq & Jane his wife & Thos. Salysburye gent. Lands in Eastwycke.
Thomas Sadleir & Mathew Smythe esq<sup>rs</sup>: Edw. Baeshe esq & Jane his wife. Manors of Affledwike *alias* Beachampes & Cosens & 6 messuages & lands in Layston, Widiall, Ansteye, Gt. Hormeade, Ware, Stansted Abbott, Hunsdon & Thundridge.
Anthony Cage senior: Edw. earl of Oxford. Manor of Great Hornemede *alias* Horemede *alias* Hormade & 80 messuages & lands in Gt. Hornemede, Little Horemede, Anstye, Barkewaye, Wallyngton, Laystone, Alswycke, Nutsted & Braughinge.

### 1579. Mich. Term. 21 & 22 Eliz.

*Henry Hewett esq: Geo. Horde gent & Cicily his wife. Lands in Aldenham & Busshie.

Robt. Nicoll: John Huntley & Rose his wife. A fourth part of two messuages & lands in Watford.
John Dards: Edw. Pulter esq & Mary his wife. Messuage & garden in Hitchin.
Peter Lyndesell: Edw. Parker lord Morley. Messuage & lands in Sabridgeworthe.
Randall Nycoll: John Hyckman & Agnes his wife. Three messuages & lands in Watford.
Edw. Norwood: Oswald Huckle. Two messuages & lands in Coddred *alias* Cottered.
John Smythe: Wm. Faroe & Margt. his wife. Moiety of a messuage & garden in St Albans.
John Fyssher: Thos. Rice & Margt. his wife. Two messuages & garden in Bushey.
Nich. Bower: John Kelynge & Margt. his wife. Three messuages & lands in Esyngden & Hertford.
Thos. Narrowld gent: John Hall & Winifrid his wife. Messuage & land in Ashwell.
Rich. Bull gent & Wm. Hartforde gent: John Lawrence. Messuage & land in St Albans.
Wm. Thrale: Thos. Appowell & Margt. his wife. Messuage in St Albans.
Geo. Samy: John Clapham & Dorothy his wife. Lands in Little Hadham.
Geo. Turfoot: Edm. Barbor & Eliz. his wife. Messuage & lands in Gt. Munden & Little Munden.
Rich. Colly gent: John Harvi & Alice his wife. Lands in Ware.
Simon Warren: Wm. Frauncis esq, Rich. Frauncis gent & Susan his wife & John Hunt jun. gent. Lands in Hytchen. A warranty against John Hunt senior, father of sd John.
Henry Sadleir esq & Dorothy his wife: Edw. Sadleir esq & Anne his wife. Manor of Hexton & 20 messuages & lands in Hexton.
Matthew Audley: Wm. Frauncis esq, Rich. Frauncis gent & Susan his wife & John Hunt jun. gent. Messuage & garden in Hitchen.
Roger Gysse & Thos. Webb: Gilbert Hyll gent. Manor of Grimbalds & 6 messuages & lands in Ware.

### 1579-80. Hilary Term. 22 Eliz.

Wm. Lodge: Wm. Sewell & Alice his wife. Two messuages & lands in Studham. A warranty against the heirs of Rich. Myckley.
Edw. Clark gent & Robt. Hackshawe: John Elmer *alias* Fylewood. Four messuages & lands in Rysden *alias* Ryshden *alias* Rushden & Bradfilde.
John Moyer & Grace his wife: Philip Clarke & Agnes his wife. A third part of a messuage & lands in Harpeden & Whethamsted.
John Bonnycke: Thos. Whyte & Agnes his wife. Messuage & lands in Long Marston & Goblecote.
Rich. Lovett: Thos. Butterfeld & Kath. his wife. Messuage & land in Flaunden.
Rich. Mounke & Philippa his wife & John Wright: John Bekke. Messuage & land in Laiston.
Robt. Newporte esq: Robt. Leghe. Three messuages & lands in Rushden, Cottered, Clottall & Bradfeild.
Patrick Roddye: Thos. Russell & Cecily his wife & Wm. Petitt & Alice his wife. Messuage & garden in Chipping Barnett.

Edw. Pulter esq: John Brokett knt & Ellen his wife. Manor of Bradfeilde *alias* Brodefcilde & 10 messuages & lands in Bradfeilde, Rushden & Codreth *alias* Cotered & the advowson of church of Bradfeilde.
John Knyghton esq & Geo. Knyghton gent son of s^d John: Edw. Sulyard esq & Anne his wife. Manors of Parkburye & Legatt & 20 messuages & lands in Kympton, Abbots Walden, Knebworthe, Codicote & Whethamsted.
Rich. Roberts gent: Wm. Anstee & Anne his wife. The Rectory of All Saints in Hertford, & all tithes belonging thereto in parish of All Saints in Hertford, Brekingdon, Stanstede, Hoddesdon, Ware, Amwell, Hertford, Brekingdon grene & Hertford Heth & the advowson of the vicarage of All Saints, Hertford.
Anthony Weldon gent & Matthew Cracherode gent: Francis Alley gent. Messuage & lands in Barkhamstede & Northchurche.
Wm. Preston: John Puckering esq & Jane his wife & John Mauchell esq & Ursula his wife. Lands in Childwicke *alias* Chilwicke, Seynt Michells, Harpeden, Sandrige & Redborne & a fourth part of the manor of Childwicke. Also 10 messuages & lands in same places.

### 1580. Easter Term. 22 Eliz.

John Barkemaker: Roger Parkes & Margery his wife. Messuage & garden in Harttingfordbery.
Ralph Radclyffe gent: John Parker & Joan his wife. Two messuages & gardens in Hutchen.
Thos. Bumpsted: John Cockerell. Messuage & land in Chesthunt.
Henry Childe: Robt. Twytchet & Agnes his wife. Messuage & lands in Sarett.
John Smythe sen: Thos. Vaughan gent. Lands in S^t Michaels near S^t Albans.
Anthony Radclyffe: Humph. Steppinge & Mary his wife. Two messuages & gardens in S^t Albans.
Robt. Spencer esq & Frances his wife: Robt. Forrest & Jeromina his wife. Messuage & land in town of Hertford.
Andrew Kynge gent & Thos. Hammond: Henry Hammond gent. Five messuages & lands in Westmyll *alias* Buntingford Westmyll.
John Myles: John Bigge & Joan his wife. Two messuages & land in Knebworth.
Henry Eyre: Rich. Gosson. Messuage & lands in Buntyngford, Widiall, Laystone, Throckyng, Aspeden & Bennyngton.
Edmund Griffyn gent: Geo. Bodwell *alias* Boydell & Thos. Bodwell *alias* Boydell son & heir apparent of s^d George. Messuage & lands in Bishops Hatfeild *alias* Kings Hatfeild.
Edw. Hunt gent: Rich. Grene gent. Messuage, two barns & lands in Braughyng.
Edw. Hunt gent: Rich. Grene gent. Messuage, barn & lands in Braughyng.
Henry Sadleir esq & Dorothy his wife: John Phillpott esq & Eliz. his wife. Manor of Aspden *alias* Aspeden & 3 messuages & lands in Aspden *alias* Aspeden.
John Brograve esq & Margt. his wife: Edw. Halfehyde gent & Anne his wife. Ten messuages & lands in Westmill & all tithes in Westmill.

### 1580. Trinity Term. 22 Eliz.

Ralph Radclyff gent: Edw. Pulter esq. Lands in Hitchyn & Polletts *alias* Ippolletts.

Thos. Hedd : Rich. Erle & Joan his wife & John Atwood. Messuage & land in Gt. Monden.

Rich. Everett : Rich. Pope & Joan his wife & John Pope. Messuage & lands in Gossams end in parishes of Barkhamsteed Marie *alias* Northchurche & Barkhamsteed S$^t$ Peter *alias* Great Barkhamsteed.

Rich. Brokeman gent : Wm. Lathum gent & Susan his wife. Manor of Lyburye *alias* Lybery & 20 messuages & lands in Little Munden, Gt. Munden, Westmell, Waltcorne, Braughinge & Yeardley.

John Pope gent & John Wharton : John Harvye gent & Margery his wife. Manor of Salmons & 4 messuages & lands in Rydge, Shenlye & Aldenham.

Henry Butler esq : Edw. Skeggs, Joan Skeggs widow & John Mathewe gent. Ten messuages & lands in Brauntfeilde, Bacheworthe Stapleford, Waterford, Watton, Bengehoe & Tuynge.

### 1580. Mich. Term. 22 & 23 Eliz.

*Thos. Hopkyns *alias* Jane & Hugh Cooke : John Buckmaster & Rich. Buckmaster. Two messuages & lands in Hemelhamsted & Feldon.

*Wm. Cecyll knt lord Burghley High Treasurer of England : Wm. Franckland & Hester his wife & Hugh Franckland. Messuage & lands in Hoddesdon, Broxborne, Amwell & Stansted. A warranty against the heirs of Wm. Franckland dec$^d$ father of the s$^d$ William.

Thos. Morison esq : Wm. Moore gent & Sarah his wife. Messuage & land in Rowgrene in Standon. A warranty against Leonard Moore gent.

John Fuller : Thos. Fuller & Eliz. his wife. Three messuages & lands in Broxborn & Hoddesdon.

Jonas Fring : Geo. Golde & Joan his wife. Four messuages & land in Watford.

Jas. Wyllmott gent : Wm. Warren. Lands in Therfeld.

Thos. Norwood gent : Clement Gunell & Agnes his wife. Lands in Ashewell.

John Hudnoll : John Jurden & Eliz. his wife. Messuage & garden in Barkhamsted.

Henry Cock knt : Wm. Knighte & Grace his wife. Four messuages & lands in Broxborne, Hoddesdon, Amwell & Wormeley.

John Gladman *alias* Grene : Rich. Davie. Messuage & lands in Kensworth.

Thos. Ancell : Rich. Francis gent & Susan his wife. Lands in Ickelford.

Jas. Pratt senior : John Richardson & Eliz. his wife & Alice Medcalfe. Lands in Clothall.

Wm. Moore : Thos. Morrison & Eliz. his wife. Lands in Sandon.

Edw. Phellippes gent & Theophilus Adams gent : Matthew Lowe gent & Anne his wife. Manor of Giffordes & 6 messuages & lands in Little Munden & Great Munden.

### 1580-1. Hilary Term. 23 Eliz.

Jas. Trystram : John Pearles & Eliz. his wife. Messuage & lands in Hutchen.

Michael Longe gent : Thos. Graveley & Joan his wife. Messuage & garden in Hutchen *alias* Hitchen.

Henry Hickman : Wm. Mylwarde *alias* Alexander esq & Kath. his wife & Anthony Brigham gent. The site of the manor of Busshey & 2 messuages & lands in Busshey & Watford & free fishery in the water of Busshey & Watford ; also the advowson of church of Busshey.

Agnes Adam widow & Francis Adam : Edw. Adam.  Two messuages & lands in Burnt Pelham.

Thos. Iverie. Rich. Humfrey, John Sibbley, John Hill & Thos. Yarrowe : Tho. Awncell & Joan his wife.  Three messuages & lands in Kings Walden.

John Dirrington : Robt. Nicolls & Eliz. his wife.  Messuage & land in Sabridgworth.

Robt. Sharpe & Eliz. his wife : Henry Geldnor gent.  Messuage & garden in Ware.

Thos. Bennett & Agnes his wife : Winefrid Thourgood & Frances Thourgood.  Two parts of a messuage & lands, in four parts divided, in Stansted Theale, Stansted Abbott & Amwell.

*To be Continued.*

# Deeds relating to Stone Hall in St. Albans.*

I. Sciant presentes et futuri quod Ego Thomas Fysshewyke de Villa Sancti Albani in Com. Hertf. Pewterer pro diversis causis & consideracionibus me moventibus, dedi concessi et hac presenti Carta mea confirmavi Henrico Fysshewyke filio meo, Totum illud Messuagium meum cum suis pertinentibus vocatum le Stonehall cum Curtilagio adjacente scituatum & jacentem in Villa de Sancto Albano exopposito le Flesshamellf in vico Sancti Petri inter tenementum nuper Monasterii Sancti Albani modo in manibus Domini Regis pertinens Officio Subcellarii nuper dicti monasterii ex una parte & terram nuper dicti Monasterii ex altera parte. Et predictum Curtilagium jacet in latitudine inter tenementum quondam Ade Stoneham nuper Bartholomei Westby ex una parte & Curtilagium nuper dicti Monasterii ex altera parte unde unum caput inde abuttat super Regiam viam & aliud caput super gardinum quondam Thome Fayreman nuper Johannis Nunny sicut mete & bunde inde se undique habent docent & demonstrant, habendum et tenendum predictum Mesuagium cum Curtilagio & suis pertinentibus prefato Henrico Fysshewyke heredibus & assignatis suis Ad usum ipsius Henrici heredum & assignatorum suorum imperpetuum De Capitalibus Dominis feodi illius per servicia inde debita & de jure consueta Et ego vero predictus Thomas Fysshewyke & heredes mei predictum Mesuagium cum Curtilagio & suis pertinentibus prefato Hensico Fysshewyke heredibus & assignatis suis Ad usum predictum contra omnes gentes warantizabimus & imperpetuum defendemus per presentes. In cujus rei etc. Datum apud Villam Sancti Albani predicti Octavo die mensis Junii Anno regni Henrici Octavi Dei gratia etc. tricesimo quinto. [1543] Seal gone. Endorsed with note of livery of seisin in the presence of Nich. Savage clerk, James Asshford, Thomas Burford, Henry Onyons & others.

II. Omnibus Christi fidelibus ad quos hæc presens carta pervenerit Ricardus Laycrofte cives & Armorer London. Salutem in Domino sempiternam Sciatis me prefatum Ricardum Laycroft pro quadam

* Now the property of Richard Gibbs, Esq., J.P., to whom I am indebted for kind permission to publish these copies and abstracts. Ed.

pecunie summa michi per Thomam Johnson de villa Sancti Albani in Com. Hertf. yoman etc., dedisse etc., prefato Thome Johnson Totum illud Mesuagium meum cum Curtilagio adjacente et suis pertinentibus vocatum le Stonehall scituatum & existens in villa Sancti Albani in Com. Hertf. in vico Sancti Petri nuper in tenura sive occupacione Henrici Fyshewyke, habendum etc. ad opus & usum ipsius Thome Johnson heredum & assignatorum suorum imperpetuum de Capitalibus Dominis etc. Dat. octavo die Januarii Anno regni Henrici Octavi dei gratia etc. tricesimo octavo. [1547] *Seal gone.* Endorsed with note of livery of seisin in the presence of Martin Vele, Henr. Gape, Robt. Braud, Will. Cowley, Thos. Somerlandes & others.

III. Omnibus Christi fidelibus etc. Thomas Johnson de Villa Sancti Albani in Com. Hertf. yoman, salutem etc., Noveritis me prefatum Thomam Johnson dedisse, concessisse etc., Georgio Butler de Villa Sancti Albani in Com. Hertf. yoman, totum illud Messuagium meum cum suis pertinentibus vocatum le Stone halle cum Curtilagio etc. inter Tenementos nuper Abbatis & Conventus Monasterii Sancti Albani modo dissoluti pertinentes Officio Subcellarii ex utraque parte etc., habendum etc., prefato Georgio Butler etc., sub ista tamen forma & condicione subsequente videlicet si predictus Georgius Butler solvat seu solvi faciat aut heredes vel executores sui solvant seu solvi faciant prefato Thome Johnson heredibus vel executoribus suis in domo Mansione ipsius Thome Johnson vocato le Bull infra dictam villam Sancti Albani sexdecim libras legalis monete Anglie in forma subscripta videlicet in festo Annunciacionis beate Marie virginis prox. etc., quousque predictam summam sexdecim librarum esse plenarie satisfactam persolutam & contentam etc. Dat. quintodecimo die Octobris Anno regni Edwardi sexti dei gratia etc., secundo [1548] Seal showing the initials T. W. Endorsed with note of livery of seisin in the presence of John Lokkey, Martin Vele, John Spencer, Thomas Est, Thomas Davis, Will. Cowley & others. Also endorsed 'Rec. of the fyrst iiij$^{or}$ pound$\ell$ w$^{th}$ wryten x$^s$.'

IV. Thomas Johnson of the town of S$^t$ Albans, yeoman, quitclaims to s$^d$ George Butler, all his estate & title, claim demand & interest in the messuage called 'le Stonehall.' Dat. 13 Nov. 5 Edw. VI. [1551].

V. George Butler of S$^t$ Albans, yeoman, for a certain sum of money, confirmed to John Alway of Kympton, co. Herts. gent. all that tenement called the Stonehall with the curtilage & a house called a Wellhouse & a well therein, in S$^t$ Albans in S$^t$ Peters Street, opposite the Flesheshambles there, between the tenement of Richard Lee knt. & the messuage lately called the Charnell house on the south & the tenement of John Laurence on the north & extends in length from the s$^d$ street on the east as far as the garden of John Nunney on the west, which premises s$^d$ Geo. Butler lately acquired by the gift & feoffment of Thomas Johnson of S$^t$ Albans by deed dated 15 Oct. 2 Edw. VI. Dated 8 Oct. 6 Edw. VI. [1552] *Seal almost gone.* Livery of seisin in the presence of Thomas Rowse gent. James Gleadall, Thomas East & others.

VI. John Alweye of Kympton, co. Herts, gent. for the sum of sixteen pounds, confirms to Francis Watson of S$^t$ Albans, yeoman, the said messuage called the Stone Hall etc., situated between the tenement of Richard Lee knt. now in the occupation of Thomas Bett & the Towne Hall on the south & the tenement of Martin Veale on the north, etc., subject to the proviso for redemption therein contained on payment ' apud mesuagium predictum vocatum le Stonehall ' of fourteen pounds at the times therein named. *Signed* Per me Johannem Alwey. Dated 18 Nov. 1 Mary [1553]. *Fragment of seal only.* Livery of seisin in presence of Robert Skepweth gent., Nich. Aylwarde, Thos. Wodwarde, Will. Lowdam & others.

VI. (a). Copy of the last deed, signed by Francis Watson. *Seal gone.*

VII. George Butler of S$^t$ Albans, yeoman, quitclaims to Francis Watson of same place, yeoman, all his estate, title, claim etc in the messuage called the Stonehall, late in the tenure of John Alwey gent. *Dated* 18 Nov. 1 Mary [1553]. *Seal gone.* Witnesses:—John Alwey, Robt. Stepney gent., Nyclas Aylwarde, Willm Lowdam & others.

VIII. Francis Watson of S$^t$ Albans, yeoman, quitclaims to John Alweye of Kympton gent. all right, title etc. in the messuage called the Stone Hall, late in the tenure of George Butler. *Dated* 24 June 1 Mary [1554]. *Seal gone.* *Signed* Per me Franciscum Watson.

IX. John Alweye of Kympton, gent. demises grants and 'to ferme letts' to Richard Grubbe of the towne & boroughe of Sainte Albanes, yeoman, all that his tenement called the Stonehaulle etc. for a term of 40 years, at yearly rent of 30s. *Dated* 1 July 1 Eliz. [1559]. *Signed* Per me Joh'em Alwey. *Seal indistinguishable.* Wit$^s$:—Thomas Rowce, gentylmā, and Jamys Gleadall.

X. John Allwaye of Sharpenho in the parish of Streteley, co. Bedf. gent. for a certain sum of money, confirms to James Thamesyn of the Borough of S$^t$ Alban, gent., the messuage called Le Stonehalle etc. situated between the tenement of Thos. Johnson gent. now in the occupation of Wm. Hannell & the Townehall on the south & a tenement formerly of Martin Veale's & now of s$^d$ Jas. Thamesin & in the occupation of s$^d$ James on the north, etc. which messuage s$^d$ John Allwaye had by bargain & feoffment of one George Butler of s$^d$ town & boroughe of S$^t$ Albans, yeoman, by deed dated 8 Oct. 6 Edw. VI. John Kylbyff & John Clarke are appointed attorneys to deliver seisin. *Dated* 20 Apr, 11 Eliz. [1569]. *Signed* Per me Joh'em Alwey. *Seal a man's head.* Livery of seisin by John Kylbiff in the presence of John Skynn' carpenter, Rich. Martyn, James Walker, Rich. Webbe, Stephan Chappell *als* Baylye servant of s$^d$ John Skynner, John Abbott, 'et mei Francisci Mantell scr.' and others.

XI. James Thomasyn of St. Albans, 'purvio$^r$' & Johan his wife, grant to Robert Spencer of St. Albans esq. their messuage & tenement in S$^t$ Albans in which s$^d$ James & Johan now dwell 'the one side thereof Lyinge to the Streete And thother side towardes the howse of one M$^r$ Weste of S$^t$ Albons aforesaid The one hedd or ende of the same abuttinge to the howse of the said Roberte And thother hedd or ende abuttinge to the howse Late one Thomas Lockeye,' subject to the proviso for redemption therein contained, on payment of £100, at the now dwelling house of s$^d$ Robert situate in S$^t$ Albans, called 'the Grenehowse' at the time therein named. Dated 20 Mch. 15 Eliz. [1573]. *Two seals gone.* Wit$^s$:—George Ferrers, Willm Angrome, Water Parry, John Sparepoynte. Livery of seisin in presence of George Ferrers & John Sparepoynte.

XII. Indenture between Richard Belfeld of S$^t$ Albones, co. Hertf. gent. of thone ptie & Thomas Spencer of London gent of thother ptie, after reciting an indenture of lease dated 13 April 38 [*sic*] Eliz. between Robt. Spencer late of S$^t$ Albones esq of the one pt. & one Rich. Gilman late of S$^t$ Albones gent on thother ptie whereby s$^d$ Robt. demised to s$^d$ Rich$^d$ Gilman all that his messuage etc. wherein one

James Thomasine & Johane his wife late dwelt (except such several Chambers parcels & rooms being then in the occupation of s^d Robt.) situate in S^t Albones, then in the occupation of one Gilbert Stoughton the younger, for a term of 41 years at a yearly rent of £4. And reciting that by an indenture dated 27 Mch. 32 Eliz. [1590] between s^d Rich^d Gilman of the one part & s^d Rich^d Belfeld of the other part, s^d Gilman assigned to s^d Belfeld the s^d lease & all his interest in s^d messuage &c. Now s^d Belfeld in consideration of £50 assigns to s^d Thos. Spencer the s^d indentures of lease & assignment & all his interest for residue of s^d term of 41 years. Dated 12 May 34 Eliz. [1592]. [*Signed*] p Ri'cum Belfeld. [*Seal indistinguishable*]. Wit^s:— Wyllya Gryffith, the m'ke of Nicholas Hartford.

XIII. Indenture dated 23 Aug. 38 Eliz. [1596], between Thomas Spencer of London, gent. of the one part & Mathew Palmer of London, gent. of the other part, whereby after reciting the before mentioned lease of 13 Apr. 28 Eliz. & the assignment of 27 Mch. 32 Eliz. to Rich^d. Belfeilde (desc^d as of Greate Gaddesdene, co. Hertf. gent) & the assignment from Belfeild to Spencer, the s^d Thos. Spencer assigns s^d lease & assignments to s^d Mathew Palmer in consideration of 'a certeine some' of money. [*Signed*] Tho. Spencer. [Seal representing a lion rampant with the initials M [or W] P.] Wit^s: Geo. Balie.

XIV. Indenture dated 9 May 2 Jas. [1604] whereby Mathewe Palmer of London, gent. in consideration of xxiij*li* x*s*. assigns to John Spencer, Esquire., all his estate & interest in the premises above described. [*Signed*] M. Palmer. [Seal, much worn, apparently the initials T. T.] Wit^s:—William Hertforde, scr.

XV. Fine. Michaelmas Term 15 Jas. [1617] between W^m. Haile, quer. & Joan Harvy widow & W^m. Harvy son & heir apparent of s^d Joan, def^s., of a messuage & a garden in the town of S^t Albans.

XVI. Indenture dated 2 June 3 Chas. [1627] between Robt. Gyllman gent one of the sonnes of Richard Gyllman, late of S^t Albans, co. Hertf. esq. dec^d & of Anne one of the sisters of John Spencer late of S^t Albans esq. dec^d of the one part & Twyford Wath of S^t Albans gent. of the other part, reciting that s^d John Spencer by will dat. 18 Aug. 1622 (amongst other things) gave to Marg^t. his wife now wife of s^d Twyford Wath for her life & after her decease to s^d Robt. Gyllman, the messuage known by the name of the Stonehall in S^t Albans in the parish of S^t Peter in a street there called S^t Peter streete over against or neare the Flesh Shambles Betwene the tenement now of Edmund Wrighte gent & late W^m. Dobsons of the one parte & a tenement late in the tenure of one Robt. Neave butcher, beinge the inheritance of the s^d Marg^t. wife of s^d Twyford Wath of the other parte, By the name of the howse wherein hee then dwelt, it was witnessed that s^d Robt. Gyllman in consideration of £72 granted s^d messuage to s^d Twyford Wath. [*Signed*] Robert Gulman. [Seal half broken away, probably same as that attached to No. 13 above]. Wit^s:—Edw. Hide, Ry. Storye, S^t John Bromhall, Nicho. Davies.

XVII. Fine. Trinity Term 3 Chas. [1627] between Twiford Wathe gent. quer. & Robt. Gillman gent. def. of one messuage & one garden in the parish of S^t Peter in S^t Alban.

XVII. Indenture dated 24 May 1649 between Henric Twyford of London, stationer, & Frances his wife & Ann Wath dau. of Twyford Wath late of S^t Albons co. Hertf. gent. dec^d of the one part & John Wolley of Raunston co. Darbie esq & W^m. Smalwood of London gent on the other part, after reciting the will of John Spencer dat.

18 Aug. 1622 & the indenture (No. 16 above) of 2 June 3 Chas. and reciting that s^d John Spencer & Margt. his wife were both dead & the s^d Twyford Wath was also dead having issue the s^d Ann Wath & Frances now wife of s^d Henrie Twyford who were daughters & coheirs of s^d Twyford Wath, it was agreed by s^d H. Twyford, Frances his wife & s^d Ann Wath to levy a fine ' sur connuzance de droit come ceo que ils ont de lour done ' whereby s^d John Wooley & Wm. Smalwood should stand seised of the premises above described to the use of the s^d Ann Wath her heirs & assigns for ever. [Signed] Henry Twyford, Francis Twyford, Anne Wathe. Witnesses to the sealing & delivery by Henry & Frances Twyford, John Wheatley, Georg ffl. . . . . ., Richard Bonner. Wit^s:—to the sealing &c. by Ann Wath, Nich. Morryon, Martha Thorp, Francis Walker.

XIX. Fine. Trinity Term 1649 between John Wolley esq. & Wm. Smalwood gent. quer^s. & Henr. Twyford & Frances his wife & Anne Wath def^s of one messuage in the parish of S^t Peter in S^t Albans.

XX. Declaration dat. [blank] June 1649 by s^d John Wolley & Wm. Smalwood that they held s^d premises in trust only for s^d Ann Wath. [Signed] John Wolley, Wm. Smalwood. Wit^s:—Nich. Morryon, Martha Thorp, Francis Walker.

XXI. Indentures of Lease and Release dat. 1 & 2 Dec. 1698 the latter made between Ann Williams of London widow & John Williams son and heir apparent of s^d Anne Williams of the one part & John Tombes of S^t Albans, co. Hertf. gent. & Anne his wife of the other part, witnessed that in consideration of £240, s^d Ann Williams & John Williams granted to s^d John Tombes & Anne his wife All that messuage or tenement situate in psh. of S^t Peters in S^t Albans now in tenure of Hannah Feild wid. & Jane Trott wid. called Stone Hall & also one messuage adjoining Stone Hall on the north part now or late in the tenure of George Rowney butcher and adjoining south on the Comon Town Hall there both which s^d premises front the public street in S^t Albans called S^t Peters Street towards the east. Covenant for quiet enjoyment free from any claim by s^d Ann Williams & John Williams ' or from by or vnder Anne Wath spinster dec^d ' except only one lease made of the premises to Wm. Butler for securing repayment of £150 with interest. [Signed] Ann Williams, Jn^o. Williams. [Seals. Arms a cross counter compony surmounted by crest, a hand holding a chaplet (?)]. Wit^s:—Bat. Shotbolt, Calamy Bayly, Daniel Tombes.

XXII. Fine. Hilary Term 8 Wm. III. [1697] between Rich. Dodwell quer. & Anne Williams, John Williams & Ellen his wife, Nich^s Bergerott & Margt. his wife def^s of two messuages & two gardens in the town of S^t Albans.

XXIII. Extract from the will of Daniel Tombes dat. 2 Aug. 1755. ' Also I give & devise to my s^d wife Sarah & to my s^d Daughter Mary & their assigns All that my Capital Messuage or Tenement situate & being in S^t Peters Street in the Town of Saint Alban aforesaid wherein I now live ' for their lives & after the death of the survivor then to the heirs & assigns of s^d dau. Mary etc. Said dau. Mary sole extrix. Proved 4 Oct. 1764 by s^d Mary Tombes spinster. On 30 Apr. 1793 administration (with will annexed) of goods left unadministered by s^d Mary Tombes was granted to Sarah Neale spinster the ad'strix with the will annexed of s^d Mary Tombes dec^d. (P.C.C. Simpson 407).

XXIV. Extract from the will of Mary Tombes of psh. of S^t Peter in S^t Alban, spinster, dat. 19 Dec. 1767. To Sarah Paul £10, also annuity of £15 out of land at Barnet Heath. To Rev^d M^r John

Wingfield of Shrewsbury £100. To Frances Wing of Salop £100. To M⁽ʳˢ⁾ Eliz. Thornton of Lawrence end £100. To Sarah Smith & Henry Tombes Smith son & dau. of Henry Smith of Mains £100 each. To Mary Secker wife of John Secker of Milman Street £100. To Mary Hudgebout of Knightsbridge & Martha Hudgebout of Ditto £50 each. To W^m. Hurst £20. Residue to Rev^d M^r W^m. Neale Jun^r of Clothall whom I appoint exor. Fifty pounds to the Poor of the Parish of S^t Peters. Proved 28 April 1779 by exor. On 30 Apr. 1793 admon. (with will annexed) of goods left unadministered by s^d Rev^d W^m. Neale the younger dec^d, granted to Sarah Neale spinster the dau. & ad'strix of the goods of s^d W^m Neale dec^d. (P.C.C. Warburton 181).

XXV. Indenture dat. 9 Oct. 1779 between the Rev^d W^m. Neale of Essenden, co. Hertf. clerk, sole exor of the will of Mary Tombes late of S^t. Albans spinster who was the sole extrix of Daniel Tombes late of S^t Albans gent. dec^d, who was the sole exor of John Tombes late of S^t Albans gent. dec^d, of the one part & W^m. Kinder of S^t Albans esq of the other part, reciting that by indenture dat. 25 July 1704 made between Matthew Iremonger of S^t Albans grocer & John Iremonger son & heir apparent of s^d Matthew Iremonger of the one part & s^d John Tombes of the other part, s^d Matthew & John Iremonger demised to s^d John Tombes All that piece & portion of wall or so much thereof with the ground & soil whereon the same stood & upon which part of the north east end of the then dwelling house of s^d John Tombes situate in S^t Peters Street in S^t Albans was erected & built, with the erections & buildings upon the same & parting & dividing the court yard of the s^d Matt. Iremonger from the s^d dwelling-house of s^d John Tombes & containing in length 26 feet, for a term of 500 years at annual rent of 5s, it was witnessed that in consideration of 5s. s^d W^m. Neale assigned to s^d W^m. Kinder s^d piece of wall &c for residue of s^d term. [*Signed*] W^m. Neale. [Seal of arms:— Or on a bend between two lions rampant sable a dragon passant, wings elevated. *Pembroke*] Wit^s:—John Taylor, John Simpson.

XXVI. Indentures of lease & release dat. 8 & 9 Oct. 1779 the latter made between Elizth Rotheram Neale of Essenden, co. Hertf. widow the Aunt & one of the heirs at law of Mary Tombes late of S^t Albans spinster dec^d, who was the only surviving dau. & heir at law of Daniel Tombes, late of S^t Albans gent. dec^d who was the only son & heir at law of John Tombes late of S^t Albans gent dec^d, The Rev^d John Tombes Wingfield of Shrewsbury, co. Salop clerk, the only son & heir at law of Ann Wingfield widow dec^d who was another of the Aunts & heirs at law of s^d Mary Tombes dec^d & Henry Tombes Smith of New Barnes in psh. of S^t Peter, co. Hertf. esq the only son & heir at law of Hannah Smith widow dec^d who was another of the Aunts & heirs at law of the s^d Mary Tombes dec^d of the one part & W^m. Kinder of S^t Albans esq of the other part, witnessed that in consideration of £530 the parties of the one part granted & confirmed to s^d W^m. Kinder, the s^d messuage called Stone Hall etc. late in tenure of s^d Mary Tombes dec^d & now or late in tenure of the Rev^d W^m. Neale clerk, s^d premises front the public street towards the east, a garden belonging to Caleb Lomax esq towards the west, a garden which was heretofore a Courtyard belonging to the dwellinghouse of Matthew Iremonger & John Iremonger dec^d or one of them & now of Martha Kentish widow towards the north & a piece or parcel of ground on which heretofore formerly stood a messuage or tenement etc formerly in tenure of

George Rowney butcher dec⁴ afterwards of Rowland Mardall butcher dec⁴ & which buildings have been lately pulled down towards the south. [*Signed*] The mark of Elizth. Rotheram Neale, John Tombes Wingfield, Henry Tombes Smith. [Seal in each case same as on last deed]. Witˢ:—to sealing by E. R. Neale & H. T. Smith, George Pembroke & Wm. Archer. Witˢ:—to the sealing by J. T. Wingfield, Robt. Pemberton & R. Sutton.

XXVII. Fine. Trinity Term 20 Geo. III. [1780] between Wm. Kinder esq & Thos. Kinder esq pltfs & Eliz. Rotheram Neale widow, John Tombes Wingfield clerk & Henry Tombes Smith esq & Susannah his wife defˢ. of two messuages, two barns, two stables, one curtilage & one garden with the appurts. in psh. of Sᵗ Peter in town of Sᵗ Albans.

XXVIII. Indentures of lease & release dat. 10 & 11 May 1782 the latter made between Henry Tombes of Hardley, co. Southampton esq of the one part & Wm. Kinder of Sᵗ Albans esq of the other part, witnessed that in consideration of £100 sᵈ Henry Tombes released to sᵈ Wm Kinder all that mess. situate in psh. of Sᵗ Peter in Sᵗ Albans formerly in tenure of Geo. Rowney butcher decᵈ, afterwards of Rowland Mardall butcher decᵈ, since of Mʳˢ Mary Tombes decᵈ & now of sᵈ Wm. Kinder, which premises front the public street on the east, a garden belonging to Caleb Lomax esq on the west, messuage of sᵈ Wm. Kinder called Stone Hall on the north & a messuage called The Town Hall on the south, subject to a yearly rent of 2s. payable to the King. [*Signed*] Henry Tombes. Witˢ:—Wm. Froud, Wm. Burgess.

XXIX. Copy Will of William Kinder of the Borough of Sᵗ Alban co. Hertf. gent. Dated 15 July 1803. To wife Ann annuity of £300, also £1000 three per cent consol. bank annuities part of the stock now standing in my name, also for life my messuage wherein I now dwell & after her decease sᵈ messuage etc to son Thos. Kinder. To son in law Benj. Rooke junʳ of town of Hertford gent. £1000. To bro. in law Wm. Hardy of Addle Street in City of London esq £2000 out of my personal estate at the death of sᵈ wife in trust to invest for benefit of my dau. Ann wife of sᵈ Benj. Rooke for her life & after her decease for her children then living. To each of my brothers & sisters £25. To granddau. Anna Kinder £100 at 21 or marriage. To my old servants Matthew Rogers & Mary his wife [marginal note says 'both dead'] annuity of £10. Residue to son Thos. Kinder. Wife, son Thomas & bro-in-law Wm. Hardy exors. [*Signed*] Wm. Kinder. Witˢ:—Jno. Cowper, Jno. Saml. Story, Jno. Cowper Junʳ. Proved in P.C.C. 26 Jan. 1805 by Thos. Kinder & Wm. Hardy, reservation to sᵈ Ann Kinder.

## Court Rolls of the Manor of Picotts otherwise Piggots in Bishops Stortford.*

**PECOTTES.**  Court of Master . . . . . . clerk holden there on Monday next before the feast of Saint Michael in the 20th year of King Richard the Second after the Conquest. [1396]

Richard Huberd tailor came to this Court and showed a certain charter by which he acquired the tenement formerly of Isabel Cobbe & did fealty to the lord which same charter is made in the form of the statute by the service of vjd. by the year & suit of court.

Fealty.

Robert Skynner came to this Court & did fealty to the lord & acknowledged that he holds of the lord five acres of land in Shepeho formerly of Nicholas Chaunbre together with a parcel of John Chaumbre, and John Bussh. And they shall render by the year xxjd. & suit of court. And he did fealty to the lord.

Fealty.

Day

It is ordered to distrain John Fullere to show his charters at the next [Court] by what services & rent [he holds] the tenement formerly of Andrew Fullere next the tenement formerly of Nicholas Hobekyn, on pain of paying the said rent. Afterwards he came & showed a charter by which he is heir of the said Andrew & he did fealty to the lord etc.

Fealty

It is ordered

It is ordered to distrain Robert Skynnere & John Thurkild to show how they hold land in Shepeho formerly of Nicholas Chaumbre & theretofore of Nicholas Large for the rent of ijd. by the year.

Mercy vjd.

John Harpe of Great Hallyngbery had a day to show at this court his charter whereby he acquired from William Turnour one tenement & 30 acres of land called Manshepe & he did not come to this court therefore he [is] in mercy. And it is ordered to distrain him against the next [Court] to show etc.

It is ordered

It is ordered to distrain against the next [Court] John Borlee in a certain grange upon Horsundich for the rent of vjd. by the year & formerly of John Ardaunt junior & theretofore of Thomas Eldemed. And to distrain Hugh Davy in one croft of land at Meesgrene† formerly of Magota Motte for the service of vjd. by the year. And to distrain the tenants of the lands formerly of John Cameswell for the rent of xd. by the year. And to

It is ordered

---

* The originals of these rolls are in the possession of Mr. J. L. Glasscock, of Bishops Stortford, to whom the Editor is indebted for kind permission to transcribe and translate them.

† The following note is interlined :—It is void, because it is not so, because the rent aforesaid is [charged] upon John Maldon.

distrain the tenants of the lands formerly of John Godpayere called Leperes for the rent of iiijd. by the year.

It is ordered       It is ordered to distrain the tenants of one acre and a half of land in the field called Brambilfeld for the rent of xviijd. by the year being in arrear. And to distrain the tenants of [Busch *interlined*] of two acres of land in Apiltonefeld for the rent of ijd. by the year. And Nicholas Tannere has a day to show how he holds 3 acres of land [called] Presteleye formerly of Sibilla Estgrene (?) next the land of the lord Bishop of London. And to distrain William Jakelay for suit of court to be done for the lands which he holds in Brambilfeld and
Suit       Heyefeld being in arrear. Afterwards he comes & does to the lord suit of court etc.

Walter Godwyne [xijd. *interlined*] puts himself [in mercy] for trespass with beasts & sheep in the lord's pasture on twelve occasions & he broke the lords pound
Mercies       therefore [he is] in mercy. Thomas Everard [vjd. *interlined*] for cows and hogs in the pasture on seven occasions, therefore in mercy. And John Godwyne [iijd. *interlined*] for trespass with sheep in the lord's pasture on two occasions therefore in mercy. And John Baldewyne [iijd. *interlined*] of Thorleye for trespass by night with his consent with horses in the lord's pasture on divers occasions, therefore in mercy. And John Botild [viijd. *interlined*] senior for trespass on two occasions with his sheep remains [in mercy?] for trespass &c. And William Spycer [vjd. *interlined*] for trespass with one horse & he broke the lord's pound. And John Cameswell [ijd. *interlined*] for trespass in the corn with his beasts. And John Stokkere [iijd. *interlined*] of Thorleye for trespass with sheep in the lord's pasture. And John Moys [viijd. *interlined*] junior for trespass with sheep in the lord's pasture, therefore in mercy. And John [vjd. Peel *interlined*] the shephard of the lord bishop of London for trespass in throwing down the lord's hedges, therefore in mercy. And William Bygge [iiijd. *interlined*] for trespass with sheep on two occasions in the lord's oats & pease. And the same William [ijd. *interlined*] because he cut down the lord's hedges in Brambilfeld, therefore in mercy. And John Botild junior [iiijd. *interlined*] for horses in the lord's pease & oats. And the same John [iiijd. *interlined*] for four horses in the [lord's] pasture. And John atte Hull [vjd. *interlined*] of Hallyngbery for colts & sheep in the lord's pasture. And Geoffrey Galyon [iijd. *interlined*] for beasts in the corn.

The Inquisition by virtue of office, present that Nicholas Tannere of Southstret, has acquired one piece of meadow in Landmed from William Clerk by the service of vijd. [xviijd. *interlined*] by the year. And
It it ordered       because he does not come to show his charter therefore it is ordered to distrain him against the next [Court]. And that John Harpe of Great Hallyngbery has acquired from William Turnour one tenement & 30 acres of land called Menshepes &c.

|         |         |
|---------|---------|
| Fealty  | William Turnour had a day to do fealty to the lord for three acres of land in P . . . agereshill acquired from John Rowhey lying next the land of the lord bishop of London rendering to the lord vjd. by the year. And he came to this court & did fealty to the lord & suit of court &c. as it is said. Afterwards he came & did fealty. |

     Affeerers { Robert Hunden, John Paleman, John Palmere } sworn

            Sum viijs.

[Endorsed] Pecott℄. Court there in the 20th year of the reign of King Richard the second.

---

**PECOTES.**  Court held there namely in the house late of Nicholas Colman on Monday in the vigil of Saint Peter that is called Advincula in the fifth year of the reign of King Henry the fifth. [1417].

Essoins. None.

Fealty To that court came William Rose & acknowledged that he held as of the Manor of Pekot℄ one acre of land in the Half Acres, lying between the land of Robert Perkot on the one part & the land of Walter Greye by the rent of vjd. by the year & one acre of land in Schepehoo between the lands of Thomas Flemyng on both parts by the rent of jd. by the year. And he did fealty.

Day As yet heretofore William Tanner has a day until the next Court to show his charters & evidences concerning two crofts called Wyndellocrofft℄ which he lately acquired within the fee of the lord there from John Veyse & Ralph Bentle &c.

Day As yet John Clopton has a day until the next Court to show how he entered in the lord's fee, namely in a certain parcel of a certain tenement with one garden in Southstret late John Beuerle's &c.

Day John Turnor of Wyndell has a day until the next court, in like manner to show the charter whereby he acquired one piece of land in Benehook containing two acres which is held of the manor aforesaid [at] vd. by the year.

Let it be inquired Let it be inquired at the next [Court] who holds or hold certain lands & tenements which formerly were Elias Blethewen's which are held of the manor aforesaid by the rent of xvd. by the year, newly withdrawn &c.

'Modo Gybbe' William Rose has a day until the next &c. to discharge himself of iijs. vjd. of rent issuing from one solar & one Gatewey of his tenement called Rodeland℄ by sufficient evidences under penalty of paying said rent &c. Afterwards he did not show his discharge but agreed to pay vd. by the year of rent & to be discharged of the residue until it can be better inquired into concerning the same fee.

Day

It is ordered It is ordered to distrain John Colyn that he may be at the next Court to do fealty for a parcel of his garden & half an acre of land formerly Philip Potager's &c. of the fee aforesaid &c.

| | |
|---|---|
| Inquisition | Taken by virtue of office by the fealty of John Cook, John Greye, John Belhom, Thomas Peion, John Goos, John Fuller, Richard Boteler, John Wryght, John Palmer, John atte Hill, William Skot & John Piper who present |
| Mercies xixd. | that The Prior of S<sup>t</sup> Bartholomew (vjd.), The Vicar of Storteford (iiijd.) John Webbe (iijd.) & John Colyn (vjd.) are suitors of the Court & make default at this day, therefore in mercy. And the aforesaid jurors have a day until the next [Court] as they asked by assent, each of |
| Day under penalty | them under paid of 13s. 4d. to return his verdict concerning certain lands & tenements which were formerly Elias Blethewen's as above & formerly John Hegyn's. |
| Attachment of the farm bailiff Mercies ijs. vjd. | John Strouge [vjd. *interlined*] senior puts himself in mercy for trespass in Parkfild with four horses on divers occasions. John [xxd. *interlined*] the farmer of Thorleyhall for trespass in the lord's wheat in the field before the manor with four score sheep on divers occasions, in mercy. The same [iiijd. *interlined*] there with twenty beasts at times, in mercy. |

[Endorsed] Pekott*e*. Court in the fifth year of the reign of King Henry V.

---

| | |
|---|---|
| **PEKOTES.** | Court held there on the Tuesday next after the feast of the translation of S<sup>t</sup> Thomas the martyr, in the ninth year of the reign of King Henry the fifth. [1421]. |
| Essoins. | None. |
| Inquisition | Taken by virtue of office by the oaths of William Tannere, Thomas Mynotte, John Cook, Thomas Flemyng, John Blanke, Thomas Pegeon, John Belham sen<sup>r</sup>, William Rose, John Fullere, John Goos, John Belham |
| Mercies iijs. | the middle one ['medii'] John Skynere, John Palmere, who present that the Prior of S<sup>t</sup> Bartholomew [xijd.], the Vicar of Storteforde [xijd,], the Tenant of the land of Manshepes [xijd.] make default of suit of Court, therefore in mercy. |
| Day | John Fullere puts himself upon the jurors aforesaid concerning xiijd. of rent having put in his claim for two messuages upon Horshondych, which he holds of the lord's fee, as it is said & as appears by the evidence of the lord & to pay at the next court if it be adjudged. |
| Mercy vjd. | John Cook has a day until this Court to show evidence to discharge himself from vjd. of rent from that piece of one tenement upon Horshondych, or to pay the said rent under penalty of [paying] double, which same John comes & shows no evidence, but in full Court by a certain charter concerning the aforesaid rent shown by the lord openly to the same John, the steward sitting, by which he agreed to pay the said rent from henceforth. And because he withdrew for 4 years unjustly he is in mercy. And it is ordered to levy it. |
| Day | William Tannere has a day until the next [Court] to discharge himself concerning jd. of rent from two acres of land in Prestlye demanded from him which he claims to hold of the tenement of Dionisia Bole etc. |

| | |
|---|---|
| Mercy ijs. | John Stronge puts himself in the lord's grace for trespass in Parkfeld with four horses & two cows. |
| Let it be inquired | Let it be inquired who holds Kyngescroft for xxd. of rent which Edmund Hert lately held at Wyndhelle & paid, now of John Bussh, as it is said. |
| Fealty | William Rose agrees that he will pay for himself & his heirs, whilst it shall please the lord for one solar one gate & one gatewey parcel of his tenement called Rodelondes & annexed thereto vd., which formerly were Bartholomew Kere's. And he did fealty. |

Affeerers { John Palmere, John Pypere } who are sworn.

---

**PEKOTES.** Court there held in the house late Nicholas Colman's, now in the hands of Nicholas Haines & Alice his wife late wife of the aforesaid Nich⁵ Colman on the Tuesday next after the feast of St Matthias the Apostle in the fifth year of the reign of King Henry VI, in the time of John Gaall & Agnes his wife etc. 1426.*

| | |
|---|---|
| Essoins. | None. |
| George Hawkynes. Fealty. | To this Court Nicholas Haines & Alice his wife late wife of Nicholas Colman came & acknowledged that they held as of the manor of Pekot( one messuage in which they dwell & four shops adjoining, formerly Thomas Petworthe's & afterwards of the said Nicholas Colman, by the rent of xvs. & suit of Court, which same messuage with appurtenances formerly was Simon Farnham's & afterwards William Takeley's. And the same Nicholas did fealty. |
| Ed. Willey Fealty | William Tannere acknowledged that he held in like manner one croft enclosed called Wyndhellecroft, where lately there were two crofts & now under one enclosure by the rent of xxjd. by the year. And he did fealty. |
| Fealty | John Cook acknowledged that he held in like manner a certain parcel of land of one Garden upon Horshondych late William Belh'm's formerly built upon, by the rent of vijd. and also one parcel of meadow called Landmed late of the said William Belh'm's by the rent of vijd. Likewise one piece of land lying in Apetonfeld abutting on Landmed towards the south, containing one acre by estimation by the rent of jd. by the year Likewise one Croft enclosed below the Moore which he had lately from John Roughey in exchange for an enclosed garden at Okkelesforde next Hokerhille, by the rent of vjd. by the year viz:—as much as he used to pay for the said garden. And so he charges himself for the aforesaid croft henceforth for ever. And he did fealty. |
| Fealty | Hugh Thacham acknowledged that he holds in like manner one garden with a certain grange at Hokyrhille, late Richard Boteler's by the rent of xijd. by the year. And he did fealty. |

\* The figures have been added by a later hand. 1427 is the correct date.

## PICOTTS COURT ROLLS.  271

Fealty — Thomas Mynot acknowledged that he holds in like manner one acre & one rood of land in Hokyrhellefeld next the Claypettes late William Janne's by the rent of iijd. by the year. And he did fealty.

Note  
Fealty — John Belh'm senior acknowledged that he holds in like manner the other half of Landmad by the rent of vijd. by the year. And he did fealty.

Fealty — William Rose acknowledged that he holds in like manner one acre of land in the Half-acres by the rent of vjd. by the year and one acre of land in Shepehoo by the rent of jd. by the year. And he did fealty.

Day — As yet the same William has a day until the feast of Easter to show his evidences in what way he holds the Garytes next his house in which he dwells.

Fealty — Thomas Pegeon acknowledged that he holds in like manner one Tenement in which he lives formerly Richard Peion's in Southstret by the rent of xiiijd. and one piece of land in Apeltonfeld containing two acres, more or less, abutting upon Landmad by the rent of ijd. by the year. And he did fealty.

Fealty  
Cheyney — Thomas Flemyng acknowledged that he holds in like manner two pieces of land lying in Benhook late Robert Kere's by the rent of xd. by the year one piece lying next the Portway & another piece lying next one piece of land late Robert Skynner's abutting upon Apiltonfeld towards the east. And the same Thomas Flemyng did fealty. [vijd. rent *added by another hand.*]

Fealty — John Clopton, Turnor, acknowledged that he holds a messuage with a garden appurtenant to it formerly John Maldon's, abutting upon Teyntoreshelle, by the rent of iijs. by the year. And the same John Clopton did fealty.

Inquisition — Taken by virtue of office by the oaths of Nicholas Haine, William Tanner, John Cook, Thomas Mynot, John Belh'm, William Rose, Thomas Pegeon, William Skotte, Thomas Flemyng, John Pypere, John Goos senior, Thomas Coupere, John Palmere, John Clerk, who say

Mercies  
vs. vjd. — upon their oath that Henry, Vicar of the church of Storteforde (vjd.), John Busshe senior (xijd.), John Skynnere senior (vjd.), Stephen Fabyan (iijd.), for the Tenement late John Wryghte's, the Tenant of the land late John Dreye's (xijd.), John Colyn (vjd.), John Turnor of Wyndhelle (vjd.), Thomas Goldston (iijd.) for a parcel of meadow at Hokyrhillebregge, the Tenant of the land of Manshepes (xijd.) make default in suit of Court.

Fealty — John Turnor of Wyndhelle acknowledged that he holds in like manner two & a half acres of land lying in Benhook, late John Skynnere's, one head abutting upon Aptonfeld, by the rent of vd. by the year. And he did fealty.

Attachments. — John Madyll (iiijd.) of Thorleye for trespass with five of his beasts in the lord's wheat in the Hyfeld, therefore in mercy.

Mercies  
vjs. ixd. — William Besemer (xiijd.) & his shepherd for trespass with a hundred & sixty sheep of his in the lord's wheat in the said field, therefore in mercy.

The same William Besemer (ijs.) for trespass with twenty-six beasts in the pasture in the stubble in Hyfeld on three occasions immediately after Autumn & in the time of John Coraunt farmer there, therefore in mercy. The same William (xld.) for trespass with four horses & four oxen, in the barley in Brambylfeld in the time of the same farmer, therefore in mercy.

Affeerers { Thomas Pegeon / John Palmere } who were sworn.

*To be Continued.*

# Subsidy Rolls for Hertfordshire.

## HUNDRED OF BRAUGHING. 1545.*

INDENTURE made the 28th October 37 Henry VIII. between Sr Henry Parker knt, Wm. Barlee, John Cock & George Hide, esquires, Commissioners appointed for the taxing & levying of the third payment of the Subsidy granted in the 34th & 35th years of Hen. VIII., etc., appointing William Hamond of Westmyll high collector of the said Hundred. The indenture recites that the Commissioners had divided the various hundreds in the County amongst themselves as follows:— Kayshoo was allotted to Sir Richard Page knt., John Conynsbye, John Brockett, Thos. Skipwith, Rich. Rayshow, Thos. Hemyng, & Henry Heydon, esqrs.; Hertford to Sr John Peryent, knt., John Cock Francis Southwell & John Kechen, esqrs.; Braughing to John Cock, Humph. Fitzherbert & the sd Sr Henry Parker, Wm. Barlee, & Geo. Hide esqrs.; Odsey to John Sewster, Geo. Hide, John Gyll & John Newport esqrs.; Bradwater to Sr John Peryent knt., Robt. Lytton, Edw. Brokett & John Kechen esqrs.; Half Hundred of Hitchen to Sr John Peryent knt, Robt. Lytton & Edw. Brokett esqrs., and Edwynstre to sd Sr Henry Parker knt., Wm. Barlee, Geo. Hide & John Gill esqrs.

STONDON. Henry Osbaston g. xijd. Rich. Norris l. ijd. John Downe g. xiiijd. Geo. Skyngull g. xiiijd. Henry Wybard l. ijd. Robt. Parnell g. xvjd. John Kyng g. xijd. Wm. Barford g. xvjd. Henry Rawsson l. vjd. John Hawkyn sen. l. viijd. Robt. Parnell g. xd. Rich. Dardℓ jun. g. ijd. Wm. Dardℓ g. iijd. Rich. Dardℓ sen. l. ijd. Agnes Skyngull, widow, g. iiijd. Agnes Gyls, wyddow, g. jd. John Gyls g. ijd. Thos. Schambroke g. ijd. John Wrytt l. vjd. Henry Barfote g. xijd. John Browne g. ijd. John Jarsay g. xijd. John Knyght g. iiijd. Wm. Skyngull g. xiiijd. Rich. Grene l. viijd. John Marschall g. iiijd. John Hawkyn, jun., g. ijd. John Wyte g. xvjd. Rich. Reynolde g. jd. Thos. Tylar g. iijd.

*The original is in the Public Record Office, the reference being "Lay Subsidies 121/171." As before, with these subsidies, I have used the letter "g" for goods, & "l" for lands.

Alse Andlaby vid. l. ij*d*. Andrew Wodrof g. iij*d*. Wm. Godfrey g. xiiij*d*. John Kyng g. xij*d*. Thos. Kyng l. ij*d*. Wm. Parnell g. xij*d*. Rich, Broke g. iiij*d*. Wm. Skatt'good g. x*d*. Wm. Lannam g. ij*d*. Steven Red g. x*d*. Humfrey Buxton g. xviij*d*. John Evenet g. ij*d*. Rich. Tylberry g. ij*d*. Thos. Mawden g. j*d*. Eliz. Charvat g. j*d*. John Arnolde g. xij*d*. Thos. Wenam l. ij*d*. John Wottun l. ij*d*. Robt. Crowche g. iiij*d*. John Gylson g. iiij*d*. Leonard Smartfot g. ij*d*. Thos. Parkar l. iiij*d*. Wm. Gren g. x*d*. Rich. Allis g. xvj*d*. Jas. Gyffyn g. j*d*. Wm. Jarsay l. ij*d*. John Bond g. iiij*d*. Thos. Chambarlayn l. iiij*d*. Thos. Lynsay g. x*d*. Humph. Isake g. xvj*d*. Robt. Bwke [? Buke] g. xij*d*. John Speryng, sen., g. x*d*. Ellyn Semar g. x*d*. Nich. Croxton g. ij*d*. Wm. Thuftyll g. ij*d*. Geo. Lavender g. xviij*d*. Nich. Barrey g. xij*d*. John Rumny g. xij*d*. Bon. Eccl'ie ij*d*. John Wilson g. ij*d*. Kath. Speryng vid. iiij*d*. Henry Stepney g. iiij*d*. Henry Vaghan g. ij*d*. Rich. Odell g. ij*d*. John Cokerell g. j*d*. Rich. Dardℇ, sen. l. ij*d*. John Hamond g. j*d*. Joan Gylson g. j*d*. John Makenest g. j*d*. Thos. Grene g. ij*d*. Robt. Broke g. j*d*. Henry Sawyer g. j*d*. John Stapull g. j*d*. Robt. Abbott g. j*d*. Wm. Lyden g. j*d*. Wm. Lyncey g. j*d*. Rich. Asmar g. iiij*d*. John Russell g. j*d*. Robt. Coke g. ij*d*. Rich Petter g. ij*d*. Edw. Godwyn g. ij*d*. Rich. Godwyn g. ij*d*.

*Pro anticipatione.* Thos. Howe l. xxxv*s*. John Manfeld xij*s* iiij*d*. Rich. Witherall xx*s*. John Skyngull xx*d*. John Adam iij*s*. iiij*d*. John Danyell iij*s*. iiij*d*. Thos. Haynes iij*s*. iiij*d*. Wm. Crowche iij*s*. iiij*d*. Rich. Crowche xij*s*. iiij*d*. Robt. Bedell, iij*s*. iiij*d*. John Bedell v*s*. iiij*d*. Robt. Grave v*s*. iiij*d*. Geffrey Smartfote iij*s*. iiij*d*. Robt. Wayte iij*s*. iiij*d*. Thos. Joyce iij*s*. iiij*d*. Thos. Mannyng iij*s*. iiij*d*. Edw. Tylar iij*s*. iiij*d*. John Senton iij*s*. iiij*d*. Wm. Archar iij*s*. iiij*d*. Thos. Crowche iij*s*. iiij*d*. Wm. Kyng iiij*s*. Rich. Fyschar xx*s*. Wm. Perry iij*s*. viij*d*. John Lamkyn iij*s*. iiij*d*. Thos. Felde iij*s*. viij*d*. Thos. Myles v*s*. John Brett xvij*s*. iiij*d*. John Parnell iij*s*. iiij*d*. Nycolas Kyrby vj*s*. viij*d*. Wm. Parnell iij*s*. viij*d*.

*Sum* xij*li*. xj*s*. vj*d*.

THUNDRIDGE. Robt. Myll xvj*d*. John Cokes x*d*. Thos. Reynolde, jun. xij*d*. Wm. Wood iij*d*. Wm. Haruey ij*d*. Thos. Brownes iiij*d*. John Brond ij*d*. Henry Cobham ij*d*. Henry Brett ij*d*. John Fust xij*d*. Nich. Grennell xij*d*. Wm. Halfhide iiij*d*. John Hawman j*d*. John Buttlar ij*d*. Alice Brond ij*d*. Bouis Ecclesie ij*d*.

*Pro anticipatione.* Wm. Reynold iij*s*. Christr. Alman v*s*. Thos. Reynold senior v*s*. iiij*d*. Thos. Hodge ij*s*. iiij*d*. John Reynold iij*s*. iiij*d*.

*Sum* xxvj*s*. iij*d*.

WIDEFORD. Rich. Spencer xij*d*. John None x*d*. Thos. Parnell xiiij*d*. Hugh Payne iij*s*. iiij*d*. John Cartar xij*d*. Thos. Lawney j*d*. Lamberd Nycholl ij*d*. Jas. Whyte xvj*d*. Hen. Whyte j*d*. John Coke j*d*. Henry Myllℇ iiij*d*. John Saranke iiij*d*. Joan Myllℇ vid. xviij*d*. Wm. Bennett ij*d*. John Wawlar ij*d*. Agnes Alyn j*d*. Eliz. Haynes ij*d*. John Ford j*d*. Steph. Adam xij*d*. Thos. Bennett ij*d*. Wm. Braunche j*d*. John Isake ij*d*. Margt. None widow l. ij*d*. Joan Parnell wid. j*d*. Robt. Gyllett xij*d*. John Fonten ij*d*. Edw. Lyster ij*d*. John Toular j*d*. Lawrence Burchat j*d*.

*Pro anticipatione.* John Addames vj*s*. Thos. Eliott v*s*. iiij*d*. Thos. Dardℇ iiij*s*. iiij*d*. Robt. Adam iij*s*. iiij*d*. Thos. Eliott iij*s*. iiij*d*.

*Sum* xxxvij*s*. v*d*.

STANSTED. John Deve g. xij*d*. John Bennett x*d*. Wm. Bredgil x*d*. Robt. Whytnall xij*d*. John Marse l. vj*d*. John Spencer xij*d*. Eliz. Grave wid. xij*d*. Joan Cheyney wid. iij*d*. Rich. Copar ij*d*. Thos. Grosshor ij*d*. John Yardlyng, Jun. j*d*. Henry Turnar ij*d*. John Taylar j*d*. Thos. Haruey j*d*. Wm. Gylderson j*d*. John Yardlyn, sen. ij*d*. Wm. Gylderson sen. j*d*. Henry Spencer j*d*. John Smythe ij*d*. Thos. Symson j*d*. Robt. Symson j*d*. Robt. Chapman ij*d*. Edm. Haruey ij*d*. Rich. Ede ij*d*. Thos. Jacobe j*d*. Nich. Jhonson ij*d*. Jas. Gylderson j*d*. Thos. Burnap xij*d*. Tho. Atkynson xvj*d*. Edw. Cornwall xviij*d*. Olyver Symson iiij*d*.

*Pro anticipatione.* John Rodes esquyer iij*li*. vj*s*. viij*d*. John Burnoppe v*s*. iiij*d*. Robt. Grave xiiij*s*. viij*d*. Thos. Nobbes v*s*. iiij*d*. Wm. Dyer v*s*. viij*d*. Wm. Grave iij*s*. iiij*d*. John Grave iij*s*. iiij*d*. Agnes Haynes wid. v*s*. iiij*d*.

*Sum* vj*li*. ij*s*. vij*d*.

GELSTON. Simon Mede g. xiiij*d*. Geo. Underwode iiij*d*. Nich. Terlyng iiij*d*. Robt. Doweshed iiij*d*. Raffe Fotte ij*d*. Thos. Fotte ij*d*. Rich. Bennett ij*d*. Humph. Parris g. ij*d*. Wm. Cramphorne j*d*. Geo. Rayston j*d*. Bonis Ecclesie iiij*d*. Wm. Dalton iij*d*.

*Pro anticipatione.* Wm. Cramphorne v*s*. viij*d*. Robt. Cooke xiij*s*. iiij*d*. Edw. Browne iiij*s*.

*Sum* xxvj*s*. iiij*d*.

HUNESDON. Thos. Howe g. xviij*d*. Henry Hyde g. iij*s*. iiij*d*. Thos. Thurgood xij*d*. Thos. Beremā iiij*d*. Thos. Wood x*d*. Nich. Wood x*d*. Edw. More l. viij*d*. Thos. Lylldey l. ij*d*. Thos. Lauender g. iij*d*. Thos. Addames g. j*d*. Agnes Dyer j*d*. Thos. Grave j*d*. Robt. Elyot l. ij*d*. John Basseley g. iij*d*. Rich. Nicholson j*d*. Rich. Ree ij*d*. Rich. Allis x*d*. Wm. Dyer l. ij*d*. Wm. Hyggynson iij*d*. Bonis Ecclesie iiij*d*.

*Pro anticipatione.* John Carye, Esq., c*s*. John Grene xiij*s*. iiij*d*. Thos. Warde xiij*s*. iiij*d*. John Rennyngton iij*s*. iiij*d*. Thos. Payvey iij*s*. iiij*d*. Rich. Grawe iij*s*. viij*d*.

*Sum* vij*li*. viij*s*. v*d*.

SABRIDGEWORTH. Rich. Garlond g. xij*d*. John Wrytte iiij*d*. Symon Turnar iiij*d*. Henry Grawe ij*d*. John Androw ij*d*. Wm. Byllyngham xiiij*d*. John Portor iij*d*. John Cooke 'de boukes' x*d*. Rich. Noke xvj*d*. Nich. Cramphorne xvj*d*. Wm. Brawne iij*s*. iiij*d*. John Addam 'de Nones' xij*d*. Rich. Haynes iiij*d*. John Wallar xiiij*d*. Kath. Pawelay j*d*. John Coke iij*d*. Nich. Thurgood ij*d*. John Perrey iij*s*. iiij*d*. Thos. Baselay ij*d*. Robt. Androw j*d*. Wm. Wallar iij*s*. iiij*d*. Edw. Beltod x*d*. Thos. Wybard xviij*d*. John Monke, sen. xij*d*. John Pryklow ij*d*. Bastian Coke j*d*. Rich. Fott j*d*. Kath. Gladwyn ij*d*. Ralph Coke xij*d*. Margt. Galloway iiij*d*. Geo. Turnar iiij*d*. John Norton ij*d*. Wm. Dewsett ij*d*. Wm. Taylar ij*d*. Geo. Cramphorne xvj*d*. Wm. Tredgeld x*d*. Joan Chawcey wid. xiiij*d*. Robt. Abbott ij*d*. Thos. Charvell xvj*d*. Rich. Beltod iij*d*. Symon Harryson ij*d*. John Monke ij*d*. John Cramphorne ij*d*. Henry Rigerbye ij*d*. John Cramphorne, Jun. iij*d*. George Whytbye ij*d*. Joan Wallar, wid. x*d*. John Corney ij*d*. Symon Turnar jun. j*d*. Thos. Payneley j*d*. Michael Wallar j*d*. Thos. Cooke ij*d*. Ralph Perrye iij*s*. iiij*d*. John Foster iiij*d*. Ralph Addam iij*d*. Geoffrey Addam ij*d*. Hugh Edward j*d*. Ralph

Crowche iij*d*. Thos. Cooke j*d*. John Wotton j*d*. Wm. Blake j*d*. John Motte iij*d*. John Turner j*d*. Nich. Fotte iij*d*. John Blake iij*d*. Nich. Browne iiij*d*. Jas. Spylman j*d*. John Broke ij*d*. Robt. Berd xvj*d*. Robt. Monke ij*d*. John Dyer ij*d*. Thomas Brikenar xvj*d*. Thos. Goodaye iiij*d*. Henry Fott ij*d*. Rich. Colloppe xvj*d*. John Crowche ij*d*. John Aylett xij*d*. Wm. Clare x*d*. Wm. Jenyn j*d*. Rich. Beltod ij*d*. John Audrow j*d*. Thos. Haruey j*d*. John Beltod ij*d*. Rich. Hadesley ij*d*. Geo. Mathew x*d*. Wm. Gune iiij*d*. John Whetnoll ij*d*. Dodman Byllay iiij*d*. Thos. Archar j*d*. Thos. Waylett ij*d*. John Hunter j*d*. Agnes Addam l. ij*d*. Wm. Grave j*d*. Wm. Perse ij*d*.

*Pro anticipatione.* John Adam of Baseles iij*s*. iiij*d*. Thos. Blake iij*s*. iiij*d*. Wm. Cramphorne xiij*s*. iiij*d*. Wm. Dowsett iij*s*. iiij*d*. Edw. Leventhropp Esq. xl*s*. John Chawcye Esq. xl*s*. Robt. Gooday xxvj*s*. viij*d*. Robt. Nodd℮ xvij*s*. iiij*d*. John Perry xiij*s*. iiij*d*. John Payne xiij*s*. iiij*d*. John Beltod xiij*s*. iiij*d*. Agnes Au'ell xiij*s*. iiij*d*. Henry Jonson xvj*s*. viij*d*. John Hellam v*s*. iiij*d*. John Dyer v*s*. iiij*d*. John Gybb iiij*s*. Dionis Adam iiij*s*. viij*d*. Rich. Hubbard iij*s*. iiij*d*.

*Sum* xiiij*li*. viij*s*. vij*d*.

WARE. John Squyer g. iij*d*. Wm. Shereleye l. viij*d*. Thos. Denten g. x*d*. Thos. More g. iij*d*. Abraham Vele xiij*d*. John Mawcome Scotte iiij*d*. Nich Adlyngton j*d*. John Haygard ij*d*. Allyn Coston ij*d*. Wm. Farrar iiij*d*. Roger Buclond iiij*d*. Thos. Hormed ij*d*. John Dyxson xij*d*. Wm. Juster x*d*. Rich. Barratt xiiij*d*. John Newton iij*s*. iiij*d*. Edw. Nicolson iiij*d*. Robt. Art xviij*d*. Nich. Browne xij*d*. Rich. Wryght xvij*d*. Morgayn Vaughan iiij*d*. Robt. Huk℮ xviij*d*. Robt. Howe iiij*d*. Robt. Grene l. ij*d*. John Ford ij*d*. Wm. Valentyne l. iiij*d*. Robt. Daye x*d*. Peter Addam j*d*. Jas. Downyng j*d*. Thos. Edmam xiiij*d*. Thos. Tollynson iiij*d*. Wm. Walkyn iij*d*. Wm. Lyan j*d*. John Wrennocke iiij*d*. Thos. Poynard iiij*d*. Rich. Browne j*d*. Rich. Dane iiij*d*. Jas. Broughton ij*d*. Wm. Gyldner Jun. xij*d*. Morgan Allott ij*d*. Geo. Beuys ij*d*. Rich. Browne iiij*d*. Thos. Stele j*d*. Edw. Awbone ij*d*. Jas. Harrison iiij*d*. John Armerer j*d*. John Crandfeld ij*d*. Wm. Taylor l. vj*d*. Rich. Bason g. x*d*. John Byse g. j*d*. Miles Gallaway iiij*d*. Rich. Jenynes g. j*d*. Wm. Yeman g. x*d*. Christr. Dixson x*d*. Henry Browne x*d*. Rich. Helbey j*d*. John Boughton j*d*. John Pekering j*d*. John Davey g. xviij*d*. Wm. Whysterd j*d*. Thos. Taylar j*d*. John Smythe j*d*. Robt. Pereson j*d*.

VPLAND. Rich. Standlay j*d*. Wm. Fesse l. iiij*d*. Robt. Joplyn xij*d*. Edw. Crosse g. xiij*s*. iiij*d*. Robt. Poynyn xiiij*d*. Wm. Danyll xiiij*d*. Robt. Dent[on?] ij*d*. Wm. Browne 'fredenyson' iiij*d*. Humph. Morris xij*d*. Thos. Cok℮ xvj*d*. Wm. Heryn j*d*. Giles Cock℮ ij*d*. John Adkyn j*d*. Rich. Odall als Fonte j*d*. Rich. Bull Jun. ij*d*. John Tunbridge ij*d*. Robt. Wilson j*d*. John Penyngton j*d*. John Cowp j*d*. John Hormede j*d*. Geo. Sawman iiij*d*. John Smyth iiij*d*. Thos. Cock℮ ij*d*. Thos. Watt℮ xij*d*. Thos. Ford iiij*d*. Henry Coles ij*d*. Wm. Clerke xij*d*. John Coryer ij*d*. John Abdell j*d*. Thos. Graue iiij*d*. Wm. Wren x*d*. Thos. Hochyn iij*d*. Wm. Mell℮ ij*d*. John Awncell xiiij*d*. John Person x*d*. John Pavye iiij*d*. Wm. Waterman iiij*d*. Ralph Thurgood ij*d*. Nich. Thurgood ij*d*. Robt. Thurgood ij*d*. Thos. Thurgood iiij*d*. Wm. Bekson ij*d*. John Hodge j*d*. Robt. Fox j*d*. Thos. Hodge j*d*. Robt. Pavye iiij*d*. Edw. Lilleye iij*d*. John Yerdley ij*d*. John

Renold sen. xiiij*d*. John Reynold iiij*d*. John Reynold jun. ij*d*. Robt. Croche ij*d*. John Bennett x*d*. Wm. Hele j*d*. John Arman j*d*. John Baseley j*d*. Wm. Renold ij*d*. Peter Gill l. ij*d*. John Androo jun. ij*d*. John Mill𐞷 de Aswellberye g. iij*s*. iiij*d*. Rich. Andro j*d*. Wm. Androw j*d*.

*Pro anticipatione.* Tho. Birche g. xiij*s*. iiij*d*. Thos. Gottred iij*s*. iiij*d*. Michael Mede iiij*s*. Thos. Pygram iij*s*. iiij*d*. John Harvye sen. xiij*s*. iiij*d*. Rich. Broke xl*s*. Edw. Atkynson xiij*s*. iiij*d*. Henry Adam xiij*s*. iiij*d*. Wm. Spencer xiij*s*. iiij*d*. John Harvye Jun. xvj*s*. viij*d*. Wm. Geldener xxxiij*s*. iiij*d*. Wm. Pike xiij*s* iiij*d*. John Marshe xvj*s*. viij*d*. John Bradley xxvj*s*. viij*d*. Thos. Pellam xiij*s*. iiij*d*. Rich. Bromleye xiij*s*. iiij*d*. Thos. Ferrer xiij*s*. iiij*d*. Thos. Gonn iij*s*. iiij*d*. John Binsted ij*s*. viij*d*. Thos. Castell vj*s*. Wm. Harvye xiij*s*. iiij*d*. Robt. Crosse xliiij*s*. John Hanford xiij*s*. iiij*d*. Oliver Franklyn lxvj*s*. viij*d*. Thos. Lenerd xiiij*s*. viij*d*. John Griffen iij*s*. iiij*d*. John Canon Jun. iij*s*. iiij*d*. John Pott iij*s*. iiij*d*. Wm. Kirbye v*s*. Thos. Kyng xiij*s*. iiij*d*. Rich. Bull xiij*s*. iiij*d*. John Cromplyn iij*s*. iiij*d*. John Androw xvj*s*. John Crouche xiij*s*. iiij*d*. John Cock𐞷 v*s*. Robt. Skyngull v*s*. Thos. Huchyn iij*s*. iiij*d*. John Spencer iiij*s*. viij*d*. Rich. Hodge iiij*s*. Wm. Spencer xvj*s*. viij*d*. Robt. Spencer xiij*s*. iiij*d*. Robt. Eliott iij*s*. iiij*d*. Geoffrey Thurgood v*s*. John Campe xiij*s*. iiij*d*. Rich. Chambour drouer vj*s*.

*Sum* xxxij*li*. xj*s*. iij*d*.

THORLEE. Thos. Ive g. xvj*d*. Agnes Willeye xij*d*. John Willeye x*d*. Robt. Ive xiiij*d*. Christr. Soles ij*d*. Wm. Osborne xij*d*. John Spratt j*d*. John Allys xij*d*. Edw. Osborn ij*d*. Rich. Valentyne j*d*. John Laye xij*d*. John Parton iiij*d*. Oswald Davye xiiij*d*. Robt. Dauye iij*d*. Thos. Selleye x*d*. Edw. Saryng xij*d*. John Bullok j*d*. John Monke j*d*. Bonis Ecclesie ij*d*. John Ive ij*d*. Elizabeth [blank] l. ij*d*.

*Pro anticipatione.* Alexander Seynt Jon Esq. xliij*s*. Thos. Tonbridge xvj*s*.

*Sum* lxxj*s*. j*d*.

WESTMYLL. Rich. Stafford g. xvj*d*. Robt. Carlet clerk l. ij*d*. Edw. Bogitt iij*s*. iiij*d*. Wm. Rede ij*d*. John Newman jun. iiij*d*. Wm. Harington xvj*d*. John Churche sen. xvj*d*. Geo. Hamond xij*d*. Philip Carter iiij*d*. Wm. Hamond de Gailers xiiij*d*. John Hamond his son j*d*. Wm. Browne xvj*d*. Joan Hodge wid. iij*d*. John Newman sen. xij*d*. Geo. Newman j*d*. Tho. Lightfote ij*d*. John Churche Jun. ij*d*. Thos. Bound x*d*. John Newman Jun. l. vj*d*. Adam Horwode iij*d*. Thos. Bennett j*d*. Francis Cromer j*d*. John Donn iiij*d*. Agnes Chepfild j*d*. Roger Hamond xiiij*d*. Wm. Scott ij*d*. John Browne xvj*d*. Geo. Daye x*d*. Rich. Cherye ij*d*. Walter Adam l. vj*d*. Joan Pascall l. vj*d*. Wm. Hamond ij*d*. Thos. Browne l. vj*d*. Nich. Halfhide xiiij*d*. Edw. Awncell xvj*d*. John Gilson j*d*. Rich. Stowton j*d*. Basill Hamond l. ij*d*.

*Pro anticipatione.* Tho. Churche iij*s*. iiij*d*. Geo. Hamond xvj*s*. John Hammond de Miles iiij*s*. Robt. Awncell iij*s*. iiij*d*. Wm. Hamond v*s*. iiij*d*. Rich. Baker xxiiij*s*. John Hamond v*s*. viij*d*.

*Sum* iiij*li*. vj*s*. vj*d*.

ESTWIKE. Humph. Kenseye iijs. iiijd. John Chamberlayne xvjd. Thos. Cramphorne xiiijd. Joan Norrys wid. iiijd. Geo. Jonson iiijd. John Sawell ijd. John Sawell jun. jd. Ralph Jorneman iijd. Joan Underhill widow ijd.

*Pro anticipatione.* Rich. Pike g. iijs. iijd.

*Sum xs. vjd.*

STORTFORD. Geo. Hawkyn g. iijs. iiijd. John South xd. John Marion jun. ijd. Matrone Graye jd. Robt. Cockͤ ijd. Rich. Master xd. Robt. Noswall ijd. John Skillyngham sen. ijd. Thos. Golborne iiijd. John Wright ijd. Thos. Marion xd. John Ive, jd. Robt. Wod ijd. Wm. Cowley jd. Thos. Nayler xijd. Thos. Eire ijd. Ralph Starkyn xvjd. Wm. Gateward xijd. John Turner jd. Henry Mervell ijd. Thos. Mede jd. Robt. Mede his son ijd. Thos. Bore ijd. John Newman ijd. John Cocckͤ ijd. Wm. Newman jd. Leonard Skillingham ijd. Geo. Warren ijd. Thos. Mede xiiijd. Thos. Goodwyn jd. Thos. Brett jd. Wm. Sparrow iiijd. John Crabbe iiijd. Rich. Crowe ijd. Peter Dowe xvjd. John Collyng-wood ijd. Lambert Marten ijd. John Jacob jun. ijd. Andrew Clifton xvjd. John Kynge iiijd. John Albert iij l. Nich. Marden iijd. Nich. Renold jd. Matthew Caladye iijs. iiijd. Rich. South l. iiijd. Thos. Wysmer ijd. Thos. Snowe iijs. iiijd. Wm. Hetton xd. Roger Trennā iiijd. Robt. Pake ijd. Robt. Goldynge ijd. Robt. Hore ijd. Rich. Tebald ijd. Thos. Gates xviijd. John Payne ijd. John Marshall iiijd. Thos. Papes ijd. Thos. Stockͤ ijd. Thos. Chaundeler Jun. xd. John Hillͤ ijd. Ralph Castell iiijd. John Snow Jun. iiijd. John Cheyneye iiijs. viijd. John Warren g. ijd. Wm. Walter ijd. Edw. Browne xvjd. John Dewyard iiijd. Thos. Helgaye iiijd. Thos. Dewyard iiijd. John Wryght ijd. Robt. Woode jd. John Jacob sen. xvjd. Geo. Jacob xijd. Edw. Colyer jd. Wm. Northfok iiijd. Rich. Gibb l. viijd. Thos. Dawson, ijd. Rich. Robert iiijd. John Snowe sen, iijd. John Boyere xd. Joan Rokell iijd. John Newman de Rystret l. viijd. Rich. Ward g. xd. Philip Marshall iiijd. Wm. White jun. iiijd. Matrone Elyott iiijd. Edw. Willey iijs. iiijd. Thos. Crabb iiijd. Wm. Pigott xd. Wm. Pilston xvjd. Bonis Ecclesie viijd. Cornelys Jon' stranger iiijd. Jas. Frauncͤ xd. Thos. Wood ijd. Matrone Ward ijd. Wm. Swetmā ijd. Matrone Nelthorpe ijd. Bruere of Hokerell ijd.

*Pro anticipatione.* Geo. Tomson xjs. iiijd. John Cramphorne iijs. iiijd. John Marion sen. xiiijs. viijd. John Smyth vs. Esabell Woode wid. iijs. viijd. Thos. Bulfame ijs. iiijd. Alice Pilsten wid. xxijs. Geo. Carleton xiijs. iiijd. John Grene iijs. viijd. John Hawkyn vs. Thos. Marshell iiijs. viijd. Isabell Whippull iijs. viijd. Nich. Redwood xiijs. iiijd. Robt. Walter iijs. iiijd. John Abbott iijs. iiijd. John Lawncey vjs. John Whippull xiijs. iiijd. Thos. Chaundeler sen. xiiijs. viijd. Rich. Glascok xiiijs. viijd. Ralph Clerke iijs. iiijd. Robt. Goodaye iiijs. iiijd. Thos. Patmer xiijs. iiijd. Thos. Carron xxiijs. iiijd. John Willeye xxijs. Rich. Bedwell xiijs. viijd. John Bayford iiijs. John Miller xijs. iiijd. John Smythe iijs. iiijd. Robt. Addessen vs. John Allys iijs. iiijd. John Eliott xijs. Rich. Marian iiijs. Thos. Payne iijs. iiijd. Rich. Pilsten xxd. Philip Monyen iijs. iiijd. Bonis Ecclesie ijs. Thos. Glascok iijs. John Jerdfild iiijs. Rich. Jerdfild.

*Sum xviijli. xvs. vjd.*

BRAUGHING. John Woode iij*d*. Wm. Mede iij*d*. John Meriton ij*d*. John Broke ij*d*. John Senior ij*d*. Wm. Pett de Darfell ij*d*. Wm. Pett Sexston ij*d*. Rich. Strange ij*d*. Wm. Phipp ij*d*. John Frenshe ij*d*. Thos. Norman ij*d*. Wm. Blossome ij*d*. Thos. Ward ij*d*. Thos. Merytong ij*d*. Henry Hare ij*d*. John Millington j*d*. Wm. Haynes j*d*. John Castell j*d*. Ralph Daye j*d*. Thos. Birle ij*d*. Hugh Pett j*d*. Robt. Bolton j*d*. Rich. Newman j*d*. John Warren j*d*. Kath. Broke j*d*. Rich. Cole j*d*. Edm. Hamond j*d*. Wm. Mathew j*d*. Wm. Bedell j*d*. John Jorden j*d*. Rich. Dawton j*d*. Wm. Gillett ij*d*. Rich. Warwyke j*d*. John Toogud ij*d*. Rich. Bryttelbanke j*d*. Rich. Byrlee j*d*. Henry Meriton j*d*. John Marsan ij*d*. Wm. Broke de le Ford l. viij*d*. Agnes Broke wid. l. viij*d*. Edw. Wharton l. iij*d*. John Roo l. iiij*d*. Wm. Hinton l. iij*d*. Bartholomew Broke l. ij*d*. Wm. Broke de [Hull?] l. ij*d*. Rich. Daye g. xvj*d*. John Roote g. xvj*d*. John Warner xvj*d*. John Hille xvj*d*. Robt. Jennyns xiiij*d*. John Holland xij*d*. Rich. Broke xij*d*. Rich. Blossme xij*d*. Wm. Wattye xij*d*. Alice Clifton xij*d*. Rich. Cocke x*d*. Thos. Held x*d*. Thos. Foster x*d*. John Thurgoode x*d*. John Meriton x*d*. Wm. Wall x*d*. Wm. Hadeleye x*d*. Wm. Lodge x*d*. Oliver Stone iiij*d*. Ralph Broke iiij*d*. John Knyght iiij*d*. Thos. de Darsall iiij*d*. Robt. Bedell iiij*d*. Robt. Crouche iiij*d*. Thos. Rede iiij*d*. Geo. Hamond iiij*d*. Agnes Hamond iiij*d*. Henry Thorne iiij*d*. John Parnell iiij*d*. Henry Clerke xij*d*.

*Pro anticipatione.* Humph. Fitzherbert esq. l. xl*s*. John Hampton vj*s*. Rich. Grene x*s*. John Gailer v*s*. Thos. Warner xv*s*. iiij*d*. Henry Edmund iiij*s*. iiij*d*. Wm. Bond v*s*. iiij*d*. John Page v*s*. iiij*d*. Wm. Danyell iij*s*. viij*d*. Joan Clifton wid. iij*s*. iiij*d*. Wm. Cote xiij*s*. iiij*d*. Wm. Bedwell iij*s*. iiij*d*.

Sum vij*li*. v*s*. ij*d*.

Sum total cxij*li*. x*s*. xiij*d*.

[*Endorsed*] Hanc certific' liberaver' hic infrano'iat' Comiss' xiij° die Nouembr' Anno xxxvij° p man. infrano'iat' Willi Barley.

# Inquisitiones Post Mortem.

### THOMAS AUNCELL.

[*Inq. p.m.* 5 *Jas.* 1, *part* 1, *No.* 146.]

Inquisition taken at Chippingbarnet, co. Herts. 2 Nov. 5 Jas. I, [1607] before Philip Glascock, esq., escheator, after the death of Thomas Auncell, by the oath of Robt. Eames, gent., Geo. Carpenter. John Besowth, Miles Gase, Wm. Alea *alias* Cooke, John Hall, Tho. Shackmaple, Tho. Gowlde, Wm. Willett, Ralph Axtell, Francis Mayne, Edw. Mayne, Rich. Whelpeley, John Brewer and Wm. Cock who say that

Thomas Auncell was seised of the manor of Ickleford and appurtenances in Ickleford, Hitchin, Shitlington, Pirton and Hollowell in the counties of Hertf. and Bedf. & of divers houses and lands belonging thereto; four barns, two 'les Hoggestyes' and three 'les Hovells' with close called Facks, containing 2 acres in Ickleford; one pightell containing one acre in Hitchin adjoining closes of meadow called Patchetts; six acres in Hitchin in Walserfeild; one water-mill called Oughton Myll *alias* Westmyll and 40 acres thereto belonging; moiety of a messuage with appurtenances in Ickleford, Shitlington & Pirton; 40 acres in Ickleford, Hitchin, Pirton, Shitlington & Hollowell late purchased of Wm. Couingsbye; 6 acres meadow and pasture in Shitlington late in tenure of Robt. Cooper; 4 acres meadow & pasture called Snayleswell in Ickleford, 10 acres arable land in divers pieces in the parish & fields of Arlesey, co. Bedf.; four acres pasture in Ickleford now in tenure of Wm. Auncell son of said Thomas; four acres in Ickleford, Hitchin, Shitlington & Hollowell also in tenure of said Wm. Auncell; and a close of pasture called Pennes in Hitchin, late purchased of [*blank*] Bowyer.

The said Tho. Auncell, before he died, conveyed to said Wm. his elder son and heir apparent a messuage in Ickleford in which one Daniel Knott now dwells & 8 acres in same tenure being part of the manor of Ickleford & the said 4 acres pasture & the 4 acres in Ickleford etc. in tenure of said Wm.

Said Tho. Auncell & one Thos. Auncell his younger son, afterwards conveyed (by deed dat. 10 July 42 Eliz. [1600] & in consideration of an intended marriage between said Thos. Auncell jun<sup>r</sup> & Alice Denton dau. of Rich. Denton of Barton, co. Bedf. yeoman & by way of jointure of said Alice) to Matthew Denton then of Barton, co. Bedf. yeoman, the messuage in which s<sup>d</sup> Tho. Auncell jun<sup>r</sup> then dwelt, being parcel of the manor of Ickleford, 4 barns etc, and Facks close, two closes of meadow called Eyres & Rivers with a grove adjoining containing 15 acres in Ickleford & Shitlington, close called Patchetts containing 5 acres in Hitchin, the said Pightell containing one acre adjacent to same & said 6 acres in Walserfeild, close called Lewyns containing 6 acres and Jewells close containing 3 roods & 40 acres in Northfeild in Ickleford, one acre & one rood in Walserfeild, 30 acres in the Homefeild in Ickleford, 28 acres in the Werkfeild in Ickleford of which 18 acres are parcel of the water mill & 40 acres above mentioned & the residue are parcel of the manor of Ickleford, 10 acres arable land in Pirton, 10 acres in field called Great Oughton bottom in Shitlington, parcel of the said mill & 40 acres, to the use of the said Tho. Auncell jun<sup>r</sup> & Alice Denton & their heirs & in default of issue, to the right heirs of said Thos. Auncell jun<sup>r</sup> for ever. And afterwards the said marriage was solemnised & said Thos. jun<sup>r</sup> & Alice became seised of said premises.

Said Tho. Auncell sen<sup>r</sup> (by deed dat. 11 July 42 Eliz.) conveyed to Wm. Furryan of Ickleford yeoman & his heirs the whole residue of the manor of Ickleford & all other his lands & tenements in Ickleford, Hitchin, Pirton, Shitlington & Hollowell (reserving to said Thos. sen<sup>r</sup> all lands in the hamlet of Cadwell in the parishes of Hollowell & Shitlington & a messuage & 6 acres in Ickleford in tenure of John Knott & 43 acres in the Northfeild in Ickleford, 6 acres in Shitlington in tenure of Robt. Cooper, 4 acres called Snayleswell, 9 acres & a half in Walserfield, 5 acres in Pirton in tenure of Laurence Hurst parcel of a piece of land called Hamberge piece, Oughton Myll *alias* Westmyll

& 12 acres in Shitlington in tenure of Wm. Furryan, miller, parcel of said Mill & 40 acres) to the use of said Thos. Auncell sen$^r$ & Agnes then his wife, for their lives & the survivor of them, remainder to Thos. Auncell jun$^r$ & his heirs male, remainder to Edward Auncell son of said Thos. Auncell sen$^r$ & his heirs male, remainder to the right heirs of Thos. Auncell jun$^r$ & Edw. Auncell for ever, by virtue of which deed said Thos. sen$^r$ & Agnes his wife were seised of all said premises. Said Agnes still survives & said Tho. Auncell jun$^r$ & Alice now his wife still survive.

Said Tho. Auncell sen$^r$ on 10 Nov. 2 Jas. [1604] in consideration of a marriage between Edward Auncell his son & Susan Rayner dau. of Richard Rayner clerk, conveyed to John Stringer & Rich. Lawndye the said messuage & 6 acres in tenure of John Knott & 30 acres parcel of the lands reserved in the last recited deed, to the use of said Edward & Susan for life & the survivor of them, & after to their heirs, with remainder to the right heirs of said Edward for ever. And afterwards the said marriage took place, by virtue of which said Edward & Susan were seised of said premises & both still survive.

Thos. Auncell sen$^r$ on 20 Nov. 2 Jas. by another deed conveyed to said John Stringer & Rich. Laundy all residue of the lands named in the second above recited indenture except as therein reserved to the use of said Thos. sen$^r$ for life & after to the use of said Edw. Auncell & his heirs for ever.

Thos. Auncell sen$^r$ made his will dated [blank] & devised said Mill called Westmill & 12 acres to said Edw. & his heirs for ever, & died 18 Sept. last past. William Auncell is eldest son & next heir & at the time of his fathers death was aged 40 years & more.

The manor of Ickleford, lands etc., are held of the Master, Fellows & Scholars of S$^t$ John's College, Cambridge, as of their manor of Ram'wyke, co. Herts. at the yearly rent of 11$d$. and are worth per ann. £5 clear. The two barns, hoggestyes & hovells & close called Facks are held of [blank] as of his manor of Doddingsell at yearly rent of 3$s$. & are worth 2$s$. per annum clear. Said pightell & 6 acres in Walserfeild are held of Margt. Elrington widow, as of her manor of Wimbley at yearly rent of 5$s$. & are worth 7$s$. per ann. clear. Oughton Mill & 40 acres etc. are held of (blank) as of the Monastery of Ramsey at yearly rent of 54$s$. 4$d$. & are worth 66$s$. 8$d$. per ann. clear. The 40 acres in Ickleford, Hitchin, Pirton, Shitlington & Hollowell late bought of Wm. Coningesby are held of the Master, Fellows & Scholars of S$^t$ John's, Cambridge at yearly rent of 12$d$. & are worth 6$s$. per ann. clear. Pasture called Snayleswell is held of Tho. Dockray esq. as of his manor of Pirton, at yearly rent of 4$d$. & is worth 4$s$. per ann. clear. The 4 acres pasture in tenure of Wm. Auncell are held of the Master etc. of S$^t$ John's College, Cambridge at yearly rent of 1$d$. & are worth . . . per ann. clear. The 4 acres in Ickleford also in tenure of said Wm. Auncell are held of Trinity College as of the manor of [blank] but by what rent is unknown. The 10 acres in the fields of Arlesey are held of Tho. Emery gent. as of his manor of Arlesey at the yearly rent of 2$d$. & are worth . . . clear. Pennes close in Hitchin is held of said Margt. Elrington as of her manor of Wembley at yearly rent of 21$d$. & is worth 4$s$. per ann. clear.

# Marriage Licences.
## Archdeaconry of St. Albans.
### By A. E. GIBBS.
(Continued from Page 240.)

**1685**

September 29. Thomas Homes of Hemsted, bachelor, and Mary Element of Hearding, maiden; at St. Albans. Walhan Element of Hearding, tailor, a surety.

October 8. Francis Harding of St. Andrews, Hertford, maltmaker, bachelor, aged about 30 years, and Ellen Hollis of All Hallows, Hertford, spinster, aged about 35 years, having neither father nor mother living; at St. Andrews or All Saints, Hertford, or the Abby Church of St. Albans. Wheeler Budd of St. Albans, a surety.

October 10. Jeremiah Gladman of King's Langley, yeoman, bachelor, aged about 29 years and Grace Young of Sandridge, spinster, aged about 21 or 22 years, daughter of [*blank*] Young, yeoman; with her parents' consent; at Sandridge or St. Albans. Richard Beach of St. Albans, victualler, a surety.

November 21. Robert Bently and Mary Briddon of Mergate Street; at St. Albans. Richard Waller and Thomas Briddon of Mergate Street, sureties.

November 30. John Bedford of Hemel Hemsted, and Mary Wildes of the same; at St. Albans. William Wildes of St. Albans, a surety.

**1685-6**

January 9. Thomas Aker of St. Stephens, and Sara Deakon of the same, spinster; at St. Stephens.

January 23. George Baldock of Stotfold, co. Bedford, "cordwainder," and Susanna Phipp of Norton; at Norton. John Bennet [*signed* Bennitt] of Stotfold, "cordwainder," a surety.

March 4. John Crouch of Wethamstead, yeoman, and Sarah Bruton, spinster, daughter of Edward Bruton of the same; at Greate Yate *alias* Lawrence Yate or Whethamstead. Phillip Marshall of Harding *alias* Harpenden, mealman, a surety.

March 5. A signed and partly filled in allegation of John Crouch of Sandridge, yeoman. Bride's name not given. Same surety.

March 17. John Hawkins of Redborne, husbandman, bachelor, aged about 21 and a half years, son of John Hawkins of the same, and Mary Shepheard of the same, spinster, aged about 22 years, daughter of Robert Shepheard, yeoman; at Redbourn, St. Michaels, or the Abby Church. Richard Smith of Redborne, husbandman, aged about 25 years, a surety.

**1686**

March 26. John Johnson of Watford, widower, and Christian Cowley of the same, spinster, aged 23 years; at Watford, Rickmersworth, Bushey or St. Stevens. Edward Kinder of St. Albans, butcher, a surety.

April 2. William Warr and Ann Roads of Winslow; at Winslow. Thomas White and Robert Mitchell [*signed* Michell] of Winslow, sureties.

April 10. James Hannell of Redbourne, grocer, widower, and Dorothy Halsey of Flamstead, maiden, daughter of Thomas Halsey; at Redbourne or St. Michaels. William Doe, a surety.

April 28. Edmund Wood, Vicar of Sandridge, bachelor, and Mrs. Bridgett Witsey of Wethamstead, spinster, aged about 22 years; with consent of her mother, Mrs. Witsey, widow; at Sandridge or St. Albans. John Seares of St. Albans, yeoman, a surety.

May 1. John Lawrence of King's Walden, bachelor, and Lidia Welsh of the same, spinster; at King's Walden or Hennell Hempstead. John Welsh of the same, yeoman, her father, and Robert Davey of St. Peters, gent., sureties.

May 1. Jeremiah Newman of Abbots Langley, yeoman, and Hester Babb, spinster; at Abbots Langley or St. Michaels. Ephraim Babb of Abbots Langley, yeoman, her father, a surety.

June 6. Daniel Foard of Abbots Langley, labourer, and Elisabeth Newman of the same; at Abbots Langley or St. Albans. Thomas Barrowson [or Borrowson] of Abbots Langley, labourer, a surety.

June 7. Jonas Boveingdon of King's Langley, yeoman, and Grace Bigg of Chesham, co. Buckingham, spinster. Richard Beech of St. Albans, glover, a surety.

June 16. John Belch of Rickmersworth and Trissip Shirt of the same; at St. Peters. John Holt of Rickmersworth, a surety.

June 25. John King of Gillingham co. Kent, yeoman, widower, aged 32 years, and Mary Francis of the same, widow, aged about 30 years; at Gillingham. Thomas Bickham of St. Nicholas of Rochester, victualler, a surety.

June 26. William Nash of Harding *alias* Harpenden, yeoman, and Mary Davis, daughter of Mary Davis of Kempton; at Harding or Kempton. Joseph Davey [*signed* Davie] of Kempton, yeoman, a surety.

June 29. Nicholas Vineall of Newington, co. Kent, cordwainer, bachelor, aged about 22 years, and Mary Lake of Milton-next-Sittenbourne, maiden, aged about 30 years; at St. Nicholas, Rochester. Richard Vinall of Rayneham, Kent, husbandman, a surety.

July 9. Walter Peacock of Redbourn, yeoman, bachelor, and Sarah Shepheard; at Redbourne or St. Michaels. Robert Shepheard of Redbourne, yeoman, her father, a surety.

July 10. Jonas Harley of Redbourne, tailor, bachelor, and Amy Moreton, spinster, daughter of Widow Moreton of Flamstead; at Redbourne or St. Peters. Gabriel Harley of Redbourne, brasier, his father, a surety.

August 4. Nicholas Kift of Deptford, co. Kent, seaman, aged about 26 years, bachelor, and Mary Pollard, spinster, aged about 20 years, daughter of John Pollard of Maidstone, co. Kent; at Maidstone or Chatham. Mathew Jurdaine of Chatham, victualler, a surety.

August 19. Francis Ewer of Watford, maltster, bachelor, and Mary Clench of the same, spinster; at Watford. John Leader of the same, carpenter, a surety.

August 28. Peter Cooke of Dunton, co. Kent, bachelor, aged about 26 years, and Patience Allen of the same, maiden, aged about 21 years; at Dunton or Dettling. Henry Austen of Maidstone, goldsmith, and John Brimpton of Rochester, shoemaker, sureties.

September 8. Richard Wood of Bridegate, co. Kent, bachelor, aged about 24 years, and Elizabeth Pausingham of the same, maiden, aged about 24 years; at Dettling or Braudherst. John Pausingham [*signed* Possingham], her father, aged about 50, husbandman, and Henry Lambert of Rochester, labourer, sureties.

September 21. Joseph Glonister of Winslow and Jane Nash of the same; at Winslow. Thomas Croft and Thomas Godwyn of Winslow, sureties.

September 25. James Rolfe of St. Stephens, yeoman, bachelor, and Sarah Harris of the same, spinster, aged 28 years; at St. Stephens. Henry Feild of the same, tailor, a surety.

October 1. John Smith of Bobbin, co. Kent, husbandman, bachelor, aged 24, and Mary Paine of Halstow, co. Kent, spinster, aged about 24; at Bobbin, Halstow or Freindesbury. John Ive of Chatham, ship's carpenter, a surety.

October 15. John Impson of Northmims, yeoman, bachelor, aged about 22, and Bridget Herbert of the same, spinster, aged 26; at Northmims. Belnap Tibballs of St. Peters, victualler a surety.

November 6. John Paton junr. of Winslow and Rebecca Grimes of Mid Claydon, co. Buckingham; at Mid Claydon or Adstock. John Croft and Thomas Bishop of Winslow, sureties.

November 6. William Bradwin of Hennell Hempstead, tailor, bachelor, aged about 30 years, and Anne Mace of Abbots Langley, spinster, aged about 22 years, having no parents living; at Abbots Langley or St. Michaels. James Halsey of Great Gaddesden, yeoman, a surety.

November 8. Edward Taylor of Flamstead, yeoman, and Mary Knowlton of St. Peters, spinster; at St. Peters. John Beamont of St. Albans, draper, a surety.

December 1. Jeremiah Carter of St. Albans, widower, and Mary Babb of St. Stephens, spinster; at the Abby or St. Stephens. Robert Eaton of St. Albans, cordwainer, and Ralph Jackson of the same, innholder, sureties.

December 4. John Anderson of Hatfeild, carpenter, bachelor, aged 21 years and a half, and Dorothy Key of Northmimes, spinster, aged 23; at Hatfeild or Northmimes. John Camfeild [*signed* Canfield] of St. Albans, innholder, a surety.

December 17. William Trott of Hexton, shepherd, bachelor, aged above 22 years, and Sarah Eason; at Hexton. Roger Hitchcock of Aston Abbotts, clerk, surety. Robert Eason of Hexton, shepherd, her father, makes the allegation.

December 23. Adam Hubbard of Abbotts Langley, blacksmith, bachelor, aged about 30 years, and Sarah Milton of Luton, co. Bedford, spinster, aged about 22 years; with consent of her mother, [*blank*] Milton, widow; at St. Albans or Abbotts Langley. John Gates of Hempstead, miller, a surety.

December 27. Andrew Wright of Ilstree, husbandman, bachelor, aged about 28 years, and Mary Cockman of the same, spinster, aged 18 or 19 years; with consent of her father, John Cockman of the same; at Ilstree. Henry Feild of St. Stephens, tailor, a surety.

1686-7

January 3. Isaac Godfry of St. Pauls Walden, bachelor, aged 40 years, and Mary Swaine of the same, widow; at Paulswalden or the Abbey, St. Albans. William Wilson signs the allegation.

January 5. William Arnold of Hitchin, bachelor, aged about 23 years, and Elizabeth Harper of Paulswalden, spinster; with consent of her father, [*blank*] Harper; at Pauls Walden or St.

Albans. Joseph Carter of Hitchin, maltster, aged about 25, and William Adams of St. Albans, tallow chandler, sureties.

January 5. John Miles of Ridge, barber, bachelor, aged about 21 years and a half, and Hester Taylor of the same, spinster, aged about 25 years; with consent of her father, Thomas Taylor; at Ridge. Henry Marston of St. Albans, husbandman, a surety.

January 15. John Nash of Ridge, husbandman, bachelor, aged about 28 years, and Ann Little of Luton, spinster, aged about 23 years; with consent of her father [*blank*] Little; at St. Albans or Ridge. Henry Marston of St. Albans, husbandman, a surety.

January 17. Ralph Heyward *alias* Howard of St. Peters, mealman, widower, and Amy Bedo of the same, spinster, aged about 23 years; at St. Peters. William Bedo of Christ Church, London, milliner, a surety.

January 26. William Matthews of Paulswalden, and Mary Parker; at St. Albans. William Maston [*signed* Marston] of St. Peters, a surety.

February 1. Thomas Dell of St. Michaels, and Anne Hickman; at St. Albans or St. Michaels. Nathaniel Prier [*signed* Pryer] of St. Michaels, a surety.

March 19. Thomas Ebgrave of Saundridge, husbandman, widower, and Alice Ffitzjohn of Whethamstead; at Saundridge. John Beamont of St. Albans, draper, a surety.

1687

March 25. James Ewer of St. Stephens and Rebeccah Abbot of the same; at St. Stephens or St. Albans. Thomas Muns of South Myms, husbandman, and John Eaton of St. Albans, shoemaker, sureties.

April 4. William Nicholas of Hillendon, co. Middlesex, husbandman, and Frances Watts of Sandridge; at St. Albans. William Mitchell, of Sandridge, husbandman, a surety.

April 5. William Stratford of Abbats Ashston, single man and Lucy Boulton of the same, single woman; at Winslow or Ashton Abbott. John Knowles, of Tring, butcher, and Richard Boulton [*signed* Bowdon] of Wingrave, co. Buckingham, butcher, sureties.

April 11. Joseph Rose of Redbourne, husbandman, and Elizabeth Morgan of the same; at Redbourne or St. Albans. David Jones of St. Albans, gardener, a surety.

April 12. John Cox of Sandrich and Sarah Sleep; at S. Albans or Sandrich. Jeremiah Hopkins of St. Albans, a surety.

April 13. Barnard Eaton of St. Peters, husbandman, and Mary Smith of Hatfeild, widow; at Hatfeild or Redbourne. William Blowes of St. Albans, gaoler, a surety.

April 16. John Durrant of Watford and Hannah Merriday of Harrow; at Harrow, Watford, or St. Albans. John Babbs and Peter Meadows both of Watford, mealmen, sureties.

April 16. John Atkinson [*signed* Adkisson] of St. Peters, husbandman, and Mary Beech of St. Stephen's, aged about 24 years. Ralph Howard of St. Peter's, mealman, a surety.

May 7. Thomas Dagnall of Abbott's Langley, widower, aged about 40 years, and Mary Bailey widow, aged about 40 years; at Sarrat, Abbott's Langley or Rickmersworth. Bellnap Tiballs, of St. Peter's, plumber, a surety.

May 7. Nicholas Hawkins of Harding, husbandman, bachelor, aged about 33 years, and Elizabeth Halsey of Redbourne, spinster, aged about 24 years; at St. Michaels or Redbourne. John Shorter of London, gent., a surety.

May 14. John Hall of Hemel Hempstead, husbandman, bachelor, aged about 26 years, and Sara Moss of the same, spinster of the same, aged 27; at St. Albans. David Jones, of St. Albans, gardener, a surety.

May 14. John Weeden of Watford, leather dresser, and Elizabeth Runnington spinster, daughter of William Runnington of Watford; at Watford. Richard Ward of Watford, leather dresser, a surety.

May 14. Thomas Feild of Hexton, husbandman, bachelor, and about 25 years and Mary Menger of Shillington, co. Bedford; aged about 24 years; with consent of her mother, Grace Menger; at Hexton. Henry Stevens of St. Albans, cooper, a surety.

June 4. John King of Watford, bachelor, aged about 23 years and Anne Hodgsdoun of the same, spinster, aged about 22 years; at Watford or Bushey. Thomas Bampton of Watford, mealman, a surety.

June 18. Ephraim Babb of Abbott's Langley, yeoman, and Joane Arnold of St. Michaels; at St. Michaels or Abbott's Langley. Edward Wallser of Abbott's Langley, a surety.

June 23. Thomas Roberts of Watford, bachelor, aged about 30 years, and Sarah Gilford of the same, spinster, aged about 24 years; at Watford or St. Albans. Ralph Williams of Watford, butcher, and Francis Hodges of the same, saddler, sureties.

June 25. Samuel Chappell of Abbot's Langley, husbandman, bachelor, and Rosamund Pooly of the same; at Abbot's Langley or St. Stephen's. Joseph Baily of St. Stephen's, yeoman, a surety.

July 12. William Goodspeede of St. Albans and Mary Wordell of the same; at St. Albans. Jeremiah Hopkins of St. Albans, dancing-master, a surety.

July 21. Roger Napkin of St. Albans, barber-chirurgeon and Hannah Bates of Tringe; at Wigginton. Jeremiah Hopkins of St. Albans, dancing-master, a surety.

September 17. William Hanniel [*signed* Hannell] of Abbot's Langley, blacksmith, and Mary Baddison of the same; at Abbot's Langley, or Redbourn.

September 18. William Willett of Berkhamsted St. Peter's, maltman, and Elisabeth Norris of Abbot's Ashton; at Abbot's Ashton or Wenslow. David Jones of St. Albans, gardener, a surety.

September 24. Thomas Cooke and Sarah Coglove. Matthew Bradley of St. Peters, shoemaker, and David Jones of St. Albans, sureties.

September 24. Richard Kempster of Watford, mealman, widower, and Martha Funge. Daniel Lovett of Watford, husbandman, a surety.

October 1. Edward Emerton of St. Albans, husbandman, and Elizabeth Grey of the same, spinster; having no father living but with her friends' consent. John Emerton of Dunstable, malster, a surety.

October 22. Daniel Evans of St. Michaels, husbandman, widower, and Mary Huddle, widow. John Chamberlaine of St. Peter's, a surety.

October 23. Robert Manning of Clothall, husbandman, and Hannah Smith of Norton, spinster; at Norton. William Plaisted of Norton, husbandman, a surety.

December 5. George Halsey of Redbourn, yeoman, and Theodosia Draper. Francis Halford of St. Albans, draper, a surety.

December 17. John Williams of Northchurch, bachelor, and Sarah Wallis of St. Peters, maid. Henry Field of St. Peters, a surety.

December 21. Thomas Weedon of Watford, bachelor, and Sarah Millard of the same. William Lockey of St. Albans, a surety.

December 26. John Cock of Abbots Langly, bachelor, and Elizabeth Gould of Bovington. Thomas Gould of Bovington, a surety.

December 29. John Floyd of Abbots Langly, bachelor, and Sarah Dunby of Hempstead; at St. Albans. Richard Floyd of St. Albans, a surety.

1687-8

January 4. Ralph Hull of Watford, bachelor, aged about 22 years, and Mary Newton of Bushey, widow, aged about 23 years; her father dead; at St. Andrew's, Holbourne. David Jones of St. Albans, apparitor, a surety.

January 9. [name torn out] and Mary Whethered. John Turpin of Redbourn & John Cock senior of St. Peters, sureties.

January 14. John Cooper of Chipping Barnet, bachelor, and Ann Saltmash of the same, maid. John Sherer of St. Albans, a surety.

February 2. William Cooper of Northchurch, bachelor, aged about 27 years, and Elizabeth Ward of Barkehamstead, maiden, aged 26, daughter of James Ward of the same; at St. Michaels.

February 6. Joseph Weeden of Watford and Sarah Ewer of Abbots Langly; at Abbots Langly. William Lockey junr, of St. Peters, a surety.

February 22. John Feild of Leggatts, Kings Walden, yeoman, bachelor, aged about 30 years, having neither father nor mother living, and Bridgett Feild, spinster, aged about 30 years, daughter of John Feild of Stopsley in Kings Walden; with consent of her father; at St. Albans, Dunstable, Hexton or Redbouene. John Feild of Kings Walden, yeoman, aged about 40 years, a surety.

February 24. Ralph Day of Rickmersworth, gent, and Elizabeth Wallington of Abbotts Langley; at St. Michaels. John Prince of St. Michaels, gent, a surety.

March 3. William Joyner of Paulswalden, yeoman, and Rebecca Ivory of the same, spinster; at Paulswalden. Henry Marston of St. Albans, yeoman, a surety.

March 24. Thomas Trott of Redbourn, lobourer, and Judith Swain. Ambrose Robinson of the same, husbandman, a surty.

March 24. John Brock of Colney Heath, parish of Northmims, bachelor, aged about 40 years, and Sarah Sleape of St. Stephens, spinster, aged about 22 years; at St. Stephens. Mathew [*signed* Mathias] Bradley of Colney, cordwainer, makes the allegation.

1688.

March 28. John Elliot of Hexton, blacksmith, and Jane Hare. John Heyward [*signed* Howard] of St. Albans, draper, a surety.

April 14. John Edwards of Hexton, bachelor, aged about 25 years, and Sarah Field, spinster, aged about 22 years; at Hexton. Joseph [*signed* Tho] Feilde of Hexton, yeoman, her brother, and Henry Steevens of St. Albans, innholder, sureties.

June 8. George Wingfield and Ann Smith of Rickmersworth. Roger Twichett of Rickmersworth, gent., a surety.

June 22. James Pope and Rachel Smith of Abbotts Langley; at Abbotts Langley. Francis Howe of Abbotts Langley, yeoman, a surety.

July 4. John Shadbolt of Sandridge, bachelor, and Mary Hunt of St. Michaels, maid; at St. Albans. Henry Hunt of St. Michaels, a surety.

July 5. Joseph Ley of Flamstead, bachelor, and Ann Impey of Redbourn, maid; at St. Albans. John Knight of Great Gaddesden, a surety.

July 6. John Busser of St. Peters, husbandman, bachelor, aged about 25 years, and Ellen Collins of Ilstree, spinster, aged about 22 years; at St. Peters or Idelstree. Mathias Bradley of Colney, parish of Shenley, cordwainer, a surety.

July 16. Jeremy Dearman of King's Walden, husbandman, bachelor, aged about 24 years, and Sarah Boustred of Sandridge, spinster, aged about 23 years; niece to Elizabeth Ebbgrave, wife of Thomas Ebbgrave by the father's side, having neither father nor mother living but with consent of said aunt; at Sandridge or St. Peters. Thomas Ebbgrave of Sandridge, husbandman, a surety.

July 18. Andrew Baldry of St. Peters, husbandman, and Anne Nicholls of Southmims, widow; at Sandridge. Bellnap Tabballs of St. Peters, plumber, a surety.

July 20. Richard Hodsdon of Watford and Alice Singfield [?] of Sarret; at Watford or Sarret. Richard Ruth of St. Albans, a surety.

July 21. James Peacocke of Redbourn, and Mary Redding of Shenley. William Morris of St. Albans, a surety.

July 26. William Jackson of St. Albans, bachelor, and Mary Hartley of the same, maid; at St. Albans. William Wattson of St. Albans, a surety.

July 28. Andrew Puddefoot of Redbourn, yeoman, and Sarah How of St. Albans; at St. Albans. John Beamont of St. Albans, draper, a surety.

September 3. Thomas Lucey of Stapleford, wheeler, bachelor, aged about 26 years, and Alice Everet of " Fower Wants " St. Peters, spinster, aged about 25 years; at St. Peters. Richard Skegg of St. Peters, blacksmith, her brother-in-law, a surety.

September 22. John Gilbert and Sarah Edwards, spinster, aged about 22 years, daughter of Robert Edwards of Aldenham; at St. Ste [unfinished]. John Gilbert of St. Stephens, wheelwright, his father, and Henry Seares of St. Albans, yeoman, sureties,

September 29. Thomas Leey, alias Ley of Sandridge, yeoman, bachelor, aged about 27 years, son of Thomas Leey, and Elizabeth Grunwin of the same, spinster, aged about 27 years, daughter of Edmund Grunwin: at Sandridge. Edmund Wood, of Sandridge, clerk, a surety. [Enclosing a letter from Edmund Wood certifying consent of friends.]

September 29. William Reeves of Rickmersworth, husbandman, aged about 24, and Mary Pert of Cheney co. Buckingham, spinster, aged about 25 years; at Watford, Abbott's Langley, or Redbourne. Thomas Walker [signed Walkvp] of Rickmersworth, husbandman, a surety.

September 29. Joseph Chambers, bachelor, aged about 30 years, son of John Chambers of Codicote, and Mary Grunwin of Wethampstead, spinster, aged about 40 years; at Sandridge. Robert Neeves of St. Peters, victualler, a surety.

October 1. William Beastney of St. Albans, aged about 22 years, and Frances Axtell of Aldenham, widow; at the Abbey or St Michaels. Jane Trott of St. Albans, widow, a surety.

October 2. John Morice of Milton Briou co. Bedford, yeoman, and Elizabeth Turner, of St. Albans; at St. Albans. John Carter of St. Albans, plumber, a surety.

October 2. Christopher Leech of Rickmersworth, yeoman, and Susan Millington; at St. Albans. David Jones of St. Albans, gardener, a surety.

October 9. Thomas Fosset of Redbourn, bachelor, and Ann Beach of the same, maid; at Luton. John Winter of St. Albans, glover, a surety.

October 9. William Dell of Hemel Hempsted, widower, and Ann Hows of St. Michaels, widow. Edward Baldwin of Abbot's Langley, a surety.

October 9. Thomas Hodsden of Carrington, bachelor, and Elizabeth Fly of St. Michaels, maid. William Dell of Hemel Hempsted, a surety.

October 10. Thomas Nash of Wethamstead, bachelor, aged about 56 years, and Mary Newell of the same, widow, aged about 40 years; at St. Peters.

October 21. Matthew Hubbard of St. Albans, innholder, single man, and Mary Clark of the same, widow; at St. Albans. Thomas [*signed* William] Knight of St. Albans, victualler, a surety.

October 22. Mark Seabrook of St. Stephens, husbandman, bachelor, aged about 24 years, and Catherine Smith of St. Stephen's, spinster, aged about 24 years; at St. Stephen's. Richard Smith of St. Michael's, husbandman, her brother, a surety.

October 27. William Boddington of Rickmersworth, yeoman, bachelor, and Rebecka Tyler, of the same, spinster, aged about 23 years, daughter of Amy Alden *alias* Tyler; at Rickmersworth or Sarrett. Richard Boddington of Amphill co. Bedford, yeoman, a surety.

October 31. Thomas Trott of St. Michaels, husbandman, single man, and Ann Long of the same, single woman; at St. Michaels or St. Albans. Joseph Carpenter of St. Michaels, victualler, a surety.

November 3. John Field of Hemel Hempsted, maltster, bachelor, and Mary Hare of St. Michaels, maid; at St. Michaels. John Prior of Hemel Hempsted, salesman, a surety.

November 3. William George of St. Michaels, miller, bachelor, aged about 26 years, and Rose Anderson, spinster, aged about 23 years, with consent of her father John Anderson of Sandridge; at Sandridge. William Pixely of Sandridge, husbandman, aged about 40 years, makes the allegation.

November 24. Richard Smith of Coddicote, husbandman, bachelor, and Martha Nash of Thatchworth; at Shephall or Codicote. Nicholas Bradwin of St. Albans, shopkeeper, a surety.

December 10. Edward Branch of St. Albans, cooper, single man, and Elizabeth Smith of Ridge, maid; at Ridge *alias* Rudge. James Bradbury of St. Albans, grocer, a surety.

December 15. Richard Smith of St. Michaels, yeoman, single man, and Sarah Elmunds of St. Stephen's, single woman; at St. Albans, St. Michaels, St. Stevens, or Abbott's Langley. Henry Smith junr. of St. Michaels, yeoman, a surety.

December 22. Robert Eves of St. Michaels, shoemaker, widower, and Gertrude Windle of the same, widow; at St. Michaels. Richard Ruth of St. Albans, chirurgeon, a surety.

December 24. Lilford Dison of Watford, gent., and Elizabeth Fishborn of the same; at St. Albans. John Ward of Watford, gent., a surety.

*To be Continued.*

# The Herts Genealogist and Antiquary.

## Transcripts of Parish Registers.

### MINSDEN.

[Minsden Chapel in the parish of Hitchin, has long been in ruins. No Registers are known to be in existence & the value of the following Transcripts is therefore exceptionally great.]

Minsden. A certificate of the Christnings and mariages since Michalmas anno 1609 vnto the sayde feast in the yeare 1610.

Thomas Manfeild and Alice Sheppard weare maried the 15th day of Octobr 1609.

Alice Rayment of Thomas Raymont and Grace his wife was baptized Decembr 3º 1609.

Marie Ryches the daughter of Rychard Ryches and Joan his wife was baptized August 5º 1610.

Judith Bray the daughter of Thomas Braye and Mildred his wife was Baptized Septembr 16º 1610.

John Huddleston, minister.
Robrt × Nash } Churchwardens.
Richerd Riches }

---

A true Register of such as haue Beene Baptized at the chapple of Minsden belonging to the Parish of Hitchin in the County of Hertford from the feast of St Mychaell Anno Dom: 1620 vnto the feast of St Mychaell Anno Dom: 1621.

#### Christnings.

John the sonne of John Hurst iu was baptised November the 5th } Anno Dom. 1621.

Adam the sonne of Adam Buckingham was baptized November the 12th } Anno Dom. 1621.

Elizabeth the daughter of Thomas Camfield was baptized November the last } Anno Dom. 1621.

Elizabeth the daughter of Richard Clifford was baptized Februarie the 4th } Anno Dom. 1621.

Robert the sonne of William Kinge was baptized Aprill the 8th } Anno Dom. 1621.

Elizabeth the daughter of Thomas Flindall was baptized July the 8th } Anno Dom. 1621.

Rebeccha the daughter of Thomas Saunders was baptized July the 15th } Anno Dom. 1621.

Agnes the daughter of John Driver was Baptized the same 15th of July } Anno Dom. 1621.

Richard Rugmer } Churchwardens.
Rychard Clifford }

A true and perfect Register of such as haue beene Baptized at the Chapple of Minsden belonging to the parish of Hitchin in the County of Hertford from the feast of S⁺ Mychaell Anno Dom. 1621 vnto the feast of S⁺ Mychaell Anno Dom. 1622.

*Christnings.*

| | |
|---|---|
| Elizabeth the daughter of John Field was baptized November the 11th | Annoq. Dom. 1621. |
| Elizabeth the daughter of John Joyner was baptized November the last | Annoq. Dom. 1621. |
| George the sonne of John Whitlie was baptized Januarie the 13th | Annoq. Dom. 1621. |
| Anne the daughter of William Page was baptized Februarie the 24 | Annoq. Dom. 1621. |
| Daniell the Sonne of Thomas Browne was baptized March the 17th | Annoq. Dom. 1621. |
| Robert the base borne sonne of John Greaues and Elizabeth Lacy was baptized September the first | Annoq. Dom. 1622. |

Jacob Twiseltō, Cu.
Thomas Saunders } Churchwardens.
John Driver

---

A true and perfect Register of all such as haue beene Baptized and of one Marriage at the Chapple of Minsden belonging to the parish of Hitchin in yᵉ County of Hertford from the feast of S⁺ Mychaell Anno Dom: 1622 vnto the feast of S⁺ Mychaell Anno Dom. 1623.

| | |
|---|---|
| John Burwell and Hester Winchester were maried November the 25 Annoq. Dom. | 1622. |

*Christnings.*

| | |
|---|---|
| Elizabeth the daughter of John Ashwood the younger was baptized November the first Annoq. Dom. | 1622. |
| Elizabeth the daughter of John Wilkshire was baptized December the 28 Annoq. Dom. | 1622. |
| George the sonne of John Hurst was baptized Februarie the tenth Annoq. Dom. | 1622. |
| Thomas the sonne of Thomas Camfield of Hill ende was baptized June the 22 Annoq. Dom. | 1623. |
| Rose the daughter of John Dryver was baptized June the 29 Annoq. Dom. | 1623. |
| Marie the daughter of John Burwell was baptized September the 25 Annoq. Dom. | 1623. |

John Wilkshire } Churchwardens.
Henrie Three

---

## MINSDEN.

A trew Register of all the Christnings from Michms. 1623 to Michms. 1624.

1623            *Baptized.*

John the sonne of Wiłłm Rayson 9 Nouem.
Thomas the sonne of Adam Buckinghā 7 Decem.
1624 Thomas the sonne of Thomas Saunder 29 Martj.

John the sonne of John Wilshire 22 April.
Thomas the sonne of John Boswell 6 Junij.
John the sonne of John Bunne 26 Septemb.
Sarah the daughter of Robt. Chamberlaine the same day.

        Stephan Peirce
       R. John Farr.

## MINSDEN.

A true Register of all Christnings
from Michms. 1624 to Mich. 1625.

*Christened.*

Richard y<sup>e</sup> sonne of John Chaukley Oct. 18.
Dorothy y<sup>e</sup> daughter of John Whitley Dec<sup>e</sup> 12.
Richard y<sup>e</sup> sonne of Will<sup>m</sup> Gutteridge  — 19.
Elizab. y<sup>e</sup> daughter of Will<sup>m</sup> Nash Jun. 8.
Mary y<sup>e</sup> daughter of John Hurst   — 30.
John y<sup>e</sup> sonne of John Driuer y<sup>e</sup> same day.
Rebecca y<sup>e</sup> daughter of Will<sup>m</sup> Mardolfe July 3.
Esther y<sup>e</sup> daughter of John Burwell Aug. 7.

       Steph. Peirce Vicar.
       Thomas Homes his × marke.

## MINSDEN.

A true Register of all the Christnings
from Michms 1625 to Michms 1626.

Hannah the daughter of Step. Burr baptized Octob. 2.
Thomas y<sup>e</sup> sonne of Thom. Flyndall baptized Octob. 16.
Mary y<sup>e</sup> daughter of Tho. Browne baptized April 23.
Jacob the sonne of Thom. Canfield baptized Junij 14.

       Steph. Pierce Cur.

## MINSDEN.

A true Register of all Christnings
frō March 25. 1626 to March 25. 1627.

Mary the daughter of Tho. Browne baptized Aprill 23.
Jacob the sonne of Tho. Canfield baptized June 14.
Thomas the sonne of Geo. Rayment baptized Octob. 1.
John the sonne of John Chauckley baptized Octob. 8.
Thomas the sonne of Jo. Willshire baptized Nouemb. 29.
Anne the daughter of Ed. Hurst baptized y<sup>e</sup> same day.
Annys the daughter of Rich. Clifford baptized Decemb. 10.
Hannah y<sup>e</sup> daughter of Th. Whistons baptized Decemb. 31
Joane y<sup>e</sup> daughter of John Bunne baptized March 11.

       Sum̄. 9.
       Steph. Peirce. Vicar.

## MINSDEN.

A true Register of all Christnings from
Mich. 1628 to Michms 1629.

Thomas the sonne of Thomas Whistons was baptized Octob. 5.
Ruth the daughter of Jason Redding was baptized Dec. 26.

Thomas the sonne of John Hurst was baptized Dec. 29.
Hannah and Rhode daughters of Thomas Browne were baptized March 18.
Mary the daughter of John Willshire was baptized July 16.

    Steph. Pierce Curat.
    The marke R of Roger Buckingham.

---

## MINSDEN.

A trew Register of all Christnings and Marriadges from Michms 1629 to Michms 1630.

*Baptized.*

The 30 day of May Robert the sonne of Robt Dixon.
The 3d day of June Mary the daughter of John Chaukley.

*Married.*

John Iuory Cler. and Elizabeth Radcliffe daughtr of Sr Edward Radcliffe. January 29.
Thomas Kydner Cler. and Grace Younge widow Aug. 24.

    Steph. Peirce.

---

## MINSDEN.

A trew Register of all Christnings from Michms 1631 to Michms 1632.

William the sonne of Wm. Hertford baptized Decemb. 28.
Daniel the sonne of John Hurst baptized March 3.
Mary the daughter of Edward Burre baptized May 4.
Joane ye daughter of Wm Page baptized Maij 31.
Mathew the sonne of Thomas Dauy baptized July 11.
Samuel the sonne of Stephan Burre baptized July 20.

*Married.*

John Reeue & Joane Hurst were married April 25.

    Stephn Peirce.
    Edward Nash } Church:
    Thomas Davie }

---

## MINSDEN.

Register from Michms 1632 to Michms 1633.

Elizabeth daughter of John Crease was baptized Oct. 3.
Richard Smyth & Agnes Riches were married Jan. 24.

    Stephn Peirce.
    Thomas Whistons } Cnurchwardens.
    Henry Roe }

---

## MINSDEN.

A trew Register of all Christnings and Marriadges frō Michms 1633 to Sept. 25. 1634.

*Christned.*

| | |
|---|---|
| James the sonne of Wm Mardolfe | Jan. 13. |
| John the sonne of John Bowstred | March 6. |
| Wm the sonne of Wm Nash | — 27. |

W^m the sonne of John Bunne     April 13.
Hannah the daughter of Tho. Buckinghm     April 20.
Elizabeth the daughter of John Hurst     July 22.

*Married.*

W^m Fowler & Grace Stallworth Feb. 13.
John Astwood & Dinis Stallworth eodem die

         Stephn Peirce.
         They mark of Richard Smith ×.
         They mark of Jeremy Smith ×.

---

## MINSDEN.

A trew Register of all Christnings & Marriadges from Michms 1634 to Michms 1635.

*Baptized.*

Susan daught^r of Thomas Dauy Nouemb. 9.
Joseph y^e sonne of John Arnoll Nou. 16. 1634.
Dorothy the daught^r of W^m Thredder the 3 day of June 1635.

*Married.*

John Burwell and Alice Heath June 24. 1635.

         Stephn Peirce.
         The mark of John Whittley ×.
         The marke of Jer. Cranwell ×.

---

## MINSDEN.

Septemb^r 29. 1635. A true register bill of all y^e baptizings burialls and mariages y^t haue bene in Minsden Hamblets from y^e daye and yeare afore named vnto y^e 19 day of October 1636.

*Christenings.*

Ruth y^e daughter of Steuen Bur was baptized y^e 8 day of Aprill.
Edward Nash y^e son of William Nash was baptized March 31.
John Simpson y^e son of George Simpson baptized y^e 7 day of Septemb^r.
Joane y^e daughter of Thomas Browne baptized y^e 24 day of Aprill.
Thomas y^e son of Thomas Buckingham was baptized May 26.

*Mariages.*

Robert Slow and Judith his wife was married July y^e 21 day of July.

*Burialls.*

Ambrose Smith was buried the 26 day of August 1636.
George Simpson was Buried the 15 day of May.
The wife and daughter of Thomas Flindel were buried y^e 20 day of September.

         M^r Lindall vicar.
         John Whitley } Churchwardens.
         Thomas Flindel }

---

A register of all y^e Christenings burialls & Marriages in y^e Cappell of Minsden from y^e 29^th of September 1636 till y^e same day 1637.

### October
The 31 day married Wiłłm Lindall Dr of Div. & Mrs Elizabeth Peirce widdow.

### December.
The 29th day baptized Jeremiah sonne of Thomas Canfeild.

### Februarie
The 23th day married John Fowler & Sarah Feild.
The same day married Christopher Marshall & Elizabeth Barker.

### March.
The 26th day baptized John sonne of George Simpson.
The 28th day baptized Edward sonne of Wiłłm Nash.

### Aprill
The 6th day baptized Joan daughter of Thomas Browne.

### May
The 18th day baptized Sarah daughter of John Arnold.

### June
The 20 day married William Page & Mary Ball.

### August
The 5th day baptized Samuel sonne of John Burwell senr.
The 20 day married Richard Dickins & Sarah Gray.

### September.
The 10th day baptized Sarah daughter of Christopher Marshall.

Wm Lindall Dr of Divinitie & Vicar of Hitchin.
John × Whitley mark, Churchwarden.

---

A register of Christenings & Marriages that haue beene in the Chappell of Minsden from the twenty fifth day of March 1637 till the same day of ye yeare 1638.

### March
The 25 day baptized Mary daughter of William Cooper *alias* Godfrey.

### May
The 18 day baptized Sarah daughter of John Arnold.

### June
The 20 day maried William Page and Mary Ball.

### August
The 5th day baptized Samuel sonne of John Burwell ye elder.
The 20 day maried Richard Dickens & Sarah Gray.

### September
The 10 day baptized Sarah Daughter of Christopher Marshall.

### October.
The 18 day baptized John sonne of John Boustred.

### November.
The 30 day baptized Elizabeth daughter of Edward Nash.

### December.
The 20 day baptized John sonne of John Cresy.

### March.
The 11 day baptized Richard sonne of Richard Smith.
The same day baptized Joan daughter of William Thredder.

William Lindall D.D. Vicar.
marke
John × Whitly.

8th Nouemb. 1638   Minsden.

*Baptismat.*

Alicia filia Thomæ Whetston baptizat. fuit May 20. 1638.

*Nuptiæ.*

Robertus Hurst et Hanna Hurst Nupt fuere May 3°.
Edward Newton et Maria Mardoll Nupt. fuere Nou. 1°

Tho Whitly  
Simon Browne } Church wardens.

Tho. Bedford Curat de Minsden.

---

April 23 Anno Dmni. 1639.

*Baptiz.*

Stephen Burr the son of Stephen Burr & Mary his wife baptised December 20. 1638.

Sarah the daughter of William Mardall & Alice his wife baptised Janu. 24. 1638.

Daniel & Sarah Simpson son & daughter of Georg Simpson & Mary his wife baptised March 24. 1638.

*Nuptiæ.*

Thomas Goldsmith & Lettice Hutchinson married March 27. 1639.
Samuel Kinsley & Elizabeth Tristram widdow married 18 of April 1639.

Thomas Bedford Curat de Minsden.
John Whitly } Churchwardens.
Simon Browne

---

Anno D'ni. 1639.

Cap. Minsden.

*Baptismat.*

Sarah Cooper filia Gulielmi Coop baptizata fuit 1° Septemb.
Johannes Boustred filius Gulielmi Boustred baptizatus erat 1° Septemb.
Johannes Canfeild filius Thomæ Canfeild Baptizatus erat 18° May.

*Nuptiæ* 1639.

Samuel Kingsly et Elizabeth Tristram nupti fuere 17° Apr.
Gulielmus Battle et Sarah Huckle nupti fuere 6° August.

William Nashe
Richerd Riches.

---

A Register bill of all Mariages & Christnings from the feast of the Annunc. Anno 1639 to the same feast 1640.

Capella Minsdenensis paroch. Hich.

*Nuptiæ.*

Johannes Poulter et Maria Sheffeild nupti fuere 27mo die Novembris 1639.

*Baptismat* 1639.

Hellena filia Thomæ Davy baptizat fuit 10mo die Octobris.
Maria Newton filia Edvardi Newton baptizata fuit 10mo die Octobris.

Joaña filia Gulielmi Thredder baptizata fuit 22ᵐᵒ die Novembris.

Guliel. Nash
Richerd Riches } Naophylaces

Thomas Bedford Curat de Cap. Minsd.

---

A register of the names of those that haue beene married & Christened in yᵉ Chapple of Minsden from yᵉ 29ᵗʰ of September 1639 till yᵉ same day tweluemoneth 1640.

1639
Octob. yᵉ 10ᵗʰ baptized Hellen daughter of Thomas Davey.
The same day baptized Mary daughter of Edward Newton.
November The 22ᵗʰ baptized Joan daughter of William Thredder.
December The 11ᵗʰ day married John Wallin a|s Poulter & Mary Shefeild.
January The 26 baptized Thomas & Robert sonnes of John Bunne.
The same day baptized Symon sonne of Dennis Browne.
1640
April The 13ᵗʰ baptized Robert sonne of a travellour.
The 26ᵗʰ baptized Mary daughter of John Heath.
May The 10ᵗʰ baptized Alice daughter of David [Alice *erased*] Clements.
July The 23ᵈ married John Muncke & Hannah Goldsmith.
September The 20ᵗʰ baptized William sonne of William Wheeler.
The 27ᵗʰ baptized Matthew sonne of John Arnold.

William Lindall.

---

Minsden. The names of these that haue bene baptized att Mynsden Chapell from the 25ᵗʰ of March 1640 vntell the 25ᵗʰ of March 1641 as falloweth.

Robart the sonne of a traveller was Baptized the 13ᵗʰ of Aprell.
Mary thee daughter of John Heath was Baptized the 26ᵗʰ of Aprell.
Alce the daughter of David Clamantes was Baptized the 10ᵗʰ of Maye.
Willyam the sonne of Wiłtm Wheller was Baptized the 20ᵗʰ of September.
Mathew the sonne of John Arnall was Baptized the 27ᵗʰ of September.
Wiłtm the sonne of John Boustrid was Baptized the 10ᵗʰ of December.
Moses the sonne of John Driuer was Baptized the 18ᵗʰ of February.

*Maryages none.*
*Burialles none.*

Edward Nash
John Heath } Churchwardens.

---

The Chris . . . . . . . . at haue beene in yᵉ Chapp. . . .
. . . . . en from yᵉ 29ᵗʰ of Septem . . . . . . . . till yᵉ same day tweluem . . . . . . 1641.

December 1641 [*sic*]
The 10ᵗʰ day baptized William sonne of John Boustred.

### February

The 18th was baptized Moses sonne of John Driver.

### May 1641

The 9th day was baptized Anne daughter of Richard Smith.

### August

The 22th was baptized Mary daughter of Dennis & Mary Browne.

### September.

The 16th was baptized Frauncis sonne of William & Mary Godfrey als Couper.

William Lindall DD.<br>marke<br>John × Carington.

---

# Church Terriers.

## DIGSWELL.

Digswell this 13th of Apr. 1638.

A pfect terrier of the Gleabe Lands appteining to the Parsonage of Digswell w^th the outer bounds therof.

Imp'mis the dwelling house is sufficient and comodius for habitation.

It. of outhousing there is one large nue Barne thatched and bourded on the outside, of length five bayes, also one hay barne and stable nue built conteining both fower bayes covered w^th tiles being all vnder one Roofe.

It. Woodlandes lying in 2 parsels one conteining by estimat three ac. lying and scituat from the Parsonage house west bounded on the lands of M^r Sedly called the green lane south     iij ac.

The other parsell conteining fower ac. by estimat lying from the Parsonage house north west and more west butting vpon other ground of M^r Sedly, called the Malmes     iiij ac.

It. of meadow and pasture grounds one close called the meadow by estimat fower acres lying at y^e head of the Parsonage house on the west. It. one other peece of pasture next the meadow on the south named y^e woodclose conteining by estimat fower ac. It. one other pasture close beehynd the orchyard lying south from the Parsonage house and is called by the name of the Dockclose conteining by estimat five ac.     xiij ac.

It. of arrable grounds one close called the Scrubbs lying west from the Parsonage house and bounded with the Kings higheway called Digswell hill on the west conteining by estimat six ac. It. one close next beelow the Scrubbs north ward bounded with fore said highway on the west by estimat conteining seven ac. It. one close more called broome close lying on the north of the Parsonage honse conteining by estimat five ac.     xviij ac.

It. The Orchyard Courtyard and Barne yarde togeather are esteemed at two acres ........ ij ac.

The total sum of ac. is xl acres.

John Champneis Parson of Digswell.

The marke × of John Cass Churchwarden
The marke of George Nash sidesman.

## ESSENDON.

Essendon in the County of Hartford being a Parsonage or a Rectory.

A Terrar giueing a Particular Accompt of the Parsonage Hovse ovthovses Homestalls Glebe Tythes and all other matters belonging to the said Rectory of Essendon.

1. The Parsonage Hovse is a Timber hovse Covered with Tyles Containing a Hall Pantry Cellar Milkhovse Washovse and one Closett all Brick floors one Waterhovse Paved with stone two Parlovrs Mealehovse and a Closett below Staires and allso a Kitchin all Boarded floors: Above Staires six Chambers a stvdy two Closetts and three Garretts. One Large Barne for Corne Containing five Bayes the threshing floor Planked all the Walls borded and Covered with Thatch a New Granary and Cowhovse adjoyning to the s$^d$ Barne boarded and Covered with Thatch one timber haye Barne and Stable Containing togeather three bayes Covered with Thatch one ovther Stable a Chochovse Carthovs one hoggs stye all Timber and Covered with Thatch Coalehovse and Privy Hovse two Little Gardens a Covrt Yarde on the East side of the dwelling hovse one Large Orchard on the West and North of the s$^d$ dwelling hovse with a Mote in itt one Large yard for Cattell fenced with pales Containing togeather one Acre and Vpwards. Two Tenements belonging to the Rectory one thereof in the present Ovccvpation of Henery Ecclesoe Now Clarke and Sexton of the s$^d$ Parish Containing fovr Lower Roomes one Chamber Covred with thatch and a stable Covered with Thatch with one yard and garding containing by Estimation sixty Poles more or less The ovther tenement now in the Ovccupation of John Pegerom, Labovrer, Containing three Lower Rooms and three vpper Roomes Covered with Tiles and a Hoggs stye containing thirty Poles and a Smiths Shopp and two Little bildings at the End of it covered with Thatch and a piece of Grovnd adjoyning to it containing forty Poles now in the Ovccupation of John Bvckel all which s$^d$ p$^r$misses doe abbvtt on the Land of the Right Hon$^{ble}$ the Earl of Salsbvry on the North and the Highway on the Sovth.
2. The Glebe Land. One Close of Arrable Land called Bacchvs Well feild containing by Estimation teen Acres be it more or lesse adjoyning to the afordsaid homestall one ovther close of Pastvre Land called the Mores containing two Acres be it more or lesse abvting on the East on the said Bachvs Well feild, one Wood containing seven acres be it more or lesse abvtting on the East of the said Mores and part of the s$^d$ Bacchvs Well feild, One Cloase of Arrable Land called Rovnd close containing two acres be it more or lesse and a Little wood adjoyning to it containing one acre be it more or lesse abovtting on the West to a Common called Warmehole,

one of Arrable Land or pastvre Land called Bellhovse close containing three acres be it more or lesse abvtting on the East to the Chvrch yard. One Close of Arrable Land called the Povnd Close containing seven acres be it more or lesse abvtting on the West to y^e Highway Leading to Hartf^d. One Ovther Close of Arrable Land called the Lower feild containing six acres be it more or lesse bvtting west to y^e same Highway and North to y^e Common Ham. One Wood adjoyning to Povnd Cloase on the East containing two Acres be it more or lesse, one cloase of Arrable Land called Leges Close abvtting on the North to y^e s^d Wood containing fovr Acres be it more or lesse. One Close called Vpor North feild Lying at West End bvting to the Common North feild East and to y^e Highway North containing fovr acres and a half be it more or lesse. One Close called North feild botton part Arrable part meadow bvtting to John Taylor to y^e Common Warmhole East to Rich^d Baker Northe containing one acre and a half be it more or lesse. One Close of Pasture Land called Warmhole Close Lying North to Warmehole Common svrrovnded with y^e Lands M^r Rich^d Ives containing half an acre more or less. Two pieces of Arrable Land Lyeing in a Common called North feild Common containing with one Healand by Estimation three acres be it more or lesse. One piece of Land Lying in a Common called Copthorn abvtting to the Land of David Mitchell Esq on the East and West containing twenty Poles more or lesse. Three pieces of Arrable Land Lying in a Common called Chvrch feild Common containing three acres be it more or lesse. Five pieces of Arrable Land Lying in a Common called the Common Ham, which said five pieces dve containe togeather by Estimation three acres be it more or lesse. Four pieces of Meadow Land Lying in a Common Meade one piece abvtting against the River on the North and to the Earl of Salisbvry Land on the East and Sovth and to Rich^d Wynn Esq West the second piece abvtting to the River North to Richd. Wynn on the East and to the s^d Earls Land Sovth and to Richd. Bakrs Land on y^e West, the third piece abvtting East to Richd. Bakers Land John Smith the West and Sovth to the Water Covrse the fovrth and Last piece abvtting to y^e Land of John Smith to the East and North to the River Sovth to Tho: Lenard Land and to y^e s^d Richd. Wynn Land West.

3^dly The Incvmbent is a Rector and Receives the Tythes in Kind of all the Parish or by Composition as the incvmbent and parishioners can agree abovt it, Excepting the Land Lyeing in Bedwell Parke within the said Parish which is Exempted from paying all manner of Tythes whatsoever

1^st being Charter Land Onely Eleven Shillings and six pence a year paid for a Moadvs Decimand for the whole payd to the Incvmbent by the Respective Owners or Occvpyers of the said Land there is noe other prescription att all.

2 Tythe is dve according to the Cvstome of all Corne and Grass (except before ex . . . . . . . . . . . Cow and Calfe or Cow in Calfe the parishoners pay to the incvmbent seven pence for Every Cow and for every Gvest Cow three pence a year). If there be teen Piggs the Minister is to have one the Owner to Choose the two first and the Minister the third. If bvt seven Piggs the Minister may have one paying to the Owner twopence halpeney for the ovther three wanting of teen and If vnder seven Piggs the owner is to pay the Minister two pence halpeney for Everey Pigg that he hath and

so in like Maner for Lambs to be pay^d at S^t Markes day. Also the tenth of the Wooll the Minister is to have, the Owner chooseing the two first fleeces, the Minister the third allowing to each other if over or vnder teen Even fleeces according as Wooll then commonly sold by the povnd, For every Henn two Eggs, for every Cock three Eggs. So in Like Manner for Dvcks to be payd at Easter. For Geese the teenth Goslin to be payd the Latter end of May, If the seventh the Minister is to pay the Owner a half peney for each Goslin of the three wanting of teen and if vnder seven the Owner to pay a halfepeney for each Goslin. The tenth of the frvit dve to the Minister.

3^d  The Svrplice fees according to the immemorial Cvstome of the parish payd for Churching a Woman Sixpence, for a Marriage the Banns being dvly pvblished for the Minister and Clark two Shillings six pence, for bvrying a Corpps in the Chvrch to the Minister three shillings and fovr pence to the Clarke and sexton three shilling and two pence, for bvrying a Corpps in the Chvrch yard to the Minister one shilling to the clerk and sexton twenty pence and fovr pence to the sexton for Ringing the Knell vpon the death of any person, for bvrying a foreigner in any of the affore said places dvble fees for the Minister and Clerk, for sarching the Register for births Christnings Marriages or bvryalls fovr pence.

4^th  Payable to the Crowne for the first frvitts Eighteen povnds to the Bishopp every Vissitation five shillings for the Arch Deacon every Lady Day for syned and Procurations teen shillings, and at S^t Michael Annualy teen shillings and six pence.

5^th  A Communion Table with two Basses two Carpetts one Tvrkey work and the other Blew Cloath a Svrplice and a Commvnion Cloth, a Green Cvshion in the Pvlpvtt one Large Bible two Common prayer Books, in the Steple five Bells, one Silver Salvar for the Commvnion one Silver Commvnion Cvpp with a Cover to it one Pewter flaggon. Noe Lands or Money in Stock for the Repares of the Chvrch. The West and Sovth side of the Chvrch yard fenced with Pales by the Incumbent the East and North side fenced with Rayls by the Chvrch-wardens togeather with the Almes Hovses, the Body of the Chvrch Repayred by the Chvrch-wardens

Signed and Approved of by R. Lee Rector

Edward Bradley } Churchwardens.
Henery Warnar }

This is a true Coppy of the Originall Terrier, taken ovt this 5^th day of Oct^r Annoq. Dom. 1724

Jn^o Webb.

---

### FLAMSTEAD.

A true Terrier of all the Gleabe lands belonginge to the Rectorie of Flamsted in the Countie of Hertf.

There is belonginge to the Rectorie of Flamsted foure score acres of arable lands all w^ch lye mixtlie amongst othere lands in the Comone feilds of Flamsted Except onelie Eight acres thereof by estimacon devided into two severall Closes w^ch are very well fenced and the gates and stiles about the same and also about the rest well mayntayned And are now in the occupacon of S^r Thoms Barrington K^t. Barronet & Dame Judith his wife or theire assigne or assignes But of what yeare lie value the same are wee cannot certeinlie sett downe, because wee never kcewe them sett or lett to any pson alone by themselves.

The Stipend of the incumbent there is vncertayne beinge altogeather at the good will of the farmers of the impropriat Tiothes there.

Henry Pryor } Church
Rathaman Ratling } Wardens.

[*Endorsed* Flamsted 1638]

### FLAUNDEN.

A true Terrier of all the gleabe land belonging to the Chappell of Flanden (nowe) in the parishe of Hemel-Hemsteed and Con. of Herford. June 25° 1639.

Imp. One house ioyneing vnto the Chappell comonely called by the name of Church house, containeing three small roumes belowe and one loft aboue.

Itm. One halfe Roode of ground or thereabouts, ioyneing vpon the Church house aforesaid, and Chappell yarde.

Ed: Winstar, Cleric.
Richard Grovere } Church Wardens.
John Nash }

*Endorsed* 'Exhibit. apud Whethamp: 26$^{to}$ Junij Anno d'ni 1639.

*A document of which the following is a copy accompanies the above terrier:—*

Junij 26$^{to}$ 1639 apud Whethamp: Flaunden saye } Rich Grover & John Nashe Chapplewardens of

That a howse wherein Richard Reade dwelleth w$^{th}$ 10 acres of land or thereabouts was given by one Nich: Pigott as they haue heard aboue twoe hundred yeeres agoe to be yeerelie in the disposicon of the preposito$^r$s there for the maintenance of the Cure at Flaunden. This from Joseph Prince.

That they haue heard that about 60 yeeres agoe in the Courte Baron for the Manno$^r$ of Hemelhemp: the Chapplewardens (a Courte beinge purchased) surrendred this howse & land to one Reade father of the s$^d$ Rich: Reade whoe was a poore man and had manie children & therefore they gaue him that land to p$^r$vent his chardge cominge vpon the hamlett. Rich: Grover hath heard that S$^r$ John Luke vpon question made by some of the Inhabit$^s$ about this land told them they had better keepe the children, then give awaye their land.

Testes:—W. Rolfe, Joseph Peter, Christopher Kent.

---

FLAUNDEN is a Chappelry in the Parish of Hemelhemsted. The Curate thereof is nominated by the Vicar of Hemelhemsted and y$^e$ said Curate hath all y$^e$ small Tithes arising within y$^e$ Chappelry.

They are generally paid in Money & amount to about five Pounds fifteen shillgs.

There's a small Chappell yard about a Rood of ground pal'd in.

The Surplice fees for marrying with Licence are a Crown. What y$^e$ Dues for Marrying with Banns or for breaking y$^e$ Ground either in y$^e$ Chappell or Chappell yard, y$^e$ present Curate is a Stranger to.

There are three Bells, a great Bible and Common prayer Book, Surplice, Pulpit Cushion and a small Cup for y$^e$ Communion.

The Chappellyard is repair'd by y<sup>e</sup> Inhabitants of y<sup>e</sup> Chappelry and y<sup>e</sup> Clerks wages is ten Shillgs.

      Robert Crowfoot, Chaplain.
      Richd Prince } Churchwardens.
      John Grover }
      William Harding
      Thomas Ashby.

[There is no date to the last document, but Robert Crowfoot who signs it is probably the person described as of Bovingdon on p. 191 of Cussans' Herts, Hundred of Dacorum & identical with the Robt. Crowfoot (M.A. of Brasenose Coll. Oxford 1700) rector of Edlesborough 1742-60.]

## GREAT GADDESDEN.

GADESDEN MAGNA   July the 4<sup>th</sup> day Anno Dom. 1638
A Terrier of the ground & portions of tythes w<sup>th</sup> other emoluments belonging to the Vicaridge of Gadesden Magna in the County of Hartford & Diocesse of Lincolne.

Imprimis the Churchyeard being a plat of ground about the Quantity of two acres the whole profits wherof are the Vicars due.

Item all profitts arising from Chauncill or Church ground wthin, as by buryalls or the like are the Vicars.

Item to the Vicar is due the whole Tythe of Wooll & Lambe & all other tythes whatsoeuer saue Corne & Hey.

Item all oblacons & Mortuaryes whatsoeuer are the Vicars too.

Item there hath bin an house formerly, whether called by the name of a church or a townehouse we cannot as yet certainly learne, but we haue heard the vicar had the benefit to dwell therein vntill he entitled the Queene someway or other thereunto & so alienated & sold it away by y<sup>t</sup> meanes. The better pt of the house was sold from of the ground & carryed quite away & y<sup>e</sup> place whereon it stood conuerted to an orchard. The Remainder of the house stands there still on the lower side of the churchyeard adioyning to the sayd Orchard, there being one gate out of the orchard & two doores out of the sayd house wth a paire of shop windowes y<sup>t</sup> open very indecently & inconueniently into the church yeard w<sup>ch</sup> (if it be not) yet happily may be occasion of much nastynes & annoyance therein.

Subscribed the day and yeare aboue written

      William Stilling vicar there.
    By us Henny Deane, John Rutlan.

# Feet of Fines for Hertfordshire.

**TUDOR PERIOD.**

(Continued from Page 259).

### 1581. Easter Term. 23 Eliz.

Julius Ferrers esq : Rich. Ferrers gent & Mary his wife. Lands in Flamstede.

Wm. Fielde : Ralph Morer & Kath. his wife. Messuage & lands in psh of S$^t$ Michaels near S$^t$ Albans.

Geo. Heigham esq : Alex$^r$ Chauncy gent & Mary his wife. Messuage & land in Sabridgeworth.

Rich. Brooke : Robt. Walton & Susan his wife. Messuage in Ware.

Edw. Peycock gent. : Rich. Bull gent & Alice his wife. Lands in Amwell. A warranty against Christr. Bull brother of s$^d$ Richard.

Rich. Smyth : Thos. Seale gent. & Eliz. his wife. Four messuages & land in S$^t$ Albans.

Edw. Bagshaw gent & Mary his wife. Simon Gardener gent & Eliz. his wife & Jas. Gardener gent. Three messuages & land in Stonden.

Henry Osbaston : Robt. Bradley & Margt. his wife. Land in Thunderidge.

Geo. Horsey esq : Geo. Burgoyne esq & Dorothy his wife. A moiety of 3 messuages & lands in Wellwyn & Diggeswell.

Thos. Fynche : John Nedham esq & Jane his wife. Messuage & lands in psh of S$^t$ Andrew's, Hertford. A warranty against the heirs of Jas. Nedham esq. dec$^d$ late father of s$^d$ John.

Rich. Stoneley esq : John Spaldynge & Margery his wife. Messuage & lands in S$^t$ Albans.

Robt. Hemynge : Wm. Shelley esq & Jane his wife & Thos. Pereson gent & Susan his wife. Manor of Chelsyn *alias* Chelson *alias* Smeremongers & 10 messuages & lands in Bengeo & Stondon.

Wm. Hamon & Robt. Hamon : Edw. Poulter esq & Mary his wife. Two messuages & lands in Pirton, Ofley & Ickleford.

John Collyn & Robt. Collyn : Nich. Collyn & Eliz. his wife & Mary Adam. Three messuages & lands in Stortforde.

John Huckle : John Ponde & Lucy his wife. Messuage & garden in Hutchyn.

Thos. Burman gent : John Smythe *alias* Howson. Two messuages & land in Hytchin.

### 1581. Trinity Term. 23 Eliz.

*Thos. Strayte : Anth. Typladye & Joan his wife. Lands in Carington & Kenseworth.

Wm. Chapman : Nich. Chapman & Mary his wife. Messuage & lands in Little Mondon & Great Mondon.

Jas. Bolton *alias* Bowlton : Robt. Watson & Joan his wife. Messuage & lands in Buntyngford *alias* Arlingestrete & Aspeden.

Edw. Chamber : John Pratt & Eliz. his wife. Messuage & land in Kympton.

Edw. Howe: Wm. Stane & Eliz. his wife. Messuage & land in Walkerne.

Wm. Bunne: Ralph Bullocke gent. & Mary his wife. Messuage & lands in Eastbrookehay & Hemelhamsted.

Rich. Kynge: Geo. Birket & Mabel his wife. Messuage & land in Hodsden in psh. of Broxborne.

John Rowe: John Tydye & Anne his wife. Messuage & land in Cheston.

Edm. Verney esq. & Henry Cheyney gent: Ralph Bullocke gent. & Mary his wife. Manor of Westbrookehay & 40 messuages & lands in Bovyndon, Hemylhamsted & Great Gaddesden.

Affabell Battell: Rich. Locke & Alice his wife, Thos Crane & Dorothy his wife. Three messuages & lands in S$^t$ Albans & the psh of S$^t$ Stephens n$^r$ S$^t$ Albans.

Wm. Kinge: Thos. Borham & Joan his wife. Messuage in Broxseborne.

Wm. Miller senior, John Miller & Geo Hawkyns junior: Paul Connyngton & Anne his wife & Geo. Jacobe & John Jacobe. Land in Stortford.

John Beckett: Robt. Holmes & Alice his wife & Wm. Holmes son & heir apparent of s$^d$ Robt. Messuage in Watford.

Wm. Lorde: Wm. Hilles & Jane his wife, Rich. Wrighte & Kath. his wife & Thos. Raynolde & Joan his wife. Messuage in Startforde *alias* Storforde

Fras. Wynche: Wm. Edlyn & Cecily his wife & John Turnor & Ellen his wife. Lands in Aldebury.

Wm. Feaste & Joan his wife: John Derington & Anne his wife & Robt. Payne & Marion his wife. Messuage in Sabridgesworth *alias* Sabridgeworth.

Thos. Waterhous: John Waterhous esq & Anne his wife. Four messuages & lands in Barkamstede Peter & Barkamstede Marye *alias* Northechurche.

Thos. Harryson gent: Humph. Connyngesbye esq & Mary his wife & Henry Foxwell gent. The site of the late Hospital of S$^t$ Julian & two messuages & lands in the parishes of S$^t$ Stephen & S$^t$ Michael near S$^t$ Albans.

Henry Frowycke gent: Geo. Duckett & Isabel his wife. Messuage in Broxseborne.

Edw. Pulter esq: Robt. Warde & Agnes his wife. Two messuages & lands in Little Wymondley & Great Wymondley.

### 1581. Mich. Term. 23 & 24 Eliz.

*Rich. More gent.: Michael Harrys gent & Marg$^t$. his wife. Six messuages & lands in Rowney, Gt. Munden, Little Munden, Stondon, Sakam, Hormeade, Leaston & Buntyngford & tithes in Gt. Munden & Little Munden.

Thos. Barnard: Wm. Necton gent & Eliz. his wife. Land in Rydge.

John Kay esq: Wm. Dalton & Clement Dalton. Two messuages & lands in Much Hadham.

Alex. Hamond gent: Ralph Sadler knt. Manor of Poppeshall *alias* Popsall & lands in Buckland & Widiall.

Wm. Lane: John Stafford esq. Lands in Yardley & Clothall.

Wm. Clerk esq & Rich. Litler gent: Henry Darcie knt & Kath. his wife. The Advowson of the church of Shenley.

Thos. Bowyer esq & Wm. Le esq: Thos. Hall gent & Marg$^t$. his wife. Two messuages & land in S$^t$ Albans.

Wm. Parnell: Steph. Wapoole *alias* Nobbes & Agnes his wife. Messuage & land in Alberye.

Thos. Hoo jun. gent: Thos. Hoo sen. esq & Lucy his wife. Manor of Hooburye *alias* Hoo & 3 messuages & lands in Powles Walden & Kympton.

Geo. Santon, John Pryor: Christr. Clay & Eliz. his wife & Fras. Santon & Lucy his wife. Messuage & land in Stortford.

John Brakenfeld: Thos. Russell & Cecily his wife. Messuage & land in Chippinge Barnett.

John Newman jun: Wm. Cuffeley & Eliz. his wife & John Newman sen. Two messuages & lands in Barkway.

Edw. Pulter gent: John Stafforde esq & Bridget his wife. Manor of Cotered *alias* Codred *alias* Codrethe & 20 messuages & lands in Cotered, Yardley, Aspeden & Bradfeild & the advowson of the church of Cotered.

Thos. Fanshawe esq. & Thos. Person gent: Robt. Leonard & Joan his wife. Two water mills, one fulling mill & lands in Ware.

Geo. Horsey esq & Thos. Docwra gent: John Lacye & Ellen his wife. Moiety of two messuages & lands in Diggeswell & Bishops Hatfeild.

John Beamount: John Harvye esq & Margery his wife. Two messuages & lands in Langley, Bovington & Sarrett.

Thos. Fanshawe esq: Henry earl of Huntingdon & Kath. his wife & Francis Hastings esq son & heir apparent of Geo. Hastings knt. Manor of Ware & 100 messuages and lands in Ware, Thundridge, Stondon, Widford, Stansted, Amwell, Hertford and Bengeo.

Christr. Snell: John Snell sen., Nich. Aunger, John Sherman gent, Thos. Barlyman and Rose his wife & Wm. Gerrye gent. Five messuages & lands in Royston, Tharfeilde, Westreade and Barkwaye.

Francis Fletcher & Wm. Handforte gents: Humph. Conyngesbye esq & Mary his wife & Edw. Sadleir esq & Anne his wife. Manor of Soppwell & Soppwellbury & 60 messuages & lands in St Albans & St Peters within and without the town of St Albans & St Stephens & the advowson of the vicarage of St. Stephens.

### 1581-2. Hilary Term. 24 Eliz.

*Robt. Ewarde & Fras. Mallorye: Jas. Hallfehyde, John Rolte gent & Judith his wife, Paul Ewarde & Ellen his wife & Alice Hallfehyde. Six messuages & lands in Yardley & Cottered.

Thos. Mylles: Geo. Bayforde & Eliz. his wife. Land in Sabrichesworth.

Robt. Yardeley: John Pollard & Alice his wife. Messuage & land in Baldock & Weston.

Thos. Rawson: John House & Agnes his wife. Land in Kings Hatfeild.

Thos. Bagsha: John Seare & Jane his wife. Lands in Northbarkamsteade.

Rich. Yonge gent: Thos. Hudson gent. Messuage & land in St Albans.

Thos. Ballarde: Geo. Dell & Agnes his wife & Edmund Smythe. Messuage & lands in Kings Hatfield *alias* Bishops Hatfield.

John Richardson & Joan his wife: John Nicholl & Eliz. his wife. Messuage & land in Little Hadham.

Edw. Skypwyth gent: Thos. Holden & Agnes his wife. Messuage & land in St Albans.

John Baet: Edward earl of Oxford high chancellor of England. Annual rent of ten pounds issuing from the park of Scales *alias* Scales Wood in psh. of Barkwey.

### 1582. Easter Term. 24 Eliz.

Rich. Mayne : Henry Mayne gent. Messuage & land in Bovyngton [*written* Dovyngton].

Thos. Osbaston : Wm. Davy & Kath. his wife. Land in Ware.

James Boulton : John Philpot gent & Eliz. his wife, Thos. Wattes & John Wattes (son of s^d Thos.) & Margt his wife. Lands in Aspeden.

Henry Randall : John Wattes & Margt. his wife, John Phylpot gent & Eliz. his wife, Jas. Boulton & Margt. his wife & Thos. Wattes. Lands in Layston & Aspeden.

Lewis Mordaunt knt, lord Mordaunt : John Tufton esq & Christian his wife. Manor of Hokenhanger *alias* Kympton & 4 messuages & lands in Kympton.

Wm. Kympton : Edm. Yardeley & Anne his wife. Lands in Chevesfyld.

Roland Beresford gent : Rich. Brokeman gent & Agnes his wife. Manor of Lyburye *alias* Libery & 20 messuages & lands in Little Munden, Gt. Munden, Westmell, Walcorne, Braughinge & Yeardley.

Michael Meade & Eliz. his wife : Oliver Crosse & Agnes his wife. Land in Ware.

Charles Moryson esq : Wm. Ewer & Eliz. his wife. Messuage & lands in Watford & Langley.

Thos. Pomfret : Wm. Pomfret & Anne his wife. Messuage & garden in Baldocke.

Henry Sare & Rich. Wood : Wm. Pyerson gent & Agnes his wife, Rich. Haysse gent & Cecily his wife & Mich. Sare & Margt. his wife. Manor of Easton *alias* Eastone & lands in Watford & Saint Stephens.

### 1582. Trinity Term. 24 Eliz.

Peter Lyndessell : Robt. Bennett & Alice his wife. Land in Sabridgworth.

Rich. Brooke : Thos. Russell & Cecily his wife. Four messuages & lands in Cheping Barnet.

Edw. Peede : Lewis Mordaunt knt lord Mordaunt. Messuage & lands in Kympton.

Rich. Savell : John Marryon & Margt. his wife. Two messuages and lands in Stortford.

Thos. Thomson citizen & haberdasher of London : Matthew Lowe gent & Anne his wife. Manor of Gifford & six messuages & lands in Little Munden & Great Munden *alias* Much Munden.

Edw. Wylkynson : Andrew Grey esq, Edw. Halfhyde esq and Anne his wife. Lands in Aspeden and Layston.

John Anderson : Thos. Myles, Messuage & lands in Gt. Munden.

Wm. Hampton & Robt. Hampton : Christopher Marshall gent & Anne his wife & Rich. Cornwell & Mary his wife. Two messuages & lands in Chesthunt & Standon, & common of pasture in Chesthunt.

John Sybley, Henry Foster, Thos. Welche, Edm. Tufnayle & Thos. Crawley : John Prydden & Eliz. his wife. Land in Kings Walden.

Thos. Humfrey & Eliz. his wife : Thos. Crane gent & Dorothy his wife. Three messuages & gardens in S^t Albans.

Edw. Wilkynson : Andrew Grey esq, Edw. Halfhyde esq & Anne his wife. Two messuages & lands in Aspeden, Layston, Cottered & Wakeley.

John Crowche : Wm. Ayloffe gent & Alice his wife, John Felton gent & Kath his wife. Messuage & lands in Layston, Awswicke, Gt. Hormeade, Little Hormeade, Westmill & Buntingforde.

### 1582. Mich Term. 24 & 25 Eliz.

*Thos. Ansell: Rich. Frauncis gent & Susan his wife. Lands in Ickleford & Hytchyn.

Rich. Corsse: John Bennett & Anne his wife. Messuage & land in Baldocke.

John Huckle clk: John Darlinge & Ellen his wife. Messuage & land in Stevenage.

Agnes Adams wid: Thos. Adams & Julian his wife. Messuage & land in Witford *alias* Widford & Great Haddam.

Henry Randall: John Roxesonne. Messuage & land in Apsten & Layston.

Wm. Godfrey *alias* Cooper: Henry earl of Derby. Lands in Stagnall *alias* Stagnow. Powells Walden & Kings Walden.

John Bowyer esq. & Geo. Graveley: Edw. Pulter esq & Mary his wife. Lands in Hitchyn *alias* Hutchyn.

Thos. Gaddesden: Edw. Pulter gent & Mary his wife. Land in Hytchyn.

Edm. Cordell: Robt. Cordell & Agnes his wife. Messuage & land in Chesthunt.

John Plomer: John Glanfield *als* Nevell & Mary his wife. Messuage & lands in Clothall, Baldock, Bygrave & Willien.

John Bowyer esq: John Godfray *alias* Cooper & Agnes his wife. Lands in Hitchyn *alias* Hutchyn & Ipolletts *als* Hypolletts.

Ralph Radclyff esq: Edw. Pulter esq & Mary his wife. Manor of Moremeade *alias* Charleton *alias* Charlton *alias* Chalton & two messuages & lands in Hutchyn *alias* Hitchyn, Ipollets & Offley.

Thos. Rudd jun: Thos. Rudd clk & Rich. Potman gent. Messuage & lands in Kings Walden, Offley & Lynley *alias* Lylley.

John Karver & Thos. Towse: Rich. Adams gent & Margt. his wife. Messuage & land in Aldenham.

John Bowyer esq: Rich. Frauncys gent & Susan his wife. Lands in Hitchin *alias* Hutchyn.

John Bowyer esq: Geo. Fertloe & Mary his wife. Lands in Hitchyn *alias* Hutchyn.

Barnard Dewhurst gent & Thos. Bennett gent: Wm. Frankland gent & Hugh Frankland gent. Manor of Baruetts & 3 messuages & lands in Broxburne, Hoddesden & Amwell.

Rich. Hale jun: Edw. Sadleir esq & Anne his wife. Tithes in certain lands in Kynges Walden, Powles Walden & Polletts.

John Clarke: Alex. Avenon. Three messuages & land in Ashwell.

John Reamount: Laurence Asheton & Eliz. his wife, Thos. Frenche & Margt his wife, Wm. Gayler & Agnes his wife, Robt. Danyell & Margt. his wife & Jas. Wheler & Agnes his wife. Two messuages & lands in Ashewell.

Thos. Dermer & Edm. Smyth: Edw. Sadleir esq & Anne his wife. Tithes arising from certain messuages and lands in Kynges Walden.

### 1582-3. Hilary Term. 25 Eliz.

John Walford: Wm. Walford & Margt. his wife. Three messuages & land in Lechworth.

Wm. Dermer *alias* Dormer: Thos. Crane gent. & Dorothy his wife. Eight messuages & land in St Albans.

Robt. Newdyck: Robt. Redwood gent. Land in Typpingdale in psh. of St Stephens.

Geo. Rotheram esq: Edw. Sadleir esq & Anne his wife. Tithes on certain lands in Kings Walden.

Thos. Moryson esq : Rich. Fitz Hughe gent & Eliz. his wife. Land in Sandon. A warranty against Rich. Fitzhughe senior & Nich⁵ Fitzhughe gents.

Wm. Glover & Bridget his wife: Wm. Davye & Kath. his wife. Messuage in Ware.

Henry Ayer : Robt. Ayer. Windwill & land in Aspeden.

Thos. Waterhous : Geo. Morton esq. Land in Barkhamsted Mary *alias* Northchurche.

Reginald Basse gent & Wm. Hertforde gent: John Barlowe & Kath. his wife. Messuage & land in S⁺ Albans.

Robt. Shadde : John Kilbyef *alias* Kilbye & Dorothy his wife & Alex. Longe. Messuage & land in S⁺ Albans & Hemelhampstede.

Geo. Waller : Henry Heigham gent & Anne his wife. Two messuages & land in Sabridgeworthe.

Rich. Peacock : Rich. Brooke & Alice his wife. Four messuages & lands in Chepinge Barnet.

Geo. Forkelooe & Lawrence Forkelooe. John Chirrye & Margt. his wife. Barn & land in Great Munden.

John Bowyer esq : Wm. Awdeley & Mark Willyams & Agnes his wife. Messuage &c in Hitchyn *alias* Hutchyn.

Wm. Rolf gent : Rich. Snowe junior & Mary his wife. Messuage & lands in Tatteridge.

James Tristram : Thos. Coker & Eden his wife. The site of the late priory of Biggin & two messuages & land in Hutchin *alias* Hitchin.

Thos. Venables esq : Degory Pyper gent. Three messuages & lands in Ware, Widford & Thundridge, to hold to s⁴ Degory for the term of one week & after that to remain entirely to Thos. Harrys of the Middle Temple esq & his heirs.

Roger Stoughton & Mary his wife : Roger Fynche & Eliz. his wife. Moiety of two water mills in psh of S⁺ Stephens near S⁺ Albans.

John Pytches : Simon Harvye & Margt. his wife & John Harvye & Cicily his wife. Land in Sandon.

Robt. Steppinge & Edw. Crawley : Edw. Sadleir esq. & Anne his wife. Tithes on lands in Kings Walden.

Wm. Wyne, Edw. Edwarde, Wm. Beane, Thos. Lyncoln, John Lyncoln & Edw. Lyncoln : Rich. Fitzhughe gent & Eliz. his wife. Three messuages & lands in Sandon.

### 1583. Easter Term. 25 Eliz.

*Thos. Wightman & Geo. Robertes : Henry Calton. Moiety of the Rectory church of Willey *alias* Willion *alias* Willinge & the moiety of an annual rent of 20 marks issuing from the vicarage of s⁴ church.

John Parrant : Wm. Parrant. Messuage in Little Hadham.

Walter Myldmay esq : Henry Adams & Agnes his wife. Lands called Marsheland *alias* Massland Wood in Wydford.

John Kirbye : Rich. Kirbye senior. Three messuages & lands in Sacombe & Little Monden.

Ralph Copcott gent & Beatrice his wife : Lawrence Eyton gent & Dorothy his wife & Edw. Eyton gent. Messuage & lands in Pyrton.

Geo. Grave senior & Geo. Grave jun^r : Robt. Leonarde & Joan his wife. Two messuages & land in Hertford & Bengeho.

Ralph Lever gent : Isaac Adames gent & Eliz. his wife. Messuage & garden in Amwell & Ware.

Wm. Brooke : Thos. Harmer. Three messuages & lands in Westone & Clottall.

Matthew Hansecombe: Lawrence Eyton gent & Dorothy his wife & Edw. Eyton gent. Messuage windmill & lands in Pyrton.

Thos. Gardiner: Thos. Hedd & Margery his wife. Messuage & land in Great Monden.

Simon Stratton: John Carter & Eliz. his wife. Messuage in Hutchin *alias* Hitchin.

John Chamber & Wm. Chamber: Ralph Radclyff esq & Eliz. his wife. Three messuages in Hytchyn.

Robt. Westley: Barnabas Elmer *alias* Fylewood & Frances his wife. Messuage in Royston.

Wm. Barrye & Wm. Warner: Anthony Daulton & Margt. his wife & Thos. Warren & Mary his wife. Messuage & land in Stondon.

Wm. Brooke: John Humberstone. Two messuages & lands in Walkorne & Bennyngton.

Thos. Dengayne gent. & Edw. Cradocke: Nich. Rande gent. & Joan his wife. Messuage & land in psh. of S<sup>t</sup> Michaels next S<sup>t</sup> Albans.

John Crouche: Thos. lord Howarde & Kath. his wife. Manors of Cornyburye & Gibcracke & 10 messuages & lands in Layston Alswicke Wydeall Throcking Aspeden & Buckland & tithes in same places & Great Hornemeade & Little Hornemeade & the advowson of the vicarage of Layston & the fair & market in Buntingford.

John Tanner: John Brennynge gent & Alice his wife. Land in Chesthunt.

Wm. Nayler: Wm. Stane & Eliz. his wife. Messuage & lands in Walkerne & Benyngton.

Lancelot Batherst: Andrew Grey esq & Anne his wife. Manor of Johnes at Pelham & six messuages & lands in Furnex Pelham.

John Brograve esq. & Margt. his wife: Thos. Howard second son of Thos. late duke of Norfolk son & heir of the most noble princess Margt. late duchess of Norfolk late wife of the said late duke daughter & heir of Thos. Audelye knt. lord Audelye de Walden & late Lord Chancellor of England & Kath. his wife. Manor of Westmill *alias* Westmilne *alias* Westmilburye & 6 messuages & lands in Westmill & the advowson of the Church of Westmill.

Henry Prannell citizen & vintner of London: John Petre knt & Mary his wife. Manors of Rookey & Water Andrewes *alias* Walter Andrewes & 10 messuages & land in Barkwaye, Anstye, Nothamsted, Barley, Buckland, Rede & Royston.

Kath. Leaper widow: John Bowier esq & Beatrice his wife, John Newman & Phyllis his wife & Tho. Newman, Messuage & land in Hichin.

Thos. Carowe gent & Thos. Bowyer: Oliver Godfrey gent & Eliz. his wife. The site of the late dissolved chantry of Baldwyn Victor & two messuages & land in Stortford.

Thos. Monday & Margt. his wife: Thos. Hoddesdon & Anne his wife. Messuage & land in Chesthunt.

Lancelot Batherst: Edw. lord Morley, baron of Rye & Eliz. his wife & Wm. Wylkes & Joyce his wife. Manors of Pelham Turnex, Johnes at Pelham, Brent Pelham *alias* Greyes & Chamberlyns & 40 messuages & lands in Pelham Furnex, Pelham Arse *alias* Brent Pelham, Gt. Hormead, Little Hormead, Stokkinge Pelham, Meesden, Aldebury, Broughing & Anstye.

Andrew Paschall sen. & Andrew Paschall jun. gents: Arthur Hevenyngham knt & Mary his wife & Thos. Barnardiston knt & Eliz. his wife & Andrew Graye esq, Andrew Malorie esq, Thos.

Hanchett esq & Anne Hanchett. Manors of Gattesburie *als* Gattisburie, Vphall & Maisters *alias* Masters & 100 messuages & lauds in Braughinge *alias* Brackinge. Gt. Hadham, Little Hadham, Westmyll, Aldeburie & Stondon.

### 1583. Trinity Term. 25 Eliz.

*Roland Watson gent & John Pryce gent: Wm. Chetwynde gent & Attalanta his wife. Lands in Chesthunt.

Geo. Hide esq: Francis Foliott esq. Messuage & land in Bradfeild, Cottred *als* Cothred & Throcking.

John Meade: Thos. Burlinge & Grace his wife. Cottage & land in Stortford.

Zachary Fowle: Wm. Bexfyeld & Eliz. his wife. Messuage & land in Bayforde.

Wm. Hampton: John Sabyne & Eliz. his wife & Rich. Clapham & Cicily his wife. Messuage in Little Hadham.

Giles Allen gent & Fortescu Clerke gent: Giles Sewester. Messuage & land in Ashewell.

Leonard Hide esq: Wm. Hide gent. Manor of Throcking & 6 messuages & lauds in Throcking, Clothall, Weston, Sondon, Layston, Cottred, Buckland, Widdiall, Barkway & Apesden *alias* Aspeden & the advowsor of the church of Throcking.

Thos. Chawkeley & Robt. Papworth: John Brockett & Julian his wife, John Lawrence & Grace his wife. Messuage & land in Great Wymondley *alias* Gt. Wymbley.

Thos. Barnard: John Somerton & Agnes his wife & Thos. Somerton & Anne his wife. Moiety of a messuage & lauds in Rydge.

Leonard Hide esq: Thos. Wiseman esq & Jane his wife. Manor of Throcking & 6 messuages & lands in Throcking, Clothall, Weston, Sondon, Laiston, Cottred, Buckland, Widdiall, Barkewaye & Aspesden *als* Aspeden & the advowson of the church of Throcking. A warranty against Wm. Wiseman, Rich. Wiseman gents & Wm. Salkins.

*To be Continued.*

## Monumental Inscriptions.

### PRESBYTERIAN CHAPEL, UPPER DAGNALL STREET, ST. ALBANS.*

Two stones remaining in Sept. 1891, both being let into the south face of the north wall of the Chapel Yard.

No. I.   LUCY | GOODLAND | 1830.

*Probably an infant dau. of John Goodland, master of the Charity School connected with the Chapel. He was a clever modeller & became Editor of a paper at Manchester.*

No. II.   EDWARD BLANLAND | Died 26 Feby 1836 | Aged 7 years.

* Communicated by Mr. John Harris, C.E.

# Abstracts of Wills.

**ARCHDEACONRY OF HUNTINGDON (HITCHIN REGISTRY).**

REGISTER III. (CONTINUED FROM PAGE 230).

f. 47 b. THOMAS BEDELL of Watton at Stone, wheeler. (*Nunc. will dat.* 26 May 1584). Wife Ellyn extrix; My six children. Wit$^s$:—Robt. Porter parson of the town & Robt. Stockwell & the wife of Wilkynson. (*Pr. but date not given*).

f. 47 b. BARTELLMEW HILL of Lytle Gadesden. (*Dat.* 10 Aug. 1584). Sons Thos., Jeames & John; Dau. Eliz. Feild & Thos. Feild her husband; Daniel son of s$^d$ Thos. Feild; Wife Joane; Son Thos. exor; Daniel Cotton my son in law overseer. Wit$^s$:—Thos. Wynsore clarke, John Eames, Wm. Gosbell, Oliver Norcote & Robt. Dyer. (*Pr.* 10 Dec. 1584 at Baldock).

f. 48. THOMAS GRAVELYE of Gravelye gent. (*Dat.* 8 Aug. 24 Eliz.). Wife Eliz. to enjoy my mansion house, lands etc at Gravelye, Chivsfild, Wymonlye & Steuenage & my leases made to me by John Mylles of Aunseburye dec$^d$. My child$^n$ Francis, Thos., & Rowland & dau Julian; Lands in tenure of John Hasten; John Moore & John Woodfilde; Francis my son & heir; Dau. Julian (under 21); Dau. Quarles; Wife & son Fras. exors; Son-in-law M$^r$ Quarrells supervisor. Wit$^s$:—Henry Aunsell, Wm Kympton & Jeames Jeve. (*Pr.* 30 Apr. 1584 by Eliz. the relict, reservation to Fras. Gravelye).

f. 49. ELIZABETH BURGES of Bengeo. (*Dat.* 10 Apr. 1584). My father Austen; my mother; Joane Yemmonger my sister; Sist. Marye; Bro. John Burges; Kinswom. Eliz. Burges; Wm. Austen my father exor; Rich. Heylye curate at Bengeo overseer. Wit$^s$:—Eliz. Speringe, Grssell Taylor, Margery Austen. Catren Pollard & W$^m$ Austen. (*Pr.* 21 May 1584).

f. 49. MARGARET GRAYE of Tharfeild. (*Dat.* 15 Mch. 1583). Son John Graye of Barkwaye & his three child$^n$ Thos., Grace & Fraunc$^e$; Kath. Smyth; Anne Wrighte; Johan Priest; Fraunc$^e$ Grayes child$^n$; Margt. Grey; John Gray the younger; Peter Wright; John Page; John Grayes children thelder; Legacy to poor of Kelsey & poor of Reede; Wm. Graye; Johan Priest & Ann her dau; Thos. Game; Dau Kath.; Mother Hazard; Grace Graye; Symon Cooles wife; Land bought of Thomas Carter of Reede; Son Francis Graye exor. Wit$^s$:—John Graye & Geo. Wren. (*Pr.* 27 Jan. 1584-5).

f. 49 b. ELIZABETH HEWARD widow, of Kensworth. (*Dat.* 28 Sep. 23 Eliz.). Son Henry Heward; Sons John & Allyn; George Heyward my son in law; Dau. Ellyn; Sons Henry, John, Allyn & Nicholas; Son Henry exor; Nich$^s$ Neele & Roger Nichols overseers. Wit$^s$. Leonard Tuke vicar, Thos. Robins. (*Pr.* 14 Jan. 1584 at Baldock).

f. 49 b. THOMAS EWER of Hemelh'msted, sholvemaker [*sic*]. (*Dat.* 29 May 1584). Wife Alice extrix; My children. Wit$^s$:—

Robt. Royse, Wm. Turner of Wards end, Jas. Gladman. (*Pr.* 15 July 1584).

f. 49 b. RICHARD ORIS of Northchurch. (*Nunc. will undated*). Son John & his mother & his brother & sisters; Eliz. Royse; Son John exor. Wit*s*:—Wm. Axtell, Henry Sere & Wm. Edlyn & W*m* Cocke. (*Pr.* 16 July 1584).

f. 50. WILLIAM STRONGE of Freesden in psh. of Burckhmsted Peter, husbandman. (*Dat*. 13 Nov. 1583). Uncle Robt. Stronge; Servant Wm. Bale & Alse Bale his grandmother; Henry Nutkyn my bro-in-law; Bro. Thos. Stronge; Land called the smythes crofts held of John Howe; Legacy to poor of Netellden; Wife Joane extrix; Mycaell Yonge & bro. Thos. Stronge overseers. Wit*s*:—John Whelplye, John Feild, Rich. How, John Munne. (*Pr*. 9 Apr. 1584).

f. 50. WILLIAM FRAUNCES of London Coney in psh of Shenley, smyth. (*Dat*. 9 Nov. 1584). Wife Anne & our three daus.; Son Francis; Wife extrix. Wit*s*:—Phillip Slep, Rich. Smyth, Wm. Heward, John Lowe. (*Pr*. at Baldock 10 Dec. 1584).

f. 50 b. JOYCE LONGE of Hartingfordbury, widow. (*Dat*. 27 Jan. 1582). Son Wm. Longe; Dau. Joane Longe; Goddau. Joyce West; Dorothy Bridgman; Eliz. Longe; Eliz. Bridgman; Margt. Bridgman; Ann West; Sybbell Longe; Son Roger Longe; Agnis Bridgman. Residue of my corn to be divided amongst 'W*ill*m, Agnis, & Jane'; M*r* Ellis exor. Wit*s*:—Phillip Lawrence minister, Thos. Sayer, Thos. Standley. (*Pr*. 30 Apr. 1584).

f. 51. BARTELLMEW HILL. Registered before at folio 47.

f. 51 b. EDWARD WILSHERE of Steuenage, yeoman. (*Dat*. 18 Mch. 1582). Youngest son Edward; Lands & tenements at Codycoate called Smyth*e* formerly in the occupation of Geo. Hattred & now of Thos. Spoarte; Land in Brok*e* valley in psh. of Steuenage w*ch* late was one W*illm* Kerbies of Hertf; Land called Gospell peece in Brok*e* valley late John Bagshaes gent; Close called Barlie Crofte in the fields of Shepall; Dunstone Wilsheer my 2nd son; Lands in Redhills in Stevenage; Close called Pynn greene & house in occ. of Geo. Heaward; Eldest son George; Grace Parker sometime my maid servant; Clemens Cotton son of Thos. Cotton of Wellwin (under 21); Ann Cotton dau. of s*d* Thos. (under 18); Wm. son of Geo. Wilsheer (under 18); Child*n* of John Parker now living at Hitchin; My three sons exors; Thos. Clarke & Wm. Gynn of Stevenage overseers. Wit*s*:—Wm. Clarke, Rich. Page, Rich. West. (*Pr*. 24 July 1584 at Baldock).

f. 52. MARKE AXTELL of Hemelhempsted, yeoman. (*Dat*. 3 June 25 Eliz.). Son Richard (under 21); Lands in Felden Heath; Wife Grace; Dau. Susan; Father Robt. Axtell; Wm. Royse of Boxwood; 'my said thre children'; Wife extrix; Bro. Thos. Axtell & Robt. Coleman overseers. Wit*s*:—Raphe Knyvet, Christr. Raye, Thos. Axtell & Robt. Coleman. (*Pr*. 15 July 1584).

f. 52. JOHN PORTER of Gravelye, yeoman. (*Dat*. 14 Feb. 25 Eliz.). Dau. Frances Porter; Son Thomas; The child*n* of John Porter & Wm. Porter *viz*. Wm. Porter & Agnes Porter &

Duglas Porter; Son Geo. Porter exor; Son John; Wm. Porter the son of John Porter; Duglas Porter the daughter. (*Pr.* 11 Feb. 1584-5 at Baldock).

f. 52 b. WILLIAM GRACE of Forde in psh. of Great Tringe. (*Dat.* 13 Mch. 1583). Son Thomas; Wife Margt.; Sons Rich. & Wm.; Dau. Eliz. Grace; Son Sebastian Grace (under 21); Sons Daniel & John; Sons Thos. & Richard exors; Cousyn Sebastian Grace & son Wm. overseers. (*Pr.* 21 May 1584 at Baldock).

f. 53. FRANCIS SEYWARD of Brickingdon, yeoman. *(Undated)*. Bur. at Alhallowes in Hertf.; Wife Alice; Sons John & Wm. exors.: Dau. Agnis (under 21); Daus. Kath., Eliz. & Joane; Wm. Heath overseer. Wit<sup>s</sup>:—Wm. Greenewood the wrighter & John Harper; Tenement & ground called Addams Hill. (*Pr.* 24 Sep. 1584).

f. 53. JOHN BLACKETT of Lytle Gaddesden. (*Dat.* 14 Dec. 1583). Son Henry; Thos. Bedford; Son John; Wife Joane; Legacies my mother gave to my sisters child<sup>n</sup> viz. to Eliz. Quarendn & to her bro. Wm. & her sisters Alice & Agnes & to Nicholas Jacson & to Robt. Waddes ij children; Cous. Wm. Garret of Hudnall exor & cous. Rich. Garret overseer. Wit<sup>s</sup>:—Thos. Godard & Thos. Wynsore. (*Pr.* 30 Apr. 1584).

f. 53 b. ROBERT GRIGGE of Kensworth. (*Dat.* 27 Dec. 27 Eliz.). Wife Joane; Son Robt; Dau. Ellyn Beamonde; Margt. Grygge; Son Thos.; Julius Herne; Wife extrix. Wit<sup>s</sup>:—Edw. Horne, Wm. Heaward & Henry Lodge. (*Pr.* 14 Jan. 1584-5 at Baldock).

f. 54. JOANE WELLS of Bovingdon, widow. (*Dat.* 4 Dec. 1583). Joane Axtell my daught<sup>r</sup> unmarried; Daus. Alice Axtell & Agnes Axtell; Timothy son of Henry Axtell my son; Jeames Heart son of Thomas Harte my son in law; Alice Hart dau. of s<sup>d</sup> Thos.; Agnis Goold dau. of Hughe Goold my son in law & John son of s<sup>d</sup> Hugh; Susan Goold dau. of s<sup>d</sup> Hugh; Anne Goolde wife of s<sup>d</sup> Hugh; Dau. Joane Hart; Son Henry Axtell exor; Thos. Axtell & Thos. Hart my son in law of Bovingdon overseers. Wit<sup>s</sup>:—Thos. Wilcocke, Richard Axtell, Thos. Hay. (*Pr.* 21 May 1584).

f. 54. THOMAS WYXE of Digswell. (*Dat.* 31 Jan. [*year omitted*]). Wife Margaret; Son Clement (under 21); Daus. Eliz & Margaret. Wit<sup>s</sup>:—Goodman Jeames Feild & John Celye; wrytten by me John Matrevers the psone of Digswell. (*Pr.* 17 June 1584).

f. 54 b. WILLIAM BRIGES of Harpeden, clarke. (*Dat.* 24 Mch. 26 Eliz.). Sons Wm. & Thos.; Dau. Agnis Briges; Dau. Alice Craulye her child; son in law Tuke his iiij children; Margaret Crane extrix; Thos. North of Hearnes & Marke Stubins overseers. Wit<sup>s</sup>:—John Style, John Stubbyns, Marke Stubbyns, Wm. Squier. (*Pr.* 29 Apr. 1584).

f. 55. KATHERYN IVORYE of Offleye. (*Dat.* 13 Feb. 1584). Thos. Derem' my son; Son Wm. Ivorye; Kath. Tobye; Johne Sebrucke; Robt. Cawdell; Frauncis Deremer, Thos. Deremer, Edw. Deremer, Mary Deremer & Aunis Deremer child<sup>n</sup> of Thos. Deremer; Alce Younge; Joane Younge; Eliz. Younge; Thos.

Younge son of Thos. Younge: Rich. Ivorye; Robt. Ivorye my husband (dec'd); Daus. Aunis & Eliz.; Dau. Joane Younge; Son W<sup>m</sup> Ivorye exor. Wit<sup>s</sup>:—Thoms. Deremer, Thos. Younge, Wm. Ivorye. (*Pr*. 17 June 1584).

**f. 55.** JOANE SERMAN of Barckh'msted Peter, widow. (*Dat*. 22 June 1584). Godson Toby West; John Aweedon; Lawrence Dycons; Henry Seare & his uncle John West; Jerome West; Henry West; Awdrie Nutkine; Raphe Nutkine of Hempsteed; Son-in-law John West; Dau. Mary Dicons; Dau. Alse West; Anne Harbarson of Dunstable; Dau. Joane Penfote; Mother Broune; Widow Rye; Goddau. Marie Whelplye; Mary Aston; Mary Stanboroughe; Goddau. at Dunstable; Son-in-law Richard Panfote exor; Son-in-law John West overseer. Wit<sup>s</sup>:—Nicholas Cleitonus, Wm. Wedon, John Whelplye. (*Pr*. 16 July 1584).

**f 55 b.** HENRY BAGWELL parson of the Rectories or parsonages of Kings Hatfeild *alias* Bushoppes Hatfeild & of Hartingfordburye *alias* Hartfordlingburye. (*Dat*. 6 June 1584). Servants Geo. Gurlye & Jeames Mitchell of Hatfeild exors.; Fouke Onsloe gent of Hatfeild overseer. Wit<sup>s</sup>:—Robt. Bristow gent, Edmound Smyth, Thos. Hauke & Peeter Joanes. (*Pr*. 2 July 1584).

**f. 56.** JOHN PENRED innholder, in the Towne of Hertf. (*Dat*. 24 Oct. 1583). Dau. Gartred (under 18); Son John; House in Westreite; Tenement in psh. of St. Andrew in Hertf. that Hardinge dwelleth in; Eliz. Bucke; Marye Garsey; John Gersey my wifes son; Ralph Gersey; Wife Mary; House that Thos. Springham now dwelleth in; Goodwife Dayne; Legacies to poor of Bengeo, St. Andrews & All Saints in Hertf.; Wife extrix; John North of Jenningesburye overseer; Mary North; M<sup>r</sup> Momford to make a sermon. Wit<sup>s</sup>:—Roger Byrchley 'hye baylye,' Edward Cason, Mich. Jerlane, Robt. Noades, Rich. Healy. (*Pr*. 24 Sep. 1584 at Baldock).

**f. 56 b.** ANTHONY REYNOLD of Baldock, yeoman. (*Dat*. 1 June 1584). Legacy to poor of Norton; Son Anthony (under age); Richard Nenell *alias* Glanfeild, Henry Spurlinge of Baldock, Frauncis Pomford, Nich. Renould & John Lawrence of Norton; Wife Agnes; Wm. Pomford of Baldock; James Lawman of Sutton & his child<sup>n</sup>; Jeames Lawman his brothers child<sup>n</sup> & ij sisters of the s<sup>d</sup> Jeames & their child<sup>n</sup>; Two Banisters of London & their sister, my sisters child<sup>n</sup>; Wm. Reanold of Norton; John Graye & Robt. Graye *alias* Butler. Wit<sup>s</sup>:— Wm. Chatburne the wrighter hereof, Frauncis Pomford & Henrye Spurlynge. Surrender of copyholds to John Pollard & Christr. Crofte to the use of his son, in the presence of Richard Knight gent, & the above witnesses. (*Pr*. 2 July 1584 at Baldocke).

**f. 57 b.** MATHUE BARKER the elder of Aldenham, yeoman. (*Dat*. 1 Dec. 1590). Son Rich. exor; Wife Izabell; Dau. Marye Barker; Mary Butterfeild dau. to John of Pullocke co. Bedf.; John Butterfeild & Joane his now wife; Richard Manning & Mathewe Barker overseers. Wit<sup>s</sup>:—Wm. Butterfield, France Bernard, Wm. Stanes. (*Pr*. 10 Dec. 1590).

f. 58. JOHN IVORYE of Walden Regis, yeoman. (*Dat.* 16 Mch. 1585). Wife Agnes; The childⁿ of my daus. Agnes. Jone & Margt; Xpofer Wellingham my son; Son Thomas (dec^d); House & land at Browneings end in occ. of John Coup: John Sibley; Margt. Sibley my dau.; Master Bristow; Eldest dau. Jone Prudden; Dorothy Jeve my sisters dau.; Thos. & Mary Wellingham & Alice Prudden my daughters childⁿ; Wife extrix. Bro. Thos. Crawley & Edw. Prudden overseers. Witˢ:—Thomas Crawley, Thos. Welche senior, Thos. Richardsonne clarke, scriptor. (*Pr.* 14 July 1586).

f. 59. WILLIAM SHEPPERD of Offley, yeoman. (*Dat.* 14 Feb. 1584). Son Richard: Child my wife now goeth with; Jhon Riches & John Headye; Thos. Woodley & Thos. Tiler; Daus. Eliz. & Annis (under 18); Wife Eliz. extrix; Bro. Bur. Witˢ:—Thos. Woodley, Thos. Tyler, Edw. Foster, John Riches. Surrender of copyholds to Thos. Woodley & Thos. Tiler to use of Robt. Burre my bro-in-law for term of 13 years for payment of legacies &c. Witˢ:—same as before & Thos. Dermer, Robt. Tyler & Robt. Burre. (*Pr.* 17 Mch. 1588).

f. 59. THOMAS MAYNARDE of Wimonlie pva, yeoman. (*Dat.* 31 Aug. 1594). Bro-in-law John Stammer; Messuage called Mayes; Robert Addames; Bro-in-law John Maynard; Grace & Eliz. Stamer daus. of John Stamer; Sist. Eliz. Stamer; Agnes Nashe dau. of Wm. Nashe; Sist. Grace Nashe; Sist. Allis Maynarde; John & Thos. sons of John Maynarde; Bro-in-law Wm. Nashe; Sisters Eliz. Grace & Allis; Grace dau. of Edmund Maynarde; John Ward; Robt. Ward the younger; Godson Thos. Pigion; Goddau. Jane Ward dau. of John Ward; Jone Ward dau. of Robt. Warde; Jone Budden widow: Agnis Fillis: Robt. Whitfield exor.; M^r Fabyan overseer. Witˢ:—John Howze clarke, Wm. Nashe. (*Pr.* 9 Oct. 1594).

f. 60 CLEMENT RUDD of Datchworth, clarke. (*Dat.* 23 May 40 Eliz.). Wife Ann; Interest in the advowson of the rectory of Datchworth; Father Thomas Rudd; Lands in a common field called Covndell known as the Dell peece; The 4 childⁿ of my bro. Rich. Rudd viz:—Annis, Wm., Eliz. & Thos.; The childⁿ of John Rudd & Robt. Rudd my brothers & of Rich. Bockett my bro in law; Bro. Wm. Rudd; Kinswoman Annis Bennet; Mother Eliz. Rudd; Wife extrix; Friends Thos. Michell & Thos. Foster of Datchworth overseers. Witˢ:— George Lewes, Thos. Michell. (*Pr.* 29 May 1598).

f. 60 b. RICHARD FEYLD of Preston in psh. of Kings Walden, yeoman. (*Dat.* 15 July 1609). Copyholds of the manor of Temple Dinsbery [*sic*]; Wife Johan; Son Thos. Feild (under 21); Land bought of Wm. Connisbye; Daus. Johan Feild & Mary, Eme & Agnes; Wife extrix. Witˢ:—John Harmar, Rich. Chawkeley, Thos. Barker & Symon Browne. Surrender of s^d copyholds by the hands of Symon Browne & Thos. Barker two customary tenants, to the uses of the will. (*Pr.* 13 Sep. 1609).

f. 61. ANNE BRADWINE of Great Gaddesden, widow.* (*Dat.* 13 Sep. 6 Jas.). Joane Childe dau. of my Son Robt. Halsey &

* This will gives considerable additions to Cussans' Pedigree of the Halseys (Hund. of Dacorum p. 122).

Mary Halsey & Amy Halsye daus. of s^d Robt.; Hester Halsey
Dorothy Halsey & Sara Seare daus. of s^d son Robt.; Goddau.
Anne Halsey wife to Wm. Halsey of Gaddesden; Anne Wells
dau. of Thos. Wells my son in law; Amy Wells, Joane Wells,
Mary Wells & Jane Wells; Son William his 4 daus. viz:—
Mary, Sara, Judeth & Rebecca; Alice Halsey wife of my son
Thos.: My son Thomas his dau.; Son Phillipp Halsey exor;
Son Robt. Halsey & Wm. Lyllington overseers. Wit^s:—Wm.
Lyllingston & Robt. Halsey. (Pr. 16 Aug. 1609).

f. 61. **JOHN EWINGTON ALIAS DARY** of Harpeden in psh. of
Whethampsted, husbandman. (Dat. 8 May 1609). Wife
Joane; Two tenements in Harpeden, one where I now dwell &
the other where old Ellis dwelleth; Son-in-law Wilm Whitt-
locke & Grace his wife; House at Bamvile wood where I now
dwell; Son-in-law John Whittlocke & Eliz. his wife my dau.;
Son-in-law Geo. Clarke of Saundridge & Margt. his wife;
Thomas Hurst; Every of my grandchild^n being the child^n of
my three daus.; Wife extrix. Wit^s:—John Starr, George
Haward & Nich. Whittlocke. (Pr. 13 Sep. 1609).

f. 62. **THOMAS BYBBESWORTH** th'elder of S^t Ippollyt^e, yeoman.
(Dat. 4 Sep. 1609). Eldest son Thomas; Lands which
descended to me from my father; Second son John; Third son
Geo.; Fourth son Wm.; Fifth son Edward; Sixth son Affabell;
Seventh son Humphrey; Eighth son Robt.; youngest son
Samuel; Hanna & Eliz. daus. of s^d Thomas the younger;
Lands in Gosmer feild late purchased of Wm. Carter; Christr.
Marshall: Land in Tuttingdall feild late purchased of Wm.
Clerke; S^r John Brockett; M^r Cooke; Robt. Draper; Edm.
Claye: Close called Hamondes; Agnes wife of son Wm.; Thos.
son of my son Wm.; Alice dau. of son Affabell; Bro-in-law
John Welch; Thos. & Geo. sons of my son Affabell; S^r Richard
Spencer; Wife Eliz. extrix. Wit^s:—John Marshall, Thos.
Gaddesden, John Gaddesden, John Welch, Edmond Maynerd.
(Pr. 4 Oct. 1609).

f. 62 b. **EDMOND EWINGTON** of Whethampsted, wheelwright.
(Dat. 5 May 1609). Daus. Avis Fletcher & Gabriell her son;
Dau. Mary wife of John Rayment; Dau. Johan Ewington; Son
Thos.: Son-in-law Wm. Fletcher; Bro. Nich. Ewington; Sist.
Johan Casson; Son Thos. exor; Bro. Rich^d Ewington overseer.
Wit^s:—Wm. Feild, Valentyne Thredder & John Facy. (Pr. 4
Oct. 1609).

f. 63. **JOHN BIGGE** of Larence Ayott, laborer. (Dat. 22 Jan. 1608).
Mary Bigge & Eliz. Bigge daus. of Wm. Bigge of Larence
Ayott my kinsman; George Feilde of Walter End; Eliz. wife
of s^d Wm. Bigge; Sist. Gray of Sanderydge; Bro. Edm. Bigge
of Sanderydge; Sist. Bettison of Sanderyege; Widow Dormer
of Ayott S^t Peter; Kinswoman Patyent Bettison; Robt.
Bettison; Thos. Heath of Larence Ayott; John Fray; Thos.
Etheryege; Said Wm. Bigge exor. Wit^s:—Thos. Porter &
Robt. Fulsebye. (Pr. 1 Jan. 1608-9).

f 63 b. **WILLIAM FREEMAN** of Great Stewkely, co. Hunt. husband-
man. (Nuncupative Dat. 11 Aug. 1609). Sons Laurence & Wm.;
Wife Eliz. & son John exors. Wit^s:—Thomas Apleyard, Dau.
Marryot & [blank] Ashton wid. (Pr. 5 Oct. 1609 at S^t Neots).

## ABSTRACTS OF WILLS.

f. 63 b. ROBERT ALPRESSE of Fenny Stanton, co. Hunt. sheaperd. (*Dat.* 22 Sep. 1609). Sons Wm. & Miles; Youngest dau. Amye Allpresse; Henry Allpresse; John son of 'my said sonne John Allpresse'; Edw. son of Thos. Sibbley; Thos. son of Edw. Jennynge; Wife Alice extrix. Wit^s:—Thos. Thodye, John Alpresse, Edw. Jeninge & Miles Arborowe. (*Pr.* 10 Oct. 1609 at Godmanchester).

f. 64. RICHARD ELLKINS of Worneditche in psh. of Kimbolton, co. Hunt. husbandman. (*Dat.* 14 Feb. 1608). Sons Richard & John Elkins; Robt. Quenby of Tylbrooke; Robt. Nicols of Tilbrooke; Son Fras Ellkins 'yf he come agayne into the countrie'; Daus. Dorothy & Mary Ellkins; Sons Rich. & John exors & Thos. Peet 'my landlord overseer; John Gray of Pertenhall; Robt. Newman of Tillbrooke. Wit^s:—Thos. Chamberlayne, Thos. Peet. (*Pr.* 6 Oct. 1609 at S^t Ives).

*To be Continued.*

# Will of John Thomas Hilocomius.

(*P.C.C. Drake* 10).

In the name of God Amen. I, John Thomas Hilocomius scholem^r of the Towne of S^t Albanes in the Countie of Hartff being sicke and weake in bodie but of perfecte mynde and memorie (praised be god) Doe make and ordeyne this my Last will and Testamente in manner and forme followinge that is to saie, ffirste I comende my soule into the handes of Almightie god, and my Bodye to be buryed w^thin the Parrishe Churche of S^t Alban in suche comelie and decent place of the same Churche as to my welbeloved wiefe shalbe thought meete and convenient. Item I doe geue vnto the poore people of the saide Towne of S^t Albons Three powndes to be distributed vnto them on the daye of my Buryall according to the discrecon of my saide wiefe and of my Lovinge kinsman M^r Westerman Clerke viccar of Sandridge. Item I doe geue and bequeathe vnto the saide M^r William Westerman All my Bookes and all my papers in my Studye, my Bookes of Accompte, the bookes of my Ephemerides and my wiefes churche Bookes excepted, the which I geue to my saide wiefe, and excepted also the Bookes of Sebastian Francke, the which I geue to my Lovinge Countryman John de Brooke. And in consideracon of the saide Legacye and bequest of my saide Bookes and papers by me to the saide William Westerman geven and bequeathed my intente and true meaninge is, and I will that the saide William Westerman w^thin sixe monthes after my decease shall paye to the Ministers and Elders of the Dutche Churche in London Tenne powndes to be by them distributed and geven amoungest the poore people of the saide Dutche Churche according to the graue and godlye discrecons of the saide Ministers and elders. And that also he the saide William Westerman shall paye and deliver to the Mayo^r and Burgesses of the saide Towne of S^t Albans for the tyme beinge Tenne powndes of lawfull english money, the w^ch I geue to the poore people of the saide Towne of S^t Albanes to be by the saide Mayo^r and Burgesses according to their best knowledge and discrecon forever employed towardes the Contynuall settinge on worke of the saide poore people. But forasmuche as dyvers stock℈ and somes of money heretofore by good and well disposed persons geven and bequeathed to the saide vse haue bene and are by necligent and evell employmente of the saide Mayo^r and Burgesses consumed and vtterlie wasted whereby not onely the saide poore people are greatelie iniuryed But also the good intente and meanynge of the givers of the saide money vtterlie frustrated Therefore my meanynge ys And I will that the saide Mayo^r and Burgesses shall enter into Bande of fifteene powndes vnto the saide William Westerman with Condicon, that the saide Tenne powndes shall from tyme to tyme forever remayne in stocke and be employed to the vse before by me in this my Will appointed accordinge to my desire mynde and intent therein. Item I will that the saide William Westerman shall enter into Bonde of fortie powndes to my Executrix for the true payment of the saide Twentye powndes aboue by me seu'allie and respectively geven to the saide poore people of the Dutche Churche and of the Towne of S^t Albanes att the tyme aforesaide before that he shall haue or take into his possession the saide Bookes and papers so to him by me gyven as aforesaide. Item I geue and bequeathe to the saide William Westerman all suche debts and somes of money whatsoever w^ch are due vnto me from one Edwarde Bowes gentleman, and all specyalties to me made concernynge the saide debte. And in regarde of the saide Legacies by me to the saide William in this my p'nte Last will and Testamente geuen and bequeathed, and of dyuers other Benefitt℈ by hym of me heretofore had and receaved, I doe earnestlie entreate and desyre the saide William Westerman according to his dutie and my greate trust and confidence in hym reposed to be att all tymes aydinge and comfortinge to my saide wiefe in all matters and occasions whatsoever to the best and vttermoste of his power and good will. Item I geue and bequeathe to my servaunte Edwarde Hitchcocke Three powndes of lawfull english money. Item I geue and bequeathe vnto Margarett my Wiefe whome I doe make and constitute Executrix of this my Last will and Testamente all and singuler the rest of my goodes and Chattelles household stuffe money Jewells and plate debts and specyalties whatsoeu' not before by me in this my p'nte Last will and Testamente geven and bequeathed. And I doe desire my very lovinge and assured good freindes M^r Thomas Woolley one of the princypall Burgesses of the saide Towne of S^t Albons, M^r Roger Williams Parson of the saide Towne of S^t Albans, and the saide William Westerman to be Overseers of this my Last will and Testamente, and to see the same executed and performed accordinge to my true intente and meanynge aboue specyfyed. In wit^s etc. Dated 18 Nov. 38 Eliz. *Signu dicti Johannis Thome Hilocomij Testatoris antedicti.* Wit^s:—Roger Williams Parsone of the Parrishe of S^t Albans, Tho. Hayward, Jan Vanden Broak and of me Richarde Easte. *Confirmation* of will 4 Dec. 38 Eliz. *Proved* 18 Feb. 1595. On the 10th. March 1596 administration *de bonis non* was granted to James Browne son of Margaret Thomas Hilocomius late relict of s^d John Thomas Hilocomius.

# Abstracts of Wills.

### ARCHDEACONRY OF MIDDLESEX ESSEX AND HERTS.

REGISTER "RAYMOND"—CONTINUED FROM PAGE 216.

f. 325 b. ALICE HALYWELL of Chesthunt, widow. (Dat. 7 Apr. 1581). To Cath. & Mary Halywell, daus. of John Halywell y^e younger late of Chesthunt dec^d a legacy which was bequeathed to s^d John by the last will of John Thomas my father (& grandfather to s^d John Halywell); Eliz^th late wife of s^d John & mother of s^d Kath. & Mary; Wm. Lowen (son of Simon Lowen late of Chesthunt dec^d) grandson of s^d John Thomas; Son Robt. Halywell & John his child; Dau. Alice; Dau. Mary; Widow Lambe; Dau.-in-law Eliz. Halywell; Dau. Rebecca extrix: Simon Williams vicar of Chesthunt overseer. Wit^s:—Symon Williams, Edw. Gowldyn. (Pr. at Ware 29 Mch. 1582).

f. 329 b. JOHN ROBERDS of Amwell, husbandman. (Dat. 17 Apr. 1582). Bur. in churchy^d of Amwell; Mother Joan Hemmyng; Bro. Thos. Roberds; A legacy bequeathed to s^d Thos. by the will of Rich^d Roberds his father; Son Thos.; Servants Henry Aylward & Awdry Alway; Wife Anne extrix. Son-in-law John Thomas overseer. Wit^s:—John Thomas, Thos. Rallins ×, Robt. Thomas. (Pr. at Stansted Abbot 26 May 1582).

f. 331 b. THOMAS CHYKKEN. (Dat. 13 Oct. 1582). Bro. Rich. Chikken & his two child^n Wm. & Rich.; Wm. Chykken my bro. Williams son & his bros. & sisters; Sister Joane; Jhonne Chapman; 'All my wyues childrens children'; Annes Sarring my maide; Richard Kinge; Thecher of Amwell; Father Hampton; Wife Margt. extrix. *Thomas Chykkyns.* Wit^s:— Xpofer Ward & Robt. Borham. (Pr. at Stansted Abbot 29 Oct. 1582).

f. 334 b. THOMAS BURTON of Hunsdon, husbandman. (Dat. 17 Dec. 1582). Bur. at Hunsdon; Wife Joane extrix; Lands in Hunsdon comon meade toward Estwicke; Son John; Eldest dau. Joan Burton; Dau. Margt. Burton; Bro. Rich. Burton of Stapleforth Tawny, co. Essex, overseer. Wit^s:—Wm. Preston parson of Hunsdon, Thos. Cramhorne, John Redyngton, John Elliot y^e younger, John Banbricke. (Pr. at Stansted Abbot 29 Oct. 1582).

f. 339. JOHN STILES of Buntingford, yeoman. (Dat. 14 June 1582). Bur. in churchy^d of Leyston; Wife Alice; My sisters son Rich. Newman of Shelford, co. Camb.; Sist. Alice; Saffron ground in Shelford; Margery & Margt. daus. of s^d sister Alice; Frances Stacye my wife's dau.; Wife extrix. Wit^s:—Lewes Reynolds minister, Thos. Watts, John Gylman, Geo. Churchix. (Pr. 17 July 1582).

f. 342 b. JOHN GRAUE of Standon. Registered before, f. 321 b.

f. 344. JOHN CHAIER of Chesthunt, singleman. Registered before, f. 320.

f. 347. WILLIAM FOSTER of Ware, channler. Reg$^d$ before, f. 322 b.

f. 347. WILLIAM BRIGGES of Laiston, gent. Reg$^d$ before, f. 319.

[*End of Hertfordshire Wills in Register "Raymond."*]

### REGISTER "BARKER."

f. 2. MATHEWE KYNGE of Barly. (*Dat.* 4 Dec. 1582). Bur$^d$ in churchy$^d$ of Barly 'amonge myne Awncestors'; Wife Kath.; Copyhold tenement in Barly called Pryors; Mathewe Kynge my systers sonne; House in Barly called Fyshers; Sister Johan Heydaye: Copyhold tenement called Hickteyke; Land in Nuttamsted; Rich$^d$ Kynge my sisters son; House called Stevens; Allyce Vmweld my mother; House & tenement called Barlyes Landes belonging to the manor of Newsells in Barkewaye; Copyholds of the manors of Rookye & Water Andrewes in Barkwaye; Copyholds of manor of Cockenhache in Barkway; Copyhold tenement of manor of Grenebury in Barlye; Rich$^d$ Kinge & his mother Johane Forham; Freeholds in psh. of Great Chissell & little Chissell, co. Essex, Nothamsted, close called Dowesemers, messuage called Fypps; To the poor of Barlye annual rent of 10s.* out of my freehold lands called Porters Peece; Marcye Ingley my sist-in-law; Grace Kynge one of my 2 sisters daus.; Margaret Kynge my sisters dau.; Anne Fordham my sisters dau; Rebecka Heydaye dau. of my sist. Heydaye; Wife extrix. Wit$^s$:—Edw. Ingley, Hen. Hawke, Wm. Kefford & others.

f. 9 JOHN RAMSAY of Stortford, malteman. (*Dat.* 8 Oct. 1561). Bur. at Stortford; Wife Alese; Son Mathew; House held of M$^r$ Parsons of the same town; Daus. Jone & Margt; Frauncis my boye; Said wife & son exors; John Maryon overseer. Wit$^s$:—John Marion, John Cramphorne, Richard Calyday 'scriptorem huius Testamenti'.

f. 15. ROBARTE EDMUNDE of Hormede. (*Dat.* 15 Mch. 1558). Bur. at Hormead; Wife Jone extrix; Sons Thomas, John, Harrye & Edward; Daus. Annys, Eliz., Margery & Kath. Wit$^s$:—Harry Edmund, Thos. Broude.

f. 27 b. WILLIAM FRYER of Puckeridge. (*Dat.* 2 May 1590). Wife Helyne; Bro. Rychard Fryer in Lankeshire, James his son; Sist. Margt. Hatton & her son John Hatton; Eliz. Knagge of Naysinge once my servant; Wife extrix. Wit$^s$:— Henry Heron, Lewes Asmall. (*Pr.* at Stansted Abbot, 30 Sep. 1590).

f. 31. HENDRY SMYTH of Braughinge. (*Dat.* 3 July 1590). Wife Jhone; Sons Hendry, Jeaspere, John, Hewe & Myhell (all under 21); Wife extrix. Wit$^s$:—John Allman, Wm. Bownest, Henry Beell, Rich. Rowe, John Headlam vicar of Broughinge. (*Pr.* at Stansted Abbot 1 Sep. 1590).

f. 31 b. ROWLAND HEARYNGE clerk, parson of the parish Church & Rectory of Throckynge. (*Dat.* 22 May 1587). Wife Elizabeth extrix. Wit$^s$:—Thos. Northop the elder, Wm. Hetes, John Plare, Wm. Clere. (*Pr.* at Stansted 22 May 1590).

* Mentioned by Mr. Cussans in his account of the Charities of Barley, but without any intimation as to its origin.

f. 32 b. JOHN SIMPSON of Puccaridg within the parish of Braughin, yeoman. (*Dat*. 9 Apr. 1590). Wife Eliz.; The late husband of my s<sup>d</sup> wife; M<sup>r</sup> Cokes parson of Throckin; M<sup>r</sup> John Headlam vicar of Braughin; Clemenc 'my baise doughter' to be brought up 'as his owne' by my bro. Simpson; Bro. Wm. Simpson exor; House wherein I dwell called the Crowne; Henry Casell. List of debts names Goodman Manning, Raphe Day, Wm. Scattergood servant of M<sup>r</sup> Thos. Godly, John Alman, Thos. Clarke of Braughinge, M<sup>r</sup> Kimpton, Thos. Hoye of Stondon. *John Simpson*. Wit<sup>s</sup>:— John Hedlam vicar of Braughling, Thos. Manyng, Wm. Simpson. (*Pr*. at Stansted Abbot 22 May 1590).

f. 33 b. JOHN BARNES the elder of Chesthunt (*Nunc. will dat*. 2 Aug. 1590). John Barnes the younger of Chesthunt. Wit<sup>s</sup>:— Christ<sup>r</sup> Clarke, Edw. Kinge & John Griffen. (*Adm*. 20 Aug. 1590).

f. 34. MARRIAN HART of Stockinge Pelham widow. (*Dat*. 24 Aug. 1590). The four daus. of my son John; Son John Hart; Dau. Johan Baucock; Dau. Betrys; Henry Hayward of Stockinge Pelham; Henry Strong & Jeames Growt of Stocking Pelham exors. Wit<sup>s</sup>:—Anthony Baucock & Henry Hayward. (*Pr*. at Stortford 11 Feb. 1590).

f. 37. THOMAS THELE of Brawghin, yeoman. (*Dat*. 13 Nov. 1590). Thomas son of my bro. John Thele; Bro. Botterell; My brothers in law; My three sisters their child<sup>n</sup> viz. sister Botterell, sist. Langdall & sist. Brampfelld; Jone wife of John Lucas; Bro. John Thele exor. List of debts names Wm. Snowe of Aspeden, Dlle [*sic*] Cramphorne, Mathewe Parrant, Wm. Bownest of Stone bury, Geo. Hyde Master Baeshes man, Jeames Boulten gentleman, M<sup>r</sup> Tomlyne parson of Aspeden, M<sup>r</sup> Cox parson of Throcking. Wit<sup>s</sup>:—John Headlame vicar of Broughin, John Langdell, Henry Botterell. (*Pr*. at Stortford 19 Dec. 1590).

f. 37 b. JAMES UMWELL of Layston. (*Dat*. 5 Sep. 1590). John Chrowch; Alse Vmwell, Eliz. Vmwell; Apprentice Wm. Eterige; My two brothers dwelling at Barkewaye & three sisters; Prudence Nunvm; Wife Jone extrix. *James Vmvell*. Wit<sup>s</sup>:—Rich. Awnsham vicar of Layston, Wm. Edridge, John Chruch. (*Pr*. at Stansted Abbot 26 Oct. 1590).

f. 38. ROBERT CROUCHE of Thunderige, yeoman. (*Dat*. 2 Apr. 1589). Dau. Eliz. now wife of Robt. Daulton & her child<sup>n</sup>; Son Robt.; Dau. Joan now wife of Wm. Bridgman & her child<sup>n</sup>; Dau. Margt. now wife of Geo. Crowche; Wife Eliz. extrix; Thos. Crouch my sonne Robert his child. Wit<sup>s</sup>:— John Semer, Als Hulden, Wm. Parker. (*Pr*. at Stansted Abbot 26 Oct. 1590).

f. 42 b. AGNES COOKE of Chesthunt, widow. (*Dat*. 2 May 1590). Youngest son Hendry Cooke; Dau. Margt. Cooke; Wm. Cooke my 2<sup>nd</sup> son; Son Robt. (dec<sup>d</sup>); Sarah Cooke dau of Thos. Cooke my eldest son; Robt. Hasellwood; Eliz. Snoden; Goodwife Foster; Margerye Jening(?); Goodwife North; John Cottiges; Eldest son Thos. exor; Son Wm. overseer. Wit<sup>s</sup>:—Thos. Betigonne scr., Henry Cannon, John Lamploy. (*Pr*. at Sabridgeworth 16 Dec. 1590).

f. 44. RAPH MODYE of Braughin, miller. (*Dat.* 13 Nov. 1590). Bro-in-law Wm. Simpson: Bro-in-law Thos. Simpson to bring up my two child[n] which I had of his sisters body; Wife Dorothy extrix. Wit[s]:—John Headlam vicar of Braughin Thos. Clarke, Wm. Meade, John Silvester. (*Pr.* at Sabridgeworth 11 Mch. 1590-1).

f. 45. JOHN HITCHMAN thelder of Wydford. (*Dat.* 1 Dec. 28 Eliz.). House called Fewterers; Wife Margt.; John Hitchman my younger son; Robt. Hitchman my elder son; The 3 child[n] of son Robt.; Wife extrix. Wit[s]:—John Hille, John Addames. (*Pr.* at Stortford 14 Jan. 1590-91).

f. 50. RICHARD PARKER of Barlye, blacksmyth. (*Dat.* 13 July 32 Eliz.) Wife Margt.; House wherein I dwell called Prestons: Son Rich[d]; Pastures called Holyewells, Preists Pikle, & Grege; Eldest son Henry; Land in Great Watrdenn; (Other lands specified); Richard Parker son of my son Henry; Younger son Rich. Parker; Dau. Margt; Dau. Jonne (married); Magdelen Dennys (under 21); Wm. Parker son of s[d] son Richard; Eliz. Socklyng; Dau. Agnes Botman; Thos. & Henry brothers of Richard (son of my son Henry) & Ellen their sister; Wife Margt. extrix. *Sign. Richard Parker.* Wit[s]:—Andrew Willett, Thos. Parker, Henry Hankes. (*Pr.* at Sabridgworthe 12 Feb. 1590-1).

f. 53. ROBERT DALTON of Barwicke in psh. of Standon. (*Dat.* 16 Nov. 1590). Sons Robt. & Joseph; Tenement at Heaven end; Son Thoby (under 21); Daus. Sarra, Mary, Martha & Bridget Dalton (under 21); Son John & Wife Eliz. exors. Wit[s]:— Geo. Crouche, Jeames Jurden & Thos. Gamble. (*Pr.* at Sabridgworth 13 Jan. 1598-9).

f. 56 b. WILLIAM KYNGE of Olde Hall grene in psh of Standon. (*Dat.* 13 Feb. 159 [*sic*]). Joane Barfoote my mother; Wife Eliz.; Sons Wm., George & John Kyng; Daus Mary, Alice & Eliz. Kynge; House in occupation of Robt. Archer; Jane Skelton; Wife extrix; Friends Wm. Parnell, Chas. Wrottinge, Thos. Weedinge & John Godfrey jun[r] overseers. Wit[s]:—the four overseers. (*Pr.* at Sabridgeworth 11 Mch. 1590-1).

f. 57 b. EDWARD BYGGE of Symonsyde in psh of Bishops Hatfield, yeoman. (*Dat.* 16 Jan. 27 Eliz.). Bur. at Hatfield; Daus. Alice, Anne, Marye & Eliz.; Thos. Chadysleye; Wife Alice extrix; Bro. Phyllype Bygge & John Duke overseers. Wit[s]:— Thos. Rawsone. (*Pr.* at Stansted Abbot 14 Apr. 1590).

f. 58 b. WILLIAM THOROWGOOD of Chesthunt, yeoman. (*Dat.* 16 Jan. 1589). Dau. Mary; House & land in Aldeburrye in psh. of Chesthunt; Son John; Servants Marye Cooke & Thos. Grat; Child[n] of my wifes dau. Johan Cranfyld; Wife Kath.; House at Turners hill in psh of Chesthunt; Wife extrix; Henry Fade & Thos. Claxton my neighbours overseers. Wit[s]:—the overseers & Symon Williams vicar of Chesthunt. (*Pr.* at Stansted 14 May 1590).

[*End of Hertfordshire Wills in Register "Barker."*

# Court Rolls of the Manor of Picotts otherwise Piggots in Bishops Stortford.

(Continued from Page 272).

**PEKOTES.** Court held there on the Monday next before the feast of S⁺ Peter which is called Advincula in the fourteenth year of the reign of King Henry VI. 1435.*

Essoins. None.

Fealty. William Tannere is distrained more often for xv$d$. of rent in arrear arising from certain lands which were formerly Elias Blethewen's viz:—from the little croft lying next Hokyrhille viz:—parcel of the same fee. And because the entire fee thereof is not unknown the same William for one croft agrees that he will pay x$d$. of rent for ever. And he did fealty.

Fealty. As yet Alice who was the wife of William Rose, widow, agrees that she will pay v$d$. for a solar, a gate & one gateway under the same form as the aforesaid Wm. Rose her husband agreed, for which iij$s$. vj$d$. were lately claimed therefor. Wherefore she is charged excessively as it is said. And she did fealty.

Inquisition. Taken by virtue of office by the oaths of twelve jurors from the tenants, who present that Stephen Fabyan (vj$d$), Robt. Smyth (vj$d$), John Colyn (vj$d$), the vicar of Storteford (xij$d$) & the Tenant of the land of Manshepes (xij$d$.) make default in suit of Court. Therefore in mercy.

Mercies iij$s$. vj$d$.

Mercies xij$d$. And they present that Rich. Pegeon (iij$d$.), John Gate (iij$d$.) and his servant, the servant of John Bussh (iij$d$.) & the servant of John Belh'm of Northstret (iij$d$.) have cut down the wood at Pekotẻ for latices without licence. Therefore in mercy.

Mercies ij$s$. ix$d$. John Everard (iij$d$.) for trespass in Westfeld with xvj sheep, Matilda Everard (vj$d$.) there with xx sheep on four occasions, Roger Pulter (vj$d$.) there with viij sheep, Thos. Stronge (iij$d$.) there with vj sheep, Nich. Tannere (iij$d$.) with iij beasts, John Baldewen (xij$d$.) of Thorle in the lord's meadow with vj beasts, on twelve occasions. Therefore he puts himself in the lord's grace.

Affeerers { Richard Pegeon } who are { John Stonhard } sworn

**PECOTES.** Court of John Leventhorp esq, Robert Canfeld, Ralph Grey & their fellows, feoffees, held there on the Friday in the morrow of Corpus Christi in the 37ᵗʰ year of King Henry VI. 1458.

* As before the date in figures is added by a later hand. It should be 1436.

|              | Land held of S<sup>t</sup> Bartholomew, land held lately by Thomas Thressher vicar of the church of Stortford, Wm. |
|---|---|
| Default of suit of court | Cursū, Thos. Saunsom, Thos. Chirchesey miller, John Folkyngham, Alice Stonard, John Hogon, John Barnton & John Ponde make default of suit of court. And further the bailiff is ordered to distrain them against the next Court to do fealty to the lords abovesaid. |

To this Court came John Palmer & did fealty to the lord for one messuage lying [*blank*] which he holds of the aforesaid lords by the rent of vj*d*. by the year & [which] came to him by right of inheritance after the death of John Palmer his father who died seised thereof. And further he pledged to the lord for Relief as much as he owed for rent.

*Fealty*

*Relief* vj*d*.

To that same Court came John Newman, Barker & did fealty for a messuage with a garden at Horshamdich, late Thomas Beu'le's, cowper at the rent of xij*d*. by the year & which he lately had by the gift & feoffment of Roger Shipman.

*Fealty.*

Wm. Drey, Thos. Bowyer, Wm. Kyng, Thos. Palmer, John Mynott, John Newman, Tanner & John Wanell did fealty to the lords aforesaid.

*Fealty*

It is ordered to distrain Henry Snowe for rent of ix*d*. for one messuage etc.

*It is ordered*

Affeerers, the whole Homage.

---

**PECOTTES.** Court of Henry Barle esquire & others, lords of this Manor, there held on Tuesday next before the feast of S<sup>t</sup> Luke the Evangelist ' anno ab inchoacione regni Regis Henrici sexti post conquestum xlix° & readepcionis sue regie potestatis Anno primo. 1422 '.*

*Essoin* Joan who was the wife of Thomas Bowyer for common suit by John Grace.

Yet as heretofore it is ordered to distrain Henry Snowe to pay to the lords, by the year ix*d*. for one messuage & one piece of land formerly Thomas Milward's & afterwards Wm. Belhom's & afterwards Hykeman Draper's lying in Kyngesbreggefeld. And for ix*d*. rent by the year for one tenement in Okelesford near Helion Blithewyn formerly said Wm. Belhom's, by the aforesaid Henry now unjustly withheld &c.

*It is ordered*

To this Court came Robert Turnor and acknowledged that he holds of the lords, one messuage, formerly Thos. Palmer's, situate in the Northstrete between the tenement of Thos. Palmer on the north part & the messuage of Rich. Markes on the south part, one head thereof abutting on the kings highway towards the east, the other head thereof abutting on Barborlane towards the west, by the service of rent to the lords vj*d*. by the year. And he did fealty to the lords.

*Ric. Feast*

*Fealty*

To this Court came Thomas Pernell & acknowledged that he holds of the lords, in right of Alice his wife, late

*Tho. Crabbe*

* Once more the figures representing the year have been added by a later hand, who has blundered seriously this time. 1470 is the correct date.

|   |   |
|---|---|
| Fealty | wife of John Clerk, one piece of land formerly Thos. Goldston's, lying in a certain field called Appeltonfeld by the service of rent to the lords ij$d$ by the year, at the usual terms of this Manor. And he did fealty to the lords. |

To this Court came John, son of Richard Marion & acknowledged that he holds of the lords a Garden with a certain Grange & a certain meadow lying at Hokerellbregge called Vnkelishawe & a certain Croft called Partrichcrofft late the aforesaid Richard his father's, who died seised thereof, by service of rent to the lords, ij$s$. by the year. And he did fealty to the lords. And because the Court is not rightly informed whether the said Richard died seised thereof or not, a day is given to the Inquisition to give the full truth thereof at the next Court &c.

*Marginal notes:* Fealty. Marrien now Savell now Godfries.* Day.

By virtue of the Steward's office the inquisition is taken by the fealty of John Tanner, Thos. Palmere, John Newman, John Palmere, Wm. King, John Bareitton, John Marion, John Warner, who say upon their fealty that The Prior of S$^t$ Bartholomew's Hospital, London, (xl$d$.), The vicar of Storteford (xij$d$.), Rich. Markes (iiij$d$.) for land formerly John Cook's, Wm. Blank (iiij$d$), the tenant of the land late Andrew Fuller's on Horsendych (iiij$d$.), the tenant of the land late Thos. Peion's, now Anne Folkyngham's for her tenement in Southstrete (iiij$d$.), John Hogon (iiij$d$.) for one acre of land in Shepho, John Chapman (iiij$d$.) ['modo Georg Cheney' *interlined by later hand*] for one piece of land in Benhook, Thomas Rotors (iiij$d$.), Thos. Samsom (not warned) for one messuage in Southstrete late John Trotte's & John Jardeuyll Jun. (not warned) for land formerly John Wanell, owe suit to this Court & now made default. Therefore they are in mercy &c.

*Marginal note:* Mercies vj$s$. viij$d$.

Item, they say that Thomas Pernell should pay to the lords by the year xij$d$ for one piece of land in Appeltonfeld, for many years by him unjustly withdrawn. And that John Hogon should pay to the lords by the year v$d$. for land late Wm. Waleys. And that the Prior of the Hospital of S$^t$ Bartholomew London should pay to the lords by the year vj$d$. for certain [lands] by him unjustly withdrawn. And that Rich. Markes should pay to the lords by the year xxj$d$. for certain parcels of land which he holds of that Manor, by him unjustly withdrawn. Therefore let them be distrained &c.

*Marginal note:* It is ordered.

Item, they say that John Folkyngham has unjustly encroached on the land of this manor by the space of five feet, with a certain hedge by him placed at Stonehill. Therefore he is ordered to remove it before the next Court.

*Marginal note:* It is ordered.

Item, they say that when the Bailiff of this Manor on Friday in the feast of S$^t$ Michael the Archangel in the 8$^{th}$ year of the reign of Edward late King of England, at Storteford within the fee of the lords, for a certain rent

---

* These marginal notes are added by later hands.

|||
|---|---|
| Mercy xx*s*. | of ij*s*. vj*d*. by the year for many years being in arrear unpaid, took a certain horse by way of distress & wished to detain it according to the law & custom of the realm of England, William Waleys of Storteford aforesaid by force & arms rescued the aforesaid horse from the possession of the said Bailiff. Therefore he is in mercy &c. |

Affeerers { Thomas Palmer
{ John Newman

---

**PECOTTES.** Court* held there on Monday next after the close of Easter in the 17th year of the reign of King Edward the 4th after the conquest. [1478]

Essoins None.

Inquisition Inquisition taken by virtue of the Steward's office by the oaths of Thos. Palmer, Wm. Newman sen*r*, Walt. Newman, Robt. Turnour, John Clerk, Thos. Sampson, Reginald Jegon, John Taillo*r*, John Jardevile jun*r* who say upon their fealty that The Prior of the Hospital of S*t* Bartholomew, London (iiij*d*), The Vicar of the church of Stortford, Richard Markes for land late John Coke's, the tenant of land late Wm. Blank's (iiij*d*.), the tenant of land late Thos. Peicon's now John Worlich† for his

Mercies tenement in Southstrete, John Hogon (iiij*d*.) for one acre of land in Shepeho, the tenant of one piece of land in Benhook, late John Chapman's, the tenant of the land late Thos. Rotor's, John Marion (iij*d*.), the tenants of the land of Manshippes, John Newman owe suit of Court & make default. Therefore they are in mercy.

Fealty 'modo le taynter barnes' To this Court came Wm. Newman senior & did fealty to the lords for one messuage in Southstrete with certain lands late Thos. Bowyer's and for one messuage formerly Wm. Kyng's.

Fealty. To this Court came Walter Newman & did fealty to the lords for one croft called Oxecroft abutting on Brambilfeld late John Baryngton's & he is admitted tenant thereof.

Fealty To this Court came John Clerk son of John Clerk of Waterlane & acknowledged that he holds of the lords one piece of land lying in Waterlane for one piece of land in Apptonfeld formerly Thos. Golston's by the rent of xij*d*. by the year, and another piece of land in the same field late the s*d* Thos. Golston's & he did fealty.

Fealty Thomas Sampson acknowledged that he holds of the lords one tenement with a garden adjoining, formerly Andrew Fuller's & afterwards John Trotte's by the rent of v*d*. by the year. And he did fealty therefor.

'Modo le George' Reginald Gegon acknowledged that he holds of the lords one messuage formerly Nicholas Colman's & four shops annexed formerly belonging to the same Nicholas by the rent of xv*s*. & suit of Court which same messuage

---

* Another Roll in Mr. Glasscock's possession contains accounts of this and the next two Courts. The writing is by a later hand and the differences, mainly in spelling, are not of sufficient importance to justify printing both copies.

† In the margin a later hand writes 'modo J. Wylly q. nuper fuit John Wolryche.'

| | |
|---|---|
| Fealty | was formerly Simon Farnham's. And he did fealty. |
| Fealty<br>'Modo Thome Wilsemar' | John Taillor acknowledged that he holds of the lords one tenement in Southstrete with the appurtenances, formerly John Piper's & before that Margaret Lavenham's,* by the rent of xviij*d*. by the year. And he did fealty to the lords. |
| 'Modo Ric. Jardevile fil.'<br>Fealty. | John Jardevile junior acknowledged that he holds of the lords three acres of land lying on Dontonhill by the rent of ij*d* by the year which same three acres of land were formerly John Wanell's & he did fealty.† |
| It is ordered<br><br><br><br><br><br><br><br><br><br><br><br><br>Distraint. | It is ordered to distrain the tenant of one piece of land in Benhook,‡ late John Chapman's to attend the Court & make satisfaction for default in suit of court & to do fealty. And that John Hogon should§ pay to the lords by the year vj*d*. for lands late Wm. Waleys', that the Prior of the Hospital of St Bartholomew London should§ pay to the lords vj*d*. by the year for certain lands in the Rental contained, that Rich. Markes should pay to the lords by the year xxj*d*. for certain parcels of land by him unjustly withdrawn, that Christian Drey should pay to the lords by the year vj*d* for one messuage in Shoprowe, that Henry Snowe should pay to the lords by the year ix*d*. for one messuage & one piece of land formerly Thos. Milwards, afterwards Wm. Belhom's & afterwards Hikman Draper's lying in Kyngesbreggefeld & ix*d*. by the year for one tenement in Okelesford near Helion Blythewyn, formerly the sd Wm. Belhom's. Therefore let them be distrained etc. |

Affeerers The whole Homage.

| | |
|---|---|
| **PECOTTES** | Court held there on Tuesday next after the feast of Holy Trinity in the 14th year of the reign of King Henry VII. 1499. |
| Inquisition<br><br><br><br><br><br><br><br><br>Mercies | Inquisition taken there by virture of the Steward's office, by the oaths of John Grace, Thos. Felde, Rich. Jardefeld, John Clyfton, Robt. Breton, John Frounceys, who say that the Master of St Bartholomew's London (vj*d*.), the Vicar of Stortford (iij*d*.), John Thomson (iij*d*.) for land late Hogyns, Reginald Rother (iij*d*), Henry Snowe (iij*d*.), Joan Bolington (ij*d*.), the tenant of lands called Manshepes, the tenant of land late John Marion's, Robt. Berdeney (iij*d*.), John Janyn (iij*d*.), Geoffrey Thurgode (iij*d*.), the tenant of land called Markes (vj*d*.), Wm. Mede, Thos. Sampson, John Taillor & John Spencer of Estwik owe suit of Court & made default. Therefore they are in mercy as appears above their names. |
| Fealty<br>'George Hawkynes' | To this Court came Thos. Felde, as in right of Joan his wife & did fealty to the lord for one messuage called the George & four Shops annexed formerly Thos. Petteworth's, held of that Manor by service of xv*s*. by the year & suit of Court. |

\* *Wenham* in second copy.
† In the margin of the second copy is written 'The Hill nexte to the Shippes.'
‡ '*Chenics*' written in margin of second copy.
§ *Redderet* in first copy. *Solebat reddere* in second.

| | |
|---|---|
| Fealty | To this Court came John Grace & did fealty to the lord for part of a messuage with a garden appurtenent thereto, formerly John Maldon's abutting on Teyntorhill, which he holds by service of xxiij*d*. by the year And two acres & a half of land lying in Benehoke, late John Skynner's abutting on Appetonfeld, by the rent of v*d*. & one piece of land lying in Appetonfeld, by service of ij*d*. by the year & suit of Court. |
| Fealty | To this Court came Robt. Breton & did fealty to the lord for one tenement lying in Northstrete formerly Robt. Turnor's, held by the rent of vj*d*. by the year & suit of court. |
| Fealty 'Ric. Feaste' 'Jo. Gybbes' | To this Court came John Fraunceys & acknowledged that he holds of the lord one Shop with a Solar formerly Wm. Rose's by the service of vj*d*. by the year & suit of Court. |
| Fealty 'Ro. Perrye' | To this Court came John Clyfton & acknowledged that he holds of the lord one Tenement in Southstrete late Edward Marssh's, by the rent of xij*d*. by the year & suit of court. |
| Fealty 'Jardfeld' | To this Court came Rich. Jardefeld & acknowledged that he holds of the lords one acre of land lying in Halfacres in one piece included at Dontonshill by the rent & service of ix*d* and suit of court. |

Affeerers The whole Homage.

---

**PECOTTES** Court held there on Tuesday the last day of March in the 21st year of the reign of King Henry VII [1506]

Essoins [None]

Inquisition taken there by virtue of the Steward's office by the oaths of John Grace, Richard Jardefeld, Andrew Clyfton, Richard Newman, Robt. Breton & Thos. Dynes who say upon their oath that Thos. Jegon, the Master of St Bartholomew, London, the vicar of the Church of Stortford, John Thomson, John Parker for land called Manshyppes Reginald Rotor, John Fychet for land late Henry Snowe's, the tenant of land late John Marion's, Robt. Berdeney, John Franceys, the tenant of the land late Thos. Markes', Joan Mede widow, Wm. Taylor, Joan Spencer* owe suit of court & make default. Therefore they are in mercy as appears above.†

| | |
|---|---|
| Fealty Now George Browne‡ | To this Court came Andrew Clyfton & did fealty to the lord for a messuage in Southstret formerly Wm. Kynge's lately purchased from John Clyfton, held of that Manor by service of xij*d*. by the year & suit of Court. |
| Fealty George Hawkins | To this Court came Richard§ Newman & did fealty to the lord for one tenement lying upon Teyntorhyll, late Thos. Sampson's held of that Manor by service of v*d*. by the year & suit of court. |

* The name of 'Thurgode' appears in the first copy.
† In the second copy the amounts are omitted, and in the earlier copy they are almost illegible.
‡ A later hand has added the name 'Robt Perrey.'
§ Nicholas in first copy.

|  |  |
|---|---|
| Fealty G. Hawkins | To this Court came Thos. Dynes* & did fealty to the lord for one tenement late John Jardefeld's lying in Southstret held of that manor by service of ij*d* by the year & suit of court. |
| Relief xv*s* George Hawkins | And that Joan late wife of John† Jegon died after the last court solely seised of & in one free messuage with a chamber a cellar & the appendages belonging to that Manor, formerly Alice Colman's & lately Thomas Thressher's called the George with the appurtenances after whose death there fell to the lord for relief xv*s*. & j*d*. Thomas Jegon is her son & next heir & of full age. |
| Distress | And that Wm. Taylor withdrew the rent of xviij*d*. by the year for one messuage in Southstret formerly John Pyper's for vij years past. Therefore it is ordered to distrain the said Wm. Taylor to be here at the next court to pay to the lord the rent aforesaid & to do fealty to the lord. |

And that John Fraunceys withdrew the rent of iij*s*. by the year for his lands & tenements. Therefore it is ordered to distrain the said John to be here at the next court to pay to the lord the rent aforesaid & to do fealty to the lord.

And that John Maryone died since the last court seised of & in one garden with a certain grange & one piece of meadow lying at Hokerell brygge called Vnueleshove‡ & formerly a Croft called Parterichscroft which he held of that Manor by service of ij*s*, after whose death there fell to the lord for Relief ij*s*. & that John Maryon is heir & but 16 years of age.

Affeerers the whole Homage.

*To be Continued.*

---

# Marriage Licences.
## Archdeaconry of St Albans.
### By A. E. GIBBS.

(Continued from Page 288).

1688-9

January 7. John Love of Watford, joiner, single man, and Elizabeth Potton of Abbott's Langley, single woman; at Abbott's Langley. John Arnett of St. Albans, turner, a surety.

January 9. John Roggers of St. Albans, shoemaker, single man, and Mary Copley of the same; at St. Albans. Richard Roggers of St. Albans, shoemaker, a surety.

---

* Denys in first copy.
† Altered to Reginald in first copy.
‡ Vnkelishawe in first copy.

January 30. John Chilton or Chiltron [*written both ways*] of St. Peters, and Sarah Young; at Redburne. Bernard Chilton or Chiltron of Hulcutt, co. Buckingham, a surety.

February 7. Richard White of St. Albans, glover, and Ann Clark of St. Michaels, spinster, aged about 40 years; at the Abbey or St. Michaels. Edward Clark [*signed* Clake] of St. Michaels, a surety.

February 10. William Halsey of Redbourn, baker, single man, and Mary Pilgrim of the same, single woman; at St. Albans. William Grove of Redbourn, sawyer, a surety.

March 2. Robert Taylor of St. Albans, miller, bachelor, and Elizabeth Johnson of the same, maid; at St. Albans. Henry Parker of St. Albans, baker, a surety.

March 6. George Stonehouse of Radley, co. Oxon, gent., and Ann Ashton of St. Albans; at St. Albans. Thomas Mottershed of Stoney Stratford, co. Buckingham, gent., a surety.

1689

March 25. Samuel Pope of Abbott's Langley, blacksmith, single man, and Rose Perry of the same, single woman; at St. Albans. Ralph Jackson of St. Peters, victualler, a surety.

March 30. John Lawrence of Watford, blacksmith, bachelor, aged about 25 years, and Mary Boddymaid of the same, spinster, aged about 22 years; at Watford. John Arnott of St. Albans, turner, a surety.

April 1. William Beech of St. Stephen's, labourer, bachelor, and Mary Wright of St. Michaels, spinster; at St. Michaels.

April 3. Thomas Atkinson of Bushey, gent., and Mary Fauson of Berkhamstead; at Bushey. Samuel Cleaver of Bushey, gent., a surety.

April 13. John Hill of St. Stephen's, husbandman, bachelor, aged about 30 years, and Mary Hunt of the same, aged about 19 years; with her father's consent; at St. Stephens. Henry Feild of St. Stephens, tailor, a surety.

April 27. Edward Babb of Watford, husbandman, bachelor, aged about 42 years, and Sarah Pudiford of Sarrat, spinster, aged about "22 years and something better"; at Sarratt, Watford, Sandridge, Bushey, or Idelstree. Henry Marston of St. Albans, husbandman, a surety.

May 16. Samuel Fley of St. James's in the City of Westminster, joiner, and Elizabeth Richardson of St. Albans; at St. Albans. John Richardson of St. Albans, brewer, a surety.

May 18. John Smith of St. Albans, maltster, and Frances Richardson of the same; at St. Albans. David Jones of St. Albans, gardener, a surety.

May 19. Henry Morgan of Ridge, labourer, single man, and Ann Oliver of North Mimms, single woman; at St. Peters. Henry Marston [*signed* Maston] of St. Peters, labourer, a surety.

May 30. John Stoakes, of Harding *alias* Harpenden, husbandman, bachelor, aged about 25 years, and Elizabeth Randall of the same, spinster, aged about 28 years; at Harding [St. Peters in allegation.] Ralph Heyward of St. Albans, mealman, a surety.

June 6. John Page of Harrow on the Hill, bachelor, aged about 30 years, and Susanna Skidmore of Rickmersworth, spinster, aged about 23 or 24 years; having neither father nor mother; at St. Albans. Henry Marston of St. Albans, husbandman, a surety.

June 6. John Prentice of Hatfield, bachelor, and Susan Ivory of St. Albans; at St. Albans, John Beaumont [*signed* Beamont] of St. Albans, a surety.

June 13. John Grover of St. Peters, yeoman, widower, and Ellen Chopping of St. Michaels, single woman, at St. Albans, St. Peters, or St. Michaels. William Chopping of St. Michaels, blacksmith, a surety.

July 31. James Baldwin of St. Peters, widower, and Mary Rench of St. Michaels, maid; at St. Albans. Edward Robinson of St. Albans, a surety.

August 16. Richard Keen of St. Albans, tailor, single man, and Ann Scrivener of St. Stevens, single woman; at St. Michaels. National Prior of St. Michaels, tailor, a surety.

August 24. Gilbert Kinder of St. Albans, butcher, single man, and Mary Sheerer of the same, single woman; at St. Albans. David Jones of St. Albans, gardener, a surety.

September 7. John Trott of Great Gaddesden, husbandman, and Sarah Dolt of Sarrett; at Sarrett. Alexander Trott of St. Albans, butcher, a surety.

September 8. Abraham Ealin of St. Stephen's, husbandman, single man, and Martha Deacon of St. Michaels, single woman; at St. Albans. David Jones of St. Albans, gardener, a surety.

September 18. Thomas Bingham of Ilstree, yeoman, bachelor, and Joane Grove *alias* Johnson of the same widow; at Ilstree or Barnet. John Seares of St. Albans, a surety.

September 18. Humphrey Aldin of St. Albans, tallow chandler, and Sarah Blood of St. Stevens; at St. Albans or St. Stevens. John Barnard of St. Albans, gent, a surety.

September 21. Joseph Hare of St. Michaels, blacksmith, singleman, and Mary Brewster of the same, widow; at St. Michaels. Robert Scott, jun., of St. Albans, draper, a surety.

October 1. Henry Woodbridge of Sarret, carpenter, bachelor, aged about 27 years, and Susanna Baldwin of Abbots Langley, spinster, aged about 40 years; at Abbots' Langley, St. Albans, or St. Peters. Thomas Scott of St. Albans, cutler, a surety.

October 2. John Cheworth and Elizabeth Stepping of Harpenden; at Harpenden; James Cheworth and Richard Man of St. Albans, sureties.

October 5. William Adamson of St. Albans, labourer, widower, and Mary Young of Kimpton, single woman; at Sandridge. Richard Ruth of St. Albans, barber-cherurgeon, a surety.

October 8. Robert Feild of St. Paul's Walden, bachelor, and Martha Buckingham of the same; at St. Paul's Walden or Codicot. William Cosens of St. Peters, a surety.

October 18. Nathaniel Young, single man, and Sarah Hind, single woman, both of St. Paul's Walden *alias* Abbots Walden; at Paul's Walden, or any other in our jurisdiction. John Tuffnell of Kimpton, yeoman, and George Baker of St. Albans, sureties.

October 19. Thomas Hawkins of St. Stephens, husbandman, single man, and Sarah Knolton of the same, single woman; at St. Stevens. William Bradwin of St. Albans, bricklayer, a surety.

October 20. William Johnson, widower, and Sarah Campion, maid, both of St. Albans; at St. Albans. Nicholas Whelpley of St. Albans, a surety.

October 24. William Metcalf of St. Michaels, husbandman, single man, and Joan Woodwards of the same, single woman; at St. Michaels or St. Albans. John Woodwards of St. Michaels, husbandman, a surety.

October 29. Alban Heyward of St. Stephens, husbandman, and Susan Dell, aged about 22 years; at St. Stephens. John Dell of St. Stephens, yeoman, her father, a surety.

December 11. John Harding of Sarratt, husbandman, and Ann Newton of Watford; at Watford or Sarrett. William Morris of St. Albans, innholder, a surety.

December 24. William Carter of St. Albans, carpenter, and Sarah Fitch of the same; at St. Albans. Jeremiah Fitch of St. Albans, baker, a surety.

1689-90

January 5. William Christmas of St. Albans, butcher, and Jane Beesney of the same, "spinster and widow"; at St. Albans. John Brinkley of St. Albans, a surety.

January 16. William Burton of St. Peters, widower, and Letice Morgan of the same, spinster, aged about 25 years; at St. Peters. James Barnes of St. Peters, innholder, a surety.

February 1. Samuel Mallitrot [*signed* Maletrat] of St. Albans, locksmith, single man, and Mary Element of the same, single woman; at St. Albans. William Hunt of St. Albans, tobacco pipe maker, a surety.

February 8. Jesper Mitchel of Northall *alias* Northaw, farmer, bachelor, and Elizabeth Hall of the same, widow. Ann Tibballs of St. Peters, widow, a surety.

February 8. Joseph Long of St. Stephens, farmer, bachelor, and Jane Kentish, aged about 23 years; with consent of her father Henry Kentish; at St. Stephens. Henry Feild of St. Stephens, "bodyes maker," a surety.

February 15. Thomas Ruth of St. Albans, cooper, single man, and Mary Ethringham of the same, single woman; at St. Albans. Richard Ruth of St. Albans, barber chyrurgeon, a surety.

February 17. John Clark of Sleapside, St. Peters, labourer, widower, and Margaret Miller of the same, spinster, aged about 40 years; at St. Peters. Ralph Heyward, parish clerk of St. Peters, a surety.

February 25. Jacob Robinson of St. Katherine Coleman, London, and Sarah Peters of St. Albans; at St. Albans or Sandridge. Robert Woodards of St. Albans, a surety.

March 3. William Partridge of Shenley, wheelwright, widower, and Mary Street of St. Albans, single woman; at St. Albans. Edward Robinson of St. Albans, victualler, a surety.

March 3. George Reeve of King's Langly, yeoman, bachelor, aged about 27 years, and Ann Shepherd of the same, spinster, aged above 21 years; having neither father nor mother living; at King's Langley or St. Albans. William Heydon of King's Langley, and William Burr of St. Albans, sureties. The said William Heydon, aged about 40 years, deposed that she had the consent of her uncle John Emes of Barkhamstead.

March 24. John Brock of Northmins, and Sarah Sleap of St. Stephens. Mathias Bradley of Shenley, cordwainer, and Robert Bradley of Ridge, yeoman, sureties.

1690

March 29. John Chownes son of John Chownes of Hexton, labourer, bachelor, aged about 30 years, and Sarah Ady *alias* Adee, spinster, aged about 25 years, daughter of Jeremiah Ady of Hitchin; at Hexton, Newnham, Norton, Shephal or Paulswalden. James Negoose of Luton, butcher, bachelor, aged about 25 years, and Henry Marston of St. Albans, yeoman, sureties. The following note is written at the bottom of the allegation sheet: John Chowneing weaver hath bin at Hitchin abt. a fortnight his last habitacon att Hexton.

April 15. John Woodward of St. Peters, husbandman, and Elizabeth Chamberlaine of the same, spinster; at St. Peters. Edward Oxton, of the same, gent., a surety.

April 19. John Poynings of Ridge *alias* Rudge, millwright, single man, and Martha Partridge of Shenley, single woman; at St. Albans or St. Michaels. William Bush of St. Michaels, brewer, a surety.

April 22. James Newton [*signed* Nuton] of Sarett, yeoman, single man, and Hannah Hunt of Rickmersworth, single woman; at St. Albans. William Morris of St. Albans, innholder, a surety.

April 22. John Blythe of Abbott's Langley, husbandman, single man, and Ruth Jennings of the same, single woman; at St. Albans or Abbotts Langley. John Turner of Abbotts Langley, husbandman, a surety.

May 21. John Nore of Great Gaddesden, husbandman, bachelor, aged about 29 years, and Rebecca Alden of Smugg Oak in the parish of St. Stephens, single woman, aged about 30 years, sister of Daniel Alden of St. Stephens; at St. Peters or St. Albans. Francis Betts of St. Peters, widow, who is a surety, alleges that Rebecca Alden was at the last time of her dwelling an inhabitant with her brother Daniel Alden.

June 3. Richard Millard of St. Albans, and Amey Robinse of St. Peters; at St. Peters. William Cosens, of St. Peters, a surety.

June 9. William Gamble of London, bachelor, and Elizabeth Swalden of Codicote, maiden; at Codicote. Richard Swalden of Codicote, a surety.

June 26. William Lea of Carington, co. Bedford, carpenter, single man, and Sarah Hughes of St. Albans, single woman; at St. Albans. Richard Finch of St. Albans, mealman, a surety.

July 6. Thomas Axtel of Hemel Hempsted, glover, widower, and Ann Gray of Redbourn, single woman; at Redbourn. Thomas Gray of Redbourn, husbandman, a surety.

July 10. William Caton of Redbourn, husbandman, single man, and Elizabeth Norris of the same, single woman; at Redbourn. William Hunt of St. Albans, tobacco pipe maker, a surety.

July 14. Thomas Thrale of Sandridge, bachelor, aged about 22, having neither father nor mother living, and Elizabeth Andrews of the same, spinster, aged about 23 years; at Sandridge, St. Peters, Redbourn, or St. Michaels. John Andrews her brother, a surety.

September 13. William Sherlocke and Anne Giles both of St. Michaels; at St. Michaels or St. Peters. Richard Childs of St. Michaels, a surety.

September 20. George Bayly, widower, and Mary Weedon, single woman, both of Watford; at Watford. Henry Weedon of King's Langley, yeoman, and William Hunt of St. Albans, tobacco pipe maker, sureties.

Septemer 22. William Swinsborn of Rickmersworth, gent., single man, and Mary Wicks of the same, single woman; at St. Albans. William Hunt of St. Albans, tobacco pipe maker, a surety.

September 22. George Rowney of St. Michaels, butcher, widower, and Elizabeth Pankhurst of the same, single woman; at St. Michaels. Nathaniel Prier of St. Michaels, tailor, a surety.

September 26. George Fidgen of Baldock, widower, aged about 34 years, and Mary Mayes of the same, spinster, aged 24 years, having neither father nor mother; at Baldock. Thomas Mayes of Haines co. Bedford, husbandman, her brother, and Henry Wharton of Gravenhurst co. Bedford, yeoman, sureties.

September 29. James Nichol, single man, and Mary Randall, single woman, both of Rickmersworth; at St. Albans, St. Stephens, or Rickmersworth. George Randall of Rickmersworth, yeoman, and John Randall of St. Stephens, blacksmith, sureties.

September 29. John Browne of Sandridge, husbandman, bachelor, and Sarah Smith, spinster; at St. Peters. Daniel Smith, of St. Peters, husbandman, her father, a surety.

September 30. William Minchin of St. Botolph's Without Bishopsgate London, haberdasher, and Mary Gilbert of St. Albans. Samuel Loft one of the Aldermen of the Borough of St. Albans, a surety.

October 4. Seth Parratt of Abbotts Langley, mealman, single man, and Sarah Porter of the same, single woman; at Abbotts Langley. Robert Rainsford of St. Albans, victualler, a surety.

October 9. Daniel Shepherd of Rickmersworth, husbandman, single man, and Martha Rampton of the same, single woman; at Sarret. Thomas Scott of St. Albans, cutler, a surety.

October 22. Thomas Wildes of Hemel Hempstead, single man, and Maria Southend of Watford, single woman; at St. Albans. William Wildes of St. Albans, boddys maker, and Samuel Lines of Great Gaddesden, blacksmith, sureties.

October 25. John Halsey of Studham, yeoman, bachelor, aged about 27 years, and Elizabeth Rose of Redbourn, spinster, aged about 22 years, daughter of Jonathan Rose; at Redbourn. William Watson of St. Albans, victualler, a surety.

October 25. John Cowley of St. Albans, baker, widower, and Mary Welsh of the same, spinster, aged about 30 years; at St. Albans or Sandridge. John Anderson of Sandridge, yeoman, a surety.

October 25. Martin Clark of Watford, yeoman, and Hannah Windsor of the same, spinster, aged about 22 years; having her father's consent; at Watford. Peter Fullwood of St. Albans, collarmaker, a surety.

November 8. George Selby of St. Peters, husbandman, bachelor, and Ann Webster, late of Welling but now of St. Peters, spinster, aged about 27 years; at St. Peter's, Sandridge or Redbourn. Henry Seares of St. Peters, a surety.

November 10. John Hodsden, single man, and Sarah Fuller, single woman, both of St. Michaels; at St. Michaels. William Hodsden of St. Michaels, husbandman, his father, a surety.

November 17. Robert Rainsford of St. Albans, gent., widower, and Elizabeth Ellis of the same, single woman; at St. Albans. William Gibson of St. Albans, shoemaker, a surety.

November 17. William Smith of Harpenden, blacksmith, single man, and Elizabeth Fribridge of Sandridge; at St. Albans or St. Peters. William Hunt of St. Albans, tobacco pipe maker, a surety.

December 27. William Clark of Watford, widower, and Mary Eeling; at Watford. William Eeling of Bushey, husbandman, her father, a surety.

1690-1

January 2. Thomas Babbs of St. Albans, bricklayer, single man, aged about 24 years, and Mary Nash of the same, single woman, of about the same age; at Sandridge or St. Albans. William Lloyd of St. Albans, gent., a surety.

January 24. Thomas Weedon of Bushy, bachelor, and Rebecca Summers of the same; at Bushy. Daniel Cocke of Bushy, a surety.

February 2. Francis Manington of Milton-next-Sittingborne, co. Kent, husbandman, and Margaret Ellvin of Ward, co. Kent; at St. Nicholas, Rochester, or Ward. John Bing of Rochester, barber, a surety.

February 20. John Chalkley of Kimpton, husbandman, single man, aged about 25 or 26 years, and Mary Nicholas, of Codicote, aged about 23 years; at St. Albans. John Nicholas of Codicote, yeoman, a surety.

February 25. William Walker of Redbourn, labourer, single man, aged about 28 years, and Mary Mayes of the same, single woman, aged about 22 years; at Redbourn. John Winter of St. Albans, glover, a surety.

February 27 [*endorsed* February 17]. John Stratford of Beerton, co. Buckingham, labourer [bachelor *erased*], and Martha Stratford of Abbats Aston, spinster; at St. Albans. Luke Beckilles of Barkhampsted, a surety.

March 14. Matthew Rogers of St. Albans, butcher, single man, aged about 23 years, and Ann Knight of the same, single woman, aged about 20 years or more; at St. Albans. Edward Rawlinson of St. Albans, husbandman, a surety.

March 14. Wendover Benbow of Winslow, co Buckingham, and Dorothy Stevens of Sheford, co Bedford, widow; at St. Peters. Zachary Cole a surety.

1691

April 10. William How of St. Albans, maltman, widower, and Ann Thrale of St. Peters, spinster, aged about 40 years; at St. Peters. Henry Sears of St. Albans, labourer, a surety.

April 22. Samuel Finch of Watford, plumber, widower, and Rachil Newman of the same, single woman; at St. Albans. Henry Kentish of Abbotts Langley, yeoman, a surety.

April 24. Richard Tuffnell of Lyley, yeoman, single man, and Sarah Peacock, single woman. William Carter of St. Albans, carpenter, a surety.

May 8. Joseph Hussey, of Paul's Walden, gent., bachelor, aged aged about 31 years, and Mary Squire, aged about 16 years; with consent of her father; at Paul's Walden. William Squire of Paul's Walden, gardener, her father, a surety.

May 10. Stephen Fullwood of St. Giles, Cripplegate, London, "calender," single man, and Elizabeth Blithman of St. Albans, single woman; at St. Albans. John Wilkinson of St. Albans, innholder, a surety.

May 16. Edward Dearmer of Market Street, cooper, and Ann Barker of Mill End, Luton, co. Bedford; with consent of her father, Jeremiah Barker. William Watson of St. Albans, innholder, a surety.

May 16. William Cock of Bednam, parish of Langley, aged about 21 years, bachelor, and Mary Pucker of St. Michaels, aged 21 years, spinster; at St. Michaels. Thomas Jacques of St. Albans, coachman, a surety.

May 25. John Hoddesdon of Bushey, shopkeeper, single man, aged about 22 years, and Susanna Messeder of the same, single woman, aged about 19 years; at St. Albans. William Hunt of St. Albans, tobacco pipe maker, a surety.

May 28. John Clark of South Mimms, gent., single man, and Katharin Roberts of Redbourn, single woman; at St. Michaels or Redbourn. Thomas Roberts of Redbourn, a surety.

May 30. Joseph Edmunds of St. Albans, tailor, single man, and Susanna Woodwards of St. Michaels; at Redbourn. Thomas Nichol of St. Peters, joiner, a surety.

June 6. Bedford Stacey of Abbots Langley, tailor, single man, and Sarah Sears of the same, widow; at St. Albans. William Hannell of Abbott's Langley, blacksmith, a surety.

June 18. James Love of Watford, victualler, single man, and Mary Lovet of the same, single woman; at St. Albans. Jonathan Love of Watford, miller, a surety.

July 6. John Fisher of [Little Harwood erased in allegation and Eddlesborrow inserted] co. Buckingham, yeoman, bachelor, aged about 30 years, and Catherine Standbridge of Studham, co. Bedford, widow, aged about 27 years; at St. Albans or St. Peters. William Robinson of Alberry, husbandman, and Michael Humphrey of Edeborrow [Eddlesboro] co. Bucks., wheelwrght, sureties.

July 25. Thomas Dagnal of Abbotts Langley, widower, and Elizabeth Cripps of Hadnam, co. Buckingham, maid. John Turner of St. Michaels, a surety.

July 25. John Pope of Watford, baker, bachelor, aged about 28 years, and Jane Benbow of the same, spinster, aged about 29 years; at Watford. John Seares of St. Albans, gent., a surety.

August 19. John Cranwell of Farnham Royall, co. Buckingham, yeoman, bachelor, aged about 22 years, and Adrey Osmond of Rickmersworth, spinster, aged about 23 years; at Rickmersworth or Sarratt. Richard Osmond of Rickmersworth, yeoman, a surety.

September 12. Samuel Halsey of Sandridge, husbandman, bachelor, aged about 23 years, and Ann White of the same, spinster, aged about 22 years; at St. Peters or Sandridge. Ralph Heyward [*signed* Howard] of St. Peters, mealman, a surety.

September 13. William Chambers of Luton, cooper, widower, and Sarah Eilot of Pauls Walden, single woman. Richard Ruth of St. Albans, chirurgeon, a surety.

September 21. William Warren of Towcester, co. Northants, innholder, widower, and Ann Woollhead of Redbourn, widow. John Turpin, of Redbourn, butcher, a surety.

September 24. Joseph Wood of Burton-on-Trent, co. Derby, husbandman, single man, and Mary Smith of St. Albans, single woman. Thomas Priestly [*signed* Pristley] of St. Albans, ostler, a surety.

October 10. John Cogdell of Abbots Langley, single man, and Elizabeth Ford of the same, single woman. Daniel Ford of Abbots' Langley, mealman, and William Hunt of St. Albans, tobacco pipe maker, sureties.

*To be Continued.*

# The Herts Genealogist and Antiquary.

## Funeral Certificates.

### SIR EDWARD BARKHAM. 1633.

The right worshipfull Sir Edward Barkham Kt. sometyme Lo: Maior of y<sup>e</sup> Cittie of London, died at his house in the parish of S<sup>t</sup> Mary Bothawe near Downegate 15 Jan. 1633 in the 82<sup>nd</sup> year of his age. His body was conveyed to his manor of Southacre in Norfolk. He was buried in the north aisle of the chancel of Southacre church under a monument erected by himself in his lifetime. He married Jane daughter to John Crowch sometime of London and after of Cornibery co. Hertf. gent by whom he had issue Sir Edw<sup>d</sup>. Barkham knt. & bart. who married Francis dau. of Sir Thos. Berney of Redeham co. Norf. kt. by whom he hath issue Edw<sup>d</sup> son and heir apparent aged about 6 years & Thos. second son about 1 year, also Jane eldest dau. died a child, Francis 2<sup>d</sup>, now aged 9 years, Margaret 3<sup>d</sup> dau. aged 7 years, Jane 4th dau. aged about 3 years & Eliz<sup>th</sup>. now youngest dau. about 2 years.

John 2<sup>d</sup> son of the defunct died an infant.

Robert 3<sup>d</sup> son married Mary dau. of ——Wilcocks of London & hath issue Edward aged about 3 years and 4 daus. Mary, Eliz<sup>th</sup> Marg<sup>t</sup>. & Jane now children.

John 4<sup>th</sup> son, Thomas 5<sup>th</sup> son & Hugh all died young without issue.

Jane eldest dau. of defunct died in infancy.

Elizabeth 2<sup>nd</sup> dau. married S<sup>r</sup> John Garrard of Lammer co. Hertf. kt. & bart. by whom she left issue at the time of her decease now living 5 sons and 7 daus., John eldest son, Nithermyll 2<sup>nd</sup>, Edw<sup>d</sup> 3<sup>d</sup>, W<sup>m</sup>. 4<sup>th</sup>, & Charles 5<sup>th</sup>, Jane eldest dau, Eliz<sup>th</sup> 2<sup>d</sup>, Isabell 3<sup>d</sup>, Marg<sup>t</sup>. 4<sup>th</sup>, Francis 5<sup>th</sup>, Anne 6<sup>th</sup>, & Mary 7<sup>th</sup>.

Suzan 3<sup>rd</sup> dau. of defunct married Robt. Walpoole of Houghton near Harpley co. Norfolk. gent. & at her decease left him living one son Edw<sup>d</sup> & 2 daus. Jane & Eliz<sup>th</sup>.

Jane 4<sup>th</sup> dau. of defunct married Sir Chas. Cæsar of Benningtou co. Hertf. kt. & being his 2<sup>nd</sup> wife hath issue by him now living 3 sons Julius, Henry & Charles & 1 dau. which died an infant.

Margaret 5th daughter of the defunct died an infant and
Margaret 6th dau. married Sr Anthony Irby of Boston co. Lincoln kt. & as yet by her being his 3rd wife hath no issue.
Certificate taken by Wm. Penson, Lancaster Herald 23 Feb. 1633 & certified by sd Sir Edwd Barkham kt. and bart. heir & one of the executors.

[Signed] Edward Barkham.

Arms :—Argent three pales gules over all a chevron or, impaling quarterly 1 & 4 Argent on a pale sable three crosses pattée or within a bordure engrailed of the second [Crouch], 2 & 3 Argent on a chevron sable three helmets or [Scot]
Crest :—Two arms in armour embowed proper in hands a sheaf of arrows banded.

# Feet of Fines for Hertfordshire.

## TUDOR PERIOD.

(Continued from Page 309).

### 1583. Mich. Term. 25 & 26 Eliz.

*Francis Flower esq. & Edw. Buggyn gent: Wm. Lee esq. & Eliz. his wife. Lands in Rydge and Shenley.
John Cleare: Wm. Snowe & Eliz. his wife. Lands in Thorley.
Robt. Woolley: Humph. Couingesbye esq. and Mary his wife. Twenty shillings yearly rent arising from lands in psh. of St. Peters near St Albans.
Thos. Fage: Anth. Fage and Ellen his wife. Messuage in Clothall.
Thos. Turner & Wm. Turner: John Hoye. Lands in Barkwaye.
Wm. Andrewes & Wm. Smythe gents: John Addams & Lucy his wife. Two messuages & lands in Hunesden, Standsted Abbot & Estwycke.
Wm. Brooke: Thos. Bagshawe & Anne his wife. Eight acres of wood in Mawdlyn.
Thos. Thorogood: Leonard Hide esq. Land in Throckinge.
John Symynge esq: Nich. Bower gent & Mildred his wife. Three messuages and lands in parishes of Essendon alias Essingden & All Saints in Hertford.
Robt. Sharpe: Thos. Barnard and Eliz. his wife. Messuage and lands in London Colney.
Thos. Roe alias Raye: Geo. Graveley & Martha his wife. Messuage in Hytchin alias Hutchin.
Jas. Odale: Rob. Dockwraye & Grace his wife. The third part of a messuage and lands in Thundriche.
Edmund Hale: Mich. Branckley & Joan his wife. Messuage & lands in Haley & Amwell.

Ralph Sadler knt.: Edw. Harbert knt & Mary his wife. Manor of Stonden *alias* Standen called the Brickeplace *alias* the Stonehouse & six messuages and lands in Stonden *alias* Standen, Puckeridge, Collyers End, Podington, Great Dorney & Braughing. A warranty against Thos. Stanley.

Edw. Hurste & Robt. Hurste: Edw. Sadler esq. & Anne his wife. Lands in Hitchin *alias* Hutchin, Hippolites & Kingeswalden. A warranty against all claiming through Ralph Sadler knt. father of s^d Edward.

Wm. Chapman: Edmund Barber & Eliz. his wife. Messuage & lands in Great Munden & Little Munden.

John Feilde: Geo. Feilde & Joan his wife. Messuage and lands in Graveley & Chisfeilde.

Matthew Hansecombe: Thos. Copcott & Cicily his wife. Lands in Pyrton.

Thos. Gylmote *alias* Gylman: Thos. Wylcockes & Margt. his wife. Messuage & garden in psh. of S^t Stephens near S^t Albans.

John Halden: Henry Osbaston & Margt. his wife. Lands in Standon.

Benedict Cocke: John Clerke & Henry Clerke. Messuage in Barkehampsted S^t Peter.

Edw. Fage, Wm. Chambers & Urias Barker gents: John Spicer *alias* Helder and Lucy his wife. Messuage in Royston.

Thos. Wolley & Wm. Hickman: Humph. Coningesbye esq. and Mary his wife. Messuage, etc., in St. Albans.

Christr. Elmeston gent: Wm. Garnett gent & Margery his wife & Henry Garnett son and heir apparent of said Wm. Messuage and lands in Bennyngton.

Henry Cocke knt. & John Goodman esq: Ambrose earl of Warwick and Anne his wife. Manor of Northawe *alias* Northall & 40 messuages and lands in Northawe and Cuffeley.

Roger Pemberton: Roger Browne & Alice his wife. Messuage in S Albans.

John Markeham gent & Alice his wife: Edw. Sadleir esq & Anne his wife. The Rectory of Kings Walden & a messuage & lands etc in Kings Walden.

## 1583-4. Hilary Term. 26 Eliz.

The Mayor & Commonalty & Citizens of the City of London governors of the possessions revenues & goods of the Hospitals of King Edward VI, of Christs, Bridewell & S^t Thomas the Apostle: Thos. Ramsey knt. and Mary his wife. Five messuages & lands in Burnt Pelham, Stoking Pelham & Reade.

Henry Clerke gent: Giles Sewester esq. Four messuages & lands in Ayshwell & Hinxworth.

Wm. Plomer: Leonard Hyde esq. Lands in Throckinge, Aspden *alias* Aspeden & Leyston.

Thos. Carpenter: John Brokett knt. Messuage and lands in Wethamsted.

Wm. Lowdam: Robt. Hallywell & Alice his wife. Two messuages in Chesthunt.

Ralph Clackson jun.: Thos. Clackson senior & Margt. his wife. Messuage and land in Ware.

Edw. Brighowse & John Goodridge: Matthew Woodward. Three messuages and lands in Hitchin.

1584. Mich. Term. 26 & 27 Eliz.

Geo. Gynne: Wm. Makeres & Kath. his wife. Messuage in Hitchin *alias* Hutchyn.

Edw. Brokett gent: Wm. Collins & Ellen his wife. Messuage in Whettamstede.

Thos. Munforde clerk: Robt. North & Joan his wife. Lands in Tewynge.

Andrew Wood: John Potter & Joan his wife. Messuage in Storteforde.

John Bowyer esq: Edw. Pulter esq. Lands in Hitchyn *alias* Hutchin.

John Martyn senior: Wm. Fynche. Messuage in Watford.

Rich. Jorden junior: Rich. Jorden senior. Two messuages & lands in Gt. Hormeade.

Wm. Nicoll & Thos. Nicoll jun: Rich. Nicoll senior & Mary his wife. Messuage & land in Tatteridge.

Ralph Browne: Christr. Perrye & Agnes his wife. Land in Sabridgeworth.

Wm. Neale: Thos. Neale & Eliz. his wife. Lands in Harpenden.

John Skyngell: Robt. Hall gent & Anne his wife. Lands in Stortford.

Robt. Wedon & Joan Pymble: John Buckberd & Walter Buckberd. Three messuages and land in Watford.

John Warner & Margt. his wife: Wm. Holland and Eliz. his wife. Messuage & lands in Great Monden.

Simon Gardener: Philip Gardener & Alice his wife. Two messuages and lands in Stondon & Watton.

Wm. Holland: Rich. Roo & Eliz. his wife. Land in Braughinge.

John Clarke: John Smythe & Eliz. his wife. Messuage in Baldock.

Robt. Nycoll & Rich. Nycoll junior: Rich. Nicoll senior & Mary his wife. Lands in Tatteridge.

John Grover: John Robynson & Eliz. his wife. Messuage & land in Barckhampsted St Peter & Northechurche.

Thos. Northe: John Brokett & Julian his wife & John Laurence & Grace his wife. Lands in Great Wymondeley.

John Harvye senior & Humph. Harvie: Robt. Coates & Agnes his wife. Three messuages & lands in Hoddesden & Broxborn.

Geo. Edwards gent: Rich. Fitzhughe gent. Manor of Greenehall & lands in Sandon.

James Oddall: Barth. Downe & Kath. his wife. A third part of a messuage & lands in Thundriche.

John Clarke junior & Alice his wife: John Easte & Mary his wife & Wm. Easte. Three messuages in St Albans.

Henry Marshe: Robt. Barbour & Agnes his wife. Manor of Sowches & two messuages & lands in Cadington.

Roger Pemberton: Thos. Holden gent. & Anne his wife & Barnabas Laurence & Mary his wife. Four messuages & land in St Albans. Warranty against the heirs of John Arnold dec<sup>d</sup>.

John Brograve esq: Thos. Hanchett esq & Mary his wife. Manor of Maisters *alias* Masters & messuage & lands in Westmill, Braughin *alias* Brackynge & Standen. A warranty against John Fitzherbert & his heirs.

Thos. Dyer: John Hunt & Joan his wife. Messuage in Watford.

Geo. Chauncey gent: Edw. Bugges gent, Henry Chauncey esq & Thos. Salysburye gent. Messuage & lands in Gedleston, Eastwycke & Sabridgeworthe.

John Stywarde & Andrew Malorye esqr<sup>s</sup>: Thos. Hanchet esq. A water mill & lands in Brawghinge, Standon & Hadham.

John Hellam senior John Hellam junior & Wm. Addams: John Addams gent & Lucy his wife & Richard Fanner & Agnes his wife. Two messuages & lands in Hunsdon, Stansted Abbatt & Estwick.

John Harvie junior. Thos. Harvie & Humph. Harvie sons of John Harvie senior & Alice his wife: The said John Harvie & Alice his wife. Three messuages & lands in Ware.

### 1584-5. Hilary Term. 27 Eliz.

Geo. Hamond: Henry Hamond junior & Eliz. his wife. Lands in Westmyll.

Wm. Swyfte: Henry Dytche. Messuage in Watford.

Wm. Hawkeshedd: Wm. Lee esq & Eliz. his wife. Lands in Ridge.

Robt. Newman: Rich. Corse & Lucy his wife. Messuage & lands in Baldock, Wyllien & Weston.

Wm. Shotbolt, Robt. Clarcke & Edw. Lyncolne: Wm. Moore gent & Sarah his wife. Messuage & lands in Sandon.

Thos. Hannam esq, John Popham esq, Jas. Clarke gent & Hugh Worthe gent: John Matthew gent & Joan Skegge widow. Manor of Pansanger *alias* Passanger *alias* Panshanger & 5 messuages & lands in Pansanger, Qwynhoe, Hertford & Hertyngfordbury.

### 1585. Easter Term. 27 Eliz.

*John Peter knt & Robt. Foorthe doctor of laws: Eliz. Riche widow. Ten messuages & lands in Stondon, Puckeridge, Brauhinge & Monden.

*Thos. Markham esq, Robt. Harington esq & Griffin Markham esq: Edm. Brudenell knt. Manor of Coleshill *alias* Stockplace & 40 messuages & lands in Coleshill & Stockplace.

Edw. Bryscoe: John Longe gent & Mary his wife. Lands in Ilstrie.

John Rawlins: Thos. Miller & Matilda his wife. Land in Much Hadham.

Rich. Franklyn & Robt. Millett: Henry Hickman & Alice his wife. Manor of Bushey Hall & 2 messuages & lands in Bushey & Watford & free warren there.

Rich. Clarke: John Davis gent & Bridget his wife. The third part of a messuage & lands in Sabridgeworthe.

John Miller: Philip Kente & Joan his wife. Messuage & lands in Bishops Stortforde.

Wm. Pygott: Geo. Moreland & Alice his wife & John Lee & Bridget his wife. Five messuages & lands in Barkwaye, Reed, Layston, Throckinge & Buntingford.

Thos. Parsons: Thos. Jarnigan & Eliz. his wife. Lands in Stortford.

Boniface Wood: Rich. Fitzhugh gent & Eliz. his wife. Lands in Sandon.

Francis Burbecke: Thos. Boreham & Joan his wife & John Addam & Margt. his wife. Two messuages & lands in Broxbourne.

Wm. Auncell: Geo. Hayward & Joan his wife & John Grunwyn & Eliz. his wife. Two parts of a messuage & lands (in three parts divided) in Herpenden.

John Hemynge: John Cherye & Kath. his wife, Robt. Hemynge, Wm. Hamond & Margt. his wife. Messuage & lands in Great & Stonden.

Nich Brockett gent & Joan his wife: Edw. Brockett esq. & Eliz his wife. Messuage & lands in Sabridgeworth.

Jas. Dixon, Rich. Fissher, Wm. Hutton, John Haynes, Thos. Colte, Rich. Warner, Jas. Orgar & Thos. Brooke: Ralph Daye & Thos. Smartfoote. Six messuages & lands in Braughinge & Stondon.

Roland Hall: John Darnall gent & Susan his wife. The fourth part of a messuage & lands in Hartingfordburye *alias* Hartfordingburye, Tewinge, Bramfeilde & the psh. of S<sup>t</sup> Andrew in Hartford.

### 1585. Trinity Term. 27 Eliz.

*Nich. Wheler & Andrew Palmer: Magdalene Chester widow. Fifty messuages & lands in Royston, Melborn, Berkwaye, Reade & Therfeld & a certain water course in the town of Royston.

*Philip Wingefield: Christr. Bavyne & Agnes his wife, Anthony Sawrey gent & Eliz. his wife. Messuage & lands in Aldenham.

*Edw. Stanhope doctor of civil law & Michael Stanhope esq: Wm. Heygate gent. Lands in Estbarnett.

Rich. Smyth & Thos. Smyth: Julius Ferrers gent & Susan his wife. Lands in Flamsted.

John Harmer: John Goodman gent & Frances his wife. Lands in Wallington.

Geo. Haynes & Agnes Haynes widow: John Haynes & Mary his wife. Three messuages & lands in Little Hadham & Much Hadham & Stondon.

Geo. Withe: John Downer & Agnes his wife. The third part of a mill & lands in Aldenham.

John Pitches: John Goodman gent & Frances his wife. Messuage & lands in Wallington.

Wm. Pygott gent: Edw. Halfhead & Beatrice his wife. Two messuages & lands in Layston, Buntingforde & Throckinge.

Ralph Warren: Jonas Fringe & Sarah his wife. Three messuages &c. in Watford.

Edm. Haynes & Agnes Haynes widow: John Hayne & Mary his wife. Three messuages & lands in Aldebury, Little Hadham & Thorley.

Christr. Preston & Geo. Perrie: Christr. Perrie & Agnes his wife. Land in Sabridgeworthe.

Thos. Harmer: Thos. Tirrell cit. & grocer of London & Leonard Hyde esq. Lands in Clothall.

Thos. Axtell: Christr. Wyngfeild & Isabel his wife, Ralph Wyngfeild & Agnes his wife. Messuage & lands in Sarrett.

Wm. Olyner: Geo. Brumley & Ellen his wife. Messuage & land in Ware.

Thos. Haydon: Edw. Streete gent. Lands in Ilstre.

John Briscoe: Edw. Streete junior gent. Messuage & lands in Idelstreete *alias* Elstrey & Aldenham. Warranty against s<sup>d</sup> Edward & his heirs & against Audry Wolde, Thos. Streete, Edw. Streete senior, John Streete & Wm. Streete.

Edw. Meade gent & Philippa his wife: Michael Meade gent & Eliz. his wife. Messuage & lands in Great Amwell, Little Amwell & All Saints in Hertford.

### 1585. Mich. Term. 27 & 28 Eliz.

John Bird: Henry Hamond gent & Eliz. his wife. Land in Westmill.

Cuthbert Lynde of London, grocer: Edward, lord Morley. Twenty messuages & lands in Pelham Furnex.

Wm. Perott: Edw. Everett & Jane his wife. Messuage & lands in Flampsted.

Rich. Parker: John Martyn senior. Messuage & land in Watford.

Thos. Hare: Thos. Copcott & Cicely his wife. Messuage & lands in Pirton.

Wm. Ancell: Henry Hamond gent & Eliz. his wife. Lands in Westmill.

John Caige: Rich. Snowe & Mary his wife. Lands in Tatteridge.
John Wryghte: Rich. Willey & Agnes his wife. Two messuages & lands in Thorley.
Thos. Harmer: Henry Hamond gent. & Eliz. his wife. Lands in Great Monden.
Roger Roose: Wm. Ewer. Messuage & land in St Albans.
Jas. Croftes: Henry Hamond gent. & Eliz. his wife. Lands in Westmill.
Geo. Nichols & Geo. Devell: John Marshe & Anne his wife. Three messuages & lands in Bocklond alias Bucklond & Tharfield & the moiety of two messages & lands in same places.
Henry Frowycke gent & Nich. Deringe gent: Humph. Conyngesbye esq. & Mary his wife. Messuages & lands in parishes of St Albans & St Peters.
Geo. Copwood gent: Robt. Poynter gent & Margt. his wife & Edmund Thymbleby gent & Sophia his wife. Lands in Tatterydge.
Griffin Davye, Wm. Aske gent & Margt. his wife. Lands in Barkcomstede Peter.
Geo. Waller: Henry Johnson. Two messuages & land in Sabridgeworth.
Wm. Smyth: Nich. Hoo & Grace his wife & Thos. Hoo gent. Three messuages & land in Busshops Hatfielde alias Kings Hatfielde.
John Brograve esq: Henry Hamond gent & Eliz. his wife. Messuage & lands in Westmill & Great Monden.
Christr. Corey: John Goodrich & Ellen his wife. Messuage & lands in the town of St Albans.
John Styward esq & Nichs Styward doctor of laws: Thomas Howard of Awdly end second son of Thos. late duke of Norfolk & Kath. his wife. Manor of Braughinge alias Braughingberrye & 10 messuages & lands in Braughinge & the Rectory & advowson of Braughinge.
Geo. Heigham esq. & Fras. Heigham gent: Rich. Josselyn esq & Henry Heigham esq. Manor of Hyde Hall & 5 messuages & lands in Sabridgworthe.

### 1585-6. Hilary Term. 28 Eliz.

*Thos. Gatward: Hasild Burye gent & Margt. his wife. Lands in Royston, Tharfeild, Westreede, Newsells & Barkewaye.
Tho Grave & Tho. Burnappe: Tho. Fuller & John Fuller gent. & Margt. his wife. Two messuages & lands in Broxborne and Hoddesden.
Michael Hall: Wm. Hall. Messuage & lands in Little Gaddesden.
John Banburye gent: Hen. Goodere esq. Annual rent of thirty pounds issuing out of the manor of Sandrydge.
Tho. Foster esq: John Daker alias Dakers & Jane his wife. Messuage in Hunsdon. A warranty against Alice Dedon widow.
Wm. Moffett gent: Hen. Clerke gent & Anne his wife. Messuage & lands in Ashewell.
Wm. Hampton gent & John Stacy: John Browne & John Stone & Winifred his wife. Messuage & land in Little Hadham.
Wm. Moffett: Wm. Wake & Lucrecia his wife. A fourth part of a messuage & lands in Northe Mymes.
John Clerke senior: Dorothy Gryme widow. Messuage & land in St Albans.
Wm. Brokett gent: Nich. Hoo gent & Grace his wife, Tho. Hoo gent & John Brokett gent. Messuage & lands in Bishops Hatfild alias Kings Hatfild & St Peters near St Albans.
John Cage: Rob. Poynter gent & Margt. his wife & Edm. Thymbleby gent & Sophia his wife. Lands in Tatteridge.

John Ponde junior gent : Tho. Gaddesden gent & Anne his wife. Two messuages &c. in Hitchin *alias* Hutchyn. Warranty against Edw. Laurence gent & Mary his wife & the heirs of sd Mary & against the heirs of John Hemyng gent decd & against Nich{s} Luke esq & his heirs.

Eustace Grubble gent. & Constance his wife : Robt. Jaynes & Joan his wife & Robt. Ockley & Agnes his wife. Two messuages & lands in Northmyms.

Andrew Kynge gent : Tho. Gaddesden gent & Anne his wife. Ten messuages & lands in Hytchyn.

John Stacy & John Parrant : John Browne, John Stone & Winifred his wife & Edw. Marshall & Sibil his wife. Lands in Little Hadham.

Edm. Bardolff & Rich Bardolff gent : Edw. Dockwra gent & Eliz. his wife & Nich. Fynche & Joan his wife. Lands in Whethamsted, Harpeden & Redbourne.

### 1586.   Easter Term.   28 Eliz.

Tho. Bennett : Hugh Flemynge gent. & Margt. his wife. Messuage & land in Hoddesdon in the psh. of Broxborne.

Rich Smythe : Robt. Austyn & Joan his wife. Messuage and land in Aldenham *alias* Auldenham.

Wm. Wroth gent : Nich. Brett & Joan his wife. Messuage & land in Stondon.

Geo. Copwood gent : Robt. Poynter gent. & Margt. his wife & Edm. Thymbleby gent & Sophia his wife. Cottage & land in Tatterydge.

John Bowier esq : Rich. Fraunc{e} gent & Susan his wife. Lands in Hitchin.

Wm. Kynge : John Adams & Margt. his wife. Two messuages, etc. in Broxbourne.

Philip Sleape : Rich. Ruthe & Joan his wife. Two messuages & land in St Albans.

John Hurste : John Godfrey *alias* Cowper & Agnes his wife. Lands in Hytchyn & Hippolitt *alias* Hippolett.

Wm. Plumer : Henry Marshall & Kath. his wife & John Marshall. Land in Aspeden.

Rich Woodwarde, clerk : Nich. Bryan & Helen his wife. Messuage & land in psh. of St Peter in St Albans.

Thos. Manestye : Thos. Bennett & Eliz. his wife. Messuages & lands in Hoddesden & Broxborne.

Edm. Bardolfe junior gent : Edm. Bardolfe senior esq. Manor of Rothamsted & 12 messuages & lands in Wethamsted & Kympton.

Andrew Kynge gent & John Hemynge : Thos. Thompson cit. & haberdassher of London. Manor of Gifford{s} & 2 messuages & lands in Great Monden & Little Monden.

Thos. Burman : Edw. Astrey gent. Three messuages & lands in Hytchyn.

Robt. Taillor esq : John Robert{s} & Susan his wife. Four messuages & lands in Northmynnes.

John Welbecke gent : Thos. Stephens gent & Dorothy his wife. Three messuages & lands in Buntingforde.

Philip Mylles : Edw. Wylley & Eliz. his wife. Lands in Thorley.

John Millett, John Jorden, Thos. Cherrye, Ralph Joyce, Thos. Dellowe, Thos. Wood & Geo. Ancell : Henry Hamond gent & Eliz. his wife. Two messuages & lands in Great Mouden & Westmyll.

*To be Continued.*

# Subsidy Rolls for Hertfordshire.

### HUNDRED OF CASHIO. 1545.

[In volume I of this magazine at page 225, was printed a copy of this subsidy, taken from a Roll in the Public Record Office, to which the official reference is 121/164 & owing to the mutilated condition of the original, a good many gaps & considerable confusion appeared in the lists of names. The Editor has recently discovered that a duplicate roll exists, the reference to which is 121/166 and although the official calendar describes it as 'imperfect' & it is defective in many places, it contains many more names than the other & the arrangement is correct. By collating one copy with the other a fairly complete roll is obtained & the confusion in the one already printed, owing to the various parchment membranes having been sewn together in a wrong order, disappears. In the following pages the text of the second roll has been followed & variations & additions supplied by the other are denoted in italics enclosed in rounded brackets.]

### HUNDRED DE CAYSHO.

HERTF. THE TOWNE OF SEYNT ALBONS. MYDDLEWARDE.
Wm. Eyre g. jd. Wm. Cartleg (*Cartlegge*) g. xijd. John Cowley g. xvjd. Uxor [*blank*] Laurence g. ijd. Wm. Laurence g. iijd (*ijd*). Wm. Holcome (*Holland*) g. xijd. Wm. Crandwell (*Cranwell*) g. iijd. Wm. Greye g. iijd. Robt. Browne g. xijd. Hugh Whithed (*Whythede*) g. ijd. Wm. Gaythorne g. iiijd. John (*Rose*) g. ijd. John Mylwood (*Mylwarde*) g. iiijd. Geo. Yongloue g. iiijd. Geo. Baker g. ijd. Geo. Waido (*Warde*) g. iijd. Jeames Colines (*Colyns*) g. xd. Nich. Foster g. xijd. Rich. Foster g. iiijd. Thos. Est g. ijd. Uxor [*blank*] Stephynsons (*Stewson Wyf*) g. xijd. Wm. Bayes g. iijd. Johane Batman widow g. iijd. Johane Feld widow g. ijd. Rich. Gregorye g. xd. Wm. Wheler g. xiiijd. Uxor [*blank*] Megers widow (g.) jd. Uxor [*blank*] Vaughan (g.) xd. Humph. Denton g. iijd. Tho. Mose (*Mosse*) g. xvjd. Tho. Robynson g. xvjd. Geo. At Hoo g. xijd. John Drue (*Drewe*) g. ijd. Rich. Grace g. xiijd. Wm. Herberd g. jd. Rich. Mason g. jd. Geo. Bate (*Batt*) jun. g. iiijd. Tho. Kyng g. ijd. Geo. Bate sen. g. xvjd. Tho. Fowle (*Foule*) g. iiijd. John Gyles g. iiijd. Nich. Studesburye (g.) xd. Jeames Smythe g. ijd. Wm. Gaskyn g. ijd. Tho. Locke (*Lockye*) g. (xijd.) John Whelpedale g. ijd. Rich. Johnson g. ijd. John (*Napton g. iiijd.*) John [Mersh?] (*g. ijd.*). W . . . . . ijd. G . . . . . ijd. L . . . . .jd. W . . . . . . ijd. John . . . . . xviijd. John . . . . . . xijd. Rich. Pe . . . . . Tho. . . . . Tho. T . . . John . . otteles . . . . . . Tho. . . . . Robt. B . . . Geo. H . . . . . John Cram . . . Alice Shadd . . . Robt. Shadd . . . . . . . Uxor. Eliz. Fysher g. . . John . . . . ner g . . . . Wm. Fytbye g. . . Thos. Harryes g. . . . Eliz. Lamb g. ijd. John Cowley g. ijd. Henry Alen g. jd. Henry Kentyshe g. jd. Henry Campyou g. jd. Albyn Hewes g. jd. Gilb.

Lyghtfote g. j*d*. Simon Lee g. j*d*. W . . . . g. j*d*. Jeames . . . by g. iij*s*. iiij*d*. Elyn Rogers g. xiij*s*. iiij*d*. Tho. Som'land g. j*d*.

Summa xlvj*s*. xj*d*.

HALYWELL WARD. Rich. Byrchmore g. ij*d*. John Thomson (*Thompson*) g. x*d*. Cuthberd Stokedall (*Stokdale*) g. x*d*. Andrew Royse g. xij*d*. John Brangwell g. ij*d*. Tho. Twhales g. ij*d*. Tho. Wood g. ij*d*. Rich. Myller g. x*d*. Lewes Capper g. iij*d*. Mother Done g. ij*d*. John Byng g. xiiij*d*. Rich. Combes (*Comes*) g. iiij*d*. Tho. Kynge g. iij*d*. John Abbot g. xiiij*d*. John Wye g. xij*d*. Jeames Locke (*Looke*) g. iij*d*. Wm. A(*mbler g. ij*d*.*) Tho. Payeke g. ij*d*. Tho. Chawney g. x*d*. Wm. Greye g. iij*d*. Hugh Est g. xiiij*d*. John Atkyns g. ij*d*. Peter Polston Wyf. g. j*d*. Robt. Baker g. iij*d*. Tho. Glewe g. iij*d*. Wm. Rychardson g. ij*d*. Wm. Murfflet g. j*d*. John Terry g. ij*d*. Roger Self g. ij*d*. John Graye g. ij*d*. Jespere Ferne g. iij*d*. Robt. Hygbye g. j*d*. Oliver Knolles g. j*d*. Rich. Cheltam g. j*d*. John Tayllor g. iij*d*. Wm. Dyckson g. ij*d*. Rich. Ruthe g. x*d*. John Dyer g. iij*d*. Rich. Tytworth g. xiiij*d*. Wm. . . . . . g. ij*d*.

[*There are six more illegible entries.*]

Summa xviij*s*. iiij*d*.

SEYNT STEPHYNS ENDE AND PARISHE. Saunder Royse g. iiij*d*. Geo. Fraunce g. iij*d*. John Redwood jun. g. ij*d*. Robt. Skele g. ij*d*. Robt. Wyndsore g. ij*d*. John Wyndsore g. j*d*. Tho. . . . . g. xiij*d*. Wm. W . . . . g . . . Robt . . . . g . . . Tho. . . . . l . . . John Wylcocke g . . . Rauf Euerye g . . . Wm. . . . . l . . ij. Tho. Trot g. xij . . Tho. Pratt g. iiij*d*. Rich. Redwoode g. j*d*. Rich. Royse g. iij*d*. John Hyll g. ij*d*. John Marshall g. iij*d*. Tho. Redwood g. x*d*. Deverys Purse widow g. iij*d*. Rich. Man. g. x*d*. Jeames Woode g. j*d*. Wm. Royse g. iij*d*. John Skele g. iij*d*. Alice Fraunce widow g. j*d*. Mother Stoke widow l. ij*d*. Henry Stoke g. ij*d*. Robt. Nutkyn g. j*d*. John Turnour g. j*d*. Elizabeth Flagge widow g. j*d*. Henry Prat g. j*d*. John Fraunce g. j*d*. Jeames Woodward g. j*d*. John Heywarde g. ij*d*. Rich. Colyns g. ij*d*. Henry Pye g. j*d*. Robt. Bosewell g. ij*d*.

Summa xj*s*. vj*d*.

SEYNT PETURS WARDE. George Vaughan g. x*d*. John Clement g. ij*d*. Joan Portor widow g. . . . Wm. Foxe g . . Henry Foster g . . . Tho. . . . .

[*Both rolls fail us at this point & I believe the names that follow in the next paragraph belong to the Fishpool Ward of St. Albans.*]

Xpofer . . . . Wm. . . . . John Cast . . . xiiij. Wm. Taylior g. x*d*. John Coke tanner g. iij*d*. Nich. Huntleye xij*d*. Tho. Carter x*d*. John Nayshe g. x*d*. John Croche g. x*d*. Tho. Crosse g. x*d*. Eliz. Robyns widow g. x*d*. Margery Chapman widow ij*d*. Alice Harvey widow g. iij*d*. Eliz. Sare widow ij*d*. John Welles g. ij*d*. Thos. Seybroke g. x*d*. John Osborne g. x*d*. Elyn Long widow g. j*d*. Thos. Lowson g. ij*d*. Wm. Stoncham g. ij*d*. Robt. Baxter g. iij*d*. Thos. Spigans g. ij*d*. John Hurst g. j*d*. Gilb. Bastion g. ij*d*. Wm. Thorneton g. j*d*. Nich. Browne g. ij*d*. Rich. Gylles g. ij*d*. Wm. Herne g. ij*d*. Rich. Daynes g. iij*d*. John Kent g. j*d*. John Blanke g. j*d*. Gawen Skelton g. j*d*. Rauf Harding g. ij*d*. Jeram Aprice g . . . Peter Marten g . . .

John Mesye g . . . Henry Bucket g . . . Robt. Benyson g . . .
Edw. Stoneham . . . Edw. Meth . . .
*Summa* . . . . . .

WAT[FORD]. Tho. G . . . . . Gyles . . . . . John
. . . Robt. . . . . Thos. . . . . . . .
Clem. . . . . . . Robt. . . . . . John . . . . . .
Ag . . . . . . . Robt. . . . . . . Laurence
More g . . . Edw. Rede g . . John Elder g. ij*d*. Wm. Greye
g. ij*d*. Wm. Harper g. iij*d*. John Throte g. j*d*. John Bate
g. ij*d*. John Skylsye g. x*d*. Rich. Sharpe g. xiiij*d*. Geo. Marshe
(*Marsche*) g. iij*d*. John Wheles (*Whelye*) g. xvj*d*. Rich. Carter
g. iij*d*. Rich. Hickman g. xvj*d*. Roger Heylot g. xvj*d*. Rich.
Esten g. iij*d*. Robt. Robson g. j*d*. Wm. Swyft g. ij*d*.
Tho. More g. iij*d*. Eliz. Dyche widow g. iiij*d*. Tho. Hele g. ij*d*.
John Barbor g. iij*d*. John Marteyn g. ij*d*. Alice Fynche (*widow*)
g. xiiij*d*. Philip Blackwell g. ij*d*. Wm. Robynson g. x*d*. Wm.
Moncke l. ij*d*. Gilbt. Wecneyll (*Weenake*) g. ij*d*. Rich. Haukyns
g. j*d*. John Hell (*Helbye*) g. j*d*. Elyn (*Elynor*) Goldsmythe widow
(*g.*) iiij*d*. Rich. Russell g. j*d*. Tho. Smythe g. j*d*. John Gardener
g. j*d*. Jeames Browne g. j*d*. Roger Wedon g. j*d*. Rich. Fleecher
g. x*d*. Tho. Saunders g. j*d*. Tho. Hocket (*Hookett*) g. ij*d*. Robt.
Foster g. ij*d*. Arthur Cannon g. xij*d*. Wm. Homes (*Holmes*) l.
xx*d*. John Bunne g. ij*d*. Geo. Harton g. x*d*. Edw. Thornton g.
j*d*. John Blackwell (*Blackhall*) g. ij*d*. Tho. Cornys g. j*d*.

*Summa* xxvs. x*d*.

CAYSHOO HAMLETT. Tho. Johnson g. xiiij*d*. (*xiij*d*). John
Hoddesdon g. iiij*d* (*iij*d*). Geo. Davyson g. iiij*d*. Xpofer Burford
g. ij*d*. Jeames Ewer g. ij*d*. Rich. Stoneham g. j*d*. Tho. Edmund
g. j*d*. (*iij*d*). Uxor [*blank*] Carter widow g. xvj*d*.

*Summa* iijs. ix*d*.

OXHEY HAMLETT. Tho. Edmund g. x*d*. Roger Weden g. ijs.
iiij*d*. Tho. Wedon g. xvj*d*. Wm. Jackett g. xiiij*d*. Robt. Edlyn
g. xij*d*. John Pople g. iiij*d*. Wm. Hill g. ij*d*.

*Summa* viijs. iij*d*.

LEVYSDEN HAMLET. Wm. Eu'ston (*Everson*) g. iij*d*. Roger
Dent g. x*d*. Wm. Hoddesdon g. ij*d*. Wm. Woodward l. xij*d*.
Wm. Ewer l. iiij*d*. Robt. Stephyn l. iiij*d*. Wm. Woodward senior
(*junior*) g. j*d*. Robt. Hill g. j*d*. Edm. Woodward g. ij*d*. Tho.
Hill g. ij*d*. Rich. Woodward g. j*d*. John Hill l. (*g.*) iiij*d*. Tho.
Woodward (*g.*) xiiij*d*. John Prat g. j*d*. John Perse (*Payse*) g. iij*d*.
John Stoke l. iiij*d*.

*Summa* vs. x*d*.

LEES LANGLEYE. John Hobbes sen. g. ij*d*. Wm. Gladman g.
x*d*. Rauf Deye l. xx*d*. Jeames Dolwyn g. x*d*. Rauf Decon g. x*d*.
Saunder Boltwell g. x*d*. Wm. Kentyshe l. iiij*d*. Margt. Kyng
widow l. ij*d*. John D(*econ g. iij*d*.*) Xpofer Besouthe g. (*xij*d*.
Robt. Catlyn g. (*x*d*. Tho. Dell g. x*d*. Wm. Heyward g. (*x*d*.
Rich. Ellf (*Gyles*) g. j*d*. John Meger l. ij*d*. John Muge (*Mugge*)
g. j*d*. John Hobbes jun. g. j*d*. (*John*) Portres sen. g. j*d*. John
Ewer jun. l. vj*d*. (*Jeames*) Heydon g. iij*d*. (*John*) Lewes g. x*d*.
. . . . Ewer de . . . brige g. x*d*. . . . Roberts . .
ij*d*. . . . . **Portres g.** ij*d*. . . . . Ewer de . . . . .

Wm. Ewer l. iiij*d*. Robt. Stephyn l. iiij*d*. Wm. Woodward senior ryge g . . . Wm. . . . . g . . . Jeames . . . l . . Tho. E . . . g. j*d*. Wm. . . . . . . g. j*d*. Wm. . . . . ster j*d*. Tho. . . . . l. ij*d*. Xpo. . . . . g. j*d*. Wm. . . . . g. j*d*. Robt. . . . g. j*d*. Tho. . . . . g. ij*d*. Wm. . . . ton g. j*d*. Henry . . . stall l. ij*d*. Tho. H . . . we g. ij*d*. John Feld g. xvj*d*. Rich. Atkyn g. j*d*. Henry Doll g. j*d*. Wm. Chapell iij*d*.

*Summa* xvj*s*. iij*d*.

SARROT. Jeames Boldewyn l. xx*d*. Robt. Johnson g. xviij*d*. John Heydon jun. g. xvj*d*. John Androwe g. x*d*. John Swetyng l. iiij*d*. Tho. Ockleye l. iiij*d*. John Watt℥ g. j*d*. John Salter g. j*d*. Tho. Knolton g. j*d*. Edm. Heydon g. ij*d*. Rich. Heydon g. j*d*. Xpofer Wynkfelde g. ij*d*. Xpofer Raye g. j*d*. Eme Aldwyn widow g. ij*d*.

*Summa* vj*s*. xj*d*.

[RIC]KMERSWORTHE TOWNE . . . ncle widow g. xiiij*d*. . . . thmer g. xiiij*d*. . . . g. xviij*d*. . . . wyn g. iij*d* . . . Dolt g. j*d*. Geo. Merydethe g. ij*d*. Roger Baldewyn g. ij*d*. Henry Awedon g. xiiij*d*. Tho. Lane g. xiiij*d*. John Colynson g. x*d*. Symon Warden g. x*d*. Barth. Awedon g. x*d*. John Fysher g. iiij*d*. Tho. Welshman g. iiij*d*. John Gardyner g. iiij*d*. Wm. Johnson g. iij*d*. Rich. Perkyns g. ij*d*. John Gybbe g . . *d*. Rich. Capon g. ij*d*. Geo. Wastell g. j*d*. Rich. Randolf g. ij*d*. Rich. Nores g. iiij*d*. Uxor [*blank*] Casylman g. ij*d*. Robt. Hethe g. x*d*. John Evelyn l. ij*d*. Uxor [*blank*] Marteyn g. ij*d*. Roger Johnson g. j*d*. John Sterope g. j*d*. Tho. Androwe . . j*d*. John Harton g. j*d*. Anne Whyt widow g. j*d*. Rich. . . . . g. j*d*. Edw. . . wbyng j*d*. John Grey g. j*d*. Wm. Turn . . g. j*d*. Wm. Gy . . . j*d*. Dorythe Wylson g. xij*d*. Uxor [*blank*] Twychet g. ij*d*. John A Dale g. iiij*d*.

*Summa* xv*s*. iiij*d*.

CHARLOWOODE HAMLETE. Rich. Wynchestr g. iij*d*. Rich. Butterfeld g. x*d*. John Davy l. ij*d*. John Awedon g. iij*d*. Edw. Awedon g. ij*d*. Wm. Wood g. xvj*d*. Xpofer Baldwyn (*Balwyn*) g. ij*d*. Rich. Davy g. j*d*. Thos. Branche g. ij*d*. John Webb (*Webbse*) g. ij*d*. John Baldwyn g. xvj*d*. John Wynkfeld g. xiiij*d*.

*Summa* vj*s*. ij*d*.

CROSSELEY (*CROXLEY*) GRENE. Uxor Holtyng g. x*d*. Roger Axstell g. iiij*d*. (*Rich*.) Clerke g. ij*d*. Tho. Hethe (*Hetch*) g. ij*d*. (*jd. ob.*) Tho. Pawltocke (*Pawlton*) g. ij*d*. (*Tho. Stan*)browe g. iij*d*. (*Rich. Baldwyn g.*) iij*d*. (*Tho. Butterfeld g. ij*d*. Codlyghasyll g*.) ij*d*. (*John Goodlyshe*) g. ij*d*. (*Rich. Pygeworth g*.) iij*d*. (*Geo. A. Wed*)on g. ij*d*. (*John Butter*)feld g. ij*d*. (*Geo. Bald*)wyn g. x*d*. Tho. He(*yward*) g. iiij*d*. (*John*) Ewer g. ij*d*.

*Summa* iiij*s*. vj*d*. ob.

WESTHIDE (HAMLET). Androwe Randoll g. xvj*d*. Wm. Awedon g. xiiij*d*. Sibell Butterfeld g. x*d*. John Randoll g. ij*d*. Rich. Gybb g. iiij*d*. Robt. Randoll g. ij*d*. Edw. Rolf g. j*d*. Eme Rolf g. j*d*. Johane Randoll g. j*d*. Geo. Whit g. j*d*. Marget Butterfeld x*d*. John Gybbe g. ij*d*. Henry Rolf g. ij*d*. John Rede g. j*d*. John Randoll l. & g. j*d*. Tho. Wedon g. j*d*. Alice Dofett (*Dofat*) g. j*d*.

*Summa* v*s*. x*d*.

**BATCHEWORTHE.** Tho. Mekyn (*Mykyn*) g. x*d*. John Knolton g. iij*d*. Tho. Awedon g. ij*d*. Rich. Stanbrught (*Stanbruth*) g. j*d*. Tho. Marteyn g. ij*d*. Rich. Marteyn g. iiij*d*. Tho. Rede g. ij*d*. Edw. Dorsett g. ij*d*. John Sympson (*Symson*) g. x*d*. Rich. Smyth g. j*d*. Wm. Bryon (*Bryan*) g. ij*d*. Uxor [*blank*] Goodwyn vid. g. j*d*. John Atkyns g. xvj*d*. John Ludlowe g. x*d*. Rich. Fynche (*Fyshe*) g. iij*d*. John Darante g. j*d*. John Fotherleye g. j*d*. Geo. Grover g. ij*d*. Henry Awedon g. ij*d*. Jeames Fotherley l. ij*d*.

Summa vj*s*. v*d*.

**ALDENHAM.** Wm. Meryon l. iij*d*. (*iiij d*). Robt. Tayllour g. xvj*d*. John Utram (*Ultram*) g. j*d*. Wm. Wygborne l. ij*d*. Simon Wayshe g. ij*d*. Wm. Downer g. ij*d*. Humph. Boraston (*Beraston*) g. xiiij*d*. Johane Grene vid. g. ij*d*. John Archer g. x*d*. Rich. Sheppd sen. g. xvj*d*. Simon Sheppd g. iij*d*. Rich. Smythe l. iiij*d*. Wm. Grene g. x*d*. Wm. Wrenche g. iiij*d*. Rich. Elsbie (*Ellysbye*) g. ij*d*. Robt. Warren g. x*d*. Thexecutors of Thoms Hamond g. xiiij*d*. Tho. Gonne (*Gune*) g. iiij*d*. John Palmer g. j*d*. Wm. Palmer g. ij*d*. Agnes Palmer g. ij*d*. (*j d*). Wm. Hyll g. ij*d*. John Goldsmyth g. j*d*. Rich. Sheppd. g. x*d*. John Brythe (*Bryght*) g. j*d*. Robt. Cherie g. ij*d*. Tho. Russell g. iij*d*. John Foster g. ij*d*. Rich. Buckberd l. vj*d*. Alice Meryden vid. j*d*. Robt. Añable g. xiiij*d*. Edw. Huddell g. xiiij*d*. Henry Heyward g. ij*d*. Tho. M . . . g . . John Downer g . . . Alice Lane widow l. ij*s*. Rich. Hall g. x*d*. Thos. Ablet g. ij*d*. Rich. Basse g. ij*d*. Rauf Sterky g. j*d*. Thos. H . . . x*d*. . . . Kytter g. j*d*. . . . s Woodward g. ij*d*. . . . .

[*The roll is much mutilated at this point*].

. . . Boraston g. iiij*d*. . . . s Packwood g. iij*d* . . . Horwell g. j*d*. [Wm.] Horwell g. ij*d*. Rauf Castell l. iiij*d*. Wm. Sterkye g. j*d*. Eliz. May g. ij*d*. Humph. Hegger g. x*d*. Eliz. Skote g. ij*d*. Humph . . . g. x*d*. Thos. Archer g. iij*d*. Wm. Redwood g. ij*d*. Hen. Plot jun. ij*d*. Elyn' Hunt wid. g. xij*d*. Thos. Basse g. ij*d*. Edw. Bristoo jun. xvj*d*. Wm. Hunt g. iij*d*. Rich. Wedon g. j*d*. Wm. Pope g. j*d*. John Redwood g. ij*d*. Wm. Whit l. ij*d*. Robt. Whitby g. ij*d*. Tho. Palmer g. ij*d*. John Bat(?) g. j*d*. Wm. Wylde g. ij*d*. Tho. Bocher g. j*d*. Tho. Fene g. j*d*. Wm. Roger g. ij*d*. Anthony Wayshe g. iij*d*. Wm. Wayshe g. iij*d*. John Kemp g. j*d*. John Russell g. j*d*. John Dericke g. j*d*. Thos. Dych g. j*d*. Robt. Russell g. j*d*. Robt. Ablet & John Oxton for the goods of John Cogdale orphant iiij*d*. Thos. Cogdale g. iij*d*. Eliz. Purueye g. xvj*d*. Elyn' Ashellwood g. j*d*. Robt. Lowson g. ij*d*. Henry Rugge g. iiij*d*. Wm. Nele g. ij*d*. John . . . g. j*d*. John Basse g. j*d*. Wm. Fabian g. ij*d*. Henry Lyon g. j*d*. Wm. Wrench sen. j*d*. Wm. Springhall j*d*.

Summa xxxiij*s*. iiij*d*.

**ILSTRE.** John Foster g. viij*d*. Rauf Hyll g. iiij*d*. John Lucke g. x*d*. Rich. Hamond g. iiij*d*. John Lane g. ij*d*. John Bygmore g. j*d*. Tho. Hunt g. ij*d*. Robt. Colavll g. ij*d*. Rich. Meryden g. ij*d*. . . . Rogers g. xij*d*. Arthur Grove j*d*. . . . King wid. ij*d*. [*The next ten names are defective*]. Wm. Lucke g. j*d*. John Rodes g. iij*d*. Rich. Hayle g. j*d*. Ralph Messynger (*Messyng*) g. j*d*. Rich. Hyll g. ij*d*. Thos. Lane g. j*d*. (*ij d*).

Summa vij*s*.

SLEPE AND SMALEFORD. John Burges (*Burgys*) g. xij*d*. Edw. (*Edmund*) Wetherhed g. xvj*d*. Luce Turnepenye (*Turpenye*) g. xij*d*. Wm. Est g. ij*d*. Geo. Est g. x*d*. Robt. Shawe g. iiij*d*. Thos. Smythe g. xiiij*d*. Philip Slepe g. xij*d*. Walter Goodvere g. iiij*d*. Tho. Clerke g. iiij*d*. Wm. Knolton g. iiij*d* John Clerke g. j*d*. Roger G(*rubbe*) g. iij*d* (ij*d*). Philip (*Est*) g. ij*d*. Wm. (*Ma*)rston jun. ij*d*. Thos. (*Cha*)pell g. ij*d*. Wm. (*Man*) g. ij*d*. John (*Hyll*) g. j*d*. John (*Brokkes*) g. xiiij*d*. Joan (*Foster*) g. xiiij*d*. Philip Holtyng) g. j*d*. Rich. (*Graye*) g. ij*d*. John (*Clerke*) g. xiiij*d*. Robt. B(*othe*) g xiiij*d*.

*Summa* viij*s* ix*d*.)

CHYLDWYKE. (*John*) Hawgood g. xiiij*d*. (*Rich*. C)ristian g. iij*d*. (*Rich*.) Myles g. ij*d*. (*Tho*.) Elles (*Ellys*) g. j*d*. (*John*) Hyll g. j*d*. (*Thos*.) Everot (*En'ate*) g. j*d*.

*Summa* xxij*d*.

WESTWIKE. Wm. Butell (*Batell*) g. xiiij*d*. Thos. Etherope g. iij*d*. Thos. Beche g. ij*d*. Rich. Marston g. j*d*. Robt. Fynche g. ij*d*. John Lagoo l. iij*d*. John Nayshe g. iij*d*. (*Gyles*) Dell g. iiij*d*. (*Robt*.) Ranshom (*Ramison*) g. xiiij*d*. Thos. Roberts g. ij*d*. Rich. Bunne g. l. ij*d*. Edm. Baxster g. j*d*. (ij*d*.) John Marston jun. g. ij*d*.

*Summa* iiij*s*. vj*d*.

KYNGESBURY. John Kentyshe g. x*d*. Robt. Bestney l. viij*d*. Walter Dewbury g. x*d*. Alice Brygge (*widow*) l. iiij*d*. Robt. Baker g. xiiij*d*. Alice Baker g. ij*d*. Josepe Eu'ton (*Em'ton*) feod. iiij*d*. Xpofer Tucke g. ij*d*. (*Robt*.) Nele g. iiij*d*. John Broke g. j*d*. Robt. Long. g. j*d*. Hugh Denyon g. j*d*. Hugh Gyfford g. j*d*. John Myles g. j*d*. Wm. Mower g. j*d*. Robt. Hollond g. j*d*. John Grencope (*Grenehope*) g. j*d*.

*Summa* v*s*. vj*d*.

WYNDERIGE. Thos. Thewer g. (*l*) ij*d*. Robt. Kentyshe l. iiij*d*. Thos. Saunders g. iij*d*. Uxor Joh'is Sybley g. iij*d*. Robt. Hariese g. ij*d*. Rich. Roding g. ij*d*. Wm. Collyn l. ij*d*. John Ewer g. ij*d*. Walter Royse g. ij*d*.

*Summa* xxij*d*.

TYTTENHANGER. Rich. Chapman g. xviij*d*. Wm. Davye g. xij*d*. Agnes Langham vid. xij*d*. Rich. Symon g. j*d*. Wm. Bestneye j*d*.

*Summa* iij*s*. viij*d*.

RUGGE. Wm. Gonstone g. xij*d*. Henry Grubbe g. xij*d*. Henry Sharp g. iiij*d*. Rich. Whyte g. x*d*. John Stannet g. x*d*. John Colyns g. iiij*d*. Wm. Bokete g. iiij*d*. Thos. Edryngton g. ij*d*. Marget Sharpe g. ij*d*. Wm. Basse g. x*d*. Wm. Tyler g. x*d*. Robt. Dell g. iiij*d*. Alice Bokete g. ij*d*. John Thomson g. ij*d*. Wm. Croseleye g. ij*d*. John Whyt g. ij*d*. Wm. Boket g. ij*d*. Henry Bokket g. ij*d*. Marion Messynger vid. xij*d*.

*Summa* ix*s*. ij*d*.

ESTBARNET. Wm. Harrison l. viij*d*. Wm. Rolf de Chasesyd xvj*d*. Thos. Rolf g. x*d*. Alice Colman vid. g. xij*d*. Joan Parkyn vid. g. x*d*. Nich. Bradeleye g. ij*d*. Thos. Hardwike g. iij*d*. Thos. Mathewe g. ij*d*. John Rolf g. ij*d*. John Smythe g. j*d*. Rich. Gylbert g. j*d*. Wm. Large g. j*d*.

*Summa* iiij*s*. x*d*.

CHEPING BARNET. Robt. Pratt g. xviijd. Thos. Love g. xviijd. John Dene g. iiijs. Wm. Oxton g. vs. Roger Burwell g. xd. John Tayllor g. ijd. [blank] Ree smythe jd. Rich. Alen g. ijd. Rich. Byrde g. xd. Xpoffer Brokke g. ijd. John Royse g. xd. Wm. Catlyn g. jd. Thos. Skynner ijd. John Vaughan g. xd. Wm. Laurence g. iiijd. Thos. Elye . . jd. John Berye . . xiiijd. Roger Pole . . ijd. Wm. B . . . . g. xd. Annes S . . . g. iijd. John S . . . . g. xd. Wm . . . . . g. ijd. John . . . . . g. iijd. Thos. . . . . g. . .d. Henry . . . . g. ijd. Thos. . . . . . g. ijd. Valentyne . . . . g. . xd. Rich. Haddo . . . . ijd. Wm. E . . . g. xiiijd. Rich. Mussag . . on g. xijd. Thos. . . . stell g. iiijd. Wm. Blackwell ijd. Robt. N . . . . an g. jd. John H . . . . g. xiiijd. John H . . . . g. jd. John . . . . . g. jd. Harman Doble bere iiijd. John Dorwood g. iijd. Alice Blakborne l. vjd. Annes Hodden g. xiiijd. Margt. Braye g. xiiijd. Ellyn Braye g. xiiijd. Annis Foxe g. xiiijd. John Bellamye g. iijd.

*Summa* xxxijs. iijd.

NORTHALL. Rich. Fyshe g. xijd. John Hyde g. iijd. Wm. Hyde g. xijd. Wm. Lowen g. ijd. Robt. Muffett sen. g. xd. John Lowen jun. g. xd. John Grubbe g. ijd. John Knight g. ijd. Thos. Foster g. ijd. Roger Noode (*Node*) g. xd. John Blake (*Bloke*) sen. jd. (*John Bloke jun. g. xd*). Robt. Muffet jun. g. xijd. Thos. Baldocke g. iiijd. Uxor Willi Hyll g. iijd. Rich. Foster g. ijd.

*Summa* viijs. jd.

SANDRYGE. John Bygge (*sen.*) g. xd. John Bygg jun. xd. Rich. Wetherhed g. xd. John Michell g. xiiijd. Thos. Lambrt g. iiijd. John Turpenye g. iiijd. Henry Porter g. iiijd. John Wetherhed g. xd. Wm. Spyngoll (*Spryngold*) g. ijd. Isabell Adyson vid. g. iiijd. Kat'yn Holt vid. g. ijd. Thos. Catlyn g. iiijd. Wm. Witherhed jun. iijd. Edw. Bygge g. ijd. Adame Brokk g. jd. John Adame (*Adams*) g. ijd. Henry Syblye (*Bell*) g. ijd. Wm. Clerke g. jd. (*John Hewett g. jd. Tho. Febrygge l. viijd.*

*Summa* vijs. xd.

REDBOURN. John Fynche g. xijd. Walter Fynche g. xijd. John Kylby g. xd. Tho. Humfrey g. xd. Tho. Heyward g. xijd. John Lasby g. iiijd. Robt. Laxbye g. ijd. Wm. Hawgoode g. xiiijd. John Fynche sen. g. xiiijd.) Wm. Saunder g. xd. Thos. Pecok g. xd. Wm. Horne g. iiijd. John Thewer g. iiijd. Rich. Cranwell (*Crandwell*) g. iiijd. Robt. Martyn jun. g. iiijd. Wm. Taylor g. iiijd. Thos. Marston g. iiijd. John Munne g. iiijd. Robt. Hawgood g. iijd. Thos. Marteyn g. iiijd. Wm. Fynche g. ijd. Rich. Hawgood g. iiijd. Robt. Bostocke g. iiijd. Anne Pecok g. ijd. Walter Fynch jun. iijd. Wm. Thewer g. jd. Nich. Fynche g. jd. Thos. Fynche g. ijd. Geo. Symond[ g. ijd. Rich. Broke g. ijd. Xpofer Hower g. jd. Robt. Burwell g. ijd. Walter Bech g. ijd. Wm. Durrant g. ijd. John Edlynn g. ijd. Robt. Marteyn sen. g. ijd. Geo. Cristmas g. ijd. John Myles (*jun.*) g. jd. (*ijd*). Thos. Strudder g. ijd. Thos. Cogdale g. ijd. John Myles sen. g. ijd. John Baker g. ijd. Robt. Beche g. iiijd. Wm. Barton g. jd. Wm. Fawdye g. ijd. Walter Hyckden g. jd. John Beeche g. jd. Jeames Parker g. jd. Henry T[ymas?] g. iijd. Wm. Turrye g. jd. Nich. Robynson ijd. Wm. Abraham ijd. Wm. Cristmas g. jd. Thos. Myles g. jd. Wm. Iverye g. jd. Hugh Cranwell g. jd. Marion Kylbye g.

j*d*. Thos. Pecok jun. j*d*. Thos. Hedge g. j*d*. Geo. Al . . . g. j*d*. Rich. Wetherhed g. j*d*. Rauf Buckmaster sen. ij*d*. Thos. Aunsell g. j*d*. Robt. Marshall g. ij*d*. Alice M'shall g. ij*d*. Wm. Fleccher g. j*d*. Rich. Burford g. ij*d*. Rich. Hickden g. j*d*. Thos. Sybleve g. j*d*. John Robynson g. j*d*. Rich. Marteyn g. j*d*. Robt. Clarke g. j*d*.

*Summa* xix*s*. viij*d*.

POLLES WALDEN. John Camfeld g. xviij*d*. Rich. Hall g. x*d*. John Yong g. x*d*. Thos. Yong of Buteslowe g. iiij*d*. Rich. Sturmyn jun. iiij*d*. John Roffe g. iiij*d*. Wm. Auncell g. ij*d*. Wm. Austen g. ij*d*. Rich. Rhyld g. ij*d*. Wm. Goodryge g. ij*d*. Jeames Yong g. iij*d*. John Hauken g. ij*d*. John Chalkley g. ij*d*. Wm. Nutting g. iiij*d*. John Jenkyns g. iiij*d*. John Ventres g. ij*d*. Thos. Overton ij*d*. John Sturmyn sen. ij*d*. Edw. Penyfather iiij*d*. Thos. Gasleye iij*d*. Wm. Chakley de Esthall g. ij*d*. John Bure g. j*d*. Xpofer Nuttyng g. j*d*. Thos. Camfelde g. j*d*.

*Summa* vij*s*. v*d*.

CODYCOTE. Edm. Darde g. iiij*d*. Edw. Younge g. xij*d*. Geo. Wylshere g. xij*d*. Wm. Kympton g. iiij*d*. Thos. Gaseleye iiij*d*. Edm. Michell iiij*d*. Edw. Michell iij*d*. Rich. Baker g. iij*d*. Jeffrey Plomer iij*d*. Alice Astry vid. iij*d*. Henry Wren g. iij*d*. John Wylsher g. ij*d*. John Hunt g. ij*d*. John Spore g. ij*d*. John Beckfeld g. ij*d*. Rich. Dardes g. j*d*. Gilbt. Triamore j*d*. Henry Darde j*d*. Wm. Style j*d*. Rich. Johnson g. j*d*. Thos. Thomson j*d*. Edm. M'shall j*d*.

*Summa* v*s*. xj*d*.

HEXTON. Mathewe Hale g. xviij*d*. John Rudd g. ij*d*. John Johnson g. ij*d*. Thos. Wakes g. ij*d*. Henry Brace g. iij*d*. Thos. Feld g. j*d*. Thos. Landes g. j*d*. Jeames Landes g. j*d*. Thos. Feld sen. x*d*. John Brace g. iij*d*. Thos. Goldsmythe g. j*d*. Henry Prior g. j*d*. Thos. Crowche (*Croche*) g. xij*d*. Henry Carter g. ij*d*. Wm. Pn'ter g. j*d*. (*Thos. Prudden g. iiijd. John Samme g. ijd. Robt. Spencer g. jd. Tho. Same g. ijd. Thos. Brace g. ijd. Henry Crowche g. iiijd. Wm. Barton g. ijd. Rich. Goldsmyth g. iiijd. Wm. Dermer g. iijd. Margt. Buckyngham ijd.*

*Summa* vij*s*. ij*d*.)

NEWNEHAM. Nich. Arthure (*Artour*) g. iiij*d*. John Geve (*Gyre*) g. iiij*d*. Hugh Hyde g. iiij*d*. Thos. Jeames g. iiij*d*. Thos. Turnor g. iiij*d*. Rich. Payne g. ij*d*. Thos. Dewnope g. ij*d*. Wm. Blowe g. ij*d*. Wm. Payne g. j*d*. Thos. Morleye g. j*d*. Thos. Reason (*Rason*) g. j*d*. John Nele (*Neley*) g. j*d*. Anthony Colfeld [*Camfeld erased*] g. j*d*. Thos. Sabt g. j*d*. Thos. Thomson g. j*d*. Edm. Wylson g. iiij*d*. Robt. Blowe g. j*d*. Thos. Newton g. j*d*. Walter Dagleye g. j*d*. Symon Blowe j*d*. Robt. Rose (*Rosey*) j*d*. Hugh Pepyn [*Pegion erased*] j*d*. Robt. Botelson j*d*.

*Summa* iij*s*. viij*d*.

NORTON. Nich. Lawman g. xviij*d*. Thos. Phipe g. vij*d*. Anth. Raynold xiiij*d*. John Wygge iiij*d*. Nich. Coke g. ij*d*. Robt. Hyll g. ij*d*. John Mosse g. iij*d*. Wm. Camoke g. ij*d*. Anth. Frankilcast' Denyzen g. viij*d*. Wm. Bell g. ij*d*. Thos. Annyson g. iij*d*. Tho. Fyppe jun. g. j*d*. Edw. Fyppe g. j*d*. Jeames Fyppe g. j*d*. Thos. Bygrave iiij*d*. Rich. Grave iij*d*. Rich. Plomer ij*d*. John Lorde j*d*. (*ijd*).

*Summa* vij*s*. ij*d*.

BRANDFELDE. Edw. FitzJohn g. xviijd. Rich. Penyfather g. xviijd. Wm. Tufnall g. xviijd. John Hyll g. xviijd. Thos. Wyge g. xijd. Wm. Hynde g. xijd. Thos. Cannon g. xd. Rich. Berkemaker g. iiijd. Tho. Tredgolde g. iijd. John Bakyn g. iijd. Rich. Grene g. ijd. Edm. Tuffnall g. iijd. Thos. Penyfather g. jd. John Culwyke g. jd. Edm. Dell g. iijd. Robt. Parke g. ijd. John Ive (*Ere*) g. ijd. Wm. Lowen g. jd. Edw. Tredgold jd. Wm. Archer g. jd. Rich. Herne g. jd. Michell Hyll g. jd.
*Summa* xjs. iijd.

SHEPHALL. Robt. Kympton g. xd. Jhon Bygge g. iiijd. John Chapman iiijd. John Hatton g. iijd. Thos. Kympton jd.
*Summa* xxijd.

Summa totalis tercie solucionis Subsidij Hundredi predicti Anno xxxvij$^{mo}$ Henrici Octavi } xxli vs vjd whereof

Allowed to the Comiss ijd de le pound and ijd to the high Collector and ijd de le pound to the petye Collector } xs Et

Sic Clar. Domino Regi xixli xvs vjd.

# Transcripts of Parish Registers.

### AYOT ST. PETER.

[*The existing Registers commence in* 1696].

Ayott pva. A true certificate taken out of the Regoster booke of all the names of thos which haue bin baptised maried or Buried within the pish of Little Aoyt in the Countie of Hartfd from the feast St Mychaell the archangell Anno Dom 1609 vnto the said ffeast 1610.

*Baptised.*

ffrances Hones was Baptised 29 day of October Anno Dn 1609.
ffrances Rament was baptised 27 day of December Anno Dn. 1609.
Margaret Chappell was baptised the 7 day of July Anno Dn. 1610.
Thomas Hicmā was Baptised the 5 day of August Anno Dn. 1610.

*Buried.*

John Addam was Buried 26 day of Januari Anno Dn. 1609.
Elisabeth Addam was Buried the 1 day of Februarie Anno Dn. 1609.

*Married none.*

John Bussie minister.
the marke of × William Conny Churchwarden.
the marke of × Thomas Dormer sidesman.

---

Ayot pva

a true certificate taken out of the Regester booke of Little . . . in the Count of Hartf of all the names of such as haue bine bapt . . . maried or buried sence S<sup>t</sup> mich . . . . in the yeare of our Lord god 16 . . vnto the same feast 1615.

*baptized.*

Marie Gine the daughter of Henrie Gine was baptized the first day of November 1614.

Robart Henes the sonne of Willā Henes was baptized the second day of Aprill 1615.

*maried none.*

John Addā the wife of Thomas Addā was buried the 9 day of June 1615.

John Bussie, minister.
the marke × of Willā Conny, churchwarden.
the mark × of Thomas Dormer sidesmā.

---

A true certificat taken out of the regester booke of the parish of Little Ayot in the Countie of Hartford of all the names of such as haue bin baptized maried or buried from the feast of mychaell the archangel 1621 vnto the said feast 1622.

*Baptized.*

Elizabeth Ruffin and Marie Ruffin gemelli were Baptized the 5 day of May 1622.

*Married none.*
*Buried none.*

John Bussie, rector.
Thomas Ruffyn.
the marke × of Richard Randall, sidesmā.

---

[*After this I omit the head notes. W.B.*]

From Mich<sup>s</sup> 1623 to Mich<sup>s</sup> 1624.

*Baptized none.*

John Haukin and Marie Conny were married the 30 day of June 1624.

*Buried none.*

John Bussie minister.
the mark × of Richard Randall churchwarden.

---

From Mich<sup>s</sup> 1624 to Mich<sup>s</sup> 1625.

*Baptizsed.*

Thomas Capmā the sonne of Thomas Capmā was baptized the 28 day of August 1625.

James Bemon was baptized the 8 day of September Anno dni 1625.

*Married.*

Williā Griffin and Marie Beule were maried the 2 day of October 1625.

John Boyse and Annis Tredder were married the 9 day of October 1625.

*Buried.*

Marie Bussie the wife of John Bussie was buried the 4 day of August 1625.

       John Bussie minyster.
the make × of Richard Fynwod churchwarden.

---

From the Feast of the Annunc. B.M. 1626 to said feast 1627.

*Baptized none.*

*Married*

John King and Elizabeth Chappel were married the 18 day of October 1626

*Buried none*

      John Bussie clark.
the mark × of Richard Fynwod churchwardin
the mark × of Thomas Barnes sidesmā.

---

Endorsed Mich⁸ 1629 to Mich⁸ 1630.

*Christenings none.*

*Marriages none.*

*Burialls none.*

      Jo. Iuory Rect. ibid.
      Jo. Beamont churchward.

---

From Mich⁸ 1631 to Mich⁸ 1632.

*Christenings not any.*

*Mariages.*

John Hawkins and Elisabeth Clerke were marryed May 10. 1632.
Robert Winch and Elisabeth Gabriell were marryed July 31. 1632.

*Burialls.*

Elisabeth Hind was buryed March 17. 1631.
Thomas Clerke was buryed April 14. 1632.

      Jo. Iuory Rect. ibid.
      Will. Conny churchward.

---

From Mich⁸ 1633 to Mich⁸ 1634.

*Christenings.*

Lewis the sonne of Mʳ Alexander Napper was baptised March 27. 1634.
Thomas the sonne of Edward Wren was bapt. March 30. 1634.
Grizzilde the daughter of Edward Abry was bapt. August 10. 1634.

*Marriages.*

George Graue and Martha Chambers were marryed October 16. 1633.

Edward Chandler and Margaret Chappell were marryed Oct. 18. 1633.
Jasper Ireland and Elisabeth Hodge were marryed Aprill 8. 1634.
*Burialls.*
Widow Chappell was buryed November 5 1633.
Thomas Dormer was buryed March 2. 1633.
M<sup>rs</sup> Mary Poulter was buryed May 11. 1634.

      Jo. Iuory Rect. ibid.
      Will. Conny churchward.

---

From Mich<sup>s</sup> 1634 to Mich<sup>s</sup> 1635.
*Christenings.*
Richard the sonne of Nicholas Wellingham bapt. Octob. 28.
Elizabeth y<sup>e</sup> daughter of John Beamont bapt. March 20. 1634.
Katherine y<sup>e</sup> daughter of Tho. Capman bap. May 10. 1635.
*Marriages.*
William Clerke and Jane Jasy marryed Nouēb. 14. 1634.
John Conny and Susan Ellis marryed June 24. 1635.
*Burialls.*
Margaret y<sup>e</sup> wife of Ed. Mullington buryed Febr. 27. 1634.
Elisabeth y<sup>e</sup> daughter of Jo. Beamont buryed March 22. 1634

      Jo. Iuory Rect. ibid.
      Nich. Hind churchward.

---

From Mich<sup>s</sup> 1635 to Mich<sup>s</sup> 1636.
*Christenings.*
Thomas y<sup>e</sup> sonne of Thomas Ansell was bapt. Nouēb. 8. 1635.
Judeth y<sup>e</sup> daughter of Edward Abry bapt. May 22. 1636.
Elisabeth the daughter of Jo. Iuory bapt. May 25. 1636.
*Marriages none.*
*Burialls.*
The Lady Purient was buryed Decemb. 6. 1635.
Jone Hanes y<sup>e</sup> daughter of Tho. Barns buryed Jan. 17. 1635.
Freeman Hind was buryed Febr. 10. Año dom. 1635.

      Jo. Iuory Rect. ibid.
      Nich. Hind churchward.
      Ed. Abry sid.

---

From Mich<sup>s</sup> 1636 to Mich<sup>s</sup> 1637.
*Christenings.*
Katherine y<sup>e</sup> daughter of Will. Haynes was bapt. Nouēb. 13. 1636.
Susan y<sup>e</sup> daughter of Jo. Conny was bapt. May 14. 1637.
*Marriages.*
Edward Wren and Elisabeth Harper were marryed Decēb. 31. 1636.
William Dawson and Elisabeth Bowles were marryed Febr. 24. 1636.
Samuell Ellement and Alice Ellis were marryed March 5. 1636.
*Burialls not any.*

      Jo. Iuory, Rect. ibid.
      Nich. Wellinghā, churchward.

### From Lady Day 1637 to Lady Day 1638.
#### Christenings.
Susan yᵉ daughter of John Conny was bapt. May 14. 1637.
Williã and John yᵉ sonnes of Tho. Ansell were bapt. Jan. 28. 1637.

#### Burialls.
Widow Dormer was buryed Octob. 27. 1637.
Williã and John yᵉ sons of Tho. Ansell were buryed the one Jan. 29 yᵉ other Febr. 6. 1637.

    Jo. Iuory Rect. ibid.
    Nich. Wellinghã Churchward.

### From Michˢ 1637 to Michˢ 1638.
#### Christenings.
William and John yᵉ sonnes of Tho. Ansell bapt. Jan. 28. 1637.
Francis yᵉ sonne of Jasper Irland was baptized Aprill 15. 1638.

#### Marriages.
Williã Bennet and Susan Hind were marryed Aprill 5. 1638.

#### Burialls.
Widdow Dormer was buryed October 27. 1637.
Williã et John sonnes of Tho. Ansell buryed yᵉ one Jan. 29, yᵉ other Feb. 6. 1637.
The wife of Richard Woodfine was buryed Septēber 9. 1638.

    Jo. Iuory Rect. ibid.
    Jo. Wells churchward.

---

### From Lady Day 1638 to Lady Day 1639.
#### Christenings.
Francis yᵉ sonne of Jasper Irland was bapt. Aprill 15. 1638.
Dorcas yᵉ daughter of Nicholas Wellingham bapt. June 22. 1638.
Mary yᵉ base daughter of Tho. Harris [? Hains] et Elis. Conny bapt. Aug. 26. 1638.
Mary yᵉ daughter of William Turner was bapt. Decēb. 16. 1638.

#### Marriages.
William Bennet and Susan Hind were marryed Aprill 5. 1633.
Richard Woodfine and Jone Bowman were marryed Jan. 28. 1638.

#### Buryalls.
Elisabeth yᵉ wife of Rich. Woodfine was buryed Septemb. 16. 1638.
John Edmunds yᵉ elder was buryed Nouemb. 9. 1638.
John Edmunds iu. was buryed Decemb. 2. 1638.

    Jo. Iuory Rect. ibid.
    Jo. Wells. Churchward.

---

### From Michˢ 1638 to Michˢ 1639.
#### Christenings.
Imp. Mary yᵉ daughter of Williã Turner baptised Decēb. 16.

#### Marriages.
Richard Woodfine and Jone Bowman marryed Jan. 28. 1638.

*Burialls.*

John Edmonds sen. was buryed Nouēb. 9. 1638.
John Edmonds iu. was buryed Decēb. 2. 1638.

Jo. Iuory Rect. ibid.
Jo. Wells. Churchward.

---

From Lady Day 1639 to Lady Day 1640.

*Christenings.*

William ye sonne of Edward Auis was baptised Nouēb. 24. 1639.
Jone ye daughter of Jasper Irland was bapt. Feb. 9. 1639.

*Burialls.*

Mary ye daughter of Tho. Capman was buryed March 12. 1639.

Jo. Iuory Rect. ibid.
Jo. Wells churchward.

---

From Michs 1639 to Michs 1640.

*Christenings.*

William ye sonne of Edward Auis was baptized Nouēb. 24. 1639.
Jone ye daughter of Jasper Ireland was bapt February 9. 1639.
John ye sonne of Tho. Ansell was bapt. July 5. 1640.

*Marriages.*

John Todd and Martha Mott were marryed Septēb. 28. 1640.

*Buryalls.*

Thomas Scott was buryed June 3. 1640.

Jo. Iuory Rect. ibid.
Nich. Hind Churchward.

---

From Lady Day 1640 to Lady Day 1641.

*Christenings.*

John ye sonne of Tho. Ansell was baptised July 5. 1640.
Sarah ye daughter of Edward Wren bapt. Jan. 13. 1641.

*Marriages.*

Jonn Todd and Martha Mott were marryed Sept. 28. 1640.

*Buryalls.*

Thomas Scott was buryed June 3. 1640.
The wife of Tho. Barnes was buryed Jan. 10. 1641.
Mary ye wife of Will. Conny was buryed Jan. 19. 1641.
Edward Mullington was buryed Jan. 26. 1641.
Nicholas Hind was buryed March 4. 1641.

Jo. Iuory Rect. ibid.
Tho. Barnes sideman.

---

From Easter 1660 to Easter 1672.

*Christenings.*

1660

May   6· Katharine daugh. of Jo. & Margery Gibson.
 ,,    7  Thos sonne of Hugh and Mary Hawkines.
July 36  Francis daught. of Henry & Fran. Pritchard.
Sep. 30  Charles sonne of James & Sarah Bealam.
Oct.  5  James sonne of Nicolas & Mary Nash.
Nov.  1  Mary daught. of Mr Witt & Mrs Mary Hale.

1660-1
Jan. 20 Edw. sonne of Edw. & Francis Griffin.
1661
Mch. 29 Emanuell sonne of Jo. & Dorcas Robards.
June 9 Thos sonne of Thos & Mary Ley.
„ 9 Sara daught. of Edw. & Mary Mitchell.
Oct. 11 Jo. sonne of Thos & Ellin Wells.
Nov. 12 Jona. sonne of Jona. & Jude Smyth.
1661-2
Jan. 3 Rowland sonne of Mr Will & Mis Mary Hale.
1662
June 22 Edw. sonne of Nicolas & Mary Nash.
Oct. 5 Dorothy daught. of Jo. & Margery Gibson.
1663
July 12 Susan daught. of Edw. & Eliz. Carter.
Sep. 20 Jo. sonne of Edw. & Mary Renn.
Oct. 27 Will sonne of Nichs & Mary Nash.
1663-4
Feb. 26 Will sonne of Mr Will & Mis Mary Hale.
Mch. 6 Sara daught. of Hugh & Mary Hawkines.
1664
Apr. 1 Mary daught. of Jo. & Dorcas Robards.
Apr. 3 Ellin daught. of Thos & Ellin Wells.
„ 17 Jo. & Thos sonns of Edw. & Francis Griffin.
1665
July 2 Rich. sonne of Thos & Mary Ley.
Aug. 13 Will sonne of Jo. & Katherine Hutchinson.
„ 27 Jasp sonne of Jo. & Hanah Goudes.
Dec. 4 Mary daught. of Jona. & Mary Smyth.
1665-6
Jan. 24 Jo. sonne of Mr Will & Mis Mary Hale.
1666-7
Feb. 6 Eliz. daught. of Will & Eliz. Abry.
„ 19 Dorcas davght. of Jo. & Dorcas Robards.
Mch. 14 Will sonne of Emanuell & Sara Clarke.
„ 17 Will sonne of Edw. & Francis Griffin.
1667
. . . 14 Frances sonne of Th[os &] Ellin Wells.
. . . 19 Sara daught. of Jona. & Mary S . . . .
. . . 16 Moses sonne of Hug[h] & Mary H . . . .
1668
. . . . Jeremie sonne of Mr Will & Mis . . . ale.
. . . . Eliz. daught. of John . . . . . . . Go . . .
. . . 31 Eliz. daught. of Edw. . . . Fran . . . .
1669
. . . 14 Jo. sonne of Jo. & . . . . . . . .
. . . 31 Edw. . . . . . . . .
. . . 31 . . . . . . . . .
. . . 5 . . . . . . . . .
1670
. . . 31 . . . . . . . . .
. . . 22 . . . . . . . . .
1671
Oct. 22 Ha . . . . . . . . .
. . . 16 Mary daught. of . . . . . . . .

. . . 18 Willᵐ sonne of W . . . & Eliz. . . . . .
Nov. 23 Willᵐ sonne of Henry & Marth.
1672
Mch. . . Jo. & Eliz. children of Jo. & Dorcas. .

*Marriages.*

1660
May 19 Willᵐ Parratt & Eliz. Ameris.
June 11 Petr Ansell & Grace Chapell.
Oct. 9. Willᵐ Scotchbrooke & Jone Burgaine.
 „ 25 Willᵐ Greeninge & Debo. North.
Nov. 5 Jo. Sheepard & Eliz. Sebrooke.
1661
June 3 Rich. Prentise & Temp. Blackden.
 „ 3 Randall Littler & Mary Bates.
Dec. 2 Jo. Aubry & Mary Seabrooke.
1663
Oct. 6 John Gouges & Hanna Nicols.
1665
Sep. 25 Daniel Gazely & Katherine Pursey.
1668
Oct. 5 Willᵐ Andrew & Mary Ward.
 „ 6 Mr Henry Feild & Mⁱˢ Martha Birch.
 „ 8 Jona. Wackett & Susan Crips.
1670
May 19 Willᵐ Wadley & Isabelle Gladman.
1670-1
Mch. 17 Edward Penny & Anne Harding.
Jan. 12 Mr Thoˢ Juce & Mⁱˢ Eliz. Birch.
1671
Oct. 10 Willᵐ Wackett & Susan Cony.
Nov. 28 Jo. Hewell & Jone Ireland.
Dec. 4 Thoˢ Watson & Eliz. Clarke Wid.

*Burialls.*

1660-1
Feb. 20 Nich. Ireland.
1661
June 14 Mary the daught. of Willᵐ Cony.
 „ 16 The Widow Iuory.
1667
Dec. 4 Mⁱˢ Mary Ellwes, Wid.
1668
June 16 Edw. Field.
1669
Nov. 10 Mⁱˢ Eliz. Birch wife of Jo. Birch Rectr
Sep. 11 Emm Cony wife of Willᵐ Cony.
1670
Nov. 11 Eliz. Ireland Wid.
Dec. 6. Geo. Cony.
1671
Sep. 4 Anne Wrenn.
 „ 19 Jude Kirke Baseborne of Jude Ansell.

John Birch Rectr
Jo. Cony Church-warden,

## Lady Day 1672 to Mich. 1673.
### Maryges.

1672
Oct 6 Tho. Field & Sarah Bayly.
,, 28 Fra. Field & Sarah Canfield.
1673
Apr. 2 Jer. Chambers & Ann Morgan.
July 9 Jo. Marston & Alice Griffin.
July 13 Phillipp Ansell & Jone Deare.

### Christenings.

1672
Mch. 31 John & Eliz. the son & Daughter of Jo. & Dorcas Roberts.
May 5 Marke the son of Tho. & Ellen Wells.
June 9 Rose the daughter of Jonathan & Mary Smith.
1672-3
Feb. 9 John the son of Jo. & Dorcas Farmer.
1673
May 25 Tho. son of Solo. Goldsmith.
June 1 Robert son of Jo. & Jone Howell.
Aug. 1 Geo. the son of Geo. & Mary Bassett.

### Buryings.

1673
June 19 Jo. Kittle.
Nov. 15 A strangers child.
,, 23 Edw. & Sarah Bland of Tatnam high crose.
,, 25 John Wrenne.
Dec. 9 Mary the wife of Will. Coney.
,, 11 Eliz Wrenne.
,, 22 Dorcas the wife of John Roberts.
,, 24 Will Coney.

Dated ye 2d of May 1674     Jo. Birch Rectr.
                            John Coney Churchwarden.
                               Exhibit 8° May 1674.

---

## From 1673 to 1677
### Marriages.

1673-4
Feb. 16 George Law & Susan Cater.
Mch. 2 Tho. Ivory & Sarah Nash.
1674
July 8 Mr Tho. Armes & Sarah Unckle.
Oct. 26 Will Cramhorne & Mary Wrenn.
Dec. 31 Mr Joseph Stanley & Judith Clinton.
1675
Apr. 5 Hugh Hawkins & Mary Heath.
Oct. 14 Ric. Clark & Hanna Halsey.
Nov. 4 Robert Watkins & Mary Morgan.
1676
May 15 Tho. Carter & Eliza. Hust.
June 15 John Randall & Anne Noads.
Aug. 28 Edw. Dauy & Susan Kimpton.
Nov. 7 Tho. Shepheard & Mary Nash.
Dec. 14 Jo. Ibgraue & Eliz. Carter.

1676-7
Feb. 2 Ric. Waller & Catherine Smith.
1677
Apr. 29 Ric. Squirge & Grace Wellinggame.
June 19 Jo. Hawkins & Anne Field.

### Christned.

1673
Oct 30 Eliz. the daughter of M<sup>r</sup> Hen. & M<sup>rs</sup> Martha Field.
1674
May 10 Phebe a strangers Childe.
July 19 Ric. son of Ric. & Catherine Richford.
1674-5
Feb. 7 Jona. & Grace of Jona. & Mary Smith.
1675
Aug. 15 Hen. son of M<sup>r</sup> Hen. & M<sup>rs</sup> Martha Field.
Oct. 20 Mary daugh. of Geo. & Mary Basset.
1676
Aug. 25 Mary daugh. of Hugh & Mary Hawkins.
" 27 Mary daugh. of Richa. & Catherin Richford.
1676-7
Mch. 9 Martha daugh. of M<sup>r</sup> Hen. & M<sup>rs</sup> Martha Field.
1677
May 27 Tho. son of Thos. & Eliz. Carter.

### Buryed.

1674
May 3 Nicolas Ivory.
Nov. 8 Rose daugh. of Jona. & Mary Smith.
" 20 Mary Kittle widd.
" 20 Sarah daugh. of Jona. & Mary Smith.
Dec. 10 Dorothy Robbinson wife of Jo. Robbinson.
1674-5
Feb. 22 Jona. son of Jona. & Mary Smith.
1675
Apr. 12 Will. Abry.
Sep. 11 Samuel Hall was found dead in our Parish.
Nov. 20 Jo. Gouds.
1676
Mch. 27 Oliver Abery.
June 9 Eliz. Smithe.
1677
Apr. 14 Mary the wife of Hugh Hawkins.

John Birch Rect<sup>r</sup> ibid.
Jo. Conney Churchwar.

---

From Lady Day 1695 to Lady Day 1696.

### Marriages.

Samuell Gue & Dorathy Canfield both of Cuddicut by virtue of a Licence.
Samuel Fletcher & Mary Banford both of Cudd. by virtue of a Licence.
Richard Freeman of Hadly & Mary Mansell of Cuddicut by virtue of a Licence.

**And none married by Banes.**

### Christenings.

Tho. York son of Tho. York Bapt.
Sarah Wells Daughter of Francis Wells Bapt.

### Burialls.

We have not had one buried within y^e time aboue specified.

Cha. Horn Rect.
Thomas Dauis Churchwarden.

---

# Notes Relating to the Family of Wyndowt.*

## WILL OF THOMAS WYNDEOUT.

[*P.C.C.* Moone 4.]

Thomas Wyndeout citezin mercer and alderman of London. (Dated 17 July 1499). 'My body to be buried in the Chapell of Saint Anne in the parish church of Saint Antouyne in the Warde of Cordewanerstreete of London yf god dispose for me to dye in London or w^tin xx^ti myles thereof and yf it fortune me to dye elleswher thenne to be buried in halowed ground by the discrecion of myne executours And yf I be buryed in the saide Chapell in Saint Antonynes Chirch I will that thenne I be layed in that place of the north syde of the same chapell where as nowgh lieth a grete stone with noon supscripcion uppon And I will that first a fore alle other thing℩ aftre my body be buried alle the Debb℩ that I owe or am bounde fore and be due of right be sette in due ordre that the creditours may be paied accordyngly as they ought to be And this to be Doon assone as it may goodly be w^tout any Respect of tyme or mynysshing of any part or parcell of the same other wise thenne is of right and coven'nt betwene the same Creditours and me in my^r lief made Also I wille that my body be brought in erthe with viij torches & iiij tapers and no moo And alsoe myne Extermes and monthes mynde doon I wil that iiij of the said torchies shall Remayne and be gevin vnto the parish Chirch or place wher I shalbe buryed And ij more of the said viij torchies I bequeth to the saide [*sic but not previously mentioned in the will*] chirch of Fulh'm in Midd. And the other ij torches Reste I bequeth to the parish and parish Chirch of owre lady of Apisden besid℩ Buntyngford where as my fader and moder lye buryed And I will that eu'y prest and seruyng [*sic*] in the Chirch where as my body shalbe buried saying and synging placebo and Dirige with other orysons accustomed aftre Salisbury use and masse of Requiem by note for my soule and for the soules of my fader and moder eu'y Day During a month next ensuyng as aftre my decesse shalhaue for ther Labo^r as folowith ffirst the Curat ther yf he

---

* Communicated by C. E. Gildersome Dickinson, Esq.

geve attendance and Doe the same to have xxs. Euery prest xiijs iiijd and eu'y Clerk xs they therewith to be content for the Day of my burying my month mynde and the meane tyme also I will ther been xiij Trentall? of masses seid and Doon for my soule and for the sowlis of Thomas my fader and Basill my moder that is to wit the first Trentall to be said the Day and tyme of my Depting and buryng and the next at my month mynd and so eu'y month aftre one And the last at my xij mouthes mynde for eu'y of whiche Trentall? so to be said and Doon I bequeth xiijs iiijd Also I woll that a good honest prest be ordeyned by myne Executours to serve w'tin the Chirch where as my body shalbe buryed by the space of xx<sup>ti</sup> yeres next ensuyng aftre my Decesse he to pray for my sowle and for the soulis of the said Thomas and Basill my fader and moder and all Crisan sowlis And that the said prest be bounde and chargeable to say thryes eu'y weke During the said xx<sup>ti</sup> yeris Placebo & Dirige with Commendacious The same prest to haue yerely for his Salarye yf he serve in London xj marc And I will that this prest be of good conu'sacion and of sadde and u'tuous guyding And els I wil that of that seruice he be deprived and Removed as ofte as myne executours or by the Curate and Churchwardeyns wher he shall so serue shall or can be thought necessarye Itm I bequeth to be gevin unto pour housholders dwelling w'in the ffranchise of London And sp'ially such as I haue been acquaynted w'talle And in the parissh of saint Antonyne afore said xx<sup>li</sup> to be distributed w'tin the yere next aftre my decesse afre the discrecion of myne Executours so that the grettist somme so gevin passe not x<sup>s</sup> that the leste not undre iijs iiijd Itm I bequeth to the iiij howsis of ffreres mendicant? of London that is to say to eu'y hous of them xl<sup>s</sup> to praye for my soule And that eu'y conuent of theym bringe my body to the chirch of my buring and ther singe Dirige for my soule Itm I bequeth to thise iiij prisons undre named that is to say Newgate Ludgate the King? Benche and Marchalsie to eu'y prisonne xl<sup>s</sup> ther to be bestowed by the Discrecion of myne Executours to the Relefe of the prisonners to haue my soule in Remembraunce Item I bequeth to the fynding and exhibicion of poore Scolers in Oxford and in Cambridgge by the discrecion of myne Executours lxvj<sup>li</sup> viij<sup>s</sup> iiij<sup>d</sup> Itm I bequeth to the mariag? of poore maydens to pray for my soule and to be distributed by the discrecion of myne Executours lxvj<sup>li</sup> xiiij<sup>s</sup> iiij<sup>d</sup> Item I bequeth to the making and bilding of Rowchestre brigge xlvj<sup>li</sup> xiij<sup>s</sup> iiij<sup>d</sup>. Goods to be divided into three parts one whereof to remain to performing this my testament, another to Kateryne my wife & the third to my children at their full age. 'To eu'y psone to the Noumb<sup>r</sup> of xx<sup>ti</sup> of my kyndrede nowe being w'tin the iij<sup>de</sup> Degre to me yf there be founde so many of them v<sup>li</sup> a pece to pray for me. To eu'y psone of my name and kynne iij<sup>li</sup> vj<sup>s</sup> viij<sup>d</sup> to the Nombre of a c psones yf ther be so many. Myne Executours shall competently fynde and exhibite to scole Roger Wyndeout nowe being at Buntyngford tyll he be of the age of xxiij yers and yf he live to the age of xxj yeris I bequeth him theme xx<sup>li</sup> of my goodes and if he die that xx<sup>li</sup> to Remayne to the next of kynne w'tin Hertfordshir. To my feliship of the Mercery of London a Cupp of the price of x<sup>li</sup>. To William Clerk xxiij<sup>li</sup> vj<sup>s</sup> viij<sup>d</sup>. To William Dyne iij<sup>li</sup> vj<sup>s</sup> viij<sup>d</sup>. To Robt Gedge besidis his wagis vj<sup>li</sup> xiij<sup>s</sup> iiij<sup>d</sup>. To Robert Horneby besides his wages vj<sup>li</sup> xiij<sup>s</sup> iiij<sup>d</sup>. To eu'y of myne Apprentise vj<sup>li</sup> xiij<sup>s</sup> iiij<sup>d</sup>. To my Maydenes Agnes and Elyn to either of them iij<sup>li</sup> vj<sup>s</sup> viij<sup>d</sup>. To Symond Ryse my s'unt I marc. The said Kat'yne my wife shall have during lief all my londes and tenementꝭ in the Towne and ffeldis of Fulh'm, co. Midd. as also my hous in Saint Pancras pissh in London whiche Thomas Kesyng of me holdith there. I make and ordeyne Executours John Wynger, Grocer, Barthilmewe Reed, Goldsmyth, Aldremen, John Style and Thomas Baldrye mercers and cittezins of London and as ouerseers Sir Raynold Bray and Sir John Shaa Knyghtꝭ.

Witnessed 22 May 1500 by Doctor Simond Foderby Mr John Reed, Henry Woodecok, notaries, Hugh Atton, Thomas Speight, Robt Kellam, Tailloirs, John Mott, Skynner and William Mannyng grocer with other.

Proved at Lamehith [no date or name of administrator.]

NOTES.— By will dated 18 Nov. 1505 (registered in the Hustings Court of London, roll 232, no. 14) Nicholas Alwyn, alderman and mercer of London, devises to the Wardens of the Mercers Company & their successors, a certain messuage in the parish of S. Antonin which he had acquired from Dean Colet, charged with the observance of an obit in the church of S. Thomas the Martyr called 'de Acon' or in the chapel thereto annexed called 'le Mercers Chapell' for the souls of Thomas Wyndout late mercer and alderman & others. (See Dr Sharpe's Calendar of Hustings Wills).

Thomas Wyndeout was alderman successively of the wards of Cripplegate and Coleman Street & served as Sheriff of London & Middlesex 1497-8.

The will of Sr Richard Haddon Kt & Alderman of London and mercer of the parish of St Olave, Hart Street, dat. 1 April 1516, proved 12 Feb. 1516-7 (P.C.C. Holder 29) mentions 'my brother Symonde Rice' & gives 'to my sonne Barthilmewe Wyndoute a like Ryng of golde of an unce.'

## WILL OF BARTHOLOMEW WYNDOWT.
[*P.C.C. Maynwaryng 22.*]

In dei nomine Amen The x Day of Septembr I Bartilmewe Wyndowt in hole mynde and memory loving be to almighty god make this my last wille first I bequeth my soule to god our savyour and to his moder our lady Saint Mary and all the holy company of hevyn and my body to be buried in cristen buriall at the discrecon of my executours I geve to the high awter for oblacions and tithes forgotten vjˢ. Item to my wife Anne Wyndowt my manor in Moch Hormede parishe called Radwells for the terme of hir lyfe Also my lande and howsing theruppon callid Hammondꝭ in Westmyll Also Antonyes and Hampstelys also that I bought of John Milys in Newe Cheping for term of hir lyffe naturall and she to doo noo waste of wodes and to kepe and maynteyn with repacions all the said howses during her lyfe orellꝭ Richard my sonne to enter and her expell of that parcell so wasted Also I will she haue all my moueable goodes except this following the which shall remayn in the maner of Hormede and she to occupye it to the tyme she decesse that is to sey thre fetherbeddꝭ wt bolsters pyllowes and Couerlettꝭ to them the hanging of the parlour two table Clothes & a towell a doseyn of Napkyns four pair of shetꝭ ij pillow berys a pott a pann a spitt a pair of cobberdꝭ And Richard my sonne when he is by the grace of god xxj yeres olde then I woll he haue a Chambr to resorte to for himself and one for his ser'untꝭ in the said Maner of Radyswell Item to Richard my sonne my howse in Buntingford with all the lande therto belonging also that lande I bought of maister Thomas Clyfford which he paieth me an annuitie for of xvjˡⁱ yerely Also the londe bought of Witton being the thirde parte of all Roger Grenes landꝭ Also all Sir Thomas Hewys land wherupon I gave him in money in partie of payment Also I giue to the said Richard a standing cup chasyd gilt And to that that my wife goith with yf it please god it be a sonne to haue my lande and howsing(e) in London And yf it be a doughter then I woll that myne Executours at hir marriage or xxj yeres of hir age geve hir a hundred m'rc(s) in money And I woll that my executors fynde both the Children and Anne my wife haue the custodye of them and myn executours to receyue all the profits of my land(es) growing to my children during their nonage and either to be the others heire And if it please god to take both them then I will the next of my bloud taking my name on them to haue it orell(s) the next Woman of my blod having a sonne bering the name of Wyndowt to haue it and so to remayn alwey in the blood taking my name on them and unto such tyme that one take my name on them and be of the age of xxj yeres I will myn executors Receyve the Rent of it except my doughter for she being maried I will she haue it till hir sonne be of the age that may bere my name and she haue no sonne she to haue it terme of lyfe and to remayn to myn executors my Mother, Symond Ryce and Anne my wife I geve to my Wyff(e) brother Humfrey a gowne lyned and other furryd and two Doblett(s) And to euery of my men a gowne and to every maide xxs in money And to Isabell my maide iiij nobles a yere During hir lyfe at Hamersmyth orell(s) out of my lande at Buntyngford. [*No witnesses recorded*]

Proved at Lamehith 20 Mch. 1521 by Anne the relict, reservation to Symon Ryce & Dame Katherine Haddon the other exors.

---

### INQUISITION POST MORTEM BARTHOLOMEI WYNDOWT.
[*Chancery Inq. p.m. 13 Hen. VIII. No. 76 & Escheators Inquests Series II. File 306 No. 1.*]

Inquisition taken at Hertford 12 Nov. 13 Hen. VIII [1521] before William Poyntz esq. escheator, after the death of Bartholomew Wyndeowt esquire, by the oaths of John Smyth of Hunnesdon, John Warde, Thos. Whyte coup, John Shelly, John Parker, John Renyngton, John Boughton, Simon Woodlyff, Christr. Galaway, Wm. Rumbolt, Wm. Abery, Thos. Geldwer & Robert Alott who say that

Said Bartholomew some while before his death was seised in fee of the manor of Raddoswell in Great Hormede and so seised, by charter, enfeoffed John Egerton, John Morton, John Mores, Simon Rice, Rich. Wye & Rich. Birde & their heirs to hold to the use of sd Bartholomew & Anne his wife for life of sd Anne, with remainder to use of the heirs of sd Bartholomew, by virtue whereof the sd feoffees became seized & afterwards sd Richard Wye died but the other feoffees yet survive.

Moreover sd Bartholomew was seized of the manor called Hamstall(s) & 100 acres of land, 100 acres of pasture & 20 acres of meadow in the psh. of Great Munden co. Herts & by his charter enfeoffed Simon Rice, Rich. Wye, John Mores, Rich. Danvers & John Wyndowt, to hold to them & their heirs to the use of the last will of sd Bartholomew & sd Rich. Wye & Rich. Danvers are dead but the other feoffees yet survive.

Furthermore John Carter, Thos. Harte & Wm. Snowe were seised of a messuage & 80 acres of land & pasture in Westmyll & Gt. Monden as feoffees of sd Bartholomew. And John Pakyngton, Simon Rice cit. & mercer of London, John Mores, gent, John Morton & James Charite held to them & their heirs to the use of last will of sd Barth.

Moreover Thos. Clifford of Aspeden & Fras. Hasylden esquires were seised of 1 messuage, 40 acres of land, 20 acres of pastures &

10 acres of meadow called Antons and Dymmantez in psh. of Great Munden & so seised, enfeoffed Rich. Haddon kt, Simon Rice, John Pakyngton, Rich. Wye & John Mores gents to the use of s^d Bartholomew. And Rich. Hadden & Rich. Wye died so seized & the other feoffees yet survive.

And on the Morrow of the Purification, 9 Hen. VIII, before Robt. Rede kt. & his fellows, justices at Westminster, a fine was levied between the s^d Barth. Wyndeowt, Simon Rice, Rich. Wye, Henry White & John Mores plaintiffs & John Miles & Kath. his wife deforciants of 1 messuage, 15½ acres of land, 3 acres of meadow & 1½ acres pasture in Bucklond, whereby the s^d John Myles & his wife acknowledged the s^d premises to belong of right to s^d Barth. as that which they the s^d Barth. Simon, Rich. & John Mores had of the gift of s^d John Miles & his wife which fine was declared to the use of s^d Barth. & his heirs for ever.

Said Barth. was also seised in fee of 1 messuage, 100 acres of land, 20 acres of meadow, 10 acres pasture & 10 acres of woodland in Buntingford, Wydyall, Rokkyng̃ & Alsewyk in s^d county & by his charter enfeoffed Rich. Haddon kt, John Pakyngton, John Mores, Rich. Wye & Henry White, by the description of all his lands in the town & fields of Buntyngford which descended to him the s^d Barth. upon the death of his father Thomas Wyndowt, to hold to them & their heirs to the use of the last will of s^d Barth., by reason whereof they were seised & the s^d Rich. Haddon & Rich. Wye so seised died & the other feoffees yet survive.

Further, the jurors say that fifteen days from Holy Trinity in the 10^th year of Hen. VIII. before the s^d Robt. Rede kt & his fellows, justices, a fine was levied between the s^d Barth, John Pakynton & John Mores plaintiffs & Christr. Witton & Ann his wife one of the daus. & heirs of Roger Grene deforciants, of the third part of 5 messuages, 100 acres of land, 140 acres of pasture, 40 acres of meadow & 40 acres of wood with the appurts. in Standon & Browhyng, whereby the s^d Christr. & Ann recognised the right of s^d third part to be in s^d Barth. as that which s^d Barth, John & John had of the gift of s^d Christr. & Ann, by reason whereof s^d Barth. was seised in demesne as of fee & the s^d John & John in demesne as of frank tenement to the use of s^d Barth. & his heirs.

Furthermore the s^d Barth. was seised as of fee of one messuage with appurts. in the psh. of Aspeden, called Howeddescroft.

The manor of Raddeswell was held of Wm. Node as of his manor of Stokes in Stevenage by fealty & 5s. per ann. for all services & worth per ann. viij^li. The manor of Hamstall̃ & lands in Gt. Munden was held of Wm. Say kt. as of his manor of Gt. Munden by fealty for all services but at what rent the jurors are ignorant & worth per ann. xlvj^s. viij^d. The messuage & tenement lately erected upon & 80 acres of pasture in Westmyll & Gt. Munden, were held of the Abbot of Towrehill as of his manor of Westmyll, by rent of xs. & fealty for all services & worth per ann. clear, iij^li. The premises called Antons were held of s^d Wm. Say kt. as of his manor of Gt. Munden by fealty but by what other services the jurors are ignorant, & worth per ann. [*blank*]. The tenement called Damannt̃ was held of the Abbot of Tourehill as of his manor of Westmyll by fealty and 10s. rent for all services & worth per ann. clear, iiij^li. The premises in Buckland & Brokkyngs were held of Katherine, Queen of England, as of her manor of Poppyshale by fealty & rent of 4d. per ann. for all services

& worth per ann. clear, 1s. The messuage & lands in Buntyngford, Wydyall, Rokkyng & Alsewyk were held of the lord prior of S$^t$ John Bapt. of Jerusalem in England, at annual rent of 18d. & fealty for all services & worth per ann. clear, vj/i. The s$^d$ third part of the tenement in Sandon & Broughyng was held of Humph. Fitzherbert & Rich. Broughyng as of their manor of Gaddisbury by fealty & annual rent of 2s. for all services & worth per ann. clear, x/i. The messuage called Howoodcrofte was held of the s$^d$ prior of S$^t$ John of Jerusalem, by fealty & 1d. per ann. & worth per annum, clear, vijs. And s$^d$ Bartholomew held no other lands of our lord the king etc.

And s$^d$ Barth. died 23 August 13 Hen. VIII. & Richard Wyndowte is son & next heir & is aged seven years & more.

# Marriage Licences.
## Archdeaconry of St. Albans.
### By A. E. GIBBS.

(Continued from Page 335).

**1691**

October 24. Thomas Briggs of Luton, husbandman, single man, aged about 30 years, and Martha Pearles of Redbourn, single woman, aged about 22 years; at St. Albans or Redbourn. Robert Thompson of Nottingham, barber chirurgeon, a surety.

October 31. Christopher Woodards of St. Peters, husbandman, bachelor, aged 22 years, and Ann Wright of Watford, spinster, aged about 21 years; at Watford or Bushey. Anthony Polkinghorne of St. Albans, innholder, a surety.

November 14. Abraham Carter of Sandridge, husbandman, single man, aged about 26 years, and Elizabeth Gray of the same, single woman, aged about 25 years; at Sandridge or Redbourn. Francis Holford of St. Albans, draper, a surety.

November 14. Thomas Roberts of Sandridge, husbandman, single man, aged about 30 years, and Mary House of Whethamsted, single woman, aged about 24 years; at Sandridge. George Chappell of Sandridge, blacksmith, a surety.

November 24. Thomas Probey [*signed* Probey] of Hunton, co. Kent, yeoman, bachelor, aged about 27 years, and Elizabeth Austen of Marsden, co. Kent, maiden, having neither father nor mother; at Hunton or St. Nicholas, Rochester. Roderick Thomas of St. Nicholas, Rochester, parish clerke, a surety.

December 25. Thomas Sage of Redbourn, wheelwright, single man, aged 20 years, and Mary Miles of the same, aged about 19 years; at St. Albans, St. Michaels or Redbourn. William Hunt of St. Albans, tobacco pipe maker, a surety.

December 30. Edward Seywell and Mary Saveel of Hodsdon; at St. Peters. Daniel Battman of St. Peters, a surety.

1691-2

January 21. Marmaduke Hubbard of Bexley, co. Kent, husbandman, bachelor, aged about 31 years, and Mary Humphrey of the same, maiden, aged about 24 years, her parents deceased; at Bexley or Rochester Cathedral. Marmaduke Weekes of Lidgeing, co. Kent, yeoman, a surety.

January 29. Marmaduke Weekes of Lidgeing, co. Kent. yeoman, widower, and Joanna Kembstey of the same, maiden; at Lidgeing or Rochester Cathedral. Richard Warman of St. Margarets, Rochester, a surety.

1692

March 25. Thomas Punn of Ridge, husbandman, single man, aged 23 years, and Mary King of St. Stephens, single woman, aged about 23 years; at Ridge or St. Stevens. John King of St. Stephens, husbandman, a surety.

March 25. Ralph Collins of Watford, husbandman, single man, and Sarah Darvall of Bovingdon, widow; at Sarrett, Watford, or Rickmersworth. John Scott of St. Albans, cutler, a surety.

March 28. Daniel Knight of St. Albans, shoemaker, single man, and Esther Wilson of the same, single woman; at St. Albans. William Hunt of St. Albans, tobacco pipe maker, a surety.

March 29. Samuel Beech of St. Albans glover, single man, and Catherine Richardson of the same, single woman, both of full age, at St. Albans. Robert Hitchen of St. Albans a surety.

March 29. William Roberts of St. Giles, Cripplegate, London, wiredrawer, single man, and Ann Carter of St. Albans, both of full age; at St. Albans. William Hunt of St. Albahs, tobacco pipe maker, a surety.

March 29. Robert Martin of St. Albans, butcher, single man, and Mary Jackson of the same, single woman, both of full age; at St. Albans. Robert Whitby [*signed* Whedbee] of St. Albans, a surety.

April 2. William Maschall of St. Albans, butcher, single man, and Elizabeth Carter of the same, single woman; at St. Albans. William Hunt, of St. Albans, tobacco pipe maker, a surety.

April 2. Joseph Edmunds of Watford, yeoman, single man, and Ann Sanders of Abbott's Langley, single woman; at St. Albans or Abbott's Langley. Bernard Sanders of Abbotts Langley, yeoman, a surety.

April 20. Edward Burr, of Wimly, co. Hertford, and Anne Davy of St. Peters; at St. Peters. John Canfeild of St. Peters, a surety.

April 21. Roger Ballard of Sandridge and Judith How of St. Peters; at St. Peters. Edward Wilson of St. Albans, a surety.

April 25. Thomas Kentish of St. Michaels, yeoman, widdower, and Mary Dell of the same, single woman; at St. Michaels or St. Albans. John Dell of St. Michaels, gent, a surety.

May 2. Stephen Hawkins of Wheathamsted, tailor, widower, and Mary Gray of St. Pauls Walden, single woman; at St. Albans. John Wiltshire [*signed* Wllsher] of St. Albans, tanner, a surety.

May 7. Robert Rainsford of St. Albans, victualler, widower, and Jane Utsenton of the same, single woman; at St. Albans. Peter Fuller [*signed* Fullwood] senr., collar maker, a surety.

May 13. John New, gent, one of the aldermen of St. Albans, widower, and Elizabeth How of Abbott's Langley, single woman; at Abbott's Langley. Joseph Dell of St. Michaels, gent, a surety.

May 14. William Clark of St. Michaels, husbandman, single man, and Elizabeth Antebus of the same, single woman; at St. Michaels. Nathaniel Pryor of St. Michaels, tailor; a surety.

May 14. Richard Smith of St. Michaels, husbandman, single man, and Sarah Spencer of Carrington, co. Bedford, single woman; at Redbourn. Henry Taylor of St. Michael's, yeoman, a surety.

May 14. John Furman of Redbourne, wheelwright, bachelor, aged about 25 years, and Elizabeth Almond *alias* Aumond of the same, spinster, aged about 25 years; at Redbourn. Thomas Furman of Battlesdown, co. Bedford, yeoman, a surety.

May 15. John Ballard, son of Roger Ballard of Sandridge, bachelor, aged about 30 years, and Dorothy Marckward of South Mims, spinster, aged about 27 years; at Sandridge. Thomas Robinson of St. Albans, innholder, a surety.

June 10. Edward Ralph of Luton, yeoman, single man, and Sarah Gasely of Redbourn, single woman; at St. Albans or Redbourn. Thomas Bull of St. Albans, labourer, a surety.

June 18. Joseph Ansell of Sandridge, yeoman, widower, and Elizabeth Ibgrave of the same, widow; at Sandridge or St. Albans. James How of St. Peters, butcher, a surety.

June 25. John Willan of Cheshunt and Alice Cooper of Sandridge; at Sandridge. Thomas Catlin of Whethamstead, a surety.

June 17. William Wigg of Great Gaddesden, gent, single man, and Rebekka Beynon of Redbourn, single woman; at Redbourn. Edward Horsell, gent., Mayor of the Borough of St. Albans, a surety.

July 29. William Floyd of St. Albans, gent., bachelor, aged about 32 years, and Ann Eggleston of the same, spinster, aged about 20 years; at St. Albans, St. Michaels, St. Peters, or Sandridge. Ralph Jackson of St. Alban's, a surety.

August 14. Thomas Shepheard of St. Stephens, blacksmith, son of Henry Shepheard of the same, waggoner, aged about 20 years, and Lowes Edmonds of the same, spinster, aged about 25 years, daughter of John Edmonds of the same, tailor, with consent of both their fathers; at St. Stephens. William Osbourne of St. Stephen's, drover, who married the daughter-in-law of Henry Shepheard, a surety.

August 31. Thomas Cooper of Coney, parish of St. Peters, widower, and Margaret Blaker of Watford, widow; at Watford. John Grevett of Watford, tailor, and Thomas Seares of St. Albans, yeoman, sureties.

September 17. Timothy Norris of Abbotts Langley, butcher, single man, and Elizabeth Priest of the same, single woman; at St. Albans or Abbotts Langley. William Hunt of St. Albans, tobacco pipe maker, a surety.

September 20. Richard Newman, of St. Michaels, yeoman, single man, and Elizabeth Shepherd of the same, single woman. John Barnard of St. Albans, gent., a surety.

September 29. John Sheerer of St. Albans, blacksmith, single man, and Ann Pheasant of the same, single woman; at St. Albans; William Hunt of St. Albans, tobacco pipe maker, a surety.

September 30. Henry Caine of Shephall, bricklayer, single man, and Sarah Martyn of Luton, single woman; at St. Albans. William Hunt of St. Albans, tobacco pipe maker, a surety.

October 1. John Deacon of Abbotts Langley, mealman, widower, and Sarah Sibley of the same, single woman; at Abbott's Langley. John Poole of St. Albans, innholder, a surety.

October 1. John Beastney of St. Albans, butcher, single man, and Mary Seabrook of St. Peters, single woman; at St. Albans or St. Peters. William Hunt of St. Albans, tobacco pipe maker, a surety.

October 8. Nehemiah Knowlton of Watford, yeoman, and Elizabeth Jenkins of Harding *alias* Harpenden, spinster; at Watford or Bushey. John Elisha of St. Albans, farrier, a surety.

October 19. Thomas Peacock of St. Albans, mealman, single man, and Elizabeth Hoyland of the same, single woman; at St. Albans. Wm. Hunt of same, tobacco pipe maker, a surety.

October 22. Richard Fisher of Flitweek, co. Bedford, "traunter," widower, and Elizabeth Parker, late of Harpenden but now of St. Peters, spinster; at Sandridge. Thomas Davy of Flitwick, warrener, a surety.

November 1. Thomas Clinton of Buntingford, Westmill, yeoman, single man, and Mary Hopkins of Coddicote, single woman; at St. Albans. Samuel Hopkins of All Saints, Hertford, tallow chandler, a surety.

November 2. John Grover, of St. Michaels. butcher, single man, and Dorothy Watts of St. Stephens; at Watford. Walter Beech of St. Albans, tallow chandler, a surety.

November 19. John Hewson, of St. Albans, laceman, single man, and Ann Babbs of the same, widow; at St. Albans. William Morris of the same, innholder, a surety.

November 21. William Mayes of St. Michaels, labourer, single man, and Elizabeth Griffin of Sandridge, single woman; at St. Michaels. Richard Griffin of Sandridge, husbandman, a surety.

December 26. Thomas Ferne [*signed* Fearn] of Aldenham and Mary Cogdell of St. Stephens; at St. Stephens. Thomas Hickman of Cadington, a surety.

December 29. John Finch of St. Albans, labourer, single man, and Katharin Roberts of the same, single woman, both of full age; at St. Albans. Joseph Marshall of St. Albans, innholder, a surety.

1692-3

February 1. John Glover of Abbotts Langley, miller, single man, and Elizabeth Pryor of St. Michaels, single woman, both of full age; at St. Michaels. Nathaniel Pryor of St. Michaels, tailor, a surety.

February 4. Thomas Hodsden of Watford, innkeeper, widower, and Elizabeth Edmonds of the same, widow; at Watford or St. Albans. Thomas Smith of Watford, malster, a surety.

February 5. William Mead [*signed* Meads] of St. Michaels, husbandman, single man, and Grace Clark of the same, single woman; at St. Michaels. William Clark of St. Michaels, husbandman, a surety.

February 20. John Randall of Watford and Hannah Louett of Wendever, co. Buckingham, maiden; at Watford or Sarrat. Nicholas King of King's Langley, a surety.

March 14. Thomas Bates of St. Michaels, labourer, single man, and Sarah Slaney of the same, single woman; both of full age; at St. Albans or St. Michaels. William Hunt of St. Albans, tobacco pipe maker, a surety.

1693

March 25. Samuel Hall of St. Peters, weaver, widower, and Ann Martin, daughter of Robert Martin of St. Albans, spinster, aged about 23 years; at St. Albans. Ralph Marston, a surety.

April 17. Thomas Townsend of St. Albans, gardener, bachelor, and Sarah Pollyn of the same, spinster; at St. Albans or St. Michaels. John Pollyn of St. Michaels, blacksmith, a surety.

April 28. Henry Collins of Idlestree, yeoman, single man, and Mary Carter of Watford, single woman, both of full age; at St. Albans. John Brinkley of St. Albans, victualler, a surety.

April 28. Richard Stannell [*signed* Stonill] of Ivinghoe, co. Buckingham, yeoman, single man, and Jane Carter of Watford, single woman; both of full age; at St. Albans. John Brinkley of St. Albans, victualler, a surety.

May 23. Matthew Street of Sandridge, husbandman, single man, and Isabel *alias* Lisbell Wethered of the same, both of full age; at St. Albans or Sandridge. Robert Ruth of St. Albans, surgeon, a surety.

June 5. Thomas Leifchild of St. Albans, vintner, single man, and Christian Kent of the same, single woman; at St. Albans. John Leonard junior of St. Albans, tailor, a surety.

June 10. Walter Chetam of St. Albans, tailor, single man, and Mary Squire of the same, single woman; at St. Albans or St. Michaels. John Beaumont of St. Albans, victualler, a surety.

June 22. Christopher Skinner of Chipping Barnet, gent, single man, and Susanna Thedder of Hemel Hempsted, single woman; at St. Albans. Richard Munn of St. Albans, tanner, a surety.

June 24. John Townsend of St. Albans, gardener, widower, and Sarah Pate of St. Michaels, single woman; at St. Albans or St. Michaels. William Hunt of St. Albans, tobacco pipe maker, a surety.

July 11. Anthony Findall of St. Peters, and Katherine Davies of the same, single woman; at St. Peters. John Heyward of St. Peters, a surety.

August 2. Jeremiah Carter of Hexton, tallow chandler, widower, and Rebecca Palmer of St. Michaels, single woman; at St. Michaels or St. Albans. William Hunt of St. Albans, innholder, a surety.

August 29. Thomas Birchmore [*signed* Burchmore] of Bushey, husbandman, single man, and Elizabeth Buckmister of St. Stevens, both above 21 years; at Watford. Francis Halford of St. Albans, draper, a surety.

September 30. Robert Wood of St. Peters, joiner, widower, and Mary Seawell of Abbott's Langley, spinster, aged about 46 years; at Abbott's Langley. Richard Pickering of St. Peters, gent., a surety.

September 30. Daniel Tidd of Bishop's Hatfield, carpenter, bachelor, aged about 24 years, and Elizabeth Kilbey of Sandridge, spinster, aged about 22 years; with her parents' consent; at Sandridge. Daniel Munn of St. Albans, sawyer, a surety.

December 3. William Archer of Hatfeild, bachelor, and Mary Turner of Bushey, maid; at St. Michaels. Nathaniel Prior of St. Michaels, a surety.

December 6. John Weedon of King's Langley, yeoman, single man, and Sarah Turner of St. Michaels, single woman; both of full age. Abraham Turner of St. Michaels, yeoman, a surety.

December 20. Thomas Halsey of Dunstable Houghton co. Bedford, malster, single man, and Mary Hughs of St. Stephens, single woman; at St. Stevens or Watford. Thomas Halsey of Houghton Regis, yeoman, a surety.

December 28. Thomas Picket of St. Michaels, husbandman, single man, and Mary Woodwards of the same, single woman; at St. Michaels. Nathaniel Hare of St. Michaels, blacksmith, a surety.

1693-4

January 13. Joseph Hurst of St. Albans, labourer, single man, and Mary Goodspeed of the same, widow; at St. Albans or St. Michaels. John Philby of St. Albans, victualler, a surety.

January 31. Valentine Rolfe of King's Langley, bricklayer, widower, and Sarah Carter of Watford, single woman; both of full age; at St. Albans or Watford. Charles Seaman of St. Albans, clerk, a surety.

1694

April 23. John Buckingham of Ridge, yeoman, single man, and Mary Hall of Solebury, co. Buckingham, single woman; at St. Albans. Nathaniel Buckingham of Ridge, yeoman, a surety.

April 25. Edward Martin of Gillingham, co. Kent, husbandman, bachelor, aged about 34 years, and Ann Cockerell of the same, spinster, aged about 25 years; at Gillingham. Thomas Canford of the same, husbandmen, a surety.

May 2. John Fothergill of St. Albans, clerk, single man, and Ann Marston of St. Albans, single woman; both of full age; at St. Albans. Charles Seaman of St. Albans, clerk, a surety.

May 19. Thomas Downes of St. Albans, schoolmaster, bachelor, aged about 21 years, and Mary Stafford of Chilleck, St. Michaels, spinster, aged about 21 years; at St. Michaels or Redbourn. William Element of St. Albans, blacksmith, a surety.

August 25. John Yarrow of Hertford, gunsmith, bachelor, aged about 30 years, and Susanna Brookes of St. Michaels, spinster, aged about 30 years, daughter of [blank] Brooks of Hornsey; at St. Michaels. Richard Yarrow of St. Michaels, tailor, a surety.

August 27. Thomas Banbery of Fenny Stratford, Bletchley, co. Buckingham, grazier, bachelor, and Charity Gleave of Chipping Barnet, spinster, aged about 22 years; at Chipping Barnet. John Poole of St. Albans, innholder, a surety.

August 29. Roger Ewer of Rickmersworth, yeoman, widower, and Susanna Partridge of the same, widow; at Rickmersworth. Joseph Dell of St. Michaels, yeoman, a surety.

September 29. William Kilbey of St. Michaels, husbandman, single man, and Bathia Chopping of the same, single woman; at St. Michaels. William Choppinge of St. Michaels, blacksmith, a surety.

November 3. James Pope of Abbott's Langley, yeoman, single man, and Rose Shepherd of the same, single woman; at Abbotts Langley, St. Michaels, or Redbourn. Robert Shepherd of Redbourn, yeoman, a surety.

December 7. Henry Barker of St. Albans, gent, single man, and Margaret Carter of the same single woman; at St. Albans. Edward Carter of St. Albans, gent, a surety.

December 20. Robert Pitheon [signed Phithen] of Abbat's Langley, and Elizabeth Jennior [?] of the same, at Abbat's Langley. William Lee of St. Michaels, a surety.

December 28. William Smith of St. Peters, yeoman, widower, and Ann Edmunds of St. Michaels, widow; at St. Michaels. Gilbert Kinder of St. Albans, butcher, a surety.

1694-5

January 12. Hugh Norman of St. Michaels, husbandman, single man, and Grizell Lloyd of the same, single woman; both without parents and at full age; at Redbourn, St. Albans, or St. Michaels. Richard Griffin of St. Michaels, gardener, a surety.

1695

March 29. Bernard Angier of Northaw *alias* Northall, gent, single man, aged about 21 years, and Sarah Weld of Ware, single woman, aged about 23 years; at St. Albans. Alexander Weld of Ware, gent, a surety.

April 29. Thomas Newton of Watford, yeoman, bachelor, aged about 28 years, and Mary Reeves of Cheneys, co. Buckingham, widow, aged about 35 years; at Watford, St. Albans, or Sarrett. Stephen Harding of St. Michaels, mealman, a surety.

April 29. John Manfield of Sandridge, husbandman, single man, and Ann Wethered of the same, single woman; at Sandridge. Walter Beech of St. Albans, tallow chandler, a surety.

May 14. Richard Fowkes of Shephall, yeoman, single man, and Judith Fensham of Wootton, co. Bedford, single woman; at Shephall or St. Albans. Richard Chetwood of Flamsted, grocer, a surety.

May 25. Joshua Runnio of Chipping Barnet, bachelor, aged about 23 years, and Susan Maurice of the same, spinster, aged about 33 years; with consent of her parents; at Chipping Barnet. Joseph Thomas of Southmims, clerk, about the age of three score and upwards, a surety. Allegation only.

May 28. William Illing of Little Harwood, yeoman, bachelor, aged about 45 years, and Elizabeth Woodward of the same, aged about 18 years; with consent of her father, James Woodward; at Greenborrow, Little Harwood, or Aston Abbotts. Robert Adams of Swanbourn, gent, a surety.

June 1. Thomas Loveday of Brackley co. Northampton, widower, and Joane Dimmock of Winslow, spinster; at Winslow. John Croft, clerk, and William Norman of Winslow, sureties.

June 5. Thomas Bond [*signed* Pond] of Rickmersworth, and Mary Halloway of Uxbridge; at Rickmersworth.

June 10. Thomas Howard of St. Albans, ironmonger, single man, and Rachel Beinon of Redbourn; at Redbourn. Charles Seaman of St. Albans, clerk, a surety.

June 15. Daniel Hill of St. Michaels, carpenter, single man, and Mary Prior of St. Albans, single woman; at St. Michaels. Nathaniel Pryor of St. Michaels, tailor, a surety.

June 26. John Turpin of Redbourn, butcher, widower, and Mary Clark of the same, widow; at Redbourn. Richard Ruth of St. Albans, barber chirurgeon, a surety.

July 13. Hugh Burrall of Winslow, butcher, widower, aged about 23 years, and Avis Aris of Buckingham, spinster, aged about 21½ years; with her parents' consent; at Winslow, Watford, or Bushey. Richard Benbow of Winslow, woolman, a surety. Consent testified to by John Hunt of Buckingham, butcher, aged 26 years.

July 17. Richard Turner of Chipping Barnet, bachelor, aged about

30 years, and Elizabeth West of High Barnet, spinster, aged about 24 years; at Chipping Barnet. Joseph Thomas, vicar, and Mary Thomas sign the bond.

July 28. John Toney of Watford, glover, single man, and Mary Bartlet of the same, single woman; at St. Albans. Richard Wyatt of Watford, farrier, a surety.

August 3. William Scurfield of St. Albans, saddler, single man, and Ellen Waller of the same, widow; at St. Albans. William Hunt of St. Albans, tobacco pipe maker, a surety.

August 13. Cornelius Chapman of Redbourne, barber chirurgeon, widower, and Elizabeth Clark of St. Michaels, spinster; at St. Michaels or Redbourn. John Beech of Redbourn, brewer, a surety.

August 31. Henry Winchester of Watford, tallow chandler, single man, and Ann Gold of St. Stevens, single woman; at St. Stevens. Randolph Winchester of Watford, mealman, a surety.

# The Hertfordshire Ancestry of Hon. Richard Olney, Secretary of State for the United States of America.*

In April 1635 there sailed a company of intending settlers in the ship Planter from London, having certificates from the minister at St. Albans.

This company was composed of about a dozen families with their servants, and a very few, who do not appear to have been servants and who were single men seeking their fortune in the new country. There were the Tuttles, who settled in Ipswich and Lynn and Boston; Allen Perley, the founder of a family widely spread in New England; Francis Peabody, the ancestor of George Peabody the great benefactor of London; Thomas Savage, who founded a most illustrious family and whose blood runs in the veins of some of the most prominent public men of the United States (including, if the writer is not mistaken, Senators Hoar and Sherman, the latter of whom is to be Mr. McKinley's Secretary of State); George Giddings, the founder of the Ipswich family of Giddings; and lastly *Thomas Olney*, styled on the record "Shoemaker, aged 35," with wife Marie aged 30, son Thomas aged 3, and son Etenetus. Nearly all these people settled in and about Salem, although some soon removed to less crowded quarters.

Thomas Olney was made freeman at Salem, 17th May, 1637, and that same year had there a grant of land, but in this year he became involved in the religious disputes of the day, and had license to depart from Massachusetts, and on the 12th March, 1638, was ordered to appear before the General Court to answer to objections against him. Six months later he was at Providence and Treasurer of the town,

* Communicated by Eben Putnam, Esq., of Danvers, Mass. U.S.A.

associated with Roger Williams. He was one of the Assistants, at ten different times, between 1649 and 1667, often Deputy and Commissioner.

His will dated the 21st March, 1679, proved the 17th October, 1682, gives to Thomas, his eldest son, all his lands and house, and mentions other children. Of his five sons Thomas, Epenetus, Nedabiah, Stephen and James, only those he brought from England left descendants.

According to Mr. Austin's "Genealogical Dictionary of Rhode Island" his wife was Mary Small, but the Registers of St. Albans Abbey show that he was married to Mary Ashton, 16th Sept., 1629, and further give the baptisms of his children as folllows:

Thomas, 6th Jan., 1631/2.

Epinetus, 14th Feb., 1633/4 (by wife Marie).

The name Olney and Oney occurs frequently in the parish register of St. Albans, and there was a family in the county who were of more or less consequence. The writer does not seek to establish any connection with other families of the name but merely to call attention to the fact of the county having given birth to, and sent forth on the same ship, to help colonize America, two men who have produced the man to whom England and the United States will eventually owe so much, and his successor, to whom will fall the duty of putting the Treaty of Arbitration into operation.

The Ashton connection also suggests an interesting query. Was James Ashton the early settler and Commissioner in Rhode Island in 1652-63, and therefore an associate of Olney, the same as that James Ashton who had several children baptised at St. Albans between 1600 and 1620, of whom Marie was baptised 25th August, 1605. Unfortunately we have no record of the children of the New England settler, though he is presumed to have been the ancestor of the Ashtons of New Jersey, and perhaps of a collateral branch with the Ashtons of Maine. The connection of Salem and Hertfordshire does not consist only through the families named above but through many others, for a large proportion of the early settlers were from Herts, and especially from St. Albans or near vicinity.

---

## Court Rolls of the Manor of Picotts otherwise Piggots in Bishops Stortford.

(CONTINUED FROM PAGE 328).

**PIGOTTS.** First Court Baron of Robert Salmon of his Manor aforesaid, held there on Wednesday, 1st Oct. 4 Jas. [1606] before Lewis Jebbe gent, steward there.

Essoins. Richard Godfrey by Francis Abell.
Thos. Chaundler by Tobias Chaundler sen.

Homage. Geo. Hawkyns, Edw. Willey, Thos. Barnarde, Geo. Browne, Wm. Parsley, John Bull, Gilbt Westhead & Isaac Palmer.

Edward, lord Morley, Robt. Hall gent vj*d*, Geo. Jacob vj*d*, W<sup>m</sup> Bendishe, clerk, vicar of Stortforde vj*d*, Andrew Calton vj*d*, Rich. Jarfeilde vj*d*, the Master of S<sup>t</sup> Bartholomew's Hospital in London vj*d*, the heir of [blank] Birde vj*d*, Henry Jernegan gent, vj*d*, John Feaste vj*d*, the heir of John Goslyn vj*d*, Robt. Spencer vj*d* & James Marden vj*d*, owe suit of court & made default. Therefore in mercy etc, except Edw. lord Morley who is exonerated according to the form of the statute etc.

Anthony Tunbridge died since last court & before his death sold a messuage held by fealty, suit of court & [blank] rent, to Tobie Chaundler junior. Bailiff is ordered to distrain s<sup>d</sup> Tobie to appear at next court to do fealty, suit of court & to pay the relief [left blank].

Thomas Willesmere died since last court & before his death sold his tenements in Stortforde, in le Southstreete, to Wm. Parseley & his heirs for ever. Said tenements are held by fealty, suit of court & 12*d*. yearly rent. Relief 12*d*.

James Bull died since last court, and held a messuage in Southstreete & a barn at le Taynter hill, by fealty, suit of court & 2*s*. 2*d*. yearly rent. John Bull is son & next heir & of full age. Relief 2*s*. 2*d*.

John Goslyn died since last court & held a tenement in Northstreete in Stortforde, now in tenure of Wm. Gladwyn jun., by fealty, suit of court & 6*d*. annual rent. Elizabeth Dauie is 'consanguinea' & next heir & aged [blank]. Relief vj*d*.

Thomas Parsons esquire died since last court & held a messuage in le North streete, now in tenure of John Norton, by fealty, suit of court & 12*d*. annual rent. Thomas Parsons son of Edmund Parsons is 'consanguineus' & next heir & under age. Relief 12*d*.

John Gybbe gent. died since last court & held three tenements in Stortforde, by fealty, suit of court & [blank] rent. John Gybbe is his son & next heir & of full age. Relief [blank].

Wm. Feaste died since last court & held a tenement in Northstreete, formerly Jarfeilds, by fealty, suit of court & 6*d*. annual rent. John Feaste is son & next heir & under age. Relief 6*d*.

John Maryon died since last court & before his death sold a barn in Hockerell & a certain meadow at Hockerell Bridge, held by fealty, suit of court & 2*s*. annual rent, to Rich. Godfrey & his heirs for ever. Relief 2*s*.

Wm. Cheney since last court sold a piece of land containing two acres, in Benhooke, held by fealty, suit of court & 4*d*. annual rent, to Thos. Barnarde & his heirs for ever. Relief 4*d*.

Edward Willey since last court sold a croft called Windell Meade, held by fealty, suit of court & 2*s*. 4*d*. annual rent, to John Meade & his heirs for ever. Relief 2*s*. 4*d*.

Andrew Calton since last court, sold a parcel of his tenement in Stortforde, held by fealty, suit of court & 2*d*. annual rent, to John Noke & James Marden & their heirs for ever. Relief [blank].

[Signed] Per me Lodovicum Jebbe Senescall. Cur. p'dce.

---

**PIGOTTES.** FIRST COURT BARON of Robert Sallmon, lord of the manor aforesaid, held there on Friday the last day of November 1649.

Homage. John Bull, Wm. Tayler, Rich. Curby, Wm. Bayford, Fras. Cramphorne & W<sup>m</sup> Barnard.

Henry lord Morley, Edw. Hawkins gent, Magister Mannyng clerk, now vicar of Stortford, M<sup>rs</sup> Morse widow, John Jacklyn, M<sup>ris</sup> Westwood widow, Henry Ladd, John Jones. Geo. Dennyson, Rich. Godfry, John Barnes, Thos. Ashby, Wm. Pallmer & Anne Wall widow owe suit of court etc. except Henry lord Morley who is exonerated etc.

Rich. Butler, clerk, late vicar of Stortford, who held by free charter a barn & garden, parcel of the vicarage of Stortford, died before this Court. —— Mannyng, clerk, is now vicar of Stortford & ought to pay relief vj*d*.

Geo. Hawkins senior died before this Court seised of a messuage called the George in Stortford & 4 shops adjoining held by free charter etc. & rent of xv*s*, also a barn at Taynter Hill held by free charter etc & rent iij*d*. Geo. Hawkins was his son & next heir & also died before this Court seised of the premises. Edward Hawkins gent. is his son & next heir. Relief xv*s* iij*d*.

Thos. Westwood gent died before this Court seised of 4 acres of land called Wyndlemeade in Stortford held by free charter etc. & by will gave same to Grisell his wife for life & after to Nich. Westwood & his heirs for ever etc. Relief ij*s* iiij*d*.

Geo. Dennyson died before this Court seised of 3 acres of land near Halfeacres above Donton Hill. Geo. Dennyson is his son & next heir etc.

Thos. Barnard after the last Court & before this Court sold to Wm. Barnard his son a piece of land lying in Benhooke containing 3 acres formerly Cheneys etc.

Henry Ladd of Hodesdon, before this Court, purchased from John Noke a tenement in Southstreete formerly Caltons, etc.

Mistress Morse widow before this court, bought from Daniel Cramphorne a tenement in Southstreete late Willesmores & afterwards Jo. Graves etc.

Rich. Godfry died before this court seised of a barn & a meadow at Hockerellbridge. Henry Godfry was his son & next heir & died also seised of the premises. Rich. Godfry is his son & next heir etc.

John Fish clerk, before this court, bought from Thos. Wall a tenement in Northstreet late Feast's, & before this court John Jacklyn bought s^d tenement from s^d John Fish, etc.

Wm. Tayler, before this court, bought from Tobie Chandler 2 acres of land in Aptonfeild & s^d Tayler died before this court seised thereof. Wm. Tayler is his son & next heir etc.

Francis Cramphorne lately bought from Avery Lucy a tenement in Northstreet late Jarfeilds & afterwards Feaste's.

Wm. Bayford, before this court, bought from Thomas . . . . ford esq a messuage in Stortford now called the Bull late in tenure of John . . . . . . .

Wm. Barnes, before this court, died seised of a tenement in Northstreet late Davye's & before Ludford's. John Barnes is his son & next heir, etc.

Thos. Ashby, before this court, died seised of a messuage in Northstreet, called the Swan, late bought from Gilbert Westwood. Thos. Ashby is his son & next heir etc.

Isaac Wall, before this court, died seised of a tenement, late . . . . . . . Wm. Wall is his son & next heir etc.

Anne Wall widow, lately bought from Robt. Spencer a tenement in Southstreet late Brands etc.

Rich. Kirby senior, before this court, bought from Edw. Ashby a tenement in Southstreet, late of Kath. Chandler & formerly Ives & Tunbridge's etc.

John Bull, before this court, died seised of a messuage in Southstreet & a barn at Taynter hill etc. John Bull is his son & next heir.

[Signed by John Rowe steward.]

**MANERIUM DE PIGOTTS** First Court Baron of Robert Dawges & Eliz. his wife held there .. July 1676 by Thomas Byrd gent. steward there.

Homage: Geo. Dennison, Rich. Godfrey, Wm. Bayford, Wm. Reade & Thos. Barnard.

All the tenants appeared at this court & none made default.

[*blank*] Manninge clerk late vicar of Stortford died seised of a barn & a garden parcel of the vicarage of Stortford, after whose death Nathaniel Croucher now vicar of Stortford held same etc.

John Wilsmore dec$^d$, in his lifetime bought from Rich. Kirbie junior son of Rich. Kirbie senior likewise dec$^d$ a tenement in Southstreet & by will gave same to Margaret his dau.

Wm. Westwood who lately held a tenement in Southstreet sold same to Alice Chapman.

Wm. Barnard who held 3 acr. of arable land in Apton feild, died so seised & Thos. Barnard is his son & next heir.

Nath. Jones who held a tenement called Searles, died so seised & Nath. Jones junior is his son & next heir.

Wm. Reade who held a tenement in Northstreet abutting on the street afores$^d$ towards the east & the tenement of Matthew Wolley gent. towards the south & the messuage called the Whitehouse towards the north, died since last court & Wm. Reade is 'nepos' & next heir.

Wm. Reade son of Wm. Reade senior bought from —— Morse widow a tenement in Stortford next the tenement of Wm. Wright towards south & the tenement of Roger Bankes towards the north, died since last court & Wm. Reade junior is son & next heir.

John Ashbie held messuage called the Swan in Stortford & died & Sarah Ashbie widow his wife did fealty etc.

John Barnes who held messuage called the Halfe Moon in Stortford before his death gave same to Thos. Barnes his son, which same Thomas by Wm. Barnes his attorney did fealty etc.

Anne Wall died since last court seised of a tenement in Southstreet & Anne Brittaine is dau. & heir.

Wm. Palmer died seised of a messuage called Shrimps in Stortford & Thos. Hayward & Martha his wife late relict of s$^d$ Wm. acknowledged that they held for the life of s$^d$ Martha etc.

Said Wm. Palmer died seised of 2 acres land in Apton feild & s$^d$ Thos. Hayward & Martha his wife hold for life of s$^d$ Martha etc.

John Payne since last court bought from Rich. Feast & Thos. Edwards & Sarah his wife sister & heir of John Bull son of John Bull son of John Bull, a messuage in Stortford.

Robert Ley bought from Thos. Edwards & Sarah his wife, sister & heir of John Bull son of John Bull the father son of John Bull the grandfather a barn in Stortford etc & because s$^d$ Robert refused to pay relief therefore proclamation is made etc.

Edw. Hawkins senior was seised of a messuage called the George in Stortford & 4 shops near the s$^d$ measuage & a barn at Taynter Hill & died & Edw. Hawkins junior was his son & heir & died before this court etc & because no one came to court to pay relief etc therefore proclamation is made etc.

[Signed by Thomas Byrd steward there.]

January the 22. 168¾.

Measured there for John Reeve gent severall parcells of Land belonging to his Mannor called Piggotts lying and being in the Parish of Bishops Stortford in the County of Hertford. And also some other Lands called Moat Lands adjoyning to the Mannor aforesaid. The names of the Closes with their contents, what is arrable and what may be made arrable in Statute measure, is as followeth, viz:

|  |  | acres | r. | p. |
|---|---|---|---|---|
| these plowed | The great Homefeild conteynes | 14 | 0 | 00 |
|  | The Middle feild conteynes | 12 | 1 | 20 |
|  | Stortford feild conteynes | 5 | 0 | 04 |
|  | Thisley or Long feild conteynes | 3 | 0 | 20 |
| Pasture | The Long Meade conteynes | 4 | 3 | 18 |
|  | The Long Ley conteynes | 2 | 0 | 0 |
|  | Stortford Meade conteynes | 3 | 0 | 12 |
|  | The Hop ground conteynes | 1 | 0 | 27 |
|  | The Little Hoppit conteynes | 0 | 3 | 00 |
|  | The Little Meade conteynes | 1 | 0 | 7 |
| Plowed | Great Moat Lands conteynes | 15 | 0 | 10 |
|  | Long Moat Lands cont. | 4 | 1 | 00 |
|  | The two little Moat Lands cont. | 3 | 1 | 10 |
|  | Mr Plumes Close conteynes | 5 | 0 | 34 |
|  | The whole sume of these Closes is | 75 | 1 | 02 |
|  |  | acres | roods | perches |

per me Hen: Dormer.

Vera Copia } The original being in paper and worne is thus coppied
A true Coppy } in 1700 anno.

---

A Rentall of the Releifes and Quit Rents paid to the Mannor of Piggotts being collected and paid in the yeare 1707 by mee Roger Boultwood tenant of the farme of Piggots als Pickets to John Lowe Esqr, which sumes of money I finde by severall old Rent Rolls were formerly paid for those estates viz.

|  | Releifes | | | Rents | | |
|---|---|---|---|---|---|---|
|  | li. | s. | d. | li. | s. | d. |
| William Pollhill Vicar of Stortford for a barne and part of a garden adjoyning to the Vicaridge of Stortford | 0 | 0 | 6 | 0 | 0 | 6 |
| Thomas Barnard for three acres of land in Beane hooke | 0 | 0 | 4 | 0 | 0 | 4 |
| John Graue for a mesuage in Southstreet | 0 | 0 | 6 | 0 | 0 | 6 |
| William Dixon (late Robert Lay deceased) for a barn at Tainter hill | 0 | 0 | 6 | 0 | 0 | 6 |
| John Reynalds for a Mesuage in South Street in possession of Wm. Stock | 0 | 0 | 2 | 0 | 0 | 2 |
| Reginald Ramsey for a Mesuage in Potters Street called Searles | 0 | 1 | 0 | 0 | 1 | 0 |
| [blank] Mott (late Edward Woods) for a Mesuage in South Street (late in possesion of Joseph Andrewes and now of [blank] Br [blank] | 0 | 0 | 6 | 0 | 0 | 6 |

| | | |
|---|---|---|
| Thomas Appleby for a Mesuage in Potters Street | 0.1.8 | 0.1.8 |
| William Bayford for a Mesuage in Potters Street called the Bull | 0.1.0 | 0.1.0 |
| William Ferguson for a Mesuage in North Street | 0.0.6 | 0.0.6 |
| John Roth (late Sarah Ashby for a Mesuage in North Street called the White Swan in possession of John Browne | 0.0.9 | 0.0.9 |
| Rachael Hockley for a Mesuage in North Street called the Halfe Moone in possession of George Church and late in possession of Charles Sandford | 0.0.6 | 0.0.6 |
| Henry Peachy for a Mesuage in South Street called Shrimps in possession of Thomas Wattner | 0.0.6 | 0.0.6 |
| Zachariah Blowes for two acres of land in Apton feild | 0.0.3 | 0.0.3 |
| William Reade for a Mesuage in North Street in possession of John Cullick | 0.1.0 | 0.1.0 |
| William Reade for a Mesuage in South Street in possession of W$^m$ Woolridge | 0.1.0 | 0.1.0 |
| William Ingram for 3 acres of Land upon Dunton Hill in possession of Richard Osborne | 0.0.9 | 0.0.9 |
| Oct$^{br}$ 1$^{st}$ 1713 M$^r$ Ferguson for a Barn at Hockerill Bridge | 0.0.6 | 0.0.6 |
| Oct$^{br}$ 1$^{st}$ 1713 M$^r$ How for a meadow at Hockeril bridge | 0.1.6 | 0.1.6 |

---

**THE MANOR OF PIGGOTTS OTHERWISE PICKETTS.** } to wit  GENERAL COURT BARON of Amey Lowe widow Lady of the said Manor there held 4 May 1752 before Peter Calvert esquire steward there.

Homage.    Ezekill Ramsey & Thomas Heath.

Robert Stileman clerk late vicar of Stortford who held a piece of ground whereon a barn formerly stood & part of a garden died so seised. W$^m$ Jackson clerk, the present vicar is his successor.

Samuel Bayford who held 3 acr. land in Beanhook late Thos. Barnards & 2 acr. land in Apton field late Zachary Blows, died so seised, having devised same to his sons David & Thomas.

John Wood sold a messuage in South Street, late John Graves, to Samuel Mason.

John Ramsey died seised of a messuage in Potters Street called Searls. John Ramsey an infant is his grandson & heir.

Said John Ramsey also died seised of a barn at Tenter Hill late Robert Lays. The same is since the last court sold to Thos. Adderly.

Benj. Reynolds sold a messuage in South Street (formerly John Reynold's, clerk) to Rob$^t$. Ayley.

Matthew Mott & Dorothy Smith sold a messuage in South Street to Thos. Heath.

Anthony Appleby died seised of a messuage in Potters Street. Eliz. Appleby is his widow & hath a right to the said premises.

Sarah Ward, widow, died seised of a messuage in Potters Street formerly called the Bull, late Wm. Bayfords And the s^d premises are descended to Sarah Clayton widow.

John Guyver died seised of a messuage in North Street, late Fergusons. Joseph Guyver is his son & heir.

Samuel Trigg sold a messuage formerly called the White Swan & now the Half Moon in North Street (late John Roths,) to Wm. Walker who is since dead having devised same to Ann Walker.

Thos. Hockley sold a messuage formerly called the Half Moon (which is now taken down) in North Street, to Ann Walker.

Wm. Ingram sold a messuage in North Street (formerly Wm. Reeds) & a messuage in South Street (formerly Wm. Reeds) to Joshua Winter esquire.

John Eyres sold 3 acr. of land on Dunton Hill to Joshua Winter esq.

Abm. Smith died seised of a barn at Hockerell late Fergusons. Joseph Smith is his eldest son & heir.

Geo. James sold a meadow at Hockerell Bridge to Thomas Drane.

---

**THE MANOR OF PIGGOTTS OTHERWISE PICKETS.** General Court Baron of William Lowe Esquire lord of the said Manor held there on Tuesday the 1st July 1760 before Wm. Lens steward there.

Homage. Ralph Phillips & Thomas Heath.

Joseph Smith gent. sold a Barn at Hockerill to Thos. Adderly gent.

John Ramsey sold a croft of ground on Tenter hill (whereon a barn formerly stood) to s^d Thomas Adderly.

Wm. Jackson clerk late Vicar of Stortford who held a piece of ground whereon a barn formerly stood & part of a garden, resigned same to the Rev^d Richard Hynd Doctor in Divinity the present vicar.

Henry Petchey sold a messuage called Shrimps in South Street, to Thos. Nash the elder.

John Ramsey sold a messuage called Searles in Potters Street to Ralph Phillips gent.

Joseph Guyver gent sold a messuage in North Street to John Phillips.

Joshua Winter esq sold a messuage in South Street to Ralph Winter esq.

Said Joshua Winter also sold 3 acr. land on Dunton Hill to s^d Ralph Winter.

# INDEX.

N.B.—An asterisk is placed after a reference when the name occurs more than once on the page.

Abbott (Abbatt), John 177, 261, 277, 347; Reb. 284; Rob. 43, 273, 274; Sus. 177; Wm. 138, 230.
Ablell, John 275.
Abell, Fras. 377; Ric. 189.
Aber(r)y, Oliver 363; Rich. 43; Wm. 367. *See Abry, Aubry.*
Ablet(t), John 12; Rob. 350; Tho. 211, 350.
Abower, Kath. 158*.
Abraham, Tho. 65; Wm. 352.
Abry, Edw. 356, 357*; Eliz. 360*; Griz. 356; Jud. 357; Wm. 360, 363. *See Aberry, Aubry.*
Adam (Addam), Adam 237; Agn. 259, 275; Alice 132*; Anab. 237; Anne 63, 65; Dion. 275; Edw. 259; Eliz. 175, 354; Fras. 259; Geof. 274; Geo. 134; Hen. 80, 276; Jane 83; Jerome 120; Joan 134; John 47*, 120, 132, 191*, 233, 237, 273, 274, 275, 342, 352, 354, 355; Margt. 80, 342, 345; Margery 47; Mary 302; Oliver 134; Peter 275; Ralph 274; Ric. 98, 132*, 172; Rob. 63, 273; Steph. 273; Tho. 120, 122, 157, 175, 233, 355; Walt. 276; Wm. 120*, 134, 148, 193.
Adams (Addam(e)s), Agn. 306, 307; Anfillis 162; Bird 84; Cath. 41; Eliz. 307; Firmin (Frimyne) 29, 75; Hen. 307; Isaac 307; Joan 32, 65; John 40, 65*, 80, 96, 181*, 238, 273, 321, 337, 342, 345; Jul. 306; Lucy 337, 342; Margt. 306; Mary 96; Ric. 306; Rob. 314, 375; Sil. 51; Theo. 258; Tho. 32, 41, 65, 102, 274, 306; Wm. 284, 342.
Adamson, Wm. 330.
Adcocke, June 159; Tho. 159.
Adderly, Tho. 382, 383*.
Addison (Addessen, Adyson), Anne 152; Isab. 352; Rob. 277.
Adee. *See Adye.*
Adkins, Hen. 3*; Isab. 2; Ric. 88.
Adkyn, John 275.
Adlard, Anth. 51.
Adler, Mr 51; Sim. 340.
Adlyngton, Nic. 275.

Adnut, Mary 167.
Ady(e) *alias* Adee, Jer. 332; John 340; Sar. 331; Thomasine 340.
Ager, Geo. 220.
Aicon, John 75.
Ailmer, Tabell 253; Theoph. 103.
Aker, Tho. 281.
Akers, Edw. 153.
Albert, John 277.
Alberye, Sim. 30.
Albrede, Cecilia 189; Walt. 189.
Albrey, John 191; Marion 191; Walt. 191*.
Albright, Ric. 31; Rob. 27, 72; Tho. 72; Wm. 72*.
Alce, Wm. 30.
Alcy, John 196*.
Alden *alias* Tyler, Amy 288.
Aldere, John 186.
Aldin (Alden), Dan. 332*; Edw. 156; Eliz. 156*; Hum. 330; John 156*; Mary 141; Reb. 332*; Ric. 156; Rob. 156*.
Aldred, Sib. 173, 177; Wm. 173, 177.
Aldrych (Aldrige, Allderiche), Anne 170; Fras. 78; Margt. 120; Zach. 170.
Aldwin (Ald(e)wyn), Dan. 182; Em. 349; Nic. 27; Rog. 45.
Alea *alias* Cooke, Wm 278.
Alee, John 27; Sus. 43.
Alewood, Mary 9.
Alexander (Allexaunder), John Michaell 227; Ric. 219. *See Mylwarde.*
Aleyne, Rob. 27.
Alford(e), Rog. 173, 174.
Alkebarow, Alice 189; John 189*; Mat. 189.
Alkeburn, John 91.
Allan, Kath. 243.
Allen (Allin, Al(e)yn), Agn. 30, 132, 273; Anys 198; Christr. 176; Giles 309; Hen. 346; John 30, 85, 121, 191; Master 235; Pat. 282; Reb. 165; Ric. 76, 96, 352; Sib. 191; Tho. 74*, 132; Wm. 30, 64, 132.
Alley, Fras. 131, 257, 339; John 132; Verney 339.
Allingsby, Rob. 247.

1

ii.  INDEX.

Allinson, Tho. 247.
Allis (Allys), John 107, 276, 277; Ric. 273, 274.
Allison, Mary 244; Mich. 244: Ric. 244.
Allott (Alott), Morgan 275; Rob. 367.
Alman (Allman), Christr. 273; John 319, 320.
Almond alias Aumond, Eliz. 371.
Alnewyk, Wm. 46.
Alpresse, Amye 316; Hen. 316; John 316*; Miles 316; Rob. 316; Wm. 316.
Alrede, Jas 30.
Alsworth, Master 235.
Alway (Alwey(e)), Awdry 318; Joan 190; John 260*, 261*; Rob. 45, 190.
Alwyn, Nich. 366.
Aman, Cath. 143; Reg. 80; Rob. 143.
Ambler, Mary 243; Wm. 126, 128, 347.
Ambrose, Alice 235; Dor. 235; El. 234, 235; Frances 235.
Ameris, Eliz. 361.
Amye, Agn. 46.
Ancell (Ansell), Anne 214; Edw. 214; Geo. 345; John 30, 358*, 359*; Jos. 371; Jud. 214, 361; Peter 361; Phil. 362; Ric. 202, 217; Sar. 202; Tho. 214, 258, 306, 357*, 358*, 359*; Wm. 155, 358*. See Auncell.
Anckell (Ankell), John 227; Wm 40.
Andelsby, Wm. 35.
Anderson, Anne 241; Bridget 241; Dor. 241; Edm 176, 220; Frances 241; Hen. 241*; John 241, 283, 288, 305, 333; Kath. 241; Margt. 241*; Mary 241*; Pen. 241; Ric. 176, 241*; Rob. 241*; Rose 288; Sam. 8; Wm. 241.
Andlaby, Alse 273.
Andrew(e) (Androw, Androo), Alice 31; Geo. 152; John 31, 177, 189, 274, 275, 276*, 349; Margt. 31: Mary 152; Ric. 276; Rob. 1, 31, 98, 274; Tho. 31, 349; Wm. 31*, 150*, 218, 276, 361.
Andrewes (Androwes), Eliz. 242, 332; Hen. 141; John 240, 332; Jos. 381; Kath. 242; Tho. 89*, 173, 184, 242; Wm. 141, 337.
Andrews alias Woodroof, John 81.
Angel (Angill), Cuth. 86; Jone 32.
Angier, Bernard 375.
Angles, Amos 168.
Angrome, Wm. 261.
Angyl(tyl)tille, John 101*.
Annable, Rob. 350.
Annesley, John 220; Letice 220.
Annyson, Tho. 353.
Ansell. See Ancell.
Anstee, Anne 257; Wm. 257.
Anterbus (Antebus), Eliz. 371; Wm. 62.
Anthony, Widow 243.
Antwissell (Antwyssell), Phil. 219; Wm. 219, 223, 253.

Apleyard, Tho. 315.
Appleby, Anth. 382; Eliz. 382; Tho. 382.
Ap(p)owell (Appowell alias Lewes, Appowell alias Powell), John 188 Margt. 77, 79, 81, 176, 217, 222, 256; Tho. 77, 79, 81, 176, 217, 222, 256.
Appryce (Aprice), Jeram 347; Sim. 119, 180.
Arborowe, Miles 316.
Archell, Wm. 73.
Archer (Archar), Alice 35, 175; Anne 41, 246; Geo. 31; Hen. 65; John 31, 35, 175, 204, 245, 246*, 350; Rob. 321; Sam. 31; Tho. 9, 31, 196, 275, 350; Val. 204; Wm. 142, 265, 273, 354, 373.
Ardaunt, John 266.
Argente, Wm. 120.
Aris, Avis 375.
Arland, Christr. 187.
Arman, John 276.
Armerer, John 275.
Armes, Tho. 362.
Armesbey, Dor. 44.
Armestronge, Mark 7.
Arnold (Arnoll, Arnall), Jas. 123; Joan 214, 285; John 223, 273, 292, 293*, 295*, 341; Jos. 202; Mat. 295*; Sar. 293*; Tho. 153; Wm. 146, 283.
Arnott (Arnot, Arnett), John 137, 328, 329; Ric. 114; Widow 116; Wm. 182.
Arrowsmith, Rob. 94.
Arryngton, Rose 79; Wm. 79.
Art, Rob. 275.
Arthure, Nich. 353.
Artur. See Fawcett.
Ashb(e)y, Anth. 41; Edw. 379; John 380: Sar. 380, 382; Tho. 301, 379*.
Ashellwood, Elyn 350.
Asheworthe, Margery 175; Rob. 175.
Ashton (Asheton), —— 315; Ann 329; Eliz. 306; Jas. 377*; Laur. 306; Mary 377*.
Ashwood, Eliz. 259; John 289; Ric. 50.
Aske, Margt. 344; Wm. 344.
Asmall, Lewes 319.
Asmar, Ric. 273.
Aspynne alias James, Eliz. 81; Tho. 81.
Asser, Edm. 24; Edw. 26.
Asshefeld (Ashefilde), Rob. 52; Tho. 34.
Asshford, Jas. 259.
Astin, Geo. 249; Jos. 181*, 182*; Tho. 181. See Austin.
Aston, Mary 313.
Astood, Nich. 202.
Astr(e)y (Astrie), Alice 353; Edw. 345; John 73, 122.
Astwick(e), John 29, 88.
Astwood, John 292.
At Felde, Alice 196*; John 196; Wm. 195, 196. See Field.

At Felde *alias* Porter, Ric. 196*.
At Hille (Atte Hille), John 145, 146*, 147, 193*, 195, 196*, 269; Rob. 146; Tho. 145, 146; Wm. 145, 193, 197* *See Hill.*
At Hoo (Atte Hoo), —— 194; Edw. 237; Geo. 346; John 193, 194*; Ric. 194; Tho. 148*, 194*; Wm. 148, 194. *See Hoo.*
Atkinson (Atkynsonne), Edw. 276; John 284; Ric. 228; Tho. 274, 329.
Atkyn, Ric. 349; Wm. 190.
Atkyn(e)s, John 72, 347, 350; Margt. 38; Wm. 78, 81.
Atridge, Ellyn 63.
Atto Watir, Ric. 191.
Atte Welle, John 192.
Atte Wyk(is), John 192*; Kath. 192; Ric. 192.
Attewynche, Alice 90; Wm. 90.
Atton, Hugh 366.
Att ye Naysh. *See Nash.*
Atwood(e), John 31, 258.
At ye Verne, Agn. 91; Alice 91; Kath. 91; Margt. 91; Sim. 91.
Aubon, Grif. 5.
Aubry, Jo. 361. *See Aberry, Abry.*
Audley (Awd(e)ley), Avis 2; Edw. 2, 230; Frances 2; Francis 165; Geo. 209; Hamlet 165; Joan 229*; John 2, 229*; Mat. 2*, 256; Tho. lord 308, 339; Wm. 229*, 307.
Aumond. *See Almond.*
Auncell (Auncill, Awncell), Agn. 280*; Alice 279; Edw. 276, 280*; Eliz. 32; Helen 153; Hen. 310; Joan 259; John 275; Mat. 153; Ric. 32; Rob. 276; Sus. 280; Tho. 259, 278*, 279*, 280*, 353; Wm. 279*, 280*, 342, 343, 353. *See Ancell.*
Aunger, Nic. 304.
Austin (Austen, Awstyn), Eliz. 78*, 369; Geo. 249; Hen. 282; Joan 76, 340, 345; John 219; Jos. 182; Margery 310; Mr 377; Rob. 78*, 340, 345; Tho. 227; Wm. 78, 248*, 249*, 310*, 353.
Austrey, Anne 42.
Avenon, Alex 306.
Averell (Au'ell), Agn. 275; Bened. 82; Hen. 173.
Avis (Auis), Edw. 359*; Jos. 164*; Wm. 359*.
Awbone, Edw. 275.
Awdery, Jonas 173.
Aweedon (Awedon), Bar. 349; Edw. 349; Geo. 349; Hen. 349, 350; John 313, 349; Tho. 350; Wm. 349. *See Weedon.*
Awmer, John 233.
Awnsham, Ric. 320.
Awsopp, Margt. 133; Rob. 133.
Awtriche, Grace 216.
Axtell (Axtill, Axstall, Axstyll), Agn. 312; Alice 312; Frances 287; Fras. 76; Grace 311; Hen. 312*; Jane 116; Joan 114, 115, 312; John 28, 74*, 115, 181; Mark 311; Ralph 278; Ric. 311, 312; Rob. 311; Rog. 349; Sar. 242*; Steph. 188, 242; Sus. 311; Tho. 27, 28, 73, 157*, 158, 173, 311*, 312, 332, 343; Tim. 312; Wm. 75, 114*, 115*, 116, 311.
Ayer, Hen. 307; Rob. 37, 102, 307.
Ayle, Tho. 231.
Aylett, John 275.
Aylewarde, Aune 77; Hen. 318; Joan 77, 219; John 77; Nic. 261*; Wm. 35, 77, 219.
Ayley, Rob. 382.
Ayloff (Ayliff), Alice 305; Em. 146; Wm. 176, 305.
Aynsel(l), Martha 83*; Mary 84; Ric. 84; Sar. 84.
Ayscough, Mary 176; Rob. 176.

Babb (Babb*), Ann 372; Edw. 329; Eph. 240, 282, 285; Hester 282; John 284; Mary 283; Sus. 149; Tho. 170, 334; Wm 139.
Bacheler (Bachelder), Edw. 158; Eliz. 121, 242*; Joan 132; Leon. 161; Mary 158; Ric. 121, 242; Wm. 132.
Bacon, Anne 34, 77, 78, 81, 173; Edw. 78; Jas. 80*, 184; Nath. 8, 78; Nic. 34, 36, 77, 78, 81*, 173*, 175, 178, 184*, 185*, 217, 254; Sus. 229.
Baddison, Mary 285.
Badger, Nic. 255.
Baeshe (Baesshe), —— 320; Edw. 34, 78, 79*, 130, 131, 133*, 177, 178*, 220, 221, 255; Jane 78, 130, 131, 133*, 178*, 221, 255; Nic. 36; Ralph 133; Thomasine 34.
Baet, John 304.
Bagerd, Phil. 199.
Bagsha(w)e, Agn. 174; Anne 337; Edw. 302; John 311; Mary 302; Mat. 81, 217; Rob. 81, 217; Tho. 304, 337.
Bagwell, Hen. 313.
Bailey (Bailie, Balie, Bayly), Alex. 28; Ann 83; Calamy 263; Christian 115; Elen 91; Ellenor 159; Eliz. 113; Esdras 163; Geo. 262, 332; Helen 141; John 115*, 159, 160*, 161, 163; Joseph 93, 95, 285; Joshua 123; Ket. 163; Margt. 114; Mary 159, 160, 284; Ralph 3*, 4; Sar. 362; Tho. 160; Wm. 187, 188, 230. *See Chappell.*
Baker, Alice 351; Anne 94; Christr. 209; Dan. 5; Eliz. 209; Geo. 330, 346; Hen. 182, 190; Isab. 233; John 74, 125, 352; Joshua 168; Mat. 236; R.G. 111; Ric. 34, 36, 95, 240, 276, 298*, 353; Rob. 126, 347, 351; Rog. 111; Wm. 189, 191, 227, 231.
Baker *alias* Machell, Isab. 236; Tho. 236.
Bakyn, John 354.

Baldock, Geo. 281; Mich. 152; Tho. 106, 352.
Baldry(e), Andr. 287; Tho. 366.
Baldwyn (Baldwin, Baldwen, Boldewyn), Alice 12*; Anne 96, 132; Christr. 349; Dan. 8; Drew 12*; Edw. 288; Geo. 349; Hen. 132; Jas. 12*, 330, 349; Jane 228; John 94, 162, 242, 267, 322, 349; Martha 161; Ralph 68; Ric. 228, 349; Rog. 349; Sus. 242, 330; Tho. 24, 139, 242.
Baldyn, John 201.
Bale, Alse 311; Wm. 311.
Bales, Christr. 218.
Ball, Mary 293*.
Ballam. *See Balloon.*
Ballard, Geo. 142; John 371; Rog. 152, 370, 371; Tho. 72, 304.
Ballawbye, John 229.
Ballett, Mary 100.
Balloon (Ballam), Laur. 158*.
Bampton, Tho. 285.
Banbricke, John 318.
Banburye (Banbery), John 344; Tho. 374.
Banford, Mary 363.
Bankes (Bancks), John 199; Ric. 254; Rog. 380; Wm. 51.
Bannester (Banister), —— 313; Alice 120; Grace 152; Hen. 73, 120; John 120*.
Barbor (Barboure, Barber, Barbur), Agn. 34, 119, 339, 341; Beat. 155; Edm. 256, 338; Eliz. 242, 256, 338; Geo. 233, 236*; Jas. 95; Jane 202; John 232, 348; Rice 216; Rich. 34, 181, 216*, 339; Rob. 31*, 173, 341; Tho. 155, 242*, 243; Wm. 146, 147, 150, 155*. *See Whitlom.*
Barcock, Ellen 246; Jas. 246*; Margt. 246; Mary 246; Peregrine 246; Sam, 246; Sar. 247; Wm. 245, 246.
Bardolfe (Bardolphe), Edm. 37, 134, 217, 218, 222, 229, 254*, 345*; Edw. 174, 220, 254; Eliz. 37, 174, 222*, 229; Geo. 249; Jas. 154; Kath. 254; Ric. 254*, 345.
Bareitton, John 324.
Barefoot(e) (Barfotte), Hen. 272; Joan 132, 321; John 132, 156; Mich. 104, 132; Nich. 156; Rob. 156; Rog. 177; Tho. 63, 72, 156*, 158*; Wm. 178, 218.
Bar(e)legge, Joan 143; Jo. 93; Ruth 93.
Barford, Wm. 152, 272.
Barkemaker, Ann 155; Eliz. 155; John 155*, 257; Jone 155; Wm. 155*.
Barker, Ann 334; Eliz. 293; Hen. 374; Isab. 313; Jenetrix 38; Jer. 334; Mary 313; Mat. 313*; Ric. 313; Tho. 314*; Urias 338.
Barkham, Edw. 336*, 337*; Eliz. 336*; Fras. 336*; Hugh 336; Jane 336*; John 336*; Margt. 336*, 337*; Mary 336*; Rob. 336; Suz. 336; Tho. 336*.
Barkley, Hen. 131.
Barley (Barlye, Barlee), Eliz. 35, 254; Hen. 323; John 254; Wm. 33, 35, 67*, 130, 132, 175, 272*, 278.
Barley *alias* Parsell, Anne 150.
Barlo(w)e, Anne 140; John 307; Kath. 307.
Barlyman, Rose 304; Tho. 304.
Barnabe, Agn. 92; Phil. 92; Ric 92; Wm. 92.
Barnard(e), Eliz. 337; Ellen 175, 178; John 39, 122, 240, 330, 371; Tho. 66, 103, 175, 178, 303, 309, 337, 377, 378, 379, 380*, 381, 382; Wm. 38*, 66, 174, 206, 378, 379, 380. *See Barnett.*
Barnardiston, Eliz. 308; Tho. 308.
Barner, Alex. 179; Bridget 179; Hen. 179; Kath. 179*; Tho. 179*; Wm. 179*.
Barnes (Barns), Agn. 86; Eliz. 37, 136; Geo. 5, 94*, 96*, 136*, 137*, 138*, 140*, 141, 166*, 167, 168, 238; Jas. 139*, 331; John 20, 22, 85*, 86*, 152, 239, 320*, 379*, 380; Tho. 86, 239, 356, 357, 359*, 380*; Wm. 173, 379, 380.
Barnet(t), John 93; Mary 244; Sim. 83; Ric. 132, 178.
Barnton, John 323.
Baron, Ric. 45, 237; Rob. 236; Wm. 218.
Barowe, John 220.
Barr(e), Agn. 215; Anne 215; Clem. 215; Edm. 215; Grace 215; Kath. 215*; Wm. 137, 215.
Barrell, Tho. 52.
Barrett (Barratt), Anne 63; Joan 63; Ric. 51, 275; Rob. 98; Urs. 63; Wm. 65*.
Barrick, Agn. 200.
Barrington (Baryngton), John 325; Jud. 299; Tho. 78, 299.
Barrowson (Borrowson), Tho. 282.
Barr(e)y, Geo. 3*; Nic. 273; Wm. 308.
Barsfoote, Kath. 62.
Bartillmew, Tho. 73*. *See Golston.*
Bartlet(t), Mary 376; Tho. 177.
Barton, Alice 204; Fras. 99; Joan 30, 199; Wm. 204, 352, 353.
Basely(e) (Basseley), Jane 30; John 274, 276; Tho. 274; Wm. 146.
Basford, Geo. 172; John 65.
Basill, Alice 150; Wm. 150.
Bason, Ric. 275.
Baspole, Rob. 177.
Basse, Anne 199; Hen. 79; John 350; Reg. 307; Ric. 350; Rob. 66; Tho. 350; Wm. 90, 351.
Basset(t), Alice 72; Geo. 362*, 363; Gilb. 72; Mary 362, 363*; Tho. 151; Wm. 195*, 196*.
Bastion, Gilb. 347.
Batchlour (Batchelder), Wm. 181*, 182.

Bate, Eliz. 162; Geo. 346*; John 348; Kath. 162; Ric. 162, 236; Rob. 85, 121; Tho. 27.
Bateman, Margery 192.
Bates, Han. 285; John 350; Mary 361; Reb. 41; Tho. 372; Wm. 11.
Batherst, Lanc. 308*.
Batman, Joan 346.
Batte, John 91; Rob. 216.
Battell (Batell, Battle), Affabell 303; Eliz. 153*; Em. 143; Jasper 214; John 229; Ralph 143; Rob. 129*, 145, 147*, 195*, 196*; Wm. 129*, 154, 294.
Battman, Dan. 369.
Battsforth, Christian 37; Tho. 37.
Baudin, Jas. 168.
Bavyne (Bavinn), Agn. 343; Christr. 343; Tho. 182.
Bawcocke (Baucock), Anth. 216, 320; Edw. 211; Hen. 10; Joan 320.
Bawnett, Hellen 33; Wm. 33*.
Bax(s)ter, Edm. 351; Rob. 347.
Baye, Agn. 75.
Bayes, Ellen 82, 134; Tho. 82, 134; Wm. 346.
Bayford, David 382; Eliz. 217, 223, 304; Geo. 217, 223, 304; Hen. 86, 104; John 40, 82, 277; Sam. 382; Tho. 382; Wm. 210, 378, 379, 380, 382, 383.
Bayland, Tho. 219.
Bazill, Wm. 98.
Beachingal (Bechonal), Rose 244; Sus. 246; Tho. 216; Wm. 246
Beadle, Christr. 12; Geo. 213; Wm. 253.
Beaff, Anne 181.
Bealam, Chas. 359; Jas. 359; Sar. 359.
Beal(e) (Beell), Agn. 157*; Helden 157; Hen. 319; Joan 157; John 250; Val. 157; Wm. 157.
Beaumont (Beamonde, Beamon, Beaman), Eliz. 357*; Ellyn 312; James 355; Jane 153; John 62*, 105*, 283, 284, 287, 304, 330, 356, 357*, 373; Mary 168; Ric. 7.
Beane, Widow 73; Wm. 307.
Beasley, Wm. 7, 140.
Beason, Ric. 228.
Bechampe, John 92, 236.
Bechaunt, Wm. 237.
Beck(e) (Bekke), John 256; Rob. 10*, 66*, 105*; Sar. 239; Wm. 75.
Beckett, John 12, 303; Widow 64.
Beckfeld, John 353.
Beckilles, Luke 334.
Becksfeld, Eliz. 74; Tho. 73.
Bedell (Bedle, Bedyll), Anne 220; Ellen 310; Geo. 34; John 206, 248, 273; Ric. 34, 81, 174, 220; Rob. 273, 278; Sim. 34; Tho. 72, 310; Wm. 278.
Bedford, Alice 242; Bridget countess of, 173; Francis earl of, 173; John 204, 205, 242, 281; Myles 205; Ric. 204, 205*, 242, 243; Tho. 294*, 295, 312.

Bedgrove, Rob. 192.
Bedo, Amy 284; Wm. 284.
Bedwell, Ambr. 11; Andr. 11; Anth. 11; Edw. 11; Eliz. 11*; John 11*; Ric. 277; Wm. 278.
Bedworthe, Nic. 64.
Beech(e) (Beach, Bech), Ann 288; Eliz. 151; Hen. 93, 125, 216; John 210, 352, 376; Mary 284; Ric. 94, 281, 282; Rob. 352; Sam 370; Tho. 351; Walt. 94, 151, 352, 372, 375; Wm. 329.
Beechernole, Mercie 242; Ric. 242; Rob. 242.
Beesbronne, John 155.
Beinon, Rach. 375.
Bekson, Wm. 275.
Belch, Joan 45; John 282; Rog. 45.
Belcher, Tho. 139.
Beldon, John 123.
Belfeild(e) (Bellfeld), Ric. 261, 262*; Wm. 27.
Belgrave, Edw. 75; Eliz. 74; Joan 74; John 75; Mary 74; Tho. 74; Wm. 74*.
Belhom (Belham, Belh'm), John 269*, 271*, 322; Wm. 270*, 323*, 326*.
Bell, Anne 244; John 130, 198, 244; Martha 244; Rob. 219; Sar. 244; Wm. 201, 353.
Bellamy (Belamye), Alice 177; Barth. 339; Ellen 78; Hen. 78, 219; Joan 219; John 352; Kath. 132, 339; Rob. 237, 339; Tho. 132; Wm. 177.
Bellingham, Rob. 7.
Belson, Ambr. 339.
Beltod, Edw. 274; John 275*; Ric. 274, 275.
Bemores *alias* Chapman, John 158.
Benbow, Jane 335; Ric. 375; Wendover 334.
Benbridge, Rob. 65.
Bendishe, Wm. 378.
Bendyng, Rog. 46.
Benn, Sar. 143.
Bennes (Benes), Annes 159, 160; Ric. 159, 160.
Bennett (Benet(t), Benyt), Abel 8; Agn. 210, 259, 340; Alice 215, 305; Angel 149; Anne 306; Annis 314; Bridget 102; Clem. 161; Eliz. 80, 176, 345; Ellen 133, 173; Geo. 133, 173; Joan 204; John 215*, 239, 274, 276, 281, 306; Kath. 215; Mary 239; Nic. 215; Ric. 216, 274; Rob. 305; Tho. 80, 87, 176*, 215*, 259, 273, 276, 306, 340, 345*; Wm. 161, 215, 273, 358*.
Benninge (Beinge), Agn. 12; Alice 12; Anne 11; Eliz. 12; Geo. 11; Hen. 11; Joan 12; John 11, 20*; Mary 11; Ric. 11, 12; Rob. 11; Tho. 11.
Benson, Elen 199.
Bently (Bentle), Ralph 268; Ric. 281.
Bentou, Andr. 63; John 44.
Benyson, Rob. 348.

Beovys, Geo. 172.
Bepset, Mat. 231, 232.
Berd, Rob. 275.
Berdeney, Rob. 326, 327.
Bereman, Tho. 274.
Beresforde, Rowl. 10, 305.
Berge, John 56.
Bergerott, Margt. 263; Nic. 263.
Bergwasch, Hen. 46.
Berkemaker, Ric. 354.
Berkley, —— 195; Lord 131.
Bernard, Fras. 313.
Bern(e)well, Custance 191\*; John 44, 191\*; Margt. 191.
Berney, Frances 336; Mr 127; Tho. 336.
Berry (Berye, Berrie), Edw. 136, 169; John 207, 352; Reb. 137.
Besemer, Wm. 271, 272.
Besonn, John 164; Peter 164.
Besouthe (Besowth), Alice 73\*; Christr. 73, 348; Edw. 40\*; Eliz. 73; Geo. 73, 88; Hen. 40; Joan 73; John 40\*, 73, 153, 278; Ronyon 40; Rose 73; Sus. 73; Tho. 73; Wm. 40\*.
Bessill, Edw. 183.
Bestney (Besteneye, Beastney, Beesney), Alice 77; Ellen 37; Jane 331; John 372; Rob. 37, 351; Tho. 77; Wm. 77, 287, 351.
Betham, Edw. 221.
Betigonne, Tho. 320.
Bett, Tho. 260.
Bettison, —— 315; Patyent 315; Rob. 315.
Betts, Eliz. 245; Fras. 332; Jo. 108\*; Leon. 4.
Beule, Mary 356.
Beverle, John 268; Tho. 323.
Bevys, Geb. 275; John 84, 86.
Bewick, John 107.
Bexfeild (Bexfyeld), Eliz. 309; John 175; Wm. 309.
Beynon, Reb. 371.
Bibbye (Bib(b)ee, Beby), John 175; Ric. 136.
Bibsworth (Bybbesworth), Agn. 315; Affabell (Amphibolus) 143, 315\*; Alice 315; Edw. 315; Eliz. 315\*; Geo. 141, 315\*; Han. 315; Hum. 315; John 315; Rob. 315; Sam. 315; Tho. 315\*; Wm. 315\*.
Bickham, Tho. 282.
Bigg(e), Agn. 30, 64\*; Alice 321\*, 351; Anne 321; Edm. 315; Edw. 184, 321, 352; Eliz. 30\*, 35, 42, 315\*, 321, 340; Ellin 30; Fras. 155, 252\*; Geo. 30, 229; Grace 282; Joan 257; John 30, 197, 257, 315, 340, 352\*, 354; Mary 209, 315; 321; Phil. 321; Tho. 64, 136, 137; Wm. 31, 35, 209, 267, 315\*.
Bigg(e)s, Elixander 112; Joan 121; John 112; Margt. 115; Mary 121, 159; Tho. 159.
Bigland, Tho. 201.

Bigott, Mary 8.
Bigrave (Bygrave), Edw. 170; Kath. 179; Tho. 353.
Bilby (Bilbie), Eliz. 112\*; John 112\*, 113; Margt. 113; Tho. 43, 112, 113.
Billing (Bilin), John 47, 48; Sus. 48\*.
Bilson, Anne 5.
Bing, John 334.
Bingham, Tho. 330.
Binns (Bins, Bynns), Arth. 112; Eliz. 163; Ric. 160, 161\*, 165; Wm. 160. *See Bennes.*
Binsted, John 276.
Birbuge, Agn. 33; Rob. 33.
Birch(e), Eliz. 361\*; Jas. 178; John 137, 361\*, 362, 363; Martha 361; Mary 137; Ric. 75; Tho. 178, 276; Wm. 8.
Birchemore (Byrchemore), Alice 79; Eliz. 6; Ellen 236; John 236; Ric. 24, 79, 122, 170, 222; Tho. 44, 373; Walt. 79, 222; Wm. 44, 154, 255.
Birde (Byrde), —— 378; Alice 37; Edw. 99; Eliz. 43; Geo. 37; Grace 37; Isab. 11, 104; John 37\*, 155, 229\*, 343; Josias 106; Margt. 8; Mary 5; Ric. 178, 352, 367; Rob. 98; Sus. 37; Tho. 380\*; Wm. 37\*, 99.
Birket, Geo. 303; Mabel 303.
Birle, Tho. 278.
Birles, Joan 37; Nich. 37.
Birt, Eliz. 51.
Birtbye, Alveraie 2\*.
Bishop (Bys(c)hop(p)), Anne 228, 254; Hen. 190, 232; John 92, 192; Margt. 156, 228\*; Mat. 160; Tho. 254, 283; Wm. 156, 228.
Bisset, Wm. 247\*.
Black. *See Blake.*
Blackden, Temp. 361.
Blackett, Hen. 312; Joan 312; John 312\*.
Blackhead (Blacheade), John 228, 340; Wm. 228.
Blacknell, Mary 228.
Blackwell (Blackhall), John 348; Phil. 348; Rob 135; Wm. 352.
Blakborne, Alice 352.
Blake (Black, Bloke), John 94, 275, 352\*; Tho. 275; Wm. 275.
Blaked, Ric. 112.
Blaker, Dor. 95; Margt. 371.
Blaket, Tho. 27.
Blakwen, John 28.
Bland, Edw. 362; Sar. 362.
Blank(e), John 269, 347; Wm. 324, 325.
Blanland, Edw. 309.
Bledlow, John 189.
Bletso, Fras. 213.
Blindell (Blindle), Eliz. 94; Wm. 94.
Blitheman (Blythman), Eliz. 334; Judith 138; Mat. 140; Wm. 220.
Blithewyn (Blethewen), Elias (Helion) 268, 269, 322, 323, 326.

Blocke, Ric. 229 ; Tho. 132.
Blofeild, Giles 123*.
Blood, Sar. 330.
Blossom(e) (Blossam), Ric. 278 ; Tho. 81, 340 ; Wm. 278.
Blounte, Ric. 79.
Blow(e), Joan 158, 223 ; John 158, 223 ; Ric. 158 ; Rob. 353 ; Sim. 353 ; Tho. 158 ; Wm. 158*, 353.
Blow(e)s (Blowse), Alice 227 ; Tho. 227* ; Wm. 284 ; Zach. 382*.
Blundell, Alice 237 ; John 237 ; Wm. 237.
Blunt, John 158.
Blysedale, Ric. 221.
Blythe, Fras. 220 ; Geo. 220 ; John 332.
Bocher, John 191, 232 ; Tho. 350.
Bockett, Ellen 93 ; Ric. 314 ; Wm. 209.
Boddington, Ric. 288 ; Wm. 288.
Boddy, Jas. 182*.
Boddymaid, Mary 329.
Bodger, John 162.
Bodwell alias Boydell, Geo. 257 ; Tho. 257.
Bogitt, Edw. 276.
Boker, John 148.
Bokete (Bokket), Alice 351 ; Hen. 351 ; Wm. 351*.
Bole, Dion. 269 ; Hen. 75, 101 ; Joan 172, 220 ; John 172, 220.
Bolington, Joan 326.
Bollamy, Kath. 220 ; Tho. 220.
Bolle, Joan 217* ; John 217*.
Bolom, Adam 233.
Bolton (Boulton, Bowlton, Boulten, Bulton), Jas. 216*, 302, 305*, 320 ; John 166 ; Lucy 284 ; Margt. 305 ; Ric. 284 ; Rob. 278.
Boltwelle, Joan 44 ; Saunder 348.
Bonam, Wm. 37.
Bond(e), Alice 231 ; John 216, 273 ; Margt. 216 ; Tho. 375 ; Wm. 278.
Boneste, Wm. 340.
Bonne, Wm. 190.
Bonner, Agn. 65 ; Ric. 263.
Bonnycke, John 256.
Bonoe, Sus. 154.
Boole, Joan 218 ; John 218.
Boone, Tho. 197.
Boorder, John 113, 115* ; Mary 113*, 115.
Boore, Serj. 72.
Boorks, Wm. 240.
Boorne (Borne), John 29, 75.
Boothe (Bouth, Bothe), Joan 176 ; John 149 ; Rob. 11, 351 ; Wm. 176.
Boram, Rob. 176.
Boruston, —— 350 ; Hum. 350 ; Margt. 217.
Bordal(e), Tho. 91, 236.
Border (Bordor), Agn. 165 ; Benj. 159, 160 ; Ralph 161 ; Tho. 159, 160, 161 ; Wm. 165.
Bordolf, Edm. 28. See Bardolf.
Bore, Tho. 277.

Bor(e)ham, Abm. 103 ; Anne 103* ; Joan 303, 342 ; John 103 ; Rob. 103*, 318 ; Tho. 303, 342 ; Wm. 103.
Borlee, John 266.
Borne, Alice 80 ; Wm. 80.
Boron, Paul 228, 229 ; Peter 228, 229.
Borough, John 155.
Borraston, Alice 340 ; Tho. 340.
Bosgrave, Jane 130 ; John 130.
Bostocke, Rob. 352 ; Wm. 6.
Boswell (Bosewell), Hen. 8 ; John 290 ; Rob. 347 ; Tho. 290.
Botelson, Rob. 353.
Botervylde, Tho. 46.
Botild, John 267*.
Botler (Boteler), John 46 ; Nich. 46 ; Ric. 269, 270 ; Rob. 189*, 232.
Botman, Agn. 321.
Botterell, —— 320 ; Hen. 68, 320.
Bottomley (Bottamlye), Christr. 201, 205 ; Kath. 79 ; Margt. 201 ; Wm. 79.
Boughton, Edw. 184 ; John 275, 367.
Boultwood, Rog. 381.
Bound, Tho. 276.
Bounty, Wm. 52.
Boure, John 148*, 193*.
Bournham, Eliz. 137 ; Ric. 137.
Bovilen (Bowden), Eliz. 47, 48 ; John 47 ; Peter 47 ; Sus. 47, 48.
Bovyngdon (Boveingdon), Kath. 132 ; Jonas 282 ; Ric. 132.
Bowdon, Ric. 284. See Bovden.
Bower (Bowre), Jeff 65 ; Mildred 337 ; Nich. 256, 337 ; Wm. 46, 47.
Bowes, Edw. 317 ; Martin 125, 126, 128.
Bowghe, Hen. 220 ; Philippa 220.
Bowghton, Edw. 132.
Bowles(se), —— 158 ; Eliz. 184, 357 ; Sar. 209 ; Tho. 81.
Bowlnest, Bernard 210.
Bowman, Hen. 177 ; Hugh 121 ; Joan 358* ; John 62 ; Maryan 198 ; Mr 216, 229.
Bownes, Margt. 40 ; Tho. 40.
Bownest, Tho. 82 ; Wm. 319, 320.
Bowstred (Boustred, Boustrid), —— 211 ; Dion. 211 ; John 291*, 293*, 294, 295* ; Sar. 287 ; Wm. 294, 295*.
Bowtell, Israell 204.
Bowyer (Bowier), —— 279 ; Beat. 308 ; Joan 323 ; John 306*, 307, 308, 341, 345 ; Tho. 303, 308, 323*, 325.
Boxer, Tho. 107.
Boxsted, Agn. 82 ; Grace 10 ; John 10*, 82.
Boydell. See Bodwell.
Boydon, Rob. 31.
Boyere, John 277.
Boyfeild, Christr. 44.
Boyle, Ric. 205.
Boyse, John 356
Brabebon, Hen. 45 ; Margt. 45.
Brace, Ellen 153 ; Hen. 353 ; John 353 ; Tho. 353.

Bradbury (Bradberye), Anne 5; Dor. 219; Jas. 168, 169, 288; Ric. 88; Tho. 219; Wm. 219.
Bradcrofte, John 46.
Bradford, Tho. 89.
Bradhurste, Ric. 204; Rob. 204
Bradley (Bradelye), Edw. 150, 299; John 276; Margery 199; Margt. 302; Mat. 285, 286, 287, 331; Nic. 351; Rob. 91, 302, 331; Wm. 199*.
Bradshaw(e), Agn. 217; Anne 242; Eliz. 137; John 242*.
Bradwell, Joan 211; Judith 211; Wm. 211.
Bradwin (Bradwyn, Braden), Anne 314; Hen. 8; Nic. 283; Rob. 159; Tho. 28; Wm. 136, 283, 330.
Bradwin *alias* Evans, John 239; Nic. 239.
Bragg, Joan 142; Tho. 52, 142.
Brakenfeld (Brekenfyld), John 80, 198, 304; June 199, 200.
Bramfield, Jas. 227.
Bramley, Dor. 158.
Brampfelld, —— 320.
Branch (Braunche), Edw. 288; Gilb. 119; Jas. 166; Joan 39; John 166; Kath. 119; Tho. 119*, 349; Wm. 12, 207, 273.
Branckley, Joan 337; Mich. 337.
Brand(e), Andr. 180; Constance 217; Mr 68; Rob. 260*; Sus. 212; Tho. 86, 179, 217; Wm. 8.
Branfelde, Mary 215.
Brangwen, Ric. 202; Rob. 202.
Brangwell, John 347.
Braunangr (Brauvangr, Braumange, Brannanttr), John 46, 91, 190, 192*.
Brawne, Wm. 274.
Bray(e), Edw. 35; Ellyn 352; Jud. 288; Margt. 352; Mary 35; Mildred 288; Raynold 366; Tho. 27, 288.
Breame, Arthur 218*.
Bredcroft, Rob. 232.
Bredgil Wm. 274.
Brennynge, Alice 308; John 308.
Breton, Elenor 45; Rob. 326, 327*; Rowl. 45.
Brett, Giles 37, 38; Hen. 273; Joan 37, 345; John 180, 222, 273; Nic. 345; Rob. 179; Tho. 222, 254, 277; Wm. 222, 254.
Brettand, Ann 83.
Brewer(e), John 46, 278; Mary 8; Roger 166.
Brewster, Mary 330.
Breykspeyr (Brekesper), Margt. 46, 47; Tho. 46.
Brian. *See Bryan.*
Briars (Brior), Andr. 244; Mary 244, 246; Rob. 244, 246; Wm. 246.
Brice, Rob. 3.
Brickland, Luke 246*; Martha 246.
Briddon, Mary 281; Tho. 281.
Bridgeman (Bredgman), Agn. 38, 311; Dor. 311; Edm. 75; Eliz. 311; Joan 320; John 75; Margt. 311; Wid. 72.
Bridges, Edw. 34; Frances 34.
Brigges (Briges, Brygges), Agn. 39*, 312; Alice 39; Anne 216; Arthur 216; Chas. 216; Joan 216; Margt. 216*; Roger 39; Tho. 43, 312, 369; Wm. 32, 73, 216*, 312*, 319.
Brigginshaw, Hen. 166.
Brigham, Auth. 258.
Brighowse, Edw. 338.
Bright (Bryght), John 232; Wm. 51.
Brightwell, Ric. 73.
Brikenar, Tho. 275.
Brimpton, John 282.
Brinkley, John 331, 373*.
Briscoe (Brysco, Briskoo), Alice 199; Edw. 122, 203, 342; Isab. 77; John 77, 80, 122, 343; Phil. 202, 203; Ralph 186; Rob. 200, 202; Tho. 77*, 228*.
Bristow(e) (Brystow, Bristoo, Bryston), Edw. 28, 350; Master 314; Nic. 130, 134; Rob. 313; Wm. 71*.
Brittaine, Anne 380.
Britte *alias* Webbe, Ric. 146.
Broadley, John 137.
Broadway (Bradway), Andr. 163; Mary 163*, 165.
Brocas, Bernard 218.
Brock(e), Barth. 87; Geo. 104; Joan 87; John 87*, 286, 331; Mich. 87; Ralph 87; Rob. 87; Tho. 168, 170; Wm. 104*.
Brockbanke, Wm. 254.
Brockett (Brokett, Brockitt), Edm. 151; Edw. 82, 132, 218, 272, 341, 342; Eliz. 339, 342; Ellen 33, 82, 257; Etheldreda 132, 218; Frances 151; Joan 342; John 26, 33, 43, 82*, 88, 122, 217, 219, 220, 222, 253, 257, 272, 309, 315, 338, 339*, 341, 344; Julian 309, 341; Kath. 82; Nich. 30, 132, 222, 342; Wm. 81, 82, 344.
Brode, John 46.
Brograve, Chas. 340; John 257, 308, 340*, 341, 344; Mr 11; Margt. 257, 308; Sim. 340.
Broke. *See Brooke.*
Brokeman, Agn. 305; Ric. 258, 305.
Brokk(e), Adam 352; Christr. 352.
Brokkes, John 351.
Bromhall, St John 262.
Bromley(e), Geo. 173, 218; John 46; Ric. 276; Tho. 173, 220.
Brond, Alice 273; John 273.
Brooke (Broke), Agn. 278; Alice 307; Barth. 278, Joan 201, 219; John 44, 216, 219, 253, 275, 278, 316, 351; Kath. 278; Margt. 253; Mother 38; Ralph 278; Ric. 273, 276, 278, 302, 305, 307, 352; Rob. 132, 273; Tho. 147*, 342; Wm. 2, 278*, 307, 308, 337.
Brookes, —— 374; Sus. 374.
Brotherton, Wm. 222.

Broude, Tho. 23, 319.
Broughton, Agn. 150; Jas. 275; Ric. 150.
Broughyng, Ric. 369.
Brouks, Martha 5.
Brouton, Anne 115.
Broweman, Mr 33, 97.
Brown(e) (Broune), Agn. 230; Alice 192, 338; Anne 103, 202, 240; Annis 74; Anth. 174; Bridget 168; Christr. 6; Clem. 203; Dan. 289; Dennis 295, 296; Dion. 39, 77; Edw. 5, 215, 274, 277; Eliz. 63, 77; Geo. 103*, 156*, 327, 377; Hannah 291; Hen. 5, 275; James 317, 348; Jane 120; Joan 62, 292, 293; John 62, 63, 120, 134, 238, 272, 276, 333, 344, 345, 382; Julian 45; Kath. 170; Laur. 39, 40; Martha 83; Mary 83, 103, 149, 203, 290*, 296*; Mother 313; Nic. 275*, 347; Ralph 341; Rhode 291; Ric. 62, 230, 275*; Rob. 168, 173, 177, 210, 346; Rog. 338; Sim. 29*, 294*, 295, 314*; Tho. 40, 51, 103*, 120, 136, 143, 276, 289, 290*, 291, 292, 293; Thomasine 177, 179; Val. 177, 179, 220; Wm. 10, 39, 69, 75, 103, 119, 130, 156, 157, 275, 276; Wistan 78, 178.
Brownes, Tho. 273.
Bruce. *See Berkley.*
Brudenell, Edm. 342.
Bruer, Griffin 42.
Brumbrogh, John 126.
Brumley, Ellen 343; Geo. 343.
Bruster, Annis 228; Edw. 228; Fras. 228; Joan 228; John 228*; Ralph 228; Tho. 228; Wm. 228*.
Bruton, Edw. 281; Geo. 142; Sar. 281.
Bryan (Bryon, Brian), —— 152; Helen 345; Margery 45; Nic. 345; Rob. 202, 205; Sus. 152; Tho. 202; Wm. 115, 350.
Bryckett, Tho. 174.
Brydon, Rob. 31.
Brygham, Tho. 173.
Bryriehurst, John 243.
Brystoo. *See Bristow.*
Brythe, John 350.
Brytnell, Annis 74; Edw. 74; Eliz. 74; Jessper 74; Joan 74; Mary 74; Ric. 34, 74; Rob. 74; Tho. 74.
Bryton, Rob. 91, 237.
Bryttelbanke, Ric. 278.
Bryttyn, Edm. 202; Sus. 202.
Bu . . ., John 28.
Buckberd, John 341; Ric. 350; Walt. 341.
Bucke, Eliz. 313; Geo. 86; John 86; Margt. 86, 120; Prud. 43; Sus. 86; Tho. 86.
Buckell (Buckle), Ann 247; Cuthb. 174; Hum. 247; John 297; Sar. 247.
Bucket, Hen. 348.

Buckhouse, Annis 229; Anth. 229; Luce 229.
Buckingham, Adam 288, 289; Han. 292; John 374; Margt. 353; Martha 330; Nath. 374; Rog. 291; Tho. 289, 292*.
Buckmaster (Buckmister), Agn. 151; Eliz. 373; John 156, 258, 340; Ralph 353; Ric. 258; Wm. 72*.
Bucknall, Wm. 50.
Buclond, Roger 275.
Budd, John 182; Wheeler 281.
Budden, Jone 314.
Budder, John 145*, 147*, 195, 196*; Tho. 145; Wm. 145*, 147*, 196*.
Bugberd, Eliz. 340; Roger 340; Wm. 201.
Bugges, Edw. 340, 341.
Buggyn, Edw. 337.
Buke, Rob. 273.
Bukney, John 23.
Bulfame, Tho. 277.
Bull(e), Agn. 157, 255; Alice 157, 302; Christr. 255, 302; Edw. 157; Eliz. 63; Geo. 39; Hen. 26, 157; Hew 157; Jas. 378; John 377, 378*, 380*; Ric. 157, 256, 275, 276, 302; Rob. 119; Tho. 371.
Bullock(e) (Bullok), Abig. 235; Christr. 235; John 276; Kath. 235; Mary 255, 303*; Mistris 235; Ralph 76, 158, 255, 303*; Rob. 235.
Bullyn, Ellen 32; Hen. 32*; Sim. 32, 72; Tho. 32*.
Bulmer, Tho. 94.
Bumsteade (Bumstedd, Bumpsted), —— 11, 63; Alice 63; Eliz. 131; Hen. 63; Joan 63; John 9, 11; Kath. 63; Tho. 11, 39, 131, 257; Wm. 63.
Bunby, John 93; Mary 5; Tho. 167.
Bunchleye, John 228*.
Bunne (Bun), Alice 143; Benj. 136; Joan 290; John 30, 182*, 243, 290*, 292, 295, 348; Ric. 351; Rob. 295; Tho. 182*, 295; Wm. 143, 255, 292, 303.
Bunnion (Bynyon), Isaac 162, 164; Margt. 162; Sar. 162.
Bunyan, Edw. 7.
Burbecke, Fras. 342.
Burch, Fras. 113, 160; Jane 163; Tho. 182.
Burchat, Lawr. 273.
Burchier & Lovayne. *See Essex & Ewe.*
Burdall, Wm. 222.
Burd(e), Edw. 51; Wm. 4, 51.
Burden, Geo. 29.
Burder, Tho. 112.
Burdit, Agn. 155; Cicely 155; John 155; Margt. 155.
Burdon, Cath. 239.
Burford, Christr. 348; Matilda 233; Ric. 353; Tho. 259.
Burgaine, Jone 361. *See Burgin.*
Burgall, Sam 48.

Burgess (Burges, Burgeys), Agn. 236;
Christian 244; Eliz. 244, 245, 310*;
Jas. 244; John 310, 351; Margt.
244; Mary 310; T. 100; Tho.
236; Walt. 236; Wm. 231, 265.
Burgh, Kath. 218; Lord Wm. 218.
Burghley, Baron of. *See Cecill.*
Burgin (Burgen, Burgaine), Anne
113, 115, 116; Frances 115; Fras.
113, 115*; Ric. 115; Tho. 11, 104:
Widow 116.
Burgoyne (Burgoine), Dor. 222, 302:
Frances 149; Geo. 78, 131, 222*,
302; Godf. 78; Rob. 186.
Burgun, John 45; Mary 45.
Burle, Alice 120.
Burley, Wm. 148, 193*.
Burlinge, Grace 309; Tho. 309.
Burman, Tho. 302, 345.
Burnap(p) (Burnoppe), John 70, 100*,
274; Tho. 274, 344.
Burr(e), Edw. 291, 370; Han. 290;
John 353; Jos. 169, 170; Margt.
181; Mary 291, 294; Rob. 74,
314*; Ruth 292; Sam 291; Sar.
96; Steph. 290, 291, 292, 294*;
Wm. 32, 68*, 70, 331.
Burrage, John 209.
Burrall, Hugh 375.
Burrell Geo. 35, 36.
Burrus, Hannah 244; Jas. 244; Wm.
244.
Bur(r)yge, Agn. 202; Rob. 200; Tho.
201.
Burt(e), Anne Phillis 114; Dan. 142;
Edm. 113, 114; Edw. 162; Ellen
114.
Burton, Alice 32, 222; Anys 193;
Cath. 42; Edm. 145, 146, 147;
Joan 318*; John 92, 137, 138*,
166, 167, 194, 318; Margt. 318;
Mary 141; Ric. 63, 318; Tho. 35,
222, 318; Thomasine 35; Wm. 5,
235, 331. *See Saunders.*
Burtweesle, Symon 143.
Burwell, Esther 290; John 289*, 290,
292, 293*; Mary 289; Rob. 352;
Rog. 352; Sam. 293*.
Bury (Burie), Edw. 87; Hasild 344;
John 104; Margt. 344.
Busawe, Gilb. 47.
Busbie, John 65.
Bush(e) (Busshe), Agn. 175; Alice
158*, 227; Edw. 4, 51; Hum 158;
John 266, 270, 271, 322; Mr 157;
Nic. 175; Ric. 227; Tho. 157, 227;
Wm. 138, 332.
Bushewe, John 180.
Busser, John 287.
Busshey (Boushey), Const. 40; Geo.
40; Hen. 40; Joan 40; Rob. 40*;
Sim. 40; Wm. 40*.
Bussie, John 355*, 356*; Mary 356.
Butell, Wm. 351.
Buthered, John 203; Rog. 203.
Butler (Buttler, Bootler), Alice 98,
130, 173; Const. 65; Fras. 138;
Geo. 260*, 261*; Grisol 220; Hellen
65; Hen. 130, 173, 220, 258; John
48, 64, 176, 273; Lord 183*; Phil.
75, 176, 219, 220; Ric. 216, 228,
340, 379; Tho. 98; Wm. 29, 181,
263. *See Grays.*
Butt, Cath. 151; Eliz. 151.
Butterfeild, Jane 42; Joan 313; John
42, 313*, 349; Kath. 256; Margt.
349; Mary 313; Ric. 76, 349; Sib.
349; Tho. 172, 256, 349; Wm. 313.
Buxton, Hum. 273; Rob. 102.
Bycton, Tho. 200.
Byggins, Tho. 227.
Bygmore, John 350.
Bylfyld, Alice 120; Rog. 120; Wm.
120.
Byll, Andr. 133; Eliz. 133.
Byllay, Dodman 275.
Byllingham, Isab. 134; John 134;
Wm. 274.
Bynckes, John 29.
Byng, John 347.
Byrcheley (Birchley, Brycheley), John
34, 80, 131, 178*, 253, 339; Kath.
77; Philippa 34, 80, 131, 178*,
253; Ric. 347; Rog. 77, 80, 178,
253, 313; Tho. 339; Wm. 180.
Byrlee, Ric. 278.
Byse, John 275.
Byworthe, Agn. 218; Ric. 218.


Cade, Hen. 77; John 82, 131, 203;
Sus. 203.
Cadwell, Ralph 131.
Cæsar, Chas. 336; Sir Chas. 108*,
109, 241, 336; Hen. 336; Jacomina
241; Jane 336; Julius 336.
Cage (Caige), Anth. 34, 255; John
344*; Rob. 35.
Caine, Hen. 371.
Caladye (Calyday), Matt. 277; Ric.
319.
Calamoche, Giles 237.
Calcott, Rob. 162, 163.
Caldecote, John 190.
Calf(e), Joan 192; Margt. 192; Tho.
192.
Calfehild, Geo 254.
Calowaye, Alice 126.
Calowe, Adam 191.
Calthorp, Chas. 176.
Calton, Andr. 378*; Hen. 307.
Calvert, Peter 352.
Camfield (Camfyle, Canfield), Anne
135; Edm. 94; Edw. 5, 135; Eliz.
288; John 283, 353; Ric. 170;
Sar. 362; Tho. 30, 288, 289*, 353.
*See Canfield.*
Camoke, Wm. 353.
Campe, Jas. 174; John 276; Wm. 103.
Campion (Campyon), Alice 10; Avis
10; Eliz. 137; Geo. 41; Hen. 346;
John 10, 66, 227; Lionel 41; Mary
213; Sam. 83; Sar. 330; Wm. 10,
79, 81.

INDEX

Campkin, Tho. 212.
Camvyle, John 195, 196.
Canfield, Dor. 363; Jacob 290*; Jer. 293; John 138, 140, 294, 370; Mary 140; Rob. 322; Tho. 290*, 293, 294, 374. *See Camfeild.*
Can(n)on, Arthur 348; Dor. 221; Edm. 150; Hen. 86, 320; John 49, 50, 81, 221, 276; Mary 49*, 93; Ric. 152; Tho. 49*, 354; Wm. 49.
Cany, John 47.
Capell, Hen. 78.
Caple, Martyn 203.
Capman, Kath. 357; Mary 359; Tho. 355, 357, 359.
Capon, Jane 31; Joan 169; John 31*; Margery 31; Ric. 349; Sar. 93; Wm. 31.
Capper, Lewes 347.
Carde, Edw. 75.
Cardinall, Wm. 237.
Carewe, Alice 35; Roger 35.
Carlell, Alice 200.
Carlet, Rob. 276.
Carleton, Geo. 277.
Carowe, Tho. 308.
Carpenter (Carpentor), Alice 230; Annas 230; Christr. 230; Frances 72; Geo. 88, 169, 230*, 278; Joan 72; Joseph 7, 169, 288; Joshua 96, 137, 167; Mary 7; Rob. 72; Tho. 63, 136, 230*, 338.
Car(r)ing(e)ton, John 157, 296.
Carron, Tho. 277.
Carte, Edw. 212.
Cartelledge (Cartleg), Steph. 35, 217; Wm. 346.
Carter (Cartar, Cartur), —— 348; Abm. 369; Agn. 91, 215; Anne 142, 370; Bridget 222; Edw. 360, 374; Eliz. 91, 235, 308, 360, 362, 363, 370; Hen. 42, 353; James 140, 161, 188; Jane 373; Jer. 283, 373; John 82, 91*, 156*, 213, 243, 273, 287, 308, 367; Jos. 137, 170, 284; Margt. 374; Mary 72, 82, 102, 373; Mat. 155*; Phil. 276; Ralph 38; Ric. 91, 153, 156, 218, 348; Rob. 26, 72, 189; Sar. 8, 374; Sus. 360; Tho. 27, 93*, 142, 156, 310, 347, 362, 363; Widow 32; Wm. 70, 72, 222, 315, 331, 334. *See Nicholson.*
Carter *alias* Ypgrave, Eliz. 87; Geo. 87; John 87; Tho. 87; Wm. 87.
Cary(e) (Carey), Henry, lord 187, 255; John 274; Wymond 80, 82, 132*, 221, 339.
Casell, Hen. 320.
Cash, Henry 243*.
Cason, Edw. 76, 217, 220, 313; Tho. 181.
Cass, John 297.
Casselden, John 137.
Casson, Joan 315.
Cast, John 347.

Castle (Castell), Ann 49; John 49, 278; Mercie 87; Ralph 277, 350; Tho. 276.
Casylman, —— 349.
Cater, Eliz. 200; John 151; Mary 138; Sar. 151; Sus 362; Wm. 6, 205.
Catlin (Cat(te)lyn, Catelyen), Agn. 32; Alice 211; Anne 154; Edw. 218; Eliz. 174, 227; Frances 227; Fras. 93; Grace 32; John 32, 174; Ric. 227; Rob. 88, 89, 185*, 348; Tho. 30, 96, 174, 210, 352, 371; Wm. 32*, 154, 210, 352.
Caton, Wm. 332.
Cauche, Joan 192; John 91, 192*. *See Caunche.*
Cauldon, Wm. 84.
Caulton, Margt. 36; Wm. 36.
Caunche (Cauche), John 45*.
Cawdell, John 153; Rob. 312.
Cawley, John 132.
Caynhoo, John 155.
Cecill (Cecyll), Wm. 34, 36, 77*, 82, 130, 133*, 174, 185, 221, 258.
Celye, John 74, 312.
Chaddisley (Chadysleye), Ric. 81; Tho. 321.
Chaire (Chayre, Chaier), Alice 40, 216; Anne 40; Eliz. 215; Joan 40; John 40*, 64, 86*, 216* 319; Kath. 40, 216; Leon. 215; Margt. 40, 216; Ric. 39, 40*, 131; Rob. 40*, 215*, 216*; Sus. 40, 216; Tho. 215, 218; Widow 86; Wm. 216.
Chalkhyll, Wm. 28.
Chalkley (Cha(u)kley, Chawkley), —— 141; Abm. 167; Agn. 29, 153; Anne 152, 209; Dor. 149; Ellin 29; Han. 143; Hen. 8, 169, 209; Joan 153; John 235, 290*, 291, 334; Kath. 29; Mary 8, 13, 291; Ric. 290, 314; Rob. 7; Sar. 136; Tho. 29*, 136, 149, 309; Wm. 5, 29, 96, 131, 152, 353.
Challis (Challas, Chalice), Ellen 9; Fras. 64; John 86; Wm. 119.
Chamber (Chambour, Chaumbre), Alice 153; Edw. 302; Eliz. 32, 221; John 266, 308; Mich. 178; Nic. 266*; Ric. 221, 276; Wm. 75, 230, 233, 308. *See Halsey.*
Chamberlaine (Chamberleyne), Anne 96; Dor. 220; Eliz. 332; Fitzralph 220; Fras. 216; John 277, 285; Rob. 216, 290; Sar. 290; Tho. 216, 273, 316; Walt. 216; Wm. 216.
Chambers, Agn. 154; Grace 143; Jer. 362; Joan 131; John 287; Jos. 287; Martha 356; Mary 2*; Ralph 2; Rob. 153; Sar. 41; Wm. 2*, 335, 338.
Chambers *alias* Halsey, Anne 92, 94; Edw. 92.
Champneis, John 297.
Chanbroke, Oliver 229.

Chandler (Cha(u)ndelour), Ambr. 109; Anth. 214; Edw. 357; Eliz. 140, 170; Giles 12; Joan 77, 81; John 11, 104*; Kath. 379; Leon. 131; Mary 167, 214; Rob. 77; Tho. 81, 277*, 377; Tobias 377, 378*, 379; Wm. 206.

Chapman, Agn. 39; Alice 135, 380; Anne 39; Brian 135; Cornelius 376; Dan. 102; Edm. 39; Fras. 67, 68; Gilb. 47; Helen 209; Hen. 121, 151; Joan 2, 92, 318; John 39*, 96, 108*, 155, 249, 250, 324, 325, 326, 340*, 354; Margery 347; Mary 302; Mich. 155; Nich. 302; Ric. 39, 351; Rob. 274, 340; Tho. 2*, 30, 76; Titus 86; Wm. 87, 302, 338. *See Bemores.*

Chappel(l) (Chapple), Angell 156; Eliz. 42, 83, 213, 356; Fras. 8, 93; Geo. 369; Grace 361; Han. 83*; John 73; Margt. 354, 357; Mary 140; Sam. 285; Tho. 42, 184, 227, 351; Widow 357; Wm. 92, 210, 230, 349.

Chappell *alias* Baylye, Steph. 261.

Charit(i)e, Hen. 339; Jas. 367; Mary 339.

Charvell, Tho. 274.

Charyat, Eliz. 273.

Chatburne, Wm. 32, 158*, 313.

Chauncy (Chawncye, Chawc(e)ye), Alex. 85*, 132, 302; Bridget 85*; Chas. 50; Eliz. 35, 77, 132; Geo. 85, 340, 341; Hen. 35, 50, 80, 177*, 178, 220, 253, 255, 341; Jane 177*, 178, 220, 253, 255; Joan 274; John 35, 77, 132, 275; Mary 85, 302; Philippa 178; Rob. 178; Rose 80; Wm. 38*, 85, 178.

Chauntrell, John 119.

Chawney, Tho. 347.

Chaworth, John 137.

Cheek, Thos. 111.

Cheltam, Richard 347.

Chepperfild. Agn. 276.

Cherry (Cherye, Cherie), John 342; Kath. 342; Ric. 69, 276; Rob. 350; Tho. 345.

Chester, Magd. 343.

Chestre, Wm. 24.

Chetam, Walt. 373.

Chettolls, Isaac 12.

Chetwood, Rich. 375.

Chetwynde, Attalanta 309; Wm. 309.

Chovelye (Cheevelye), John 204; Tho. 199, 204; Widow 205.

Cheworth, Jas. 330; John 330.

Cheyney(e) (Cheyne, Cheanie), —— 248*, 271; Agn. 66; Frances 43; Fras. 76; Geo. 66*, 324; Hen. 44, 220, 303; Jane 220; Joan 274; John 66*, 76, 277; Mr 22; Peter 195*; Rob. 43, 44; Tho. 44; Wm. 66, 378. *See Persmythe, Webbe.*

Child(e) (Chyld), Agn. 10; Bennet 10; Edw. 214; Eliz. 136; Hen. 10*, 257; Joan 314; John 24, 26*, 73, 143; Tho. 210.

Childer, Anne 154; Eliz. 154.

Childersbee, Anne 243; John 243; Tho. 243.

Childmere, Andr. 191; Emma 191; Joan 191; Rose 191; Tho. 191.

Childs, Richard 332.

Chilterton, Alice 29; Wm. 29*.

Chilton (Chiltron), Bernard 329; John 329.

Chipp, Margery 154; Wm. 154.

Chirchesey, Tho. 323.

Chirrye, John 307; Margt. 307.

Chopping(e), Bathia 374; Ellen 330; Wm. 330, 374.

Chowne, Eliz. 33; Nic. 33.

Chownes (Chowneing), John 331* 332.

Chreesey, Tho. 33*.

Christian, John 230*; Tho. 32.

Christie, Nich. 75.

Christmas, Wm. 167, 170, 331.

Chudsdon, Frances 169.

Church(e), Agn. 38; Geo. 382; John 135, 276*; Tho. 276.

Churchix, Geo. 318.

Chykken, Joan 318; Margt. 318; Ric. 318*; Tho. 318; Wm. 318*.

Chylderbye, Tho. 199.

Chyvall, Wm. 36.

Clackesonne. *See Claxton.*

Clapham, Cecily 309; Dor. 103*, 256; John 256; Martha 103; Rich. 309.

Clare, Reg. 237; Wm. 275.

Clark(e) (Cler(c)ke), —— 142; Agn. 142, 192*, 256; Alice 39, 86, 133, 324, 341; Anis 161; Anne 12, 95, 329, 344; Beat. 217, 219; Christr. 86, 320; Edm. 164; Edw. 1, 29, 256, 329, 339; Eliz. 215, 244, 246, 247, 356, 361, 376; Eman. 8, 360; Fortescu 309; Geo. 42, 63, 87, 131, 206, 315; Grace 372; Han. 164; Hen. 278, 338*, 344; James 182, 342; Jasper 244, 247; Joan 2, 39; John 3, 29*, 30, 33*, 45, 65, 67, 97, 104, 122*, 133, 152, 160, 165, 169, 170, 172, 176, 182, 188*, 207, 218, 235, 237, 244, 245, 246*, 247, 261, 271, 306, 324, 325*, 331, 335, 338, 339, 340, 341*, 344, 351*; Justina 46; Kath. 176; Margt. 45, 315; Martin 333; Mary 39, 48, 84, 136, 288, 375; Mr 67; Nich. 100*, 142, 192*; Petronilla 192; Phil. 256; Ralph 277; Ric. 182*, 209, 218, 220, 342, 349, 362; Rob. 33, 97, 342, 353; Roger 27; Sar. 360; Tho. 1, 29, 39*, 75, 86, 182, 217, 219, 311, 320, 321, 351, 356; Walt. 46, 104, 232; Wm. 4, 29, 30, 33*, 34, 39, 64, 78, 82, 97*, 151, 173, 232, 267, 275, 303, 311, 315, 334, 339, 352, 357, 360, 365, 371, 372. *See Smythe, Haris.*

Clarke *alias* Deane, Jane 43.

Claxton (Claxstone, Clax(s)on(ne), Clackeson), Ann 48; Fras. 48; John 170; Margt. 36, 220, 338; Mary 84; Ralph 95, 338; Tho. 36, 85, 220, 321, 338; Wm. 84.
Claye, Christr. 304; Edm. 315; Eliz. 11, 304; Joan 179, 211; Mary 211; Rand. 11.
Clayton, Sar. 383.
Cleare, John 337.
Cleaver (Clever), Mark 114; Sam. 329.
Cleiton(ns), Nich. 156, 313.
Clement, John 347.
Clements (Clamantes), Alice 295*; David 295*; Wm. 95.
Clench, Mary 282.
Clenton, Kath. 202.
Clere, Anne 81, 222; Edw. 81; Tho. 81, 222; Wm. 37, 97, 319.
Clifford (Clyfforde), Annys 290; Eliz. 288; Lady 28; Ric. 288, 290; Tho. 366, 367.
Clifton (Clyfton), Alice 278; Andr. 34, 277, 327*; Joan 278; John 326, 327*.
Climson, John 110.
Clinton, Eliz. 211; John 152, 211*; Jud. 362; Margt. 153; Rob. 248; Sam. 134; Tho. 372.
Clobbe, Agn. 190; John 190.
Clopton, Felice 237; Hen. 237; John 237, 268, 271*; Rob. 232; Wm. 82*, 130*, 179.
Clotheman, Tho. 189.
Clypsone, John 205.
Coates, Agn. 9*, 341; Rob. 9*, 341.
Cobb(e), Eliz. 42; Isab. 143, 266; Peter 143; Tho. 82*.
Cobem, John 30*.
Cobetts, Edw. 10.
Cobham, Hen. 273.
Cock(e) (Co(c)kes, Cokke, Coockes), Anne 339; Benedict 338; Bennet 156; Dan. 334; Eliz. 120; Geo. 75, 180; Giles 275; Hen. 133, 172, 173, 223, 258, 338; Joan 180; John 31, 44, 75, 86, 106*, 120, 139, 180, 218, 272*, 276, 277, 286*; Margt. 31; Nich. 12; Ralph 75; Ric. 31*, 278; Rob. 31, 154, 209, 277; Sam. 139; Sim. 339; Thos. 44, 149, 160, 161, 174, 214, 275; Tim. 166; Ursula 173; Wm. 31, 40, 75, 133, 156*, 179, 190, 216*, 228, 232, 278, 311, 335.
Cocken, Steph. 230.
Cockens, Kath. 170.
Cocker, Alice 199.
Cockerel(l) (Cokerell), Ann 374; Eliz. 180; Hen. 86; John 257, 273; Rob. 146, 147, 195.
Cockford, Eliz. 84.
Cockinge, Wm. 153.
Cockman, John 283; Mary 283.
Codd, Richard 3*.
Codgell, Agn. 10; Tho. 11*.
Codlyghasyll, 349.
Coe, Wm. 75.

Cogdell (Cogdele, Cogdale), Eliz. 239; John 182, 220, 335, 350; Mary 372; Tho. 350, 352.
Cogger, Joan 254; Tho. 254.
Coghill, John 5.
Coglove, Sar. 285.
Cokdall (Cokdelle), Anne 45; John 45; S. 28.
Coke, Bastian 274; John 145*, 273, 274, 325, 347; Nic. 353; Ralph 274; Rob. 273; Tho. 23, 218.
Coke alias Lee, Tho. 28.
Coker, David 198; Eden 307; Eliz. 340; Tho. 307; Wm. 72, 340.
Colborne, Mary 204.
Colby(e), Tho. 31, 89, 186.
Cole, John 28; Mary 247; Ric. 278; Tho. 247; Zach. 334.
Coleman (Co(l)man), Alice 138, 270, 328, 351; Jer. 139, 168; Mary 141; Nic. 268, 270*, 325*; Rob. 311*; Wm. 73, 138, 182.
Coles, Anne 94; Hen. 275; Jos. 239; Rob. 138.
Colet, Dean 366.
Colfeyld, Anth. 353. See Tokefield.
Coll(e), Isab. 91; Jone 198.
Colles, —— 207; Wm. 38.
Collett, Geo. 138.
Collins (Colines, Colyns), Ellen 287, 341; Hen. 373; Jas. 346; John 142, 351; Margt. 65; Ralph 370; Ric. 65, 347; Wm. 239, 341.
Collopp(e), Christr. 66*; John 64; Ric. 275.
Colly, Hum. 77, 221; Ric. 256.
Collyer (Collier, Colyer), Alice 243; Edw. 277; Frances 85; Joan 202; John 202; Sar. 48.
Collyn (Colyn), Eliz. 302; John 268, 269, 271, 302, 322; Nic. 302; Rob. 302; Wm. 82, 351,
Collyngwood, John 277.
Colston, Alice 222; Gab. 222.
Colsyll, Rob. 350.
Colt(e), Edw. 9, 62, 66; Eyon 10; John 177; Kath. 63; Mary 172, 178; Rob. 78; Rog. 78, 79, 172, 177, 178; Tho. 342.
Coltman, Andr. 10.
Colwell, John 191; Tho. 191.
Colyns, John 27.
Colynson, John 349.
Combes, Ric. 27, 347.
Comodall, John 221.
Compton, Nich. 120.
Conaway, Freeman 200.
Conningford, John 72.
Conny (Cony, Coney), Eliz. 358; Emm. 361; Geo. 361; John 357*, 358, 361, 362, 363; Mary 355, 359, 361, 362; Ric. 47, 90; Sus. 357, 358, 361; Wm. 105*, 355*, 356, 357, 359, 361*, 362*.
Connyes, John 254.
Connyngesby(e) (Conygesbye, Connisbye), Eliz. 80, 222; Hen. 79*, 80,

122, 222; Hum. 23, 24, 35, 78, 80, 130*, 133, 173, 176, 234, 303, 304, 337, 338, 344; John 26, 28, 272; Mary 35, 78, 130*, 133, 173, 176, 303, 304 337, 338, 344; Tho. 82, 131; Wm. 279, 280, 314.
Connyngton, Anne 303; Paul 303.
Conyers, John 174.
Coo(e), John 76, 218; Kath. 218; Tho. 109.
Cook(e), Agn. 40, 320; Anth. 174*; Cath. 41; Edm. 75; Edw. 2; Eliz. 50*, 121; Geo. 9, 106; Hen. 47, 121*, 218, 320; Hugh 253; Joan 30; John 2, 38*, 93, 121*, 269*, 270, 271, 274, 324; Margt. 121, 320; Martha 137; Mary 121, 168, 321; Mat. 218; Mr 315; Peter 245, 282; Phil. 3; Ric. 31, 174, 228; Rob. 31, 121*, 274, 320; Sar. 320; Tho. 23, 30, 31, 121*, 274, 275, 285, 320*; Walt. 167; Wm. 9*, 66, 121*, 126, 174, 320*. *See Dabenys, Foster, Alea.*
Cooles, John 112; Symon 310; Wm. 112.
Cooley, —— 207; Tho. 206.
Cooper, —— 65; Anne 244; Aug. 79, 81; Alice 130, 371; Chas. 244; Edm. 156; Eliz. 198, 229, 245; Hum. 244; Joan 214; John 32, 72, 123, 137, 204, 214, 286, 314; Lewes 230; Mary 246; Ric. 229, 246; Rob. 228, 229, 279*; Sar. 150, 294; Sim. 206; Sus. 246; Tho. 371; Wm. 130*, 204, 227, 230, 286, 294. *See Godfrey.*
Cooper *alias* Godfrey, Wm. 293.
Copcot(t), Beat. 307; Cecily 173, 217, 338, 343; John 2; Ralph 307; Tho. 173, 217, 338, 343.
Cope, Edw. 175*; Joan 175*; Ralph 175.
Coper (Copar), John 29; Ric. 274.
Copley, Mary 328.
Coppocke, Eliz. 166; Ric. 166.
Copwood, Geo. 344, 345; Wm. 218.
Coral, Sar. 83.
Coraunt, John 272.
Corbett, Andr. 218; Anne 223; Hum. 223, 340.
Corbye, Anne 212*.
Cordell (Cordall, Cordle), Agn. 306; Edm. 119, 306; Guthlac 133; Hen. 85, 119, 180; Joan 119, 180; John 11, 86, 119*; Mary 119; Rob. 40, 119, 306; Sym. 85; Tho. 119; Wm. 119*, 174, 215.
Corey, Christr. 344.
Corior, Margt. 45.
Corneford, Tho. 96.
Cornellus, Lewis 150.
Cornewall (Cornewell), Edw. 274; John 64; Mary 305; Ric. 222, 305.
Corney, John 274.
Cornishe, Agn. 39; John 39, 151.
Cornys, Tho. 348.

Cors(n)e, Lucy 342; Ric. 306, 342.
Coryer, John 275.
Cosen (Cosyn), Gerard 219; Wm. 213.
Cosens, Wm. 330, 331.
Cost(e), John 151; Prud. 151; Tho. 142.
Coston, Allyn 275; Tho. 140.
Cote, Wm. 278.
Cotes, Dor. 37; Rob. 37.
Coton, John 191; Laur. 200.
Cotteis, John 121.
Cottiges, John 320.
Cotton, —— 192; Agn. 203; Ann 311; Clem. 311; Dan. 310; Esther 138; Jane 104; John 203; Josias 138*; Rob. 201; Sybbell 200; Tho. 311*.
Cotum, Agn. 238.
Couchman, Ezech. 204.
Couldeham, Tho. 34.
Coule, Joan 30.
Coulter, Peter 66.
Couper(e) (Cowper), Joan 191; John 147, 191*; Tho. 146, 271; Wm. 191*.
Course, Tho. 63.
Courtman, John 26.
Courtney (Cortneye), Ric. 120, 121.
Covill, Edw. 142.
Cowdon, John 227.
Cowell, Alice 189; Joan 189; Wm. 9, 10, 180.
Cowlburne, Nic. 12.
Cowley, Christian 281; Jer. 167; John 333, 346*; Tho. 96; Wm. 260*, 277.
Cowper, —— 243; Aug. 121; Christr. 132; Jas. 37; Joan 37, 340; John 81, 189, 232, 236, 237, 265*, 275; Mary 189; Mat. 121*; Ric. 79; Rog. 340; Wm. 236.
Cox(e) (Cokes), Agn. 121; Alice 121; Eliz. 121; Giles 121; Jane 163; John 180, 273, 284; Jone 95; Margery 121; Mary 163, 207; Mat. 121; Mr 320*; Peter 121; Tho. 121, 163, 180, 207*, 208, 275; Wm. 181.
Coxall, Wm. 244.
Crabb(e), John 277; Tho. 134, 253, 277, 323.
Crabtree, John 205.
Cracherode, Matthew 257.
Cradocke, Edw. 308.
Craicall, Geo. 172.
Cramphorne (Cramporne, Chramphorne), Dan. 379; Dennis 38; Dlle 320; Eliz. 39; Fras. 378, 379; Geo. 39*, 215, 274; Grace 39; Joan 39, 180; John 39, 274*, 277, 319; Kath. 39; Mary 39; Nic. 274; Ric. 248; Rob. 181; Tho. 38, 39, 85, 277, 318; Wm. 274*, 275, 362.
Crane, Anth. 134; Dor. 303, 305; Margt. 312; Rob. 250; Tho. 303, 305; Wm. 217.

Cranfeild (Cran(e)fyld, Crandfeld), Alice 131; Jas. 198; Joan 321; John 52, 131, 275; Julian 77; Ric. 77, 217; Wm. 82.
Cranwell (Crandwell), Hen. 207; Hugh 352; Jer. 292; John 335; Ric. 352; Wm. 108, 346.
Crasbey, Alice 49.
Crathorne, Mrs. 2.
Craven, John 51*.
Crawley (Craulye), Alice 312; Edw. 307; Eliz. 210; John 96; Judith 209; Mary 94; Tho. 29, 305, 314*; Wm. 36, 94.
Crease, Eliz. 291; John 291.
Crecy (Creacy), Alice 44; Edw. 53; Eliz. 44; Isab. 44; Math. 44; Wm. 44. See Cressey.
Crede, Anth. 121, 180.
Credy, Joan 145; John 145*.
Cre(e)ke, Alice 47; Jas. 8; Olave 133; Ric. 47; Steph. 133.
Cressel, Jas. 4.
Cressett, John 173.
Cressey (Cresy, Cressie), Constance 186*; Edm. 186; Geo. 181*; John 186*, 293*; Mat. 186; Nic. 186; Wm. 28. See Crecy.
Crew, Edw. 52; Eliz. 246*, 247*; Ric. 52; Tho. 246, 247.
Crip(p)s, Eliz. 335; Frances 161; John 161*; Sus. 361.
Cristian, Rich. 351.
Cristmas, Geo. 352; Wm. 352.
Cristmas alias Wilversey, Christr. 80; Joan 80.
Croche, John 347; Rob. 276.
Crofte, Christr. 313; Gab. 202; Jas. 155, 229; John 283, 375; Percival 202; Ric. 122; Tho. 283.
Croft(e)s, Jas. 344; Rob. 2*, 233.
Crofton, Rob. 231; Wm. 44, 236.
Croile, Sim. 46, 91.
Cromer, Francis, 276.
Cromplyn, John 276.
Crosbye (Cros(se)bie, Crosbee), John 65*; Mary 65.
Croseleye, Wm. 351.
Crosfield, Gowing 6.
Crosier, Tho 181.
Cros(se), Agn. 305; Edw. 82, 275; Eliz. 7; Laur. 92; Margt. 82; Oliver 255, 305; Rob. 236, 276; Tho. 347.
Croucher, Nath. 380; Ric. 196.
Croute, Tho. 151.
Crowche (Crou(t)ch(e), Chrowch, Chruch), Alice 216; Anne 102*; Eliz. 235*, 320; Eman. 119; Geo. 119*, 216*, 320, 321; Hen. 353; Jane 336; Joan 102, 119, 216; John 77, 90, 102, 119, 143, 206, 216, 275, 276, 281*, 305, 308, 320*, 336; Margt. 86, 320; Mary 102; Mich. 102*, 216; Ralph 275; Ric. 102*, 119, 167, 235*, 248*, 250*, 273; Rob. 181, 273, 278, 320*; Tho. 102, 109, 119*, 216*, 273, 320, 353; Wm. 90, 273.
Crowchley (Croutchly), Eliz. 246*; Jer. 246; Tho. 246*.
Crowder, Lewis 68.
Crowe, Rich. 277.
Crowfoot, Mr. 182; Rob. 301*.
Croxall, Wm. 198.
Croxon, Audr. 104; Eliz. 104; Geo. 104; Joan 104; John 104; Margt. 104.
Croxton, Nich. 273.
Croyle (Croile), Sim. 190*.
Crumwyne, Rich. 230.
Cry(o)ke, Jas. 202; John 202*.
Cryspe, Rob. 202; Sim. 202.
Cuckow(e), Edm. 75; John 75*.
Cuddington, Ellenor 246.
Cuffeley, Eliz. 304; Wm. 304.
Cullicke, John 31, 382.
Culwyke, John 354.
Cuppedge, Ric. 12; Sib. 12.
Ourb(e)y, Ric. 378; Sar. 235.
Curle (Curll, Courle), Frances 223; Mr. 86; Wm. 26, 157, 223, 229*.
Curlewes (Curlewis, Curloawes, Curlesse), Fulke 38, 119; Joan 119; Wm. 29, 31.
Cursum, Wm. 323.
Curteyn, Sam. 143.
Curtis (Curt(e)ys), Agn 201; Dor. 85; Eliz. 85; Geo. 4; Hen. 85, 87; Margt. 85; Ric. 205; Sus. 4; Tho. 121; Wm. 199, 205, 254.
Cushie, Dan. 151.
Cussans, Mr 319.
Cussen, Alex. 3*.
Cuthbert (Cuttbertt, Cutberd), Alice 62*; Isab. 62; Walt. 62; Wm. 138
Cutterwoode, Parnelle 179*.
Cut(t)ler, Sar. 240; Tho. 160.
Cutts (Cutt, Cut), Ann 4, 51*, 173; John 83, 122, 173; Mary 51; Nic. 51; Rob. 28; Sus. 51; Tho. 32; Wm. 88, 230.

Daben(e)ye alias Cooke, Jas. 75*; John 75.
Dacres, Eliz. 77; Geo. 77; Lady 51.
Dagleye, Walt. 353.
Dagnall (Dagnole), Ann 48; Eliz. 48*, 217; Goodwife 158, 227; John 27, 47, 48*, 142, 159, 164*, 217; Sam. 115; Tho. 284, 335.
Daker(s), Jane 344; John 344; Mr 86.
Daldarne, Henry 214.
Dale (A Dale), John 349; Val. 34, 36.
Dalemore, Wm. 6.
Dalling(e), Hen. 10; John 52.
Dalton (Daulton(ne), Anth. 181, 303; Barnabas 181; Bridget 321; Clem. 303; Eliz. 181, 320, 321; Frances 181; John 181*, 321; Jos. 321; Margt. 308; Martha 32; Mary 181, 321; Rob. 181, 320, 321*; Sar. 321; Thoby 321; Thomas 181; Wm. 181*, 274, 303.

Damporte, Rand. 215.
Dance, Jo. 105.
Dane, Richard 275.
Danvers, Rich. 367*.
Danyell (Daniell), Eden 121; John 34, 85, 121*, 273; Jonas 211; Kath. 121; Margt. 306; Rob. 306; Tho. 111; Wm. 194, 275, 278. *See Humberstone.*
Darante, John 350.
Darawaye, Jone 98.
Darby, John 243*; Pernell 243.
Darcie, Hen. 303: Kath. 303.
Darrknoll, Rob. 34.
Dard(e)s (Deards).—228; Edm. 81, 219, 353; Hen. 353; John 151, 252, 256; Ric. 272*, 273, 353; Rob. 155; Tho. 273; Wm. 272.
Darlin(ge) (Darlyng), Ellen 306; Joan 177, 217; John 177, 210, 212, 217, 306; Rob. 212.
Darmer, Ralph 135.
Darnell, Edw. 93; Han. 93.
Darrell, Ann 140.
Darsall, Tho. 278.
Darvall (Darvell), Anne 139; Edw. 200; Hen. 200; John 139, 343; Mary 169; Sar. 169, 370; Sus. 343.
Dary, John 32; Mich. 32.
Daughton, Anth. 31.
Dauncer, Hen. 27.
Dav(e)ney, John 22*, 46; Tim. 20, 21.
Davis (Dav(i)es), Abig. 137; Bridget 342, Cassandra 202; Elianor 164; Geo. 159, 161*, 162*, 164; Jas. 150; John 167, 177, 342; Kath. 373; Mary 159, 162, 177, 282*; Nich. 262; Ric. 162, 340; Sar. 162, 167; Tho. 159, 260, 364; Wm. 159, 162*, 218. *See Dawes.*
Davison, Sus. 83.
Davy(e) (Davie, Davey), Alice 254; Anne 370; Dennis 77; Edw. 362; Eliz. 378; Ellen 114, 163; Geo. 114*, 134, 163; Griffin 344; Helen 294, 295; Hugh 266; John 114, 181, 238, 275, 349; Jos. 282; Kath. 305, 307; Oswald 276; Ric. 254, 258, 349; Rob. 276, 282; Sar. 163; Sus. 292; Tho. 45, 91. 112, 291*, 292, 294, 295, 372; Wm. 112, 179, 305, 307, 351.
Davyson, Geo. 348.
Dawbeney, Rob. 221.
Dawber, John 3.
Dawes, Clem. 176; Eliz. 112; Margery 176.
Dawes *alias* Davis, Anne 150.
Dawges, Eliz. 380; Rob. 380.
Dawlton, Goodwife 38; John 85.
Dawlyn, Anne 201.
Dawney, Joan 46; John 46.
Dawson, John 143; Rob. 24, 26; Tho. 203, 277; Wm. 357.
Dawton, Rich. 278.
Day(e) (Daie), Alice 91; Chas. 162; David 100; Edw. 4; Fras. 63;

Geo. 276; John 46; Martha Mary 83; Perse 38; Ralph 63*, 278, 286, 320, 340, 342; Ric. 63, 278; Rob 275; Roger 46*; Tho. 91, 156; Walt. 91; Wm. 63*, 120, 136.
Daye *alias* Palmer, John 254; Margt. 254.
Dayne, Goodwife 313.
Daynes, Richard 347.
Dayntye, Moses 203; Roger 203.
Deacon (Deakon), Audry 76; Dion. 210; Eliz. 41; Joan 76, 138; John, 76, 151, 170, 348, 371; Margt. 76; Marion 158; Martha 330; Mary 76; Ralph 348; Roger 76, 113; Sar. 281; Tho. 7, 76*, 168; Wm. 139.
Deane (Dene), Anne 142; Henny 301; John 352; Margt. 135; Mary 43; Mr 29; Mother 347; Rob. 47; Tho. 42. *See Clarke.*
Dearman, Jer. 287.
Dearmer (Deremer, Dearmore), Edw. 334; Jone 158; Mary 168; Wm. 96. *See Dermer.*
Dedon, Alice 344.
Dedyleston, Henry 147.
Deere (Deare), Geo. 242; John 155*; Jone 362; Margt. 242; Rich 242.
Delawood, Fras. 216.
Dell, Agn. 304; Anne 135; Edm. 354; Edw. 93; Eliz. 93; Geo. 133, 304; Giles 351; Han. 164; Hen. 163*, 164, 239, 349; John 123, 167, 331, 370; Joseph 370, 374; Mary 6, 163*, 181, 243, 370; Mat. 112; Ralph 157; Rob. 351; Sar. 137; Sus. 331; Tho. 23, 284, 348; Wm. 112, 288*.
Dellow(e), Eliz. 230; Joan 229; John 229; Margery 229; Mary 229; Ric. 213; Tho. 230*, 345.
Denevett, Even 205.
Dengayne, Tho. 308.
Denny, Edw. lord 187, 188; Edw. 221, 340; Mary, lady 187.
Dennys (Denys), Magd. 321; Wm. 197.
Dennyson, Geo. 379*, 380.
Dent, Roger 348.
Denton (Denten), Alice 279*; Edw. 36, 78, 179; Ellen 51; Hum. 346; John 51; Joyce 36, 179; Mat. 279; Ric. 63, 279; Rob. 275; Tho. 275; Wm. 78.
Denyon, Hugh 351.
Derby, Henry earl of 306; Margt. countess of 171.
Dericke (Derycke), Eliz. 35; John 35, 350.
Deringe, Nic. 344.
Derington, Anne 303; John 303.
Dermer (Deer(e)mer), Agn. 41; Alice 213; Annis 312; Ed. 312; Frances 42; Fras. 312; Joan 41; John 230; Mary 312; Rob. 27, 42; Tho. 73*, 213, 306, 312*, 313, 314; Wm. 353. *See Dearmer.*

Dermer *alias* Dormer, Wm. 306.
Devell, Geo. 344.
Dewberry (Dowberie, Dewbury), —— 65, 207; Walt. 351.
Dewey, Thos. 111.
Dewhurst, Barnard 174, 306.
Dewnope, Thos. 353.
Dewsett, Wm. 274.
Dewyard, John 277; Tho. 277.
Dey(e), Isab. 190; John 147, 190, 192, 195, 274; Ralph 348; Rob. 219; Roger 190. *See Ketheringe*.
Diason, John 39, 86, 216.
Dicenson, Tho. 212.
Dickes (Dixe), Margt. 30; Wm. 42.
Dickins (Dickens), Grace 149; Mary 140; Ric. 293*.
Dickinson, C. E. G. 364.
Dighton, Agn. 76, 131, 176; Hen. 76, 158, 176, 228; Ric. 131; Tho. 229.
Dikes, Roger 42.
Dimmock, Joan 375.
Diuton, —— 164; Eliz. 113, 114; John 113*, 114; Mary 114.
Dirrington, John 259.
Dison, Lilford 288.
Dixon (Dyx(s)on, Dyckson), Agn. 143; Anne 7, 34, 80, 104, 172; Christr. 275; Edw. 7; Jas. 342; John 104*, 275; Jos. 101; Margt. 48; Mary 94; Phil. 104*; Ralph 34, 80, 104, 172; Rob. 291*; Sar. 143; Sus. 101; Tho. 101; Wm. 38, 40, 85*, 121, 347, 381.
Doble, Harman 352.
Dobson, Joan 85; Rob. 40, 85; Wm. 262.
Docklee, Henry 212.
Docwra (Dockwraye, Dock(e)ray(e)), Edw. 345; Eliz. 345; Grace 337; Mildred 35; Rob. 337; Tho. 34, 35, 72, 82, 280, 304.
Dod(de)s (Dod), Barth. 222; Charity 222; Hugh 108; Kath. 177; Nath. 109; Wm. 79*, 177, 195*, 219, 233.
Dodkin, Joan 211; Wm. 153.
Dodkin *alias* Saunders, —— 211.
Dodwell, Rich. 263.
Doe, Joan 140, 239; Wm. 282.
Dofett, Alice 349.
Dogelas, Wm. 231.
Dogget (Doggat, Doget, Doggdat), Alice 218; Joan 42, 46, 114; John 20*, 21*, 22*, 42, 46*; Ralph 168; Ric. 168; Rob. 159; Sar. 244*; Tho. 168, 218, 228, 244.
Dolling(e), Hen. 239; Jas. 239.
Dollwyn *alias* Dollyng, Tho. 77.
Dolt(e), —— 349; Ric. 30; Sar. 330; Wm. 227.
Dolton, Jane 162.
Dolwyn, Jas. 348.
Done (Donn), John 37, 276; Ranulphe 185.
Done [? Doue], Joan 133; John 133.
Dorman, Anne 203.
Dormer, Hen. 381; Tho. 355*, 357; Widow 315, 358*. *See Dermer*.

Dorrington, Anne 246; Fras. 246; Mary 246, 247; Sar. 245.
Dorsett (Dossit), Christian 136; Edw. 350; John 136*.
Dorwood, John 352.
Dossett, John 94; Sar. 94.
Doubtley (Dowtley), Jos. 166.
Dove. *See Done*.
Dover, Alice 228; Dan. 163*; Eliz. 114, 165; Han. 162; Hester 116; John 161, 162, 163*; Mary 161*; Ralph 160, 161*, 162*, 163*; Ric. 113, 114, 116; Sar. 160; Wm. 237.
Dowdale, Hen. 242; Mary 242; Nath. 242.
Dowde, Tho. 23.
Dowe, Peter 277.
Dowell, John 86.
Doweshed, Rob. 274.
Dowman, Hen. 132; Jas. 185, 219; Joan 219; Margt. 132.
Downe, Barth. 341; John 272; Kath. 341.
Downer, Agn. 343; John 343, 350; Martha 95; Wm. 350.
Downes, Phil. 173; Sib. 12; Tho. 374. *See Staffords*.
Downyng(e), Agn. 340; Jas. 275; John 340.
Dowse, Wm. 52.
Dowsett(e), Joan 133; John 133, 219; Wm. 275.
Drable, Alex. 148*.
Drables, Nich. 28.
Drane, Tho. 383.
Draper, Christr. 78; Edm. 214; Grace 247; Hykeman 323, 326; Jane 50; John 5; Margt. 78; Mary 209; Rob. 2, 315; Theodosia 285.
Drew (Drue), John 346; Kath. 96.
Drey(e), Christian 326; John 271; Wm. 323.
Driver (Dryver), Agn. 288; Ellen 177; John 288, 289*, 290*, 295, 296; Moses 295, 296; Nic. 119; Rose 289; Tho. 177.
Drury(e), Drugo 176; Eliz. 176; Tho. 254.
Duck, Eliz. 245; Jas. 244; Mary 245; Tho. 12; Wm. 12.
Duckett, Geo. 303; Isab. 303.
Dudley, Deb. 5; Elisha 5.
Duke, Edw. 8; Eliz. 8; John 321.
Dukesonn, Rob. 2.
Dunby, Sar. 286.
Duncombe, John 12; Jud. 12; Ric. 27, 28; Rob. 21*.
Dunham, Rich. 173.
Dun(n)e, Anne 76; Edw. 81; Hugh 189; Peter 76; Sar. 93; Wm. 76, 219, 248, 249.
Dunnill, Tho. 6.
Dunton (Donton), Jane 159; John 159*, 160.
Dunwell (Dunwill), John 30, 80.
Duram, John 117.
Durdan, Agn. 45; John 45; Walt. 45.

Durrant, Alse 113; Edw. 114, 160, 164; John 10*, 164*, 284; Joyce 114; Mary 164; Sim. 113*; Sus. 113, 164; Urs. 114; Widow 116; Wm. 164*, 352.
Durren, Jone 199.
Duxford, Rob. 219.
Dwight, Tho. 115.
Dych(e) (Dytche), Eliz. 348; Hen. 342; Tho. 28, 350; Wm. 236.
Dychefeld, Steph. 231.
Dyckynson, Hugh 205.
Dycons (Dicons), Laur. 313; Mary 313.
Dyer (Dier(e)), Agn. 192, 274; Cicily 192; Edw. 230; Geo. 81; Joan 82, 177, 219; John 81, 177, 192*, 219, 275*, 347; Margt 192; Nic. 82, 177; Petronilla 192; Phil. 4; Ric. 192; Rob. 310; Tho. 341; Wm. 274*.
Dykeswelle, Margt. 117; Rob. 117.
Dymoke, Joan 135; Wm. 135.
Dyne, Wm. 365.
Dynes, Tho. 327, 328.
Dytton (Ditton), John 237; Kath. 237.
Dyxe, Tho. 178.
Dyxy, Wm. 233.

Ealin, Abraham 330.
Ealing, Rose 168.
Eames (Emes), John 80, 81, 310, 331; Rob. 27, 278; Sar. 166; Wm. 5.
Earle (Erle), Alice 79; Eliz. 213; Hen. 228; Joan 258; Ric. 258; Tho. 79.
Eason, Edw. 228; John 151; Rob. 283; Sar. 283.
East (Este), Agn. 156; Geo. 94, 351; Hugh 347; John 341; Jud. 136; Mary 341; Phil 351; Ric. 317; Tho. 260*, 346; Wm. 157, 341, 351.
Eastgate, Eliz. 2*; John 2.
Eastland, John 3.
Eates, John 244; Mary 244; Sar. 244.
Eaton, Barnard 284; John 284; Jos. 5; Mary 168; Rob. 5, 283; Tho. 169.
Eb(b)grave, Eliz. 287; Tho. 284, 287*.
Ecclesoe, Hen. 297.
Edden (Eddon), Rob. 170; Sus. 170; Wm. 170.
Ede, Ric. 274.
Edgerton, Ralph 173.
Edlin (Ed(e)lyn), —— 147; Cecily 222, 303; Isab. 198; Jas. 12; John 12, 196*, 352; Rob. 348; Rose 12; Sar. 92; Sic. 12; Sus. 12; Tho. 196*; Wm. 12*, 42, 222, 303, 311.
Edmam, Tho. 275.
Edmonds (Edmundes, Edmonce), Ann 375; Annys 319; Edw. 319; Eliz. 38, 319, 372; Ellen 113; Hen. 38*, 218, 278, 319*; Joan 38, 319; John 6, 38, 143, 319, 340, 358*, 359*, 371; Jonas 112; Jonath 93; Jos. 250, 335, 370; Kath. 38. 319; Lowes 371; Margery 38, 319; Mary 7; Ric. 10; Rob. 319; Roger 190; Sar. 288; Tho. 38, 319, 348*; Wm. 30, 112*.
Ednam, Eliz. 132; Hen. 132.
Edrych, Benedict 237, 238*.
Edryngton, Tho. 351.
Edward(e) Clemence 191; Edw. 307; Hugh 274; John 189*; Marion 189; Tho. 191.
Edwards, —— 4; Agn. 175; Dr. 105; Eve 49; Geo. 42, 339, 341; Giles 42; Hen. 210; John 49*, 182*, 286; Jone 49; Mat. 175; Ric. 49*, 72; Rob. 153, 287; Sar. 287, 380*; Tho. 380*.
Eedes, John 96.
Eeling(e), Mary 334; Wm. 139, 334.
Egerton, John 367.
Eggleston, Ann, 371.
Egleton, Edw. 164.
Eilot, Sarah 335.
Eive, Anth. 121; Mary 121.
Elborne, Wm. 248.
Eldebury, John 90; Ric. 90; Rose 90.
Eldemed, Tho. 266.
Elder, John 348.
Elderbek, Rob. 146*.
Ele, John 91; Thomasine 91.
Eleanor, Queen, 117.
Element (Ellement), Martin 8; Mary 281, 331; Sam. 357; Walhan 281; Wm. 374.
Eliott (Eliatt, Ellyotte, Elat), Geo. 175, 176, 255; Joan 175; John 78, 277, 286, 318; Julian 78; Matrone 277; Rob. 274, 276; Tho. 42, 176, 273*; Wm. 146*, 198, 215.
Elisha, John 138, 372.
Ellaby, Sus. 244.
Elles, Richard 348.
Ellis (Ellys, Elles), —— 315; Alice 357; Austen 242; Eliz. 333; Joan 242; Martha 150; Mr 311; Rob. 65; Sus. 357; Tho. 75, 138, 174, 242, 351.
Ellis alias Wayte, —— 150.
El(l)kins, Dor. 316; Fras. 316; John 316*; Mary 316; Rich. 316*.
Ellvin, Margt. 334.
Ellwes, Mary 361.
Elmer alias Fylewood, Barnabas 308; Frances 308; John 256.
Elmeston, Christr. 338.
Elrington, Margt. 280*.
Elsbie, Rich. 350.
Elsynge, Hen. 79.
Elton, Grace 202.
Ely(e), Bishop of 197*; John 73, 238; Tho. 352.
Elynge, Rob. 204.
Elys(e), Edm. 92; John 233.

Emerton, Edw. 242, 285; Eliz. 242; Joan 242; John 285.
Emery, Tho. 218, 280.
Emyn, Wm. 64.
Emyn *alias* Robson, Anne 64.
Enderbie, Edw. 143; Eliz. 143.
Englishe, Rich. 181.
Entwessell, Wm. 76.
Erberd, Walter 192.
Erbury (Earbury), Wm. 136.
Erle. *See Earle.*
Esgae, Peter 29.
Essex, Rob. 11; Walter earl of 131*.
Essex & Ewe, Henry earl of 36; Mary 36.
Esten, Rich. 348.
Estgreue, Sib. 267.
Estridge, John 186.
Estwood, Edm. 104.
Etheridge (Etheryege), Abig. 138; Agn. 120; Isab. 120; Joan 120; John 120*; Margt. 120; Tho. 120, 214, 315; Wm. 120.
Etherope, Tho. 351.
Ethringham, Mary 331.
Etridge (Eterige, Edridge), John 86; Wm. 320*.
Eustes, Eliz. 161.
Evans, —— 12; Anne 166; Dan. 285; Dor. 6; Jane 2; Jonath. 238; Rich. 207; Wm. 138, 166. *See Bradwin.*
Eve, Rich. 239; Sar. 239.
Evelin(ge) (Evelyn), —— 10; John 349; Ursula 42.
Evenet, John 273.
Everard, John 322; Matilda 322; Tho. 267.
Evered, Edw. 74.
Everesdone, Agn. 238; John 238; Matilda 238; Wm. 238.
Everet(t) (Everot), Alice 287; Edw. 343; Jane 343; Ric. 258; Tho. 351; Wm. 63.
Everston (Eu'ston), Wm. 348.
Everton (Eu'ton), Jos. 351.
Everye, Ralph 347.
Everyngame, Eliz. 198*.
Eves, Mary 202; Rob. 138, 288.
Evyn, Hugh 204*, 205*.
Ewarde, Ellen, 304; Paul 304; Rob. 304.
Ewer (Ewyer), —— 348; Alice 64, 310; Anne 76, 187, 188*, 189; Bridget 64; David 187, 188*, 189*; Eliz. 6, 305; Fras. 282; Hen. 187*, 189; James 284, 348; Jane 64; John 64, 76, 220, 318, 349, 351; Jos. 5, 7, 94, 96, 137, 187, 239; Mary 187, 188*; Nich. 64; Ralph 27; Roger 64, 374; Sam. 166; Sar. 286; Sim. 132; Tho. 64, 75, 156, 187*, 188*, 189*, 310; Wm. 64, 76, 188, 255, 305, 344, 348, 349.
Ewington, Edm. 315; Joan 315; John 135; Nic. 240, 315; Ric. 315; Tho. 315*.

Ewington *alias* Dary, Joan 315; John 315.
Excestr, John Duke of 231.
Exsoll, Alice 205.
Exton, John 249, 250*.
Eydon, Eliz. 201.
Eyer, Wm. 87.
Eylat, Margery 221; Nich. 221.
Eyms, Tho. 221.
Eyre (Eire), Hen. 257; Tho. 277; Wm. 346.
Eyres, John 383.
Eytou, Dor. 307, 308; Edw. 307, 308; Laur. 307, 308.

Fabyan (Fabian), Mr. 314; Steph. 271, 322; Wm. 350.
Facy, John 315.
Fader, Wm. 23.
Fades, Hen. 321.
Fage, Anne 77; Anth. 31, 337; Edw. 134, 338; Ellen 337; Geo. 77; Tho. 337.
Faireclough (Fayrclough, Fayrecloth), Agn. 9; Edw. 141; Geo. 9; Giles 9; John 50; Margery 9; Ric. 9; Sym. 208.
Fairedough, Jo. 51.
Falsebye, Rob 315.
Falthropp, Tho. 111.
Fanche, John 75.
Fanne, Rich. 120*.
Fanner, Agn. 342; Rich. 178, 181, 220, 342.
Fanshawe, Hen. 26; Tho. 178, 304*.
Farand, Anne 142.
Fardean, Mary 239.
Farmer, Dorcas 362; Geo. 141; John 362*.
Farnecombe, Joan 232.
Farnefold, Rich. 134.
Farnham, Sim. 270, 326.
Faroe, Margt. 256; Wm. 256.
Farr, John 211, 290; Rob. 154; Wm. 151.
Farrar, John 158; Wm. 275.
Farrine, Kath. 244.
Farrington, Roger 215.
Farthing(e), Mary 132, 177; Mrs 2*; Roger 132, 177.
Fassett, John 152.
Faunces, Mr 181.
Fauntoner, Agn. 90; Tho. 47, 90.
Fauson, Mary 329.
Fawcett *alias* Artur, Jud. 213; Mary 213.
Fawdye, Wm. 352.
Fawkener. Mary 119.
Fawkland. *See Carye.*
Fawson, Frances 168.
Fayr(e)fax(e), Hum. 34; Tomysoune 198.
Fayreman, Tho. 259.
F(e)arn(e)sly, Rich. 138.
Feaste, Joan 303; John 378*; Ric. 323, 327, 380; Wm. 303, 378.

Febridge (Febrygge), —— 141 ; Tho. 352.
Feilder, John 76.
Fells, Han. 7 ; Wm. 7.
Fellowe (Felowe,) Dan. 152 ; John 231 ; Rob. 201 ; Sus. 162* ; Wm. 152, 162.
Felton, John 176. 305 ; Kath. 176, 305 ; Mr. 2.
Fenc, Thomas 350.
Fenney, Tho. 211 ; Ursula 211.
Fensom (Fens(h)am). Hen. 83 ; Jud. 375 ; Tho. 93.
Fenton, Thos. 51.
Feroby, ——234 ; Tho. 233.
Fer(e)ys, John 190, 232.
Ferguson, Mr. 382 ; Wm. 382.
Fermer, Adam 45 ; Joan 31 ; John 34 ; Tho. 214.
Ferne (Fearn), Jespore 347 ; Tho. 372.
Ferneley, Bridget 34 ; Wm. 34.
Fernes, Margt. 4.
Fernesly, Bridget 222 ; Wm. 222.
Ferrer, Thos. 276.
Ferrers, Fras. 131 ; Geo. 37, 176*, 261* ; Julius 302, 343 ; Knighton 111 ; Margt. 37, 176 ; Mary 302 ; Ric. 131, 302 ; Sus. 343.
Ferris, Alice 10 ; Edw. 10 ; Eliz. 10 ; Jone 10 ; Sam. 10 ; Sus. 10 ; Tho. 10.
Fertloe, Geo. 306 ; Mary 306.
Fesa(u)nte, Cicily 86 ; Joan 229 ; John 229.
Fesse, Wm. 275.
Fest, Eliz. 62.
Fidgen, Geo. 333.
Fidgharbor, Edm. 47 ; Nich. 47.
Field (Feild, Fe(e)lde, Feyld, At Felde) Abm. 168 ; Agn. 314 ; Alice 73, 165, 166, 192 ; Ann 51, 238 ; Arth. 253 ; Bridget 286 ; Cath. 73 ; Dan. 228, 310 ; Edw. 36, 212, 250, 361 ; Eliz. 30*, 83, 99, 140, 152, 214, 289, 310, 363 ; Eme 314 ; Frances 170 ; Fras. 362 ; Geo. 155, 228, 315, 338 ; Grace 152 ; Han. 263 ; Hen. 88, 170, 283*, 285, 329, 331, 361, 363* ; Jas. 312 ; Jane 41 ; Jer. 182 ; Joan 217, 314*, 338, 346 ; John 24, 27, 30*, 42, 73, 84, 143, 150, 152, 181, 213, 228, 244*, 246, 286*, 288, 289, 311, 338, 349 ; Joseph 286 ; Josias 143 ; Leon. 51* ; Martha 363* ; Mary 73, 99, 136, 167, 200, 213, 314 ; Phil. 147 ; Reb. 139 ; Ric. 123, 192, 314 ; Rob. 166, 330 ; Sam. 48 ; Sar. 42, 166, 286, 293 ; Sus. 239, 244, 246* ; Tho. 9, 12, 27, 29, 45, 51, 73, 74, 76, 155, 273, 285, 310, 314, 326*, 353*, 362 ; Wm. 30, 73, 95, 99, 166, 216, 228, 302, 315.
Fillis, Agn. 314.
Finch (Fync(h)e), —— 32 ; Alice 105, 348 ; Edw. 52*, 223 ; Eliz. 81, 105, 119, 136, 181, 223, 307 ; Frances 10 ; Isaac 7 ; Isab. 181 ; Joan 10, 181, 345 ; John 10*, 24, 26, 76, 105, 181, 352,*, 372 ; Jos. 238 ; Margt. 223 ; Margery 76 ; Mary 136, 242*, 243 ; Nic. 345, 352 ; Ric. 139, 332, 350 ; Rob. 351 ; Rog. 307 ; Sam. 334 ; Sar. 52 ; Tho. 32, 81, 223, 254, 302, 352 ; Walt. 81, 352* ; Wm. 23, 105, 181, 242, 341, 352.
Findall, Anth. 373 ; Eliz. 288 ; Tho. 288.
Finton, Alice 216 ; Margt. 216 ; Margery 216 ; Martha 216 ; Mary 216.
Fishborn, Eliz. 288
Fishe (Fysshe), Alice 214 ; Edw. 99 ; Geo. 174 ; John 379* ; Leon. 174 ; Margt. 79 ; Ric. 352 ; Rog. 79 ; Sar. 5 ; Tho. 214.
Fisher (Fysher, Fyschar), Anne 157, 219 ; Anth. 242 ; Edm. 157 ; Edw. 157*, 158*, 177 ; Eliz. 346 ; Isab. 242 ; Jacob 242 ; John 102, 157, 182, 256, 335, 349 ; Mary 181 ; Ric. 273, 342, 372 ; Tho. 157.
Fitch, Jer. 331 ; Sar. 139, 331.
Fitzherbert, Hum. 272, 278, 369 ; John 341. *See Fidgharbor.*
Fitzhugh(e), Eliz. 307*, 339, 342 ; Nich. 34, 80, 307 ; Ric. 80, 307*, 339, 341, 342.
Fitz John, Alice 281 ; Edw. 79, 354 ; John 146*.
Fitzraff, Wm. 186.
Flagge, Eliz. 347.
Flayle, Agn. 120.
Flemyng(e), Hugh 345 ; Margt. 345 ; Tho. 268, 269, 271*.
Fletcher (Fle(e)cher), Agn. 121 ; Anne 120 ; Avis 315 ; Eliz. 176 ; Fras. 304 ; Gab. 315 ; John 176 ; Maud. 119 ; Ric. 119, 120, 348 ; Rog. 119 ; Sam. 363 ; Wm. 28, 176, 181, 315, 353.
Flete, Wm. 91.
Flexmere (Flexmore), Anne 247 ; Joan 92 ; Mary 245 ; Wm. 247*.
Flindel (Flindal, Flyndall), Tho. 29*, 292* ; Wm. 83.
Flinden, Griseld 32.
Floure, Wm. 191.
Flower, Agn. 73 ; Basill 73 ; Fras. 337 ; John 73*, 230 ; Rob. 73 ; Wm. 73.
Floyd, John 286 ; Rich. 286 ; Wm. 371.
Fly (Fley), Eliz. 288 ; Sam. 329.
Foderby, Sim. 366.
Folden, Blanch 43.
Foliott, Francis 309.
Folkyngham, Anne 324 ; John 323, 324.
Fonte. *See Oda.l.*
Foote (Fot(t)e), Alice 233 ; Anth. 120 ; Hen. 275 ; John 120* ; Margt. 120 ; Nich. 275 ; Ralph 274 ; Ric. 274 ; Tho. 274.

Ford(e) (Foard), Dan. 282, 335; Eliz. 335; John 234, 273, 275; Mary 167; Tho. 102, 119, 275; Widow 39.
Fordham (Forham), Agn. 75; Anne 319; Eliz. 75; Joan 75*, 319; Margt. 75; Phil. 75; Rob. 64; Sar. 75; Sus. 102; Tho. 75; Wm. 75*.
Forester, Madam 249*, 250*, 251*; Pulter 251.
Forkelooe, Geo. 307; Laur. 307.
Forrent, Jeromina 257; Rob. 134, 257; Wm. 104.
Forsett, John 84.
Forster, Beat. 76; Edw. 76; John 76*, 195, 196; Margt. 221; Mich. 76; Peter 147; Ric. 81, 192; Rob. 147, 148, 194*; Tho. 221; Walt. 92. *See Gamelin.*
Fortescu(e), Alice 220; Fras. 212; John 220; Sir John 148*, 193.
Forth (Foorthe), John 34, 36; Rob. 342.
Fortho, John 90*.
Fortune, Christian 75; Ellen 75; Grace 75; Tho. 75.
Fosset, Tho. 288.
Foster, Agn. 143, 216; Alice 230, 339, 340*; Edw. 314; Eliz. 216; Emme 216; Geo. 115; Goodwife 320; Hen. 35, 305, 347; Isott 81; James 198, 216; Jane 216; Joan 114, 221, 351; John 24, 27*, 111, 114, 122, 149, 161*, 274, 350*; Martha 114; Mary 7; Mat. 102; Mr. 110*, 111; Nic. 346; Ric. 81, 133, 161*, 175, 236, 339, 340*, 346, 352; Rob. 348; Tho. 37, 175, 221, 252*, 253, 278, 314, 344, 352; Wm. 175, 213, 216, 319.
Foster *alias* Cooke, Geo. 254; Scolastica 254.
Fothergill, John 374.
Fotherley(e), Jas. 350; John 350; Tho. 12*, 65*.
Foull, John 253.
Fountayne (Founteine, Fonten), Joan 217; John 10, 273; Wm. 217.
Fowk(es) (Fowlk), Edm. 8; Edw. 7, 8, 93*, 95, 137, 139, 166; Fras. 84; John 48*; Ric. 375; Widow 243.
Fowle, Tho. 346; Zach. 309.
Fowler, Gab. 176; John 293; Nic. 87; Sar. 170; Wm. 292.
Fownell, John 149.
Fox(e), Adonia 243; Annis 352; Chas. 100; Geof. 186; John 72; Rob. 275; Sam. 101; Steph. 72; Wm. 347. *See Oxton.*
Foxcrofte, Tho. 65.
Foxon, Rich. 94.
Foxwell, Henry 303.
Francis (Fraincis, Fraunce(y)s), —— 120; Alice 347; Anne 311; Fras. 311; Geo. 347; Hen. 23, 170; Jas. 277; Jeff. 32; John 326, 327*, 328, 347; Mary 282; Ric. 256*, 258, 306*, 345; Sus. 256, 258, 306*, 345; Tho. 120; Wm. 28, 256*, 311.

Francke, Sebastian 316.
Francks, Ric. 88.
Frankilcast', Anth. 353.
Frankland (Franckelande), Edm. 80, 81; Hester 258; Hugh 175, 258, 306; Wm. 35, 36, 79, 81, 135, 175, 258*, 306.
Franklyn (Franckeleyn), Isab. 45; Margt. 198; Mary 169; Oliver 276; Ric. 45, 312; Rose 199; Tho. 199, 200; Wm. 177.
Fray(e), Lady Agnes 117*; Jas. 153; John 102, 117, 315.
Frebarn, Wm. 189.
Fre(e)man, Anne 49; Bette 50; Eliz. 315; Isaac 93, 139; Jas. 240*; John 315; Laur. 315; Ralph 70; Ric. 42, 139, 363; Rob. 49*; Tho. 142; Wm. 27, 315*.
French(e) (Frenshe), Const. 80; John 278; Margt. 306; Nic. 150; Tho. 306; Wm. 80.
Frend, Isab. 92; John 92.
Frenschman, Janyn 47.
Fribridge, Eliz. 333.
Fring(e), Jonas 258, 343; Sar. 343.
Friour, Mabel 189.
Frith (Fryth), Aug. 72; Rob. 80; Tho. 98; Wm. 28.
Frobisher, Alice 50.
Frone [? Froe], Anne 42.
Frost, Hum. 229; Rob. 250.
Froud, Wm. 265.
Frowe, Kath. 45, 91.
Frowycke, Hen. 303, 344.
Fryer, Helen 319; Jas. 319; Ric. 319; Wm. 319.
Fulkember, Mich. 198.
Fuller(e), Andr. 266, 324, 325; Eliz. 258; Geo. 85; John 30, 258, 266, 269*, 344; Margt. 344; Ric. 45; Sar. 333; Tho. 115, 116, 258, 344; Wm. 237.
Fullwood, Peter 6, 333, 370; Steph. 334; Wm. 200, 201.
Funge, Jas. 8; Martha 285.
Furman, John 371; Tho. 371.
Furryan, Wm. 279, 280.
Fust, John 273.
Fychet, John 327.
Fylewood. *See Elmer.*
Fyllyan, Tho. 198.
Fylyan [Fyliam] *alias* Russhelyn, Edw. 24, 26*.
Fylys, Agn. 190; Anice 190; Wm. 190.
Fynell, Joan 92; John 92.
Fynwod, Rich. 356*.
Fyppe, Edw. 353; Jas. 353; Tho. 353. *See Phippe.*
Fysshewyke, Hen. 259*, 260; Tho. 259*.
Fytbye, Wm. 346.


Gaall, Agn. 270; John 270.
Gabriel(l), Eliz. 142, 356.

Gaddes . . . , —— 27.
Gad(de)sden, Anne 345*; John 218, 315; Mary 214; Tho. 306, 315, 345*.
Gaell, Geo. 51.
Gailer, John 278.
Gale, Richard 182.
Galloway (Gal(l)away, Gallewey), Christr. 367; Margt. 274; Miles 24, 275.
Galyon, Geof. 267.
Gamble, Tho. 64, 321; Wm. 332.
Game, Ralph 143; Tho. 310.
Gamelyn *alias* Forster, Rob. 194.
Gape, Anne 186, 187; Henry 260; Joan 186*, 187; John 7, 186*, 187*; Mary 7.
Gardener (Gardiner, Gard(y)ner), Alice 341; Anne 216, 246; Edw. 72; Eliz. 216, 302; Frances 81; Hen. 119; James 77, 302; Jane 216; John 46, 198, 216, 233, 348, 349; Margt. 216; Phil. 341; Sar. 246; Sim. 302, 341; Sus. 216; Tho. 216, 249, 308; Wm. 81, 216, 246.
Garlond, Rich. 274.
Garnett, Hen. 338; Jasper 103; Margery 133*, 338; Wm. 131*, 133*, 338*.
Garnons, Alice 34; Tho. 4, 34.
Garrard, Anne 336; Chas. 336; Edw. 336; Eliz. 336*; Fras. 336; Isab. 336; Jane 336; John 336*; Margt. 336; Mary 336; Nithermyll 336; Wm. 336.
Garrell (Garroll, Garill), Anne 151; John 140.
Garret(t), Joan 228; John 42, 70; Rich. 312; Tho. 228; Wm. 228, 312.
Gascoign, Thos. 173.
Gase, Miles 278.
Gaseley(e) (Gazeley), Anne 142; Dan. 361; John 220; Mary 140; Sam. 140; Sar. 371; Tho. 353*.
Gaskyn, Tho 218; Wm. 346.
Gate, Hester 115; John 322.
Gates John 283; Tho. 277.
Gat(e)ward, Tho. 344; Wm. 277.
Gawton, Rich 30, 74.
Gayler, Agn. 306; Wm. 306.
Gaythorne, Wm. 346.
Geary(e) (Geery), Anne 245; Ben. 8; Hen. 161, 164*; John 115*, 116; Jos. 159, 160*, 161, 162, 163*, 164*; Mary 43, 163*; Sar. 162; Sus. 163, 164.
Gedge, Rob. 365.
Gedney, Rob. 194*.
Geffus, Helen 45; John 45*.
Gefray, Tho. 233.
Gegon. *See Jegon.*
Geldener (Geldnor, Gyldner), Anne 131; Hen. 259; Wm. 131, 275, 276.
Geldwer, Tho. 367.
Gennyns. *See Jennings.*
Genyn, Anne 218; Wm. 218.

George, Eliz. 210; Wm. 288. *See Wright.*
Gerneys, John 192.
Ger(r)ard(e), Gilb. 88, 173, 174, 185; Joan 237; Phil. 91; Wm. 339.
Gerrye, Wm. 304.
Gersey (Garsey), John 313; Mary 313; Ralph 313.
Geve, John 353.
Ghy, Ane 198.
Gibbons, A. 144.
Gibb(e)s (Gibbe, Gybb(e), —— 268; Hen. 209; Joan 178; John 178, 194, 275, 327, 349*, 378*; Nic. 12*; Ric. 259, 277, 349; Rob. 192; Rog. 41; Wm. 165.
Gibson, Dor. 360; Jas. 137; Jo. 359, 360; Kath. 359; Margery 259, 360; Wm. 8, 139, 333.
Giddings, Geo. 376.
Giffs, Leonard 103.
Gilberd, —— 212; Mary 212.
Gilbert (Gylbert), Agn. 33, 97; John 287*; Mary 333; Rich. 351.
Giles (Gy(l)l(e)s), Agn. 130, 272; Anne 332; Hen. 130; John 64, 272, 346; Ric. 347; Tho. 200, 201, 228.
Gilet, Audrey 41; John 41*.
Gilford, Sarah 285.
Gill (Gylle), John 78, 177, 178, 215, 272*; Margt. 38; Peter 276; Tho. 243.
Gillett, (Gyllett), Rob. 273; Wm. 278.
Gillman (Gylman), Alex. W. 144; Anne 262; Eliz. 153; John 318; Nic. 75; Ric. 261*, 262*; Rob. 262*.
Gilpin, Thos. 22.
Gilson. *See Gylson.*
Gilver, Edw. 64.
Ginns, Mary 41. *See Gynne.*
Gippes, Christian 104; Eliz. 104; Hen. 104; Nic. 104; Rob. 104; Tho. 104; Wm. 104.
Gipson, Jane 214.
Gittings, Eliz. 137.
Gladin, Joan 11; Tho. 11*; Wm. 11.
Gladman, Anne 139; Isab. 361; Jas. 311; Jer. 281; John 222; Mary 239; Nathan 141; Seth. 93; Wm. 348.
Gladman *alias* Grene, John 258.
Gladwyn, Jane 131; John 236; Kath. 274; Tho. 131; Wm. 378.
Glandvile, Rich. 87.
Glanfeeld [Glandfyld] *alias* Nevell [Nevill], Ellen 306; John 134, 229, 306; Ric. 158
Glas(s)co(o)k(e), J L. 266, 325; Joan 104, John 104; Phil. 278; Ric. 24, 277; Tho. 24, 26, 277, 339.
Glasyer, Reg. 232.
Glawdin. Rob. 227.
Gleadall, Jas. 260, 261.
Gleave, Charity 374; John 247.
Glen(n)ester (Glenister), Edw. 20, 114; Hugh. 170; Jane 75; Jos. 283; Wm. 20, 21.

Glewe, Thos. 347.
Glover, Alex. 134 ; Bridget 307 ; John 372 ; Master 235 ; Wm. 307.
Gnoton, Rich. 32.
Goard, Bridget 208.
Gobet, Rich. 146.
God(d)ard (Godderd), Joan 113 ; John 27 ; Rog. 230 ; Tho. 223, 312.
Godfr(e)ye, —— 324 ; Anne 64 ; Eliz. 308 ; Ellyn 64 ; Hen. 379 ; Isaac 283 ; John 41, 64, 227*, 321 ; Kath. 244 ; Mary 64 ; Nic. 64 ; Oliver 308 ; Ric 91, 377, 378, 379*, 380 ; Sar. 213 ; Tho. 64, 243, 244* ; Wm. 181, 273.
Godfrey alias Cooper, Agn. 306, 345 ; Alice 74 ; Anne 42 ; Eliz. 74 ; Fras. 220, 296 ; Joan 214 ; John 74, 134, 178, 306, 345 ; Josana 178, 220 ; Joyce 134 ; Mary 296 ; Ric. 81 ; Tho. 74 ; Wm. 74, 134, 178, 220, 296, 306.
Godlington, Rich. 158.
Godly, Thomas 320.
Godman, John 137, 140.
Godpayere, John 267.
Godrych, John 116.
Godthank(e), Margery 192 ; Margt. 192 ; Ric. 192* ; Tho. 45*, 192 Wm. 192.
Godwin, Abednego 83, 84* ; Edw. 273 ; John 267 ; Ric. 273 ; Sus. 48, 84 ; Tho. 283 ; Walt. 267.
Golborne, Thos. 277.
Gold(e), Ann 376 ; Geo. 131 ; Joan 131 ; John 27 ; Tho. 27. See Gould.
Golding (Goldynge, Goulding), Dam. 138 ; Joan 46 ; John 46 ; Rob. 277. See Gouldin.
Goldsmith (Gouldsmith), — 213 ; Agn. 212 ; Elyn 348 ; Frances 213 ; Han. 295 ; John 350 ; Mary 239 ; Ric. 353 ; Sam. 212 ; Sol. 362 ; Tho. 152, 294, 353, 362.
Gol(d)ston, Tho. 271, 324, 325*.
Golston alias Bartelmewe, Anne 222 ; Tho. 222, 228.
Gonn(e), Tho. 276, 350.
Gonson, Benj. 78.
Gonstone, Wm. 351.
Goodacres, James 79.
Goodall, Prisc. 244 ; Tho. 53.
Goodaye (Goodday), Dion. 81 ; Rob. 275, 277 ; Tho. 81, 178, 275.
Goodchild, John 86.
Goode, John 213.
Goodes, Edw. 223.
Goodiere (Goodyer, Goodders), Anne 184, 185 ; Frances 175 ; Fras. 90, 125*, 184 ; Hen. 89*, 90, 175, 185*, 186, 344 ; John 134 ; Tho. 185* ; Ursula 90 ; Walt. 351 ; Wm. 185*.
Goodin, Geo. 5.
Goodland, John 309 ; Lucy 309.
Goodlyshe, John 349.
Goodman, Dr. 29* ; Edm. 156 ; Frances 343* ; John 81, 222, 338, 343* ; Wm. 175.

Goodrich(e), Ellen 344 ; John 344 ; Wm. 157.
Goodrick, Sar. 153.
Goodridge (Goodryge), John 338 ; Wm. 353.
Goodsonne, Alice 198.
Goodspeed(e), Mary 374 ; Tho. 96 ; Wm. 285.
Goodwin (Goodwyne), — 350 ; Edw. 255 ; Eliz. 4, 255 ; John, 76, 81, 130, 131, 180 ; Tho. 277 ; Wm. 101, 141.
Goold(e), Agn. 312 ; Anne 312 ; Hugh 312* ; John 75, 76, 157, 312 ; Sus. 312.
Goore, John 255.
Goos, John 269*, 271.
Gootheridge, John 213.
Gosbell, Prisc. 143 ; Wm. 310.
Goslyn, John 378*.
Gosmolde, John 135.
Gosson, Rich. 257.
Gottred, Thos. 276.
Goud(e)s, Han. 360 ; Jasper 360 ; John 360, 363.
Gouges, John 361.
Gould (Gowlde), Eliz. 286 ; Geo. 258 ; Joan 258 ; Judith 154 ; Sym. 154 ; Tho. 278, 286 ; Tim. 187. See Golde.
Gouldin (Gowldyn), Edw. 318 ; Mary 170. See Golding.
Goule, John 190.
Gowin, Barb. 149.
Grace, Agn. 163 ; Bastian 217 ; Dan. 312 ; Edw. 80 ; Eliz. 312 ; John 312, 323, 326, 327* ; Margt. 312 ; Nic. 176 ; Ric. 163, 312*, 346 ; Sam. 163 ; Sebastian, 312* ; Tho. 83, 312* ; Wm. 27, 223, 312*.
Grand, Wm. 233.
Grat, Thos. 321.
Gra(u)nge, John 243 ; Tho. 27.
Grave, — 65 ; Agn. 78, 130, 176, 178, 216 ; Bridget 29 ; Edm. 176 ; Edw. 29, 216 ; Eliz. 274 ; Frances 221 ; Geo. 29, 81, 176, 307*, 356 ; Hen. 29, 84 ; Jas. 174, 226 ; Joan 174 ; John 29*, 72, 153, 216, 274, 318, 381, 382 ; Kath. 29 ; Margt. 29 ; Ric. 353 ; Rob. 29*, 35, 37, 174, 181, 214, 221, 273, 274 ; Tho. 29*, 35, 37, 78, 86, 103, 130, 157, 174, 178, 274, 275, 344 ; Wm. 24, 29, 178, 274, 275.
Graveley, Eliz. 310 ; Fras. 310* ; Geo. 306, 337 ; Joan 258 ; John 133, 134, 174 ; Julian 310* ; Martha 337 ; Rowl. 310 ; Tho. 258, 310*.
Gravenor (Gravener), Edm. 228 ; Rob. 35, 174, 175 ; Wm. 174.
Graves, Hugh 230 ; Jane 166 ; Jo. 379 ; Tho. 142.
Grawe, Hen. 274 ; Ric. 274.
Gray(e) (Graie), — 315 ; Alice 223 ; Andr. 308 ; Ann 332 ; Eliz. 11, 369 ; Fras. 310* ; Grace 310* ; Helen 209 ; Ivo 133 ; Jeremy 80, 132 ; John 223,

310*, 313, 316, 347; Kath. 310;
Lewes 12; Margt. 64, 310*; Mary
75, 94, 370; Matrone 277; Ric.
351; Rob. 25*; Sar. 293*; Tho.
164, 310, 332; Walt. 25, 26; Wm.
164, 310.
Graye *alias* Butler, Rob. 313.
Graynger, Rich. 254.
Greaues, John 289; Rob. 289.
Green (Gren, Greine), — 212; Agn.
95; Dor. 12; Geo. 52; Gilb. 30;
Grace 208; Hen. 242; Joan 350;
John 64*, 65*, 99, 197, 202, 274,
277; Laur. 78; Margt. 191; Mary
170, 242; Ric. 73, 78, 257, 272,
278, 339, 354; Rob. 275; Rog. 366,
368; Sar. 212; Tho. 147, 228, 273;
Val. 242; Wm. 72, 98, 273, 350.
*See Gladman*.
Greenhill, Mary 239; Tho. 51, 187.
Greeninge, John 100; Tho. 211; Wm.
361.
Greenwood (Greenewod, Greneho(o)d),
Anne 149; Kath. 46; Ric. 232;
Wm. 312.
Gregory (Gregorie, Grigorie), Dan. 6,
243; Fr. 52; Grace 243; John 75,
138; Ric. 346; Rob. 168; Tho. 6,
243; Wm. 228.
Gregorie *alias* Redhead, Edw. 214.
Grenehope, John 351.
Grennell, John 86, 120; Nich. 273.
Greswell, Geo. 51*.
Gretham, Alice 192; Rob. 192.
Grevett, John 371.
Grey(e), Andr. 35, 220, 305*, 308;
Anne 308; Eliz. 285; Ivo 33; John
269, 349; Ralph 322; Walt. 268;
Wm. 346, 347, 348.
Griffe (Gryffe), Margt. 215*.
Griffin (Griffen, Gryffyn), Agn. 103*;
Alice 36, 362; Edm. 257; Edw.
360*; Eliz. 103*, 372; Frances
360*; Jas. 36; John 84, 103, 200,
276, 320, 360; Jone 103; Mary 83;
Ric. 372, 375; Rob. 220; Tho. 360;
Wm. 356, 360. *See Gurley*.
Griffith (Gryffythe), Alice 175; Jas.
175; Mary 48; Rowland 126; Wm.
262.
Grigg(e) (Grygg, Grige, Grigs), Eliz.
204; Joan 312; John 84*, 167;
Margt. 312; Mary 84; Rob. 221,
312*; Tho. 312; Wm. 28, 32, 136*.
Grimes, Reb. 283; Syb. 244.
Gronwynne, Ric. 88; Tho. 88. *See
Grunwin*.
Groom(e), John 6; Sam. 102.
Grossbor, Thos. 274.
Grot(e)more, Ric. 23, 234*.
Grove, Arth. 350; Barb. 160, 161,
162, 163; Edm. 76; Edw. 162;
Hen. 160, 161*, 162, 163; Jas. 163;
John 231; Jos. 8; Mary 8; Sar.
161; Wm. 329.
Grove *alias* Johnson, Joan 330.

Grover(e), Anne 162; Gatheriche 170;
Geo. 330; Han. 164; Hen. 161,
164*; Hester 163; John 164, 301,
330, 341, 372; Mary 114; Reb. 114,
163; Ric. 73, 93, 114*, 115, 152,
161, 163, 164*, 227, 300*; Rob. 73;
Sus. 168; Tho. 140, 164; Wm. 164.
Growt, Jas. 320
Grub(be) (Grobbe), — 206; Abig. 7;
Agn. 149; Anne 7; Const. 345;
Dor. 123; Eliz. 131, 158, 173, 228;
Eustace 123*, 345; Geo. 122*, 123,
142; Hen. 28, 122*, 351; Joan 195,
228; John 123*, 195, 352; Nath.
154; Ric. 24, 122*, 228, 261; Rob.
27; Roger 131, 173, 351; Sar. 94;
Tho. 41, 239; Wm. 30, 41.
Grunnill (Grunell), Ann 7; John 253;
Ralph 253.
Grunwell, Thos. 40.
Grunwin (Grunwyn, Grunwind), Edm.
287; Edw. 96; Eliz. 287, 342;
John 342; Mary 287; Sar. 95. *See
Gronwynne*.
Gryme, Dor. 219, 344; Hen. 219.
Grymesdyche (Grymsditch), Eliz. 221;
Tho. 78, 175, 177, 178, 221, 254.
Gue, Edw. 10; Sam. 363.
Guet, John 161.
Guise (Guyse), John 167; Wm. 166.
Gun(n)e, Rich. 218; Wm. 275.
Gun(n)ell, Agn. 258; Clem. 34, 258;
John 79; Mary 246; Wm. 246*.
Gunstone, Thos. 183.
Gunthorpe, Ralph 12*.
Gunttyune, Wm. 104.
Gurley (Gurlye), Geo. 313; Leon. 30;
Rob. 30; Wm. 30.
Gurley *alias* Griffin, Geo. 30.
Gurnett, Sus. 5.
Gurney, Anth. 244; John 95.
Guthre(e), Rob. 62, 65, 103.
Gutteridge, John 208; Mary 208;
Rich. 290; Wm. 290.
Guye, Rob. 27.
Guyver, John 383; Jos. 383*.
Gyfford, Hugh 351.
Gyffyn, James 273.
Gylderson, Jas. 274; Wm. 274.
Gyles, Gylles. *See Giles*.
Gyllett. *See Gillett*.
Gylmote *alias* Gylman, Tho. 338.
Gylnar, Edm. 73; Eliz. 73; Joan 73;
John 73; Lettis 73; Nic. 73;
Ralph 73; Rob. 73; Tho. 73*, 74;
Wm. 73.
Gylson (Gilson), Joan 273; John 273,
276.
Gyner, Roger 199.
Gynn(e) (Gin(n)e), Geo. 24, 151, 341;
Hen. 134, 355; Jane 178; Joan
134, 154; Mary 355; Sim. 29;
Tho. 154; Walt. 178; Wm. 1, 311.
*See Ginns*.
Gyssee, Roger 256.
Gyssyng, John 231.

Hackman, Rich. 199.
Hackney, Joseph 101.
Hackshaw(e), Hum. 235; Rob. 256.
Haddon, John 122; Kath. 367; Ric. 352, 366, 368*.
Hade, Alice 242; Steven 242; Tho. 242.
Hadeley(e), Geo. 339; Wm. 278.
Hadesley, Rich. 275.
Hadie. *See Maple*.
Hadley, Cecily 81; Rob. 81.
Hagar, Hen. 86; Wm. 79.
Hagarthe, Geo. 173.
Hagger, Alice 33, 97.
Haine, Nich. 271.
Hakes, John 229.
Halden (Haldon), John 179, 338; Tho. 179.
Hale (Haile), Agn. 134, 189; Alice 209; Edith 192; Edm. 134, 337; Grace 213; Hen. 238; Jer. 360; Joan 189; John 44, 78, 90*, 163, 189*, 236*, 238, 360; Margt. 236; Margery. 238; Mary 359*, 360*; Mr 105*, 106; Ric. 134, 149, 153, 218, 225, 238*, 306; Rob. 213*; Rowl 360; Sam. 211; Sim. 189; Tho. 90*, 238; Walt. 44, 90, 236; Wm. 90, 187, 192, 206, 236, 262, 359, 360*.
Hales, Alice 80; Jas. 80; Reb. 95.
Half(e)head (Halfhedd), Anne 79; Beat. 343; Edw. 79, 343; Rich. 53*.
Half(e)hide (Hallfehyde), Alice 304; Amy 177; Anne 222, 257, 305*; Dennis 230*; Edw. 134, 177, 221, 222, 257, 305*; Eliz. 230*; Ellen 227; Ezech. 43; Hen. 151; Jas. 1, 304; Joan 230; John 206, 230*; Kath. 230; Leon. 178; Lettice 178; Margery 173; Nic. 276; Ric. 173; Wm. 43, 273.
Halford, Fras. 169, 285, 373.
Halingdale, Sam. 66.
Hall(e), Anne 8, 221, 340, 341; Cic. 12; Edm. 174; Edw. 230; Eliz. 180, 331; Fras. 20*, 22; Geo. 176; Joan 31, 104; John 31*, 35, 95*, 96, 135, 155*, 166, 180, 215, 246, 256, 278, 285; Joseph 52; Margt. 31, 202, 303; Martha 114; Mary 31, 82*, 166, 374; Mich. 314; Mordecai 246; Reb. 246; Ric. 180, 203, 340, 350, 353; Rob. 180, 221*, 341, 378; Roland 343; Sam. 363, 373; Sus. 214; Tho. 6, 93*, 136, 138, 139, 142, 303, 340; Wm. 344; Winif. 31, 256.
Hallam, Thos. 76, 156.
Halloway, Mary 375.
Hal(l)ywell (Hallewell), Alice 318*, 338; Cath. 318; Eliz. 87, 318; John 87, 318*; Kath. 87; Mary 87, 318*; Reb. 318; Rob. 80, 87, 318, 338; Tho. 179.
Halse, John 32.

Halsey (Hawlsey), Alice 315; Amy 315; Anne 315; Dan. 151; Dor. 282, 315; Edw. 169; Eliz. 95, 284; Fras. 167; Geo. 285; Grace 210; Han. 362; Hester 315; Isaac 7; Jas. 240, 283; John 27, 169, 186, 333; Judith 239, 315; Lucy 169; Margt. 174; Mary 6, 315*; Mordecai 186; Phil. 315; Reb. 315; Ric. 28*, 169; Rob. 27, 143, 159, 314, 315*; Sam. 335; Sar. 6, 92, 315; Tho. 8, 135, 169, 174, 208, 282, 315*, 374*; Wm. 27, 315*, 329.
Halsey [Halsye] *alias* Chamber(s). — 43; Margt. 35; Ric. 75*; Rob. 31; Tho. 35, 79. *See Chambers alias Halsey*
Halton, Agn. 80; Hen. 80.
Hamant, Leonard 32.
Ham(m)ond(e), Agn. 156*, 157, 278; Alex. 303; Basill 276; Clemens 157; Edm. 278; Edw. 227; Eliz. 342, 343, 344*, 345; Geo. 63, 157, 276*, 278, 342; Henry 156, 157, 180, 257, 342, 343*, 344*, 345; Joan 156; John 68, 69*, 153, 155, 156, 157, 209, 230, 273, 276*; Margt. 156, 157, 342; Margery 157; Marryon 63; Martha 8; Peter 42; Ric. 350; Rog. 156, 276; Tho. 84, 257, 350; Wm. 1, 156*, 157*, 272, 276*, 342.
Hamon, Eliz. 340; Geo. 340*; Hen. 340*; John 218, 340; Maurice 340; Rob. 302, 340; Tho. 340; Wm. 302, 340.
Hampden, Edw. 34; Mich. 34.
Hampton, —— 12, 318; Grace 12; John 103, 278; Ric. 12; Rob. 216, 305; Wm. 216, 305, 309, 344.
Hanchett, Anne 309; Julian 218; Mary 341; Mr 11; Tho. 131, 309, 341*.
Hancocke, Sus. 96.
Hand, Eliz. 150.
Handforte, Wm 217, 254, 304.
Handkyn, Geo. 158.
Handlye, John 158.
Hanford, John 276.
Hankes, Hen. 321.
Hankyn (Hankin), Chas. 249; John 192, 355.
Hannam, Thos. 342.
Han(n)ell (Hanniel), Jas. 169, 282; Tho. 140; Wm. 261, 285, 335.
Hanscom(b)e (Hanscombe, Hanscowie), Eliz. 32, 149; John 245, 246*, 247; Mary 247; Math. 73, 210, 308, 338; Rob. 32; Sus. 246, 247; Thos. 149.
Harbarson, Anne 313.
Harbert, Edw. 338; Mary 338.
Harbinger, Edw. 12.
Hardewyn, Agn. 46*; Wm. 46.
Harding(e) (Hardyng), —— 313; Agn. 63; Anne 361; Christr. 64

76; Edw. 217; Eliz. 151; Fras.
281; Geo. 63*, 228; Hugh 126;
Joan 63, 228; John 149, 165, 331;
Mary 63; Mich. 151; Rauf 347;
Steph. 375; Sus. 48, 228; Wm. 301.
Hardwen, Giles 181.
Hardwike (Hardewyk), Tho. 351;
Wm. 237.
Hardy(e), Hen. 148, 194; Phil. 199;
Wm. 265*.
Hare, Fras. 99; Hen. 278; Jane 286;
John 5; Jos. 330; Mary 288; Nath.
374; Rob. 222; Tho. 343.
Harford Martha 95.
Haris *alias* Clarke, Rog. 160.
Harley, Gab. 282; Jonas 282.
Harlowe, Bridget 203.
Harmer (Harmar), Alice 76, 132;
Joan 76; John 76, 99, 132, 175*,
314, 343; Peter 76*; Tho. 76*,
307, 343, 344.
Harmon (Harman). Edw. 219; Isab.
219; Joan 36; Kath. 34; Peter 36;
Roger 34; Tho. 28.
Harpe, John 266, 267.
Harper (Harpur), —— 283; Eliz.
283, 357; John 312; Ric. 210;
Rob. 211; Wm. 140, 348.
Harris (Harrys, Harryes, Haris, Hares,
Hariese), Agn. 41; Ann 168, 244,
246*; Edw. 202, 206; Jas. 202;
John 37, 112*, 244, 309; Margt.
303; Martha 170; Mary 358; Mich.
303; Peter 244, 246*; Reb. 142;
Ric. 182*; Rob. 122, 351; Rog.
96; Sar. 246, 283; Tho. 156, 307,
346, 358; Wm. 83, 88, 126, 128.
Harrison (Harryson), Christian 113*;
Jas. 142, 275; John 50; Rob. 113;
Sym. 274; Tho. 303; Wm. 351.
Harrod, Mary 115, 151; Ric. 115;
Wm. 151. *See Lawrance.*
Harroden, Mary 180; Tho. 180*.
Harrolde, Edw. 2.
Harrop (Harrip, Harrup), Ann 247;
Eliz. 246; Hen. 244, 246; Tho.
246; Wm. 7.
Har(r)yngton (Harrington), Fras. 174;
Isab. 77, 221; John 77, 174, 221;
Rob. 342; Wm. 276.
Hart (H(e)arte), Alice 312; Anne 244;
Beatrice 320; Eliz. 137; Jas. 3 2;
Joan 312; John 39, 244, 246*, 320*;
Marrian 320; Martha 246; Mary
244; Tho. 312*, 367.
Hartbard *alias* Rogers, Clem. 9; Wm.
9*.
Hartelye, Agn. 157; Mary 287;
Rouland 157.
Hartford(e) Nic. 262; Wm. 256.
Hartin, Wm. 168.
Harton, Geo. 318; John 349.
Hartwell, Edw. 202; Isab. 202.
Harvey (Harvye, Harvie), Agn. 158*;
Alice 63, 256, 342*, 347; Cecily 255,
307; Edm. 274; Gyles 158; Hum.
341, 342; Joan 63, 158, 262*; John

63, 77, 99, 188*, 189, 218, 255*, 256,
258, 276*, 304, 307, 339, 341, 342*;
Margery 255, 258, 304; Margt. 63,
307; Ralph 158; Ric. 63; Rob.
158*; Sam. 150; Sim. 176, 255,
307; Tho. 63, 158, 274, 275, 342;
Wm. 63*, 138, 262, 273, 276.
Harwarde, Christr 205; Mary 205.
Harwood, Eliz. 43; Joan 43.
Haskins, Abig. 150.
Hassarde, Edw. 31.
Hasten, John 310.
Hastings, Fras. 304; Geo. 304.
Haaye (Hasey), Ric. 29; Rob. 29.
Hasylden, Fras. 367.
Haaylwood (Hassellwood), Nevell 174;
Rob. 320; Tho. 215.
Hutch, Cath. 152; Mary 137.
Hattley, Rob. 120; 123*.
Hatton, John 319, 354; Lucy 10;
Margt. 319; Mr. 158; Ric. 212;
Rob. 72, 158.
Hattred, Geo. 311.
Havers, John 66.
Haward(e), Anne 10; Gee. 315;
Roland 178.
Hawden, John 232.
Hawes (Hawse), —— 156; Tho. 84*,
227; Wm. 86, 227.
Hawfehende, Ell. 2; John 2.
Hawgood, Agn. 32; Alice 32; Emm.
32; Fras. 32; Jas. 137; John 32*,
63, 351; Margt. 32; Nic. 63; Ric.
32, 352; Rob 352; Sar. 137; Tho.
63; Walt. 137; Wm. 352.
Hawke, Hen. 40, 319; Ric. 38.
Hawkes (Haukes), John 30; Mary 93;
Rob. 42; Tho. 313; Wm. 34.
Hawkeshedd, Wm. 342.
Hawkins (Haukins, Hawkyn(e)s),
Agn. 72; Edw. 378, 379, 380*;
Geo. 212, 270, 277, 303, 326, 327,
328, 377, 379*; Hellen 41, 104;
Hugh 359, 360, 362, 363*; Joan 104;
John 9, 72, 104, 142, 153, 213, 239,
272*, 277, 281*, 356, 363; Mary 170,
359, 360, 363*; Mistress 119; Nic.
104, 284; Peter 72; Reb. 169;
Ric. 139, 169, 348; Sar. 360; Steph.
143, 370; Tho. 72, 100, 330, 359.
Hawkswell, Leon. 44.
Hawman, John 273.
Haword, Peter 101.
Hay, Thomas 312.
Haydie, John 32.
Haydon (Hayden), Frances 131, 222;
Francis 131, 222; Ralph 134; Tho.
343.
Hayes, Thomas 240.
Haygard, John 275.
Hayle, Rich. 350.
Haylocke, Mr. 72.
Haylye, Rich. 73, 74.
Haynde, Wm. 46.
Haynes (Haines, Hayne), Agn. 274,
343*; Alice 270*; Edm. 343; Eliz.
273; Geo. 343; John 177, 242, 342,

343*; Jone 357; Kath. 357; Mary 343*; Nic. 270*; Peter 242; Philis 242; Ric. 274; Tho. 273; Uxor 233; Wm. 150, 278, 357.
Hayrse, Cecily 305; Ric. 305.
Hayward(e), Geo. 342; Hen. 329*; Hum. 122; Joan 342; Martha 380*; Rob. 12, 339*; Roland 79, 223; Tho. 41, 43, 317, 380*; Walt. 82; Wm. 43, 339.
Hayworth, Thos. 33.
Hazard, Mother 310.
He . . . . , Rich. 28.
Head, John 48; Peter 48.
Headey (Headye), John 73, 314.
Headlam(me), Bridget 11; John 11*, 33, 40, 85, 97, 120, 319, 320*, 321; Kath. 11; Wm. 11.
Heald, Ann 83.
Heale, Luke 202; Nic. 202; Phil. 201; Wm. 201.
Healy, Richard 313.
Heare, Henry 228.
Hearne, Wm. 158*.
Hearynge, Eliz. 319; Rowland 319.
Heathe (Hethe, At Hethe); Agn. 143; Alice 292; Fulk 175; Greg. 138; Jeff. 205; John 30*, 295*; Mary 295*, 362; Ric. 201; Rob. 177, 349; Roger 146*; Tho. 87, 214, 315, 349, 382*, 383; Wm. 312.
Heatly, Hellenor 49.
Heaward, Geo. 311; Sam. 239; Wm. 312.
Heblethwet(t), Rowl. 112, 113.
Hebson, John 75.
Hecheman, Alice 192.
Hedd, Margery 308; Tho. 258, 308.
Heddeson, Geo. 74; Ralph 74; Tho. 74.
Hedge, Thos. 177, 353.
Hedgekin, Francis 75.
Heel (Hele), Hen. 246; John 246; Kath. 246; Mary 246*; Tho. 348; Wm. 276.
Hegger, Hum. 350.
Heggs, Eliz. 94.
Hegyn, John 269.
Heigham, Anne 307; Fras. 344; Geo. 302, 314; Hen. 255, 307, 344; Martha 222.
Helbye (Helbey, Hell), John 348; Ric. 275.
Held, Thos. 278.
Helder, John 73; Ric. 73. *See Spicer*.
Helder *alias* Spicer, Frances 210; Rob. 210.
Helgaye, Thos. 277.
Helham (Hellam), John 181, 275, 342*.
Hely(e), Agn. 222; John 150, 222.
Hemerford, Andrew 81.
Hemminge (Hemynge), Ellen 39; Joan 39, 178, 318; John 39, 178, 342, 345*; Rob. 302, 342; Tho. 272.
Hemyngwaye, Adam 216.
Henchman, Thos. 72.
Henes, Frances 354; Rob. 355; Wm. 355.

Henman, Wm. 169.
Hennage, Jas. 35; Margt. 35.
Henrye, Hary 204.
Herberd, Wm. 346.
Herbert, Bridget 283; Goodman 50; Walt. 238.
Herde, —— 89, 90; Eliz. 217, 219; Geo. 89, 217, 219; John 120.
Herdman, Gartered 39; John 39; Margt. 39; Tho. 39.
Hereford, Geo. Cooke bishop of 106; Walt. visc. 82.
Herne, Julius 312; Oliver 216; Ric. 354; Wm. 186, 347.
Heron, Hen. 319; John 118.
Hert, Edm. 270; John 23.
Hertforde, Wm. 262, 291*, 307.
Herwell, Agn. 47.
Heryn, Wm. 275.
Hetes, Wm. 319.
Hetton, Wm. 277.
Hevenyngham, Arthur 308; Mary 308.
Heward, Allyn 310*; Eliz. 310; Ellen 310; Hen. 310*; John 310*; Nic. 310; Wm. 311.
Hewell, Jo. 361.
Hewes, Albyn 346.
Hewett (Hewitt), Eliz. 27, 51; Hen. 255; Hester 135; John 352; Nath. 51*; Wm. 219.
Hewson, Christr. 340; Eliz. 340; John 372.
Hewys, Thos. 366.
Heydaye, Joan 319; Rob. 319.
Heydon, Alice 12; Dor. 74; Edm. 349; Frances 82; Fras. 82*; Hen. 26, 272; Jas. 114, 348; John 74, 349; Ric. 349; Sar. 142; Tho. 74; Wm. 331*.
Heygate, Wm. 343.
Heylot, Roger 348.
Heylye, Rich. 310.
Heyne, Thos. 91.
Heynes, Fras. 203; Geo. 203.
Heyward(e) (Heyworde), Agn. 10; Alban 331; Edw. 31; Eliz. 8, 31, 136, 168; Geo. 10, 310; Hen. 350. Hum. 176; John 31, 72*, 190, 347, 373; Jonas 239; Lawr. 230; Margt. 94; Matth. 239; Ralph 329, 331, 335; Ric. 27; Rob. 75, 166, 190*; Sisley 72; Tho. 28, 31*, 349, 352; Wm. 31, 348.
Heyward *alias* Howard, John 286; Ralph 284.
Heyworthe, —— 26.
Hiccox, Thos. 239.
Hickden, Rich. 353.
Hickford, Tho. 140.
Hickman (Hickeman, Hyckeman, Hicman), Agn. 132, 256; Alice 342; Anne 284; Edw. 132; Eliz. 35; Hen. 33, 82, 187, 253, 342; Joan 82; John 244, 246, 256; Mary 214; Ric. 35, 348; Sar. 244, 246; Tho. 65, 207, 208, 228, 246, 351, 372; Wm. 338.

Higate, Mrs 51; Tho. 34.
Higbit, Emme 156; Fras. 155.
Higbyde, Rob. 34.
Higbye (Hygbye), Rob. 347; Wm. 42.
Higden, Julian 157; Walt. 149.
Higgs, John 136.
Highland, Mary 245.
Hill(e) (Hyll, Hills), Abig. 141; Agn. 142; Anne 141, 167, 223; Barth. 310, 311; Chas. 113*, 115, 162; Dan. 375; Dor. 62; Edw. 62, 141; Eliz. 93*, 139; Geof. 28; Geo. 183, 184, 200; Gilb. 77, 118, 178, 256; Han. 166; Isab. 46, 190; James 310; Jane 303; Joan 152, 310; John 76*, 98, 109, 115, 148*, 190, 196, 223, 237, 259, 277, 278, 310, 321, 329, 347, 348, 351*, 354; Lettice 113, 115; Margt. 153, 200, 201; Mary 141; Mich. 354; Ralph 350; Ric. 30, 62, 350; Rob. 46, 147, 340, 348, 353; Tho. 23, 139, 210, 211, 310*, 340, 348; Wm. 62, 140, 235, 303, 348, 350, 352. *See At Hills.*
Hilocomius. *See Thomas.*
Hilton, John 90, 208.
Hind(e), Dion. 134; Edm. 134; Eliz. 94, 154; Fras. 132; John 166; Nic. 105*; Tho. 132; Wm. 166. *See Hynde.*
Hinksman, Wm. 123.
Hinoue, Wm. 87.
Hinton, Wm. 278.
Hipworthe, John 36.
Hitchcocke, Edw. 317; Jos. 167; Margt. 162; Rog. 283; Wm. 167.
Hitche (Hytch), Wm. 120, 218.
Hitchin (Hitchen), Edw. 212; Isab. 212; Joan 150; Rob. 370.
Hitchman, John 321*; Margt. 321; Rob. 321*.
Hix, Sarah 168.
Hoar(e), Senator 376; Sus. 167.
Hobbes, Jack 107; John 348*; Josias 210; Tho. 12.
Hobekyn, Nich. 266.
Hobley (Hopley), Jas. 6.
Hobson(e), Tho. 1; Wm. 143.
Hobyll, John 87.
Hocheson, Gilbert 159.
Hochyn, Thos. 275.
Hochynson, Christr. 174; Kath. 174.
Hocket (Hookett), Tho. 348.
Hockley, Rachel 382; Tho. 383.
Hodden, Annes 352.
Hod(de)sden (Hodsdon), Anne 215, 308; John 333, 335, 348; Mary 138; Ric. 287; Sar. 44; Tho. 40*, 215, 288, 308, 372; Wm. 333, 348.
Hode, John 28.
Hodge, Christr. 38; Eliz. 357; Isab. 38; Joan 276; John 275; Kath. 38; Margt. 38, 133; Ric. 276; Sam. 38; Sar. 38; Tho. 24, 38, 273, 275.

Hodgekins, Rob. 155.
Hodges, Fras. 285; Wm. 120.
Hodgeson, Eliz. 9; Hester 9; John 9; Millicent 9.
Hodgsdoun, Anne 285.
Hodierne, Thos. 94.
Hodson, Eliz. 246*; Jos. 5; Ric. 246.
Hogg(e), Agn. 80; Anne 64; John 80; Tho. 136.
Hog(ge)kyn, John 90; Mich. 234.
Hogou (Hogyn), —— 326; John 323, 324*, 325, 328.
Holbem, Agn. 40.
Holbydge (Holbidge, Holebydge), Amey 242; Edw. 204; John 202, 204, Tho. 242*; Widow 243.
Holcome, Wm. 346.
Holden, Agn. 304; Anne 341; Joan 176; Tho. 176, 253, 304, 341.
Holder, Hugh 121.
Holford(e), Fras. 369; Hen. 94; Ric. 35.
Holiday (Hollydaye), Sar. 8; Tho. 75.
Hollam, Dor. 120; John 120; Wm. 120.
Holland, Eliz. 341; John 232, 278; Mary 135; Rob. 126*, 351; Tho. 255, 339; Wm. 341*.
Holling(s)worth, Anne 244, 245, 246*; Chas. 244, 246; Edw. 245; Eliz. 213; Martha 247; Sar. 244, 245; Wm. 247.
Hollis, Ellen 281.
Hollye, Alice 227; Geo. 227; John 227; Mary 227; Rach. 227.
Hol(l)yman (Holiman), Edw. 113*, 114, 160*, 161*, 163, 164; Eliz. 114, 161; Fras. 114; Jude 113; Judeth 161; Lettis 113; Mich. 113.
Holm, Hen. 54.
Ho(l)mes, Alice 35, 236*, 303; Clem. 200; Edw. 155; John 73, 211; Mother 73; Rob. 35, 303; Tho. 236, 281, 290; Wm. 303, 348.
Holond, Helen 92; John 92.
Holstok, John 147.
Holt(e), Jas. 152; John 282; Kath. 352.
Holtyng, —— 349; Phil. 351.
Homarston. *See Humberston.*
Honor, Eliz. 152.
Hoo, Agn. 237; Grace 344*; John 148, 237*; Lucy 304; Nic. 217, 344*; Petronilla 237; Steph. 237*; Tho. 132, 237, 304*, 344*; Wm. 237. *See At Hoo.*
Hoode, Margt. 38*.
Hooker, Mary 95.
Hooper, Hum. 134, 173.
Hooton, Mary 51.
Hope, Edw. 7.
Hopkins, Avis 238; Jer. 284, 285*; John 73; Mary 372; Sam. 372.
Hopkyns *alias* Jane, Tho. 258.
Hopley. *See Hobley.*
Hoppie, Jas. 143.
Hopwoode, Rob. 205.

Horde, Cecily 255 ; Geo. 255.
Hore, Rob. 277.
Horevod, —— 181.
Hormed(e), John 275 ; Tho. 275.
Horn(e), Chas. 364 ; Edw. 80, 312 ; Julian 221 ; Margt. 80 ; Wm. 352.
Horneby, Rob. 365.
Horrwoode (Hoorewood), Cecily 31 ; John 86 ; Rob. 31. *See Horwoode.*
Horsell, Edw. 139, 371.
Horseman, Tho. 82*, 95, 130*, 179.
Horsey (Horsie), Geo. 79*, 82, 88, 302, 304, 339.
Horskeper, Nic. 126.
Horslye, Abr. 230*.
Horton, John 132 ; Mary 132.
Horwood(e), Adam 276 ; Hen. 236. *See Horrwoode.*
Horwell, —— 350 ; Wm. 350.
Howard(e), John 246 ; Kath. 308*, 339*, 340*, 344 ; Mary 246 ; Ralph 240*, 284 ; Thos. lord 308*, 339*, 340*, 344 ; Thos. 375 ; Wm. 245, 246. *See Heyward.*
How(e), Abig. 149 ; Agn. 82, 158 ; Allen 62 ; Audry 339 ; Dan. 186 ; Edm 210 ; Edw. 75, 82, 303 ; Eliz. 42, 370 ; Fras. 286 ; Hen. 179*, 229 ; Jas. 83, 371 ; Joan 75 ; John 8, 27, 39*, 75*, 93, 122, 135, 156, 220, 311 ; Jud. 370 ; Kath. 179 ; Leon. 179 ; Luce 75 ; Margt. 339 ; Mary 8 ; Matt. 3 ; Mich. 156 ; Mr. 382 ; Ric. 35, 75*, 240, 311, 339 ; Rob. 75* 275 ; Roger 179* ; Sar. 8, 237 ; Tho. 74, 75, 82, 157, 179, 227, 273, 274 ; Wm. 8, 110, 179, 220, 240, 334.
Howell, Jo. 362 ; Jone 362 ; Ric. 234 ; Rob. 362 ; Tho. 243.
Hower, Christr. 352.
Howghton, Jas. 135 ; Ric. 135.
Hows(e) (House, Howze), Agn. 304 ; Ann 288 ; Eliz. 136 ; John 304, 314 ; Mary 369 ; Tho. 110.
Howson, Mary 155. *See Smythe.*
Hoye, Edw. 158* ; Eliz. 158 ; John 158, 181, 337 ; Mary 216 ; Tho. 320.
Hoye *alias* Odye, Joan 176 ; Rob. 176 ; Tho. 134.
Hoyland, Eliz. 372.
Hubberd(e) (Hubbard, Hubbert), Adam 283 ; Anne 42, 227 ; Edw. 35, 134, 220 ; Hen. 42, 227 ; Jane 220 ; Joan 218 ; John 86, 218 ; Marm. 370 ; Matt. 288 ; Ric. 266, 275 ; Wm. 86.
Hubhull, John 189.
Huchin (Huchyn), John 12 ; Tho. 276.
Huckle, Basell 230 ; John 302, 306 ; Oswald 256 ; Sar. 154, 294 ; Tho. 214.
Huckle *alias* Hurst, Jane 142.
Hucksley, Eliz. 154.
Huddell (Huddle), Const. 228 ; Edw. 228*, 350 ; Eliz. 228 ; John 65* ; Mary 285 ; Tho. 228 ; Wm. 228.

Huddleston (Huddelston(e), Huddilston), Dor. 77 ; Edm. 77 ; Isab. 254 ; John 245, 246*, 288 ; Mary 246 ; Ric. 254.
Hudding, Sar. 240.
Hudgebout, Martha 264 ; Mary 264.
Hudnall (Hudnoll, Hudnole), Hen. 19, 20*, 21*, 42, 81, 113, 228* ; John 228*, 258 ; Ric. 21, 42 ; Syb. 228 ; Wm. 228.
Hudson (Hoodsone), —— 182, 213 ; Christr. 255 ; Edw. 204 ; Fras. 204 ; John 95, 200 ; Tho. 176, 304, 340 ; Wm. 154.
Huett, Wm. 35.
Huff, George 12.
Huggins (Huggens), Steph. 95, 240.
Hugh, Hen. 148, 194.
Hughes, Mary 374 ; Rouland 158 ; Sar. 332.
Hukes, Rob. 275.
Hulden, Als 320.
Hull (Atte Hull), John 267 ; Ralph 286.
Hulme, Jas. 96
Humberstone (Humbarston, Hummerston, Homberston, Homarstone), —— 4 ; Agn. 33*, 97*, 98* ; Alice 1*, 2*, 3, 98, 99* ; Anne 3*, 4, 50*, 51*, 98*, 99, 100*, 101* ; Avice 1 ; Barbara 1, 99 ; Barnabas 1 ; Beatrice 1 ; Cath. 98, 100 ; Chas. 53 ; Cicily 52, 97, 99 ; Dan. 102 ; Dor. 1, 50, 51, 99 ; Edm. 4*, 51* ; Edw. 2, 3*, 4, 33, 49, 51*, 52, 53, 97*, 98*, 99, 100, 101*, 214 ; Eliz. 1*, 2*, 4, 49*, 50, 51*, 53, 98*, 99, 101, 102* ; Ell. 4*, 98 ; Em. 50 ; Frances 100 ; Fras. 2, 4, 50*, 51, 98, 99, 101 ; Garnons 4, 53 ; Geo. 4*, 33, 51*, 53, 97*, 98, 101, 102* ; Grace 98, 101, 102 ; Gyles 2, 3*, 4, 50*, 51, 53, 97, 98 ; Henry 2*, 3*, 4*, 52, 53, 97, 98, 100 ; Hugh 3, 4 ; Jas. 4, 51*, 53* ; Joan 1*, 49, 52, 53 ; John 1*, 2*, 3*, 4*, 33*, 49, 50*, 51, 52, 80, 97*, 98*, 99*, 100*, 101*, 102, 308 ; Kath. 98 ; Leon. 1*, 2, 50, 52, 53, 87, 97, 98 ; Lewis 98* ; Margt. 1*, 2, 3, 51, 53, 99, 101 ; Margery 52 ; Mary 2*, 3*, 50*, 51, 53*, 99, 100*, 101*, 102* ; Miles 53 ; Mr 108* ; Osmond 3* ; Peter 4*, 51, 52 ; Ric. 2*, 3, 4, 97, 102, 156 ; Rob. 2*, 4, 50, 53, 98*, 99*, 100 ; Sar. 3, 50, 51, 52, 101, 102 ; Sislie 33 ; Sus. 2, 50, 99* ; Theodocia 3 ; Tho. 1*, 2, 3*, 4*, 49, 50, 51*, 53, 98*, 99*, 100*, 101*, 102* ; Timothy 101* ; Wm. 1, 2*, 3*, 4*, 33*, 49*, 50*, 51*, 52*, 53, 97*, 98*, 99*, 100*, 102. *See Reeve.*
Humberstone *alias* Daniell, Beatrice 52.
Humberstone *alias* Finch, Sar. 52.
Humferstone (Humfreystone), Wm. 228, 247.

Humfrey (Humfrie, Humphrey), Dan. 158; Eliz. 32, 305; Fras. 164; John 158; Lucy 158; Mary 370; Mich. 335; Ric. 259; Tho. 305, 352; Wm. 158.
Hunden, Robt. 268.
Hundsdon, Sam. 169.
Hunsdon, Lord 228. *See Carey.*
Hunt(e) (Hounte), Agn. 1; Alice 1, 199; Avis 1; Bathshuah 242; Edw. 257*; Eliz. 5, 244; Ellen 32, 237, 350; Han. 8, 332; Hen. 286; Jas. 199; Joan 341; John 158*, 178, 201, 256*, 341, 353, 375; Mary 245, 286, 329; Nic. 93; Rog. 27; Sar. 41; Sus. 242; Tho. 8, 198, 350; Wm. 32*, 199, 219, 237, 242, 245, 331, 332*, 333*, 335*, 350, 369, 370*, 371*, 372*, 373*, 376.
Hunter, John 275.
Huntewade, John 146*.
Huntingdon (Huntingtou), Hen. earl and Kath. countess of 174, 178, 304.
Huntley(e), John 256; Nic. 347; Rose 256.
Huntman, John 216.
Hurry, Ann 83; Sar. 48.
Hurst(e) (Hyrst), Agn. 212; Anne 290; Dan. 154, 291; Ed. 290, 338; Eliz. 209, 292; Geo. 212, 289; Graveley 151, 210; Han. 294; Joan 291; John 153, 213, 288, 289, 290, 291*, 292, 345, 347; Jos. 374; Jud. 151; Kath. 169; Laur. 279; Mary 8, 290; Rob. 43, 81, 294, 338; Sar. 142; Sus 209; Tho. 209, 291, 315; Wm. 72, 143, 155, 264. *See Huckle, Monks.*
Husee, Mary 81; Wm. 81.
Huss, Wm. 169.
Hussey, Joseph 334.
Hust(e), Eliz. 64, 362; John 64.
Husted, Jer. 244; Mary 244; Sar. 244.
Hutchyn (Hutchine), Eliz. 215; John 121; Tho. 38, 120; Wm. 40.
Hutchynson (Hutc(h)inson, Hucchynsone), Doctor 205; John 72, 360; Kath. 360; Lettice 152, 294; Nic. 28; Ric. 205; Tho. 92; Wm. 360.
Hutt, Joan 96.
Hutton, Wm. 63, 342.
Huyck, Rob. 173; Tho. 173.
Hyckden, Walt. 352.
Hyde (Hide), Edw. 222, 262; Eliz. 43, 104, 223; Geo. 223, 272*, 309, 320; Hen. 274; Hugh 353; John 104, 352; Leon. 223, 309*, 337, 338, 343; Ric. 84; Rob. 253; Sir Thos. 20*, 21*; Tho. 104; Wm. 33, 77, 78*, 80, 87, 102, 223, 244, 309, 352.
Hyggnson, Wm. 274.
Hynd(e), Edw. 31, 183*; Eliz. 356; Freeman 357; Nic. 357*, 359*; Ric. 383; Sar. 330; Sus. 358*; Tho. 30; Wm. 354. *See Hinde.*

Ibgrave, Eliz. 371; Jo. 362. *See Ebgrave.*
Ibotsonne, John 12.
Idonbrace, John 147, 196; Tho. 146 147*, 196.
Illing, Wm. 375.
Impey, Ann 287; Geo. 151; Sar. 151.
Impson, John 283.
Ince, Rowl. 202; Wm. 202.
Ingham, John 231.
Ingley, Edw. 319; Marcye 319.
Ingram, Eliz. 175; John 175; Wm. 382, 383.
Inshoo, Ric. 83.
Inskip, Henry 211.
Ipgrave (Ypgrave). *See Carter.*
Irby, Anth. 337; Margt. 337.
Ir(e)land(e) (Jerlane), Eliz. 361; Fras. 358*; Jasper 357, 358*, 359*; Jo. 105; Jone 359*, 361; Mich. 80, 313; Nic. 361.
Iremonger, John 264*; Matt. 139, 140, 158, 264*.
Isacke (Isa(a)ke), Eliz. 40; Geo. 40; Hum. 273; John 40, 87, 273; Kath. 40; Tho. 156; Widow 85.
Ism(y)e, Margt. 203; Val. 197.
Issard, Thos. 150.
Izard, Mary 210; Wm. 155, 211.
Izard *alias* Draper, Hannah 210.
Ive, John 23, 276, 277, 283, 354; Rob. 276; Tho. 276.
Ive *alias* Munne, Mary 142.
Ives, Richard 298.
Ivory(e) (Ivery(e), Ivorie), Agn. 314; Annis 73, 313; Eliz. 73, 210, 313, 357; John 34, 74, 106, 222, 291, 314, 356*, 357*, 358*, 359*; Kath. 312; Nic. 210, 363; Reb. 169, 286; Ric. 73*, 313; Rob. 73, 93, 313; Sus. 330; Tho. 28, 73*, 222, 259, 314, 362; Widow 361; Wm. 73, 87, 312, 313*, 352.

Jackest, Thos. 87.
Jackett, Wm. 348.
Jacklyn, John 378, 379.
Jackson (Jac(ke)son), Agn. 200; Anth. 187, 204; Barth. 215; Christr. 6; Geo. 119; John 138; Mary 370; Nic. 312; Penelope 96; Ralph 283, 329, 371; Rob. 203; Roger 119*; Sar. 167; Wm. 140, 203, 204, 287, 382, 383; Zach. 2.
Jacob(e), Ellen 133; Geo. 133, 277, 303, 378; John 277*, 303; Tho. 274.
Jakelay, Wm. 267.
James (Jeames, Jeamys), Audry 31; Geo. 383; Joan 31, 131; John 26, 28, 122; Tho. 31*, 353; Wm. 131. *See Aspynne.*
Jane. *See Hopkyns.*
Janne, Wm. 271.
Janyn, John 326; Tho. 236.
Jaques (Jacques), Fras. 42; Mary 160; Tho. 335.

Jardfeild (Jarfeild, Jardeuyll, Jardevile), John 219, 324, 325, 326, 328; Ric. 326*, 327*, 378. *See Jerdfelde.*
Jarsie (Jarsay), Jane 151; John 272; Wm. 273.
Jasy, Jane 357.
Jaynes, Joan 345; Rob. 345.
Je....s, Agn. 28.
Jebbe, Lewis 377, 378.
Jebson, Clem. 131; Leon. 131.
Jee, Joan 239.
Jeffes, Joyce 151; Rob. 169.
Jegon, Joan 328; John 328; Reg. 325*; Tho. 327, 328.
Jenkins (Jenkyn(s)), Alice 238; Eliz. 372; John 353.
Jennings (Jennyns, Jennens, Gennyus), —— 63, 125; Barnard 89, 125, 126, 128; Dor. 89; Geo. 176; John 103, 104, 215, Margery 320; Ralph 89*, 125, 184, 185*; Ric. 275; Rob. 278; Ruth 332; Tho. 63, 103, 316*; Wm. 83, 275.
Jennior, Eliz. 374.
Jenoure, Andr. 135; Grezagon 135.
Jerdfelde (Jerdfild), John 132, 277; Ric. 277. *See Jardfeild.*
Jerlane, Mich. 313. *See Ireland.*
Jermyn. *See Londines.*
Jernegan (Jernygan, Jarnigan), Anne 255; Eliz. 177, 254*, 342; Henry 255, 378; Tho. 177, 254*, 342.
Jeve, Dor. 314; Jas. 174, 310.
Jewell, John 206*.
Jewet(t), Dor. 43; Eliz. 6; Tho. 151; Wm. 43.
Jingould, Agn. 104; Tho. 104; Wm. 104*.
Joellye (Joyllye), Dor. 204; John 204*; Ric. 204.
Johns, Mr 121.
Johnson (Jhonson), Alice 9, 63; Anne 9, 53, 93; Eliz. 210, 329; Grace 77; Hen. 63, 81, 255, 344; Jas. 135, 175; Joan (John) 237; John 9*, 63, 281, 353; Jud. 240; Mary 9; Nic. 132*, 274; Petronilla 175; Ric. 9, 166, 346, 353; Rob. 66, 349; Rog. 349; Tho. 11, 37, 104, 168, 237, 260*, 261, 348; Wm. 9, 20*, 21*, 53, 164*, 237, 330, 349. *See Grove.*
Jole, Wm. 140.
Jon', Cornelius 277.
Jones (Joanes), Anne 242; David 284, 285*, 286, 288, 329, 330*; Eliz. 48; Griffith (Griffin) 6, 136, 242; Hugo 190; John 219, 379; Kath. 242; Marreddeth 242; Nath. 380*; Peter 313; Ric. 242; Steph. 242; Tho. 94; Wm. 190.
Jonson, Geo. 277; Hen. 275; John 72, 158.
Jonys, Thos. 231.
Joplyn, Rob. 275.
Jopson, Anne 65, 66; Jas. 214.

Jordan (Jordaine, Jordeyne, Jurda(i)ne, Jurde(i)ne), Dan. 84; Dor. 212; Edw. 46, 48*; Eliz. 258; Ellyn 119; James 321; Jaques 119; John 155, 213, 237, 258, 278, 340, 345; Kath. 121*; Mat. 282; Mich. 69*, 150; Mother 73; Ric. 121, 216, 341*; Tho. 83*, 121*.
Jorneman, Ralph 277.
Josselyn (Jooselyn), Hen. 78; Ric. 344.
Joyce (Joyse), Ralph 345; Tho. 273; Wm. 218.
Joye, John 103.
Joyner, —— 150; Eliz. 289; Geo. 152; Grace 150; John 289; Wm. 169, 286.
Juce, Thomas 361.
Judd(e), John 79, 81; Kath. 79, 81; Nic. 185; Rob. 64.
Jurnyman, Kath. 220; Tho. 220.
Jury, Mislen 73.
Juster, Wm. 275.
Jyngkynson, John 203.

Kakis, Wm. 75.
Karver, John 306.
Kay(e), John 303; Rob. 179.
Kechen, John 272.
Keen, Rich. 330.
Kefford(e), Wm. 120, 319. *See Kifford.*
Kell, Thos. 207.
Kellam, Rob. 366.
Kellett (Kellat), Anys 198; James 198; Jane 201.
Kelsey, Alice 75; Anne 94; Cecily 75; Dan. 94; Wm. 75*.
Kelynge, John 256; Margt. 256.
Kembstey, Joan 370.
Kemp(e), Barth. 89*, 173, 184, 254; Eliz. 244; Geo. 244; Honner 244; John 245, 350.
Kempster, Rich. 239, 285.
Kempton. *See Kimpton.*
Kendall, Margt. 135; Wm. 135.
Kene, Rich. 28.
Kenseye, Humph. 277
Kent, Christian 373; Christr. 300; Hen. 29; Joan 342; John 29*, 98, 176, 223, 347; Mary 76, 181; Phil. 342; Rob. 72; Tho. 70, 100, 108*, 149; Walt. 136; Wm. 76*.
Kentish(e) (Kentysch), Agn. 12; Damaris 167; Eman. 93; Hen. 24, 96, 331, 334, 346; Jane 41, 331; John 351; Martha 264; Mary 96; Ric. 41; Rob. 141, 351; Sar. 96; Tho. 137, 138, 370; Wm. 12*, 82, 95, 140, 167, 190, 348.
Kentsham, Eliz. 243.
Kepe, John 91.
Kerbye, John 74; Rose 74; Wm. 311.
Kere, Barth. 270; Joan 178; Robt. 271; Tho. 178.
Keron, Thos. 193*.
Kesyng, Thos. 366.

Ketcher, John 65.
Ketheringe *alias* Deye, Agn. 36; Wm. 36.
Kettere, Roger 45.
Ketyll, Thos. 27.
Kevyll, Rog. 193; Wm. 148, 193*.
Key(e), Dor. 283; Mr 85.
Keyford, Wm. 40.
Kiffett, Edw. 142.
Kifford, Eliz. 64*; John 64; Rob. 64; Tho. 64. *See Kefford.*
Kift, Nicholas 282.
Kilby(e) (Kylby, Kylbe, Kilbey), Eliz. 95, 373; Geo. 210; John 92, 141, 352; Marion 352; Mary 141; Nic. 33*, 75; Wm. 28, 374. *See Kilbyfe.*
Kilbyfe (Kylbyff), Dor. 134, 307; John 134, 261*, 307.
Killinglie, Robt. 153.
Kimpton (Kympton, Kemptou), —— 211; Agn. 10; Anne 211; Cath. 141; Edw. 218; Eliz. 10; Geo. 10, 101, 106*, 252*, 339; Grace 217; Grizild 143; Honer 245; Jeane 115; John 132; Margt. 10; Mat. 115, 116; Mr 320; Ralph 149*; Ric. 98, 211, 212, 217, 252*, 253*; Rob. 354; Sus. 10, 212, 362; Tho. 252*, 340, 354; Wm. 10*, 35, 80, 305, 310, 353.
Kinder, Ann 265*; Edw. 281; Gilb. 330, 375; Tho. 265*; Wm. 264*, 265*.
King(e) (Kyng). —— 350; Alice 149, 321; Andr. 180*, 257, 345*; Ann 83; Dan. 167; Dor. 38; Edw. 320; Eliz. 39*, 180*, 211, 321*; Fras. 182*; Geo. 157*, 321; Grace 180*, 319; Helen 209; Hen. 45, 81, 173; Isab. 180; Jane 48; Joan 39*, 63, 120, 180; John 9, 23, 39*, 62, 79, 82, 121, 157, 180*, 182*, 272, 273, 277, 282, 285, 321, 356, 370; Jonath. 182; Joyce 72; Jud. 157; Kath. 82, 91, 199, 319; Margt. 38, 66, 180, 319, 348; Martha 98; Mary 83, 321, 370; Mat. 72, 91, 319*; Mr 126; Nic. 27, 150, 372; Ric. 9, 66*, 303, 318, 319*; Rob. 11, 39, 63, 66, 104, 288; Sar. 149; Sus. 180; Tho. 10, 39*, 66, 126, 180, 273, 276, 346, 347; Wm. 38*, 41, 243, 273, 288, 303, 32*, 323, 324, 325, 327, 345; Zach. 182.
Kingman, Ben. 246; Mary 246; Wm. 245, 246.
Kingsbury, Peter 245.
Kingsl(e)y, Sam. 153, 294.
Kinsley, Sam. 294.
Kinwood, Widow 4.
Kirby (Kirbie). —— 151; Eliz. 151; John 65*, 307; Mary 209; Nic. 273; Ric. 217, 307, 379, 380*; Sam. 69; Tho. 26; Wm. 276.
Kirke, Alice 235; John 235; Jude 361; Tho. 234, 235.

Kirkeby, John 148.
Kitchin, Thos. 214.
Kittle, Jo. 362; Mary 363.
Knagge, Eliz. 319.
Knevet(t), Geo. 12; Mary 8; Tho. 12.
Knight (Knyght, Knite), Anne 4, 51, 93, 334; Christr. 209, 248*, 249; Dan. 370; Edm. 250*; Geo. 213; Grace 213, 258; Hester 154; Joan 168; John 27, 64, 272, 278, 287, 352; Ric. 27, 32, 313; Tho. 288; Wm 82, 136*, 258, 288.
Knolles, Oliver 347; Tho. 174.
Knott, Dan. 279; Edm. 132; Eliz. 210; Joan 209; John 280.
Knowlewater, Eliz. 210.
Knowling, Andrew 48*; Ann. 48*.
Kno(w)lton, John 32, 350; Mary 283; Mr. 182; Neh. 372; Sar. 330; Tho. 187, 188, 349; Wm. 351.
Knyghte *alias* Brother, Val. 131.
Knyghton, Geo. 178, 257; John 34, 145, 148, 178, 195, 257*.
Knyvet, Ralph 311.
Kw, Richard 231.
Kydner, Thos. 291.
Kyghtley, Thos. 34.
Kyiforde, John 119; Kath. 119; Tho. 119*; Wm. 119.
Kynaston, Margery 221; Ric. 221.
Kynoe, Wm. 77.
Kynwelmershe, Anne 134, 135, 221, 223; Edm. 135; Ric. 186; Rob. 134, 135, 221, 223.
Kypple, Margt. 200.
Kytewelde, John 190; Walt. 190.
Kytfeld, John 233; Margery 233; Thos. 233.
Kytter, —— 350.

Lacon, —— 43; Jane 43.
Lacy(e), Eliz. 289; Ellen 304; John 179, 254, 304.
Ladd, Henry 379*.
Lagoo, John 351.
Laico(c)k(e), Agn. 39; John 37, 39*.
Lake, John 33; Mary 282; Wm. 33*.
Lamun, Thomas 192.
Lamb(e), Eliz. 346; Prud. 199; Widow 318; Wm. 187.
Lamberde, Alice 121; Edw. 121; Grace 121; John 121; Ric. 121.
Lambert, Anne 35; Anth. 103, 181*; Hen. 283; Tho. 35, 352.
Lambky, Thos. 119.
Lame, Sarah 11.
Laminge, Wm. 3.
Lamkyn, John 38, 273; Tho. 85.
Lamploy, John 320.
Lancaster, Annis 158; Ellin 242, 243; Jane 158; Mary 242; Tho. 158; Wm. 242, 243.
Lanchestr, Adam 232.
Lander, Jas. 353; Tho. 353.
Lane (Laine), Alice 219, 350; Barth. 176*, 220; Chas. 84*; Edw. 3;

Eliz. 139, 227*; Isaac 170; John 83, 219, 227, 237, 350; Jone 227; Rob. 30; Tho. 219, 349, 350; Wm. 33, 303.
Laneham, Agn. 197*; John 195*; Tho. 236; Wm. 147, 197.
Langdale (Langdell), —— 320; John 230*, 320.
Langford, Hugh 236, 237.
Langham, Agnes 181, 351.
Langhton, Alice 172; John 172.
Langley, Eliz. 174; Frances 83; Hen. 174; John 79, 178, 194; Ric. 205.
Lannam, Wm. 273.
Lansdale. See Lawrence.
Lapadge, Jasper 153.
Lapley, John 52; Ric. 52*.
Large, —— 180; Jone 200; Nic. 266; Wm. 351.
Larke, George 32.
Larle, George 32.
Lasby(e), John 352; Rob. 352.
Latham (Lathom, Lathum), Margt. 90*; Sus. 258; Tho. 90, 125*; Wm. 258.
Latimore (Lattemore) Jer. 169; Tho. 5.
Laundey, Edw. 213; Mary 213; Ric. 280. See Lawndye.
Lavender, Geo. 273; Nic. 85; Tho. 274.
Lavenham, Margt. 326; Tho. 45.
Law(e), Geo. 362; John 2, 158*; Lucy 2.
Lawford, Marion 72.
Lawghton, Ellen 219, 340; Tho. 219, 340.
Lawman, Alice 103; Anne 103; Eliz. 103*; Jas. 313*; Joan 103; John 103; Kath. 103; Nic. 103*, 353; Wm. 103, 189.
Lawncey, John 277.
Lawndye, Rich. 280.
Lawney, Thos. 273.
Lawrance alias Harrod, Mercy 214.
Lawrence (Laurence, Larrence), —— 346; Agn. 119; Anne 119, 150; Awdry 139; Barnabas 341; Edw. 119, 345; Geo. 136; Grace 309, 341; Han. 243; Jas. 141; Joan 10; John 35, 38, 72, 96, 109, 177, 218, 247, 256, 260, 282, 309, 313, 329, 341; Mary 154, 246*, 247, 341, 245; Oliver 32; Phil. 75, 311; Ric. 38*, 119; Sus. 214; Tho. 65*, 150, 186, 228, 240; Wm. 10, 39, 41, 119, 246, 247, 346, 352; Winif. 119.
Lawrence alias Lansdale, Joan 10.
Lawton, Wm. 92.
Laxton, Joan 77.
Lay, Robt. 381, 382.
Layche, Kath. 78, 79; Ralph 78, 79.
Laycroft(e), Rich. 259*.
Laye, John 276.
Laysby, Robt. 187.
Layton, Anne 149; Joan 242; John 242*; Tho. 149.
Leach (Leech), Anne 139; Christr. 288; Tho. 96.

Leader, John 282.
Leake, John 181.
Leate, Father 181.
Lee (Lea, Le), Bridget 342; Eliz. 85, 337, 342; John 28, 85, 342; Mary 166; R. 299; Ric. 35, 78, 79, 81, 130*, 133, 173, 260*; Rob. 133, 135, 173; Sim. 347; Tho. 168; Wm. 79, 80, 221, 303, 332, 337, 342, 377. See Coke.
Leeys, Thos. 46.
Legat(e), John 237; Margery 237; Thos. 147.
Legg, Thos. 7.
Leifchild, Thos. 373.
Leigh (Leghe), John 96; Master 235; Rob. 236.
Leman (Lemmon), Lady 83; Lucy 83; Rob. 95.
Lens, Wm. 383.
Lenthall, John 36.
Lenthrope, Gabriel 121.
Leonard(es) (Lenerd), Joan 304, 307; John 42, 95, 137, 373; Rob. 304, 307; Tho. 77, 276, 298; Wm. 12.
Leper (Leaper), Joan 237; Kath. 308; Tho. 203.
Lerie (Learey), John 33; Wm. 3.
Le(t)cheworthe, Alice 36; Jas. 36, 175; Sus. 79, 80; Tho. 36, 79, 80.
Leuse, Sus. 44.
Leventhorpe, Dor. 78; Edw. 275; Gab. 177; Geo. 174; John 322; Tho. 78, 178, 215*.
Lever, John 93, 94; Ralph 307.
Levett, —— 181.
Levison, Wm. 65.
Lewes (Lewys), Alice 229; Geo. 253, 314; John 32, 46, 64*, 84, 348; Ralph 84; Ric. 64; Tho. 229. See Appowell.
Lewkenor, Edw. 81, 178, 222; Suz. 81, 222.
Lewyn, Agn. 65; Alice 65; Eliz. 65; Lydia 65; Tho. 65*; Wm. 65.
Ley (Leey), Hester 141; Jos. 287; Mary 360*; Ric. 360; Rob. 380; Tho. 287*, 360*.
Leycetre, Joan 190; Wm. 190.
Lightes, Eliz. 92.
Lightfo(o)te, Gilb. 347; Martha 65; Mary 6, 65; Ric. 65; Tho. 276.
Lightwood, Eliz. 95.
Lillingston, Mary 44; Wm. 44.
Lilly (Lilley, Lylly), Edw. 275; John 142; Rob. 12*.
Lincoln (Lyncolne), Agn. 79, 81, 155; Alex. 40; Anne 155; Edw. 307, 342; Eliz. 31; Geo. 31*, 40*, 155; Hen. 31; John 155, 307; Margt. 155; Mary 155; Ralph 155; Rob. 155*; Tho. 307; Wm. 79, 81, 155.
Lindall, Mr 292; Wm. 293*, 295, 296.
Linden, Agn. 153.
Lines, Sam. 333.
Ling, Wm. 3.

Lingwood (Lingewode), John 38; Wm. 188.
Lishman, Alice 243.
Little, —— 284; Ann 284.
Littlepenig, Sam 181*, 182*.
Lit(t)ler, Randall 361; Ric. 303.
Lloyd (Loyde), Evan 33; Giles 33; Grizell 375; Jane 235; Ric. 93; Tho. 142; Wm. 334.
Locke (Lok), Alice 303; Freman 199; Jas. 347; John 196, 233; Ric. 303; Tho. 346.
Lockey(e) (Lokkey), John 129, 260; Ralph 177; Ric. 177; Tho. 261; Wm. 286*.
Loddington, Sarah 140.
Lodge, Emma 143; Hen. 72, 312; Mich. 28; Tho. 143; Wm. 256, 278.
Loft, Sam. 333.
Lokley, John 194*.
Loksmyth, Rob. 190.
Lomax, Caleb 264, 265.
Londines alias Jermyn, Eliz. 33
London, Bishop of, 66, 67, 118*, 267, 268.
Long(e), Agn. 157; Alex. 307; Anne 167, 288; Annis 11; Dor. 149; Edm. 157*; Edw. 167; Eliz. 131, 239, 311; Elyn 347; Esther 6; Joan 311; John 11*, 27, 157, 167, 239, 342; Jos. 331; Joyce 311; Margt. 11; Marion 11; Mary 168, 342; Mich. 72, 229, 258; Ralph 136, 157; Ric. 131, 218; Rob. 157*, 351; Roger 311; Sim. 11; Sybbell 311; Tho. 157*; Widow 72; Wm. 157*, 187, 311.
Lord(e), John 238, 353; Wm. 303.
Lorrymer alias Renolds, Margt. 152.
Lostrige, Anne 228; Joan 228*; Rob. 228; Wm. 228.
Lottie, George 11.
Lotton, Thos. 77.
Loue, Richard 33.
Louth(e), Ric. 147; Rob. 24, 195*, 197*.
Lovayne. See Essex and Eve.
Love, Jas. 335; John 328; Jonath. 335; Tho. 352.
Loveday, Thos. 375.
Lovelace, Wm. 88.
Loveland, Jos. 3.
Lovell, Greg. 238; Prud. 238; Tho. 36.
Lovet(t), Alice 156; Dan. 285; Han. 372; Mary 335; Ric. 156*, 172, 256; Ursula 172.
Lowdam, Margt 86; Wm. 86*, 121, 261*, 338.
Lowe, Amey 382; Anne 305; John 311, 381; Mat. 258, 305; Nath. 154; Rob. 9; Wm. 383.
Lowen (Lowin, Lowyn, Leowyn), Agn. 85, 86, 180; Alice 180*; Anne 66, 211; Eliz. 64*; Fras. 180*; Geo. 76; Joan 64, 180; John 46*, 62, 64, 66*, 85, 91, 180*, 352; Kath. 64; Lucy 180; Margt. 46; Margery 62; Nic. 66, 85, 180; Ric. 9*, 86, 180; Roger 46, 192; Sim. 85, 86, 120, 192*, 196, 318; Tho. 11, 62, 64, 85, 86*, 104, 180*, 192; Tristram 64; Wm. 46, 62*, 85, 86*, 157, 180, 192, 318, 352, 354.
Lowson, Rob. 350; Tho. 347.
Lucas, Alice 192; Anne 245; Edw. 210; Eliz. 214; Father 64; Joan 320; John 119*, 213, 320; Mary 214; Rob. 165; Roger 192*; Tho. 165.
Lucke, Hum. 228; John 350; Wm. 350.
Lucye (Lucey), Avery 379; Eliz. 29; Hen. 29; Tho. 253, 287.
Luddeford, Alice 197; Hen. 145², 146*; John 146*, 196*; Margery 145.
Luddington, Nich. 77.
Ludlowe, John 350; Tho. 10*.
Luke, Grace 39; John 41, 114, 300; Nic. 345.
Lundon, Elen 91; Tho. 91.
Lurchyn, John 194, 195; Wm. 195.
Luthyngton, John 145, 148, 195.
Luyck, Margery 174; Rob. 174.
Lyden, Wm. 273.
Lyle, Anne 2; Mary 2; Nic. 2*.
Lylldey, Thos. 274.
Lylling(s)ton, Wm. 315*.
Lynd(e), Cuthb. 343; Joan 236; John 158*; Tho. 236; Wm. 236.
Lyndsell (Lyndessell), Peter 40, 120*, 256, 305.
Lynsay (Lyncey), Tho. 273; Wm. 273.
Lyon (Lyan), Hen. 350; John 177; Rob. 158; Wm. 275.
Lyonell, Margt. 199.
Lyons, Jer. 169.
Lyster, Edw. 273; Wm. 195.
Lytherland, Anne 243.
Lyttell, Gyles 181; Ric. 181; Wm. 181.
Lytton (Litton), Rob. 272; Rowland 179, 252.

Mabbe, John 176, 221.
Mabbotts, Eliz. 166.
Mace, Anne 283; Eliz. 240.
Machell (Mauchell), Frances 34; John 34, 257; Ursula 257. See Baker.
Ma(c)keres, Kath. 341; Wm. 340, 341.
Madle, Mother 180; Ralph 180.
Madyll, John 271.
Maho, Dor. 230; Eliz. 230; Hen. 230; Jane 230; Lawr. 230; Rob. 230.
Maid, Mary 245.
Maior, Edw. 63; Wm. 63.
Maiot, Henry 189.
Makeholme, John 237.
Makenest, John 273.
Malcom. See Scott, John Mawcome.

Maldon (Malldon, Mauldon), Alice 9; Joan 9*; John 9, 30, 65, 266, 271, 327; Mary 65*; Wm. 9, 11, 66*, 104.
Malin, John 170.
Mallett, Matthew 34.
Mallitrot (Maletrat), Sam. 331.
Mal(l)orye (Malorie), Andr. 308, 341; Fras. 304.
Mallowes, Wm. 173, 220.
Mande, Andrew 30.
Manfield (Manfeild), Ann 84; Edw. 209; Esther 240; Fras. 152; John 273, 375; Mary 94, 152; Tho. 288.
Manger, John 4; Sar. 4.
Manington, Francis 334.
Manison, John 31.
Man(ne), Alice 173; Anne 96; John 252*; Mary 212; Mich. 173; Ric. 330, 347; Rob. 26; Tho. 158, 212; Wm. 351.
Manning (Man(n)yng), Goodman 320; John 90; Mr. 378, 379, 380; Ric. 313; Rob. 285; Tho. 63, 273, 320; Wm. 366.
Mannistie (Manisty, Manestee, Manustie), Clem. 122, 132; Nath. 105, 235; Tho. 345; Wm. 26.
Mans, Wm. 104.
Mansell, Mary 363.
Mansfield (Mansfeild), Fras. 211; John 48*; Mary 83.
Mantell, Eliz. 35, 217; Fras. 261; Hugh 35, 133, 217.
Manyngson, John 32.
Maple, James 84.
Maple alias Hadie, Jane 153.
Maples, Joan 85.
Mapleton (Mapulton), John 87; Rog. 237.
Marche, John 157; Margt. 157; Wm. 157*.
Marckward, Dor. 371.
Marden, Jas. 378*; Nic. 277.
Mardall (Mardell, Mardoll), Alice 294; Eliz. 213; John 10, 29; Maria 294; Rowland 265*; Sar. 294; Wm. 294.
Mardolfe, Jas. 291; Reb. 290; Wm. 290, 291.
Marfflet, Wm. 347.
Marham, John 137.
Markes, Ric. 323, 324*, 325, 326; Tho. 327.
Markham (Markeham), Alice 338; Frances 79; Fras. 178; Griffin 342; John 338; Mary 178; Tho. 342; Wm. 79, 208.
Marret, Wm. 44.
Marryot(t), — 315; Rob. 174.
Marse, John 274.
Marsey, Eliz. 10.
Marsh(e) (Marsah, Mershe), Abig. 243; Alice 242; Anne 80, 344; Edw. 327; Eliz. 176, 244*, 245; Fras. 175; Geo. 348; Hen. 31, 339, 341; John 35, 80, 176, 187, 201, 276, 344; Jos. 242; Margt. 239; Ric. 133; Rob. 162; Roger 188, 200; Sus. 7, 199; Tho. 27, 133, 242, 339; Wm. 244, 245.
Marshall (Marschall), Adria 222; Agn. 32; Alice 255*, 353; Anne 210, 240, 305; Christr. 33, 293*, 305, 315; Edm. 353; Edw. 6, 72, 230, 345; Eliz. 32*, 168; Hen. 221, 345; Joan 32*; John 32*, 44, 45, 272, 277, 315, 345, 347; Jos. 7, 136, 239, 372; Kath. 221, 345; Margt. 216; Nic. 222; Olive 213; Phil. 277, 281; Rob. 188, 353; Sar. 293*; Sibil 345; Tho. 226, 277; Wm. 50, 213, 255*.
Marson (Marsan), Fras. 82; John 278; Tho. 24, 32; Wm. 82.
Marston, Ann 374; Eliz. 10, 36; Geo. 122; Giles 186; Hen. 284*, 286, 329*, 332; John 36, 186, 187*, 351, 362; Ralph 373; Ric. 351; Tho. 352; Wm. 10*, 123, 139, 284, 351.
Martin (Marte(y)n, —— 349; Agn. 91; Alice 91, 103, 191; Ann 373; Christian 45; Dor. 339; Edw. 374; Eliz. 30; Hen. 133; Jas. 6, 170; John 8, 91, 191, 195, 196*, 341, 343, 348; Jos. 239; Lambert 277; Laur. 45; Mary 8, 116; Nath. 167; Nic. 32, 63*, 64, 339; Peter 347; Ric. 91, 191, 261, 350, 353; Rob. 352, 370, 373; Sar. 371; Steph. 78; Sus. 101; Tho. 45, 159, 189*, 350, 352; Wm. 30*, 154, 168.
Marvell (Marvyle), Dor. 2; Mary 49; Rob. 2; Wm. 49.
Maryon (Marion, Marian, Marryone), Christian 91; John 277*, 305, 319*, 324*, 325, 326, 327, 328*, 378; Margt. 305; Ric. 91, 277, 324*; Tho. 277.
Mascall (Maschall), John 244, 246; Mary 244*, 246; Ralph 244; Ric. 246; Wm. 370.
Mashall, Eliz. 96.
Maskoll, Eliz. 42.
Mason (Masen), John 46, 190, 191*, 237, 255; Phil. 200; Ric. 82*, 346; Sam. 382.
Massingberd, Dor. 82*, 130*, 134, 179; John 82*, 130*, 134, 179.
Master, Ric. 277; Wm. 244.
Mathison, Kath. 340.
Mat(t)hew(e), Ellen 101; Fras. 36; Geo. 275; John 66, 95, 96, 136, 255, 258, 342; Margery 36; Nath. 99; Tho. 351; Wm. 255, 278. See Santon.
Matthew(e)s, John 92, 94*, 95, 139, 140, 168*; Mary 94; Tho. 8, 107; Wm. 284.
Matrevers, John 74, 312.
Maunder, Harry 11, 104.
Maundevyle (Ma(w)ndevile), John 146; Ric. 190, 191.
Maurice, Sus. 375.

Mawden, Thos. 273.
Mawe, —— 126.
May . . ., Rich. 28.
May (Maie), Alice 32*; Bridget 32; Eliz. 350; Kath. 32; Margery 39.
Maydwell, Rich. 35.
Mayes, Mary 333, 334; Tho. 333; Wm. 372.
Mayhoe, Rich. 110.
Mayle, John 65.
Maylin, Fras. 137.
Maynard(e), Allis 314; Edm. 314, 315; Grace 247, 314; John 90, 125*, 314*; Margery 37, 81, 90; Ralph 77*, 81, 89, 90, 176, 184; Sim. 198; Tho. 314*.
Mayne, Edw. 278; Fras. 278; Hen. 76, 82, 227, 305; Ric 27, 206, 305.
Meacock, Frances 243.
Me(a)de, Anne 223, 254; Edw. 343; Eliz. 131, 177, 223, 305, 343; Hum. 223, 254; Joan 327; John 309, 378; Mich. 76, 131*, 177, 223, 276, 305, 343; Philippa 343; Rob. 277; Sim. 274; Tho. 172, 175, 277*; Wm. 278, 321, 326, 372.
Meadew, Tho. 8.
Meadowes (Meddowes, Meadwees), Ann 138; Mary 136, 138, 240; Peter 240, 284.
Me(a)ger, —— 166, 346; Eliz. 166; Grace 285; John 348; Mary 285.
Meares, Margt. 4; Ric. 4.
Medcalfe, Alice 258.
Mede. *See Meade.*
Meedlay, John 51.
Meek, Wm. 247.
Mekyn, Thos. 350.
Melles, Phil. 77; Wm. 275.
Meppesale, Geo. 146*.
Mercham, John 47.
Meridithe, —— 151; Eliz. 151.
Meriton (Meritown(g)e, Merytong), Agn. 85; Hen. 278; Joan 85; John 278*; Margt. 85; Mich. 86, 339; Tho. 85, 278.
Merridsy, Hannah 284.
Mersh, John 346.
Merston, Wm. 174.
Mervell, Hen. 277.
Mery, Thos. 196.
Meryden, Alice 350; Ric. 350.
Merydethe, Geo. 349.
Meryon, Wm. 350.
Messeder, Sus. 335.
Messynger, Marion 351; Ralph 350.
Mesye, John 348.
Metcalf, Wm. 330.
Meth, Edw. 348.
Meverell, Sampson 218.
Michaell, Rob. 62.
Micheley, Rob. 104.
Michell. *See Mitchell.*
Mid(d)leton (Middelton), Anth. 185*; Tho. 3, 4, 149; Wm. 33, 76, 97, 109.
Miland, John 46.
Miles (Myles), Alice 216; Anne 85*,
210; Eliz. 36; Em. 30; Hen. 85*; Isab. 30; Joan 216; John 206, 210, 216*, 257, 284, 351, 352*, 368*; Kath. 368*; Mary 369; Nath. 95; Ric. 351; Rob. 206; Tho. 30, 36, 273, 352; Ursula 85; Walt. 30.
Mille (Mylle), John 46; Matilda 46; Rob 273; Tho. 231, 232.
Miller (Millar, Myller), Eliz. 139; John 38, 77*, 277, 303, 342; Margt. 201, 331; Matilda 342; Ric. 347; Tho. 342; Wm. 38.
Millett, John 345; Rob. 342.
Millington, Chas. 242*; Joan 242; John 3, 278; Sus. 288.
Mills (Mylles, Milys), —— 229; Edw. 64; Geo. 106; Hen. 273; Joan 273; John 65, 176, 182, 276, 310, 366; Lettice 65; Oliver 65*; Phil. 345; Tho. 65, 304.
Milton, —— 283; Ric. 196*; Sar. 283; Wm. 195, 196.
Milward (Millard), Edm. 45; Matthias 243; Ric. 332, Sar. 286; Tho. 323, 326; Wm. 93. *See Mylicarde alias Alexander.*
Minchin, Wm. 333.
Minors, Wm. 100.
Mitchell (Michell, Mychell), —— 141, 211; David 298; Edm. 353; Edw. 353, 360; Eliz. 211; Hugh 95; Jas. 313; Jesper. 331; John 179, 352; Joseph 238; Mary 360; Ric. 123; Rob. 9, 281; Sar. 360; Tho. 137, 167, 252*, 253*, 314*, 340; Wm. 229, 230*, 284
M'kyn, Wm. 119.
Moate, Jo. 105.
Modle, Henry 10.
Modye, Dor. 321; Ralph 321.
Molloy, Eliz. 245.
Momford, Mr. 313.
Monday (Mondie, Monedaie), Margt. 308; Tho. 38, 40*, 86, 308.
Mone, Rich. 186.
Mongett (Mungett), Annis 76; John 76; Jonas 76; Margt. 76; Tho. 76.
Monke (Mounke, Mongke, Muncke), Anne 213; Eliz. 2, 218; John 92, 218, 274*, 276, 295; Philippa 221, 256; Ric. 221, 256; Rob. 35, 275; Sus. 153; Wm. 2, 156, 348.
Monke *alias* Hurste, Susan 213.
Monoxe, Rich. 27.
Montford, Alice 151.
Monyen, Philip 277.
Moore (More), —— 84; Agn. 236; Edw. 274; Eliz. 119; Hugh 84; John 310; Laur. 348; Leon. 258; Ric. 149, 303; Sar. 258; Tho. 275, 348; Thos. F. 83; Tristram 39; Wm. 136, 236, 258*.
Moor(e)s (Mores), Agn. 75; Alice 6; John 156, 367*, 368*; Wm. 8.
Mo(o)rco(c)k(e), John 221; Steph. 192*.

Moor(e)ton, Amy 282; John 139, 152; Widow 282.
Mordaunt, Lewis, lord. 82*, 305*.
Mordon (Moorden), Alice 192; John 189, 192*, 231; Wm. 194.
Moreland, Alice 342; Geo. 255, 342.
Morer, Kath. 302; Ralph 302.
Moret, Thos. 198.
Morewell, John 145, 147*, 195*, 196.
Morgan, Ann 362; Eliz. 284; Fras. 339; Hen. 329; Hugh 177; Jane 79, 81, 255; John 85; Letice 331; Mary 362; Nic. 255; Tho. 339; Walt. 79, 81.
Morley (Morlie), Edm. 243; Edw. lord 308, 343, 378*; Eliz. 308; Etheld. 151; Henry, lord 378, 379; John 222; Tho. 353. See Parker.
Morrell, Esther 83.
Mor(r)is (Morice, Moryce, Morys), Alice 112; Anne 3; Edm. 198; Faith 3; Frances 137; Hen. 113, 137; Hum. 275; Jas. 83, 172; John 104*, 287; Margt. 198; Ric. 112, 113, 160; Sus. 162; Wm. 8, 170, 240, 287, 331, 332, 372.
Morrisbee, Thos. 52.
Mor(r)ison (Moryson), Chas. 131, 173, 206, 208, 305; Eliz. 258; Mr. 110; Tho. 223, 258*, 307.
Morryon, Nich. 263*.
Morse, John 139; Mrs 378, 379.
Morton, Geo. 307; Hen. 139; John 367*.
Morynge, Christian 132; Wm. 132.
Mosell. See Mussell.
Mos(s)e, Jane 158; Joan 151; John 122, 353; Sar. 285; Tho. 346.
Mott(e), — 381; Eliz. 235; John 166, 167, 275, 366; Magota 266; Martha 359*; Matth. 382; Tho. 235.
Mottershed, Thos. 329.
Mounson, John 219; Rob. 33.
Mountague, Sam. 167.
Moun(t)ford, Mr 228; Tho. 229.
Mower, Wm. 351.
Mowse, Mary 154.
Moyer, Grace 256; John 172, 256.
Moys, John 267.
Moyser, Hugh 36.
Moythen (Moython), Ric. 162, 163; Sus. 163*.
Muffett (Moffett, Mowffett), Rob. 199, 352*; Tho. 174, 254; Wm. 339, 344*.
Mugge, John 348.
Mulle, Wm. 45.
Mullington, Ed. 357, 359; Margt. 357.
Munde, Anne 236; John 31; Matilda 236; Nic. 236; Tho. 236.
Munforde, Thos. 341.
Mun(ne) (Mone), Anna 162; Dan. 373; Jas. 75*, 143; Joan 113; John 140, 168, 311, 352; Mary 94; Ralph 113*; Sam. 163*; Wm. 168. See Ive.
Muns, Ric. 373; Tho. 284.
Munt, John 166; Mary 166; Sam. 101.
Mussag . . on, Rich. 352.
Mus(s)ell (Mosell), Eliz. 160; Faith 160; Geo. 113, 114; Jane 159.
Mutchett, Joseph 140.
Myckley, Rich. 256.
Myldmay(e), Walt. 37, 174, 307.
Myllyan, Wm. 200.
Mylwarde alias Alexander, Kath. 258; Wm. 258.
Mylwood, John 346.
Mynne, Geo. 175.
Mynott(e), Alice 10; Anne 10; Annis 10; Hen. 10*; John 323; Lettice 10; Margt. 10; Rob. 10; Tho. 269, 271*.
Myse, Isab. 237; Tho. 237.
Myston, Anne 35; John 35.
Mytt, Rich. 186.

Napier, John 110.
Napkin, Roger 285.
Napper, Alex. 356; Lewis 356.
Napton, John 346; Wm. 133.
Narrowld, Thos. 256.
Nash(e) (Att ye Naysh), —— 152; Agn. 314; Anne 141, 142; Blase 33, 97; Cisley 64; Edw. 71, 229, 291, 292, 293*; 295, 360; Eliz. 6, 150, 290, 293; Geo. 64, 297; Grace 314; Gyles 63; James 359; Jane 283; John 63, 95, 284, 300*, 347, 351; Margt. 132; Martha 288; Mary 48, 334, 359, 360*, 362; Mich. 63; Nic. 359, 360*; Rob. 132, 288; Sar. 362; Sus. 93, 112, 152, 160; Tho. 64, 150, 153, 169, 288, 383; Tristr. 63; Walt. 112, 162; Wm. 63, 64, 199, 237, 282, 290, 29.*, 292, 293, 294, 295, 314*, 360.
Nason, Thos. 103.
Nayler, John 174; Tho. 174, 277; Wm. 308.
Neale (Ne(e)le), Edw. 186; Eliz. 341; Eliz. R. 264, 265*; Geo. 41, 168; Joan 140, 198; John 182*, 353; Nic. 310; Ric. 96; Rob. 351; Sar. 93, 263, 264; Tho. 157, 341; Wm. 93, 95, 264*, 341, 350.
Neave, Rob. 262.
Neaves (Ne(e)ves), Fras. 96; Mary 169; Rob. 169, 287.
Necton, Eliz. 178, 303; Wm. 178, 303.
Nedham, James 302; Jane 302; John 179, 302.
Negoose, James 332.
Nel(l)son, John 38, 40, 120.
Nelthorpe, Matrone 277.
Nevell alias Glanfeild, Ric. 313. See Glandfyld.
Newce, Clem. 179*, 219, 221; Mary 221; Wm. 221.

Newdegate, Fras. 82; John 82; Martha 82; Tho. 82.
Newdyck, Rob. 306.
New(e), John 7*, 370; Rob. 123.
Newell (Newill), Dr 106; Edw. 135; Mary 288.
Newlin, Jane 84.
Newman (Numan), Alice 157, 189, 229*; Ann 83, 172; Bridget 221; Eliz. 41, 282; Ellen 157; Geo. 156, 157, 229*, 276; Helen 189; Jane 229; Jer. 282; John 42, 197, 229*, 276*, 277*, 304*, 308, 323*, 324, 325*; Kath. 229; Margt. 229; Mary 140; Mat. 48; Nath. 136; Phyllis 308; Rach. 334; Ric. 140, 253, 278, 318, 327*, 371; Rob. 189, 209, 316, 342; Tho. 46, 110, 166, 182*, 190, 221, 308; Walt. 325*; Wm. 74, 77, 229, 237*, 253, 277, 325*.
Newport(e), John 272; Rob. 175, 256.
Newton, Ann 331; Edw. 294*, 295; Jas. 332; John 275; Mary 286, 294, 295; Mrs 52; Ric. 9; Rose 150; Tho. 353, 375.
Newys, Rob. 221; Scolastica 221.
Nicholas, John 334; Mary 334; Wm. 284.
Nicholl (Nycholl, Nicol(l), Nycoll), Alan 34; Dan. 242; Eliz. 222, 304; Ellen 177; Jas. 333; Joan 242; John 23, 191, 192, 222, 239, 304; Jud. 42; Lamberd 273; Mary 341*; Petronilla 34; Randall 256; Ric. 42, 242, 341*; Rob. 198, 222, 256, 341; Tho. 122, 151, 236, 335, 341; Wm. 34, 92, 177, 192, 198, 222, 341.
Nicholls (Nic(k)holes, Nycolls), Agn. 11; Anne 154, 287; Eliz. 11, 154, 210, 259; Freeman 188; Geo. 80, 133, 344; Hamond 133; Han. 361; Jas. 210; Joan 11, 210; John 42, 188; Jos. 167; Margt. 227; Marrian 42; Ranulph 340; Ric. 11; Rob. 11*, 259, 316; Roger 63*, 88, 310; Rose 95; Sar. 11; Thos. 8, 32, 88, 170, 340; Wm. 95, 112, 139, 150.
Nicholson, Edw. 85, 275; Ric. 274.
Nicholson alias Carter, Wm. 26.
Nobbes. See Waypole.
Nobby, Sim. 84, 86; Tho. 274.
Noble, Bevis 202, 203; Mr. 108, 109; Roger 202, 203.
Noblers, Thos. 159.
Nod, Agn. 190; John 190*; Kath. 190; Tho. 190.
Node (Noode), John 147, 148, 194, 195*.
Nodes (Noad(e)s, Nodden), Anne 362; Edm. 134, 174, 178; Eliz. 174; Geo. 101; John 101, 157, 206; Rob. 275, 313; Rog. 122, 352; Tho. 157*; Wm. 368.
Noke, John 378, 379; Ric. 274.
None, Jon 273; Margt. 273.

Norburye, Thos. 30.
Norcote, Oliver 310.
Nore, John 332.
Nores, Rich. 349.
Norfolk, Margt. duchess of 303, 339; Tho. duke of 303, 339, 344.
Norman, John 66; Rob. 198*; Tho. 278; Wm. 375.
Norres, Rob. 122.
Nor(r)ice, Geo. 31; Wm. 134.
Norris (Norrys), Agn. 30, 42; Anne 5; Christr. 30*; Edw. 157; Eliz. 31, 242, 285, 332; Henry, lord 131; Joan 30, 277; John 30, 170, 212; Joyce 43*; Margt. 30; Mary 31, 218; Ric. 272; Rob. 218; Sar. 210; Sus. 242; Tho. 30, 31, 185, 210; Tim. 31; Wm. 30*, 218.
North(e), Agn. 33, 91; Anne 30, 48*; Chas. 252; Deb. 361; Edw. 86, 229*; Eliz. 229*, 242; Frances 74; Geo. 150; Goodwife 320; Hugh 229; Joan 74, 341; John 30*, 70, 73, 74*, 91, 145, 146, 147, 157, 196, 313; Margt. 33; Mary 30, 313; Oliver 229; Ric. 242; Rob. 74*, 341; Sus. 242; Tho. 29, 33, 73*, 230*, 312, 341; Tim. 74; Wm. 74, 94, 175, 229*.
Northadge, Wm. 104.
Northampton, Anne, marchioness of 36.
Northappe, Thos. 216. See Northup.
Northcote, Edw. 167.
Northey, Alice 90; Martin 90.
Northfok, Wm. 277.
Northup (Northop), Tho. 120, 319. See Northappe.
Norton, Anne 227; Eliz. 143, 227, 228; Hugh 375; Jane 143; Joan 243; John 27, 203, 274, 378; Lettice 43; Luke 43; Mary 227; Widow 203; Wm. 198, 203*, 227*.
Norway, Master 235.
Norwich, Edw. earl of 187*, 188, 189.
Norwood, Edw. 29, 256; Tho. 80, 258.
Noswall, Robt. 277.
Note, Wm. 134.
Nottingham, John 87*.
Nunn(e)y, John 259, 260.
Nunvm, Prud. 320.
Nutkyn, Awdrie 313; Hen. 311; Ralph 313; Rob. 24, 347.
Nuton, Anne 168.
Nuttinge, Christr. 353; Edw. 150, 154; Nath. 141; Wm. 353.

Oaker, John 121.
Ock(e)ley (Okely), Agn. 345; Amy 73; Eliz. 42; Margt. 99; Ric. 99; Rob. 345; Tho. 42, 73*, 349.
Odale (Oddall), Jas. 337, 341.
Odall alias Fonte, Ric. 275.
Odell, Ric. 273; Tho. 5.
Odye. See Hoye.
Okyng, Joan 28.

Oldfeild, John 214 ; Mary 214.
Oliver (Olyver, Olliuer), Ann 329 ; Christr. 134 ; Edw. 157*; Frns. 157 ; Giles 100 ; John 101, 102, 157 ; Johnan 157 ; Ric. 157 ; Tho. 157 ; Wm. 343.
Olney (Oleney, Oney), Epinetus (Etenetus) 376, 377* ; Jas. 377 ; John 233 ; Martha 83* ; Mary 242, 376 ; Nedabiah 377 ; Oshea 48 ; Ric. 376 ; Steph. 377 ; Tho. 239, 242*, 376*, 377*.
Oncle. See Uncle.
Onge, Thomas 7.
Onslo(w)e, Fulk 131, 174, 229*, 313 ; Mary 131, 174.
Onyous, Henry 259.
Orger (Orgar), Eliz. 63 ; Hen. 63* ; Jas. 63, 342 ; Joan 63 ; Tho. 63, 209.
Oris, John 311* ; Ric. 311.
Osbaston (Osbostone), Hen 120, 272, 302, 338 ; Margt. 32, 338 ; Nic. 120 ; Tho. 305.
Osbo(u)rne, Anne 175 ; Edw. 175, 276 ; John 347 ; Jos. 6 ; Peter 78, 175 ; Ric. 382 ; Wm. 276, 371.
Oscroft, Robt. 232.
Osman, Edw. 6 ; Jos. 239.
Osmond, Adrey 335 ; Ric. 335 ; Wm. 169.
Osnard, Clem. 192 ; Nic. 192.
Otway, Mr 11.
Overman, John 83.
Overton, Ric. 133 ; Tho. 353.
Oviatt (Ovyatt), Eliz. 161 ; Jane 114 ; Joan 134 ; Roger 134.
Owen (Owyn), Frances 242 ; Gruf. 11 ; Hary 199 ; Henry 242 ; John 154, 204* ; Ric. 51 ; Sar. 242 ; Tho. 50 ; Wm. 8.
Oxenford, Thos. 96.
Oxenfort, Eliz. 6.
Oxford, Edw. earl of 255*, 304.
Oxley, Sar. 142 ; Wm. 142.
Oxton, Edw. 332 ; John 239, 350 ; Tho. 169 ; Wm. 352.
Oxton (Oxston) alias Foxe, — 206 ; John 177 ; Phil. 154 ; Sus. 154.
Oyle, Eliz. 240 ; Geo. 240 ; Ric. 240.
Oytes, Sarah 199.

Pacey, Dorcas 169.
Packer, Recka 6.
Packwood, — 350.
Pa(c)kyngton, John 367, 368* ; Thos. 79.
Padbery, — 128 ; Ric. 126.
Page (Payge), — 7 ; Ann 84, 85, 289 ; Eliz. 7, 83, 167 ; Fras. 85 ; Geo. 85 ; Hen. 85 ; Hum. 85* ; Joan 291 ; John 77, 278, 310, 329 ; Mary 85* ; Ric. 119, 272, 311 ; Rob. 79, 243* ; Wm. 48*, 177, 289, 291, 293*.
Pake, John 3 ; Ric. 29 ; Rob. 277 ; Wm. 201.

Paleman, John 268.
Palmer (Palmare), — 128 ; Agn. 236, 350 ; Andr. 343 ; Eliz. 240 ; Felex 65 ; Henry 177 ; Herb. 67 ; Isaac 377 ; Jane 177 ; John 201, 246*, 268, 269*, 270, 271, 272, 323*, 324, 350 ; Mary 246 ; Mat. 262* ; Reb. 157, 373 ; Ric. 244 ; Sylas 137 ; Tho. 236, 237, 246, 247, 323*, 324, 325*, 350 ; Wm. 42, 157, 219, 230, 350, 379, 380*.
Palynge, Agn. 204 ; Hugh 204.
Panfote, Rich. 313.
Pankhurst, Eliz. 333.
Papes, Thos. 277.
Papworth, Jo. 165 ; John 72 ; R. 165 ; Rob. 76, 229*, 309 ; Wm. 229.
Parant. See Parrant.
Pare, Gilb. 27 ; Ric. 27.
Parget, Matth. 157.
Pargeter, Jas. 33 ; Kath. 33.
Parish(e), Alice 10 ; Bennet 10 ; Ralph 10.
Parke, Robt. 354.
Parker (Parkar), — 65 ; Agn. 135 ; Edw. 155, 254, 256 ; Eliz. 254, 372 ; Ellen 321 ; Grace 311 ; Han. 48 ; Hen. 73, 272*, 321*, 329 ; Hugh 199 ; Jas. 352 ; Joan 257 ; John 139, 257, 311, 327, 367 ; Margt. 321* ; Margery 147 ; Mary 284 ; Phil. 176 ; Ralph 339 ; Ric. 321*, 343 ; Roland 209 ; Sus. 48 ; Tho. 273, 321* ; Wm. 132, 135, 175, 223, 320, 321.
Parkes, Margery 257 ; Roger 257.
Parkins (Parkyns), Cecily 221 ; Mary 164 ; Tho. 221.
Parkinson, Geo. 248.
Parkyn, Joan 351.
Parmyter, John 219.
Parnell (Pernell), Alice 323 ; Joan 77, 273 ; John 77, 273, 278 ; Margt. 63 ; Paul 63* ; Rob. 272* ; Tho. 273, 323, 324 ; Wm. 73, 273*, 304, 321.
Par(r)ant, Jas. 104* ; John 307, 339, 345 ; Mat. 320 ; Ric. 104 ; Tho. 104 ; Wm. 104*, 307.
Parrat(t) (Parrott, Parrot), Jane 34 ; Joan 254 ; John 6, 34, 64 ; Margt. 64 ; Mich. 169 ; Nic. 254 ; Sar. 169 ; Seth 333 ; Tho. 155 ; Wm. 63, 64, 76, 361.
Parris (Parrys), Alice 34 ; Eliz. 177 ; Hum. 274 ; John 34 ; Robt. 177 ; Tho. 34, 229*.
Parry, Water 261.
Parsell, Wm. 150. See Barley.
Pars(e)ley, Wm. 377, 378.
Parson, Frances 242 ; Jane 242 ; Tho. 242.
Parsons, Edm. 378 ; Joseph 83 ; Mr 319 ; Tho. 84*, 342, 378*.
Parton, John 276.
Partridg(e) (Parterigge, Patridg, Pattrig), Alse 113 ; Dor. 6 ; Edm.

157; Eliz. 113*; Em. 74; Enoch 113; John 27; Martha 332; Mary 221; Roger 41; Sam. 21*; Sus. 374; Tho. 221; Wm. 112*, 113*, 331.
Pasc(h)all, Andrew 308*; Joan 276.
Passemonteyn, Agn. 193; John 148.
Pate, Nic. 28; Sar. 373.
Patmer (Patmare), Peres 30, Tho. 277; Wm. 77.
Paton, John 283.
Pattinson, Robt. 75.
Patyngmaker, Marion 237; Rob. 237.
Paul, Sarah 263.
Paulyn, Alice 195.
Pauper, Walt. 91; Wm. 91.
Paupett, Edw. 123.
Pausingham (Possingham), Eliz. 282; John 282.
Pavye, John 275; Rob. 275.
Pawclay, Kath. 274.
Pawltocke, Tho. 349.
Payne (Paine), Anys 227*; Barth. 28; Edm. 220; Edw. 77; Eliz. 227; Frances 214; Fras. 227; Harry 227; Hugh 273; John 77, 154, 224*, 225*, 226, 227, 254, 275, 277, 380; Margt. 178; Marion 303; Mary 283; Ric. 353; Rob. 227, 303; Tho. 178, 227, 277; Wm. 227, 353.
Payneley, Thos. 274.
Payntor, John 197*.
Payse (Payes), Barth. 28; John 31; Ric. 27.
Payton, Eliz. 141; John 65. See Peyton.
Payvey, Thos. 274.
Peabody, Fras. 376.
Peacham, Henry 157.
Pe(a)chye (Peachie, Petchey), Alice 80; Hen. 382, 383; Rich. 80, 178, 220.
Peacocke (Pecock), Alice 170; Andr. 240; Anne 139, 352; Eliz. 50, 170; Geo. 29; Jas. 287; Joan 255; Kath. 139; Ric. 78, 222, 255, 307; Rob. 29; Sar. 136, 334; Steph. 7; Tho. 155*, 190, 352, 353, 372; Walt. 282; Wm. 29*, 66, 188, 190.
Peake (Pe(ac)ke), Dor. 163; Fras. 112, 159, 160*, 163*; Harry 163; Hen. 112; Joan 114; John 159, 234*; Joyce 163.
Pearles, Eliz. 258; John 258; Martha 369.
Pearpointe, Moses 212.
Pearse (Pearce, Pierce, Peirce), Arthur 212; Eliz. 293; Ellen 114; Isab. 114; Mark 39, 217, 223; Mary 160, 161; Ric. 162; Rob. 238; Steph. 290*, 291*, 292; Sus. 212; Tho. 182*; Wm. 48. See Russell.
Pedder, Alice 31; Hen. 31; Ric. 31*; Tho. 135.
Peede, Edw. 26, 223, 305; John 154; Tho. 223.

Poel(e), Christr. 84; Edw. 151; Hen. 204*; John 267.
Peer(e)man, Ann 49; Edw. 49*, 50.
Peet, Thos. 316*.
Pegeon (Pei(e)on), Ric 271, 322*; Tho. 269*, 271*, 272, 324, 325.
Pegot, Laur. 191; Margt. 191.
Pegrim (Pe(a)grome, Peagrem, Pegerom, Pygrame, Peygrym), Alice 157, 180; Dion. 180; Eliz. 180, 218; Frances 180; Geo. 180; John 297; Ric. 222, 254; Tho. 180, 218, 276.
Pegsworth, Eliz. 164.
Pekering, John 275.
Pelham (Pellam), Edm. 10; Tho. 276.
Pelle, John 20; Wm. 20, 21.
Pem(b)erton (Pemartonne), Eliz. 199, 200; Mary 206; Raph. 206; Rob. 265; Roger 338, 341; Val. 198.
Pembroke, Geo. 265; Wm. 137.
Penbury, Alice 24; John 24.
Pend(e)red, Mr 110; Wm. 169.
Pendreth, Fras. 253; Miles 253.
Penfote, Joan 313.
Penger, John 47.
Pen(ne) (Atte Pennes), Alice 233*, 234*, 235; Anne 25*, 26*; Charity 235*; Chevall 235*; Dor. 25*, 26*, 234; Elen 234*; Eliz. 234, 235*; Fras. 234*, 235*; Jas. 95; Joan 233; John 24*, 26, 27, 233*, 234*, 235; Jonathan 234, 235*; Lucy 24*, 26, 234; Margt. 233; Mary 235; Ralph 23*, 24*, 233*; Rob. 24*, 25*, 26*, 234*, 235; Sar. 235; Sim. 234*, 235; Sus. 25, 26*; Tho. 24, 26*, 233, 234*, 235*; Wm. 234*, 235*.
Pennant, Master 235.
Penny, Edw. 361.
Pen(n)yngton, John 1, 275; Ric. 1*.
Pen(n)yston(e), Anth. 3; Eliz. 82; Tho. 78, 82.
Penred, Gartred 313; John 313*; Mary 313.
Penruddocke, Anne 133; Geo. 133.
Penrye, Eliz. 98.
Penson, Wm. 337.
Penton, Eliz. 131*; Wm. 131*.
Peny, John 91; Mat. 91.
Penyfather, Edw. 353; Jas. 98; John 32; Ric. 354; Tho. 354.
Peppercorne, Eliz. 1; Henry 121.
Pepwell, Ed. 156.
Pepyn, Hugh 353.
Per(e)son, John 275; Rob. 275; Sus. 302; Tho. 302, 304.
Peris, John 45.
Perkins (Perkyns), Ric. 349; Searles 6.
Perkot, Rob. 268.
Perle, Rob. 27.
Perles, Wm. 218.
Perley, Allen 376.
Permenter, Agn. 40*; Geo. 40*; John 40; Mary 40; Tho. 40.
Pernell. See Parnell.

Per(r)ott, Edw. 95; Jn. 235; Wm. 343.
Perry(e) (Perrie, Perrey, Perryn), Abm. 103*; Agn. 341, 343; Christr. 120*, 180, 341, 343; Dan. 219; Frances 167; Geo. 120, 180, 343; John 120, 180, 274, 275; Margery 120, 180; Mary 137; Ralph 120, 223, 274; Rob. 120, 180*, 327; Rose 329; Sam. 223; Wm. 121, 273.
Perse, John 348; Wm. 275.
Persmythe *alias* Cheyney, John 175.
Pert(e), Joan 173; Mary 287; Ralph 74, 173.
Pery, Aug. 78; Geo. 103; John 78.
Peryent, Dor. 129; John 272*; Tho. 128; Wm. 129. *See Purient.*
Peter (Petre, Peeter), Alles 198; Hermon 198; John 177, 308, 342; Jos. 300; Mary 308.
Peters, Sarah 331.
Peterson, Daniel 207.
Pett(e), Eliz. 82; Hen. 215*, 339; Hugh 278; Ric. 40*; Rob. 82; Tho. 3, 215; Wm. 278*.
Petter, Richard 273.
Pettit (Pettyte), Alice 256; Rob. 9, 120*, 181*; Roger 191; Wm. 256.
Petworth (Pettewborth), Tho. 270, 326.
Pewterer, Winif. 209.
Peycock, Edw. 302.
Peyton, Eliz. 241; J. 46; John 91, 241; Ric. 78; Rob. 241. *See Payton.*
Pheasant, Ann 371; Reb. 139.
Philby, John 374.
Philer, John 98.
Phil(l)ip(p)es (Phelip(pes). —— 65; Agn. 62; Edw. 258; Eleanor 84; Frances 220; Geo. 240; John 27, 62, 147, 383; Ralph 383*; Ric. 62*; Tho. 38, 62*, 78, 79; Tob. 62; Wm. 62, 89, 186, 208, 220.
Phil(l)pot(t), Eliz. 130, 254, 257, 305; John 254, 257, 305*; Ric. 130.
Phip(pe), John 143; Sus. 281; Tho. 70, 353; Wm. 278. *See Fyppe.*
Phippes, Eliz. 218; John 218.
Picker (Picking) John 86*.
Pickering(e), Christr. 180; Ric. 373.
Picket, Thos. 374.
Pickman, John 103*; Winif. 103.
Pigion, Thos. 314.
Pike, Ric. 277; Wm. 85, 276.
Pilgrim, Mary 329.
Pillie, Thos. 85.
Pillis, Rich. 38.
Piper (Pypere, Pypar), Degory 307; John 269, 270, 271, 326, 328; Ric. 80; Wm. 46.
Pitches (Pytches), John 32, 106, 307, 343.
Pitheon (Phithen), Rob. 374.
Pitkin, Fras. 43*, 110; Mr 181.
Pixeley, Wm. 288.
Plaisted, Wm. 285.
Plare, John 319.

Plate, John 73.
Platt, John 44; Ric. 37, 217.
Plomer, Jeff. 353.
Plompton. Wm. 217.
Plot, Henry 350.
Ploughe, Thos. 184.
Plowewryt, Wm. 186.
Plumbe, Thos. 213.
Plume, Mr 381; Wm. 73.
Plummer, Eliz. 209; Hannah 240*; John 106, 219, 306; Ric. 353; Sam. 240, 248*; Wm. 68*, 142, 249, 338, 345.
Pn'ter, Wm. 353.
Pnycke, Thos. 347.
Pockthrope, — 74.
Podmer, Mary 216.
Podyfat. *See Puddifatt.*
Pole, Roger 352. *See Poole.*
Poley, Joan 189; John 189; Kath. 189; Lawr. 189*; Margt. 189; Ric. 189; Tho. 189*.
Polkinghorne (Paulkkinghoorne), Anth. 96, 369.
Pollard (Pollerd), Alice 304; Catren 310; Dor. 200; Eliz. 103, 201; Hen. 226; John 176, 282, 304, 313; Mary 282; Nic. 103; Ralph 206.
Pollhill, Wm. 381.
Pollyn (Pollin, Pallen). John 139, 373; Sar. 373.
Polston, Peter 347.
Pomford, Fras. 313*; Wm. 223, 313.
Pomforth, Fras. 176.
Pomfret, Anne 305; Tho. 305; Wm. 305.
Ponde, John 302, 323, 345; Lucy 302; Wm. 216. *See Bond (Thomas).*
Poole, Alice 77; Eliz. 77; Hen. 77; Joan 243; John 372, 374; Mary 48, 84; Tho. 77. *See Pole.*
Pool(e)y, Mary 92; Rosamund 285.
Poor, John 40.
Pope (Poope), Agn. 158; Anne 158; Eliz. 143; Jas. 286, 374; Joan 258; John 27, 158, 186, 217, 227, 254, 258*, 335; Kath. 220; Margery 161; Paul 133, 220, 254; Ralph 175; Reb. 42; Ric. 75, 258; Rob. 35; Rog. 161; Sam. 329; Sar. 83; Tho. 147; Wm. 73, 350.
Popham, John 342.
Pople, John 348.
Porter (Portor), Agn. 120, 311; Alice 75, 120; Duglas 312*; Ellen 120; Frances 311; Fras. 223; Geo. 206, 255, 312; Grace 120; Hen. 352; Jas. 120; Joan 192, 347; John 63, 120, 192, 255*, 274, 311*, 312*; Jos. 83*; Love 223; Margt. 62; Mary 120; Mrs 38; Ric 196; Rob. 38*, 310; Sar. 333; Sybell 120; Tho. 63, 255, 311, 315; Wm. 311*, 312. *See At Felde.*
Portres, — 348; John 348.
Potager, Philip 268.
Potkins, Mr 51.

Potkyn, Ben. 134, 173 ; Sus. 173.
Potman, Rich. 306.
Pott, John 276.
Potter, Alice 42 ; Edw. 51*; Eliz. 154; John 42, 157, 341; Jone 75, 341; Kath. 157; Steph. 195; Widow 201; Wm. 157, 201.
Potten (Potton), Edw. 222, 223; Eliz. 328; Margt. 93; Tho. 93.
Pot(t)relle, John 215; Margt. 215.
Potts, Nich. 255.
Poulett, Giles lord 36.
P(o)ulter. *See Pulter.*
Pounfreyt, John 231.
Pounte, Rich. 37*.
Powell, Nic. 121. *See Appowell.*
Powlter. *See Pulter.*
Powre, Francis 36.
Powter, Edward 178.
Poynard, Thos. 275.
Poynings, John 332.
Poynter, Margt. 344*, 345 ; Rob. 344*, 345.
Poynts, Wm. 367.
Poynyn, Robt. 275
Pran(n)ell, Hen. 255, 308.
Prat(te). Alice 112; Andr. 31; Arnet 113, 162; Aug. 202, 203, 204, Bettres 162; Cath. 142, 159; Dan. 182; Eliz. 149, 157, 302; Em. 202, 203; Hen. 347; Isaac 182*; Jas. 258; Joan 12; John 103, 114, 157*, 161, 302, 348; Mary 53; Nic. 157; Ric. 72, 186; Rob. 12, 352; Sar. 168; Tho. 204*, 205, 347; Wm. 4, 46, 63, 112, 113, 152, 162*.
Prentice (Prentise, Prentyce), John 330; Ric. 194, 361.
Presson, Oades 204; John 204.
Preston, Ann 240; Christr. 343; Eliz. 95; Frances 254; Geo. 84; Jane 227; Mary 123*; Ric. 6*, 141; Tho. 7, 48, 83*, 84; Wm. 39, 123, 254, 257, 318.
Prestwoode, Geo. 202, 204; Sus. 204.
Price (Pryce), Eliz. 38*, 216; Gab. 203, 204; Hen 154; Hugh 38: John 38, 309; Marian 80; Tho. 216; Zach. 137.
Priest (Preist), Ann 310; Eliz. 371; Jas. 75; Joan 310*; John 93; Mary 153; Tho. 153.
Priestly, Thos. 335.
Prince (Prynce), John 286; Jos. 300; Ric. 27, 301.
Pritchard, Frances 359*; Hen. 359.
Probey, Tho. 369.
Prounce, — 194.
Prudden, Alice 314; Edw. 314; Jone 314; Tho. 353.
Prydden, Eliz. 305; John 305.
Pryklow, John 274.
Pryor (Prior), Anne 210; Anth. 33, 210; Deb. 244; Dor. 227; Eliz. 10, 83, 372; Fras. 227; Hen. 300, 353; Jas. 211; John 7, 42, 92, 288, 304; Jos. 48; Luke 166, 238; Margt.

33; Mary 375; Nath. 7, 135, 137, 168*, 169, 284, 330, 333, 371, 372, 373*; Tho 227*; Wm. 83, 227.
Pucker, Mary 335.
Puckeringe, Jane 178, 257; John 178, 257.
Pudd(i)fast, Ric. 32*.
Puddifat(t) (Puddiford(e), Puddyfat, Pudephat, Pudefatt, Pudifoote, Podyfate), Agn. 156; Amye 156; Andr. 287; Edw. 156; Geo. 76; Hen. 137; Hum. 182; Isab. 30; Joan 45; John 30*; Mary 138; Nic. 156; Ralph 156; Ric. 156; Rob. 156; Sar. 329; Sisley 156*; Tho. 140, 156*, 233; Walt. 45.
Pulfforde, Thos. 184, 185.
Pullyson, Thos. 254.
Pulter (Poulter, Powlter), Edw 157*, 218, 256, 257*, 302, 303, 304, 306*, 341; John 294; Kath. 36; Mary 218, 256, 306*, 357; Rog. 322; Wm. 36. *See Wallen.*
Punchon, Thos. 233.
Punn, Thos. 370.
Purbart, Margt. 136.
Purient, Lady 357. *See Peryent.*
Purratt, Bridget 115.
Purrye, Robt. 211.
Purse, Deverys 347.
Pursey, Eliz. 152; Kath. 361; Mary 152; Thos. 94, 214.
Purslack, Eliz. 204; Odes 202, 203, 204.
Purveye (Purevey), Eliz. 350; John 36, 174; Mr 1; Wm. 10.
Put(t)nam, Eben 143, 376; Hen. 182; John 143, 181, 182*; Rob. 186; Tho. 22*; Wm. 182
Pycard, Rich. 186.
Pye, Henry 347; Margt. 1; Ric. 12; Rob. 207; Wm. 4*.
Pyerson, Agn. 305; Wm. 305.
Pygesworth, Rich. 349.
Pyg(g)ot(t), — 193; Agn. 175; Eliz. 229; John 229; Nic. 300; Ric. 194, 195, 228*; Rob. 148, 175, 193*, 194*; Tho. 194, 223, 228*; Wm. 277, 342, 343.
Pykes, John 47; Wm. 46.
Pylston (Pilsten), Alice 277; Joan 134*; Ric. 277; Wm. 134*, 277.
Pym, Edmund 102.
Pymble, Joan 341.
Pynke, Wm. 148*.
Pynknye (Pinkenye, Pynkanie), John 39*; Wid. 86.
Pyper. *See Piper.*

Quarendn, Agn. 312; Alice 312; Eliz. 312; Wm. 312.
Quarles (Quarrells), — 310: Jas. 177; Joan 177; Mr 310.
Quarrington, Alice 113
Quenby, Robt. 316.
Querryngton, Wm. 173.
Qvynowe, Eliz. 39.

# INDEX.

Radcliffe (Radclyff), Anth. 177, 257; Edw. 291; Eliz. 291, 308; Ralph 179, 253, 257*, 306, 308.
Rafe, Rich. 215.
Railyng, Thos. 39.
Rainsford, Robt. 333*, 370.
Ralfe, Thos. 29.
Rallins, Thos. 318.
Ralph, Edw. 371.
Rampton, Martha 333.
Ramridge, Jas. 6, 166.
Ramsay (Ramsey), Alice 319; Ezech. 382; Joan 319; John 319, 382*, 383*; Margt. 319; Mary 338; Mat. 319; Reg. 381; Tho. 338.
Rance, Wm. 7.
Rand (Rande), Joan 308; Nic. 308; Rob. 214.
Randall (Randoll, Randyll), Andr. 349; Edw. 95, 176; Eliz. 329; Geo. 333; Hen. 68, 69, 305, 306; Joan 349; John 12, 72, 333, 349*, 362, 372; Mary 333; Ric. 355*; Rob. 349; Vincent 117; Wm. 142.
Randolf (Randolphe, Randulf), Isab. 45; John 192, 213; Ric. 349; Tho. 192; Wm. 45.
Ranshom, Robt. 351.
Ransome, Chare 201.
Raper, Frances 245.
Rason, Thos. 72.
Rasshe, Thos. 189.
Ratchurche, Beat. 29.
Ratling, Rathaman 300.
Rattin, Thos. 209.
Ravens, Cath. 102; Eliz. 102*; Mary 102; Ric. 102.
Ravenscroft, Mrs 245.
Ravis, Thos. (bishop) 105.
Rawlin, Conan 62*; Margery 62.
Rawlins, Edm. 5; Han. 5; John 342; Jos. 213; Mary 213; Wm. 92.
Rawlinson, Edw. 334.
Raws(s)on(e), Hen. 272; Tho. 304, 321.
Ray(e), Christr. 311, 349; John 6. *See Roe.*
Rayment (Raymont, Reamount, Rament), Alice 229, 288; Frances 354; Geo. 290; Grace 288; Isab. 33, 97; John 306, 315; Mary 315; Tho. 212, 288, 290.
Raymonde, Tho. 85; Wm. 85, 87.
Rayner, Chas. 165; Dan. 227; Ric. 280; Sus. 280.
Raynes, Eliz. 34; Wm. 34.
Raynshawe (Rayshow), Ric 26, 272.
Raynton, Mr 2.
Rayson, John 289; Wm. 289.
Rayston, George 274.
Rea, Agn. 65*; Nic. 65*.
Reade (Red(e)), Anne 214; Barth. 366; Edw. 12, 348; Eliz. 41; Geo. 12; Hugh 12; Innocent 130, 219; John 349, 366; Nic. 174; Ric. 12, 133, 300*; Rob. 368*; Steph. 273; Sus. 12; T. 70; Tho. 278, 350; Wm. 12, 276, 380*, 382*, 383*.

Re(a)dhead, George 12; Hen. 158. *See Gregorie.*
Reading(e), Mat. 152; Ric. 240.
Reason, Thos. 353.
Red(d)all, John 104*, 210.
Redding(e), Eliz. 7; Jason 290; Mary 96, 287; Ruth 290; Sar. 239.
Redington (Redyngton), John 31*, 318.
Redishe (Redich), Geo. 40, 86.
Redman, Annah 162; John 162; Rob. 114.
Redwood (Reddwood, Redewood), John 12, 24, 219, 347, 350; Nic. 277; Ric. 347; Rob. 306; Tho. 206, 347; Wm. 350.
Ree, —— 352; Ric. 274.
Re(e)ve, Christr. 62; Ellen 112; Geo. 29, 112*, 161, 331; Joan 62*; John 112*, 113, 114*, 164*, 291, 381; Martha 114; Nath. 188; Nic. 62; Reb. 113, 114; Rob. 62; Sam 53; Sus. 163*; Tho. 62*, 182*; Wm. 112*, 161, 163, 165; Zach. 170. *See Humberstone.*
Reeves, Mary 375; Wm. 287.
Refed, George 30.
Refham, Rich. 238.
Reignolds, Alice 38; Ric. 38
Rench, Mary 330.
Renn(e), Edw. 360; Jo. 360; Mary 168, 360.
Ren(n)yngton, John 274, 367.
Retchford, Joan 143.
Revett, Wm. 133.
Re(y)nold(es) (Raynoldes, Rainolds, Reanolds), Agn. 313; Anth. 313*, 353; Benj. 382; Christian 208; Dan. 229; Geo. 211; Grace 38; Isab. 38; Joan 38, 152, 189, 303; John 23, 189, 229, 273, 276*, 381, 382; Kath. 38; Lewys 86, 120, 216, 318; Nic. 277, 313; Ric. 272; Rob. 110; Tho. 40*, 95, 273*, 303; Wm. 38, 273, 276, 313. *See Lorrymer.*
Rhodes (Roads) Ann 169, 281.
Rhyld, Rich. 353.
Rice (Ryse), Margt. 256; Sym. 365, 366, 367*, 368*; Tho. 256. *See Appryce.*
Richard(s), Edm. 33; Marion 33; Mary 140; Sar. 169; Tho. 7, 140*.
Richardson(ne) (Ritchardson, Rychardisson), Cath. 370; Eliz. 258, 329; Eub. 160*; Frances 329; Jas. 239; Joan 304; John 95, 136, 258, 304, 329, 340; Ric. 136, 137; Rob. 154, 235; Tho. 74*, 237, 314; Wm. 347.
Riche, Edw. 340; Eliz. 342; Joan 340.
Riches, Agn. 291; Joan 288; John 314*; Mary 288; Ric. 288, 294, 295.
Richford, Cath. 363*; Mary 363*; Mary 363.
Richmond, Frances 243; Margt. countess of 171; Mary 52; Wm. 96.

Rickeson, Mary 5.
Rickett, Emma 212 ; Tho. 212.
Riddell, Cadwallader 213.
Ridgedale, Thos. 72.
Rigerbye, Henry 274.
Risse, John 70.
Rithe, Ezechiel 222.
Roache, Joan 208.
Robards, Dorcas 360*; Em. 360 ; Jo. 360*; Mary 360.
Robarth, John 24.
Robert, Rich. 277.
Roberts, (Roberds), —— 348 ; Anne 178, 318 ; Cath. 151 ; Dan. 140 ; Dorcas 362*; Edw. 212 ; Eliz. 362 ; Fras. 131, 218*; Geo. 307 ; Jack 20 ; John 143, 178, 209, 318, 345, 362*; Kath. 335, 372 ; Ric. 190, 257, 318 ; Rob. 27 ; Sus. 345 ; Tho. 28*, 94, 122, 157, 285, 318*, 335, 351, 369 ; Wm. 370.
Robey, James 48.
Robins (Robyns), Amey 332 ; Edw. 31 ; Eliz. 347 ; John 27, 130 ; Joseph 93, 95 ; Mary 93 ; Rob. 31*; Tho. 310 ; Wm. 3*, 72, 88.
Robinson (Robynson), Ambrose 286 ; Ann 84 ; Benj. 94 ; Christr. 134 ; Dor. 93, 363 ; Edw. 330, 331 ; Eliz. 341 ; Hen. 204 ; Jacob 331 ; John 169, 341, 353, 363 ; Kath. 204 ; Nic. 352 ; Owen 134 ; Ric. 161, 162*, 163*; Rob. 7, 140 ; Sar. 7 ; Sus. 134 ; Tho. 139, 205, 339, 346, 371 ; Wm. 335, 348.
Robotham, Eliz. 65 ; John 65.
Robson(ne), Anne, 64 ; Eliz. 64 ; Geo. 218 ; Jonas 12*, 64*; Nic. 168 ; Ric. 134 ; Rob. 348 ; Wm. 64. *See Emyn.*
Roby, Sarah 83.
Roche, Hen. 37 ; Rob. 158 ; Wm. 158.
Rocheford(e), Ellen 131 ; Tho. 91, 181.
Rockett (Rokitt), Tho. 201 ; Wm. 65, 66.
Roddye, Patrick 256.
Roder (Rutter), Steph 147*.
Rodes, John 274, 350 ; Sus 150.
Roding, Rich. 351.
Roe, Hen. 291 ; Steph. 169*.
Roe *alias* Raye, Tho. 337.
Rofe, Dan. 6 ; Wm. 30.
Roffe, John 353.
Roger, John 27 ; Wm. 350.
Rogers (Roggers, Rotgers), — 350 ; Edw. 138 ; Elyn 347 ; Jas. 35 ; John 328 ; Leon. 36 ; Mary 139, 265 ; Mat. 265, 334 ; Ric. 140, 328 ; Rob. 150 ; Tho. 156, 239.
Rogerson, Agn. 121 ; Rob. 121 ; Wm. 121*.
Rokell, Joan 277.
Roker, Thos. 83.
Rolfe (Rolff), Alice 30 ; Bray 65 ; Dor. 65 ; Edw. 349 ; Eliz. 11 ; Eme 349 ; Frances 179 ; Grace 66 ; Hen. 349 ; Hugh 66 ; Jas. 65*,

168, 188*, 283 ; John 27, 65, 169, 351 ; Margt. 30 ; Margery 30 ; Mary 139 ; Mich. 66 ; Rich. 30*, 63, 104 ; Rob. 30*, 74 ; Tho. 11, 30, 88, 89, 186, 351 ; Val. 374 ; W. 300 ; Wm. 24, 30*, 65*, 66, 99, 136, 179, 307, 351.
Rolte, John 304 ; Judith 304.
Romayne, Mr 121.
Roo, Eliz. 341 ; John 278 ; Ric. 340, 341 ; Wm. 33.
Rood(e)s, John 112 ; Ursula 112.
Rooke, Ann 265 ; Ben. 265.
Rookes, John 234 ; Sim. 215.
Roos, Edw. lord 172 ; Gilb. 186.
Roose, Mother 126 ; Roger 344.
Rooste, George 230.
Roote, John 278.
Roper, Rob. 190.
Rose, Agn. 238 ; Alice 44, 322 ; Eliz. 333 ; Geo. 8 ; Joan 141 ; John 238, 346 ; Jonath. 333 ; Jos. 234 ; Kath. 7 ; Rob. 353 ; Wm. 268*, 269, 270, 271*, 322*, 327.
Rosewell, Dor. 34 ; Pet. 34.
Rosse, George 230.
Roth, John 382, 383.
Rother(h)am, Agn. (Anne) 143 ; Geo. 34, 176, 254, 306 ; Jane 34 ; Sus. 142 ; Tho. 94 ; Vertue 93.
Rotor(s) (Rother), Anice 91 ; Reg. 326, 327 ; Tho. 324, 325.
Rowe, Anne 178 ; Eliz. 81, 152 ; John 45*, 64, 91, 192, 303, 380 ; Ric. 81, 319 ; Sim. 178 ; Wm. 86.
Rowell, Anne 51 ; Chas. 136.
Rowhede, Alice 45 ; Hen. 45 ; Tho. 45 ; Wm. 45.
Rowhey (Roughey), John 268, 270.
Rowlett (Rowlatt), —— 129 ; Affabell (Amphabell) 125*, 126, 127, 128*, 129 ; Dor. 125*, 127, 184 ; Eliz. 126*, 127*; Margt. 185 ; Ralph 77*, 87*, 88*, 89, 124*, 125*, 126*, 127*, 128*, 129, 184.
Rowley, John 205 ; Mary 143 ; Moses 108
Rownale, Alice 189.
Rowney, George 263, 265*, 333.
Rowse (Rowce), Tho. 260, 261.
Rowsom, Eliz. 2 ; Sus. 2.
Roxesonne, John 306.
Royce (Royse), Agn. 199 ; Andr. 347 ; Eliz. 311 ; Jas. 6, 41 ; John 231, 352 ; Ric. 41, 236, 347 ; Rob. 311 ; Saunder, 347 ; Tho. 236 ; Walt. 351 ; Wm. 24, 311, 347.
Royne, Mary 64.
Royston (Roiston), Margt. 37 ; Ric. 121*; Rob. 37 ; Tho. 8, 93.
Rudd, Agn. 44 ; Ann 314 ; Annis 314 ; Clem. 314 ; Eliz. 314*; John 314, 353 ; Ric. 2, 44, 206, 252*, 314 ; Rob. 213, 314 ; Temp. 2 ; Tho. 2*, 306, 3.4*; Wm. 252, 314*.
Rudston, Eliz. 212.
Ruffin (Ruffyn), Eliz. 355 ; Mary 355 ; Tho. 355.

Rugg(e), Hen. 350; Nic. 211.
Rugmore (Rugmer), Eliz. 143, 162; Geo. 208; Ric. 288; Wm. 161*, 162.
Rugsby, Mary 138.
Rumbold, Joan 172, 216; John 130, 172; Rob. 206.
Rumbolt, Wm. 367.
Rumford (Roomforde), Margery 201; Rob. 166; Wm. 201.
Rumny, John 273.
Runnington, Eliz. 285; Wm. 285.
Runnio, Joshua 375.
Rush, Oliver 224*, 225*, 226.
Rush(e)ley (Rusley), Alice 31; Anne 12, 64; Audry 31, 157, 228; Beat. 12; Bennet 31*; Eli.. 31*; Geo. 12, 64; Hen. 24, 28, 31*, 221, 228; Jerom 12; John 12*, 31, 64*, 206; Mary 12*, 64*; Tho. 31; Venice 12, 64; Wm. 31*, 62.
Russell, Anne 79, 112; Annis 113, 115; Cecily 256, 304, 305; Dionis 91; Edw. 77; Isab. 114; James 115*, 157; Jane 137; John 112, 113*, 115, 137, 160, 273, 350; Kath. 77, 91; Nath. 212; Ric. 348; Rob. 350; Tho. 36, 79, 80, 91, 256, 304, 305, 350; Wm. 39*.
Russell *alias* Pearse, Wm. 220.
Russhelyn. *See Fylyan.*
Rustat(t), Mary 253; Sam. 103; Wm. 253.
Rusten, Wm. 4.
Ruth, Joan 345; Ric. 287, 288, 330, 331, 335, 345, 347, 375; Rob. 373; Tho. 331.
Rutlan, John 301.
Rutland, Alice 161, 162; Joshua 163; Mary 160; Phillis 163; Tho. 114, 160, 161, 162, 163.
Rutter, Mary 10; Steph. 147, 195; Wm. 43, 161. *See Roder.*
Rye, Edw. lord Morley, baron of 308; Widow 313.
Ryman, John 28.
Ryngsoll, John 27.
Ryppyngton, Barth. 28.
Rysleye, Rich. 227.
Rytchemont, Alles 198.
Rythe, Christr. 36; Kath. 36.

Sabbe, Agn. 236; Eliz. 255; Fras. 255; John 45, 236; Walt. 45.
Sabisford, Thos. 92.
Sabt, Thos. 353.
Saburne, John 10*.
Sabyne, Eliz. 309; John 309.
Sadle(i)r (Sadleyer), Anne 130, 256, 304, 306*, 307, 338*; Dor. 256, 257; Edw. 78, 130, 256, 304, 306*, 307, 338*; Hen. 254*, 256, 257; John 249; Ralph 35, 79, 303, 338*; Ric. 38; Tho. 78, 133, 178, 249, 255.
Sage, Sar. 84; Tho. 369.
Saggers, Thos. 48.

Saggs, Susan 245.
St Albans, Abbot of 24.
St Bartholomew, London, Master of, 326, 327, 378; Prior of 269*, 324, 325, 326.
St John (Seynt Jon), Alex. 276; Oliver, lord 78; Oliver 78.
St Peters, Westminster, Abbot of 186.
Sale, Eliz. 39; John 236; Sam. 101; Wm. 39.
Salisbury (Salysburye), Earl of 106, 297, 298; Tho. 253, 255, 340, 341.
Salkins (Salkyns), Jane 78; Wm. 78, 309.
Sal(l)mon, Edm. 134; Lettice 9; Ric. 9; Rob. 377, 378; Wm. 9.
Salter, Edw. 110; John 349; Rob. 211; Tho. 110*.
Saltmash, Ann 286.
Sam(me), Eliz. 154; Geo. 79; John 76, 353; Mary 167; Ric. 79; Tho. 353.
Samonde, Thos. 122.
Sampson(ne), Anne 201; Eliz. 198; Isab. 200; John 201; Tho. 201, 325*, 326, 327.
Samsom, Thos. 324.
Samwayes, Wm. 218.
Samy, George 256.
Sanders. *See Saunders.*
Sanders *alias* Burton, John 34.
Sandes (Sondes), Anne 130; Hen. 20, 21; Mr 21; Rob. 130; Tho. 130.
Sandford, Charles 382.
Sannatt. *See Stannope.*
Sansum, John 45.
Santon, Fras. 304; Geo. 304; Lucy 304.
Santon (Saunton) *alias* Mathewe, Fras. 177; Geo. 132.
Saranke, John 273.
Sare, Eliz. 347; Hen. 305; John 28, 133; Margt. 305; Mich. 305.
Saringe (Saryng, Sarring), Annes 318; Edw. 276; John 104; Wm. 62.
Satterthwaite, Hum. 51.
Saule, John 210.
Saunder(s), Agn. 339; Anne 63, 243, 370; Bernard 370; Edw. 185, 218; Eliz. 218; Emma 154; Geo. 152; Isab. 34; Jane 173, 221, 222, 223, 253; John 34, 41, 63, 73, 139, 174, 255; Jos. 139; Nath. 170; Reb. 288; Tho. 126, 173, 221, 222, 223, 253, 288, 289 *,348, 351; Walt. 73; Wm. 254, 352. *See Dodkin.*
Saunsom, Thos. 323.
Savage (Savege), Nic. 259; Rob. 34; Tho. 376.
Saveel, Mary 369.
Saverye, Susan 199.
Savill (Savell), —— 324; Anne 82*, 130*; Ric. 305; Rob. 82*, 130*.
Sawell, Eliz. 210, 244; Hen. 141; John 244, 277*; Kath. 244.
Sawer, Ellin 6.
Sawger, John 47.

Sawman, George 275.
Sawrey, Auth. 343 ; Eliz. 343.
Sawtry, Henry 232.
Sawyer, Agn. 159 ; Felice 190 ; Hen. 232, 273 ; John 190 ; Rob. 64.
Say(e), John 116, 145, 148, 193, 195 ; Tho. 229 ; Wm 31, 368*.
Sayer, Roger 37 ; Tho. 311
Sayvll, John 1.
Saywell, Kath. 246 ; John 149, 246 ; Mary 246.
Scapisworth, Wm. 1.
Scarbrough (Skarborowe). Dor. 29 ; Edw. 242 ; Han. 242 ; Margery 29 ; Sar. 29 ; Sus. 242 ; Wm. 3, 29.
Scattergood (Skattergood). Wm. 273, 320.
Scogge, John 32 ; Tho. 32.
Schambroke, Thos. 272.
Sciner, Annis 33* ; Eliz. 33 ; Wm. 33.
Scotbrut, Tho. 70.
Scotchbrooke, Wm. 361.
Scot(te) (Skotte), Alice 39 ; Eliz. 350 ; Hen. 62 ; Isaac 94, 137 ; John 107, 187, 254, 370 ; John Mawcome 275 ; Martha 229 ; Rach. 240 ; Ric. 254 ; Rob. 6, 135, 238, 240*, 330 ; Tho. 96, 136, 157, 330, 333, 359* ; Wm. 269, 271, 276.
Scoun, Robt. 46.
Sc(o)urfeild, Goddard 151 ; Wm. 376.
Scrivener, Ann 330 ; Mr 108.
Scudamore, Bethia 167.
Se(a)bro(o)ke (Seybrooke, Seibroke, Sebrucke), Alice 230 ; Amy 230 ; Dennys 2 ; Edw. 7, 96, 230* ; Eliz. 230*, 361 ; Joan 230 ; John 7, 73, 230 ; Kath. 230 ; Mark 288 ; Mary 136, 361, 372 ; Ric. 230 ; Rob. 33*, 151, 220 ; Tho. 5, 8 ; Wm. 96.
Seale, Eliz. 37, 302 ; Ric. 37 ; Rob. 37, 185 ; Tho. 302.
Seaman, Chas. 374*, 375 ; Sar. 138.
Seare, Agn. 217 ; Alice 217 ; Anne 138 ; Hen. 168, 313 ; Jane 217, 304 ; John 217, 304 ; Sar. 315 ; Tho. 217.
Seares (Seers), Anne 244 ; Hen. 287, 333, 334 ; Jer. 244 ; John 239, 282, 330, 335 ; Ric. 244 ; Sar. 335 ; Tho. 245, 371 ; Tim. 138.
Searle, Geo. 31 ; John 202 ; Kath. 31, 202 ; Tho. 226.
Seawell, Mary 373 ; Ric. 70.
Seayre, Mary 168.
Secker, John 264 ; Mary 264.
Sedly, Mr 296*.
Seely, Alice 243 ; Kath. 86.
Segrave, Nic. 134.   *See Berkley.*
Selby, George 333.
Self, Roger 347.
Selioke, Mich. 168.
Sell(e), Rog. 91 ; Sar. 101 ; Wm. 176.
Selles, John 101.
Selleye, Thos. 276.
Sellwood, Anne 211 ; Eliz. 211.
Semer (Semar), Ellyn 273 ; John 320.

Sende, Robt. 27.
Sene, Robt. 122.
Senior, Agn. 72 ; Eliz. 72 ; Geo. 72 ; Isab. 72 ; Jas. 72* ; John 278 ; Sar. 72 ; Wm. 72.
Senton, Rich. 48.
Seowell, Wm. 155.
Sepset, Math. 44.
Seracoale, Mr 2.
Sere, Eliz. 113 ; Hen 311.
Serman, Joan 313.
Serrey, Thos. 240.
Seuter, Anne 210.
Seward(e), Cecily 218 ; John 195*, 218 ; Wm. 26.
Sewell, Alice 256 ; Wm. 256.
Sewer, Robt. 191.
Sew(e)ster, Giles 309, 338 ; John 272.
Sexteyn, John 146.
Seybroke, Thos. 347.
Seye, Thos. 173.
Seyman, John 174.
Seymir, Ed. 110.
Seyward, Agn. 312 ; Alice, 312 ; Eliz. 312 ; Fras. 312 ; Joan 312 ; John 312 ; Kath. 312 ; Wm. 312.
Seywell, Edw. 369.
Shadbo(u)lt, John 286 ; Tho. 78, 99*.   *See Shotbolt.*
Shad(d)e, Agn. 30 ; Alice 346 ; Dor. 30 ; John 30, 35, 132, 134 ; Margt. 35, 132, 134 ; Rob. 30, 74*, 134, 307, 346 ; Roger 35.
Shakemaple (Shackmaple), Agn. 42 ; Ric. 82 ; Tho. 278.
Shakespeare, Eliz. 95 ; Wm. 95.
Shakevyle, John 237.
Shaldon, Mary 179.
Shambroke (Shambrooke), Eliz. 86 ; Joan 39 ; John 39, 86* ; Marion 158 ; Mary 86 ; Nic. 75 ; Ric. 86 ; Wm. 158.
Shank, Thos. 232, 233.
Shardley, Wm. 24.
Sharnbrooke (Sharrenbrooke), Eliz. 104* ; Rose 104 ; Susan 104 ; Tim. 10, 104 ; Wm. 104.
Sharparowe, Rich. 199.
Sharp(e), Dr 366 ; Eliz. 259 ; Ellen 244 ; Hen. 206, 351 ; Margt. 351 ; Ric. 348 ; Rob. 259, 337 ; Tho. 188 ; Wm. 39, 244*.
Shaw(e) (Shaa), Ben. 84 ; John 366 ; Rob. 351.
Shawarden, John 133.
Sheather, —89, 90 ; Wm 89.
Sheerer, John 140, 167*, 170, 286, 371 ; Mary 330.
Sheffeild (Shefyeld), Mary 294, 295 ; Ric. 201 ; Tho. 213.
Shelfourthe, Edm. 155 ; Eliz. 155* ; Margt. 155.
Shell(e)y, Jane 302 ; John 215, 367 ; Wm. 35, 302.
Shelton, Alice 126 ; Eliz. 95.
Shenton, Margt. 137.

# INDEX.

Shepherd (Sheepheard, Shepperte, Shepperd).—4; Alice 288; Ann 331; Annis 314; Clare 114; Dan. 333; Edw. 206; Eliz. 314*, 371; Hellen 44; Hen. 142, 371*; Jas. 33, 97; Joan 64; John 72, 79, 94, 95, 154, 181, 182, 213, 361; Margery 79; Ric. 123, 188, 243, 314, 350*; Rob. 114*, 281, 282, 374; Rose 151, 374; Sam. 181; Sar. 282; Sim. 350; Steph. 182; Sus. 138; Tho. 64, 114*, 362, 371; Wm. 64, 314.
Shepperd *alias* Touthe, Tho. 215.
Shergott, Nich. 186.
Sherley (Shereleye), Anne 36; Ellen 203; Tho. 36; Wm. 275.
Sherlocke, Wm. 332.
Sherman, John 304; Senator 376.
Sherodd, Eliz. 49; Geo. 49.
Sherwood, Wm. 185, 206, 223.
Shettleworth, Anne 242; Wm. 242*.
Shipman, Roger 323.
Shirt, Trissip 282.
Shittleton, Nich. 213.
Shorte, John 153.
Shorter, John 284; Margt. 37; Tho. 37*.
Shot(t)bolt (Shodbolte, Shatbolt, Schotbolt), Bat. 263; Geo. 252; Jas. 227*; Mary 100, 227; Tho. 173, 176, 227*, 254; Wm. 47, 102*, 190, 254, 342. *See Shadbolt.*
Shreve, Agnes 43.
Shrimpton (Shrympton), Alice 140, 339; Rob. 135, 176, 339.
Shutte, Robt. 132.
Shuttlewo(o)rth, John 205; Kath. 204; Laur. 202*, 204, 205; Nic. 200.
Sibley (Sibbley, Sybleye, Sible), Anne 29; Edw. 43, 316; Eliz. 32*, 150, 152, 248; Fras. 29; Geo. 32; Hen. 352; Joan 29; John 32, 74*, 93, 259, 305, 314, 351; Margt. 29, 314; Mary 152; Nic. 88; Salom. 32; Sar. 372; Tho. 243, 316, 353; Wm. 43.
Siggin, Thos. 150.
Siggines, Nic. 98; Rob. 138, 239.
Sigrave, Kath. 121; Wm. 121.
Sill(s), Fras. 130, 133.
Silverlock(e) (Syllverlock), Ric. 188, 202, 205, 206; Tho. 202.
Silvester, Eliz. 39; John 321.
Simon, Nic 243; Peter 243.
Simonds, Joan 240; Tho. 240.
Simpson, Dan. 294; Eliz. 320; Geo. 292*, 293, 294; John 154, 264, 292, 293, 320; Mary 294; Sar. 294; Tho. 321; Wm. 320*, 321.
Singfield, Alice 287.
Sive, Robt. 229.
Skaldwell, Hen. 201.
Skanmer, Wm. 209.
Skattergood, Wm. 273.
Skegg(es), Edw. 35, 258; Joan 258, 342; John 91; Ric. 287.

Ske(e)le, Alice 44; Anne 169; John 347; Rob. 347; Tho. 44; Wm. 44.
Skelton, Gawen 347; Jane 321; Sar. 151; Wm. 6.
Skid(a)more, Sar. 166; Sus. 329.
Skillingham, John 277; Leon. 277.
Skingle (Skyngell, Skingegell), Agn. 272; Annis 216; Geo. 272; Hen. 38, 119; Joan 216; John 64, 75, 220, 253, 273, 341; Rob. 216, 276 Tho. 38, 119, 216; Wm. 272.
Skipwith (Skypwythe, Skepweth),—— 125, 129; Alice 175; Edw. 175, 185*, 218, 222, 304; Eliz. 82; Frances 223*, 254; Hen. 185, 218, 222; Joan 90; Mary 174, 223; Ralph 173, 175, 185, 218; Ric. 133, 173, 174, 220, 223; Rob. 261; Tho. 26, 90, 125*, 126, 128, 272; Wm. 23 37, 82, 89*, 90, 133, 174, 178, 185*, 218, 219*, 222, 223*, 254.
Skylsye, John 348.
Skynner(e) (Skinner), Christr. 373; J. 165; Joan 62; John 62, 221, 261*, 269, 271*, 327; Ralph 71; Rob. 266*, 271; Tho. 83, 221, 352.
Slacforde, John 201.
Slacher, Anne 246*; Ric. 246.
Slade, Sam. 182*.
Slaney, Sarah 372.
Slater, Eliz. 1; Rob. 1.
Sle(a)p(e), Fras. 95; Geo. 122*; John 64; Margery 80; Phil. 64, 122, 311, 345, 351; Sar. 284, 286, 331; Tho. 187.
Slocome, John 75.
Slow(e). Anne 154; Geo. 142; Hugh 28; Jud. 292; Mich. 94; Rob. 292; Tho. 93; Wm. 94, 155.
Slynger(e), John 232; Margery 91; Ric. 91*; Wm. 91.
Smal(e)wod, Tho. 35; Wm. 262, 263*.
Small, Mary 377.
Smallbones, Eliz. 238.
Smart. John 21*, 46; Wm. 22*.
Smartfo(o)te, Geff. 273; Goodman 38; Joan 3; Leon. 273; Tho. 339, 340, 342.
Smethwicke, Robt. 340.
Smewyn, Annis 10; Edw. 203; Jane 10; Sar. 10; Wm. 10.
Smith(e), Smyth(e), —— 66, 141; Abm. 383; Agn. 150; Alice 45, 46, 90, 170, 179; Ambr. 292; Anne 3, 245, 246, 286, 296; Cath. 288, 363; Christr. 78; Dan. 64, 139, 333; Dor. 254, 382; Edm. 304, 306, 313; Edw. 64, 74, 104, 122, 159, 176, 186, 254; Eliz. 3, 65, 74, 80, 84, 94, 150, 179, 212, 245, 246*, 253, 288, 341, 363; Ellen 223*, 255; Fras. 245; Geo. 152; Grace 84*, 363; Han. 264, 285; Hen. 8, 84, 103, 141, 170, 264, 288, 319*; Henry Tombes 264*, 265*; Hugh 104*, 138, 319; Isab. 159*, 179; James 346; Jane 84, 135; Jasper 80, 319;

Jer. 167*, 292; Joan 173, 174, 176, 200, 220, 221, 319; John 2, 3*, 24, 26, 28, 32*, 45*, 46, 72, 84*, 90, 115, 174, 176, 182*, 188, 191, 232*, 237, 240, 244, 245, 253, 256, 257, 274, 275*, 277*, 283, 298*, 319, 329, 341, 351, 367; Jonath. 360*, 362, 363*; Jos. 246, 383*; Jude 360; Kath. 35, 310; Margt. 78; Margery 84; Martha 141; Mary 96, 170, 210, 246, 284, 335, 360*, 362, 363*; Mathew 255; Mathy 65; Mich. 319; Nic. 65; Peter 179; Phil. 210; Rachel 286; Ralph 45, 91, 192; Ric. 35, 96, 192, 220, 223, 281, 288*, 291, 292, 293*, 296, 302, 311, 343, 345, 350*, 371; Rob. 6, 93, 159*, 179, 186, 322; Rose 175, 191, 362, 363; Sar. 262, 333, 363; Sol. 93, 95, 137; Sus. 95, 265; Tho. 24, 26, 29, 31, 84, 94, 95, 101, 119, 135, 147, 149, 175, 219*, 220*, 223*, 255, 343, 348, 351, 372; Walt. 191, 245; Wm. 28, 65*, 87, 122, 123, 137*, 145, 159*, 164*, 167, 176, 178, 182*, 186, 246*, 247, 333, 337, 344, 375; Zach. 35.

Smothe, John 180.
Smythe *alias* Clarke, Joan 80, 172; Rob. 172.
Smythe *alias* Howson, John 302.
Snape, George 215.
Snaw, John 237.
Snell, Christr. 304; Dor. 212; John 304.
Snell *alias* Wheeler, Joan 12; Margt. 12; Nic. 12; Rand. 12; Tho. 12*.
Snoden, Eliz. 320.
Snow(e), Anne 72; Dan. 130; Eliz. 337; Geo. 245; Henry 323*, 326*, 327; Jas. 69; John 68*, 69*, 277*; Mary 307, 314; Ric. 307, 344; Tho. 28, 277; Wm. 133, 223, 254, 320, 337, 367.
Snugg(s), Clem. 138; Elen 139.
Socklyng, Eliz. 321.
Soke, John 146.
Sole, Joan, 254; John 155, 254.
Soles, Christr. 276.
Somerlandes (Som'land), Tho. 260, 347.
Somerton, Agn. 175, 178, 309; Anne 175, 309; John 175, 178, 309; Tho. 175, 309.
Somes, Sarah 166.
Som(m)er, John 80, 177, 223.
Sommersham, Eliz. 132; Hen. 132.
Sonder, John 146, 147, 148, 195; Nic. 145*, 146*, 147, 195, 197*.
Songer, John 47.
Soon, Thomas 192.
South(e), John 277; Leon. 40, 85; Ralph 156; Ric. 277.
Southcot(t)e, John 88, 89, 185.
Southend(e), John 27; Marie 333.
Southwell, Fras. 272.
Southwode, John 194; Wm. 194.

Southen (Sowthen), Agn 30; Annis 74; Eliz. 149; Helen 30; Hugh 30, 74; Joan 30, 74; John 74; Ralph 149; Ric. 30, 74; Tho. 30, 74*; Wm. 30, 74*, 156, 227.
Spaldynge, John 302; Margery 302.
Spanby, John 233.
Spanner, John 91; Mat 91.
Sparepoynte, John 261*.
Sparke, Rog. 146; Tho. 155
Spark(e)s, Cath 245; Edw. 167; John 94; Mary 136; Ric. 150.
Sparlin(g), Hugh 135; John 141; Nic. 135, 138, 141.
Sparrow(e), Barn. 133; Wm. 277.
Speares, Eliz. 136, 137.
Specer, Wm. 84.
Speed, Wm. 32.
Speight, Thomas 366.
Spencer (Spenser), Agn. 189; Ann 262; Ben. 23; Chas. 64; Eliz. 85*; Frances 257; Hen. 200, 201, 274; Hugh 172; Hum. 95; Joan 78, 85, 211, 327; John 78, 85, 95, 96, 260, 262*, 263, 274, 276, 326; Margt. 262, 263; Margery 46; Mary 241; Ric. 46, 121, 273, 315; Rob. 26, 206, 241, 257, 261*, 276, 353, 378, 379; Sar. 371; Tho. 180, 261, 262*, 340; Wm. 40, 62, 121, 241, 276*.
Spendlove, John 233.
Spering (Sperynge), Eliz. 310; John 273; Kath. 273.
Spicer (Spycer), Edw. 213; John 192; Tho. 38*; Wm. 267.
Spicer *alias* Helder, John 36, 338; Lucy 338; Ric. 36.
Spig(g)ins (Spyggyns, Spidgens, Spigans), Alse 114, 160, 163; Eliz. 115; Ezech. 115; John 112, 115*, 160, 163; Mary 160; Prisc. 114; Ranulph 132; Tho. 347; Wm. 112, 113.
Spilman, Robt. 38.
Spoarte, Thos. 311.
Spooner, Thos. 94.
Spore, John 353.
Spoure, John 212.
Spragg, Edw. 52.
Spranger, Edw. 100.
Spratt, John 276.
Sprigge, Eliz. 174; John 174; Wm. 120.
Spriggines, John 162; Prisc. 162.
Springhall, Wm. 350.
Springham, Anne 73; Eliz. 73; John 31*, 73*; Judith 73*; Sus. 73; Tho. 313.
Spurling (Spurlynge), Hen. 313*; John 133, 175, 253.
Spylman, Jas. 275.
Spyngoll, Wm. 352.
Squire (Squier, Squyer), Edw. 129, 209*; Fras. 8; John 275; Mary 334, 373; Ric. 32; Wm. 158*, 312, 334.
Squirge, Rich. 363.

Stacey (Stacye), Bedford 335; Frances 318; John 182, 199, 201, 205, 344, 345; Jone 200, 201.
Stacforde, John 204*.
Stafford(e), Bridget 304; Hen. 215; Hum. 175; John 303, 304; Mary 374; Ric. 276; Wid. 4.
Stafforde alias Downes, Hen. 215.
Stal(l)ibras(se), Kath. 86, 180; Ric. 86; Wm. 180.
Stal(l)worth, Dinis 292; Grace 292; John 147; Wm. 147.
Stamford, Ann 246; Mary 246, 247; Tho. 246.
Stammer, Agn. 153; Edw. 209; Eliz. 209, 314*; Grace 314; John 314*; Rob. 153.
Stanboroughe (Stanbrowe), Mary 313; Tho. 349.
Stanbrught, Ric. 350.
Standbridge, Cath. 335.
Standley (Staudlay), Ric. 275; Sir Tho. 248; Tho. 311.
Standysshe, Hen. 221.
Stane, Eliz. 303, 308; Wm. 303, 308.
Stanes, Joan 172; Ric. 172; Tho. 215; Wm. 313.
Stanet, Wm. 190.
Stanford (Staunford), Christian 242; John 202, 242; Rob. 35, 175, 177; Steven 242; Sus. 202.
Stanhope, Edw. 343; Mich. 343.
Stanley, Jos. 362; Tho. 81, 338.
Stannell, Ric. 373.
Stannet, John 351.
Stannope alias Sannatt, Edw. 62; Joan 62; John 62.
Stanton, Andr. 204; Christr. 202, 204; Nic. 4; Wm. 40, 215.
Stape, Jane 62.
Staple (Stapull), Anne 6; Cecily 34; John 34, 273.
Starkyn, Ralph 277.
Starr(e), Geo. 176; John 248, 315; Margt. 176; Ric. 176; Wm. 224, 226.
Staunford. See Stanford.
Staynes, —— 86.
Stele, Thos. 275.
Stephens, Der. 345; Edw. 92, 138; John 48; Sus. 247; Tho. 345; Wm. 93.
Stephyn, Rob. 348, 349.
Stephynson, —— 346.
Stepneth (Stepnythe), Anne 130; John 130; Leon. 79; Paul 12; Ric. 175; Rob. 130, 176; Sar. 12.
Stepn(e)y, Geo. 6; Hen. 273; Isaac 8, 136; Rob. 30*, 261; Tho. 170; Wm. 141.
Stepping(e), Anne 137; Eliz. 330; Hum. 257; Mary 257; Rob. 307.
Stere, Alice 38; John 38; Rob. 38*.
Sterky, Ralph 350; Wm. 350.
Sterman, John 216.
Sterope, John 349.

Stevens (Stevyns), Anne 242, 244; Dor. 141, 334; Eliz. 242; Hen. 7, 285, 286; John 244; Kath. 221; Margt. 167; Nath. 244; Ric. 84*; Rob. 221; Tho. 242; Wm. 95, 141.
Stevenson, Cuthb. 228; Tho. 96.
Stevyn, Matilda 45; Ric. 45.
Steyinges, Jas. 216.
Stibbyng, Anth. 131.
Stile (Style), Hen. 76; John 73, 312, 366; Tho. 42, 254; Wm. 353.
Stileman, Robt. 382.
Stiles (Styles), Alice 318; Eliz. 246*; John 246, 217, 318; Tho. 167; Wm. 246*, 247.
Stilling, Wm. 301.
Stockam, Kath. 204.
Stock(e), Kath. 64; Wm. 381.
Stockes, Tho. 277; Walt. 113.
Stockwell, Robt. 310.
Stodeley, John 231.
Stokedall, Cuthbert 347.
Stokes (Stoakes), Hen. 347; John 329, 348; Lucy 35; Mother 347; Rog. 132; Tho. 23; Wm. 35.
Stokeshille, Rich. 191.
Stokhere, John 267.
Stondon, Sir Ric. 124, 125, 126*.
Stone, Alex. 30*; Eliz. 30, 92; John 176, 227*, 340, 344, 345; Oliver 278; Sib. 340; Winif. 344, 345.
Ston(e)ham, Adam 259; Edw. 348; Ric. 232, 348; Wm. 347.
Stonehouse, Geo. 329.
Stoneley, Rich. 302.
Stonhill (Ston(n)ell), Hen. 161*; Ric. 151.
Stonill. See Stannell.
Stonore, Wm. 24.
Stopes, Clem. 103; Jas. 103*; John 103*; Margery 103; Zacre 103.
Storer, Anne 50.
Stort(e)ford, Henry, vicar of 271; Vicar of 269*, 322, 324, 325, 326, 327.
Story(e), Hen. 4; John S. 265; Ric. 262.
Stoughton, Gilb. 217, 262; Mary 132, 307; Rog. 132, 307.
Stovering alias Stringer, Xpof. 2.
Stowe, Hen 41; Ric. 41.
Stowell, Edw. 37, 178; Joan 37, 178.
Stowton, Rich. 276.
Straighte (Strayte), Hen. 63; Joan 31; Ric. 31; Tho. 218, 302; Wm. 31.
Strampro, Eliz. 178; John 178.
Strange, Rich. 278.
Stratford, John 334; Martha 334; Wm. 284.
Strat(t)on, Ann. 49; John 49; Mary 49; Sim. 308; Wm. 49, 50, 111.
Strayearne, Wm. 50.
Strayne, Edward 8.
Stredder, Reb. 135.
Streete (Strett), Streate), —— 207; Edw. 343*; Joan 139, 343; Mary

331; Mat. 373; Rog. 23; Tho. 343; Wm. 73, 229, 343.
Stretele, John 45; Ric. 45; Tho. 45; Wm. 45.
Stret(e)man, Tho. 46, 91, 190, 192*.
Stretter, Master 235.
Stringer (Strynger), Jane 48; John 90, 280*. *See Stovering.*
Stronge, Hen. 320; Joan 311; John 269, 270; Mercy 63; Rob. 311; Tho. 311*, 322; Wm. 311.
Stubbinge (Stubbyns, Stubins), John 312; Mark 230, 312*.
Stubbe(s), Joan 35; John 35, 176.
Studesburye, Nic. 346.
Studley, John 238.
Sturges (Sturgis), John 96; Sus. 96, 138; Tho. 167.
Sturley, Martha 96.
Sturman, Tim. 134. *See Waters.*
Sturmyn, John 353; Ric. 353.
Sturton, Abm. 164; Erasmus 4; Margt. 167; Mary 164.
Styward(e), Edw. 33; John 341, 344; Nic. 344.
Suerties, Nath. 151.
Sulyard, Anne 257; Edw. 257.
Summers, Reb. 334.
Surmar, Wm. 112.
Suttell, Amy 211; Wm. 211.
Sutton, Anne 243; Mary 243; R. 265; Tho. 243; Wm. 78.
Swalden, Eliz. 332; Ric. 332.
Swallowe, Edm. 219; Hum. 219; Jane 175; Joan 219; Rob. 175.
Swansey, Joan 209.
Swanson (Swansom), Wm. 10, 11, 104*.
Swatthorpe, Tho. 46.
Swayne (Swaine), Eliz. 77; Hen. 77; Jud. 286; Mary 283.
Sweane, Rich. 204.
Sweete, Nic. 86; Wm. 86*.
Swe(e)tinge, John 66, 254, 349.
Swenstone (Swinston), Rob. 5, 140, 169; Tho. 5.
Swetman, Wm. 277.
Swinsborn, Wm. 332.
Swyfte, Ric. 217; Wm. 342, 348.
Swynowe, Eliz. 133; Wm. 133.
Swynsed, Thos. 121.
Sybburne, Rich. 180.
Sybsey, Edw. 156.
Sybthorpe, Geo. 103; John 223.
Sydney, Barb. 174; Tho. 174.
Syewell, Mary 217; Wm. 217.
Sykes, Hen. 71; John 251*.
Symes, Edm. 230.
Symkyns, John 201.
Symms, Joan 86; John 86; Tho. 86.
Symon, Rich. 351.
Symond(e)s, —— 63; Fras. 24; Geo. 352; Wm. 28.
Symons, Abm. 86; Edw. 249; John 66*; Margerie 66; Ric. 221; Sus. 66.
Sym(p)son, Christr. 129; John 350; Margt. 132; Oliver 274; Rob. 274; Tho. 132, 274; Wm. 76.

Symynges, John 337.
Syster, Wm. 27.

T......, John 28.
Tacker, John 170.
Tafte, John 203.
Tagell, Joyce 103; Wid. 103.
Takeley, Wm. 270.
Tangley, Eliz. 114; John 114; Miriam 115; Tho. 113, 114*, 115.
Tanner(e), John 90, 308, 324; Mary 135; Nic. 267*, 322; Wm. 268, 269*, 270, 271, 322*.
Tapp, Robt. 142.
Tappe. *See Willett.*
Tarbox(e), Dan. 8; John 209; Jos. 136, 139, 168.
Tarrye, Wm. 352.
Tatam, Eliz. 154.
Tatham, Alice 8.
Tatnell, Annis 75.
Tattenham, James 137.
Tattersale (Tatterson), Rob. 72, 227*.
Taverner, Ellen 133; Hum. 133; Joan 153; John 44, 46, 145, 146*; Margery 44.
Tawerneyr, John 45.
Taylor (Tayler, Taylar, Taylior, Tailor), Alice 167; Christr. 6; Edw. 80, 141, 283; Elianor 52; Eliz. 103; Fras. 240; Goody 4; Grissel 310; Hen. 80, 371; Hester 284; John 24, 32*, 94, 103*, 135, 138, 181, 192, 207, 240, 264, 274, 298, 325, 326*, 347, 352; Joyce 103; Kath. 80*; Margt. 52; Marion 90, 199; Mary 94; Nic. 30; Ric. 52*, 68; Rob. 65, 329, 345, 350; Rog. 215; Sar. 95, 136; Tho. 7, 275, 284; Tim. 154; Wm. 85, 134, 216, 274, 275, 327, 328*, 347, 352, 378, 379*.
Tebald, Rich. 277.
Terlyng, Nic. 274.
Terry, John 347; Wm. 192.
Tewar, Tho. 41.
Tey(e), John 23, 186.
Thacham, Hugh 270.
Thackham, Bridget 43.
Thamesyn, James 261*. *See Thomasyn.*
Tharold(e), Margaret 82*, 130*. *See Thorold.*
Tharpe, John 200; Wm. 168.
The(a)l(l)e, John 215*, 320*; Margery 215; Tho. 215*, 320*.
Thebridge, Tho. 6, 93; Wm. 6.
Thecher, —— 318.
Thedder, Susan 373.
Thewer, John 150, 352; Mary 150; Tho. 351; Wm. 352.
Thodye, Thos. 316.
Thomas, John 318*; John Hilocomius 316, 317*; Jos. 375, 376; Margt. 317*; Mary 376; Rob. 318; Roderick 369.
Thomasyn (Thomasine), Jas. 134, 261, 262; Joan 134, 261, 262. *See Thamesyn.*

Thomalyn, Rich. 192.
Thomkest, Rich. 103.
Thom(p)son, Alice 246; Ann 246, 247; Hen. 76; John 52, 122, 246, 326, 327, 347, 351; Margt. 11; Rob. 369; Roger 121; Sim. 11; Tho. 241, 305, 345, 353*.
Thorne, Cicily 142; Fras. 182; Gab. 339; Geo. 339; Hen. 278; Joan 143; Margt. 339; Rob. 339; Wm. 339.
Thorn(e)le, Andr. 199; Tho. 199.
Thorn(e)ton, Edw. 348; Eliz. 264; John 27,168,219; Ric. 177; Wm. 347.
Thornhill, Rich. 77.
Thorold (Thoralde), Edw. 210; Margt. 219. *See Tharolde.*
Thor(ow)good (Th(o)urgo(o)de, Th(r)ou(g)hgood), Christr. 133; Eliz. 142; Frances 259; Geoff. 276, 326; Geo. 121; Hen. 186; John 12*, 72, 77*, 85*, 229, 278, 321; Kath. 321; Margt. 77; Mary 321; Nic. 2*, 85, 274, 275; Ralph 275; Reb. 340; Rob. 275; Sar. 340; Tho. 274, 275, 337; Val. 215; Wm. 72, 133, 173, 176, 18:*, 220, 321; Winefrid 259.
Thorp(e), Adrian 186; Jos. 247; Martha 263*; Wm. 138.
Thrale, Ann 334; Margt. 8; Mary 95; Tho. 185, 332; Wm. 256.
Thredder, Christian 150; Dor. 292; Em. 150; Joan 293, 295*; John 101; Val. 315; Wm. 292, 293, 295*.
Three, Henry 289.
Thres(a)her, Thos. 200, 323, 328.
Thrikelt, John 216.
Thro(c)kmorton (Throkmerton), Anth. 218, 220, 340; Kath. 220, 340.
Thrope, Geo. 205.
Throte, John 348.
Thrustle, Robt. 140.
Thuftyll, Wm. 273.
Thurbie. Alice 75*; Annis 75; Joan 75; John 75; Tho. 75*.
Thurkild, John 266.
Thurlye, Margt. 227.
Thurston, Wm. 210.
Thwychyn, Hugh 192; Joan 192.
Thymbleby (Thymylbye), Edm. 344*, 345; Sophia 344*, 345; Steph. 219.
Tibballs (Tibbalts, Tabballs), Ann 331; Belknap 95*, 135, 137, 166, 169, 170, 240, 283, 284, 287.
Ticheler, Rich. 95.
Tidd (Tit), Dan. 115, 373; Mary 115*.
Tiddar, Louria 213.
Tidswell, S. W. 47.
Tilby, John 95.
Tilcocke, Eliz. 213.
Tilyard, Benj. 94.
Timmins, Rich. 166.
Tiplar. Abm. 68*.
Titmouse (Tytmos), Edw. 229; John 99, 229; Joyce 229; Lawr. 229; Margt. 229; Ric. 279; Rob. 149; Wm. 229.

Tobye, Kath. 312.
Todd(e) (Tod, Toode), Ann 83: Edw. 84; Grace 210; John 30, 210, 359*; Leon 181*; Margt. 30; Sar. 48; Tho. 30*.
Toddington, Wm. 140.
Tokefield (Tokfylde, Tockfield, Tofield, Colfeyld), Alice 32; Annis 32; Dan. 32; Hen. 32*, 72, 80; Jane 32; John 161, 162, 163; Jone 32; Jos. 138; Leon. 32; Martha 163; Mary 114; Paul 228; Tho. 32; Wm. 32, 163, 239.
Toky, John 145, 147, 148*, 195, 196, 197; Wm. 148.
Toller, Thos. 102.
Tollynson, Thos. 275.
Tombes, Anne 263*; Dan. 263*, 264; Hen. 265*; John 263*, 264*; Mary 263*, 264; Sar. 263.
Tomkins, Mich. 239.
Tomkyn, Rob. 32.
Tomlyn(e), Mr. 320; Ralph 155.
Tom(p)son, Eliz. 72; Geo. 277; John 122, 250*; Kath. 157; Reb. 142; Rob. 35, 80.
Tonbridge (Tonbrigge), Nich. 146; Tho. 276. *See Tunbridge.*
Toney, John 376.
Toogud, John 278.
Tooke (Toocke), Alice 219; Angeleta 36; John 123; Mary 200, 255; Walt. 36, 76, 88, 122, 219; Wm. 88, 122, 219, 229, 254, 255.
Totnam, Agn. 180; Hen. 9, 180*; Joan 180*.
Touthe. *See Shepperd.*
Toular, John 273.
Towe, Wm. 207.
Towersend, Thos. 96.
Towler, Jas. 85.
Townkes, Edw. 242; Margt. 242; Philad. 242.
Townley, Fras. 188.
Townsend (Tounsend, Towensend), Edw. 5; Hen. 137; John 373; Roger 80; Tho. 5, 205, 373.
Towrehill, Abbot of 368*.
Towse, Thos. 306.
Trace, Wm. 233.
Tratman, John 243*; Ric. 243.
Treacher, Dan. 140.
Tredder, Annis 356.
Tredgolde (Tredgeld), Barb. 38; Edw. 354; Joan 38; John 38; Margt. 38; Tho. 354; Wm. 274.
Tredway (Treadway), Eliz. 114, 159, 163; John 165; Margery 163; Ric. 114, 161*, 163, 173, 221, 254; Wm. 161.
Trennam, Roger 277.
Trentham, Christr. 236; Petronilla 236; Ric. 236; Rob. 236; Tho. 218.
Treswell, Mr. 108*.
Trewbody, Evace 91.
Trewe, Joan 46.
Triamore, Gilb. 353.

Trigg, Sam. 383.
Tristram (Trystram), Cecily 253; Eliz. 153, 294*; Jas. 258, 307; John 253; Law. 165.
Trott(e), Alex. 138, 330; Hen. 42; Jane 263, 287; Joan 42; John 120, 324, 325, 330; Sol. 123; Tho. 146, 286, 288, 347; Wm. 283.
Trowell, Margt. 153.
Trowghton, Jane 36; Ric. 36.
Trulock(e), John 63*.
Trundeye, Rach. 227; Ric. 227.
Trustram (Trustrum), Eliz. 214; Frances 210; John 168; Laur. 210, 214*; Mary 214.
Tryant, Wm. 167.
Trylle, John 45.
Tu, Wm. 156.
Tucke, Christr. 351; Mr. 9.
Tuf(f)nell (Tuffnaile, Tufnayle, Tufnall), Agn. 211; Edm. 305, 354; John 330; Ric. 334; Tho. 6; Wm. 354.
Tufton, Christian 219, 223, 305; John 219, 223, 305.
Tuke, —— 312; Leon. 310.
Tuker, Jone 51.
Tunbridge, Anth. 37, 180, 378; John 275. See Tonbridge.
Tunke, Kath. 32.
Turfoot, Geo. 256.
Turne, John 194.
Tur(ne)penye, John 352; Luce 351.
Turner (Turnar, Turno(u)r), Abm. 373; Anne 142; Edw. 66*, 242; Eliz. 99, 133, 219, 287; Ellen 303; Geo. 30, 31, 73, 274; Hen. 274; Isab. 138; Jas 5; Joan 66, 229; John 47, 66*, 99*, 104*, 105, 133, 158, 227, 236, 268, 271*, 275, 277, 303, 332, 335, 347; Jud. 212; Kath. 11, 104*; Margt. 152, 242; Mary 99, 169, 358*, 373; Nic 11, 64, 65, 104; Ric. 74, 87, 203, 207, 217, 219, 242, 375; Rob. 323, 325, 327; Sam. 92*, 167; Sar. 373; Sim. 274*; Tho. 40, 95, 199, 236, 337, 353; Wm. 9, 11, 63, 64, 66*, 89, 104, 138, 149, 266, 267, 268, 311, 337, 358*.
Turney, Margt. 153; Wm. 247.
Turpin, Ann 140; Hen. 96; John 286, 335, 375.
Turstwell, Rich. 40.
Turvere, Eliz. 200; Tho. 201.
Turvey, John 37.
Twhales, Thos. 347.
Twiford (Twyford), Frances 263*; Hen. 262, 263*; Martha 6.
Twiselton, Jacob 289.
Twitchell, Wm. 76.
Twitchett (Twychett), —— 349; Agn. 257; John 167; Mary 139; Rob. 257; Roger 139, 286.
Twydy, John 95.
Twynyho, Edm. 131; Eliz. 131.
Tyders, Cadw. 229.

Tydye, Anne 216*, 303; Jas. 229; John 303.
Tylberry, Rich. 273.
Tyler (Tylar, Tiler), Ann 83; Edw. 48; Eliz. 150; Geo. 75, 107; John 46, 150, 169, 195; Margt. 46; Mary 149; Reb. 288; Ric. 12, 46; Rob. 314; Sar. 46; Tho. 46*, 126, 147, 149, 272, 314*; Wm. 351. See Alden.
Tylston, Wm. 173.
Tymas, Henry 352.
Tymberlak, Christian 12; Ezech. 12; Rob. 12; Tho. 12*.
Tymperley, Leon. 80.
Tyndale, Thos. 34*.
Tynderalye, Sus. 200; Uxor 201.
Tynslye, Wm. 200.
Typladye, Anth. 302; Joan 302.
Typtoo, Wm. 28.
Tyrrell (Tirrell), Tho. 78, 343.
Tytworth, Rich. 347.

Umwell (Umweld), Alice 319, 320; Eliz. 320; Jas. 320*; Joan 320.
Uncle (Unckle), Annys 230; Eliz. 141; John 141; Kath 230; Rach. 238; Sar. 362.
Under, Edw. 198.
Underhill, Joan 277.
Underwood, Agn 42; Geo. 44, 206, 274; Grace 44; Mich. 205.
Usher, Alice 211; Dionisia 153; John 111, 153, 211.
Utram, John 350.
Utsenton, Jane 370.
Utterridge, Frances 83.

Valaunce, Peter 194.
Vale, Rich. 29.
Valentyne, Ric. 276; Wm. 275.
Vales, Alice 121; Tho. 121*.
Vanden Broak, Jan 317.
Vanderlas, Barth. 4.
Varney, Eliz. 150, 160; Grevil 150.
Vass, Sarah 83.
Va(u)ghan, —— 346; Anne 253; Edw. 78; Geo. 347; Hen. 273; John 253, 352; Morgan 275; Ro. 235; Tho. 81, 172, 257.
Vaus(s)e, Ric. 29, 73, 230.
Ve(a)le, Abm. 275; Martin 260*, 261; Ric. 219.
Venables, Rob. 229; Tho. 307.
Ventam, Christr. 219.
Ventres, John 353.
Veranderfeild, Eliz. 246*; Peter 246.
Verdesans, Agn. 237.
Verney, Edm. 81, 303; John 24; Letice 222; Urias 222.
Vessey (Veseye), —— 119; Eliz. 255; Goodman 121; John 90*, 231*, 232; Ric. 216*, 255.
Veyse, John 268.
Vicars, Edw. 40.

## INDEX.

Viccas, Agn. 86; Hen. 86; Joan 86; John 86; Kath. 86; Mary 86; Prud. 86; Sus. 86.
Vin(e)all, Nic. 282; Ric. 282.
Vinogradoff, —— 118.
Vogge, Joan 44.
Vyneyarde, John 131; Kath. 131.

Wabie (Wabye), Edw. 141; Tho. 212; Wm. 217, 254.
Wable, Lucy 245.
Wacket(t), Amy 83; Jas. 84; Jonath. 71, 361; Tho. 48, 84; Wm. 361.
Wadde, Robt. 312.
Waddell, Abm. 202.
Wadley, Wm. 361.
Waide, Geo. 346.
Waight, Wm. 229.
Wake, Luc. 344; Wm. 344.
Wakefield, Thos. 181.
Wakeham, Eliz. 220; Wm. 220.
Wakeland, —— 52; Geo. 52.
Wakeman, John 130.
Waker, Amys 198; Lawr. 180.
Wakes, Thos. 353.
Walcupp (Walcope), Ableing 95; Mary 94.
Walden(ne), —— 146. *See Audelye.*
Waler, Henry 243.
Waleys, Wm. 324, 325, 326.
Walford, John 306; Margt. 306; Wm. 306.
Walgrave, Edw. 339; Eliz. 339.
Walgrave *alias* Waldegrave, Tho. 172.
Walker, Ann 383*; Edw. 39; Eliz. 11*, 104*; Fras. 263*; Hen. 206; Jas. 261; John 11*, 104*; Kath. 11; Mary 96, 142; Moses 3; Nath. 96; Rob. 11, 104*; Tho. 28, 287; Wm. 11*, 76, 104*. 334, 383.
Walkvp, Tho. 287.
Walkyn, Sam. 104; Wm. 275.
Wall, Anne 379*, 380; Isaac 379; Joan 39; John 39; Mary 173*; Nic. 173; Ric. 39*; Tho. 379; Wm. 278, 379.
Wallen (Wallin) *alias* P(o)ulter, Anne 214; Isaac 214; John 295.
Waller (Wallar), Ellen 376; Geo. 215*, 223, 307, 344; Joan 215, 274; John 215, 274; Joyse 215; Margt. 215; Mary 215; Mich. 215, 274; Mr 67; Owen 80; Ric. 281, 363; Wm. 274.
Walleys, Wm. 219.
Wallington, Eliz. 286.
Wallis (Wallice), Giles 51, 100; John 70, 249; Sar. 285.
Wallser, Edw. 285.
Walpoole, Cæsar 11*, 63, 104; Edw. 336; Eliz. 336; Jane 336; Mr 11, 104; Rob. 336; Sus. 336.
Walrond, Edw. 173.
Walsall, Anne 210.
Walsch, Joan 91.
Walter, Rob. 277; Sim. 196; Wm. 76, 277.

Walters, Sarah 83.
Walton, Dan. 51*; Rob. 302; Sus. 302.
Wanell, John 323, 324, 326.
Warby, Mary 238.
Warcop, Anne 243.
Ward(e), Agn. 35, 303; Ann 40, 85; Christr. 318; Edw. 35, 105; Eliz. 40, 85, 164, 286; Geo. 190; Hen. 40, 85; Jas. 286; Jane 314; Joan 33, 105, 314; John 35, 181, 212, 213, 236, 288, 314*, 367; Josias 105; Jud. 212; Margt. 40, 85; Mary 255, 361; Matrone 277; Nic. 105; Ric. 130, 255, 277, 285; Rob. 303, 314*; Sar. 383; Sus. 103; Tho. 79, 170, 221, 274, 278; Walt. 87; Wm. 33, 39, 85*, 105*, 121, 164.
Warden, Sym. 349; Tho. 131.
Wardroppe, Polidore 62.
War(e)man, —— 146; Agn. 155; Edw. 155; John 155*; Margt. 155; Ric. 370; Wm. 155.
Warfeilde, Roger 254.
Warkup, John 149.
Warman. *See Wareman.*
Warne, Eliz. 28.
Warner, Agn. 180; Frances 180; Hen. 158, 212, 243, 299; John 187*, 188*, 230, 278, 324, 341; Kath. 199; Margt. 341; Ric. 342; Rob. 76, 133, 156, 158; Sus. 83; Tho. 156, 179, 180*, 206, 278; Wm. 79, 207, 308.
Warr(e), Eliz. 161, 162; Tho. 161; Wm. 281.
Warren (Ware(y)n), Alice 45; Athoma 78; Cath. 41; Geo. 277; Hen. 45; Isab. 219; Jesper 78; Joan 45, 219, 253; John 40, 45, 219, 277, 278; Mark 227; Mary 308; Master 235; Ralph 343; Rob. 219, 350; Sim. 132, 256; Tho. 141, 308; Wm. 253, 258, 335.
Warren *alias* Wood, John 212.
Warryner (Warrenner), John 220; Kath. 220; Margt. 209; Margery 201; Wm. 200, 205.
Warthe, Widow 86.
Warwick (Warwyke), Ambrose earl of 338; Anne 338; Edw. earl of 172; Ric. 278.
Washington (Washenton), Amph. 47, 48; Eliz. 47; Laur. 47*; Wm. 47.
Wastell, Geo 349.
Waterhouse (Waterhows), Anne 303; John 27, 303; Tho. 303, 307, 339.
Waterman, Anne 212; Good. 106; John 29; Ric. 209; Sol. 212; Wm. 275.
Waters, Eliz. 220; Geo. 220; Grace 153; Mr. 47, 48.
Waters *alias* Sturman, Eliz. 153.
Waterton, —— 209; Edw. 138; Eliz. 209; Sam. 167, 168, 169.
Watford, John 118.

Wath(e), Agn. 85; Alice 39, 85, 133; Ann 262, 263*; Christr. 39; Faith 85; Joan 39; Kath. 85; Margt. 262*; Ric. 39, 133; Sar. 85; Twyford 262*, 263*.
Watkins, Rob. 362; Tho. 213.
Wattner, Thos. 382.
Watts (Wattes), Dor. 372; Eliz. 213; Frances 284; John 216, 305*, 349; Margt. 305*; Tho. 80, 86, 119, 143, 213, 216*, 275, 305*, 318; Wm. 167.
Wat(t)son, Alice 155; Anne 32; Eliz. 32; Flor. 32; Francis 260, 261*; Hen. 32*; Jane 32; Joan 32, 302; John 32*, 103; Mary 32; Mother 38; Rob. 32, 130, 227, 302; Roland 309; Tho. 104, 361; Wm. 32*, 287, 333, 334.
Wattye (Wattie), Hen. 78, 87, 340.
Wawlar, John 273.
Way, Mr. 106.
Waylett, Tho. 275.
Wayneman, Alice 64.
Waypole alias Nobbes, Agn. 304; Sim. 37; Steph. 304.
Wayshe, Anth. 350; Sim. 350; Wm. 350.
Wayte, Rob. 273; Wm. 157. See Ellis.
Wealsheman, Hugh 198.
Webb(e) (Webe), Adam 49; Alice 35, 217; Annis 230; Charlton 244; Dan. 164; Edw. 72, 250*, 251; Eliz. 244; Hen. 35, 217; Jas. 150; Jerom 12; John 43*, 49, 155, 164*, 244, 255, 269, 299, 349; Kath. 244; Leon. 49; Mary 49; Ric. 261; Rob. 12; Sar. 164; Sim. 91; Sus. 12, 49*, 50; Tho. 12, 134, 173, 179*, 219, 256; Walt. 145; Wm. 78. See Britts.
Webbe alias Cheyne, Walt. 146*.
Webster, Ann 333; Tho. 63.
Wecneyll, Gilb. 348.
Weddell, Thos. 98.
Weeden (We(e)don, Wedun), Annes 114; Barth. 158; Eliz. 93, 230; Hen. 332; Jas. 4, 239; John 167, 230, 248, 285, 373; Jos. 286; Mary 332; Ric. 350; Rob. 341; Roger 348*; Tho. 130, 286, 334, 348, 349; Wm. 137, 158, 253, 313. See Aweedon.
Weedinge, Tho. 321.
Weekes, Marmaduke 370*.
Welbecke, John 345.
Weld, Alex. 375; Sar. 375.
Weldon, Anth. 257.
Weles, Wm. 40.
Welld, Humph. 110.
Well(e)s (Wellis), — 209; Agn. 201; Alice 142; Amie 161, 315; Anne 142, 315; Avys 230; Eliz. 209; Ellin 360*, 362; Fras. 102*, 360, 364; Geo. 27; Jane 315; Jerram 230; Joan 2, 79, 230, 312, 315; John 79, 91, 347, 358*, 359*, 360; Mark 362; Mary 315; Sar. 364; Tho. 63, 74, 207, 230, 315, 360*, 362; Wm. 85.
Wellingham (Wellinggame), Christr. 314; Dorcas 358; Grace 363; Mary 314; Nic. 105*, 106, 357*, 358*; Ric. 357; Tho. 314.
Wellor, Rich. 158.
Welshe (Welche), — 213; Agn. 74; Alice 74; Edw. 74*; Grace 209; Joan 74; John 42, 74, 209, 282, 315*; Lidia 282; Mary 333; Olife 74; Rob. 209; Sar. 213; Tho. 42, 74*, 210, 305, 314; Wm. 74*.
Welshman, Thos. 349.
Welwys, Helen 190.
Wen(h)am, Agn. 152; Gregory 152; Joan 33; Rob. 38*; Tho. 273; Wm. 37.
Wenlok, John, lord 147*, 148*.
Wenman, Isab. 131; Ric. 131.
Wermyngton, Rich. 90.
West, Alice 313; Ann 311; Edw. 32; Eliz. 32, 174, 376; Ellen 78, 81, 206; Geo. 143; Hen. 313; Jerome 313; Joan 132; John 32*, 72, 73, 194, 313*; Joyce 311; Julian 46; Kath. 198; Mr. 22*, 261; Nic. 34, 35, 78, 132*; Ric. 174, 311; Rob. 32; S-l. 32; Tho. 46; Toby 313; Wm. 32, 46, 78, 81, 132.
Westbury, Tho. 231.
Westby, Barth. 259; Edm. 232.
Westerman, Wm. 316*, 317*.
Westhead, Gilb. 377.
Westl(e)y, (Westlie), John 39; Radygun 39; Rob. 308; Wm. 39.
Westminster, Abbot of St. Peters, 24.
Weston, Wm. 118.
Westwo(o)d(e), Geo. 40; Gilb. 379; Grisell 379; John 206, 223; Joice 40; Margery 238; Mary 96; Mrs 379; Nic. 379; Tho. 379; Wm. 380.
Wetherall, Goodwife 2.
Wetherhead (Wetherede, Witherhead, Wetherd, Whethered), Abig. 167; Ann 375; Edw. 351; Eliz. 213, 239; Fras. 221; Isab. 373; Jer. 96; John 112, 187, 352; Mary 286; Reb. 149; Ric. 352, 353; Wm. 7, 28, 51*, 110, 153, 213, 352.
Wetheryngame, Eliz. 198.
Wett(e), Jane 85; Joan 133; Tho. 133.
Weybyn, Thos. 91.
Whale, Joan 85.
Wharton, Edw. 278; Hen. 333; John 258.
Wheatl(e)y(e), Anth. 155; Edw. 214; John 263.
Whe(e)ler, Agn. 306; Alice 192; Jas. 306; Mary 163; Nich. 343; Sam. 167; Wm. 295*, 346.
Wheles, John 348.
Whelpedale, John 346.

Whelp(e)ley (Whellple), Bridget 155; Christr. 207; Eliz. 156; John 75, 158, 227, 228, 311, 313; Mary 313; Nic. 8, 330; Ric. 156, 278; Rog. 75; Tho. 156*; Wm. 155.
Whethamsted, John 231.
Whetston. See Whistons.
Whippull, Isab. 277; John 219, 277; Wm. 219.
Whistons (Whetston), Alice 294; Han 290; Tho. 290*, 291, 294.
Whitbread alias More, John 175.
Whitby, Rob. 350, 370.
Whitchurch, Grace 165.
Whitcroft (Whetcroft), Hen. 140.
White (Whyte, Whight), Agn. 256; Alice 168, 199; Anne 7, 95, 335, 349; Dor. 150; Edw. 9, 152, 230; Eliz. 42; Ellyn 230; Geo. 77, 349; Hen. 273, 368; Jas. 42, 273; Joan 199; John 75, 138, 230*, 351; Mary 214; Ric. 29, 96, 329, 351; Rob. 168; Roger 238; Tho. 30, 162*, 192, 212, 238, 255, 256, 281, 367; Wm. 29, 46*, 277, 350.
Whit(e)he(a)d, Hugh 346; Mary 247; Rob. 101; Wm. 120.
Whitf(i)elde, John 122; Rob. 314.
Whitley (Whitlie, Whytley), Dor. 290; Eliz. 49; Geo. 289; John 289, 290, 292, 293*, 294; Ric. 28, 159; Tho. 49, 294; Wm. 28.
Whitlom (Whytlome) alias Barbor, Jas. 133, 254.
Whitlocke (Whittlocke, Whytlok), Alice 73; Anne 79; Edw. 73; Eliz. 73, 201, 315; Geraud 73; Grace 315; Hum. 79; Joan 73; John 73*, 141, 167, 315; Nic. 315; Sar. 210; Wm. 315.
Whitman, Edw. 22.
Whitmore, Joan 221; Wm. 221.
Whit(t)aker(s), (Whitacres), Ann 150; Eliz. 246*, 247; Joan 218; John 246, 247; Mary 247; Wm. 218.
Whittamore (Whyttamore), Tho. 77, 143, 221.
Whitten, Tho. 205.
Whylye, Joan 204; Ric. 204.
Whysterd, Wm. 275.
Whytbye, Geo. 274.
Whytle, Anne 221; Nic. 221; Ric. 221.
Whytnall (Whetnoll), Anne 221; John 275; Ralph 221; Rob. 274.
Whyttyngstall alias Whittenstall, Eliz. 131; Ric. 131.
Wick(e)s, (Wyxe), Clem. 312; Eliz. 312; Margt. 312*; Mary 332; Ric. 32; Rob. 228*; Tho. 312; Wm. 245.
Wiff, Rog. 161; Tho. 161.
Wigg, Wm. 371.
Wigginton, Abm. 115; Amy 160; Frances 159; Jas. 159, 160, 161, 163*; Josias 165; Mary 113, 115, 163, 165; Ric. 159; Rob. 160; Sus. 161, 163*; Tho. 113*, 115, 159, 160, 163; Wm. 160.

Wightman, John 194, 196*; Nic. 148, 194*; Tho. 307.
Wild(e), (Wylde), Mr 184; Ric. 243; Wm. 350.
Wildes, Mary 281; Tho. 333; Wm. 281, 333.
Wilkinson (Wylkynson), —— 310; Alice 211; Edw. 305*; Eliz. 255; Ellen 140; John 334; Ric. 99; Tho. 99; Wm. 140, 255.
Wilkoxe (Wylcockes, Wilcockes), —— 336; John 24, 347; Margt. 338; Mary 336; Tho. 312, 338.
Wilkshire. See Wilshire.
Willan, John 371
Willbraham, John 151.
Willet(t), Alice 75; Andr. 321; Anne 43, 153; Cath. 75*; John 75, 150, 160; Paul 75; Wm. 74, 75*, 278, 285.
Willett alias Tapps, Anne 153.
Willey(e), Agn. 276, 344; Ed. 270, 277, 377, 378; John 276, 277; Ric. 344.
Willgrasse, Mary 51; Sam. 51.
Williams (Wyllyams), Agn. 229, 307; Anne 263*; Ellen 263; Geo. 94; Jas. 27, 229; Joan 229; John 6, 132, 205, 263*, 285; Kath. 132; Mark 307; Ralph 285; Ric. 139; Rob. 102; Rog. 62, 317*, 377; Sim. 9, 38*, 39, 40*, 84, 86*, 87, 119, 120, 121*, 180*, 181, 215, 216, 318*, 321; Tho. 198.
Williamson (Wyllyamson), Agn. 73, 255; Cath. 73; Christr. 255; Joan 73*; John 73, 210; Nic. 209; Rob. 73; Tho. 73; Wm. 73*.
Williatt (Wylliatt), Margt. 62; Tho. 62*.
Willoughbye, Fras. 82*.
Wil(l)shire (Wilshere, Wylshe(y)re, Wilkshire), Beat. 211; Dunstone 311; Edw. 75, 311*; Eliz. 289; Ellen 339; Geo. 311*, 353; John 289*, 290*, 291, 353, 370; Lawr. 198; Lettice 151*; Mary 291; Ralph 154; Ric. 104, 339; Tho. 290; Wm. 98, 211, 311.
Willsmere (Wilsemar, Wilsmore), John 380; Margt. 380; Tho. 326, 378.
Wilson (Wilsonne, Willson, Wylson), Adam 34, 36; Agn. 1; Amy, 63; Anne 96; Dor. 349; Edm. 353; Edw. 1, 29, 87, 106*, 254, 370; Ellen 2; Esther 370; Geo. 177; Goodwife 181; Hen. 138, 170; Isab. 36; Jas. 31; John 36, 273; Kath. 36; Margt. 72; Marion 254; Mary 5; Ric. 107; Rob. 2, 275; Tho. 63, 143; Wm. 1, 137, 283.
Wilversey. See Cristmas.
Winch(e), (Wynch(e), Ann 159, 190; Bennet 20*, 21*, 22*; Ric. 190; Rob. 142, 356; Wm. 188, 190. See Wynche.

Winchester (Wynchester), Hen. 376; Hester 289; Rand. 376; Ric. 349; Tho. 119; Wm. 12.
Winckfold (Wynkfelde), Christr. 349; John 349; Nic. 75; Tho. 192*.
Windle, Gertrude 288.
Windsor (Wyn(d)sore), Han. 333; Hen. 149*; John 347; Mary 244; Rob. 347; Tho. 30, 167, 310, 312.
Wing, Frances 264.
Wingfe(i)ld (Wyngfeld, Winfeild), Agn. 343; Anne 239, 264; Christr. 343; Geo. 286; Isab. 343; John 8, 95, 264; John Tombes 264, 265*; Phil. 219, 343; Ralph 343; Rob. 174; Th. 196; Wm. 137.
Winstanley (Wistautly, Wen Stanley) Eliz. 62; Hen. 163*; Ric. 50, 62*.
Winstar, Ed. 300.
Winter (Wyntir), Edw. 202; John 202, 288, 334; Joshua 383*; Margt 236; Ralph 383*; Ric. 236; Wm. 243.
Wiseman (Wyseman), Edm. 34; Jane 309; John 24; Ric. 78, 309; Tho. 80, 309; Wm. 309.
Witborn, Elen 233.
Witham, Wm. 104.
Withe (Wythe), Geo. 82, 343; Ric. 82, 172.
Witherall, Ric. 273.
Withers, Eliz. 100.
Withroll, Ric. 104.
Witsey, Bridget 282; Mrs. 282; Ric. 157.
Witton, Ann 368; Christr. 368.
Wolde, Audry 343.
Wolf, John 119.
Wolferston, Sampson 176.
Wol(l)ey (Wollie, Woolley), Benj. 206; Ellen 206*; Joan 206; John 206, 207, 262, 263*; Matt. 380; Ric. 206, 207*, 208*; Rob. 80, 81, 132, 175, 206*, 207*, 208*, 337; Sar. 244*; Tho. 65*, 205*, 206*, 207*, 208*, 244, 317, 338.
Wolmer, Dor. 340; John 75; Tho. 340.
Wolryche (Worlich), John 325*.
Wolvey, Tho. 231.
Womwell, Alice 86; Felix 86*, 87; Phil. 121; Wm. 86*.
Wood(e) (Wod), Alice 115; Andr. 178, 341; Boniface 342; Dan. 42; Edm. 282, 287*; Edw. 381; Esabell 277; Jas. 347; John 85, 103, 115, 116, 159, 161*, 206, 278, 382; Jos. 335; Margt. 244; Mary 161; Nic. 274; Ric. 282, 305; Rob. 10, 43, 277*, 373; Sus. 83, 112, 162; Tho. 203, 274, 277, 345, 347; Wm. 30, 273, 349. *See Warren.*
Woodans, Sarah 169.
Woodbridge, Henry 330.
Woodcocke (Woodecok),——51; Hen. 366; Tho. 173; Thurstan 173.
Woodfield (Woodfilde), John 310; Mich. 48.

Woodfine, Eliz. 358; Ric. 105*, 106, 358*.
Wo(o)dhouse, John 72*.
Woodlande, Alice 2.
Woodley, Anne 244*; Tho. 314*; Wm. 244.
Woodlyff, Sim. 367.
Woodnet, Thos. 172.
Woodnoth, Eliz. 140.
Woodroofe (Woodruffe). Alice 130; Andr. 273; Dionis 177; John 130; Mary 6; Rob. 177; Steph. 78, 176. *See Andrews.*
Woodshawe, Edw. 219, 223.
Woodwards (Wod(e)ward(e), Woodards),——350; Alice 90; Christr. 369; Edm. 348; Eliz. 375; Frances 220; Jas. 8, 347, 375; Joan 47, 50, 331; John 47, 331, 332; Lawr. 156; Margerie 156; Mary 138, 374; Matt. 338; Ric. 345, 348; Rob. 220, 331; Rose 170; Sus. 335; Tho. 7, 151, 156*, 261, 348; Wm. 348*, 349.
Woollhead, Ann 335.
Woolridge, Wm. 382.
Woorten (Woorton),——207; Jane 38.
Wo(o)tton, Rich. 238.
Wordell, Mary 285.
Worland, Joan 131, 132; Ric. 131, 132; Sar. 119.
Worrell, John 12.
Worsencroft, Sus. 52.
Wortley, Ri. 107.
Worthe, Hugh 342.
Wos(ay)ter (Wosetor), Wm. 74, 142, 159.
Wotsonne, John 216.
Wottun, John 273, 275.
Wraste, Edw. 154; Martha 154; Wm. 29.
Wrattyng(e) (Wrottinge, Wrottyng), Alice 38*; Chas. 38*, 321; John 46, 47.
Wrawby, Henry 3.
Wrenche, Jas. 198; Wm. 350*.
Wren(ne), Agn. 227; Anne 361; Barth. 175; Christian 190; Edw. 356, 357, 359; Eliz. 100, 362; Geo. 227*, 310; Hen. 190, 353; Jeff. 85; Joan 190; John 190, 227, 249, 362; Kath. 121; Leon. 211; Mary 362; Reginald 190*; Rob. 121*; Sar. 359; Tho. 227, 356; Wm. 121, 227, 275.
Wrennocke, John 275.
Wrey, Christr. 78.
Wright (Wryg(h)te, Write), Andr. 283; Anne 99, 310, 369; Christian 91; Christr. 180; Edm. 262; Edw. 246; Eliz. 180; Frances 152; Fras. 247; Jasper 131; John 91, 120, 140, 146*, 199, 218, 246, 256, 269, 271, 277*, 344; Kath. 303; Margery 180; Mary 140, 212, 329; Moses 31; Peter 310; Phil. 243; Ralph

## INDEX.

119; Ric. 219, 220, 275, 303; Rob. 180, 251\*; Sam. 99; Sus. 245, 246; Tho. 67, 68, 81, 93; Wm. 145, 146\*, 195, 196, 380.
Wright *alias* George, Alice 212.
Wrothe, Mary 133; Rob. 175; Tho. 133, 175; Wm. 175, 254, 345.
Wrottinge. *See Wrattynge.*
Wrytt(e), John 272, 274.
Wyan, John 198.
Wyatt, Rich. 376.
Wyberde (Wybard), Hen. 272; Reynold 86; Tho. 274.
Wye, John 347; Ric. 367\*, 368\*.
Wygan, Joan 81; John 81.
Wygborne, Wm. 350.
Wyg(g)e, John 353; Tho. 354.
Wykes, John 131\*; Kath. 131\*.
Wylcock, Anne 255; Ric. 255.
Wylforde, Mary 219; Tho. 219.
Wylkes, Joyce 308; Wm. 308.
Wyley, Edw. 345; J. 325; Margery, 9; Ric. 134\*.
Wyllan, Hen. 39.
Wyllester. —— 27.
Wylley (Willye), Eliz. 345.
Wyll(i mot(t), Jas. 258; Sim. 179.
Wylyot, Rich. 232.
Wymburshe, —— 129.
Wymond, Margt. 91; Wm. 91.
Wynche, Fras. 221, 303; Wm. 47. *See Winche.*
Wyndam, Fras. 177.
Wyndeout (Wyndeowt), Anne 366, 367\*; Barth. 366\*, 367\*, 368, 369; Basill 365\*; John 367; Kath. 365, 366; Ric. 366\*, 369; Rog. 365; Tho. 364, 365\*, 366\*, 368.
Wyngate, Edw. 36.
Wynkeburn, Joan 190; John 190\*.

Wynkefeld. *See Winckfeld.*
Wynn(e), Wm, Wyne, Hen. 69; Jane 134, John 134; Ric. 298\*; Tho. 227; Wm. 307.
Wynterforde, Hen. 91.
Wynterton, Tho. 92.
Wyre, Agn. 176; John 176.
Wysmer, Tho. 277.
Wyte, John 272; Rob. 191.
Wythe. *See Withe.*
Wytton, Edw. 81.
Wyttymore, Anne 34; Tho. 34.

Yardley (Yeardly), Anne 305; Edm. 305; John 176, 275; Rob. 44, 304.
Yardlyn(g), John 274\*.
Yarrow(e), John 374; Ric. 374; Tho. 259.
Yates, Ann 246; John 246; Mary 246.
Yeman, Wm. 275.
Yemmonger, Joan 310.
Yerlynge, John 35.
Yongloue, Geo. 346.
York(e), (Yeorke), Alice 33, 75; Christian 75; Geo. 33, 75; John 2; Tho. 364\*; Wm. 33, 75.
Youing, Rich. 20\*, 21.
Yo(u)nge, Alice 312; Anne 49; Dan. 238; Edm. 24; Edw. 340, 353; Eliz. 312; Frances 211; Grace 281, 291; Jas. 353; Joan 312, 313; John 82, 200, 353; Mary 330; Mich 110, 186, 311; Nath. 330; Phil. 65; Ric. 222, 304; Sar. 329; Tho. 25\*, 63, 211, 239, 313\*, 353; Wm. 27, 49\*, 149.
Yoward, Frances 137; John 136.
Ypgrave. *See Ipgrave.*

## ERRATA.

| | | | | |
|---|---|---|---|---|
| Page | 11. | Line 12 from top. | Delete full stop after *son*. |
| ,, | 85 | ,, 8 ,, bottom. | For *Chaney* read *Chancy*. |
| ,, | 206. | ,, 11 ,, top. | For *Woiley* read *Wolley*. |
| ,, | 225. | Headnote. | For *Feet of Fines* read *Church Terriers*. |
| ,, | 236. | Line 5 from top. | For *sale* read *sole*. |
| ,, | 259. | ,, 10 ,, bottom. | For *Hensico* read *Henrico*. |
| ,, | 265. | ,, 7 ,, ,, | For *Kindor* read *Kinder*. |
| ,, | 309. | ,, 21 ,, top. | For *advowsor* read *adcowson*. |
| ,, | 343. | ,, 21 ,, bottom. | For *Olyner* read *Olyuer*. |

CPSIA information can be obtained
at www.ICGtesting.com
Printed in the USA
LVHW022340221220
674915LV00031B/886